PARTNERSHIP TAXATION
THIRD EDITION

LexisNexis
GRADUATE TAX SERIES

PARTNERSHIP TAXATION

THIRD EDITION

RICHARD M. LIPTON, ESQ.
Partner, Baker & McKenzie LLP

PAUL CARMAN, ESQ.
Partner, Chapman & Cutler LLP

CHARLES FASSLER, ESQ.
Of Counsel, Bingham Greenebaum Doll LLP

WALTER D. SCHWIDETZKY
Professor of Law
University of Baltimore School of Law

ISBN: 9780769849034 (casebook)
ISBN: 9780327176190 (e-book)

NOTE TO USERS

To ensure that you are using the latest materials available in this area, please be sure to periodically check the LexisNexis Law School web site for downloadable updates and supplements at www.lexisnexis.com/lawschool.

Editorial Offices
121 Chanlon Rd., New Providence, NJ 07974 (908) 464-6800
201 Mission St., San Francisco, CA 94105-1831 (415) 908-3200
www.lexisnexis.com

MATTHEW◊BENDER

Dedication

To Wally Blum, Cynthia Holcomb Hall and Sharon King, who taught me how to be a tax lawyer. And to my wonderful wife and family, who have come to understand and cope with my love of tax law and golf (not necessarily in that order).

—Richard M. Lipton

To my loving wife and daughters, who wisely discourage me from talking about tax at home.

—Paul Carman

Dedicated to the memory of Ajaan Mun.

I wish to acknowledge my indebtedness to Professors Stephen Lind, Stephen Schwarz, Daniel Lathrope, and Joshua Rosenberg, authors of Fundamentals of Partnership Taxation. I taught from their text for many years and it influenced my own approach to this effort.

—Walter D. Schwidetzky

TABLE OF CONTENTS

TABLE OF CONTENTS

TABLE OF CONTENTS

TABLE OF CONTENTS

TABLE OF CONTENTS

TABLE OF CONTENTS

TABLE OF CONTENTS

TABLE OF CONTENTS

TABLE OF CONTENTS

TABLE OF CONTENTS

TABLE OF CONTENTS

TABLE OF CONTENTS

TABLE OF CONTENTS

TABLE OF CONTENTS

Introduction

THE SPIRIT OF PARTNERSHIPS AND PARTNERSHIP TAXATION

Most of this textbook focuses on the rules concerning partnership taxation — when a partnership exists, the tax treatment of contributions to a partnership, the basis of partnership assets and interests in a partnership, how income is allocated to the partners, the tax treatment of distributions, the consequences of partnership liabilities, partnership mergers, the retirement of a partner, and dissolution of the partnership. There also is significant attention paid to the numerous "anti-abuse" rules that have been adopted by Congress and the Internal Revenue Service ("IRS") over the past several decades, including the disguised sale rules, the treatment of "mixing-bowl" transactions, the complex rules to prevent basis abuse, and the overriding "partnership anti-abuse regulations" adopted by the IRS. These rules are embodied in the Code,[1] the Regulations, rulings from the IRS and numerous precedents, all of which are explored and discussed below. Put simply, this textbook contains a thorough discussion of the rules of partnership taxation.

In addition, this textbook explores one of the fundamental questions which always arises in partnership taxation: is a partnership to be treated as a separate taxable entity or an aggregate of its partners? The tension between entity and aggregate treatment of a partnership is one of the recurring issues in determining the tax consequences of partnership transactions. Indeed, it can be argued that Congress created perpetual uncertainty when it decided in 1954 that for tax purposes a partnership was not solely an aggregation of its partners or a separate legal entity, but at times one and at times the other. Many of the questions addressed in this textbook arise, at their heart, because of the bifurcated nature of a partnership as both a separate entity and an aggregate of its partners. Some of the more complex areas in partnership taxation (like the TEFRA rules governing partnership controversies) arise because of Congress' unwillingness to draw the line between treating a partnership as a separate entity versus an aggregation of its partners.

However, this introduction focuses on a third aspect of partnership taxation — the spirit of partnerships and partnership taxation. The concept that individuals and corporations will, in the furtherance of legitimate business enterprise, want to enter into partnerships is one of the unspoken axioms of the tax law. The practical

---

[1] References to the "Code" and "I.R.C." are references to the Internal Revenue Code of 1986, as amended.

consequences of people coming together is the focus of the complex rules governing partnership taxation, but the underlying reason why people want to combine their efforts is not addressed frequently. People coming together to promote their individual and collective self-interests is what underlies every partnership.

In order to understand partnership taxation, you need to take into account the fact that partnerships are one of the fundamental building blocks of human economic interaction. Partnerships have long existed, and they will continue to exist, although the success of partnerships may depend upon the tax rules applicable to them. The rules concerning partnership taxation need to be judged by whether they further or inhibit this basic goal. In other words, as you read each of the chapters below, you should consider not only the technical partnership tax issues that are discussed, but also whether the rules are consistent with the undiscussed spirit of partnerships and partnership taxation. If the rules further these goals without fostering abuse, then the rules may be considered to be "spiritually" appropriate. On the other hand, if out of a desire to prevent some perceived abuse, the rules make it harder for people to combine their resources and energy, or result in uncertain or disproportionately inappropriate tax consequences, then the wisdom of the rule needs to be carefully considered.

Why Are there Partnerships? Anyone who wants to consider the origin of partnerships (and partnership taxation) needs to go no further than prehistoric times, as men banded together to hunt. The cave drawings found in Southern France all illustrate groups of men joining together to slay beasts, whether for food or protection. The proceeds of these efforts were shared by the hunters (partners), although a written agreement was not needed to determine how a slaughtered animal would be divided.

Indeed, it can be argued that the entire impetus of the change in civilization from a hunter/gatherer society to one in which people primarily lived in cities was a result of partnerships being formed. Although cities furthered economic growth and development by allowing individuals to exchange their efforts and goods, the impact of this interchange was greatly magnified as people joined together to increase the impact of their efforts. Partnerships provided the means for people to work together, and the law quickly developed to address the legal relationship of partners.

A survey of the laws of antiquity indicates that partnerships have been present for a long, long time. Dating back to the time of Sumer, there was a complex commercial system that included business partnerships. The transactions of these partnerships were recorded on clay tablets, some of which have been found in temple complexes.[2]

In his book on Mesopotamian contracts, Paul Halsell highlighted two contracts from the reign of Nebuchadnezzar II (c. 568–564 BC). In the first contract, Nabu-adki-iddin was an investor — a member of the great Egibi family. He contributed four manas of capital to a partnership, while Bel-shunu, who was to carry on the business, contributed one half mana and seven shekels, whatever property he

---

[2] Paul Guisepi & F. Roy Willis, History-World.org/sumeria, 2003.

might have, and his time. Any expenses in excess of four shekels was considered to be extravagant and had to be paid by Bel-shunu from his own pocket. The contract was witnessed by three men and a scribe. In another partnership, entered into four years later, there were no initial contributions, but each of the partners drew 20 shekels of income one year later, and additional funds were used by the partnership to pay its obligations.[3]

This business model was carried over to ancient Greece and Rome. In Rome, in particular, "associations" were formed which functioned as partnerships. Partnerships were used, especially for transmarine transactions in which risk sharing was necessary in an age before insurance. Cato advised a capitalist not to fit out a single ship but, in concert with 49 other capitalists, to send out 50 ships and to take an interest in each to the extent of a fiftieth part.[4]

When Rome fell, and "darkness" spread upon the West, partnerships continued in the thriving intellectual climate in the Arab world. Indeed, partnerships were the primary form of business enterprise because interest is forbidden in the Koran. Partnerships were regularly used to compensate the party who provided money to a venture, using a variable rather than a fixed rate of return. Indeed, there were different types of partnerships for the situation where one person contributed money and another contributed labor (Mudararah) and the situation in which both persons contributed capital (Musharakah).[5]

Even in the so-called Dark and Middle Ages, partnerships were the primary vehicle of commerce. For example, in 1235, a Jew (Saltell) and a Christian (Berenguer) formed a partnership to operate a mill. They originally agreed that Saltell would have one quarter of the income and bear one quarter of the losses. Seven years later a dispute arose, with Saltell claiming he was owed money as a result of a premature disposition of the mill, and Berenguer claiming that there was a loss for which he was entitled to compensation. The matter was submitted to jointly accepted arbitrators, who found in favor of Saltell and awarded him monetary damages.[6]

The emergence of the West from the Dark Ages was accompanied by the growth of mercantile partnerships. Indeed, on his voyage of discovery, Christopher Columbus formed a partnership with the Spanish crown and Italian investors, in which he shared the proceeds from his discoveries.[7] The explorations by Sir Francis Drake were supported by partnerships of investors.[8] And the great growth of trade in the Netherlands during the sixteenth century can be directly traced to

---

[3] Paul Guisepi & F. Roy Willis, History-World.org/sumeria, 2003.

[4] THEODOR MOMMSEN, THE HISTORY OF ROME, BOOK III.

[5] M.A. MANNAN, ECONOMIC DEVELOPMENT AND SOCIAL PEACE IN ISLAM (1989); M.U. CHAPRA, TOWARDS A JUST MONETARY SYSTEM (1986).

[6] MEDIEVAL SOURCEBOOK: A BUSINESS PARTNERSHIP BETWEEN A JEW AND A CHRISTIAN IN BARCELONA, 1235–1242, based on ARXIU CAPITULAR DE BARCELONA 1-6-3475.

[7] Wikipedia.org, "Columbus' Campaign for Funding."

[8] "The Beginning of the End: The Drake-Norris Expedition, 1589," www.loc.gov/rr/rarebook/catalog/drake.

partnerships in which investors held shares and entrusted their capital to the hands of active partners.[9]

The use of partnerships is also inextricably linked to the founding of this country. Although the original Virginia Company that founded the Jamestown settlement was a corporation chartered by the Crown, the Pilgrims who landed at Plymouth Rock conducted their enterprise as a partnership. There were "Adventurers" who provided the capital and supplies needed for the settlement. The settlers themselves were often described as "partners in land" who would be entitled to a sharing of the proceeds with the Adventurers.[10]

Partnerships were so common that they could be found in everyday conversation and in famous literature. For example, in *A Christmas Carol*, when Ebenezer Scrooge and Jacob Marley left to form their own business, they formed a partnership, Scrooge and Marley. Shakespeare referred to partners in business enterprises in several of his plays.[11]

The story goes on and on. People joining together to collectively promote their interests — to form partnerships — are a fundamental part of the history of man. Partnerships are simply a part of fundamental human relationships — people enter into partnerships in order to conduct commercial enterprise, with the hope that this will improve their lives.

Why Are There Separate Tax Rules for Partnerships? If partnerships are such a fundamental building block for human relations, why is it necessary to have separate tax rules for partnerships? This seemingly simple question can be answered with an equally simple statement — our tax system focuses on income, and income eventually goes to the people who receive it. The income tax originally applied only to individuals, and the taxation of partnerships was always focused on the taxation of the people who formed those partnerships.

There is, needless to say, a long history of partnership taxation that pre-dates the current income tax. However, for much of antiquity, there was no income tax (as we currently understand such taxes), although partnerships would have been subject to wealth, property, and similar taxes. However, as far back as 519 B.C., King Darius of Persia established a tax system that was based on the anticipated yield of land. Although this was not a true "income" tax, the tax was imposed upon the source of production of income. Even earlier, in ancient Sumer and Babylon, professional workers had to pay "taxes" to royal collectors in order to remain employed. Thus, both individuals and partnerships have long had tax burdens, although much of this taxation was not directly related to income.[12]

Of course, it also is possible to tax business entities, as the tax treatment of corporations shows. Arguments have been made that all business entities — corporations, partnerships, limited liability companies, business trusts — should be

---

[9] Jan de Vries, *The Dutch Atlantic Economies, in* Coclanis Books, at 10 (2005).

[10] "The Present [1624] Estate of New Plymouth," from the Mayflower Web Pages, Mayflo1620.

[11] *See, e.g.,* The Winter's Tale act 4, sc. 2; Coriolanus act 5, sc. 6.

[12] Michael Hudson, *Mesopotamia and Classical Antiquity — Taxation History*, Am. J. Econ. & Soc. (Dec. 2000).

directly subject to taxation. The difficulty with this argument is that there is little difference between a sole proprietorship, which is difficult to tax as a separate business entity, and a two-person general partnership. The distinction becomes even harder to discern when families are involved. For example, if a woman sets up a business in her home and it is not taxable, but then brings her daughter into the business to help her and gives her daughter an ownership interest in the business, would the former not be a business entity subject to taxation but the latter would? Unless every business entity of any size, and without regard to the number of owners, is subject to entity-level taxation, there will always be some business entities that are effectively taxed to their owners directly and not to the entity itself.

Moreover, some state and local governments (and some foreign countries) currently tax partnerships as business entities, so it is clear that there is no fundamental cosmic reason why a partnership could not be subject to taxation. But in the United States, as a general rule, a partnership has been viewed not as a separate taxable entity but, instead, as a "pass-through" entity in which its owners (and not the partnership itself) are subject to taxation. This axiom — that income tax is paid by the partners of a partnership, and not the partnership itself — underlies many of the issues that will be discussed herein.

Aggregate versus Entity Treatment. The assumption that a partnership will be treated as a pass-through entity that is not directly subject to income taxation does not answer the question whether the calculation of income will be imposed at the partner or partnership level. In other words, even if the partners in the partnership (and not the partnership itself) are directly subject to taxation on income, the computation of income can be made either at the entity level (by treating the partnership as a separate entity for purposes of computing the income that is taxable to its owners) or at the partner level (by disregarding the partnership and treating it as an aggregation of its owners, each of whom determines his own income separately).

There is no clearly "correct" way to determine how a partnership should be treated, i.e., both entity and aggregate treatments are appropriate at different times. Many of the chapters that follow will illustrate the tension between aggregate and entity treatment of partnerships in calculating the income that is taxable to the partners in a partnership. This is particularly evident in the various anti-abuse rules that have been adopted by Congress or promulgated by the IRS. Most of the anti-abuse rules address situations in which treating a partnership as a separate taxable entity results in more favorable tax consequences than would occur if the partnership were treated as an aggregation of its owners — the anti-abuse rules frequently treat the partnership as an aggregate in order to "correctly" determine the taxable income of its partners.

Where Do Substance and Form Fit In? If simplicity is ever to be achieved in the area of partnership taxation, then "substance" and "form" will remain significant determinants of the tax consequences of partnership transactions. It can be argued that much of the complexity in the more recent legislation and Regulations concerning partnership taxation are the result of Congress and the IRS not trusting that the courts will look at the substance (rather than the form) of partnership transactions. Many of the more recent rules appear to be designed to address situations in which the form of the transaction differed from its substance. It is possible that some of this complexity could be eliminated if Congress and the IRS would simply allow the courts to do their job in weighing the bona fides of partnership transactions.

For example, consider the decision in *ASA Investerings Partnership v. Commissioner.*[13] The case involved the application of the installment sale rules under I.R.C. § 453 in the context of a partnership with foreign and domestic partners. The partnership was formed so as to cause an allocation of income (resulting from the installment sale) to the foreign partner. To address this transaction, the court could not rely upon the technical words in the Code, because these rules supported the taxpayer's position. Instead, the court had to look at the substance of the transaction (rather than its form) to find that the foreign party was not a "partner" to whom income could be allocated.

What About Anti-Abuse Rules? Recent years have seen significant legislative and regulatory developments in the partnership area. Many of the newest rules can only be described as "anti-abuse" provisions which are intended to address one particular transaction or another that was considered to be abusive. The result is that the laws concerning partnership taxation have metamorphosed from the broad, general principles that were established in the 1950s into particularized rules that attempt to address every potential abuse. Of course, it is impossible to cover every conceivable situation, so Congress and the IRS have crafted numerous rules that unfortunately can be aptly described as "heads I win, tails you lose."

Several examples illustrate the approach taken by Congress in these new rules. For example, I.R.C. §§ 737, 721(b), and 731(c) all provide for the potential recognition of gain, but not loss, in certain situations. If the transaction is an appropriate event to trigger the recognition of gain, why is it not also an appropriate event for the recognition of loss?

Likewise, the basis rules in I.R.C. §§ 734 and 743 were amended in 2004 to address situations in which an election is not made under I.R.C. § 754 to adjust the basis of partnership assets. Basically, the amendment functions so that: (1) if there would be a basis increase that would potentially benefit partners, an election must be filed, and if no election is timely filed, the partners could face double recognition of gain, but (2) if there is a loss that would result in a basis reduction (which benefits the IRS), an election will be deemed to have been filed except in some very limited circumstances. This provision is a classic "heads I win, tails you lose" situation[14] and is representative of the approach taken in recent legislation and Regulations.

How Do the Tax Rules Affect Partnerships? Any practitioner who has worked with partnerships is well aware that the tax laws affect every single transaction. It would be naïve to assume that a partnership would be formed, enter into transactions, distribute its profits, bring in new partners and redeem old ones,

---

[13] 76 T.C.M. (CCH) 325 (1998), *aff'd*, 201 F.3d 505 (D.C. Cir. 2000), *cert. denied*, 531 U.S. 871 (2000).

[14] This provision was enacted to address a transaction, undertaken by Enron Corporation prior to its demise, in which a failure to make an I.R.C. § 754 election resulted in basis duplication.

incur liabilities, and (eventually) dissolve without looking at the applicable tax rules each and every step of the way. In fact, because partnerships receive more favorable tax treatment than corporations (one level of taxation instead of two), it is possible that even more attention is paid to the tax consequences of partnership transactions than to corporate ones.

The impact of the tax rules can be seen in everyday transactions. For example, assume that Jack wants to contribute property to a partnership, and Jill wants to contribute money. The contributing partners will need to consider numerous tax issues in forming their partnership, including the impact of any built-in gain or loss with respect to the contributed property, the manner in which basis will be allocated and depreciation calculated, the potential application of the disguised sale rules as distributions are made to Jack, the allocation of liabilities that encumber the property, and on and on. Even the simplest transaction can result in significant confusion.

If the goal of partnerships is to allow people or corporations to pool their efforts for the common good, then partnership tax rules should be judged by whether they make it easier or more difficult to attain this goal. Many of the more complex rules in the Code will certainly fail to meet this goal. Indeed, the most significant issue in partnership taxation is the complexity, much of which arises from more recent rules and Regulations.

Take, for example, the potential application of the disguised sale rules to the partnership formed by Jack and Jill. Even a simple transaction, in which one partner contributes property and the other contributes cash, will need to be carefully reviewed to make sure that the transaction is not treated as a disguised sale. Moreover, all distributions by the partnership to Jack and Jill will need to be carefully monitored for at least seven years to make certain that Jack is not treated as having engaged in a "mixing bowl" transaction. Thus, the simple contribution of property to a partnership can result in years of diligence. This complexity is one of the banes of the partnership tax rules at the present time.

The Spirit of Partnership Taxation. If there is an underlying "spirit" to partnerships, it is people getting together to conduct business in a manner which provides mutual benefits. This is how partnerships have always been used, and this is why partnerships have generally been treated as non-taxable entities, because it is the partners (and not the partnership as an entity) that should be subject to income taxation.

The tax rules for partnerships should be approached with the intention of furthering this goal by allowing persons to enter into mutually beneficial economic arrangements, the tax consequences of which can be simply (and definitively) determined. Moreover, the tax results should be self-evident to both the partners in the transaction and their tax advisors. The spirit which underlies partnership taxation should be the same as the spirit underlying partnerships — partnerships should be taxed in a manner which reflects the underlying business arrangements of the partners. If partnerships are a "basic" form of human economic organization, the tax rules for partnerships should also be built on the "basics" that tax consequences should be related to the underlying economic relationships of the partners.

The remainder of this book will be filled with discussion of the actual rules for partnership taxation. You will encounter complex rules, with exceptions, exceptions to the exceptions, and "heads I win, tails you lose" anti-abuse rules. We will leave it to you to determine whether each of these rules — particularly the more recent statutory and regulatory limitations on partnerships and their transactions — are consistent with or contrary to the underlying spirit of partnerships and their transactions.

The foregoing said, it is purely wishful thinking to believe that the partnership tax rules can return to the days of yore, in which there were a few simple rules and general principles guiding partnership taxation. Complexity is here to stay, and the ongoing trend is to make the rules more complex rather than simpler. Moreover, as tax practitioners find ways to take advantage of the rules, it can be anticipated that Congress and the IRS will continue to attempt to make the rules for partnership taxation more one-sided than ever.

How Practitioners Can Further the Spirit of Partnerships and Partnership Taxation. The following chapters will illustrate many of the aspects of partnership taxation. You will learn about the definition of a partnership, the tax consequences of forming a partnership, the effect of contributions to the partnership and distributions by the partnership, the determination of basis and the tax treatment of partnership liabilities, the calculation and allocation of partnership income, the disposition of partnership interests and the tax treatment of retiring partners, the tax treatment of transactions between a partnership and its partners, partnership mergers and divisions, and the myriad anti-abuse rules that are now part of the partnership tax universe. Each of these areas has its own rules, some of which are instinctual, some of which are artificial, and many of which are subject to complex rules and Regulations.

As a tax practitioner in the partnership area, you will need to be fully conversant with the rules that are discussed herein. But you also need to have a fundamental understanding of the "spirit" which underlies these rules, which is that a partnership provides a means for different persons to jointly conduct economic arrangements. The tax consequences of the partnership should be linked inextricably to the underlying economic arrangement, and although the rules are complex, they are generally intended to reach that result. Indeed, it is most likely that an anti-abuse rule will apply any time that the partnership tax rules lead to a result which is non-economic or does not appear to be consistent with the underlying economic arrangement of the partners. And in those situations which happen to lie outside of one of the anti-abuse rules, it is still possible that a court would attempt to recharacterize the transaction — whether under substance over form principles or simply on the basis of "economic reality" — so as to cause the tax consequences of the transaction to comport with the economic arrangement of the partners.

When you are advising partnerships, therefore, you should always be mindful of the underlying economic arrangement. The partnership agreement, and all of the other documents evidencing the partnership and the arrangements of the partners, should be drafted so as to clearly embody and further the partners' intent. Indeed, it often is best to state clearly in the agreement both the intended economic effect and intended tax consequences of the partnership transaction. If it cannot be stated clearly and succinctly, or if the partners are not willing to allow their intent to see the light of day, then the practitioner should be concerned about the substance of the transaction and the resulting tax consequences. However, if the partners' economic arrangement is clear and the intended tax consequences flow inevitably from the partners' economic arrangement, then it is likely that both will be respected. The practitioner's goal should be to create partnership arrangements and transactions where, notwithstanding the complexity of the Code, the Regulations, the rulings, and the case law, there is little doubt as to what the tax consequences will be.

Chapter 1

DEFINING PARTNERSHIPS AND PARTNERS FOR TAX PURPOSES

§ 1.01 INTRODUCTION

Chapter 1 will focus on the definition of a partner and a partnership for U.S. federal income tax purposes. It will analyze the *Culbertson-Luna* factors and similar criteria and provide an introduction to the check-the-box Regulations.[1] This chapter will also consider contractual alliances that are taxed as partnerships and compare other contractual arrangements, such as leases, loans, and tenancies in common to partnerships, and address other similar issues. In addition, this chapter will introduce the aggregate and entity theories of partnerships. Publicly traded partnerships will also be discussed.

§ 1.02 THE EXISTENCE OF A BUSINESS ENTITY

This text is about the U.S. federal income taxation of business entities classified as partnerships. The rules governing the taxation of partnerships are provided in the Code, the Regulations promulgated by the Department of the Treasury interpreting and implementing the Code (the "*Regulations*" or "*Treas. Reg.*"), and cases and rulings interpreting and applying the Code and Regulations. The portion of the Regulations dealing with entity classification is commonly called the "check-the-box" Regulations, because these Regulations provide an election to change the tax treatment of some types of entities by "checking the box" and filing the appropriate form. Under the check-the-box Regulations, one must first have determined that a business entity exists before one can conclude that a partnership exists.[2]

Many times, the existence of a business entity will be apparent. If a partnership or a limited liability company (an "*LLC*") is formed under a U.S. domestic state law with a valid business or financial purpose on other than a transitory basis, there is likely to be little question that a business entity exists. Controversies may develop, however, as to whether the entity has been formed for a valid business or financial purpose and whether the entity has been formed other than on a transitory basis.[3]

---

[1] Treas. Reg. §§ 301.7701-1 to -4 as modified in 1995 and subsequently.

[2] Treas. Reg. § 301.7701-2.

[3] *See, e.g.*, Commissioner v. Tower, 327 U.S. 280 (1946); ASA Investerings Partnership v. Commissioner, 201 F.3d 505 (D.C. Cir. 2000).

For example, in *Andantech L.L.C. v. Commissioner*,[4] a Wyoming LLC was disregarded by the Tax Court because the LLC was not formed for the purpose of carrying on a business. In *Andantech*, the LLC was formed to enter into a series of sale-leaseback transactions with a lessor of computer equipment subject to existing leases.[5] The LLC then entered into a series of transactions in which income was theoretically accelerated into a year in which tax indifferent partners[6] were allocated the income by the LLC. In a later year, a loss was recognized by the LLC, which was allocated to the U.S. taxable partners. In disregarding the LLC, the court concluded in the alternative that: (i) a valid business activity does not include an activity whose sole purpose is tax avoidance and (ii) the structure should be collapsed together as transitory under the step-transaction doctrine. Under either approach, the LLC could be disregarded because it was not formed by persons for the purpose of carrying on a trade or business or sharing in the profit or loss from the transaction.[7]

Similarly, if a partnership is formed merely to reallocate income from one spouse to the other spouse, the partnership will be ignored and the spouse who produced the income will be taxable on the entire income.[8] In *Commissioner v. Tower*, the U.S. Supreme Court noted that spouses could be partners for tax purposes as well as for other purposes, if each spouse invests capital originating with the contributing spouse, contributes substantially to the control and management of the business, or otherwise performs essential services to the entity.[9] However, if a spouse contributes none of the items just listed, an issue is raised as to whether the partners truly intended to join together for the purpose of carrying on business and sharing in the profits or losses or both.[10]

On the other hand, it is also possible to create a business entity for U.S. federal income tax purposes without creating an entity for state law purposes. Treas. Reg. § 301.7701-1(a)(2) provides that a "joint venture or other contractual arrangement may create a separate entity for federal tax purposes if the participants carry on a trade, business, financial operation, or venture and divide the profits therefrom." A continuing question arises as to whether "other contractual arrangements" create a business entity for tax purposes.

---

[4] T.C.M. (RIA) ¶ 2002–097 (2002), *aff'd*, 331 F.3d 972 (D.C. Cir. 2003).

[5] A sale-leaseback transaction is a transaction in which the owner of property sells the property to a buyer and then leases the property back.

[6] Tax indifferent partners are partners that are either not subject to U.S. tax on the type of income allocated to them or which have so many net operating losses or tax credits that they have a very low effective tax rate.

[7] *Andantech* at 541.

[8] Commissioner v. Tower, 327 U.S. 280 (1946).

[9] *Id.*

[10] *Id.*

§ 1.03   CLASSIFYING PARTNERSHIPS FOR TAX PURPOSES

A.   The Nature of Partnerships

I.R.C. §§ 761(a) and 7701(a)(2) define a partnership as a syndicate, group, pool, joint venture, or other unincorporated organization, through or by means of which any business, financial operation, or venture is carried on, and which is not a trust or estate or a corporation. The definition is quite broad and, as mentioned above, the definition may cause some undertakings that are not business entities for state law purposes to be treated as partnerships for federal tax purposes. However, not every joint undertaking gives rise to a partnership for federal tax purposes. The definition may also be applied to cause an entity treated as a business entity for state law purposes to be disregarded as an entity for federal tax purposes.[11]

In order for a federal tax partnership to exist, the parties must, in good faith and with a business purpose, intend to join together in the present conduct of an enterprise and share in the profits or losses of the enterprise. For these purposes, whether the entity exists or does not exist under state law does not determine whether or not it exists for federal income tax purposes.[12] The existence of a valid partnership depends on all of the facts, including the agreement of the parties, the conduct of the parties in execution of its provisions, their statements, the testimony of disinterested persons, the relationship of the parties, their respective abilities and capital contributions, the actual control of income and the purposes for which it is used, and any other facts throwing light on the parties' true intent (the factors just listed are known as the "*Culbertson factors*"). The analysis of the *Culbertson* factors shows whether the parties in good faith and action, with a business purpose, intended to join together for the present conduct of an undertaking or enterprise.[13]

In *Luna v. Commissioner*,[14] the Tax Court distilled the principles of *Tower* and *Culbertson* to the following factors as being relevant in evaluating whether parties intend to create a partnership for federal income tax purposes (the "*Luna factors*"):

> the agreement of the parties and their conduct in executing its terms; the contributions, if any, which each party has made to the venture; the parties' control over income and capital and the right of each to make withdrawals; whether each party was a principal and coproprietor, sharing a mutual proprietary interest in the net profits and having an obligation to share losses, or whether one party was the agent or employee of the other, receiving for his services contingent compensation in the form of a percentage of income; whether business was conducted in the joint names of the parties; whether the parties filed Federal partnership returns or

---

[11] Reinberg v. Commissioner, 90 T.C. 116 (1988); Bussing v. Commissioner, 88 T.C. 449 (1987).

[12] Commissioner v. Tower, 327 U.S. 280 (1946).

[13] Commissioner v. Culbertson, 337 U.S. 733 (1949); ASA Investerings Partnership v. Commissioner, 201 F.3d 505 (D.C. Cir.), *cert. denied*, 531 U.S. 871 (2000).

[14] 42 T.C. 1067 (1964).

otherwise represented to respondent or to persons with whom they dealt that they were joint venturers; whether separate books of account were maintained for the venture; and whether the parties exercised mutual control over and assumed mutual responsibilities for the enterprise.[15]

None of the *Culbertson* factors or the *Luna* factors is conclusive of the existence of a partnership. In *Culbertson*, the U.S. Supreme Court rejected the notion that there exists a set of specific criteria for determining whether or not a partnership exists for tax purposes. Instead, all of the facts must be considered to determine whether the parties "intended to join together in the present conduct of the enterprise."[16]

Although the Regulations concerning the classification of entities have changed radically since the time of the *Culbertson* and *Luna* decisions, the decisions are still relevant for the purposes of: (i) determining whether a relationship that is not formed as an entity for state law purposes should be treated as a business entity for federal tax purposes and (ii) determining whether an entity formed under state law should be ignored as a business entity for federal tax purposes.

B.   The Classification of Domestic Business Entities

Once it is determined that a domestic business entity[17] has been formed, under the check-the-box Regulations the entity must be classified as a disregarded entity, a partnership, or a corporation.[18]

If a business entity has only one owner, the entity will generally be treated as a corporation, if formed as a corporation, or as a disregarded entity, if not formed as a corporation.[19] A disregarded entity is one that is ignored for federal tax purposes. Thus, an LLC owned by an individual would, for federal tax purposes, ordinarily be treated as if the individual owned the assets of the LLC (i.e., typically as a sole proprietorship). Note that for state law purposes, the LLC remains an independent juridical entity with a full liability shield.

If a domestic business entity has more than one owner (for federal tax purposes), the entity may not be a disregarded entity. In other words, the entity must either be a corporation or a partnership. In general, under the check-the-box Regulations, whether a business entity with more than one owner is treated as a corporation or a partnership is determined by whether the entity has been formed as a corporation.[20] If a domestic entity is an unincorporated business entity with more than one owner, the default classification of the entity will be a partnership.

---

[15] *Id.* at 1077–78. *See also* Estate of Kahn v. Commissioner, 499 F.2d 1186 (2d Cir. 1974).

[16] 337 U.S. at 742.

[17] In this context, a "domestic" business entity means created or organized in the United States or under the laws of the United States or of any state. I.R.C. § 7701(a)(4). In Notice 2010-31, 2010-16 I.R.B. 594, the IRS indicated that a domestic partnership may be treated as a foreign partnership for the purposes of identifying the U.S. shareholders of a controlled foreign corporation.

[18] Treas. Reg. § 301.7701-2.

[19] *Id.*

[20] *Id.*

Whether an entity has more than one owner is determined under federal tax principles, rather than solely under state law. For example, a domestic LLC with more than one member for state law purposes may be a disregarded entity if one of its members is itself a disregarded entity owned by the other member.[21] Similarly, an LLC with two members for state law purposes was treated as a disregarded entity where one of the members had no economic rights in the LLC.[22] Under the check-the-box Regulations, a domestic unincorporated business entity may also elect to be treated as a corporation.[23] It would be unusual to make an election to be taxed as a C corporation with its double taxation, but it sometimes happens that an election is made to be taxed as an S corporation. Why not just form a corporation to begin with? Some prefer the more modern statutory architecture of LLCs, but now we digress into a topic best left for a business organizations course.

One exception to the general rule that domestic business entities with more than one owner may not be treated as disregarded entities is a spousal partnership. I.R.C. § 761(f) provides that a husband and wife who operate a joint venture may elect not to treat the joint venture as a partnership; in other words, they may treat it as a disregarded entity. In order to qualify, both spouses must materially participate in the business of the entity, and they must file a joint return. Rev. Proc. 2002-69[24] also allows spousal partnerships to be disregarded in community property states without regard to the material participation standard.

Some states have enacted legislation that provides for series LLCs. A series LLC is generally an LLC that has internal series or divisions that may have separate members, managers, assets, liabilities, business purpose, etc. In PLR 200803004 (Jan. 18, 2008), the IRS issued its first private letter ruling on the classification of a series LLC. In that Private Ruling, certain series LLCs that had only a single owner would not elect to be taxed as a corporation. Other series, which had more than one member, would not elect to be treated as other than a partnership, whereas a third group of series LLCs would be treated as corporations. The Private Ruling contained a number of representations by the taxpayer, including that each member's share of the profit and loss of a series would be based solely upon the items of income and loss of that series, that each series would consist of a separate pool of assets, liabilities, and earnings, but upon a redemption, liquidation, or termination of the series, the members of that series would only share in the assets of that series and that the creditors of each series would be limited to the assets of that series. The Private Ruling held that those series which had a single member would be treated as a disregarded entity (in the same manner as a single member LLC), that those series with multiple owners which did not elect to be taxed as other than a partnership would be taxed as a partnership, and that those series which elected to be classified as a corporation would be so classified. In effect, the Private Ruling stands for the proposition that each series would be treated as a separate entity for federal income tax purposes,

---

[21] Rev. Rul. 2004-77, 2004-2 C.B. 119.

[22] PLR 199911033 (Mar. 22, 1999).

[23] Treas. Reg. § 301.7701-3.

[24] 2002-2 C.B. 831.

and that each series need not have the same tax classification. In September 2010, the IRS proposed Regulations under Reg. § 301.7701-1 that would generally follow the same pattern of analysis as reflected in PLR 200803004.

For a detailed discussion of series LLCs, see § 1.08.

C.   The Classification of Non-U.S. Business Entities

The classification of non-U.S. entities must, again, start with the question of whether or not the entity is a business entity. The question is somewhat complicated because the system of classification of entities in other countries is often different from that of the United States.

To provide clarity as to the classification of a variety of non-U.S. entities, the check-the-box Regulations provide a list of non-U.S. entities that will be treated as corporations and are not eligible to elect to be treated otherwise.[25] The preamble to the originally proposed version of the check-the-box Regulations indicates that it was the intent to give *per se* corporation treatment to entities that would have unavoidably been classified as corporations under the prior entity classification Regulations.[26]

If a non-U.S. business entity is not *per se* classified as a corporation under the check-the-box Regulations, an analysis is applied which is very similar to that applied to domestic unincorporated business entities, except that the starting place is generally a default classification of the entity as a corporation.[27] In other words, a non-U.S. entity that is not a *per se* corporation may elect to be either a disregarded business entity or a partnership for U.S. tax purposes, depending upon whether the entity has one owner or more than one owner.

If the liability of all owners is limited, the default classification for a non-U.S. business entity is as a corporation. If the liability of any owner of the entity is not limited, the default classification of the entity is either as a disregarded entity, if the entity has only one owner, or as a partnership, if the entity has more than one owner.[28] Like domestic disregarded business entities and partnerships, such non-U.S. entities may elect to be treated as corporations for U.S. tax purposes, if such treatment is desired.[29]

---

[25] Treas. Reg. § 301.7701-2. For example, all Canadian companies are *per se* corporations, unless the liability of at least one member is not limited.

[26] Notice of Prop. Rulemaking, 61 F.R. 93, 21989 (May 13, 1996). Under the prior entity classification Regulations, an entity was classified as an association taxable as a corporation if it had more than two of the following four factors: (i) centralized management, (ii) perpetual life, (iii) free transferability of interests, and (iv) limitation of liability. Treas. Reg. § 301.7701-2 prior to amendment by T.D. 8697, 61 F.R. 244, 66584 (Dec. 18, 1996). *See also* Kintner v. United States, 107 F. Supp. 976 (D. Mt. 1952). Many of the *per se* corporations are usually publicly held.

[27] Treas. Reg. §§ 301.7701-2, -3.

[28] Treas. Reg. § 301.7701-3(b)(2).

[29] Treas. Reg. § 301.7701-3(a).

D. Reclassifying Partnerships as Corporations

1. An Election Under Treas. Reg. § 301.7701-3

As mentioned above, if an entity is initially classified as a partnership, the entity may still elect to be treated as a corporation. Under current Regulations, the election is made by filing Form 8832 with the IRS. The election may be retroactive up to 75 days prior to the time the election is filed. Upon the effectiveness of an election to be treated as a corporation, the partnership is treated as transferring all of its assets to a newly formed corporation and then liquidating.[30]

2. Publicly Traded Partnerships

If a business entity would otherwise be treated as a partnership, but its interests are publicly traded on an established securities market or are readily tradable on a secondary market (or the substantial equivalent), then, in general, the entity is treated as if it were a corporation for federal income tax purposes.[31] However, if at least 90% of the gross income of the partnership for each taxable year after 1987 is comprised of interest, dividends, real property rents, gain from the sale or disposition of real property, income and gain derived from the exploration, development, mining or production, processing, refining, transportation (including pipelines transporting gas, oil, or products thereof) or the marketing of any mineral or natural resources (including fertilizer, geothermal energy, and timber), any gain from the sale or disposition of a capital asset (or property used in a trade or business) held for the production of income described in this sentence and, for certain partnerships, income and gain from commodities (not treated as inventory) or futures, forwards, and options with respect to commodities, then the partnership will still be treated as a partnership.[32]

The interests in the partnership are considered readily tradable on a secondary market or the substantial equivalent if, taking into account all of the facts and circumstances, the partners are readily able to buy, sell, or exchange their partnership interests in a manner that is comparable, economically, to trading on an established securities market.[33] The Regulations provide an extensive list of circumstances under which interests will be deemed to be readily tradable on a

---

[30] Treas. Reg. § 301.7701-3(g)(1)(i).

[31] I.R.C. § 7704.

[32] I.R.C. § 7704(c). The 90% of gross income exception does not apply to any partnership which would be described in I.R.C. § 851(a) (relating to regulated investment companies) if such partnership were a domestic corporation. However, to the extent provided in Regulations, the regulated investment company exception to the 90% of gross income exception will not apply to any partnership which has as a principal activity the buying and selling of commodities (not treated as inventory) or options, futures, or forward contracts with respect to commodities. To date, no Regulations have been promulgated that provide for the commodity trading exception. The qualification of commodities-type income for the 90% of gross income exception only applies to partnerships that have as a principal activity the buying and selling of commodities (not treated as inventory) or options, futures, or forward contracts with respect to commodities.

[33] Treas. Reg. § 1.7704-1(c)(1).

secondary market or the substantial equivalent thereof.[34]

Interests in a partnership are not deemed to be readily tradable on a secondary market or the substantial equivalent thereof unless: (i) the partnership participates in the establishment of the market or the inclusion of its interests thereon or (ii) the partnership recognizes the transfers made on the market by redeeming the transferor partner or admitting the transferee as a partner or otherwise recognizing any rights of the transferee.[35] Also, subject to certain limitations, interests in a partnership are not readily tradable on a secondary market or the substantial equivalent thereof if all interests in the partnership were issued in a transaction (or transactions) that was not required to be registered under the Securities Act of 1933[36] and the partnership does not have more than 100 partners at any time during the taxable year of the partnership.[37]

3.   Taxable Mortgage Pools

Although not publicly traded, a taxable mortgage pool may also be treated as a corporation. Primarily related to mortgage securitizations, if an entity is treated as a taxable mortgage pool, then the entity is treated as a separate corporation that is not entitled to participate in a consolidated group. In general, an entity will be considered a taxable mortgage pool if: (i) substantially all of its assets are debt obligations, 50% or more of which are real estate mortgages, (ii) the entity is the obligor under debt obligations with two or more maturities, and (iii) payments on the debt obligations under which the entity is the obligor bear a relationship to payments on the debt obligations that the entity holds as assets.[38] If less than 80% of the assets consist of debt obligations (or interests therein), then less than substantially all of the assets of the entity consist of debt obligations (or interests therein).[39]

Although taxable mortgage pools are subject to tax as corporations, most transactions that would otherwise have been subject to the taxable mortgage pools rules are now formed as real estate mortgage investment conduits.[40]

§ 1.04   DISTINGUISHING PARTNERSHIPS FROM OTHER CONTRACTUAL ARRANGEMENTS

As mentioned above, one of the classic definitions of a partnership is when the parties join together in the present conduct of an enterprise and share the profits or losses of the enterprise.[41] This approach raises questions as to whether a

---

[34]   Treas. Reg. § 1.7704-1(c)(2).

[35]   Treas. Reg. § 1.7704-1(d).

[36]   15 U.S.C. § 77a.

[37]   Treas. Reg. § 1.7704-1(h).

[38]   Treas. Reg. § 301.7701(i)-1(b)(1).

[39]   Treas. Reg. § 301.7701-1(c)(2)(ii).

[40]   *See* I.R.C. § 860A and sections following. A discussion of real estate mortgage investment conduits is beyond the scope of this text.

[41]   Commissioner v. Tower, 327 U.S. 280 (1946).

partnership exists whenever there is an arrangement to share profits or losses of an enterprise. Not all profit-sharing arrangements result in the creation of a partnership for tax purposes.

A. Distinguishing Partnerships from Loans

Agreeing to pay a party advancing funds a percentage of the revenues of a venture should not result in a tax partnership without further evidence of the intent to create a partnership.[42] In *Williams*, a spouse made no contribution to the capital of a venture, assumed no risk, and provided no services. The promise by the spouse operating the venture to pay her half of the profits did not transform the loan into a partnership interest. Similarly, subject to some limitations, when a portion of the interest on an instrument that would otherwise be characterized as debt is based upon the appreciation of the value of property of the borrower, the shared appreciation aspect does not automatically cause the loan to be recharacterized as an equity instrument.[43]

When one party to a transaction only receives a return based upon the period of time the loan is outstanding and is shielded from the risks of the transaction, the party is not a joint venturer.[44] In *O'Hare*, a lender required the purchaser of property to obtain a credit enhancer and place the property in the credit enhancer's name. The credit enhancer treated itself as being entitled to capital gain treatment on the ultimate disposition of the property rather than recognizing ordinary income in the form of interest or a guarantee fee. The credit enhancer asserted that it had the risk of loss on the loan advanced and so should be treated as having an interest in the property. The Tax Court found that the credit enhancer's actual risk was the same as any lender's.

The analysis of *O'Hare* was recently affirmed in *ASA Investerings Partnership v. Commissioner*.[45] In *ASA Investerings Partnership*, the Tax Court first disregarded several parties as mere agents in determining whether the parties had formed a valid partnership. In reaching its conclusion that the remaining parties did not intend to join together in the present conduct of an enterprise, the court found that one of the parties was in substance a lender.[46]

On the other hand, where a purported lender is not obligated to be paid in all events but only has a right to be paid out of 50% of the net profits of the venture,

---

[42] Commissioner v. Williams, 256 F.2d 152 (5th Cir. 1958). *See also* Astoria Marine Construction Co. v. Commissioner, T.C.M. (RIA) ¶ 45,083 (1945).

[43] Rev. Rul. 83-51, 1983-1 C.B. 48. In one case, *Farley Realty Corp. v. Commissioner*, 279 F.2d 701 (2d Cir. 1960), the court held that the appreciation rights could be treated separately from the remaining instrument treating part of the instrument as debt and part as equity. Rev. Rul. 83-51 appears to be a concession that the holding of *Farley Realty Corp.* is not the general rule.

[44] O'Hare v. Commissioner, T.C.M. (RIA) ¶ 80,034 (1980), *aff'd*, 641 F.2d 83 (2d Cir. 1981); Astoria Marine Construction Co. v. Commissioner, T.C.M. (RIA) ¶ 45,083 (1945).

[45] T.C.M. (RIA) ¶ 98,305 (1998), *aff'd*, 201 F.3d 505 (D.C. Cir. 2000), *cert denied*, 531 U.S. 871 (2000).

[46] Of particular importance to the decision that the relationship was not a partnership, the court found that ABN's (the purported partner) interest was limited to a specified return (approximately LIBOR plus 75 basis points) and that AlliedSignal (the other purported partner) effectively protected ABN from loss on the transaction.

the lender was treated as a partner for tax purposes.[47]

B.   Distinguishing Partnerships from Service Agreements

The owner of a business may agree to compensate a hired manager or key employee with a percentage of the income of the business, or a broker may be retained to sell property for a commission based on the net or gross sales price without creating a partnership for tax purposes.[48]

In *Estate of Smith*,[49] an investment manager characterized the contracts with its customers as joint venture agreements. Although the agreements gave the investment manager a percentage of the profits, the court found that the investment manager had no economic interest in the capital or commodities purchased, no right to withdraw funds, and no right to a distribution on termination of the relationship. Under these circumstances, where the parties did not display an intent to create a partnership, no partnership was created for tax purposes.

Similarly, there was no partnership where the taxpayer was to receive a percentage of the renewal commissions from an insurance policy he had designed in exchange for his management services to the insurance company where the facts indicated that the parties intended a commission relationship rather than a partnership.[50]

C.   Distinguishing Partnerships from Leases

A working interest in an oil and gas lease is often held to be an interest in a partnership. In *Bentex Oil Corporation v. Commissioner*,[51] where each part owner of a working interest in an oil and gas lease was responsible for their proportionate share of the expenses of the exploration and production, the co-owners could separately commit or not commit to any exploration and the co-owners took their proportionate share of the production in kind and sold it separately, the court held that there was "no doubt" that the arrangement was a partnership.[52]

In contrast, non-energy-related leaseholds do not have the same presumption of partnership status. For example, where a landlord and tenant under a crop-share lease split the cost of seed, fertilizer, limestone, herbicides, insecticides, soil tests, and grain drying and the rent paid was 50% of farm production, no tax partnership was created when the parties did not intend to create a partnership, neither held itself out as a partner and neither undertook the other's expenses or

---

[47]   Hartman v. Commissioner, T.C.M. (RIA) ¶ 58,206 (1958).

[48]   Comtek Expositions, Inc. v. Commissioner, 85 T.C.M. (CCH) 1280 (2003).

[49]   313 F.2d 724 (8th Cir. 1963).

[50]   Luna v. Commissioner, 42 T.C. 1067 (1964).

[51]   20 T.C. 565 (1953).

[52]   It may also be significant that the co-owners of the lease filed partnership returns for three years. Working interests in oil and gas leases are also often viewed as partnerships for state law purposes. *See, e.g.*, Wagner Supply Co. v. Bateman, 18 S.W.2d 1052 (Tex. 1929).

responsibilities.[53]

Rents may be based upon a percentage of the gross receipts of a tenant without causing the rents or the lease to be recharacterized.[54] But if the "landlord" controls all of the receipts of the "tenant" and pays all the expenses of the tenant's operation, the lease may be ignored and the "rent" recharacterized as partnership income.[55]

D. Distinguishing Partnerships from Other Co-Ownerships

A mere co-ownership of property does not create a partnership for federal income tax purposes.[56] A co-ownership of property that is maintained, kept in repair, and rented or leased does not constitute a business entity for tax purposes absent other activities of the co-owners.[57] However, co-owners may also be partners if they or their agents carry on sufficient business activity. The distinction between mere co-owners and co-owners who are partners for income tax purposes lies in the degree of business activity of the co-owners or their agents.[58] For example, a separate entity exists for federal income tax purposes if co-owners of an apartment building lease space and in addition provide services to the occupants either directly or through an agent.[59]

However, in Revenue Ruling 75-374,[60] two parties each owned an undivided one-half interest in an apartment building. A management company retained by the co-owners managed the building. Customary tenant services, such as heat, air conditioning, trash removal, unattended parking, and maintenance of public areas, were provided at no extra charge. Additional services were provided by the management company for a separate charge. The IRS ruled that the customary services were not extensive enough to cause the co-ownership to be treated as a partnership. In addition, because the management company was not an agent of the owners and the owners did not share in the fee for non-customary services, the non-customary services did not cause the co-ownership to be treated as a partnership.

On the other hand, where a sponsor acquires property, negotiates a master lease on the property, and arranges for financing, the relationship between the sponsor (or persons related to the sponsor) and the co-owners may cause the co-ownership

---

[53] Harlan E. Moore Charitable Trust v. United States, 812 F. Supp. 130 (C.D. Ill. 1993), aff'd, 9 F.3d 623 (7th Cir. 1993), acq. 1994-2 C.B. 1. The language of both the trial court and the appellate court suggests that the intent was to create a special rule for sharecropping, rather than create a general rule for interpreting leases.

[54] See H.R. Conf. Rep. No. 100-495, 947, Omnibus Budget Reconciliation Act of 1987, Pub. L. No. 100-203, 1987 U.S.C.C.A.N. 2313, 1693.

[55] Campise v. Commissioner, T.C.M. (RIA) ¶ 80,130 (1980).

[56] See Estate of Appleby v. Commissioner, 41 B.T.A. 18 (1940), aff'd, 123 F.2d 700 (2d Cir. 1941).

[57] Treas. Reg. § 301.7701-1(a)(2).

[58] Cusick v. Commissioner, 76 T.C.M. (CCH) 241 (1998).

[59] Treas. Reg. § 301.7701-1(a)(2).

[60] 1975-2 C.B. 261.

to be treated as a partnership. In *Bergford v. Commissioner*,[61] 78 investors purchased "co-ownership" interests in computer equipment subject to a seven-year net lease. The co-owners authorized the manager to arrange financing and refinancing, purchase and lease the equipment, collect rents and apply those rents to the notes used to finance the equipment, prepare statements, and advance funds to participants on an interest-free basis to meet cash flow. Under some circumstances, the manager could decide to sell the property. Based upon the authority given to the manager, the court held that the co-ownership was a partnership for tax purposes.

Similarly, the sharing of the output of the venture may be the equivalent of sharing in the profits of the venture, creating a partnership for tax purposes.[62] In *Madison Gas & Electric Co.*, three utility companies joined together to build and operate a nuclear power plant. The Tax Court held that the venture was a partnership because the parties had joined together to produce a common product with economies of scale and take the product in kind.

To provide some clarity in one aspect of the distinction between partnerships and other co-ownerships, the IRS promulgated Revenue Procedure 2002-22,[63] under which taxpayers who are co-owners of real estate may apply for a ruling that the co-ownership does not constitute a partnership for federal tax purposes. To qualify for a ruling, a taxpayer must satisfy a number of technical requirements, including the following:

Each of the co-owners must hold title to the property (either directly or through a disregarded entity) as a tenant in common under local law.

The number of co-owners must be limited to no more than 35 persons.

The co-owners must retain the right to approve, by unanimous vote, the hiring of any manager, the sale or other disposition of the property, any leases of a portion or all of the property or the creation or modification of a blanket lien. Management agreements may not last more than one year.

In general, each co-owner must have the right to transfer, partition, and encumber the co-owner's undivided interest in the property without the agreement or approval of any person.

Each co-owner must share in all revenues generated by the property and all costs associated with the property in proportion to the co-owner's undivided interest in the property.

All leasing arrangements must be bona fide leases for federal tax purposes.

---

[61]   12 F.3d 166 (9th Cir. 1993).

[62]   Madison Gas & Electric Co. v. Commissioner, 72 T.C. 521 (1979).

[63]   2002-1 C.B. 733.

§ 1.05 DETERMINING WHO IS A PARTNER

The *Culbertson-Luna* factors again become relevant in determining who are the partners in a venture once it is determined that a partnership exists. In *Tower*, *Culbertson*, and *Luna*, part of the issue being addressed by the court was whether persons who claimed to be partners were partners.

As mentioned above, in *Tower*, the U.S. Supreme Court noted that spouses could be partners for tax purposes as well as for other purposes, if each spouse invests capital originating with the contributing spouse, contributes substantially to the control and management of the business, or otherwise performs essential services to the entity.[64] However, if a spouse contributes none of the items just listed, an issue is raised as to whether the partners truly intended to join together for the purpose of carrying on business and sharing in the profits or losses or both.[65] In *Culbertson*, the court concluded that the sons were not partners because they did not have a present commitment to contribute capital or services to the business.[66] In *Luna*, the taxpayer was not a partner although he was to receive a percentage of the renewal commissions from an insurance policy he had designed in exchange for his management services to the insurance company where the facts indicated that the parties intended a commission relationship rather than a partnership.[67]

If a purported partner's only interest is a fixed return with a fixed maturity date, which is insulated from the success or losses of the venture, the "partner" may in substance be a lender.[68] But where a purported lender is only payable out of 50% of the net profits of the venture, the "lender" is in substance a partner.[69]

Although the Supreme Court in *Tower* suggested that a partner must have contributed capital originating with the partner, under current law a person is recognized as a partner if the person owns a capital interest in a partnership in which capital is a material income-producing factor, whether or not such interest was derived by purchase or gift from any other person.[70] Whether or not ownership of the partnership interest has been transferred will be determined by all the facts and circumstances, including: (i) the degree of direct or indirect control retained by the transferor, (ii) the ability of the transferee to participate in management, (iii) the right of the transferee to receive distributions of the income of the venture, (iv) the participation of the transferee in the conduct of the business of the venture, (v) the age and competence of the transferee, and (vi) whether the transferee is

---

[64] 327 U.S. at 290.

[65] *Id.* at 287.

[66] Commissioner v. Culbertson, 337 U.S. 733 (1949). However, it should be noted that the Supreme Court was divided in the decision and a concurring opinion stated that the sons' contributions to capital, their participation in the income, and their commitments to return to the ranch or otherwise to render service to the partnership were among the material factors to be considered.

[67] Luna v. Commissioner, 42 T.C. 1067 (1964).

[68] ASA Investerings Partnership v. Commissioner, 76 T.C.M. (CCH) 325 (1998), *aff'd*, 201 F.3d 505 (D.C. Cir. 2000).

[69] Hartman v. Commissioner, T.C.M. (RIA) ¶ 58,206 (1958).

[70] I.R.C. § 704(e)(1).

motivated by tax-avoidance.[71]

In January 2003, the Treasury released Proposed Regulations[72] to add a new Prop. Treas. Reg. § 1.761-3 that would provide tests to determine whether a noncompensatory option should be treated as an interest in a partnership. Such Proposed Regulations will be discussed in greater detail in Chapter 10.

§ 1.06   ELECTING OUT OF SUBCHAPTER K

The members of an unincorporated organization may elect to have the organization excluded from the application of Subchapter K.[73] An unincorporated organization may only make such an election if it is availed of: (i) for investment purposes only and not for the active conduct of a business, (ii) for the joint production, extraction, or use of property, but not for the purpose of selling services or property produced or extracted, or (iii) by dealers in securities for a short period for the purposes of underwriting, selling, or distributing a particular issue of securities.[74]

Investors in investment property may elect out of Subchapter K if: (i) they own the property as co-owners, (ii) the co-owners reserve the right to separately take or dispose of their shares of any property acquired or retained, and (iii) the co-owners do not actively conduct a business or irrevocably authorize some person or persons to purchase, sell, or exchange such investment property. The Regulations would allow, however, a delegation of the right to purchase, sell, or exchange the property for a period of not more than one year.[75]

Where the participants engage in the joint production, extraction or use of property, the participants may elect out of Subchapter K if: (i) they own the property as co-owners, either in fee, under lease or under another form of contract granting exclusive operating rights, (ii) the co-owners reserve the right separately to take in kind or dispose of their shares of any property produced, extracted or used, and (iii) they do not jointly sell services or the property, produced or extracted, although each participant may separately delegate authority to sell for periods of not more than one year.[76]

The election may be made explicitly by a statement attached to Form 1065 not later than the time for filing the return (including extensions),[77] or the election can be made implicitly if all parties consistently treat the co-ownership as not being a

---

[71] Treas. Reg. § 1.704-1(e)(2).

[72] REG-103580-02, 68 Fed. Reg. 2930 (Jan. 22, 2003).

[73] Subchapter K includes I.R.C. §§ 701–777.

[74] I.R.C. § 761(a).

[75] Treas. Reg. § 1.761-2(a)(2)(iii). It should be noted that it is the position of the IRS that an entity that is recognized for state law purposes does not constitute a co-ownership that may make an election out of Subchapter K. Rev. Rul. 2004-86, 2004-2 C.B. 191. This Ruling concluded that beneficiaries of a trust classified as a partnership for federal income tax purposes could not elect out of Subchapter K under I.R.C. § 761 because the assets were not owned by the beneficiaries as co-owners under state law.

[76] Treas. Reg. § 1.761-2(a)(3).

[77] Treas. Reg. § 1.761-2(b).

partnership.[78] An implicit election is indicated if either of the following facts is true: (i) at the time of the formation of the organization, there is an agreement among the members that the organization will be excluded from Subchapter K beginning with the first taxable year of the organization; or (ii) the members of the organization owning substantially all of the capital interests report their respective shares of the items of income, deductions, and credits of the organization on their respective returns in a manner consistent with the exclusion of the organization from Subchapter K beginning with the first taxable year of the organization.[79]

If a valid election out of Subchapter K is made, the co-ownership is not generally treated as a partnership for purposes of Subchapter K, but the definitional provisions of I.R.C. § 7701 and the check-the-box Regulations still generally apply for the purposes of the remainder of the Code.[80] In other words, the election out of Subchapter K does not change the nature of the partnership and will apply to a section of the Code outside of Subchapter K only if the section is interdependent with Subchapter K.[81]

§ 1.07   AGGREGATE AND ENTITY THEORIES OF PARTNERSHIP TAXATION

The modern concept of partnerships derived originally from common law concepts of joint ownership and joint obligation.[82] U.S. tax law has moved away from this historical treatment, but still uses a combination of two seemingly contradictory approaches to partnerships: treating partnerships sometimes as entities and sometimes as aggregates of their partners. Under the "entity" theory, (i) a partnership is viewed as a separate entity from the partners, (ii) the incidence of taxation is determined at the partnership level, (iii) the income of the partnership is then allocated among the partners, (iv) partners do not have a direct interest in partnership assets or attributes, and (v) each partner's interest in the partnership is viewed as property separate from the underlying assets and operations of the partnership.[83] In contrast, under the "aggregate" theory, (i) a partnership is viewed as an aggregation of partners, (ii) the partnership is viewed as a mere conduit passing the income through to the partners, and (iii) each partner is viewed as having a direct interest in each partnership asset.[84]

The Code has adopted a combination of the two approaches. Partnership income is determined at the partnership level, recognizing the partnership as an entity for the purposes of income reporting, but the aggregate rule is applied for contributed

---

[78]   Treas. Reg. § 1.761-2(b)(2)(ii).

[79]   *Id.*

[80]   Bryant v. Commissioner, 46 T.C. 848 (1966), *aff'd*, 399 F.2d 800 (5th Cir. 1968); Rev. Rul. 65-118, 1965-1 C.B. 30.

[81]   *See* Bryant v. Commissioner, 46 T.C. 848 (1966), *aff'd*, 399 F.2d 800 (5th Cir. 1968).

[82]   Helvering v. Smith, 90 F.2d 590 (2d Cir. 1937).

[83]   *See* United States v. Basye, 410 U.S. 441 (1973).

[84]   *See* Helvering v. Smith, 90 F.2d 590 (2d Cir. 1937).

property with pre-contribution appreciation.[85] A limited aggregated approach is forced upon the partners in regard to partnerships with unrealized receivables or inventory and in connection with the sale of a partnership interest by a controlled foreign corporation.[86] In addition, elections are also provided causing the basis of partnership assets to be increased or decreased based upon the basis of the transferee of a partnership interest[87] and to not have Subchapter K apply to the entity.[88] But as noted above, the election out of Subchapter K only applies to Subchapter K itself and other provisions of the Code that are integrated with Subchapter K. For other provisions of the Code, even a partnership that wants to be treated as an aggregate must often be treated as an entity.

Partially due to the hybrid approach taken in the Code, the issue of whether an entity or aggregate approach should be applied in a section of the Code that does not make the matter explicit has been a continuing issue of controversy. The U.S. Supreme Court seemingly expressed its frustration that the entity-aggregate issue was still an issue in *United States v. Basye*.[89] Apparently hoping to settle the issue, the court held that a partnership is recognized as an independent entity for the purposes of calculating its income and determining the character of income. After the income is calculated, the court held that a partnership is then treated as a conduit through which the income must pass.

However, taxpayers and the IRS continued to argue over whether the entity or the aggregate approach was most appropriate in particular circumstances. For example, in *Brown Group Inc. v. Commissioner*,[90] the taxpayer argued that the entity approach should be applied to determine whether a partnership (and its partners) recognized Subpart F income,[91] and the IRS took the aggregate approach. The Court of Appeals for the Eighth Circuit agreed with the taxpayer, citing *Basye* for the proposition that the income of a partnership is determined as an independently recognizable entity apart from its partners. Then, the IRS responded by modifying the Regulations governing Subpart F to provide that a controlled foreign corporation's distributive share of any item of income of a partnership is Subpart F income to the extent that it would have been Subpart F income if received directly by the controlled foreign corporation — applying an aggregate approach.[92]

---

[85] S. Rep. No. 1622, Report of the Committee on Finance to Accompany HR 8300, The Internal Revenue Act of 1954, 2d Sess. 89 (1954).

[86] I.R.C. §§ 751, 954(c).

[87] I.R.C. § 754.

[88] I.R.C. § 761(a). However, as noted above, the courts have limited the effect of an election out of Subchapter K to sections of the Code that are interdependent with Subchapter K, causing the partnership to continue to be treated as an entity for other sections of the Code. *See* Bryant v. Commissioner, 46 T.C. 848 (1966), *aff'd*, 399 F.2d 800 (5th Cir. 1968).

[89] 410 U.S. 441 (1973).

[90] 77 F.3d 217 (8th Cir. 1996).

[91] Subpart F income is defined in I.R.C. § 952. Roughly speaking, Subpart F income includes certain types of passive income and certain types of income derived from transactions with related parties where there is a foreign corporation controlled by U.S. shareholders involved.

[92] Treas. Reg. § 1.952-1(g)(1).

Thus, in areas in which there is no existing authority as to whether the entity or aggregate approach should be applied, there is still substantial uncertainty as to what is the most appropriate approach.

§ 1.08 SERIES LLCs

A. Introduction

Following the lead of Delaware, a number of states have enacted "series" LLC legislation.[93] We will mostly focus on the legislation in Delaware. The legislation in the other states is usually quite similar.

The basic concept is that an LLC operating agreement may provide for "series" to be established by the LLC. Each series has its own liability shield. Thus, everything else being equal, a liability of a particular series may only be satisfied by the assets allocated to that series, and not by the assets of other series. Thus, not only does a series LLC have the LLC liability shield, but it can create multiple additional liability shields within itself. Why do that instead of just creating additional LLCs? It is mostly about convenience and possibly about cost. Creating a new series may not require an additional filing with the state and/or federal government. The additional fees that must be paid for new series, if any, may be less than the fees required for creating new LLCs. However, this varies by state, and the cost advantages may not be very significant.

Series LLCs have not yet been very popular, because it is unclear whether the series liability shield will be respected by nonseries states[94] or in bankruptcy.[95] It is also unclear how series will be treated for regulatory, licensing, and nontax purposes generally. Further, until recently, it was also unclear how each series would be classified for federal income tax purposes. We now have guidance in the form of Proposed Regulations, discussed below. Although there are only proposed, not final Regulations, there is now a measure of certainty as to tax classification. This may induce more states to adopt series legislation, which, in turn, may make their use more widespread.[96] Until that happens, the questions on how a series will be treated in a nonseries state are almost endless. Here is a sampling: Will the series liability shield be respected? May a series by itself qualify to do business? Can a series contract in its own name? How will environmental liabilities be assessed? How will sales taxes be applied? How will employment laws be applied?

---

[93] As we got to press, the following states have adopted series LLC legislation: Delaware, Illinois, Iowa, Nevada, Oklahoma, Tennessee, Texas, Utah, and Puerto Rico. Delaware previously permitted series business trusts, and now also permits series limited partnerships. *See* Carter Bishop, The Series LLC: Tax Classification Appears in Rear View, 130 Tax Notes 315 (2011).

[94] *See* GxG Management LLC v. Young Brothers and Co., Inc., 2007 U.S. Dist. LEXIS 12337 (D. Me. 2007); Butler v. Adoption Media, LLC, 2005 U.S. Dist. LEXIS 46208 (N.D. Cal. June 21, 2005) (both cases are unreported).

[95] *See* Shannon Dawson, *Series LLC and Bankruptcy: When the Series Finds Itself in Trouble, Will It Need Its Parent to Bail It Out?*, 35 DEL. J. CORP. L. 515 (2010).

[96] *See* Michael Mcloughlin and Bruce Ely, *IRS Issues Long-Awaited Guidance on Series LLCs, Will the States Soon Follow?*, 20 J. MULTISTATE TAX'N & INCENTIVES 8 (2011).

How will state income taxes be applied? Can it be fraud on creditors to transfer an asset from one series to another? A similar list could be created at the federal level for bankruptcy law, pension law, and securities law.

To date, series LLCs have mostly been used by investment funds and in certain debt offerings, where the existence of the series liability shield is of little importance, and where authority for series investment trusts gave practitioners sufficient confidence about the tax classification. Investment funds, for example, like to use series LLCs because they can create series to house new funds while operating under a single registration under the Investment Company Act of 1940.

The notice that must be provided in Delaware in order for a series to be respected is minimal. All that is required is that notice be given in the certificate of formation that the LLC is taking advantage of the series legislation that limits the liability of a series; Delaware specifically provides that there is no requirement that any specific series of the LLC be referenced in the notice.[97] Further, (1) the operating agreement must provide for the establishment of one or more series and the series limited liability, and (2) records must be maintained for each series accounting for the assets associated with that series separately from the other assets of the LLC, or any other series.[98] If these steps are taken, then the debts, liabilities, obligations, and expenses incurred by a series are enforceable against the assets of that series only, and not against the assets of the LLC generally or any other of its series.[99]

Assets may be "associated" with a series "directly or indirectly"; they may be held in the name of the series, in the name of the LLC, through a nominee or otherwise.[100] Records maintained for a series that reasonably identify its assets, including "by specific listing, category, type, quantity, computational or allocational formula or procedure (including a percentage or share of any asset or assets), or by any other method where the identity of such assets is objectively determinable, will be deemed to account for the assets associated with such series separately from the other assets of the LLC, or any other series thereof."[101] Thus, if the LLC books show assets titled in the name of the LLC as belonging to a particular series, those assets should be protected from the claims against other series. Note that asset ownership can thus be largely anonymous. Further, assets may be assigned to more than one series, though it is unclear how the claims against one series would affect the rights of creditors of other series which are also allocated a portion of the assets.

Each series may carry on any lawful business, except banking, whether or not for profit.[102] Each series can contract, hold title to assets, grant liens and security

---

[97] Del. Code Ann. Tit. 6, § 18-215(b).

[98] *Id.*

[99] *Id.*

[100] *Id.*

[101] *Id.*

[102] Del. Code Ann. Tit. 6, § 18-215(c).

interests, and sue or be sued in its own name.[103] Different LLC members may have different rights, or none at all, in different series; it is perfectly permissible to allocate all of the rights in a particular series to a single person.[104] Further, the LLC itself may own series. If different members have different rights in the various series, and if some assets are allocated to the LLC itself, the LLC is, in effect, just another series. On the other hand, if the LLC owns all of the series, the LLC is a holding company. Note that in latter case, it would be important for the LLC itself to engage in minimal activities, since a creditor of the LLC would have access to all of the assets of the LLC, including the various series.

Delaware law does not provide any rules for the names of various series. Often they are named alphabetically, series A, series B, etc.[105]

Not only may members associated with a series vary, so may managers, along with their powers and duties.[106] Some member or manager rights may be senior to others, and voting rights among members and managers can vary or be taken away altogether, including the right to vote on an amendment to the LLC agreement.[107] In the absence of an agreement, the management of a series is vested in the members associated with the series in proportion to their interests in the profits of the series, with a majority vote controlling.[108] The typical series LLC (perhaps as a consequence of all that flexibility) is manager-managed.[109] How fiduciary duties apply across series is unclear and should be addressed in the LLC operating agreement. The economic interests in a series are assignable, absent a contrary provision in the LLC agreement.[110] Termination of a series has no effect on other series or the LLC itself.[111] The liability shield of an LLC series doing business in Delaware, but formed in another state, is respected.[112]

All of these rules pose major problems for third parties dealing with a series LLC, who would be well-advised to get detailed disclosure of what series they are dealing with, what assets are held by the series, and who manages the series. This is true even if the third parties reside, and the underlying business of the series LLC takes place, in a nonseries state, since while it is not clear that the series liability shield will be respected, it is also not clear that it will not be. And indeed, full disclosure may often be in the best interest of a series LLC that wants its separate series liability shield recognized in a nonseries state (and perhaps even in another series state, as series statutes vary). The language of the statute notwithstanding, good planning would require that the series LLC keep very

---

[103] *Id.*

[104] Del. Code Ann. Tit. 6, § 18-215(e), (f).

[105] Illinois law, on the other hand, requires that a series contain the name of the parent LLC and a distinguishable identifier. 806 Ill. Comp. Stat. 180/37-40(c).

[106] Del. Code Ann. Tit. 6, § 18-215(d).

[107] *Id.*

[108] Del. Code Ann. Tit. 6, § 18-215(f).

[109] *Id.*

[110] Del. Code Ann. Tit. 6, §§ 18-215(j), 18-702.

[111] Del. Code Ann. Tit. 6, § 18-215(k).

[112] Del. Code Ann. Tit. 6, § 18-215(n).

precise records of which assets and liabilities are associated with which series. Separate books and records for each series might be wise. The advisor also needs to ask: Can I trust my client to keep this straight?

Like most states, Delaware has specific rules on when LLCs may make legal distributions to members. Broadly speaking, distributions may not be made if they would prevent the LLC from paying its creditors. Delaware applies these rules to series LLCs at the series level. Thus, even if the LLC as a whole is "under water," a given series may make a distribution as long as after the distribution the fair value of the series' assets exceed its liabilities.[113]

While Delaware went to great lengths to make its series statutes flexible, series still should not be thought of as miniature LLCs. Series cannot exist independent of an LLC, but only as part of an LLC. A series, by itself, may not merge with another LLC, convert to another entity, or domesticate. Further, dissolution of the LLC dissolves the series. Delaware law is silent on the question of whether a series is a separate entity, but given its dependence on the organizing LLC, the answer for state law purposes would appear to be no.[114] That said, at least in its home state a series has most of the capacities of a typical entity, including the right to own property, sue, and be sued.

B.   Tax Classification and the Proposed Regulations

1.   Overview

In understanding how the Proposed Regulations classify series, it is important to understand the fundamentals of entity classification for federal tax purposes discussed earlier in this chapter.[115] Recall that tax classification does not depend upon whether an organization is treated as a separate entity for state law purposes.

Generally, the Proposed Regulations treat a series as a separate entity.[116] The classification of the series is then determined under the check-the-box regulations. Further, while we will focus on series LLCs, the Proposed Regulations apply to other types of series entities as well, including series limited partnerships, series

---

[113]   Del. Code Ann. Tit. 6, § 18-215(i).

[114]   Illinois and Iowa specifically provide that a series is a separate entity, though their series too are dependent on the organizing LLC. 805 Ill. Comp. Stat. 180/37-40(b); Iowa Code Ann. § 489.1201. The California Franchise Tax Board takes the position that each series in a Delaware series LLC is a separate entity for California income and franchise tax purposes, and each series must qualify in California (and pay separate fees) if it is registered or transacting business in California. Instructions to Form 568, 2005 Limited Liability Company Tax Booklet.

[115]   Our discussion of the Proposed Regulations draws extensively from an article on the Proposed Regulations co-authored by one of our co-authors, Paul Carman. *See* Paul D. Carman, Steven G. Frost & Kelley M. Bender, *First Steps — Proposed Regulations on Series LLCs Provide Clarity*, 113 J. Tax'n 325 (Dec. 2010).

[116]   The ABA Section of Taxation has recommended that a series organization that has *de minimis* assets, perhaps because its members are associated with all of its series, at least in some circumstances be treated as a nominee or title owning arrangement and not as a separate entity. *See* ABA Section of Taxation Comments on REG-119921-09 Proposed Regulations on Series of a Domestic Series Organization (Apr. 29, 2011).

business trusts, and series protected cell companies, among others.[117]

2. Definitions

The Proposed Regulations use a very specific vocabulary, and some of the terms have not generally been used in tax practice before. The definitions are found in Prop. Reg. § 301.7701-1(a)(5)(viii).

Series organization. A series organization is a juridical entity that establishes and maintains a series, including, of course, series LLCs.[118] The LLC (or other series organization) has sometimes been called the "top entity," the "umbrella entity," or the "holding company."

Series. A series is a segregated group of assets and liabilities that is established pursuant to a series statute by agreement of a series organization.[119]

Series statute. As series are subject to the Proposed Regulations only if they are established under a series statute, the definition of a series statute is critical. The Proposed Regulations define a series statute as a statute of a state or foreign jurisdiction that explicitly provides for the organization or establishment of a series of a juridical person and explicitly permits: (1) members or participants of a series organization to have rights, powers, or duties with respect to the series, (2) a series to have separate rights, powers, or duties with respect to specified property or obligations, and (3) the segregation of assets and liabilities such that (with minor exceptions) none of the debts and liabilities of the series organization or of any other series of the series organization are enforceable against the assets of a particular series of the series organization.[120]

With minor exceptions, the Proposed Regulations apply to series organizations created in the United States.[121]

3. Starting Gate

Treas. Reg. § 301.7701-1(a) provides that whether or not an organization is "an entity separate from its owners for federal tax purposes is a matter of federal tax law and does not depend on whether the organization is recognized as an entity under local law." Whether a series is an entity under local law, therefore, would seem to be of no great import. But Prop. Treas. Reg. § 301.7701-1(a)(5)(i) contains a somewhat opaque provision that provides that whether or not a series is a "juridical person for local law purposes, it is treated as an entity formed under local

---

[117] A number of states have enacted protected cell company statutes that are typically used by the investment and insurance industries. These are essentially series-type entities with different nomenclature, separating (typically) different investments into different cells, with each cell protected against the liability of other cells.

[118] Prop. Treas. Reg. § 301.7701-1(a)(5)(viii)(A).

[119] "Series" does not include a segregated asset account of a life insurance company. *See* I.R.C. § 817(d)(1); Treas. Reg. § 1.817-5(e).

[120] The exceptions involve liabilities to the state or foreign jurisdiction related to the organization or operation of the series organization, such as franchise fees or administrative costs.

[121] *See* Prop. Treas. Reg. § 301.7701-1(a)(5)(i), (ii).

law." Why do the Proposed Regulations feel obliged to make this reference? While not free from doubt, it may be an effort to invoke the presumptions of *Moline Properties, Inc. v. Commissioner.*[122] In *Moline Properties*, the Supreme Court noted that, so long as a corporation was formed for a purpose that is the equivalent of business activity, or the corporation actually carries on a business, the corporation remains a taxable entity separate from its shareholders. Thus, organizations that are recognized as separate entities under local law generally are also recognized as separate entities for federal tax purposes.[123] By treating a series as an entity formed under local law, the Proposed Regulations may be trying to provide further support for its position that a series can be recognized as a separate entity for federal tax purposes. It also sets up a subsequent provision of the Proposed Regulations that provides that whether a series that is "treated as a local law entity" under Prop. Treas. Reg. § 301.7701-1(a)(5)(i) "is recognized as a separate entity for federal tax purposes is determined under this section [i.e., Prop. Treas. Reg. § 301-7701] and general tax principles."[124] That in turn brings a series within the check-the-box Regulations. Under those rules, a series is classified as a disregarded entity if it has one owner or a partnership if it has two or more owners, unless it elects to be taxed as a corporation.[125] (Note, somewhat counter-intuitively, that separate entity status is a condition precedent to classification as a disregarded entity.) While ultimately the Proposed Regulations arrive at the goal at which IRS wanted them to arrive, the path taken appears a bit tortured.

The Preamble to the Proposed Regulations indicates that the IRS considered other approaches to the classification of series for federal tax purposes. In particular, they considered whether series should be disregarded as entities separate from the LLC. Such an approach might be suggested by the fact that, the discussion above notwithstanding, series are not generally considered entities for local law purposes.[126] In addition, while the statutes enabling series LLCs grant series significant autonomy, under no current statute do series possess all of the attributes of independence that entities recognized under local law generally possess. As noted previously, series generally cannot convert into another type of entity, merge with another entity, or domesticate in another jurisdiction independent of the LLC. In addition, the dissolution of an LLC generally will terminate all of its series.

The Preamble to the Proposed Regulations states that the IRS believes that, overall, the factors supporting separate entity status for series outweigh the factors in favor of disregarding series as entities separate from the LLC and other series of the LLC. Additional factors they note that argue in favor of separate entity status: Managers and equity holders are "associated with" a series, and their rights,

---

[122] 319 U.S. 436 (1943).

[123] A state law entity may be disregarded if it lacks business purpose or any business activity other than tax avoidance. *See* Chapter 1 and Bertoli v. Commissioner, 103 T.C. 501 (1994); Aldon Homes, Inc. v. Commissioner, 33 T.C. 582 (1959).

[124] Prop. Treas. Reg. § 301.7701-1(a)(5)(iii).

[125] Treas. Reg. §§ 301.7701-3(b)(1)(i), (ii), 301.7701-3(a), (c).

[126] Except, potentially, under the statutes of Illinois and Iowa, where a series may be treated as a separate entity to the extent set forth in the articles of organization.

duties, and powers with respect to the series are direct and specifically identified. Individual series may (but generally are not required to) have separate business purposes and investment objectives.[127] The rule provided in the Proposed Regulations would provide greater certainty to both taxpayers and the IRS regarding the tax status of series. In effect, taxpayers that establish domestic series are placed in the same position as persons that file a certificate of organization for a state law entity. The Preamble to the Proposed Regulations indicates that the IRS believes that the approach of the Proposed Regulations is straightforward and administrable, and is preferable to engaging in a case-by-case determination of the status of each series that would require a detailed examination of the terms of the relevant statute.

As noted previously, the Delaware statute provides that the series liability limitation provisions do not apply if the series does not maintain records adequately accounting for the assets associated with each series separately from the assets of the LLC or any other series. The Preamble to the Proposed Regulations indicates that the IRS considered whether a failure to elect or qualify for the liability limitations under the series statute should affect whether a series is a separate entity for federal tax purposes. The Preamble notes, however, that limitations on liability of owners of an entity for debts and obligations of the entity and the rights of creditors to hold owners liable for debts and obligations of the entity generally do not alter the characterization of the entity for federal tax purposes. For example, an owner may form a wholly owned LLC to hold assets or operations of a business. The owner either may take advantage of the limited liability offered by the LLC, or may waive limited liability and be personally liable for the debts and obligations incurred by the LLC. In either event, the check-the-box Regulations still govern. As a consequence, the Proposed Regulations provide that an election, agreement, or other arrangement that permits debts and liabilities of other series or the LLC to be enforceable against the assets of a particular series, or a failure to comply with the recordkeeping requirements for the limitation on liability available under the relevant series statute, will not prevent a series from meeting the definition of "series" in the Proposed Regulations.

Under Treas. Reg. § 301.7701-2(b), various entities are automatically classified as corporations for federal tax purposes. While it would not be common, series could fall within these rules. For example, a series that is wholly owned by a state government would be treated as a per se corporation under Treas. Reg. § 301.7701-2(b)(6).

The Proposed Regulations also provide that, for federal tax purposes, ownership of interests in a series and ownership of the assets associated with a series is determined under general tax principles. An LLC is not treated as the owner of a series or of the assets associated with a series merely because the LLC holds legal

---

[127] The ABA Section of Taxation has recommended that the final Regulations provide additional guidance and examples of what the required threshold should be in order for series organization members to be considered to be associated with, and thus, for example, partners in a series, and what the threshold should be in order for assets to be considered to be associated with, and thus an asset of, a series. *See* ABA Section of Taxation Comments on REG-119921-09 Proposed Regulations on Series of a Domestic Series Organization (Apr. 29, 2011).

title to the assets associated with the series. For example, a state statute might not permit a series to hold assets in its own name. Its LLC, therefore, would hold the legal title to assets associated with the series. Nonetheless, the Proposed Regulations provide that the series will be treated as the owner of the assets for federal tax purposes if it bears the economic benefits and burdens of the assets under general federal tax principles. Similarly, for federal tax purposes, the obligor for the liability of a series is determined under general tax principles.

In general, the same legal principles that apply to determine who owns interests in other types of entities apply to determine the ownership of interests in series and LLCs. These principles generally look to who bears the economic benefits and burdens of ownership.[128] Furthermore, common law principles apply to the determination of whether a person is a partner in a series that is classified as a partnership for federal tax purposes under Treas. Reg. § 301.7701-3.[129]

4. Single Entity/Multiple Entities

In some circumstances, questions may arise as to whether an LLC and its series should be treated as a single entity or multiple entities. In many situations, the answer will be clear. If the documents state that the series are owned by and associated with the LLC, and the members are only allocated income and loss from the parent LLC, the LLC and the series are collectively treated as a single tax entity. On the other hand, if members take their return from each series separately, without reduction or increase by losses or income from other series, and the documentation states that groups of members are associated with particular series, there would be little question that the series should be treated as multiple tax entities.

Where the answer is less certain is when the documentation treats groups of members as being associated with particular series, but there is a substantial overlap of the membership interest in the various series. Should the series LLC be seen as multiple entities or a single entity? This same issue exists under current law with entities other than series. The mere presence of common ownership does not generally cause multiple entities to be collapsed into a single entity for federal income tax purposes.[130] For some purposes, tax authorities allow multiple entities to be combined as a single entity on an elective basis. For example, under the passive activity loss rules, multiple entities may be grouped as a single activity if they have sufficient common ownership.[131] Similarly, the Code allows corporations with sufficient common ownership to elect to file a consolidated return, which treats the included corporations as a single entity in some respects.[132] The Preamble to the check-the-box Regulations states that the issue of whether common ownership

---

[128] *See, e.g.*, Rev. Rul. 55-39, 1955-1 C.B. 403.

[129] *See, e.g.*, Commissioner v. Culbertson, 337 U.S. 733 (1949), and Commissioner v. Tower, 327 U.S. 280 (1946), discussed above.

[130] *See* Southern Pacific Transportation Company v. Commissioner, 75 T.C. 497 (1980) (the mere fact of common ownership and operations would not justify disregarding distinct corporate entities).

[131] Treas. Reg. § 1.469-4(c).

[132] *See* Treas. Reg. § 1.1502-13(a)(2).

creates a single entity for federal income tax purposes was an issue when those Regulations were finalized.[133] It also provides that although the determination of whether an organization has more than one owner is based on all the facts and circumstances, the fact that some or all of the owners of an organization are under common control does not require the common parent to be treated as the sole owner.[134] Thus, the Proposed Regulations do not provide a definitive answer, with each case being decided on its own facts and circumstances.

5. Who Are the Owners?

A related question is who the owners are of each entity that is recognized as a separate business entity for federal tax purposes. Generally, as we discussed earlier in this chapter, parties intending to be treated as partners must contemplate sharing the profits of a venture treated as a partnership for federal income tax purposes. Just as whether an entity is recognized for federal income tax purposes is not determined by state or local law, whether a person is treated as a partner also is not determined by state or local law.[135] In several Revenue Rulings, the IRS recognized as partners persons who could not be partners under local law.[136] State law determines whether a given set of circumstances creates a right or interest; federal law then determines the federal tax consequences of the presence or absence of the right or interest.[137]

---

[133] The Preamble indicates that some commentators, relying on Rev. Rul. 93-4, 1993-1 C.B. 225 (declared obsolete by Rev. Rul. 98-37, 1998-2 C.B. 133), suggested that if two wholly owned subsidiaries of a common parent were the owners of an organization, those owners would not be respected as bona fide owners and the organization would be treated as having only one owner (the common parent).

[134] State law also may provide circumstances under which multiple entities may be disregarded or treated as a single entity with a common parent. One of the most common approaches to this issue under state law is "veil piercing." Delaware law provides requirements for veil piercing, and the case law reveals that to pierce the corporate veil based on an alter ego theory, a plaintiff must demonstrate a misuse of the corporate form along with an overall element of injustice or unfairness. NetJets Aviation, Inc. v. LHC Communications, LLC, 537 F.3d 168 (2d Cir. 2008) (citing Harco Nat'l Ins. Co. v. Green Farms, Inc., 1989 Del. Ch. LEXIS 114 (Sept. 19, 1989)). In short, the test applied under Delaware law is two pronged: (1) Whether the entities in question operated as a single economic entity, and (2) Whether there was an overall element of injustice or unfairness. See id.; Medi-Tec of Egypt Corp. v. Bausch & Lomb Surgical, 2004 Del. Ch. LEXIS 21 (Mar. 4, 2004) (citing Mobil Oil Corp. v. Linear Films, Inc., 718 F. Supp. 260 (D. Del. 1989)); cf. Alberto v. Diversified Group, Inc., 55 F.3d 201 (5th Cir. 1995). This two-pronged test was recently described by the Second Circuit as follows: "Stated generally, the inquiry initially focuses on whether those in control of a corporation did not treat the corporation as a distinct entity; and, if they did not, the court then seeks to evaluate the specific facts with a standard of fraud or misuse or some other general term of reproach in mind, such as whether the corporation was used to engage in conduct that was inequitable, or prohibited, or an unfair trade practice, or illegal." NetJets Aviation, Inc., supra (internal citations and quotations omitted) (citing and quoting Mobil Oil Corp. v. Linear Films, Inc., supra; David v. Mast, 1999 Del. Ch. LEXIS 34 (Mar. 2, 1999); Martin v. D. B. Martin Co., 88 A 612 (Del. Ch. 1913)). Thus, both for state law and current federal tax purposes, commonality of ownership does not generally cause multiple entities to be treated as a single entity.

[135] Sommers v. Commissioner, 195 F.2d 680 (2d Cir. 1952); Rupple v. Kuhl, 177 F.2d 823 (7th Cir. 1949); Forman v. Commissioner, 199 F.2d 881 (9th Cir. 1952); Klein v. Commissioner, 18 T.C. 804 (1952).

[136] Rev. Rul. 58-243, 1958-1 C.B. 255; Rev. Rul. 77-137, 1977-1 C.B. 178; Rev. Rul. 77-332, 1977-2 C.B. 483.

[137] See, e.g., Drye Family 1995 Trust v. United States, 152 F.3d 892 (8th Cir. 1998); CCA 199930006 (Apr. 2, 1999).

Under the Delaware statute, classes or groups of members or managers associated with a series may have such relative rights, powers, and duties as the LLC agreement provides.[138] Neither the Delaware statute nor the Proposed Regulations specify how members are to be "associated" with a particular series. It is left up to the LLC agreement.[139]

Some guidance can be found in I.R.C. § 704(e). As we discuss in Chapter 5, this section provides that someone who owns a capital interest[140] will be recognized as a bona fide partner, regardless of whether the interest was acquired by purchase or gift, if the interest is in a partnership in which capital is a material income-producing factor.[141] Under Treas. Reg. § 1.704-1(e)(1)(iii), a donee or purchaser of a capital interest in a partnership is not recognized as a partner under these principles unless the interest is acquired in a bona fide transaction, not a mere sham for tax avoidance or evasion purposes, and the donee or purchaser is the real owner of such interest. To be recognized, a transfer must vest dominion and control of the partnership interest in the transferee. The existence of such dominion and control is to be determined from all the facts and circumstances. A transfer is not recognized if the transferor retains such incidents of ownership that the transferee has not acquired full and complete ownership of the partnership interest. Transactions between members of a family will be examined closely, and the circumstances — not only at the time of the purported transfer but also during the periods preceding and following it — will be taken into consideration in determining the bona fides of the purported gift or sale (or lack thereof).

Treas. Reg. § 1.704-1(e)(2) lists a series of factors to be considered in determining whether a partner is, in fact, the real owner of a capital interest in a partnership. The factors to be considered, which are illustrative rather than exhaustive, break down into five categories: Retained controls (including retention of control of assets essential to the business); indirect controls; participation in management; income distributions; and conduct of partnership business. Tax advisors with clients who have series in which capital is a material income-producing factor will plan with this Regulation in mind. While all the facts and circumstances must be taken into consideration, the rights of the parties may be designed to intentionally meet the five factors of Treas. Reg. § 1.704-1(e)(2).

---

[138]   Del. Code Ann. Tit. 6, § 18-215(e).

[139]   Informal comments of a Treasury representative at a recent ABA Tax Section meeting in Toronto (9/23-25/10) indicate that it was not the intent of Treasury that a special allocation of income would, by itself, be sufficient to create a separate series and associate members with the series for federal tax purposes.

[140]   Under Treas. Reg. § 1.704-1(e)(1)(v), for purposes of I.R.C. § 704(e) a capital interest in a partnership means an interest in the assets of the partnership, which is distributable to the owner of the capital interest on his withdrawal from the partnership or on liquidation of the partnership. The mere right to participate in the earnings and profits of a partnership is not a capital interest in the partnership. *See* § 8.08A.

[141]   The Code does not speak to the issue if capital is not a material income-producing factor. *See* Chapter 5 for discussion. Treas. Reg. § 1.704-1(e)(1)(iv) provides, in part, that for purposes of I.R.C. § 704(e)(1), capital is a material income-producing factor if a substantial portion of the gross income of the business is attributable to the employment of capital in the business conducted by the partnership. Capital is ordinarily a material income-producing factor if the operation of the business requires substantial inventories or a substantial investment in plant, machinery, or other equipment.

An understanding of the rights and obligations of owners under state law is essential to correctly assessing ownership for federal tax purposes. For example, under the Delaware statute, assets may be "associated" with a series. Assets associated with a series may be held directly by the series or indirectly in the name of the series LLC or in the name of a nominee. Also, members or managers of the series LLC may be "associated" with a series, in which event they have the rights, powers, and duties specified in the LLC agreement. Unless the operating agreement provides otherwise, management of the series is vested in members associated with the series in accordance with the interests of the members in profits owned by all of the members associated with the series.[142] Thus, to refine what we discussed above, practitioners may draft agreements so that: (1) the series LLC is associated with (under state law) and the owner of (under tax law) the series, and members of the series LLC, indirectly share in profits and losses of the series through their membership interests in the series LLC, (2) members of the series LLC are associated with (under state law) and the direct owners of (under tax law) the series, or (3) some combination thereof. A creditor with a claim against the series LLC will have a right against the series LLC's interests in its wholly owned series in alternative (1), will have no claim against the series in alternative (2), and may be able to satisfy the claim in part against the series in alternative (3).

6. Liabilities and Tax Collection

There are differences in local law governing series. For example, rights to hold title to property and to sue and be sued are expressly addressed in some statutes but not in others. These differences may affect how creditors of series, including state taxing authorities, may enforce obligations of a series. The Proposed Regulations provide that, to the extent federal or local law permits a creditor to collect a liability attributable to a series from the LLC or other series of the LLC, the LLC and those other series may be considered the taxpayer from whom the tax assessed against the series may be collected pursuant to administrative or judicial means. Similarly, when a creditor may collect a liability attributable to an LLC from any of its series, a tax liability assessed against the LLC may be collected directly from one of its series by administrative or judicial means.

7. Information Statements

The Proposed Regulations require each series and each series LLC to file an annual statement containing identifying information with respect to each series or the series LLC.

The Preamble explains that Treasury and the IRS are contemplating what information should be required in these statements, but information being considered includes:

(1) The name, address, and taxpayer identification number of the series LLC and each of its series and status of each.

(2) The jurisdiction in which the LLC was formed.

---

[142] Del. Code Ann. Tit. 6, § 18-215(g).

(3) A statement of whether the series holds title to its assets or whether title is held by another series or the LLC and, if held by another series or the LLC, the name, address, and taxpayer identification number of the LLC and each series holding title to any of its assets.

8. Questions and Issues

Status of LLC. Neither the Proposed Regulations nor the Preamble explicitly indicate whether a series LLC that has no assets, business, or owners (but whose series do) would be required to obtain its own taxpayer identification number. The IRS has specifically requested comments on the characterization of an LLC that has no assets or activities separate from its series. Under current Treas. Reg. § 301.7701-1, it might well be determined that such a series LLC was not a separate entity for federal income tax purposes, although the Proposed Regulations do not explicitly provide guidance one way or the other.

The effect of previous check-the-box elections. Generally, when final Regulations become effective, taxpayers that have treated series differently for federal tax purposes than series are treated under the final Regulations will be required to change their treatment of series. In this situation, an LLC that previously was treated as one entity with all of its series may be required to begin treating each series as a separate entity for federal tax purposes. General tax principles will apply to determine the consequences of the conversion from one entity to multiple entities for federal tax purposes. See, for example, Chapter 9's discussion of I.R.C. § 708 for rules relating to partnership divisions.

Service LLCs. As mentioned above, the Proposed Regulations define a series as a segregated group of assets and liabilities that is established pursuant to a series statute by agreement of a series LLC. The Proposed Regulations do not address service LLCs, as such. An LLC in the business of providing services would have contractual rights and receivables, which are assets that may be segregated and associated with a particular series under a series statute. In the start-up phase a series may only have the contribution of future services by its members. Informal comments by Treasury representatives at an ABA Tax Section meeting[143] indicated that it was not the intent of Treasury to exclude service organizations from the application of the series guidance. The Treasury has informally indicated that comments on this issue would be welcome.[144]

Continued existence for state law purposes with no members. The Preamble indicates that for state law purposes it may be possible for a series to continue after no members are associated with the series. If the series no longer has any assets or business, it would seem that it would be deemed liquidated for federal income tax purposes. See § 7.09. A more complex issue arises when no members are associated with the series for state law purposes, but the series still has assets and business operations. The Delaware statute explicitly provides that a series does not

---

[143] The meeting took place in Toronto from 9/23-25, 2010.

[144] The ABA Section of Taxation has recommended that the final Regulations specifically address service organizations. *See* ABA Section of Taxation Comments on REG-119921-09 Proposed Regulations on Series of a Domestic Series Organization (Apr. 29, 2011).

automatically terminate when members are no longer associated with a series. The statute does not appear to require both members and assets and liabilities to be associated with a series. If there were never any members associated with a series, but assets and liabilities are associated with a series, one would assume that the series LLC or whoever has rights to the assets in the particular series, even if they are not LLC members, may effectively be the persons "associated with the series." For federal income tax purposes, one generally would need to determine who has the benefits and burdens of ownership of the series.

Employment and employee benefit purposes. For both employment and employee benefit purposes, a variety of issues arise if a series is treated as the employer for federal tax purposes, but the series LLC is treated as the employer for state law purposes. The Preamble to the Proposed Regulations notes that several requirements must be satisfied to be treated as an "employer." It is not clear how the requirements should apply to series. The Treasury has requested comments on how these issues should be addressed.

How is property titled to a series? This may be of particular importance for real estate, where it may be important for tax and nontax reasons that a series formally hold title.

9. Practical Considerations

Structuring ownership. An important issue is ownership of interests in a series. In the experience of the authors, practitioners have not clearly articulated the rights and benefits of persons who are to be "associated" with the series. Attention to this detail is particularly important if taxpayers want to create a structure in which the LLC is a holding company with multiple wholly owned series that are to be disregarded as separate entities for federal tax purposes. The relevant agreements should clearly indicate that the series LLC has all of the management rights for the series and owns all the economic interests of the series.

Effectiveness of the liability shield. Many have expressed the view that the liability shield of a series should be respected in a nonseries state, as most states' LLC statutes provide that the "internal affairs" of an LLC will be governed by the law of the state of formation. As Professor Daniel S. Kleinberger has noted, however, the internal affairs doctrine may not provide the hoped-for protection. For example, section 801(a) of the Revised Uniform Limited Liability Company Act (2006) provides that "[t]he law of the state or other jurisdiction under which a foreign LLC is formed governs: (1) the internal affairs of the company; and (2) the liability of a member as member and a manager as manager for the debts, obligations, or other liabilities of the company." Most states have similar provisions in their partnership and LLC statutes. The liability that is of concern in a series LLC, however, is not the liability of a member or manager for debts of the company; it is the liability of one part of the company for the debts of another part of the company. Thus, the internal affairs doctrine may not provide the needed authority.[145]

---

[145] *See* CARTER G. BISHOP & DANIEL S. KLEINBERGER, LIMITED LIABILITY COMPANIES: TAX AND BUSINESS LAW ¶ 14.06[1][c] (Warren Gorham & Lamont, 1994; Supp. 2011-2).

Establishment of a series. It is important to pay careful attention to detail when establishing a series. For example, in Delaware the LLC statute includes several requirements that must be satisfied to establish a series with limited liability. Specifically, the statute requires that: (1) the agreement establish or provide for the establishment of series, (2) the records maintained for any series must account for the assets of the series separately from the other assets of the LLC and any other series, (3) the agreement must provide that the debts, liabilities, obligations, and expenses incurred, contracted for, or otherwise existing with respect to a particular series will be enforceable only against the assets of that series and not against the assets of the LLC or other series of the series LLC, and (4) notice of the limitation on liabilities of a series as referenced in the statute must be set forth in the certificate of formation. It is obviously important that the LLC documentation fully meets each of these requirements.

C.   Conclusion

To quote Yogi Berra, this is a little like "déjà vu all over again." Practitioners' use of LLCs got ahead of tax authority. Then tax authority was clarified, leaving many state law uncertainties. Gradually, the states caught their statutes up, and LLCs emerged as an innovative vehicle that is now a standard business tool.

Similarly, the use of series LLCs, while still limited, has gotten ahead of tax authority. Tax authorities supporting a variety of positions can be found, and taxpayers have been taking conflicting positions. The Proposed Regulations on series do not provide all of the answers, but they do provide valuable guidance. Of course, Proposed Regulations do not have formal legal force until they are finalized, but in the absence of other reliable guidance, practitioners often rely on them.

Even when the Proposed Regulations are finalized, many state law uncertainties will likely remain, most importantly whether a series LLC will be respected in a nonseries state. History may continue to repeat, with more and more states adopting series LLC statutes, and more and more practitioners using series. But perhaps history will not fully repeat itself. The very flexibility of the series LLC may be its undoing.[146] Third parties will need to get extensive disclosures to be safe, may decide that it is not worth the candle, and refuse to deal with series LLCs. Given the record keeping requirements of series LLCs, businesses may prefer the safer confines of multiple LLCs. In any event, until series LLC statutes are widespread, the use of series LLCs (and other series organizations) is likely to be limited, at least for those for whom the additional liability shield are important. They will continue to prefer multiple LLCs.

---

[146] *See* Thomas Geu, *A Single Theory of Limited Liability Companies: An Evolutionary Analysis,* 42 SUFFOLK U. L. REV. 507 (2009).

§ 1.09   COMPARISON OF PARTNERSHIPS WITH S CORPORATIONS

In general, if a corporate entity exists and qualified shareholders have filed a valid S corporation election, the corporation is an S corporation until the election is terminated. However, qualification as an S corporation is subject to a variety of rigid rules. The corporation may have no more than 100 shareholders. It may have only one class of stock (disregarding voting rights). Only certain persons may be shareholders.

In contrast, for domestic entities, there is no election that needs to be filed for an unincorporated business entity to be treated as a partnership. There is no formal limitation on the number of partners a partnership may have, but the 100-partner safe harbor of the publicly traded partnership rules places a practical limitation on many partnerships. A partnership may have as many classes of interests as the partners agree to, and there are no restrictions on who may be a partner.

Although unexpected treatment as a partner may have surprising consequences to the unintended partner, an unexpected shareholder of an S corporation may cause the S corporation election to terminate imposing corporate level tax on the entity and changing the character of distributions. For this reason, the IRS has promulgated Regulations with significant safe harbors that will generally prevent lenders, option holders, and other holders of contract rights against an S corporation from being treated as a shareholder unless a tax avoidance purpose is present.

For a more detailed discussion, see Chapter 16.

§ 1.10   READING, QUESTIONS AND PROBLEMS

A.   Reading

CODE:

I.R.C. §§ 761, 7701(a)(2), 7701(i), 7704.

TREASURY REGULATIONS:

Treas. Reg. §§ 1.761-2, 301.7701-1 to -4(d), 1.7704-1.

Prop. Treas. Reg. §§ 1.761-3, 301.7701-1(a)(5).

CASES:

Commissioner v. Culbertson, 337 U.S. 733 (1949).

Estate of Smith v. Commissioner, 313 F.2d 724 (8th Cir. 1963).

Madison Gas & Electric Co. v. Commissioner, 72 T.C. 521 (1979).

RULINGS AND OTHER INTERPRETATIONS:

Rev. Proc. 2002-22, 2002-1 C.B. 733.

B. Questions and Problems

1. a. Abbey, Bahir, and Cho are students in a tax LL.M. program. In the current semester, they are all in the same classes for Individual Taxation, Partnership Taxation, and Corporation Taxation. They have decided to meet regularly during the semester and discuss their classes. Would a study group such as the one proposed by Abbey, Bahir, and Cho be classified as a partnership for federal tax purposes?

b. A few weeks into the semester, Abbey, Bahir, and Cho decide to expand the responsibilities of the study group. Each member of the study group will prepare a course outline for one of the courses that they are taking together, and, at the end of the semester, they will exchange outlines.

   i. Does the production of the outlines cause the study group to be classified as a partnership for federal tax purposes? What are the other possible characterizations? How can you distinguish the study group from *Madison Gas*?

   ii. Does it make a difference if the agreement among the three members is that none of the three will give the outlines to anyone else without the consent of the other two members?

   iii. If the study group is a partnership, would it be eligible to make an explicit or implicit election out of Subchapter K?

c. After the semester is over, Abbey, Bahir, and Cho discover that they all received "As" in all three classes. After some discussion, they decide that their outlines contributed significantly to their success. With the consent of the others, Abbey creates a web site that offers the outlines for sale. The three agree to divide the net proceeds equally. They also agree not to give the outlines to anyone who does not buy them.

   i. The study group is over, but do the three members still, or now, have a partnership for tax purposes?

   ii. If the group is a partnership, is it eligible to make an explicit or implicit election out of Subchapter K?

   iii. Would your answer to c.(i) change if the agreement was that each member was entitled to all of the net proceeds from only the outline which that individual authored?

2. David and Ebony both work at law firms. Not feeling adequately challenged by their jobs, they also remodel houses. To be specific, they purchase a house as tenants-in-common, move into the house as their principal residence and remodel the house in a two- to three-year time span. They each contribute their labor and capital in approximately equal amounts, and their agreement is that they will split the proceeds of any sale 50/50 (with a presumption that the proceeds will be used in whole or in part to purchase the next house).

a. Are David and Ebony partners for federal income tax purposes?

b. Would David and Ebony be eligible to make an explicit or implicit election out of Subchapter K?

c. I.R.C. § 121 provides an exclusion of $250,000 for individuals on the sale of their principal residence (subject to some restrictions). Section 121 makes no reference to partnerships. If David and Ebony are a partnership and make an explicit or implicit election out of Subchapter K, would they be eligible for the section 121 exclusion?

d. Would David and Ebony be eligible to obtain a ruling that they are not a partnership under Rev. Proc. 2002-22?

3. Fai recently sold a parcel of investment real estate and intends to obtain a new parcel in a like-kind exchange transaction under I.R.C. § 1031. Fai's new lender insists that the replacement property be acquired in a special purpose entity that is bankruptcy remote. Fai suggests that the replacement property be acquired in a single member LLC, but the lender wants the LLC to have at least two members. The LLC is structured so that Fai holds 100% of the economic interests of the LLC, but an entity chosen by the lender is also a member for state law purposes even though the noneconomic member has no rights to current distributions or distributions in liquidation. Is the LLC a partnership for tax purposes?

4. Big Bank has loaned money to S Corp. In addition to receiving a note, Big Bank also receives an option to acquire S Corp stock exercisable at 1¢ per share (the value of S Corp stock is currently $1 per share). The loan is commercially reasonable to S Corp. Is Big Bank treated as a shareholder of S Corp by reason of holding the option?

5. Gena, Haji, Inez, Jacob, and Kady have purchased Office Tower as tenants-in-common. Each has reserved the right to sell his or her interest separately. They vote on the approval of any leases. All leases will be triple net leases with the owners providing no more than customary services. There is no management agreement, but from time to time one of the five is appointed temporarily to have the authority to sign the leases.

a. Are the owners eligible to obtain a ruling that their ownership is not a partnership under Rev. Proc. 2002-22?

b. Suppose that the owners operated under the name Office Towers Partners. Would they be eligible to get a ruling under Rev. Proc. 2002-22? If they met the other criteria of Rev. Proc. 2002-22, would they be eligible to make an explicit or implicit election out of Subchapter K?

6. Lars, Maria, Nabil, Odina, and Paki have purchased Big Plane as tenants-in-common. Each has reserved the right to sell his or her interest separately. They vote on the approval of any leases. All leases will be triple net leases with the owners providing no more than customary services. There is no management agreement, but from time to time one of the five is appointed temporarily to have the authority to sign the leases.

a. Are the owners eligible to obtain a ruling that their ownership is not a partnership under Rev. Proc. 2002-22?

b. If they met the other criteria of Rev. Proc. 2002-22, would they be eligible to make an explicit or implicit election out of Subchapter K? Does your answer change if there are 40 co-owners? 105? 1000?

7. Ren is an investment manager. Her usual fee is 2% of the gross value under management and 1% of the net appreciation in value. Is she a partner with her customers?

8. The Main Street Investment Club makes investments jointly. They meet together once a month to discuss their current investments and make decisions about new investments. They hold an account at a brokerage house in the name of the Club under the Social Security number of one of the founding members. The Club is operated on an all-or-nothing basis: in other words, each member of the Club holds a partial interest in each investment the Club makes. The terms of the Club have been formalized in a document that the members call the "charter agreement" that describes the responsibilities and rights of the members. No partnership returns have ever been filed. When the member whose Social Security number has been given to the brokerage house receives the Form 1099s, she sends out 1099s to the other members for their proportionate share and reports only her share. Is the Club a partnership for tax purposes? Have the members effectively elected out of Subchapter K?

9. EunSook, Jabar, and Natasha form a Delaware LLC. The certificate of formation discloses that the LLC may create separate series that will not be subject to the claims of the creditors of other series or the LLC generally. EunSook, Jabar, and Natasha each contribute $100 of cash, and the LLC buys BlackAcre, WhiteAcre, and YellowAcre. Absent other facts, how many business entities have EunSook, Jabar, and Natasha formed?

10. The same facts as Problem 9. In addition, the LLC Agreement provides that by affirmative vote of the three members, the LLC can create a new series and associate assets with such series. If a series is created, then the LLC will maintain separate books and records for the series, and, to the extent permitted under local law, title assets in the name of the series. Absent other facts, how many business entities have EunSook, Jabar, and Natasha formed?

11. The same facts as Problem 10. In addition, EunSook, Jabar, and Natasha agree by written resolution that three series are to be created and that BlackAcre, WhiteAcre, and YellowAcre will each be associated with a separate series. The LLC creates separate books and records for each series, and, to the extent permitted under local law, titles the properties in the name of the series. Absent other facts, how many business entities have EunSook, Jabar, and Natasha formed? How many partnerships have EunSook, Jabar, and Natasha formed?

12. The same facts as Problem 11. In addition, EunSook, Jabar, and Natasha have agreed that EunSook will manage BlackAcre; Jabar will manage WhiteAcre; and Natasha will manage YellowAcre. For each property, the member who manages the property will receive an allocation of 20% of the cash flow before the members split the remaining cash flow one-third apiece. Absent other facts, how many partnerships have EunSook, Jabar, and Natasha formed?

13. The same facts as Problem 12, except that in respect of each of the series the members sell 50% of the interests associated with the particular series to outside investors. Although there is some overlap between the investor pools, there are substantial differences between the ownership interests in the three series. Absent other facts, how many partnerships have EunSook, Jabar, and Natasha formed?

Chapter 2

FORMATION OF THE PARTNERSHIP

§ 2.01 INTRODUCTION

Chapter 2 will address the issues which arise upon the formation of a partnership. With respect to the contributing partner, this includes the issue of whether the contributing partner recognizes a gain or loss on receipt of the partnership interest, including discussion of the nature of the property contributed, investment companies, the receipt of cash or other property from the partnership in addition to the receipt of the partnership interest, and the effect of the partnership assuming a liability of the contributing partner, or acquiring property from the contributing partner subject to a liability. Also discussed is the issue of the contributing partner's basis for her partnership interest as well as the holding period of her partnership interest. There is also the question of potential recognition of gain by the partnership or the historic partners upon a contribution, the partnership's basis for the contributed property, as well as the partnership's holding period for the contributed property. The character of gain or loss resulting from the subsequent sale by the partnership of the contributed property is also discussed. Lastly, there is a discussion of the treatment of the organization and selling expenses incurred by the partnership upon formation.

§ 2.02 TRANSFER OF PROPERTY TO PARTNERSHIP

When the current scheme of partnership taxation was introduced in the Internal Revenue Code of 1954, partnerships were mostly used for small businesses and professional practices. The provisions were drafted in such a fashion as to make it easy for taxpayers to go in and out of partnerships without incurring taxation. That same framework continues in effect today, with some limitations and modifications, although partnerships (in particular LLCs taxed as partnerships) are used for sophisticated, large businesses and often as part of tax shelters.

A. General Rules

The general rule regarding the transfer of property to a partnership is very simple. Under I.R.C. § 721(a), no gain or loss is recognized by: (i) the transferring partner, (ii) the recipient partnership, or (iii) any of its partners, when property is contributed to a partnership in exchange for an interest in the partnership. Despite the simplicity, several points are worth noting. First, it does not matter whether the property is contributed to a newly formed partnership or an existing partnership. Second, there is no requirement, such as exists in I.R.C. § 351(a) (dealing with transfers to corporations) that the transferring partner(s) receive any specific percentage ownership in the partnership.[1]

B. What Constitutes Property

As indicated above, I.R.C. § 721(a) only applies to contributions of "property" to a partnership. The question becomes, therefore, what constitutes property for this purpose.

1. Cash

It is clear that cash is property for purposes of I.R.C. § 721, although that is probably of little consequence, since the contributing partner could not have a gain or loss upon the contribution of cash (other than a currency exchange gain or loss if a foreign currency were involved). It is relevant for purposes of the partnership, however, because in the absence of I.R.C. § 721(a), a partnership receiving cash could have taxable income.

2. Contract Rights

In general, contract rights are considered property for purposes of I.R.C. § 721(a).

a. Promissory Notes

i. Contributor's Promissory Note

If a partner contributes his or her own promissory note to the partnership (i.e., a promissory note of which the partner is the maker and the partnership is the payee), it is likely that such transaction would not be considered a transfer of property at that time, although the law is unclear on this issue. The transaction could be viewed as if the contributing partner contributed zero basis property to the partnership. There are authorities which have taken this position in the context of transfers to corporations covered by I.R.C. § 351.[2]

When the partner makes payments on the promissory note, it likely will be considered a capital contribution made by the partner at that time. This is consistent with the rules relating to maintenance of capital accounts.[3]

ii. Third-Party Note

It is clear that the contribution of a third-party note to the partnership would be treated as property for purposes of I.R.C. § 721(a).

---

[1] Treas. Reg. § 1.721-1(a).

[2] *See, e.g.*, Rev. Rul. 80-235, 1980-2 C.B. 229; Rev. Rul. 68-629, 1968-2 C.B. 154. *But see* Peracchi v. Commissioner, 143 F.3d 487 (9th Cir. 1998).

[3] Treas. Reg. § 1.704-1(b)(2)(iv)(d)(2). *See* § 5.02.

iii.   Installment Note

Treas. Reg. § 1.721-1(a) makes clear that the contribution of an installment obligation constitutes a contribution of property for purposes of I.R.C. § 721(a). The partnership will step in the shoes of the contributing partner with respect to the recognition of gain upon the receipt of payments on the installment obligation.[4] This is contrary to the general rule that a disposition of an installment obligation results in recognition of gain or loss.[5]

In addition to the provisions of Treas. Reg. § 1.721-1(a) providing for non-recognition of gain upon the transfer of an installment obligation to a partnership, Treas. Reg. § 1.453-9(c)(2) specifically provides that transfers covered by I.R.C. § 721 do not result in the recognition of gain.[6]

If the installment note is an obligation of the partnership to which it is transferred (i.e., the partnership was the purchaser in the installment sale and the contributing partner was the seller), the result is likely to be different. As a result of the partnership following the contribution being both the obligor and the obligee, the installment obligation would cease to exist by virtue of the doctrine of merger. In this situation, the installment obligation is likely to be considered to have been "satisfied" for purposes of I.R.C. § 453B(a).[7] Under I.R.C. § 453B(a)(2), if an installment obligation is satisfied, gain or loss is recognized, measured by the difference between the basis of the installment obligation and the fair market value of the obligation.[8]

iv.   Partnership's Indebtedness to the Partner

If a partnership is indebted to a person, whether they are already a partner or not, and the indebtedness is cancelled in consideration for the issuance of a partnership interest, an issue is presented as to whether such transaction is covered by the nonrecognition rule of I.R.C. § 721(a). Had the partnership repaid the indebtedness and then the obligee turned around and contributed the cash received in payment of the obligation as a capital contribution, it is clear that if those transactions are viewed as independent steps, no gain or loss would be recognized by either the partnership or the person acquiring the partnership interest. Should the result be different if instead of paying the debt and then making a cash contribution, the indebtedness is simply cancelled in exchange for a partnership interest?

---

[4] Under I.R.C. § 704(c), however, the gain recognized at the partnership level will be allocated solely to the contributing partner. *See* § 5.05.

[5] I.R.C. § 453B(a).

[6] Although Treas. Reg. § 1.453-9(c)(2) was promulgated prior to the enactment of I.R.C. § 453B, the result should be the same under current law. *See* PLR 9620020 (May 17, 1996).

[7] I.R.C. § 453B(f)(1) provides that if an installment obligation is cancelled or otherwise becomes unenforceable, the obligation is treated as if it was disposed of in a transaction other than a sale or exchange. *See also* Jack Ammann Photogrammetric Engineers, Inc. v. Commissioner, *341 F.2d 466 (5th Cir. 1965)*.

[8] If the obligor and obligee are related persons (within the meaning of I.R.C. § 453(f)(1)), the fair market value of the obligation is deemed to be not less than its face amount. I.R.C. § 453B(f)(2).

If the partnership's indebtedness is cancelled by virtue of the partnership issuing a profits interest or capital interest in the partnership to the creditor, I.R.C. § 108(e)(8) provides that the partnership is treated as having satisfied the indebtedness with an amount of money equal to the fair market value of the interest issued. Thus, if the fair market value of the interest issued is less than the amount of the indebtedness cancelled, the partnership will recognize discharge of indebtedness income. I.R.C. § 108(e)(8)(B) further provides that if any discharge of indebtedness income is recognized by reason of the partnership issuing a capital interest or profits interest in exchange for debt, the discharge of indebtedness income must be allocated to the partners who were partners immediately before the discharge (i.e., the discharge of indebtedness income cannot be allocated to the former creditor who is now a partner).

Regulations[9] have been issued which provide a safe harbor for determining the fair market value of the partnership interest issued by the partnership to a creditor in exchange for debt. Under the safe harbor, the fair market value of the partnership interest is equal to the liquidation value of the partnership interest issued. Liquidation value means the amount of cash that would be received with respect to the partnership interest issued if, immediately after the issuance of the partnership interest, the partnership sold all of its assets for cash equal to the fair market value of those assets and then liquidated, but only if: (i) the creditor, the partnership, and its partners treat the fair market value of the indebtedness as being equal to the liquidation value of the partnership interest issued for purposes of determining the tax consequences of the debt-for-equity exchange, (ii) the debt-for-equity exchange is an arm's-length transaction, and (iii) subsequent to the debt-for-equity exchange, the partnership does not redeem, nor does any person related to the partnership purchase, the partnership interest issued as part of a plan which has as its principal purpose the avoidance of the cancellation of indebtedness income by the partnership. If the safe harbor requirements set forth above are not met, then all the facts and circumstances are considered in determining the value of the partnership interest issued.

Under both I.R.C. § 108(e)(8)(B) and the Regulations, if the partnership is solvent and the contributor receives a capital account credit equal to the face amount of the indebtedness, it would not appear that there should be any discharge of indebtedness income because the contributor has in fact received a capital interest with a value equal to the debt discharged. If, however, the contributing party does not receive a capital account credit in connection with the contribution of the indebtedness (or receives a capital account less than the face amount of the indebtedness), then under the Regulations and the law preceding their promulgation, a facts and circumstances test applies, not all of the ramifications of which can always be predicted.[10] What is certain is that there will be discharge of indebtedness income and, by reason of the liabilities of the partnership decreasing

---

[9] Treas. Reg. § 1.108-8(b)(2).

[10] Unless the debt was owed proportionately to each of the partners and each of the partners made the capital contribution, there would be a change in the economics which would have to be explored. For example, if the partner canceling the debt as a capital contribution was related to the other partners, there may be gift issues involved.

as a result of the cancellation of the debt, there will be a deemed distribution to the existing partners of the partnership.[11]

The discussion above has been limited to the partnership's side of the transaction. It is also necessary to consider the effect on the contributing partner. Generally, the contribution of the partnership's debt should be treated as a contribution of property on which no gain or loss is recognized by virtue of I.R.C. § 721(a). If, however, the indebtedness is the result of services performed by the contributor for the partnership, or goods sold by the contributor to the partnership, additional issues come into play. In the case of services rendered, if the contributor has not previously included the amount in income and the contributor receives a capital account credit, then the contributor should be subject to tax to the extent of the capital account credit. On the other hand, if the contributor was on the accrual method of accounting and already included the amount in income, then the normal rules of I.R.C. § 721(a) should apply. If the provider of the services does not receive a capital account credit for forgiving the debt, then the transaction should be viewed the same as if a profits interest was issued for services, with the result that no income should be recognized by the contributor.[12]

The Regulations deny the contributing partner a loss on the contribution of a partnership's debt to the partnership when the contributing partner receives a partnership interest in exchange for the contribution.[13]

b. Right to Acquire Property

In many instances, a party has an option to acquire real property or has entered into a contract to purchase real property. The option or contract may then be transferred to a partnership which will acquire the property subject to the option or contract. It would appear that the contributing party's rights under the option or contract should constitute property for purposes of I.R.C. § 721(a). The IRS has proposed a Regulation dealing with contributing contracts. Under the Proposed Regulation, if a partner contributes a contract to a partnership and the partnership subsequently acquires property pursuant to that contract, the acquired property is treated as section 704(c) property with the same amount of built-in gain or built-in loss as the contract.[14] This would imply that the contract could be contributed to the partnership without the recognition of gain.

In *United States v. Stafford*,[15] the taxpayer contributed a letter of intent with respect to the lease of land for the construction of a hotel and the financing of same. The court first held that the letter of intent was not an enforceable obligation. In connection with its decision with respect to whether the letter of intent constituted property for purposes of I.R.C. § 721, the court stated the following:

---

[11] *See* I.R.C. § 752(b) and § 3.04.

[12] *See* § 2.02.B.4.

[13] Treas. Reg. § 1.721-1(d).

[14] Prop. Treas. Reg. § 1.704-3(a)(8)(iii).

[15] 727 F.2d 1043 (11th Cir. 1984).

An enforceable contract would perhaps be assured of property status; but the absence of enforceability does not necessarily preclude a finding that a document, substantially committing the parties to the major terms of a development project, is property.[16]

The court ultimately concluded that the letter of intent had a sufficient bundle of rights to constitute property for purposes of I.R.C. § 721.

3. Services

It is clear that services (whether performed or to be performed) do not constitute property for purposes of I.R.C. § 721(a).[17] Thus, if a partner receives a capital interest in the partnership for services, the partner will be subject to tax. Proposed Regulations would also tax the issuance of profits interests to the service provider in some circumstances. We discuss this important area in detail in Chapter 8.

4. Assignment of Income

One of the bedrock principles of federal income tax law is that income must be taxed to the earner of the income and that an assignment of the right to the income will not transfer the incidence of taxation.[18] Thus, there is a question as to whether the assignment of income doctrine would cause a taxpayer to be taxable if the taxpayer assigned to a partnership amounts owed the taxpayer for services rendered, or amounts due the taxpayer from the sale of property, in exchange for a partnership interest. Today this is probably an academic question. This is because I.R.C. § 704(c)(1) now requires[19] that its provisions are mandatory and specifically covers income items. Under I.R.C. § 704(c)(1), the contributing partner cannot transfer the incidence of taxation on the income by virtue of a transfer of such income items to a partnership.[20]

5. Right to Use Property

The term "property" as used in I.R.C. § 721(a) must be distinguished from the right to use that property. For example, a partner owning a computer may allow the partnership to use the property, although the partner would continue to own the computer. Treas. Reg. § 1.721-1(a) clearly distinguishes between a contribution of property and merely allowing the partnership to use property. If a partner receives a capital account and profits interest in exchange for agreeing to allow the partnership to use the computer, the value of the partnership interest received by the partner should generally be taxable (i.e., rental income). The situation is effectively the same as if the partnership made a payment to the partner to lease the computer which the partner then contributed back to the partnership. The exact

---

[16] *Id.* at 1051–52.

[17] Treas. Reg. § 1.721-1(b)(1); *see* § 8.08.

[18] Lucas v. Earl, 281 U.S. 111 (1930); Helvering v. Horst, 311 U.S. 112 (1940).

[19] Prior to the Tax Reform Act of 1984 (Pub. L. No. 98-369), I.R.C. § 704(c) was an elective provision and only applied to depreciation, depletion, or gain or loss.

[20] *See* discussion at § 5.05.

parameters of this rule are unclear.[21] Where a partner retains ownership of property and allows a partnership to use it, the transaction is treated as one between a partnership and a partner not acting in his capacity as a partner in accordance with the provisions of I.R.C. § 707(a).[22] Not only does the contributor of the use of property have income as a result thereof, the partnership would be entitled to an equivalent deduction (unless the amount was required to be capitalized).

6. Recapture Property

Upon the disposition of certain depreciable property and mineral property, taxpayers generally are required to recognize as ordinary income (i.e., recapture) the depreciation, intangible drilling and development costs, exploration expenditures, and mine development expenditures previously deducted.[23] Under these recapture provisions, the amount that is recaptured is the excess of the amount realized, if the disposition is a sale or exchange, or the fair market value of the property, in any other disposition, over the adjusted basis of the property, but not greater than the particular type of recapture expense previously deducted. The nonrecognition rule of I.R.C. § 721, however, overrides these rules.[24]

7. Inventory and Unrealized Receivables

It is clear that inventory and accounts receivable constitute property which is covered by the nonrecognition provisions of I.R.C. § 721(a). This is consistent with the provisions of I.R.C. § 724, which provides that any gain or loss recognized by a partnership on the disposition of unrealized receivables contributed to the partnership by a partner, or inventory items contributed by a partner to a partnership, is treated as ordinary income or loss. In the case of accounts receivable of a cash method taxpayer, the anticipatory assignment of income doctrine is potentially applicable, but as indicated at § 2.01.B.5, as a result of changes made to I.R.C. § 704(c), the anticipatory assignment of income doctrine should not be applicable and when the accounts receivable are collected by the partnership, the income resulting therefrom would be allocated to the contributing partner.[25]

8. Recapitalizations

Often partnerships have different classes of interest. In a limited partnership, there are always at least two classes, the general partner and the limited partners. In many more complex partnership arrangements, there are often a variety of classes, each of which has different rights and preferences. If a partner changes the

---

[21] A carved out oil payment has been held to be "property" for purposes of I.R.C. § 351 in *H.B. Zachry Co. v. Commissioner*, 49 T.C. 73 (1967), *appeal dismissed* (5th Cir. 1968), as has a nonexclusive patent license in *E.I. Dupont de Nemours & Co. v. United States*, 471 F.2d 1211 (Ct. Cl. 1973).

[22] Treas. Reg. § 1.707-1(a).

[23] *See* I.R.C. §§ 1245, 1254.

[24] *See* I.R.C. §§ 1245(b)(3), 1250(d)(3), 1254(b)(1).

[25] *See* Rev. Rul. 80-198, 1980-2 C.B. 113, involving transfers of unrealized receivables to a corporation in a transaction governed by I.R.C. § 351.

class of interest they own (e.g., the general partner becomes a limited partner, or a Class A Member of an LLC becomes a Class C Member), or if the partnership recapitalizes and issues different classes of interest to its existing partners in exchange for the classes they previously held, an issue arises as to whether such transactions are taxable transactions in which the transferring partner recognizes gain or loss. Such transactions might well be exchanges under I.R.C. § 1001.

In Rev. Rul. 84-52,[26] a general partnership proposed to convert to a limited partnership. Two of the four partners would become general partners and the other two partners would become limited partners. The Ruling holds that although two of the partners have changed their general partner interests in the general partnership for limited partner interests in the limited partnership, no gain or loss will be recognized by the partners by virtue of I.R.C. § 721.[27] A Private Ruling[28] involved a situation in which an LLC taxed as a partnership had A Units outstanding. The LLC intended to designate A Units as B Units, create C Units, D Units and E Units, each of which had different rights, preferences, privileges, and restrictions, and then allow its members to convert A Units into other Units. Relying on Rev. Rul. 84-52, the IRS held that no gain or loss would be recognized by the members of the LLC upon the designation of the A Units as B Units or the conversion of Units into other classes of Units.

The IRS has now issued Proposed Regulations dealing with both convertible partnership interests and debt convertible into partnership interests. These are discussed at § 10.04.

C.   When Is Property Contributed

I.R.C. § 721(a) only applies to a "contribution" of property to a partnership in exchange for a partnership interest. Thus, it becomes necessary to determine what constitutes a "contribution."

Treas. Reg. § 1.721-1(a) makes clear that I.R.C. § 721(a) only applies in situations in which the contributor is acting in his or her capacity as a partner (or partner-to-be) and not if the contributor is acting in their individual capacity. Thus, a partner may sell property to the partnership or lease property to the partnership, and such transactions would not be tax-free transactions by virtue of I.R.C. § 721(a). The Regulations further provide that if a transfer of property by a partner to the partnership results in the partner receiving money or other consideration (including a promissory note of the partnership), the transaction will be treated as a sale or exchange, rather than a contribution to which I.R.C. § 721 applies.[29]

---

[26]   1984-1 C.B. 157.

[27]   The IRS has held in a number of Private Rulings that a conversion of a general partnership to an LLC was a transaction to which I.R.C. § 721 applied. See, e.g., PLR 9809003 (Mar. 18, 1997); PLR 9841030 (July 14, 1998).

[28]   PLR 200345007 (Aug. 7, 2003).

[29]   Treas. Reg. § 1.721-1(a).

In an attempt to avoid characterization as a sale, taxpayers have attempted to structure transactions in two steps. In the first step, the taxpayer contributes property to the partnership in exchange for a partnership interest to which the taxpayer takes the position that I.R.C. § 721(a) applies, and at a somewhat later date receives a cash distribution from the partnership and takes the position that such distribution is governed by the distribution provisions of I.R.C. § 731(a). There were a number of cases dealing with this type of factual situation.[30] In an effort to treat such transactions in accordance with their substance, rather than their form, Congress enacted I.R.C. § 707(a)(2).[31]

In *MAS One Limited Partnership v. United States*,[32] a partner guaranteed the interest on a partnership loan. The partner desired to terminate its interest in the partnership, but the lender was unwilling to release the taxpayer's guarantee. On December 28, the taxpayer abandoned its interest in the property. On December 29, the property was sold, the proceeds paid to the lender and the taxpayer paid $8.3 million to the lender in satisfaction of the loan. The court held that the payment made by the taxpayer was not a capital contribution, because the payment did not result in the taxpayer receiving an interest in the partnership (which it had abandoned before). This being the case, the payment did not qualify as a capital contribution to which I.R.C. § 721(a) applied, with the result that the payment by the taxpayer to the lender constituted taxable income to the partnership.[33]

D. Effect on Depreciable Assets

As indicated above, no depreciation recapture is required if depreciable assets are contributed by a partner to a partnership. As indicated below, the partnership's basis for property contributed by a partner is a carryover of the contributing partner's basis in the property contributed. Although generally a new taxpayer begins a new depreciation schedule with respect to property acquired, in the case of a contribution of depreciable property to a partnership to which I.R.C. § 721 applies, the partnership steps into the shoes of the contributing partner and the partnership continues to depreciate the property in the same manner as the contributing partner would have depreciated the property.[34] With respect to the depreciation deductions for the year of the contribution, if the contributing partner and the partnership have the same taxable years, the depreciation for the year is allocated to each based upon the number of months each owned the property.[35] If the contributing partner and the partnership have different taxable years, the contributing partner's depreciation deduction for the year of contribution is the same as it would be if both the contributing partner and the partnership had the

---

[30] *See, e.g.*, Otey v. Commissioner, 70 T.C. 312 (1978), *aff'd per curiam*, 634 F.2d 1046 (6th Cir. 1980); Communications Satellite Corp. v. United States, 625 F.2d 997 (Ct. Cl. 1980).

[31] *See* § 8.05.

[32] 271 F. Supp. 2d 1061 (S.D. Ohio 2003).

[33] *See also* Twenty Mile Joint Venture, PND, Ltd. v. Commissioner, 200 F.3d 1268 (10th Cir. 1999).

[34] I.R.C. § 168(i)(7); Prop. Treas. Reg. § 1.168-4(d)(5).

[35] Prop. Treas. Reg. § 1.168-5(b)(4)(i).

same taxable year, but adjustments are made with respect to the depreciation deduction to which the partnership is entitled to take account of its taxable year.[36]

E.   Stock of Corporate Partners

If a corporation transfers its own stock to a partnership in exchange for a partnership interest, it is clear that such stock would be treated as property for purposes of I.R.C. § 721. The real question presented is the corporation's basis for its partnership interest and the partnership's basis for the corporate stock, as well as the manner in which I.R.C. § 704(c) operates in this situation.

F.   Disregarded Entity Becoming Partnership

As a result of the check-the-box Regulations,[37] an entity which has a single member (typically an LLC) is normally treated as a disregarded entity. What happens if the single member entity gets a new member, with the result that the entity is now treated as a partnership (assuming it has not elected to be taxed as an association taxable as a corporation)? The answer to this question was provided in Rev. Rul. 99-5.[38]

That Ruling discussed two situations. In one situation, a new member was added to the single member LLC by means of a capital contribution by the new member to the LLC. In the other situation, the new member became a member by virtue of purchasing a portion of the interest in the LLC previously owned by the single member. Rev. Rul. 99-5 holds that in the first situation the single member is deemed to have contributed all of the assets of the LLC to a newly formed partnership, simultaneously with the capital contribution made by the new member. The deemed capital contribution made by the former single member is treated the same as if an actual capital contribution had been made to a partnership in exchange for a partnership interest, with the result that I.R.C. § 721(a) applied to the transaction.

In contrast, in the second situation, the transaction is treated as if the former single member sold a portion of the assets owned by the LLC, subject to the liabilities of the LLC, to the purchaser and then both the former single member and the new member made capital contributions to a newly formed partnership. In this situation, although the capital contribution made by the former single member was subject to the provisions of I.R.C. § 721(a) (with the result that no gain or loss is recognized by the former single member), gain or loss was recognized by the former single member on the deemed purchase by the new member of a portion of the assets of the LLC. This conclusion makes sense, since in the second situation, the former single member has the cash from the purchaser, whereas in the first situation it is the LLC which has the cash from the new member.

In addition, there will be a difference in the partnership's basis for its assets. In the first situation, the partnership has a carryover of the former single member's

---

[36] *See* Prop. Treas. Reg. § 1.168-5(b)(5).

[37] Treas. Reg. §§ 301.7701-2, -3, -4.

[38] 1999-1 C.B. 434.

basis for the assets of the LLC, while in the second situation the partnership has a basis equal to the former single member's basis for the assets deemed contributed by the former single member, and a carryover of the purchasing member's basis for the assets deemed purchased by the new member (which will reflect fair market value).

G.   Underwritten Partnership Interests

Sometimes partnership interests are issued in offerings in which underwriters acquire the partnership interests and then resell them to their customers. If a taxpayer acquires a partnership interest from an underwriter pursuant to a "qualified underwriting transaction," then the taxpayer is deemed to have acquired the partnership interest directly from the partnership in exchange for the partnership interest.[39] A "qualified underwriting transaction" is a transaction in which partnership interests are issued for cash to an underwriter where the underwriter is either acting as agent of the partnership or the underwriter's ownership of the partnership interests is transitory.[40]

§ 2.03   TRANSFERS TO INVESTMENT COMPANIES

A.   Taxability of Transfer

Notwithstanding the general rule of I.R.C. § 721(a), gain is recognized on a transfer of a property to a partnership which would be treated as an investment company if the partnership were incorporated.[41] For purposes of determining whether a partnership would be an investment company if it were incorporated, the rules of I.R.C. § 351(e)(1) apply. I.R.C. § 351(e)(1) provides that in determining whether a corporation is an investment company, there is taken into account all stock and securities held by the corporation and by treating cash and other financial instruments as listed in I.R.C. § 351(e)(1)(B) as stock or securities. This provision does not do much to illuminate what makes a corporation an investment company. This hole is filled by the Regulations.

Treas. Reg. § 1.351-1(c)(1) provides that a transfer is considered to be a transfer to an investment company if: (i) the transfer results in diversification of the transferor's interest, *and* (ii) the transferee is, insofar as here relevant, a corporation more than 80% of the value of whose assets are held for investment and are stock or securities (taking into account the provisions of I.R.C. § 351(e)(1)(B)). In determining whether the corporation is an investment company, the circumstances in existence immediately after the transfer in question are taken into account.[42]

---

[39] Treas. Reg. § 1.721-1(c).

[40] *Id.*

[41] I.R.C. § 721(b).

[42] Treas. Reg. § 1.351-1(c)(2). The list of assets that are considered held for investment has been expanded by I.R.C. § 351(e) subsequent to the promulgation of Treas. Reg. § 1.351-1(c)(2).

Normally, determining whether the 80% test has been met is not difficult. The more difficult issue is whether the transfer results in diversification.

Treas. Reg. § 1.351-1(c)(5) provides that a transfer ordinarily results in diversification if two or more persons transfer non-identical assets to a corporation in the exchange. It further provides, however, if one or more of the transfers involves assets which, taken in the aggregate, constitute an insignificant portion of the total value of the assets transferred, that transfer will be disregarded in determining whether diversification has occurred. What constitutes an insignificant transfer is not a mathematical test. In examples, the Regulations indicate that 1% would be disregarded.[43]

In Rev. Rul. 87-9, 1987-1 C.B. 133, the IRS held that the transfer of cash representing 11% of the assets transferred was not considered insignificant. In PLR 9504025 (Oct. 28, 1994) and PLR 20006008 (Sept. 30, 1999), it was held that so long as the non-identical assets did not exceed 5% of the total assets, the transaction would not be covered by I.R.C. § 721(b). The Regulations further provide that if transactions which result in diversification are structured in such a manner as not to appear to result in diversification (such as a delayed subsequent transfer), the transaction will be treated as resulting in diversification.

Treas. Reg. § 1.351-1(b)(2)(6)(i) provides that if each transferor transfers a diversified portfolio of stocks and securities, such transfers will not be treated as resulting in diversification. A portfolio of stocks and securities is diversified if it meets the 25% and 50% tests of I.R.C. § 368(a)(2)(F)(ii). The 25% test requires that not more than 25% of the total assets be invested in the stock or securities of any one issuer, and the 50% test requires that not more than 50% of the value of the total assets be invested in the stock and securities of five or fewer issuers.[44] In determining total assets, cash and cash items as well as Government securities are excluded.

A number of issues are raised in this context. First, is the definition of "Government securities." Presumably, this refers to the U.S. government, and not state or local securities.[45] Second is the question of who is the "issuer" when different agencies of a state government issue bonds. Is it the state or the separate agency?

§ 2.04 EFFECT OF RECEIPT OF BOOT

There are many nonrecognition sections of the Code which provide for tax-free treatment of the receipt of stock (or other property) and then contain a separate provision governing the receipt of property not entitled to be received tax-free.[46] These provisions typically operate to provide for taxable treatment for some or all

---

[43] Treas. Reg. § 1.351-1(b)(7), example 1. In PLR 200006008 (Sept. 30, 1999), 5% non-identical assets did not result in diversification.

[44] I.R.C. § 368(a)(2)(F)(ii).

[45] See T.D. 8662, 1996-1 C.B. 101, in which it is assumed that the term "Government securities" only applies to U.S. government obligations for purposes of I.R.C. § 368(a)(2)(F)(ii).

[46] See I.R.C. §§ 351(b), 356(a)(1), 1031(b).

of the boot received as gain from the sale or exchange of the property given up in the exchange.

I.R.C. § 721 does not contain a comparable provision. Rather, the normal rules regarding partnership distributions are applied to determine the tax consequences of the distribution.[47] Of course, the receipt of boot in connection with a contribution of property to a partnership could result in the disguised sales provisions of I.R.C. § 707(a)(2) becoming applicable.[48] Absent such recharacterization as a disguised sale, if any gain is to be recognized by virtue of the receipt of a distribution, it will be treated as gain recognized from the sale of a partnership interest, not the contributed property.

§ 2.05 BASIS OF PARTNERSHIP INTEREST TO PARTNER

I.R.C. § 722 provides that the contributing partner's basis for a partnership interest acquired by a contribution of property to the partnership is the amount of money and the adjusted basis of other property contributed by the contributing partner.[49] As we discuss next, however, liabilities can increase or decrease a partner's basis.

§ 2.06 EFFECT OF LIABILITIES

We discuss liabilities in detail in Chapter 3, but some discussion is appropriate here. In many instances, the partnership will either assume liabilities of a partner, or will acquire property the partner contributes subject to liabilities. For example, a partner may contribute real property which is subject to a mortgage to a partnership in exchange for a partnership interest, with the partnership either assuming the mortgage debt or merely taking the real property subject to the mortgage.

Subchapter K does not have a counterpart to I.R.C. § 357(c). I.R.C. § 357(c) generally provides that a contributing shareholder will recognize gain, even if I.R.C. § 351(a) otherwise provides tax-free treatment, if the corporation assumes liabilities of the shareholder or takes property the shareholder contributes subject to liabilities, and the total of the liabilities exceeds the shareholder's basis in the contributed property. The amount of the gain is the excess of the liabilities over basis. Subchapter K does, however, have a significant scheme for dealing with liabilities, and in some cases a contributing partner can also recognize gain.

Under I.R.C. § 752(b), any decrease in a partner's individual liabilities by reason of the deemed or actual assumption by the partnership of those individual liabilities is treated as a cash distribution to the partner by the partnership. Under I.R.C. § 752(a), any deemed or actual assumption of partnership liabilities by a partner is treated as a contribution of money by the partner to the partnership. If a partner

---

[47] *See* § 7.02, where the effect of partnership distributions are discussed.

[48] *See* § 8.05.

[49] In the case of a taxable transfer to an investment company under I.R.C. § 721(b), the basis is increased by the amount of gain recognized by the contributing partner. I.R.C. § 722.

transfers property to a partnership and the partnership assumes any of the partner's liabilities, or acquires the contributed property subject to liabilities, the amount of such liabilities is treated as a distribution to the contributing partner. The Regulations make clear that if as a result of a single transaction a partner incurs both an increase in the partner's share of the partnership's liabilities and a decrease in the partner's share of the partner's individual liabilities, only the net decrease is treated as a distribution from the partnership.[50] If that distribution exceeds the contributing partner's basis in her partnership interest, she recognizes gain to the extent of the excess under I.R.C. § 731(a)(1).[51] Assume partner A contributes property to a partnership with a basis of $10,000, but subject to a liability of $20,000, in exchange for a partnership interest. Under I.R.C. § 722, A's "starting basis" is $10,000. If these are the partnership's only liabilities, and $15,000 of the liabilities are allocated to other partners, under I.R.C. § 752, A's individual liabilities will be reduced by $20,000 and increased by $5,000, for a net decrease of $15,000. Under I.R.C. § 752(b), there will be a deemed distribution of cash of $15,000 to A. Under I.R.C. § 731(a)(1), A will recognize $5,000 of gain ($15,000 − $10,000). More to come in Chapter 3.

§ 2.07   HOLDING PERIOD OF PARTNERSHIP INTEREST

The general rule regarding the holding period of property to a taxpayer who engages in an exchange in which the property received has a basis determined by reference to the property exchanged is applicable in the case of a contribution of property to a partnership.[52] Thus, if the property transferred to the partnership is a capital asset or a section 1231 asset, then the holding period of the partnership interest will include the period during which the partner held the property under I.R.C. § 1223(1). This is commonly called taking a "tacked" holding period, or simply "tacking." If a partner does not contribute those types of assets, the holding period in the partnership interest begins when it is acquired (i.e., no tacking).

What happens if a partner contributes both assets that qualify for tacking and those that do not? The answer is that the partner takes a "split holding period." The IRS has issued Regulations in this regard. Under these Regulations, the portion of a partnership interest to which a holding period relates is determined by a fraction, the numerator of which is the fair market value of the portion of the interest received in the transaction to which the holding period relates, and the denominator of which is the fair market value of the entire partnership interest.[53] The Regulations illustrate the application of this rule in the situation in which a partner contributes $5,000 in cash and a capital asset having a basis of $5,000 and a fair market value of $10,000. The example indicates that since one-third of the taxpayers interest was received with respect to the contribution of cash, one-third of the taxpayer's holdings begins the day after the contribution and the taxpayer has a holding period for two-thirds of the partnership interest which includes the period

---

[50]   Treas. Reg. § 1.752-1(f).

[51]   It is also possible for the transaction to be treated as a disguised sale; *see* § 8.06.

[52]   I.R.C. § 1223(1).

[53]   Treas. Reg. § 1.1223-3(b)(1).

during which the taxpayer held the contributed property.[54]

While the result reached in the Regulations seems appropriate in connection with initial contributions to partnerships, in the case of ongoing capital contributions, it reaches results which were surprising to most practitioners. For example, assume that a partner has held a 10% partnership interest in partnership ABC for a number of years. Partnership ABC requires additional capital and each of the partners makes a pro rata capital contribution to the partnership, the taxpayer contributing $5,000. If at the time the taxpayer made the capital contribution, the fair market value of the taxpayer's partnership interest (immediately prior to the contribution) was $45,000 and the taxpayer, within one year of the date of the making of the $5,000 capital contribution were to sell the taxpayer's partnership interest, 10% ($5,000 ÷ $50,000) of the gain realized would be treated as short-term gain.

To ameliorate, to some extent, this harsh result, Treas. Reg. § 1.1223-3(b)(2) provides that if a partner makes cash contributions to the partnership and receives distributions from the partnership during the one-year period ending on the date of the sale or exchange of a partnership interest, the partner may reduce the cash contributions made during the year by cash distributions received. Furthermore, for this purpose, deemed capital contributions resulting from an increase in a partner's share of partnership liabilities, and deemed distributions resulting from a decrease in a partner's interest in partnership liabilities, are generally disregarded.[55]

If a partner sells all of the partner's partnership interest, the capital gain or loss is divided between long-term capital gain and short-term capital gain in the same proportions as the holding period of the partnership interest is divided. If a partner sells less than all of the partner's partnership interest, the holding period of the transferred interest is divided between long-term capital gain and short-term capital gain in the same proportions as would be the case if the partner sold the partner's entire interest in the partnership.[56]

§ 2.08 PARTNERSHIP'S BASIS FOR CONTRIBUTED PROPERTY

The partnership's basis for property contributed to the partnership by a partner is the contributing partner's adjusted basis for the property contributed (increased by the amount of gain recognized in the case of transfers to investment companies).[57] This basis is not affected by changes to the contributing partner's basis for the partnership interest received, such as would result from a net relief of liabilities.

---

[54] Treas. Reg. § 1.1223-3(f), example 1.

[55] Treas. Reg. § 1.1223-3(b)(3).

[56] Treas. Reg. § 1.1223-3(f)(c).

[57] I.R.C. § 723.

§ 2.09　PARTNERSHIP'S HOLDING PERIOD FOR PROPERTY RECEIVED

The partnership's holding period for the contributed assets is determined under the general rules of I.R.C. § 1223. Under I.R.C. § 1223(2), in determining the period for which a taxpayer has held property, there is included the holding period of the transferor if the property has a basis in the hands of the taxpayer determined by reference to the basis of the property in the hands of the contributor. Since the partnership would have a basis for contributed property equal to the basis of the contributing partner, the partnership has a holding period which includes the holding period of the contributing partner.

§ 2.10　CHARACTER OF GAIN OR LOSS FROM SALE OF CONTRIBUTED PROPERTY

If a partner holds ordinary income property, the taxpayer might seek to obtain capital gain treatment upon its sale by first contributing the property to a partnership which would hold the property as a capital asset, rather than as an ordinary income asset. Alternatively, if a taxpayer holds a capital asset which has a built-in loss, the taxpayer might attempt to obtain ordinary loss treatment by transferring it to a partnership which would hold the property as an ordinary income asset. To prevent partnerships from being used in such a fashion, I.R.C. § 724 was enacted.

A.　Contributions of Ordinary Income Assets

1.　Unrealized Receivables

If a partner contributes property to a partnership which was an unrealized receivable in the contributing partner's hands, any gain or loss recognized by the partnership on the disposition of such property is treated as ordinary income or ordinary loss, as applicable.[58] For this purpose, the term "unrealized receivable" has the meaning given such term in I.R.C. § 751(c) (except that any reference therein to the partnership refers to the contributing partner).[59] Under I.R.C. § 751(c), the term "unrealized receivable" includes, to the extent not previously included in income, any rights to payment for: (i) goods delivered (or to be delivered) to the extent the proceeds would not be treated as amounts received from the sale or exchange of a capital asset, or (ii) services rendered or to be rendered.

2.　Inventory Items

If a partner contributes property which constituted an inventory item in his or her hands, then any gain or loss recognized by the partnership on the disposition of such property during a five-year period beginning on the date of the contribution is

---

[58]　I.R.C. § 724(a).

[59]　I.R.C. § 724(b)(1).

treated as ordinary income or ordinary loss, as applicable.[60] For this purpose, the term "inventory item" has the meaning given such term in I.R.C. § 751(b) (except that references to the partnership instead refer to the contributing partner).[61] I.R.C. § 751(b) defines the term "inventory item" to mean: (i) property described in I.R.C. § 1221(a)(1), or (ii) any other property which on its sale or exchange would be considered property other than a capital asset and other than property described in section 1231.[62]

B. Contributions of Capital Loss Property

If the property contributed by the partner was a capital asset in the hands of the contributing partner, then any loss recognized by the partnership on the disposition of such property during the five-year period beginning on the date of the contribution is treated as a loss from the sale of a capital asset to the extent that the contributing partner's adjusted basis for the property at the time of the contribution exceeded the fair market value of the property at such time.

C. Tax-Free Transfers

To discourage partnerships from trying to eliminate the taints provided by I.R.C. § 724, if any property described in that section is disposed of in a nonrecognition transaction in which the partnership has a substituted basis in the property received in such transaction, such property is treated in the same fashion as the property disposed of.[63] The foregoing rule does not apply, however, if the partnership contributes such property to a C corporation in a transaction to which I.R.C. § 351 applies in which the partnership receives stock of a C corporation.[64]

§ 2.11   ORGANIZATION AND SELLING EXPENSES

A. Selling Expenses

No deduction is allowed to a partnership or a partner for the costs incurred to sell interests in a partnership.[65] Such expenses include brokerage fees, registration fees, legal fees of the underwriters, securities advice (including advice concerning tax disclosures in offering documents), printing costs, etc.[66]

---

[60] I.R.C. § 724(b).

[61] I.R.C. § 724(b)(2).

[62] For this purpose, I.R.C. § 1231 is applied without regard to any holding period provided in that section. I.R.C. § 724(d)(2).

[63] I.R.C. § 724(d)(3)(A).

[64] I.R.C. § 724(d)(3)(B).

[65] I.R.C. § 709(a).

[66] Treas. Reg. § 1.709-2(b).

B. Organization Expenses

Expenses of organizing the partnership generally are nondeductible, but there is an election available to amortize organization expenses.[67] To qualify as an organization expense, the expense must be: (i) incident to the creation of the partnership, (ii) properly chargeable to capital accounts, and (iii) of a character which, if incurred in connection with the creation of a partnership having an ascertainable life, would be amortizable over that life.[68] In order to be incurred incident to the creation of the partnership, the expense must be incurred during the period beginning a reasonable time before the partnership begins business and ending with the due date for the partnership's taxable year (without extension) during which the partnership begins business.[69] The Regulations give as examples of organization expenses, legal fees relating directly to the organization of the partnership, such as negotiation and preparation of the partnership agreement, accounting fees for services incident to the organization of the partnership, and filing fees.[70]

Under I.R.C. § 709(b)(1), if the partnership elects, it may deduct up to $5,000 of organization expenses incurred by it, reduced on a dollar-for-dollar basis by organization expenses in excess of $50,000. Any amount which the partnership is not permitted to deduct under the preceding sentence may be amortized. Pursuant to I.R.C. § 709(b)(1)(B), such expenses may be deducted ratably over a period of not less than 180 months beginning with the month in which the partnership begins business. If the partnership is liquidated before the end of such 60-month period, the expenses which have not as yet been amortized may be deducted as a loss to the extent provided in I.R.C. § 165.[71]

Treas. Reg. § 1.709-1(b)(2) provides that the partnership is deemed to have made the election to amortize organizational expenses under I.R.C. § 709(b) for the taxable year in which the partnership begins business. If the partnership does not wish to make this election, it may do so by clearly electing to capitalize its organizational expenditures on a timely filed return for the taxable year in which the partnership begins business.

The determination of the day the partnership begins business is a question of fact that must be determined based upon all of the facts and circumstances. Ordinarily, however, a partnership begins business when it starts the business operation for which it was organized. This usually requires the acquisition of operating assets which are necessary to the type of business which the partnership intends to conduct.[72]

In the case of syndication expenses, and in the case of organization expenses if the election to amortize such expenses has not been made, the partnership would

---

[67] I.R.C. § 709(b).

[68] Treas. Reg. § 1.709-2(a).

[69] *Id.*

[70] *Id.*

[71] I.R.C. § 709(b)(2).

[72] Treas. Reg. § 1.709-2(c).

not be entitled to a deduction for such expenses at the time of its liquidation.[73] Inasmuch as organization and syndication expenses are required to be capitalized,[74] they should not constitute an expenditure described in I.R.C. § 705(a)(2)(B), with the result that the partners need not reduce the bases of their partnership interests by the amount of the nondeductible organization and syndication expenses. Consequently, the costs will benefit the partners at the time the partnership is liquidated and liquidating distributions are made to the partners, giving them less gain or more loss.[75]

C. Start-Up Expenses

I.R.C. § 195(a) denies a deduction for start-up costs. However, I.R.C. § 195(b) specifically allows the taxpayer to elect to treat these costs as deferred expenses and amortize them over a period of not less than 180 months beginning with the month in which the active trade or business begins.

I.R.C. § 195(c) provides the definitions of the terms "start-up costs" and "beginning of trade or business." Start-up costs are costs for creating an active trade or business or investigating the creation or acquisition of an active trade or business. Start-up costs include any amounts paid or incurred in connection with any activity engaged in for profit or for the production of income before the trade or business begins, in anticipation of the activity becoming an active trade or business. The expenditures must be of such a nature that they would be deductible if they had been incurred in the operation of an existing business.

When an active trade or business is purchased, start-up costs include only costs incurred in the course of the general search for or preliminary investigation of the business. Costs incurred in the attempt to actually purchase a specific business are capital expenses and are not amortizable under I.R.C. § 195. Investigatory expenses are those incurred in the review of a prospective business before a decision to acquire the business has been made.

As in the case of organizational expenditures, Treas. Reg. § 1.195-1(b) provides that a taxpayer is deemed to have made the election under I.R.C. § 195(b) to amortize start-up expenditures for the taxable year in which the active trade or business to which the expenditures relate begins. If the taxpayer does not wish to have the election apply, the taxpayer may do so by clearly electing to capitalize its start-up expenditures.

A partnership using the cash basis cannot take an amortization deduction until the start-up cost has been paid. If such costs are paid in a year after the business has begun, they should be treated as incurred on the date the I.R.C. § 195(b) election is effective. The amount of the expenses that are deductible in the year should equal their total amount multiplied by a fraction, the numerator of which is the number of months since the I.R.C. § 195(b) election was made and the denominator is 180 (the number of months in the amortization period). Thus, the

---

[73] Temp. Treas. Reg. § 1.709-1T(a)(3).

[74] *See* H.R. Rep. No. 1515, 94th Cong., 2d Sess. 42 (1976).

[75] Rev. Rul. 87-111, 1987-2 C.B. 160.

amount of amortization on items paid in subsequent years should be allowed to catch up to the amortization on costs paid in the initial election year.

§ 2.12   READING, QUESTIONS AND PROBLEMS

A.   Reading

CODE:

   I.R.C. §§ 108(e)(8), 168(i)(7), 351(e)(1), 368(a)(2)(F), 453B, 709, 721, 722, 723, 724, 751(b), 751(c), 1223(1), 1223(2).

TREASURY REGULATIONS:

   Treas. Reg. §§ 1.351-1(b), 1.351-1(c), 1.709-2, 1.721-1, 1.722-1, 1.1223-3(b), 1.1223-3(f).

CASES:

   Jack Ammann Photogrammetric Engineers, Inc. v. Commissioner, 341 F.2d 466 (5th Cir. 1965).

   United States v. Stafford, 727 F.2d 1043 (11th Cir. 1984).

   MAS One Limited Partnership v. United States, 271 F. Supp. 2d 1061 (S.D. Ohio 2003).

   Otey v. Commissioner, 70 T.C. 312 (1978), *aff'd per curiam*, 634 F.2d 1046 (6th Cir. 1980).

RULINGS AND OTHER INTERPRETATIONS:

   Rev. Rul. 80-198, 1980-2 C.B. 113.

   Rev. Rul. 84-52, 1984-1 C.B. 157.

   Rev. Rul. 87-9, 1987-1 C.B. 133.

   Rev. Rul. 99-5, 1999-1 C.B. 434.

   PLR 9504025 (Oct. 28, 1994).

   PLR 9809003 (Mar. 18, 1997).

   PLR 200345007 (Aug. 7, 2003).

B.   Questions and Problems

1. A, B, C, and D form Partnership ABCD in January 2012. The partners contributed the following:

		Adjusted Basis	FMV
A	Cash	$200	$200
	Securities	100	800

		Adjusted Basis	FMV
B	Land	100	200
	Building	400	800
C	Installment Note	300	700
	C's Promissory Note	-0-	300
D	Cash Basis Receivables	-0-	500
	Goodwill	-0-	500

a. 80% of the securities contributed by A were acquired more than one year ago and 20% were acquired less than one year ago.

b. The building contributed by B was acquired by B in January 2010 and was depreciated by B using a 39-year straight-line method.

c. The installment note contributed by C was issued to C in 2011 upon the sale of a capital asset having a basis of $300. The first payment on the note (both principal and interest) is due in June 2012.

d. The cash basis receivables contributed by D represent receivables for services rendered by D through his sole proprietorship. The goodwill contributed by D is associated with D's sole proprietorship.

    i. Do any of the partners recognize any gain on the transfer to the partnership?

    ii. What are the partners' bases and holding periods for their partnership interests?

    iii. What is ABCD's basis and holding period for each of the assets contributed to it?

    iv. How does ABCD depreciate the building?

    v. Who is taxed when the appreciated contributed property is sold/collected? What is the character of the income?

2. A and B form AB Partnership in 2012. The partners contributed the following:

a. Land which A had been selling as a residential subdivision. Approximately 60% of the original land owned by A has already been sold.

b. Cash which will be used to construct a strip mall on the land.

    i. If the strip mall is sold in 2016, will the gain be ordinary income or capital gain?

    ii. If the strip mall is sold in 2026, will the gain be ordinary income or capital gain?

3. A purchased land for $200. He borrowed $800 to construct a building on the land. When A's basis for the land and building has been reduced to $700, and the mortgage debt is still $800, A contributes the land and building to partnership AB for a 50% interest in the partnership. Assume that under

I.R.C. § 752 and its Regulations 50% of the mortgage debt is included in A's basis.

    a. What is A's basis for his partnership interest?

    b. What is the partnership's basis for the land and building?

4. C agrees to perform services for partnership AB in exchange for a 10% interest in AB.

    a. Does C recognize income?

5. a. A contributes 20 marketable securities, each of equal value, to partnership AB in exchange for an 80% interest in AB.

    a. B contributes five marketable securities, each of equal value, to partnership AB in exchange for a 20% interest in AB.

        i. Does either A or B recognize gain on the transfer?

        ii. If, instead, A's contribution gave him a 98% interest and B had a 2% interest, what effect?

        iii. Would it make a difference if A contributed the same five marketable securities of equal value as B contributed?

        iv. Would it make a difference if B contributed cash rather than marketable securities?

        v. Would it matter if the securities contributed by B were shares of a closely held corporation?

Chapter 3

OUTSIDE BASIS AND ALLOCATION OF LIABILITIES

§ 3.01 INTRODUCTION

Chapter 3 will focus on a partner's basis for the partner's partnership interest, as opposed to the partnership's basis for its assets. A partner's basis for the partner's partnership interest is typically referred to as "outside basis," whereas a partnership's basis for its assets is referred to as the partnership's "inside basis." This chapter will discuss the relevance of a partner's outside basis and the manner of computing such basis. A significant portion of this chapter will be devoted to the effect of partnership liabilities on a partner's basis for the partner's partnership interest.

§ 3.02 RELEVANCE OF OUTSIDE BASIS

A. Gain or Loss

If a partner sells her partnership interest, it is necessary to determine whether the partner realizes a gain or loss with respect to such sale. Under the general rule for determining the amount of gain or loss under I.R.C. § 1001(a), gain or loss is measured by the difference between the amount realized in the sale and the adjusted basis for the property sold as determined pursuant to I.R.C. § 1011. Under I.R.C. § 1011(a), the adjusted basis of property for determining gain or loss from the sale or other disposition of that property is the basis of the property, determined under I.R.C. § 1012 or, insofar as here relevant, the rules of Subchapter K of the Code. I.R.C. § 1012 provides that the basis of the property is the cost of the property except as otherwise provided, insofar as here relevant, in Subchapter K of the Code. Thus, in order to determine whether a partner recognizes gain or loss upon the sale of his partnership interest, it is necessary to know the partner's basis for his partnership interest.

B. Limitation on Loss

As discussed in detail in Chapter 4, a partnership is a pass-through entity for federal income tax purposes so that the items of income, gain, loss, and deduction are taken into account by the partners of the partnership, rather than being subject to tax at the partnership level. I.R.C. § 704(d) of the Code sets forth a limitation on the ability of a partner to deduct losses of the partnership passed through to the partner. Under I.R.C. § 704(d), a partner may only deduct the partner's distributive share of partnership loss to the extent of the partner's adjusted basis for the partner's partnership interest at the end of the taxable year in which the loss is incurred. Thus, in order to know whether a partner may currently deduct the partner's distributive share of a partnership's loss, it is necessary to know the partner's basis for her partnership interest.

C. Effect of Distributions

1. Cash Distributions

I.R.C. § 731(a) provides that if a partnership distributes cash to a partner and the amount of the cash exceeds the partner's adjusted basis for his partnership interest immediately before the distribution, then gain will be recognized. Similarly, I.R.C. § 731(a)(2) provides that while a partner generally does not recognize loss upon the receipt of a distribution from a partnership, where only money and certain other kinds of property described in I.R.C. § 731(a)(2)(B) is distributed, the loss is recognized to the extent the partner's adjusted basis in the partner's partnership interest exceeds the amount of money and the distributee partner's basis for the other specified property. Thus, in order to determine whether there is any gain or loss recognized by a partner upon the receipt of cash distributions, it is necessary to know the partner's basis for her partnership interest.

2. Property Distributions

Under I.R.C. § 732(a)(1), if a partnership makes a nonliquidating distribution of property other than cash (or, in some cases, marketable securities) to a partner, the recipient partner's basis for his partnership interest generally is irrelevant. In such case, the partner's basis for the property distributed is a carryover of the partnership's basis. I.R.C. § 732(a)(2) provides, however, that the partner's basis in the distributed property may in no event exceed the partner's adjusted basis for her partnership interest.

In the case of a liquidating distribution by a partnership, I.R.C. § 732(b) provides that the basis of the property distributed by the partnership is equal to the partner's adjusted basis for his partnership interest. Thus, in order to know what a partner's basis is for property distributed in liquidation by a partnership, it is necessary to know the partner's basis for her partnership interest.

§ 3.03 GENERAL RULES FOR COMPUTING BASIS

A. Starting Point

There are four principal manners in which a partner can acquire a partnership interest. A partner can make a capital contribution directly to the partnership in exchange for a partnership interest as was discussed in Chapter 2. Alternatively, a taxpayer could purchase a partnership interest from someone who is already a partner of the partnership. A person who is a partner of a partnership may make a gift of the partnership interest to a taxpayer during their lifetime. Lastly, a taxpayer may receive a partnership interest upon the death of an existing partner.

1. Capital Contributions

As indicated in § 2.05, if a taxpayer becomes a partner by virtue of making a capital contribution directly to the partnership, the contributing partner's basis for the partnership interest acquired is the amount of money and the adjusted basis of other property contributed by the contributing partner.[1] If a person receives a capital interest in a partnership by virtue of having performed services for the partnership, then the person's basis for the partnership interest received is equal to the taxable income recognized by the partner as a result of the receipt of such partnership interest.[2]

2. Purchase of a Partnership Interest

If a person purchases a partnership interest from a third party who is already a member of the partnership, then the normal rule of I.R.C. § 1012 applies, namely that the partner's basis for his partnership interest is the cost of the partnership interest purchased.

3. Gifts

If a partnership interest is received by gift, the normal rules with respect to the receipt of gifts apply. Under I.R.C. § 1015(a), the basis of the partnership interest in the hands of the recipient is generally the same as the basis of the partnership interest in the hands of the donor, subject to the loss limitation rules of I.R.C. § 1015(a). If the donor pays any gift tax with respect to such gift, the donee's basis is increased by an amount which bears the same ratio to the gift tax as the net appreciation in value of the gift (if any) bears to the amount of the gift (but not in excess of the gift tax paid).[3] The net appreciation is the amount by which the fair market value of the gift exceeds the donor's basis immediately before the gift.[4]

4. Inherited Partnership Interest

If a partnership interest is inherited from a decedent, the basis of the partnership interest inherited is equal to the fair market value of the partnership interest on the date of the death of the decedent or the alternate valuation date if that has been elected (excluding any value attributable to income in respect of a decedent, which includes depreciation recapture) subject to adjustment for the recipient's share of partnership debt.

---

[1] I.R.C. § 722.

[2] Treas. Reg. § 1.722-1. The amount of the income would be the fair market value of the partnership interest. Treas. Reg. § 1.721-1(b)(1).

[3] I.R.C. § 1015(d)(6)(A); *see* Treas. Reg. § 1.1015-5(c).

[4] I.R.C. § 1015((d)(6)(B).

B.   Adjustments to Basis of Partnership Interest — Generally

I.R.C. § 705 sets forth the general rules for determining a partner's basis for her partnership interest. The general philosophy of I.R.C. § 705(a) is that a partner's basis for his partnership interest should reflect the partner's share of the economic activity of the partnership from the time the taxpayer acquired the partnership interest. Thus, a partner's adjusted basis for her partnership interest will be increased by the partner's distributive share of partnership taxable income and is decreased by distributions received by the partner and the partner's distributive share of partnership losses. In addition, if a partner makes any capital contributions to the partnership subsequent to the dates the person became a partner, the partner's basis for her partnership interest will be increased as provided in I.R.C. § 722.

The adjustments provided for in I.R.C. §§ 705(a)(1)(A) and (2)(A) are necessary to ensure the single level of tax which is at the heart of Subchapter K of the Code. If taxable income were recognized by a partnership, the partners paid tax on that partnership income and the basis of their partnership interest did *not* increase, then at some point the distributions made by the partnership would exceed the partner's basis for his partnership interest and there would be a second level of tax at the partner level. The adjustment provided for in I.R.C. § 705(a)(1)(A) prevent this from happening. Likewise, the adjustment provided for in I.R.C. § 705(a)(2)(A) prevents a partner from claiming a double loss.

C.   Special Adjustments

1.   Tax-Exempt Income

I.R.C. § 705(a)(1)(B) provides that a partner's basis for her partnership interest is increased by the amount of tax-exempt income. This adjustment is necessary so that what is otherwise tax-exempt income does not become taxable when it is distributed to a partner. If the partner's basis for his partnership interest did not increase by the amount of the tax-exempt income recognized by the partnership, then when that income is distributed (or ultimately at liquidation), the partner would receive distributions in excess of the partner's basis for her partnership interest, resulting in the partner being taxed on what is intended to be tax-exempt income.

2.   Natural Resources Property

I.R.C. § 705(a)(1)(C) provides that a partner's basis for her partnership interest is increased by the excess of the deductions for depletion over the basis of the property subject to depletion. This provision is only applicable to partnerships engaged in natural resources businesses and then only if percentage depletion is used, rather than cost depletion.[5] This adjustment is necessary because if such an

---

[5] With the percentage depletion method, deductions for depletion may be claimed even though the amount of the depletion deductions in the aggregate exceeds the taxpayer's basis for the property.

adjustment were not made, the benefit of percentage depletion would ultimately be lost. It also eliminates a disparity between inside basis and outside basis, which would otherwise occur because the partnership's basis for its assets is not reduced by excess depletion.

Another special rule relating to natural resources is provided in the case of depletion with respect to oil and gas properties. Under I.R.C. § 613(a)(c)(7)(D), percentage depletion with respect to oil and gas properties is determined separately by each partner, not by the partnership. In recognition of this fact, I.R.C. § 705(a)(3) provides that a partner's basis for her partnership interest is decreased by the amount of the partner's deduction for depletion with respect to oil and gas property to the extent the deduction does not exceed the partner's proportionate share of the adjusted basis of the property allocated to that partner under I.R.C. § 613A(c)(7)(D).

The Regulations provide that a partner's basis for his partnership interest is also adjusted to reflect any gain or loss to the partner resulting from the disposition by the partnership of an oil and gas property.[6]

3. Nondeductible Expenditures

I.R.C. § 705(a)(2)(B) provides that a partner's basis for his partnership interest is reduced by expenditures of the partnership that are not deductible in computing its taxable income and not properly chargeable to capital accounts. The purpose of this section of the Code is to prevent a taxpayer from having an unintended loss from nondeductible expenditures, much like the increase in basis for tax-exempt income is intended to avoid inappropriate income recognition. There is little guidance concerning the specific items which are covered by I.R.C. § 705(a)(2)(B). It is likely that this section of the Code includes losses disallowed under I.R.C. §§ 267(a)(1) or 707(b),[7] life insurance premiums which are not deductible by virtue of I.R.C. § 264, and interest expense disallowed under I.R.C. § 265. It is unclear whether amounts paid to promote the sale of partnership interests by the partnership which are rendered nondeductible by I.R.C. § 709 are included within the provisions of I.R.C. § 705(a)(2)(B), but it would appear that they should be included.

Under I.R.C. § 702(a)(4), charitable contributions made by a partnership are separately taken into account by the partners. The IRS has held that if a partnership makes a charitable contribution of property, each partner's basis for her partnership interest is decreased by the partner's share of the partnership's basis for the property contributed.[8]

---

[6] Treas. Reg. § 1.705-1(a)(5).

[7] Rev. Rul. 96-10, 1996-1 C.B. 138.

[8] Rev. Rul. 96-11, 1996-1 C.B. 140.

4. Distributions

I.R.C. § 705(a)(2) provides that a partner's basis for the partner's partnership interest is decreased by distributions by the partnership as provided in I.R.C. § 733. I.R.C. § 733 provides that in the case of a nonliquidating distribution by a partnership to a partner, the adjusted basis of the partner's partnership interest is reduced by the amount of any money distributed and the adjusted basis of property other than money distributed.

D. No Negative Basis

I.R.C. §§ 705(a)(2), (3), and 733, when referring to reductions in a partner's basis for her partnership interest, contain the parenthetical phrase "(but not below zero)." This, when combined with the prohibition on a partner claiming losses in excess of the partner's basis for his partnership interest contained in I.R.C. § 704(d) and the limitation on the basis of distributed property contained in I.R.C. § 732(a)(2), prevents a partner from ever having a negative basis for her partnership interest. Instead, gain is recognized in the case of cash distributions and the basis of property received by the partner is limited in the case of distributions of property other than cash.

Sometimes practitioners refer to a partner having a negative basis. In actuality, what is meant is that the partner has a negative capital account.

E. Time for Computing Basis

As can be seen from the above, because of the various adjustments that must be taken into account by a partner in determining the partner's basis for her partnership interest, if a partner were always required to determine the adjusted basis of her partnership interest, it would be extremely burdensome. To avoid this, Treas. Reg. § 1.705-1(a)(1) provides that a partner must determine the adjusted basis of his partnership interest "only when necessary for the determination of his tax liability or that of any other person." That Regulation further provides that ordinarily the determination need only be made at the end of a partnership taxable year. To avoid having to determine a partner's adjusted basis for her partnership interest mid-year when distributions are made by a partnership during the year, Treas. Reg. § 1.731-1(a)(1)(ii) provides that advances or drawings against the partner's share of income is treated as current distributions made on the last day of the partnership's taxable year.[9]

F. Ordering Rules

In addition to knowing when computations must be made of a partner's adjusted basis for his partnership interest, it is also important to know the order in which the adjustments are made. This can be extremely important. It is clear that allocations of income are made to partners prior to distributions reducing the basis

---

[9] In Rev. Rul. 94-4, 1994-1 C.B. 196, it was held that a deemed distribution of money under I.R.C. § 752(b) resulting from a decrease in a partner's share of partnership liabilities is treated as a distribution on the last day of the partnerships taxable year pursuant to Treas. Reg. § 1.731-1(a)(1)(ii).

of the partnership interest. This is the very purpose of Treas. Reg. § 1.731-1(a)(1)(ii).

In determining the applicability of the loss limitation rule of I.R.C. § 704(d), the partner's basis for her partnership interest is first increased under I.R.C. § 705(a)(1) and then decreased under I.R.C. § 705(a)(2) (other than with respect to losses of the taxable year and losses previously disallowed).[10]

§ 3.04   EFFECT OF PARTNERSHIP LIABILITIES

A.   General Rules

I.R.C. § 752(a) provides that an increase in a partner's share of partnership liabilities is a contribution of money by such partner to the partnership. This is a unique characteristic of partnership taxation which has resulted in entities taxable as partnerships often being the preferred vehicle for tax shelters. The ability of a partner to include partnership liabilities in her basis for her partnership interest enables the partner to claim deductions flowing through the partnership in excess of the amount contributed by the partner to the partnership, notwithstanding the limitation of I.R.C. § 704(d). The ability to increase a partner's basis for his partnership interest by his share of the liabilities of the partnership is one of the major distinguishing characteristics between a partnership and an S corporation.

The theoretical purpose of allowing a partner to increase her basis in her partnership interest is to put the partner in the same place the partner would have been in had the partner directly conducted the activity being conducted by the partnership as an individual, rather than through a partnership.[11] In effect, this is the use of the aggregate theory of partnerships.

To illustrate, if an individual purchased an office building for $1,000,000, paying $200,000 in cash and borrowing $800,000 on a mortgage loan, the individual would have a $1,000,000 basis for the office building. The individual would be permitted to depreciate the entire cost of the office building, even though the individual only paid $200,000 out of pocket. If instead of that individual purchasing the office building, that individual and another individual formed a partnership to purchase the office building, the partnership's basis for the office building would also be $1,000,000, the same as in the case where the individual purchased it. If the individuals were not permitted to increase their bases for their partnership interests by the amount of the mortgage loan, however, because of the loss limitation of I.R.C. § 704(d), the losses which could be claimed by the partners would be limited to $200,000. To remedy this situation, I.R.C. § 752(a) allows the partners to increase the bases of their partnership interests by the $800,000 mortgage loan, thereby permitting them to claim losses of up to $1,000,000.

I.R.C. § 752(c) provides that for purposes of I.R.C. § 752, a liability to which property is subject is considered as a liability of the owner of the property to the

---

[10] *See* Rev. Rul. 66-94, 1966-1 C.B. 166.

[11] *See* Crane v. Commissioner, 331 U.S. 1 (1947); Commissioner v. Tufts, 461 U.S. 300 (1983).

extent of the fair market value of the property. The effect of this provision is that partners can increase the bases of their partnership interests not only for recourse indebtedness of the partnership, but also for nonrecourse indebtedness of the partnership.

To round out the statutory scheme, I.R.C. § 752(b) provides that a decrease in a partner's share of a partnership's liabilities is treated as a distribution to that partner. Lastly, I.R.C. § 752(d) provides that in the case of a sale or exchange of a partnership interest, liabilities are to be treated in the same manner as liabilities in connection with the sale of property other than a partnership interest.[12] As can be seen above, the statutory provisions dealing with liabilities in partnerships are fairly simple, consisting of four subsections, each of which is a single sentence. Notwithstanding the brevity of the Code provisions, the Regulations implementing this Code provision are extremely lengthy and complex.

A partner's interest in a partnership's liability can change in a number of ways, some of which relate to activities between the partner and the partnership and others which have no relation to activities between the partner and the partnership. Thus, a new borrowing by the partnership will result in an increase in a partner's share of the partnership's liabilities, while the repayment of partnership debt will result in a decrease in a partner's interest in partnership liabilities.

B. Definition of Recourse and Nonrecourse Liabilities

The Regulations have a very different scheme for allocating recourse liabilities of a partnership from that applicable to the allocation of nonrecourse liabilities of a partnership. For that reason, it is extremely important to know whether a liability is a recourse liability or a nonrecourse liability for purposes of the Regulations.

1. Definition of Liability

Before you can distinguish between a recourse liability and a nonrecourse liability, it is first necessary to know what is included in the term "liability." For purposes of I.R.C. § 752, an obligation is a liability to the extent that the incurring of the liability: (i) creates or increases the basis of the obligor's assets (including cash), (ii) gives rise to an immediate deduction to the obligor, or (iii) gives rise to an expense that is not deductible and not properly chargeable to capital.[13]

2. Definition of Recourse Liability

Treas. Reg. § 1.752-1(a)(1) provides that a "liability is a recourse liability of a partnership to the extent that any partner or related person bears the economic risk of loss for that liability under § 1.752-2."

---

[12] Generally, when a taxpayer sells property, liabilities assumed by the purchaser, as well as liabilities to which the property sold is subject, are treated as part of the amount realized.

[13] Treas. Reg. § 1.752-1(a)(4)(i).

Before we explain regulatory rules to you, some basics: Economic risk of loss speaks to bottom-line obligation on a recourse debt, after taking into account all facts and circumstances, including rights of contribution among partners. Assume a general partnership, that is not a limited liability partnership, has two partners, one who holds a 60% interest and one who holds a 40% interest. Generally, and unsurprisingly, they will usually share the economic risk of loss on any partnership recourse debt 60/40. Now assume a limited partnership, where A is the general partner and B is the limited partner. Again unsurprisingly, generally the general partner has all of the economic risk of loss on any partnership recourse debt and the limited partner has none. It is possible for a limited partner to voluntarily take on some part of that economic risk of loss, however, by making an agreement to that effect with the lender and/or the general partner. Limited partners often want to do this to increase their bases in their partnership interests, allowing them to deduct more losses.[14]

We also need to preview "capital accounts," a topic on which we go into excruciating detail in Chapter 5. Usually, each partner has a capital account. For now, think of a capital account as a measure of a partner's economic investment in the partnership. Generally, they are increased by money contributed, the fair market value (not basis) of property contributed, and income. They are decreased by money distributed, the fair market value of property distributed, and losses. Note that liabilities do not go into the calculation of capital accounts, unlike basis. Tax basis can never be negative — one of the few rules in tax without an exception. Capital accounts can be negative, however. One way this can happen is if debt increases the tax basis of a partner's partnership interest. Initially, the partner's tax basis will exceed his capital account. Deductions allocated to a partner, say for depreciation, can reduce the partner's tax basis in his partnership interest and his capital account. Since the tax basis was higher to begin with, the capital account will go negative before the tax basis is "used up." Generally, partners may have negative capital accounts to the extent they have an obligation to pay to the partnership any negative balance no later than the liquidation of the partnership interest or the partnership has nonrecourse debt allocable to the partner. A partner may have economic risk of loss on debt to the extent the partner has an obligation to restore a negative capital account, since the money he is obligated to pay to the partnership can be used to pay recourse debt.[15]

Further, the partnership also keeps track of its properties for economic or what is more commonly called "book purposes." Thus, if property is contributed to the partnership, the partnership accounts will show its carryover tax basis under I.R.C. § 723. But the partnership accounts will also show the property's "book value" (or what one of the authors — uniquely — likes to call book basis). The book value of a property is its fair market value on acquisition by the partnership, though as we will learn in Chapter 5, that figure can sometimes be adjusted downstream for value changes. If the partnership pays cash for a property, its tax basis and book value in

---

[14] Under I.R.C. § 704(d), a partner cannot deduct losses in excess of his basis in his partnership interest.

[15] Though it may not increase his "at risk" amount. *See* § 4.07.B; Hubert Enterprises, Inc. v. Commissioner, T.C. Memo 2008-46.

the property will be the same. Further, in calculating the partners' capital accounts, gains and losses from property are calculated using book value.

For example, if A contributes land to a partnership with a tax basis of $1,000 and a fair market value of $1,500, A's tax basis in her partnership interest goes up by $1,000, but A's capital account goes up by $1,500. The partnership's tax basis in the land is $1,000, but its book value is $1,500. If the partnership sells the land for $2,000, there is $1,000 of tax gain and $500 of book gain.

On to the Regulations: Treas. Reg. § 1.752-2(b)(1) provides that a partner or related person bears the economic risk of loss with respect to a liability if: (i) the partnership constructively liquidated, (ii) as a result of such constructive liquidation, the partner or related person would be obligated to make a payment to any person because the liability became due and payable, and (iii) the partner or related person would not be entitled to reimbursement from another partner or a related person to another partner.

In a constructive liquidation, the following events are deemed to have occurred simultaneously:

(i) all of the partnership's liabilities become payable in full;

(ii) all of the partnership's assets, including cash, have a value of zero, other than property contributed by a partner to secure a partnership liability;

(iii) the partnership disposes of all of its property in a fully taxable transaction for no consideration other than the release of liability with respect to nonrecourse liabilities; book values are commonly used for this calculation, since capital accounts are calculated using book values;

(iv) all items of income, gain, loss, etc. are allocated among the partners; and

(v) the partnership liquidates.[16]

As indicated above, in the constructive liquidation, property is generally considered to be sold for no consideration. The exception to this rule is the case of liabilities where a creditor's right to repayment is limited solely to one or more assets of the partnership (i.e., a nonrecourse liability). In that case, the property subject to that debt is treated as sold for an amount equal to the liability and gain or loss is recognized depending upon the partnership's basis for the asset subject to the debt. A loss is recognized to the extent of the partnership's remaining tax basis for its assets.[17]

In determining the extent to which a partner has an obligation to make a payment, all of the facts and circumstances are taken into account. This includes all statutory and contractual obligations, and includes obligations imposed by the partnership agreement, as well as those imposed outside of the partnership agreement. Thus, there is taken into account such items as guarantees, indemnifications, reimbursement agreements, obligations to make capital contributions to restore deficit capital accounts upon liquidation, and obligations imposed by state

---

[16] Treas. Reg. § 1.752-2(b)(1).

[17] Treas. Reg. § 1.752-2(b)(2).

law.[18] Even if a partner is obligated to make a payment, the partner's obligation to make the payment is reduced to the extent that the partner or a person related to the partner is entitled to reimbursement from another partner or a person related to another partner.[19] In determining whether a person has a payment obligation, it is assumed that all partners and related persons who have obligations to make payment actually perform those obligations, notwithstanding their net worth, unless there was a plan to "circumvent or avoid the obligation."[20] Notwithstanding this general rule, if the partner is a disregarded entity,[21] then different rules apply. In this case, the payment obligation is only taken into account to the extent of the net value of the disregarded entity as of the date on which the determination of the partner's share of partnership liabilities is determined.[22] If the owner of the disregarded entity is required to make a payment with respect to an obligation, however, then this rule does not apply.[23] The net value of a disregarded entity is equal to the fair market value of all of the assets of the disregarded entity that may be subject to creditor's claims under local law (excluding the disregarded entity's interest in the partnership in question), less obligations of the disregarded entity.[24]

Treas. Reg. § 1.752-2(c)(1) provides a general rule that a partner also bears the economic risk of loss for a partnership liability to the extent the partner or related person has made a nonrecourse loan to the partnership and the economic risk of loss with respect to such loan is not borne by another partner. In order to facilitate financial institutions making loans to partnerships in which they are a partner, the Regulations contain a *de minimis* exception to the above rule. Thus, if the partner's interest in each item of partnership income, gain, loss, etc. for every taxable year is 10% or less, and that partner or a person related to that partner makes a loan to the partnership which constitutes qualified nonrecourse financing within the meaning of I.R.C. § 465(b) (determined without regard to the type of activity financed), then the partner is not deemed to bear the economic risk of loss.[25] Generally, qualified nonrecourse financing means financing by a person regularly engaged in the business of lending who is not a related person, or from a government or guaranteed by a governmental agency, which is secured by real property, with respect to which no person is personally liable for repayment and which is not convertible debt.[26]

There is also a *de minimis* exception with respect to the general rule. In the case of a partner having less than a 10% interest in each item of partnership income, gain, loss, etc., a guaranty by that partner of a loan that otherwise would be

---

[18] Treas. Reg. § 1.752-2(b)(3).

[19] Treas. Reg. § 1.752-2(b)(5).

[20] Treas. Reg. § 1.752-2(b)(6).

[21] A disregarded entity is generally a business entity other than a corporation which has a single owner. A disregarded entity is treated as a sole proprietorship if it is owned by an individual and as a division if it is owned by another entity. Treas. Reg. §§ 301.7701-2(c)(2), 301.7701-3(b)(1)(ii).

[22] Treas. Reg. § 1.752-2(k)(1).

[23] *Id.*

[24] Treas. Reg. § 1.752-2(k)(2).

[25] Treas. Reg. § 1.752-2(d)(1).

[26] I.R.C. § 465(b)(6)(A).

qualified nonrecourse financing if the guarantor had made the loan to the partnership is not treated as recourse debt.[27]

As indicated above, in determining whether a partner bears the economic risk of loss for a partnership liability, it is necessary to take into account the obligations of a "related person." The term "related person" means a partner and a person who bears a relationship to that partner that is specified in I.R.C. § 267(b) or 707(b)(1), except that: (i) 80% is substituted for 50%, (ii) brothers and sisters are excluded, and (iii) I.R.C. § 267(e)(1) and (f)(1)(A) are disregarded.[28]

3. Assumption of Liability

As indicated above, a partner's assumption of a partnership liability is treated as a contribution of money by that partner to the partnership and the assumption by a partnership of an individual partner's liability is treated as a distribution of money to that partner. A person is treated as assuming a liability only if: (i) the assuming person is personally obligated to pay the liability and (ii) the creditor knows of the assumption and can directly enforce the partner's (or related persons) obligation and no other partner or related person to another partner would bear the economic risk of loss for the liability immediately after the assumption.[29] In the case of property contributed by a partner to a partnership, or distributed by a partnership to a partner, which is subject to a liability, the transferee is treated as having assumed the liability to the extent the liability does not exceed the fair market value of the property at the time of the contribution and distribution.[30]

4. Definition of Nonrecourse Liability

The definition of a nonrecourse liability is very simple. It is any liability which is not a recourse liability (i.e., one for which no partner or related person bears the economic risk of loss).[31] Typically, nonrecourse liabilities are secured by one or more assets of the partnership, such as a mortgage on real property. In the case of entities where no owner has personal liabilities for the obligations of the entity (such as LLCs or limited liability limited partnerships), it is possible for an obligation of the entity to be a nonrecourse liability even though the obligation by its terms does not so state.[32] In such a case, liabilities can be allocated among the partnership's property in any reasonable manner so long as the debt allocated to a particular property does not exceed the property's fair market value.[33]

---

[27]   Treas. Reg. § 1.752-2(d)(2).

[28]   Treas. Reg. § 1.752-4(b)(1).

[29]   Treas. Reg. § 1.752-1(d).

[30]   Treas. Reg. § 1.752-1(e).

[31]   Treas. Reg. § 1.752-1(a)(2).

[32]   PLR 200120002 (Dec. 14, 2001).

[33]   PLR 200340024 (Apr. 10, 2003).

5.   Bifurcated Liability

It is possible for a liability to be both a recourse liability and a nonrecourse liability. For example, a partnership may borrow $800,000 from a bank to purchase some property. The property acts as security for the loan, but the loan is otherwise nonrecourse to the partnership. If one of the partners guaranty $300,000 of the mortgage debt, the liability will be bifurcated into a $300,000 recourse liability and a $500,000 nonrecourse liability, and the liability will be allocated accordingly.[34]

C.   Allocation of Recourse Liabilities

Treas. Reg. § 1.752-2(a) provides that a partner's share of the recourse liabilities of a partnership is equal to the portion of the liability for which the partner or related person bears the economic risk of loss. As indicated in § 3.04.B.1, this is determined under the constructive liquidation analysis.

The operation of the regulatory scheme for determining a partner's share of the recourse liabilities of a partnership may be illustrated by several examples.

Example (1). Assume that A and B are equal partners in a general partnership. Each of the partners contribute $10,000 to the partnership and the partnership borrows $80,000 to purchase a $100,000 building.

Since A and B are general partners, under state law A and B have an obligation to satisfy the liability. This being the case, the liability is a recourse liability. In determining the manner in which this $80,000 recourse liability is allocated among the partners, the constructive liquidation rule is applied. Under this rule, if the partnership had no assets and an $80,000 liability, each of the partners under state law would be obligated to contribute one-half of that amount to satisfy the liability. Thus, A and B would each bear the economic risk of loss for $40,000 of the $80,000 obligation.

Example (2). Same facts as in Example 1, except that the partnership is a limited partnership, A is a general partner, and B is a limited partner.

Since A is a general partner, under state law A has an obligation to satisfy the liability whereas B, as a limited partner, does not have such an obligation. Thus, the liability is a recourse liability. Since A would be required to fully satisfy the liability if the partnership had no other assets, all of the $80,000 liability is allocated to A.

Example (3). Same facts as in Example 2, except that B, the limited partner, is the guarantor of the $80,000 liability.

The liability is still a recourse liability because both A and B now have payment obligations. How the liability will be allocated depends upon whether B would be subrogated to the rights of the lender against the partnership. If B would be subrogated to the rights of the creditor, then B would have a right to be paid by A if B made payment on the guaranty, with the result that B would not be considered to bear the economic risk of loss. Thus, all of the liability would be allocated to A. If, on the other hand, B, upon making payment on the guaranty would not be

---

[34]   Treas. Reg. § 1.752-1(i).

subrogated to the right of the creditor, then B would not have a right against A and the entire liability would be allocated to B.

Example (4). Same facts as in Example 1, except that partnership losses are allocated 75% to A and 25% to B and under the terms of the partnership agreement a partner with a deficit capital account balance is obligated to restore that deficit to the partnership.

The liability is still a recourse liability. If the partnership sold all of its assets for no consideration, the partnership would have $100,000 loss. This loss would be allocated $75,000 to A and $25,000 to B, resulting in A having a deficit capital account of $65,0000, and B having a deficit capital account of $15,000. Since both A and B would have an obligation to make a payment to the partnership, they share the liability in proportion to their deficit capital accounts (i.e., $65,000 to A and $15,000 to B).

Example (5). Same facts as Example 1, except that instead of a general partnership, an LLC taxable as a partnership is the borrowing entity.

Since, in the case of an LLC, the members are not obligated to satisfy the obligations of the LLC, no member of the LLC bears the economic risk of loss. This being the case, the liability is now a nonrecourse liability.

In determining the extent to which a partner or related person bears the economic risk of loss, it is necessary to take into account when the payment obligation is required to be satisfied. If the obligation to make a payment is not required to be satisfied within a reasonable time after the liability becomes due, or the obligation to make a contribution to the partnership is not required to be satisfied before the later of: (i) the end of the year in which the partnership interest is liquidated, or (ii) 90 days after the liquidation, then the liability is only taken into account to the extent of its value.[35] If the obligation to make a payment does not meet the above requirements, but the obligation bears interest at a rate at least equal to the applicable Federal rate (within the meaning of I.R.C. § 1274(d)), then the value of the obligation is its face value. If, however, it does not bear interest at such rate, then the value of the obligation is discounted to present value using the applicable Federal rate.[36]

D. Allocation of Nonrecourse Liabilities

Nonrecourse liabilities are allocated based upon a three-tier formula set forth in Treas. Reg. § 1.752-3(a). Nonrecourse liabilities are allocated in the following order of priority:

(i) First, there is allocated to the partners their respective shares of partnership "minimum gain." Minimum gain is determined in accordance with the rules of Treas. Reg. § 1.704-2(d)(1) and a partner's share of minimum gain is determined in accordance with Treas. Reg. § 1.704-2(g)(1).[37]

---

[35] Treas. Reg. § 1.752-2(g)(1).

[36] Treas. Reg. § 1.752-2(g)(1).

[37] *See* Chapter 5.

(ii) Second, the nonrecourse liability is allocated to the partners to the extent of their share of the taxable gain that would be allocated to the partner under I.R.C. § 704(c) (or in the same manner as I.R.C. § 704(c) in the case of revalued partnership property) if the partnership disposed of the property which is subject to the nonrecourse liability in satisfaction of that liability and for no other consideration. If multiple properties are subject to a single nonrecourse liability, the partnership may allocate the liability among the multiple properties under any reasonable method. The method is not reasonable, however, if the amount allocated, when added to other liabilities burdening a property, is in excess of the fair market value of the property.[38]

What does that mean in English? Well, to fully understand it, you will need to read Chapter 5. To get you by for now, we offer the following example:

Assume partner A contributes property to a partnership with a fair market value of $1,000, a tax basis of $100, and the property is subject to a nonrecourse debt of $400. There is no minimum gain here, as minimum gain only exists to the extent that the nonrecourse debt exceeds "book value." Here book value is $1,000. See Chapter 5 for the fascinating details. Under the second tier of the allocations, however, $300 of the nonrecourse debt is allocated to partner A (i.e., the amount by which the nonrecourse debt exceeds tax basis, $400 − $100 = $300).

(iii) Third, there is allocated to the partners their share of the balance of the nonrecourse liabilities (referred to as excess nonrecourse liabilities) in accordance with the partners' shares of partnership profits.

The partners' interest in profits is determined by taking into account all of the facts and circumstances relating to the partners' interests in the partnership. The Regulations allow the partnership agreement to specify the partners' interest in partnership profits for purpose of allocating excess nonrecourse liabilities so long as the interests are reasonably consistent with allocations that have substantial economic effect of some other significant item of partnership income or gain.[39]

The Regulations also permit excess nonrecourse liabilities to be allocated among the partners in accordance with the manner in which it is expected that nonrecourse deductions will be allocated. In addition, the Regulations permit excess nonrecourse liabilities to first be allocated to a partner to the extent of the built-in gain that is allocable to the partner under I.R.C. § 704(c)(2), or property for which reverse section 704(c) allocations are applicable, to the extent that gain exceeds the gain allocated to them in the second tier. To the extent the excess nonrecourse liabilities are not fully allocated under the previous sentence, then the balance of the excess nonrecourse liabilities must be allocated using one of the other methods in Treas. Reg. § 1.752-3(a)(3).[40]

The allocation of nonrecourse liabilities may be illustrated by an example.

---

[38] Treas. Reg. § 1.752-3(b)(1).

[39] Treas. Reg. § 1.752-3(a)(3).

[40] *Id.*

Example: A and B form an LLC, A contributing $10,000 and B contributing $190,000. The LLC obtains an $800,000 interest only loan and purchases a $1,000,000 building. The Operating Agreement provides that losses are allocated entirely to B, that income is allocated entirely to B until such time as the allocations of income are equal to prior allocations of loss, and thereafter income is allocated 40% to A and 60% to B. The Operating Agreement provides that excess nonrecourse liabilities are allocated 40% to A and 60% to B. During each of its first 10 years of operations, the LLC has a $25,000 loss, all of which is attributable to the depreciation of the building.

During the first eight years, the basis of the property would be equal to or greater than the amount of the nonrecourse liability. This being the case, there is no minimum gain. Based upon the provisions of the Operating Agreement, the excess nonrecourse liabilities would be shared 40% by A and 60% by B.

At the end of year nine, however, the LLC's basis for the building would have been reduced to $775,000, resulting in $25,000 of minimum gain. Assume that A's share of the minimum gain is $1,250 and that B's share of the minimum gain is $23,750. At the end of year nine, $311,250 of the nonrecourse liability is allocated to A [$1,250 + 40% × ($800,000 − $25,000)], and $488,750 of the liability is allocated to B [$23,750 + 60% × ($800,000 − $25,000)].

E.   Contributions and Distributions of Encumbered Property

As indicated in § 3.04.A, an increase in a partner's share of partnership liabilities is treated as a contribution of money by the partner to the partnership, and a decrease in a partner's share of partnership liabilities is treated as a distribution of cash to that partner. If a partner contributes property to a partnership and the partnership assumes liabilities of the contributing partner, or if the property contributed is subject to a liability, there may be both deemed cash distributions to the partner, as well as deemed cash contributions by the partner. Similarly, if a partnership distributes property to a partner and a partner assumes a partnership liability, or the property distributed is subject to debt, there can be deemed cash contributions and distributions.

Treas. Reg. § 1.752-1(f) provides that where the same transaction produces both an increase and decrease in a partner's share of partnership liabilities, only the net increase is treated as a contribution of money by the partner and only the net decrease is treated as a distribution of money to the partner. That Regulation further indicates that the contribution of property subject to a liability, or the distribution of property subject to a liability, will require such netting, as will the termination of the partnership or merger or consolidation of partnerships. The effect of this netting rule can be demonstrated by the following example.

Example: A contributes real property with a fair market value of $1,000,000, subject to an $800,000 liability, to a general partnership in exchange for a 25% interest in the partnership. A's basis for the real property is $700,000.

Since A continues to have personal liability with respect to the mortgage, the mortgage is a recourse liability. If, under state law, each of the partners of the partnership would be required to make a payment in proportion to their interests upon a constructive liquidation, A's share of the mortgage would be $200,000. Since A's personal liabilities would decrease by $800,000 on the contribution of the real property subject to the debt, but would increase by $200,000 as a result of A's share of the partnership liability, there is a deemed distribution to A of $600,000. This deemed distribution would reduce A's $700,000 basis for his partnership interest to $100,000, but A would not be required to recognize any gain at this point. This is true, even though the amount of the liability to which the contributed property was subject was in excess of A's basis for the property at the time of the contribution. Had A made the same contribution to a corporation, A would have recognized gain of $100,000 under I.R.C. § 357(c)(1) (assuming no other properties were contributed).

When a property which is subject to a nonrecourse liability is contributed to a partnership, the allocation of that liability is far more complicated. The IRS has addressed this situation, however, in Rev. Rul. 95-41.[41] In that Revenue Ruling, A contributed depreciable property with a fair market value of $10,000 to a partnership in exchange for a 50% interest in the partnership. The property was subject to a nonrecourse liability of $6,000, and A's basis for the property was $4,000. The Revenue Ruling first notes that as a result of the contribution, A's individual liabilities decrease by $6,000. It was then necessary to run through the Regulation's three-tier allocation scheme to determine A's share of the partnership's nonrecourse liability.

Since minimum gain is determined by reference to book value, rather than adjusted basis,[42] there is no minimum gain, even though the fair market value of the property exceeds its adjusted basis.[43] Thus, there is no allocation under the first tier. Under the second-tier allocation, if the property was disposed of for an amount equal to the amount of the liability, a $2,000 gain would be recognized ($6,000 − $4,000). For book purposes, however, there would be a $4,000 loss, allocated $2,000 to each of the partners. The manner in which the liability is allocated under the second tier is dependent upon the method used for purposes of I.R.C. § 704(c). If either the traditional method or the traditional method with curative allocations is used, $2,000 of the nonrecourse liability would be allocated to A under the second tier.

The excess nonrecourse liabilities are allocated under the third tier and, as indicated above, there are a variety of means in which that allocation could occur. Because the amount of the section 704(c) gain was $4,000, and only $2,000 of that gain was allocated under the second tier, the partners could agree to allocate an additional $2,000 of the liability to A and allocate the balance of the liability one-half to each of A and B.

---

[41] 1995-1 C.B. 132.

[42] *See* Treas. Reg. § 1.704-2(d)(3). *See also* Chapter 5.

[43] Under the Regulations promulgated under I.R.C. § 704(b), when property is contributed to a partnership the partner's capital account is credited with the fair market value of the property, not its basis. Treas. Reg. § 1.704-1(b)(2)(iv)(d)(1).

F. Tiered Partnerships

In many instances, economic activity is conducted at a partnership level and one of the partners is itself a partnership. This is referred to as tiered partnerships. The partnership which is the partner in another partnership is referred to as the "upper-tier partnership," and the partnership having a partnership as a partner is referred to as the "lower-tier partnership." Where there are tiered partnerships, it is necessary to know how the liabilities of the lower-tier partnership will be shared by the partners of the upper-tier partnership.

The general rule is that the upper-tier partnership's share of the liabilities of the lower-tier partnership is treated as a liability of the upper-tier partnership.[44] Thus, the normal rules may then be applied with respect to how the deemed liability of the upper-tier partnership is to be allocated.

In determining the upper-tier partnership's share of a recourse liability of the lower-tier partnership, there is taken into account: (i) the economic risk of loss that the upper-tier partnership bears with respect to the liability, plus (ii) any other amount of the liability with respect to which the partners of the upper-tier partnership bear the economic risk of loss.[45]

G. Sales of Partnership Interests

As indicated above, I.R.C. § 752(d) provides that in the case of a sale or exchange of a partnership interest, liabilities are treated in the same fashion as in the case of an exchange not involving a partnership interest. Outside of the partnership context, if a taxpayer sells property and the purchaser assumes a liability of the seller, or takes the property subject to a liability, the amount of the liability is deemed an amount realized for purposes of computing gain or loss from the sale. Although a transfer of a partnership interest may not directly result in the selling partner's liabilities being formally assumed, and the partnership interest itself may not be subject to liabilities, nevertheless the liabilities of the partnership must be taken into account. This is the purpose of I.R.C. § 752(d). Assume a 25% partner of a partnership has a basis for her partnership interest of $20,000 and her basis includes her 25% share of the $100,000 liabilities of the partnership (i.e., $25,000). If she were to sell her partnership interest for $15,000, the gain or loss recognized by the partner would not simply be the difference between her basis for her partnership interest and the amount of cash received. If that were all that were considered, the partner would have a loss (i.e., $20,000 − $15,000). The amount realized in this situation, however, would include her $25,000 former share of the partnership's liabilities for which she no longer has a share. Thus, the amount realized would be $40,000 ($15,000 + $25,000). Thus, a gain in the amount of $20,000 ($40,000 − $20,000) would be recognized.

With respect to a partner who acquired his interest in the partnership by making a contribution to the partnership, for the partner to have a basis for his partnership interest which is less than his share of the partnership liabilities, the

---

[44] Treas. Reg. § 1.752-4(a).

[45] Treas. Reg. § 1.752-2(i).

partner would have had to previously been allocated deductions and/or received distributions in excess of the capital contributed by the partner (i.e., a negative capital account). Where a partner has a negative capital account, the amount of gain realized upon a sale of the partnership interest is generally equal to the consideration received plus the amount of the negative capital account. Practitioners will often use this as a short cut means of determining the gain or loss.

To illustrate, assume that A and B each contribute $10,000 to the AB Partnership and the AB Partnership borrows $80,000 and constructs a building for $100,000. The AB Partnership has losses for the next two years in the amount of $30,000 per year, which results in A and B having negative capital accounts of $20,000 each. A then sells her partnership interest to C for $50,000 (reflecting the increased value of the building).

A's basis in her partnership interest initially would be $50,000 ($10,000 plus $40,000 share of the liability). As a result of the losses passed through to A, her basis would be reduced to $20,000. Her amount realized would be $90,000 ($50,000 cash and $40,000 reduction in liabilities), resulting in a gain of $70,000. This is the same as the $50,000 cash received plus the $20,000 negative capital account.

H. Anti-Abuse Rule

In an effort to fight tax shelters, the IRS has issued Regulations relating to the inclusion of partnership liabilities in a partner's basis. Treas. Reg. § 1.752-7 is designed to prevent the acceleration or duplication of loss through the assumption of certain types of obligations.[46] Prior to the promulgation of Treas. Reg. § 1.752-7, taxpayers would transfer assets to a partnership and have the partnership assume a contingent liability (such as a potential environmental liability). The taxpayer would take the position that the assumed liability was not a liability for purposes of I.R.C. § 752 and, therefore, the taxpayer was not required to reduce the basis of the taxpayer's partnership interest. The taxpayer would then sell the partnership interest to a third party for an amount which was significantly less than the taxpayer's basis (because the purchaser would take the liability into account) and claim a loss. When the liability was paid, the partnership would claim a deduction. Thus, the same liability would produce a double deduction.[47]

In order to be able to understand the application of Treas. Reg. § 1.752-7, it is necessary to understand a number of defined terms which are set forth in Treas. Reg. § 1.752-7(b). The most important term is a "§ 1.752-7 liability." This is defined as an obligation which is either not described in Treas. Reg. § 1.752-1(a)(4)(i), or (ii) the amount of the obligation exceeds the amount taken into account under Treas. Reg. § 1.757-1(a)(4)(i).[48] The term "obligation" is defined to mean any fixed or contingent obligation to make a payment without regard to whether the obligation

---

[46] Treas. Reg. § 1.752-7(a).

[47] *See* Notice 2000-44, 2002-2 C.B. 255.

[48] Treas. Reg. § 1.752-7(b)(3).

is otherwise taken into account for purposes of the Code.[49]

1. Assumption by Partnership

Treas. Reg. § 1.752-7(c) provides that I.R.C. § 704(c)(1)(A) and (B) and the Regulations thereunder apply to a § 1.752-7 liability. The § 1.752-7 liability is treated under the principles of I.R.C. § 704(c) as having a built-in loss equal to the amount of the § 1.752-7 liability as of the date of the partnership's assumption of the § 1.752-7 liability.[50] Thus, items of deduction or loss with respect to the § 1.752-7 liability must be allocated to the partner from whom the partnership assumed the § 1.752-7 liability to the extent of the built-in loss. Deductions or losses in excess of such amount are allocated among the partners in accordance with the normal rules of I.R.C. § 704(b).[51]

The amount of a § 1.752-7 liability is the amount of cash that a willing assignor would pay to a willing assignee to assume the § 1.752-7 liability in an arm's-length transaction.[52] Typically, a § 1.752-7 liability is a contingent liability.

Treas. Reg. § 1.752-7(c)(2) contains an example which illustrates the applicability of Treas. Reg. § 1.752-7(c). In the example, A contributes property with a fair market value and bases of $400, subject to a § 1.752-7 liability of $100 for a 25% interest in a partnership. B and C contribute $300 and $600, for a 25% and 50% interest, respectively, in the partnership. A's capital account is credited with $300 (the $400 value of the property less the $100 § 1.752-7 liability). At a later date, the partnership satisfies the § 1.752-7 liability by paying $200 with such amount being deductible by the partnership. The example indicates that $100 of the deduction is specially allocated to A and the remaining $100 deduction is allocated $25 to A and B and $50 to C. If the partnership satisfies the § 1.752-7 liability over a number of years, all of the deduction would first be allocated to A until such time as there has been allocated $100 to A and any deduction subsequently available would be allocated to the partners in accordance with the normal rules.

a. Transfer of Partnership Interest

If the § 1.752-7 liability partner were to transfer her partnership interest prior to the satisfaction of the § 1.752-7 liability, the rule of Treas. Reg. § 1.752-7(c) would not prevent the § 1.752-7 liability partner from having an excessive basis. To eliminate this problem, Treas. Reg. § 1.752-7(e)(1) provides that if a § 1.752-7 liability partner disposes of her partnership interest, the basis of the § 1.752-7 liability partner's partnership interest is reduced immediately prior to the disposition. The amount of the reduction is referred to as the § 1.752-7 liability reduction. The § 1.752-7 liability reduction is equal to the lesser of (i) the excess of the § 1.752-7 liability partner's basis in the partnership interest over the adjusted

---

[49] Treas. Reg. § 1.752-1(a)(4)(ii).

[50] Treas. Reg. § 1.704-3(a)(12).

[51] Treas. Reg. § 1.752-7(c)(ii).

[52] Treas. Reg. § 1.752-7(b)(3)(ii).

value of that interest, or (ii) the remaining built-in loss associated with the § 1.752-7 liability.[53]

If only a portion of the § 1.752-7 liability partner's interest in the partnership is disposed of, the § 1.752-7 liability reduction is prorated.[54] The term "adjusted value" means the fair market value of the partnership interest increased by the partner's share of partnership liabilities under Treas. Reg. §§ 1.752-1 through 1.752-5.[55]

If there is a liquidation of the § 1.752-7 liability partner's partnership interest, the § 1.752-7 liability partner's basis for his partnership interest is reduced by the § 1.752-7 liability reduction.[56]

b.　　Assumption of § 1.752-7 Liability

If a partner other than the § 1.752-7 liability partner assumes a § 1.752-7 liability while the § 1.752-7 liability partner is still a partner of the partnership, the § 1.752-7 liability partner's basis in the partnership interest is reduced by the § 1.752-7 liability reduction.[57] In addition, the partnership is required to reduce the bases of its assets by the remaining built-in loss associated with the § 1.752-7 liability.[58] Lastly, no deduction or capital expense is allowed to the assuming partner on the satisfaction of the § 1.752-7 liability assumed from the partnership to the extent of the remaining built-in loss associated with the § 1.752-7 liability.[59]

There are two exceptions to the rules of Treas. Reg. § 1.752-7(e), (f), and (g). First, those sections do not apply if a partnership assumes a § 1.752-7 liability as part of a contribution to the partnership of a trade or business with which the liability is associated and the partnership continues to carry on that trade or business after the contribution.[60] Second, those sections do not apply if immediately before the date of the transaction described in Treas. Reg. § 1.752-7(e), (f), or (g), the remaining built-in loss with respect to all § 1.752-7 liabilities assumed by the partnership is less than the lesser of 10% of the gross value of the partnership's assets or $1,000,000.[61]

---

[53]　Treas. Reg. § 1.752-7(b)(7)(i).

[54]　Treas. Reg. § 1.752-7(b)(7)(ii).

[55]　Treas. Reg. § 1.752-7(b)(2).

[56]　Treas. Reg. § 1.752-7(f)(1).

[57]　Treas. Reg. § 1.752-7(g)(2).

[58]　Treas. Reg. § 1.752-7(g)(3).

[59]　Treas. Reg. § 1-752-7(g)(4).

[60]　Treas. Reg. § 1.752-7(d)(2)(A).

[61]　Treas. Reg. § 1.752-7(d)(2)(B).

§ 3.05   READING, QUESTIONS AND PROBLEMS

A.   Reading

CODE:

I.R.C. §§ 702(a)(4), 704(d), 705, 722, 731, 732, 733, 752.

TREASURY REGULATIONS:

Treas. Reg. §§ 1.705-1(a)(1), 1.722-1, 1.731-1(a)(1)(ii), 1.752-1, 1.752-2, 1.752-3, 1.752-4, 1.752-7.

RULINGS AND OTHER INTERPRETATIONS:

Rev. Rul. 66-94, 66-1 C.B. 166.

Rev. Rul. 94-4, 1994-1 C.B. 196.

Rev. Rul. 95-41, 1995-1 C.B. 132.

Rev. Rul. 96-10, 1996-1 C.B. 138.

Rev. Rul. 96-11, 1996-1 C.B. 140.

PLR 200120020 (Feb. 13, 2001).

PLR 200340024 (Apr. 10, 2003).

B.   Questions and Problems

1. A and B form Partnership AB. A contributes property with a fair market value of $15,000 and an adjusted basis of $10,000, in exchange for a 75% interest in AB. B contributes $5,000 for a 25% interest in AB. During the first year of operations, the following occurs:

   a.   Taxable income of $20,000

   b.   Charitable contributions of $1,000

   c.   AB borrows $10,000

   d.   Tax-exempt income of $2,000

   e.   Distributions of $30,000, $22,500 to A and $7,500 to B

      i.   What are A's and B's bases for their partnership interests at the end of the year?

2. A and B form general partnership AB. A contributes real property with a fair market value of $100,000 subject to a recourse mortgage of $60,000, in exchange for an 80% interest in the partnership. The basis of the contributed property is $20,000. B contributes $10,000 in exchange for a 20% partnership interest. Assume there is a state law assumption of the mortgage by the partnership.

a. What are A's and B's bases for their partnership interests immediately following the formation of the partnership?

b. Does A recognize any gain upon the contribution of the property?

3. Same as Problem 2, except A and B form an LLC rather than a general partnership and there is no deficit restoration obligation.

4. Same as Problem 2, except B guarantees the mortgage, B has no right of contribution against A or AB if she is called upon to make payment on the guaranty, and if A is required to make payment on the mortgage, A is entitled to reimbursement from B.

5. Same as Problem 2, except B indemnifies A with respect to 20% of the mortgage.

6. Same as Problem 2, except the mortgage was a nonrecourse mortgage.

Chapter 4

OPERATION OF THE PARTNERSHIP: CALCULATION OF PARTNERSHIP TAXABLE INCOME

§ 4.01 INTRODUCTION

Chapter 4 will address the issues which arise in determining the taxable income of a partnership and how that income is taken into account by the partners. This will include a discussion of how the partnership computes its taxable income, which items must be separately passed through to the partners, which elections are made at the partnership level as opposed to the partner level, and where intent is a factor in making a tax analysis, whether it is the intent of the partnership or the partner which is relevant. Also discussed will be how a partnership must determine its taxable year and the limitations on the ability of partners to claim losses or deduction of the partnership.

§ 4.02 PASS-THROUGH NATURE OF PARTNERSHIP

As indicated above, an entity treated as a partnership for federal tax purposes is not itself taxable. Rather, the partners are taxed on the economic activity that occurs at the partnership level.[1] Thus, it is important to understand how the economic activity which occurs at the partnership level affects the partners.

There are two ways in which the economic activity which occurs at the partnership level could be passed through to the partners. Under one method (referred to as the aggregate method), each partner can be considered to own an undivided interest in each asset of the partnership and then all of the calculations could be made at the partner level. The second alternative (referred to as the entity theory) would treat the partnership as an entity for purposes of determining items of income, gain, loss, deduction, and credit and then having those amounts passed through to the partners to report on their own income tax returns. The Code does not adopt either of these principles in total, but in general, in the area of computing the income, gain, loss, deductions, and credits of the partnership, the entity theory predominates.

---

[1] I.R.C. § 701.

93

§ 4.03 COMPUTING INCOME, GAIN, LOSS, DEDUCTIONS, AND CREDITS OF PARTNERSHIP

A. Generally

The Code provisions dealing with the computation of the economic activity at the partnership level are very simple. I.R.C. § 702(a) requires that each partner, in determining their income tax, take into account their "distributive share" of various partnership items.[2] Note that distributive share does not mean *distributed* share. A partner has income irrespective of whether or not any amount is distributed to the partner. The Code could have (and perhaps should have) said allocable share. I.R.C. § 702(a) contains a list of seven items which are to be taken into account separately, with the balance of the taxable income or loss of the partnership, excluding the separately stated items, included as a single number (the so called bottom line allocation).

B. Taxable Income of the Partnership

I.R.C. § 703(a) provides that the taxable income of a partnership is computed in the same manner as in the case of an individual, with certain stated exceptions. The first exception is that those items described in I.R.C. § 702(a)(1) through (8) are separately stated. The second exception is a list of six types of deductions which are not to be taken into account by the partnership.[3] These exceptions are: (i) the personal exemption provided for in I.R.C. § 151, (ii) the deduction for foreign taxes paid, (iii) the deduction for charitable contributions provided in I.R.C. § 170, (iv) the net operating loss deduction provided for in I.R.C. § 172, (v) the additional itemized deductions allowed individuals in I.R.C. §§ 211 through 223, and (vi) the deduction for depletion with respect to oil and gas wells provided for in I.R.C. § 611.

To round out the statutory scheme, I.R.C. § 702(b) provides that the character of any item of income, gain, loss, deduction, or credit with respect to the items required to be separately stated pursuant to I.R.C. § 702(a)(1) through (7) is to be treated as if such item were realized directly from the source from which it was realized by the partnership, or incurred in the same manner as it was incurred by the partnership.

C. Separately Computed Items

1. Gains and Losses from Sales

I.R.C. § 702(a)(1) through (3) require that three types of gains or losses from sales or exchanges be separately stated. The types of gains or losses referred to in those sections are long-term gains or losses, short-term gains or losses, and section

---

[2] A partner is required to include her distributive share of the partnership's income in her income even in situations in which there are disputes among the partners and the income of the partnership is being held in escrow. Burke v. Commissioner, T.C. Memo 2005-297, *aff'd*, 485 F.3d 171 (1st Cir. 2007).

[3] I.R.C. § 703(a)(2).

1231 gains or losses. Under the Regulations, rather than being required to include the partner's distributive share of each long-term gain or loss or each short-term gain or loss, the long-term gains or losses are netted and only a single long-term gain or net long-term loss is included.[4] Similar rules are provided with respect to net short-term capital gains or losses[5] and net section 1231 gains or 1231 losses.[6] Although a net section 1231 gain is treated as a long-term capital gain,[7] even if a partnership has a net section 1231 gain and capital gains, such amounts are not combined.[8] This is because if a partner has other section 1231 gains or losses, the section 1231 gains or losses passing through from the partnership need to be combined with the other section 1231 gains or losses to determine whether there is a net section 1231 gain (which would be treated as a long-term capital gain), or a net section 1231 loss (which would be treated as an ordinary loss).

2. Charitable Contributions

I.R.C. § 702(a)(4) require that the partners' shares of the charitable contributions of the partnership be separately taken into account by the partners. The Regulations indicate that each class of charitable contribution (e.g., cash contributions, property contributions to public charity, property contributions to private foundations, etc.) be separately stated.[9] This is necessary because there are different limitations under I.R.C. § 170 for different types of charitable contributions.

3. Dividend Income

I.R.C. § 702(a)(5) provides that dividend income must be separately stated. That section specifically refers to dividends with respect to which I.R.C. § 1(h)(11) or I.R.C. §§ 243–247 apply. This separate statement of dividend income is necessary because currently certain dividends are taxed at preferential rates[10] and during the history of the Code there have been many instances in which special treatment was provided with respect to dividends received by noncorporate taxpayers. In addition, corporations are often allowed a dividends received deduction with respect to the receipt of certain dividends.[11]

4. Foreign Taxes Paid

I.R.C. § 702(a)(6) requires that foreign taxes paid by a partnership be separately stated. This is because foreign taxes paid may be treated as either a deduction under I.R.C. § 164, or as a credit under I.R.C. § 901(a).

---

[4] Treas. Reg. § 1.702-1(a)(2). Items subject to different I.R.C. § 1(h) long-term capital gain rates should be stated separately.

[5] Treas. Reg. § 1.702-1(a)(1).

[6] Treas. Reg. § 1.702-1(a)(3). Items potentially subject to different I.R.C. § 1(h) long-term capital gain rates should be stated separately.

[7] I.R.C. § 1231(a)(1).

[8] *Id.*

[9] Treas. Reg. § 1.702-1(a)(4).

[10] I.R.C. § 1(h)(11).

[11] I.R.C. § 243

5. Other Items

I.R.C. § 702(a)(7) authorizes the IRS to promulgate regulations which would require the separate statement of items other than those provided for in I.R.C. § 702(a)(1) through (6). The IRS has exercised this authority. Treas. Reg. § 1.702-1(a)(8)(i) contains a list of items which must be separately stated. These items are: (i) recoveries of bad debts, prior taxes, and delinquent amounts; (ii) gains and losses from wagering transactions; (iii) soil and water conservation expenditures; (iv) non-business expenses described in I.R.C. § 212; (v) medical, dental, etc. expenses; (vi) expenses for care of certain dependents; (vii) alimony payments; (viii) taxes and interest paid to cooperative housing corporations; (ix) intangible drilling and development costs; (x) mine exploration expenditures described in I.R.C. § 617; (xi) gain or loss recognized by the partnership under I.R.C. § 751(b); and (xii) any item of income, gain, loss, deduction, or credit subject to a special allocation under the partnership agreement which is different from the allocation of bottom-line taxable income or loss.

Treas. Reg. § 1.702-1(a)(8)(ii) requires that each partner take into account separately the partner's distributive share of any partnership item which, if separately taken into account by any partner, would result in an income tax liability for that partner, or for any other person, different from that which would result if that partner did not take the item into account separately. That Regulation lists three specific items to which it applies. First, if any partner is a controlled foreign corporation, items of income that would be subpart F income if separately taken into account by the controlled foreign corporation must be separately stated for all partners. Second, if any partner is a resident of a foreign country who may be able to avail himself of the exclusion provided for under I.R.C. § 911 with respect to certain earned income, the earned income of the partnership for all partners must be separately stated. Third, in determining the applicability of I.R.C. § 183 (the hobby loss provision), all relevant items of income or deduction of the partnership must be separately stated for all partners.

It is clear, however, that there are many other items which will be required to be separately stated. Schedule K of Form 1065 requires that the following additional items be separately stated:

i. Net income or loss from rental real estate activities.

ii. Net income or loss from other rental activities.

iii. Portfolio income (including interest income, dividends, royalty income, and gains and losses).

iv. Deductions pursuant to I.R.C. § 179.

v. Deductions related to portfolio income.

vi. Low-income housing credit.

vii. Qualified rehabilitation expenditures.

viii. Expense on investment debts.

ix. Net earnings from self-employment.

x. Adjustments and tax preference items with respect to the alternative minimum tax.[12]

xi. Expenditures described in I.R.C. § 59(e)(2).

xii. Tax-exempt interest income.

xiii. Recapture of low-income housing credit.

D. Bottom Line Profit or Loss

After taking into account all of the items required to be separately stated, the remaining net profit or loss of the partnership is determined.

§ 4.04 ELECTIONS

There are many elections which a taxpayer must make in order to determine the taxpayer's taxable income or loss. I.R.C. § 703(b) provides that elections required to be made in computing the taxable income of the partnership are made at the partnership level rather than at the partner level. Elections relating to methods of accounting, manners of computing depreciation, treatment of soil and water conservation expenses, and the option to deduct intangible drilling and development costs are all made at the partnership level.[13] Other elections which are made at the partnership level, rather than at the partner level, include (i) the reinvestment of condemnation proceeds,[14] (ii) the election out of the installment method,[15] (iii) whether to deduct and/or amortize organization fees in accordance with I.R.C. § 709(b)(1),[16] and (iv) the election provided for in I.R.C. § 754. Under I.R.C. § 703(b), the elections under I.R.C. §§ 108(b)(5) and (c)(3), 617, and 901 are made at the partner level.

Some elections potentially have application both at the partnership level and at the partner level. For example, I.R.C. § 179 permits taxpayers to elect to treat the cost of section 179 property[17] as an expense not chargeable to a capital account. I.R.C. § 179(b)(1) has a dollar limit of the maximum amount of aggregate cost of section 179 property that may be taken into account in a single year.[18] I.R.C. § 179(b)(2) has a reduction of the dollar limitations of I.R.C. § 179(b)(1) if the aggregate cost of section 179 property exceeds certain thresholds.[19] Treas. Reg. § 1.179-2(b)(3)(i) provides that in applying the dollar limitation of I.R.C. § 179(b)(1), an I.R.C. § 179 expense allocated to the partner is aggregated with any non-

---

[12] This is required by Treas. Reg. § 1.58-2(b).

[13] Treas. Reg. § 1.703-1(b)(1).

[14] Demirjian v. Commissioner, 457 F.2d 1 (3d Cir. 1972).

[15] *See* Treas. Reg. § 15A.453-1(d)(3)(i).

[16] Treas. Reg. § 1.709-1(c).

[17] Section 179 property is tangible property to which I.R.C. § 168 applies, and certain software, which is used in an active trade or business. I.R.C. § 179(d)(1).

[18] The maximum varies depending upon the calendar year in which the expenditures are incurred.

[19] Like the maximums of I.R.C. § 179(b)(1), the thresholds for the reductions in the maximums vary depending upon the calendar year.

partnership I.R.C. § 179 expenses of the partner. However, the same paragraph states that the cost of I.R.C. § 179 property placed in service by the partnership is ignored for the purposes of determining the excess I.R.C. § 179(b)(2) property placed in service. The example in subsection (ii) of Treas. Reg. § 1.179-2(b)(3) illustrates this by taking the $5,000 of I.R.C. § 179 expenses allocated to a partner into consideration by the partner in calculating the partner's I.R.C. § 179(b)(1) limitation, but ignoring both the $150,000 cost of the I.R.C. § 179 property placed in service by the partnership and the $5,000 allocated to the partner for the purposes of determining the excess I.R.C. § 179(b)(2) property placed in service by the partner.

§ 4.05   ACCOUNTING METHOD

As indicated above, a partnership elects its own accounting methods. Generally, there is no requirement that the accounting method chosen by the partnership be the same as that of its partners. Thus, a partnership may use the cash receipts and disbursements method of accounting (assuming that method is available taking into account the partnership's business activities), even though the partners use the accrual method, and vice versa.[20] There are, however, restrictions on the ability of a partnership to use the cash method.

A.   C Corporation Is Partner

Under I.R.C. § 448(a)(1), a C corporation generally may not use the cash method. In order to prevent C corporations from doing indirectly that which they cannot do directly, I.R.C. § 448(a)(2) provides that a partnership which has a C corporation as a partner may not use the cash method.

1.   Farming Business

There are several exceptions to the rule regarding a C corporation as a partner. First, the prohibition on the use of the cash method does not apply in the case of a farming business.[21] "Farming business" means the trade or business of farming within the meaning of I.R.C. § 263A(e)(4), but also includes the raising, harvesting, or growing of trees to which I.R.C. § 263A(c)(5) applies.[22]

2.   Qualified Personal Service Corporation

Under I.R.C. § 448(b)(2), a partnership having a C corporation as a partner is not prohibited from using the cash method if the C corporation is a qualified personal service corporation. "Qualified personal service corporation" means a corporation: (i) substantially all of the activities of which involve the performance of services in the field of health, law, engineering, architecture, accounting, actuarial science, performing arts, or consulting, and (ii) substantially all of the stock of which is held,

---

[20] Fong v. Commissioner, 48 T.C.M. (CCH) 689 (1984), aff'd, 816 F.2d. 684 (9th Cir.), cert. denied, 484 U.S. 854 (1987).

[21] I.R.C. § 448(b)(1).

[22] I.R.C. § 448(d)(1).

directly or indirectly, by employees performing services for the corporation in connection with the activities referred to in (i) above, retired employees who had performed such services for the corporation, the estate of an individual described above, or any other person who acquired such stock by reason of the death of an individual described above.[23]

Employees of a corporation are involved in the performance of services in the fields described above only if 95% or more of the time spent by employees of the corporation is devoted to the performance of such services.[24] In order to qualify as services performed in the field of health, the services must be performed by physicians, nurses, dentists, and other similar health care professionals.[25] In order to be performing services in the field of performing arts, the services must be performed by actors, actresses, singers, musicians, entertainers, and similar artists.[26] The performance of services in the field of consulting means the provision of advice and counsel.[27]

3. Small Corporations

A partnership having a C corporation as a partner is not prohibited from using the cash method if the C corporation meets the $5 million gross receipts test.[28] In order to meet this test, the corporation's average annual gross receipts for the three-taxable-year period ending with the immediately preceding taxable year must not exceed $5 million.[29] If the corporation was not in existence for three taxable years immediately preceding the year in question, then the test is applied based upon the period during which the entity was in existence.[30] If any of the immediately three preceding taxable years was a short taxable year, then the gross receipts for such taxable year are annualized.[31]

Under I.R.C. § 448(c)(2), all persons treated as a single employer under I.R.C. §§ 52(a), 52(b), 414(m), or 414(o) are treated as one person. I.R.C. § 52(a) is applicable to controlled groups of corporations. The term "controlled group of corporations" has the meaning given that term by I.R.C. § 1563(a) except (i) 50% is substituted for 80% in I.R.C. § 1563(a)(1), and (ii) I.R.C. § 1563(a)(4) and (e)(3)(C) are not taken into account. Under I.R.C. § 1563(a), the term "controlled group of corporations" means a parent subsidiary controlled group, a brother-sister controlled group, or a combined group. A parent-subsidiary controlled group is one or more chains of corporations connected through stock ownership with a common parent corporation if stock representing 80% of the voting power or value of each

---

[23] I.R.C. § 448(d)(2). In the case of stock acquired by reason of the death of an employee, such person may only hold the stock for the two-year period beginning on the date of death of such individual.

[24] Treas. Reg. § 1.448-1T(e)(4)(i).

[25] Treas. Reg. § 1.448-1T(e)(4)(ii).

[26] Treas. Reg. § 1.448-1T(e)(4)(iii).

[27] Treas. Reg. § 1.448-1T(e)(4)(iv).

[28] I.R.C. § 448(b)(3).

[29] I.R.C. § 448(c)(1).

[30] I.R.C. § 448(c)(3)(A).

[31] I.R.C. § 448(c)(3)(B).

corporation, other than the parent corporation, is owned by one or more corporations, and the common parent corporation owns stock representing 80% of the voting power or 80% of the value of at least one of the other corporations.[32] A brother-sister controlled group exists when two or more corporations are owned by five or fewer persons who are individuals, estates, or trusts who own at least 80% of the voting power or value of the stock of each of the corporations and 50% of the voting power or value of each of the corporations is owned by such individuals, taking into account the stock ownership of each person only to the extent of their identical ownership.[33] A combined group involves a group which has both a parent-subsidiary controlled group and a brother-sister controlled group.[34]

I.R.C. § 52(b) refers to trades or businesses which are under common control. Whether trades or businesses are under common control is to be determined applying the principles of I.R.C. § 52(a). Trades or businesses that are under common control generally refer to sole proprietorships, partnerships, trusts, estates, and corporations.[35] I.R.C. § 414(m) refers to affiliated service groups. An "affiliate service group" means a group consisting of a service organization: (i) a service organization which is a shareholder or a partner of the first service organization and regularly performs services for the first service corporation or is regularly associated with the first service corporation in performing services for third parties, and (ii) any other organization if a significant portion of the business of such organization is the performance of services for the first service organization or an organization described in (i) above and 10% or more of the interest in such organizations is held by persons who are highly compensated employees of the first service organization or an organization described in clause (i) above.[36]

The general thrust of I.R.C. § 448(c)(2) is to prevent an end-run around the $5 million gross receipts test through the use of multiple organizations.

The term "gross receipts" means the gross receipts of a taxable year in which the receipts are properly recognized under the taxpayer's method of accounting.[37] Gross receipts include all receipts from sales, net of returns and allowances, and is not reduced by cost of goods sold or the cost of the property sold.[38] In the case of sales of capital assets or property used in a trade or business, gross receipts are reduced by the taxpayer's adjusted basis for the property sold.[39] In the case of sales tax, if the tax is imposed on the purchaser of the goods and the taxpayer is only a collection agent for the governmental agency, then gross receipts do not include such sales tax, whereas if the tax is imposed on the taxpayer, then gross receipts include the sales tax.[40]

---

[32] I.R.C. § 1563(a)(1).

[33] I.R.C. § 1563(a)(2).

[34] I.R.C. § 1563(a)(3).

[35] Treas. Reg. § 1.52-1(b).

[36] I.R.C. § 414(m)(2).

[37] Treas. Reg. § 1.448-1T(f)(2)(iv)(A).

[38] *Id.*

[39] *Id.*

[40] *Id.*

B. Tax Shelters

1. Registered Offering

I.R.C. § 448(a)(3) provides that a tax shelter may not use the cash method. The term "tax shelter" has the meaning given such term by I.R.C. § 461(i)(3).[41] I.R.C. § 461(i)(3) defines a tax shelter to mean: (i) any enterprise if at any time interests in such enterprises have been offered for sale in an offering required to be registered with any federal or state securities regulating agency, (ii) any syndicate (within the meaning of I.R.C. § 1256(e)(3)(B)), and (iii) any tax shelter (within the meaning of I.R.C. § 6662(d)(2)(C)(ii)).

An offering is required to be registered with a federal or state agency if, under applicable law, the failure to register the offering would result in a violation of the applicable law, whether or not the offering is, in fact, registered.[42] An offering is also considered to be required to be registered with a federal or state agency if under applicable law the failure to file a notice of exemption from registration would result in the violation of applicable law, whether or not the notice is actually filed.[43]

2. Syndicate

I.R.C. § 1256(e)(3)(B) defines the term "syndicate" to include a partnership if more than 35% of the losses of the partnership during the taxable year are allocable to limited partners or limited entrepreneurs. A limited entrepreneur is a person other than a limited partner who does not actively participate in the management of the enterprise.[44] For this purpose, the losses of a partnership mean the excess of the deductions allowable to the partnership over the amount of income recognized by the partnership under the partnership's method of accounting, except that gains and losses from sales of capital assets or property used in a trade or business are not taken into account.[45]

An interest in a partnership is not considered to be held by a limited partner or a limited entrepreneur if: (i) the interest is held by an individual who actively participates at all times in the management of the partnership, (ii) the interest is held by the spouse, children, grandchildren, and parents of an individual who actively participates in the management of a partnership, (iii) the partnership interest is held by an individual who actively participated in the management of the partnership for a period of not less than five years, or (iv) the interest is held by the estate of an individual who actively participated in the management of the partnership.[46] In the case of the trade or business of farming, rather than using the rules of I.R.C. § 1256(e)(3)(C) for purposes of determining whether a person is a

---

[41] I.R.C. § 448(d)(3).

[42] Treas. Reg. § 1.448-1T(b)(2).

[43] *Id.*

[44] I.R.C. § 464(e)(2).

[45] Treas. Reg. § 1.448-1T(b)(3).

[46] I.R.C. § 1256(e)(3)(C).

limited partner or limited entrepreneur, the rules of I.R.C. § 464(c)(2) are applied.[47]

The IRS has issued a number of private rulings which have held that in the case of an LLC taxable as a partnership which is engaged in a professional practice (e.g., law or accounting), if the entity has never had losses, and does not expect to have losses in the future, that the entity does not constitute a syndicate for this purpose.[48]

3.   Tax Shelter

I.R.C. § 6662(d)(2)(C)(ii), insofar as here relevant, defines "tax shelter" to mean a partnership if a significant purpose of the partnership is the avoidance or evasion of federal income tax. There is very little guidance covering the scope of this provision, although most tax advisors would say that *everything* they do has a purpose of tax avoidance (clients do not pay to *increase* their tax liability). Treas. Reg. § 1.448-1T(b)(4) contains a presumption that marketed arrangements involving farming activities are presumed to have the principal purpose of tax avoidance if borrowed funds are used to prepay a substantial portion of their farming expenses.

C.   Farming Partnerships

1.   Partnerships having corporations as partners

Under I.R.C. § 447(a), a partnership engaged in the business of farming must generally use the accrual method of accounting if the partnership has a corporation as a partner. This general rule does not apply if the corporation is an S corporation or if the corporation meets the gross receipts test of I.R.C. § 447(d)(1).[49] The gross receipts test of I.R.C. § 447(d)(1) generally requires that for each prior taxable year beginning after December 31, 1975, the corporation and any predecessor corporation did not have gross receipts exceeding $1 million. In making this determination, all corporations which are members of the same control group of corporations within the meaning of I.R.C. § 1563(a) are treated as a single corporation. In the case of a family corporation, however, instead of being limited to $1 million of gross receipts, the corporation is limited to $25 million of gross receipts and the period in respect of which the test must be met changes to the taxable years beginning after December 31, 1985. A family corporation is a corporation in which at least 50% of the voting power and at least 50% of all other classes of stock of the corporation are owned by members of the same family and certain closely held corporations.[50] A closely held corporation for this purpose is defined in I.R.C. § 447(h).

---

[47]   Treas. Reg. § 1.448-1T(b)(3).

[48]   *See, e.g.*, PLR 9501033 (Oct. 5, 1994); PLR 9407030 (Nov. 24, 1993).

[49]   I.R.C. § 447(c).

[50]   I.R.C. § 447(d)(2)(C). The members of the same family are defined in I.R.C. § 447(e).

2. Farming syndicate

I.R.C. §§ 464(a) and 464(b) contain accounting method rules applicable to farming syndicates. A farming syndicate means, insofar as here relevant, a partnership engaged in the trade or business of farming if at any time interests in the partnership have been offered for sale in any offering required to be registered with any federal or state securities regulating body or if more than 35% of the losses during any period are applicable to limited partners or limited entrepreneurs.[51] As indicated above, I.R.C. § 464(c)(2) contains rules for determining when a person is not a limited partner or limited entrepreneur in the case of certain active management and ownership.

§ 4.06 CHARACTERIZATION

As indicated above, I.R.C. § 702(b) provides that separately stated items under I.R.C. § 702(a)(1) through (7) should be determined as if they were realized directly from the source from which the partnership realized the item, or incurred in the same manner as it was incurred by the partnership. Although this language is not a model of clarity, it is fairly clear that generally partnership-level characterization prevails.[52]

Treas. Reg. § 1.702-1(b) also indicates that characterization is determined at the partnership level. It indicates that a partner's distributive share of gain from the sale of depreciable property used in a trade or business be considered as gain from the sale of depreciable property in the hands of the partner, without regard to how it would be treated if the partner directly sold the property in question.

A. Dealer Status

The determination of whether property held by a partnership is inventory or property held for sale to customers in the ordinary course of business (i.e., dealer property) is made at the partnership level, not the partner level.[53] Thus, it would be possible for a dealer in real estate to be a partner of a partnership which holds real property for investment or used in a trade or business, and upon the sale of that property for the dealer to recognize capital gain. In order to prevent abuse in this area, however, I.R.C. § 724(a) and (b) prevent a person from contributing property which was inventory in their hands and obtaining capital gain treatment from its sale if the property is sold within five years after the date of the contribution. Similarly, I.R.C. § 724(a) provides that if a person contributes unrealized receivables to a partnership, any gain or loss recognized by the partnership on the disposition of the unrealized receivables is treated as ordinary income or ordinary loss. Finally, I.R.C. § 724(c) provides that if property which was a capital asset in the hands of a partner is contributed to the partnership, any loss recognized by the partnership on the disposition of such property within five years

---

[51] I.R.C. § 464(c)(1).

[52] *See* United States v. Basye, 410 U.S. 441 (1973).

[53] Podell v. Commissioner, 55 T.C. 429 (1970); Grove v. Commissioner, 54 T.C. 799 (1970); Barham v. United States, 301 F. Supp. 43 (M.D. Ga. 1969), *aff'd per curiam*, 429 F.2d 40 (5th Cir. 1970).

after its contribution is treated as a capital loss to the extent that the adjusted basis to the property at the time of the contribution exceeded the fair market value of the property on such date. These rules are designed to prevent the partnership level characterization rule from being used to convert ordinary income to capital gain, or a capital loss to an ordinary loss.

B. Holding Period

It is clear that the determination of whether there is a long-term or short-term holding period for properties sold by a partnership is determined by reference to the partnership's holding period, not the holding period of a partner for the partnership interest.[54]

C. Hobby Loss Rules

I.R.C. § 183(a) limits the deductions which can be taken by an individual or an S corporation if the activity is not engaged in for profit. Although the Code, by its terms, only applies to individuals and S corporations, the authorities are uniform in holding that I.R.C. § 183 applies to partnerships as well and that the determination of whether the activity was engaged in for profit is determined at the partnership level, not the partner level.[55]

D. Like-Kind Exchanges and Involuntary Conversions

Under I.R.C. § 1031, a taxpayer is permitted to exchange property held for use in a trade or business or for investment for like-kind property without the recognition of gain. Since it is the partnership which is the taxpayer, if the partnership disposes of the property, it is the partnership, not the partners, which is required to effect the exchange.[56] A similar rule applies in the case of an involuntary conversion of partnership property and a subsequent reinvestment in property similar or related in service or use under I.R.C. § 1033.[57]

E. Discharge of Indebtedness Income

If a partnership's debt is forgiven, the partnership will recognize discharge of indebtedness income. I.R.C. § 108(d)(6), however, provides that in the case of a partnership, I.R.C. § 108(a), (b), (c), and (g) are applied at the partner level. Thus, discharge of indebtedness income must be separately passed through to each of the partners, and is not a part of the bottom line profit or loss.

Under I.R.C. § 108(a)(1), gross income does not include discharge of indebtedness income if the discharge occurs in a Title 11 case, when a taxpayer is insolvent, when the indebtedness discharged is qualified farm indebtedness or

---

[54] Rev. Rul. 68-79, 1968-1 C.B. 310.

[55] *See* Polakof v. Commissioner, 820 F.2d 321 (9th Cir. 1987); Tallal v. Commissioner, 778 F.2d 275 (5th Cir. 1985); Brannen v. Commissioner, 722 F.2d. 695 (11th Cir. 1984).

[56] *See* PLR 9818003 (Dec. 24, 1997).

[57] Rev. Rul. 66-191, 1966-2 C.B. 300.

when the indebtedness discharged is qualified real property business indebtedness. Thus, even if the partnership is in bankruptcy or insolvent, if the partner is not in bankruptcy or is solvent, those exclusions will not be available to the partner. Under I.R.C. § 108(b), if discharge of indebtedness income is not included in income by reason of one of the exceptions contained in I.R.C. § 108(a), then the taxpayer is required to reduce the taxpayer's tax attributes as provided in I.R.C. § 108(b)(2). As a result of the provisions of I.R.C. § 108(d)(6), the attribute reduction required by I.R.C. § 108(b)(2) will be made at the partner level, not the partnership level.

If the partnership's indebtedness is cancelled by virtue of the partnership issuing a profits interest or capital interest in the partnership to the creditor, I.R.C. § 108(e)(8) provides that the partnership is treated as having satisfied the indebtedness with an amount of money equal to the fair market value of the interest issued. Thus, if the fair market value of the interest issued is less than the amount of the indebtedness cancelled, the partnership will recognize discharge of indebtedness income. I.R.C. § 108(e)(8)(B) further provides that if any discharge of indebtedness income is recognized by reason of the partnership issuing a capital interest or profits interest in exchange for debt, the discharge of indebtedness income must be allocated to the partners who were partners immediately before the discharge (i.e., the discharge of indebtedness income cannot be allocated to the former creditor who is now a partner). *See* § 2.08.B.2.a.iv.

§ 4.07   LOSS LIMITATION RULES

A.   Basis Limitation

I.R.C. § 704(d) provides that a partner's share of the partnership's loss (including capital loss) is allowed only to the extent of the partner's adjusted basis at the end of the partnership's taxable year in which the loss has occurred. Any loss which is disallowed by reason of the foregoing provision is carried over and may be deducted when the partner's basis for his partnership interest is positive.[58]

As indicated in greater detail in § 3.04, under I.R.C. § 752(a), a partner is able to increase the partner's basis for the partnership interest by the partner's share of the partnership's liabilities. The ability of a partner to include partnership liabilities in her basis for her partnership interest enables a partner to claim deductions passed through from the partnership in excess of the amount contributed by the partner to the partnership, notwithstanding the limitation of I.R.C. § 704(d).

In determining a partner's basis in his partnership interest, basis is first increased by those items referred to in I.R.C. § 705(a)(1), and then decreased by the items referred to in I.R.C. § 705(a)(2) (other than the loss for the taxable year and losses previously disallowed under I.R.C. § 704(d)).[59] If the partner's distributive share of items of loss specified in I.R.C. § 702(a)(1), (2), (3), (7), and (8)

---

[58] I.R.C. § 704(d); Treas. Reg. § 1.704-1(d)(1).

[59] Treas. Reg. § 1.704-1(d)(2).

exceed the partner's basis for her partnership interest, the limitation on losses provided for in I.R.C. § 704(d) must be allocated to the partner's distributive share of each of such losses. This allocation is determined by taking the proportion that each loss bears to total of all such losses.[60] It should be noted that the items referred to in I.R.C. §§ 702(a)(4) (charitable contributions) and 702(a)(6) (foreign taxes) are not referred to in Treas. Reg. § 1.704-1(d)(2).[61]

B. At Risk Rules

1. Limitations on Losses to Amount at Risk

Under I.R.C. § 465(b), an individual and certain closely held C corporations may only deduct losses from an activity to the extent they are "at risk" with respect to the activity at the end of the taxable year. While I.R.C. § 465(c)(1) lists five specific activities to which the at risk limitation rules apply, I.R.C. § 465(c)(3) provides that the activities to which the at risk limitation applies includes any activity engaged in by the taxpayer in carrying on a trade of business or for the production of income. Thus, the at risk limitation effectively applies to all activities for the production of income. Activities that are not carried on for the production of income may be limited by the hobby loss rules, discussed above.

2. Calculations of Amount at Risk

Under I.R.C. § 465(b), a taxpayer is generally at risk regarding an activity with respect to (i) the amount of money and adjusted basis of property contributed by the taxpayer to the activity, and (ii) amounts borrowed for use in the activity to the extent that the taxpayer is personally liable for repayment of the amount borrowed or has pledged property, other than property used in the activity as security for the borrowed amount (to the extent of the net fair market value of the pledged property).[62]

Notwithstanding the provisions of I.R.C. § 465(b)(2), a taxpayer is not considered to be at risk with respect to borrowed amounts if the amount is borrowed from a person who has an interest in the activity or from a person related to a person who has an interest in the activity.[63] For this purpose, a related person means one who bears a relationship to a person specified in either I.R.C. § 267(b) or 707(b)(1), but substituting "10%" for "50%."[64] A person is also a related person if they are engaged in trades or businesses under common control within the meaning of I.R.C. § 52(a) or (b).[65]

---

[60] *Id.*

[61] The IRS has in at least one ruling concluded that I.R.C. § 704(d) does not apply to charitable contributions. PLR 8405084 (Nov. 3, 1983).

[62] I.R.C. § 465(b)(2).

[63] I.R.C. § 465(b)(3)(A).

[64] I.R.C. § 465(b)(3)(C).

[65] I.R.C. § 465(b)(3(C)(ii).

The taxpayer's at risk amount with respect to an activity is reduced to the extent that the taxpayer claims a loss from the activity which is not disallowed under the at risk rules.[66] The taxpayer's amount of risk is also decreased by cash withdrawn from the activity, but is increased by the taxpayer's share of income from the activity.[67]

In *Hubert Enterprises, Inc. v. Commissioner*,[68] the Tax Court held that a deficit restoration obligation contained in an operating agreement of an LLC taxed as a partnership did not result in the members being at risk with respect to the recourse liabilities of the LLC because: (i) the deficit restoration obligation would only be effective if the LLC liquidated, and even then there was no assurance that the amount of the deficit restoration obligation would be equal to the amount of the unpaid recourse debt, (ii) under the terms of the operating agreement, the amount paid under the deficit restoration obligation could be paid to members with positive capital account balances, rather than to creditors, and (iii) the creditors had no enforceable right to collect any unpaid debt directly from the member by reason of the deficit restoration obligation.

3. Nonrecourse Financing

Notwithstanding the general rule set forth above, I.R.C. § 465(b)(4) contains an overriding principle that a taxpayer is "not considered at risk with respect to amounts protected against loss through nonrecourse financing, guarantees, stop-loss agreements, or other similar arrangements." There is, however, an exception to the overriding rule in the case of qualified nonrecourse financing. Under I.R.C. § 465(b)(6), a taxpayer engaged in the activity of holding real property is considered at risk with respect to the taxpayer's share of any qualified nonrecourse financing which is secured by real property used in that activity.

The term "qualified non-recourse financing" generally means nonconvertible, nonrecourse debt which is borrowed with respect to the activity of holding real property and which is: (i) borrowed from a government or instrumentality thereof, (ii) guaranteed by a government, or (iii) borrowed from a person regularly engaged in the business of lending money who is neither a person related to the taxpayer, a person from whom the taxpayer acquired the property (or related persons to such person), nor a person who receives a fee with respect to the taxpayer's investment in the property (or related person to such person).[69] There is an exception to the rule prohibiting loans from related persons. Funds borrowed from related persons will be taken into account if the related person financing is commercially reasonable and on substantially the same terms as loans involving unrelated persons.[70]

Pursuant to I.R.C. § 465(b)(6)(C), if the qualified nonrecourse financing is incurred by a partnership, a partner's share of the partnership's qualified nonre-course financing is determined on the basis of the partner's share of liabilities of the

---

[66] I.R.C. § 465(b)(5).

[67] Prop. Treas. Reg. § 1.465-41, example 2.

[68] T.C. Memo 2008-46.

[69] I.R.C. § 465(b)(6)(B).

[70] I.R.C. § 465(b)(6)(D)(ii).

partnership incurred in connection with such financing.

4. Carryover of Disallowed Losses

If the taxpayer is prohibited from taking a loss by reason of the applicability of the at risk limitation, the amount disallowed is treated as a deduction applicable to that activity in the succeeding taxable year, but the deductibility of such loss is still subject to the at risk limitation in such subsequent year.[71] Where the activity is conducted through a partnership, if a loss of the partnership is not deductible by a partner by reason of the basis limitation contained in I.R.C. § 704(d), then even if the loss would also be nondeductible by reason of the at risk limitation, the at risk rules will not apply to such loss since the loss was nondeductible without regard to the at risk rules. Thus, the amount will not be carried over pursuant to I.R.C. § 465(a)(2), but will carry over under I.R.C. § 704(d) (but subject to the at risk rule in the carryover year).

5. Applicability to Partnerships

The at risk rules are applied at the partner level, not the partnership level. While I.R.C. § 465(a)(1) refers to the amount the taxpayer is at risk at the close of the taxable year, where the activity is engaged in through a partnership, it is the close of the taxable year of the partnership which governs, not that of the partner.[72] This rule could make a difference where the partner and the partnership have different taxable years.

A partner's at risk amount and the partner's basis for her partnership interest generally are the same, except that the partner's share of partnership liabilities which cannot be taken into account under I.R.C. § 465(b)(3) (after taking into account the special rule for qualified nonrecourse financing) must be excluded. A partner's at risk amount may also be reduced for stop loss and similar arrangements that may not be taken into account in determining a partner's basis.[73] The amount the taxpayer is at risk, however, does not deal with the partnership per se, but rather deals with each activity engaged in by the partnership. (An "activity" is not defined for this purpose, but it is defined for purposes of the passive loss rules of I.R.C. § 469, discussed below.) Thus, it is possible for a partner's at risk amount with respect to the partnership to be greater than the loss applicable to the partner, but if some of that at risk amount was attributable to an activity other than the activity which generated the loss, the loss may nevertheless be non-deductible.

There are, however, certain cases in which aggregation of activities is permissible. Under I.R.C. § 465(c)(2)(B)(i), if the activities are conducted by a partnership and consist of leasing section 1245 property which is placed in service in the same taxable year, the activities are aggregated. Also, under I.R.C. § 465(c)(3)(B), in the case of the activities described in I.R.C. § 465(c)(3)(a) (i.e., all activities other than those specified in I.R.C. § 465(c)(1)), if the activity constitutes a trade or business and the trade or business is carried on by a partnership, and 65% or more of the

---

[71] I.R.C. § 465(a)(2).

[72] Prop. Treas. Reg. § 1.465-1(a).

[73] I.R.C. § 465(b)(4).

losses for the taxable year are applicable to persons who actively participate in the management of the trade or business, then the activities may be aggregated.

6. Disposition of Activity or Partnership Interest

If a partner disposes of all or a portion of the partner's partnership interest, or if a partnership engaged in an activity to which the at risk rules apply disposes of an activity, any gain resulting from such disposition is treated as income from the activity.[74] Thus, if a partner has previously had losses disallowed by reason of the at risk limitation, those losses are generally allowed in the year of the disposition of the activity or the partnership interest in the partnership conducting the activity.

There is a special rule with respect to certain carryover basis transactions. If: (i) a partner transfers the partner's interest in a partnership, (ii) the basis of the transferee is determined in whole or in part by reference to the basis of the transferor, (iii) the transferor has suspended losses by virtue of I.R.C. § 465(a) at the time of the transfer, and (iv) at the close of the taxable year in which the transfer occurs the amount of the transferor's loss from the activity is in excess of the transferor's amount at risk in the activity, the excess is added to the transferor's basis in the activity.[75] This rule is applied solely for the purpose of determining the basis of the property in the hands of the transferee.

There is another special rule which is applicable to transfers of partnership interest. If: (i) a partner transfers a partner's entire interest in the partnership, (ii) the basis of the transferee is determined in whole or part by reference to the basis of the transferor, and (iii) the transferor has an amount at risk which is in excess of losses from the activity, then at the close of the transferor's taxable year in which the transfer occurs, the transferor's amount at risk in the activity is added to the transferee's amount at risk.[76] In addition, in the case of a gift of a partnership interest, the transferee's amount at risk is increased by the amount that the donee's basis is increased under I.R.C. § 1015(d) (relating to gift tax paid by the transferor).[77]

C. Passive Loss Limitation

1. Loss Disallowance Rule

Even if a partner's losses from a partnership are not limited by the basis limitation or the at risk limitation, the partner's share of the partnership's losses may be disallowed under the passive loss rules. In the case of individuals, estates, trusts, closely held C corporations, and personal service corporations, I.R.C. § 469(a) disallows the deduction of a passive activity loss or the claiming of a passive activity credit. Any loss or credit disallowed by virtue of I.R.C. § 469(a) is treated as a deduction or credit applicable to the activity in the next taxable year (i.e., the

---

[74] Prop. Treas. Reg. §§ 1.465-66(a), 1.465-12(a).

[75] Prop. Treas. Reg. § 1.465-67.

[76] Prop. Treas. Reg. § 1.465-68.

[77] Prop. Treas. Reg. § 1.465-68(b).

disallowed loss or credit is carried over).[78]

2. Passive Activity

I.R.C. § 469(d)(1) defines the term "passive activity loss" to mean the amount by which the aggregate losses from all passive activities of the taxable year exceed the aggregate income from all passive activities for such year. The key, therefore, is what constitutes a passive activity. I.R.C. § 469(c)(1) defines the term "passive activity" to mean any activity which involves the conduct of a trade or business and in which the taxpayer does not materially participate. There are a number of special rules applicable to rental activities and working interests in oil and gas property.[79]

It is clear that certain income and expenses are not taken into account in determining the income or loss from a passive activity. These items are attributable to investment activities, rather than trade or business activities. Thus, gross income from interest, dividends, annuities, or royalties not derived in the ordinary course of a trade or business, and gain or loss not derived in the ordinary course of a trade or business which is attributable to the disposition of property producing income of the type referred to above or held for investment, is not taken into account. Likewise, expenses, other than interest, which are clearly and directly applicable to such gross income, and interest expense properly applicable to such gross income, is not taken into account.[80]

If a deduction from a passive activity is disallowed under the basis limitation rule of I.R.C. § 704(b) or the at risk limitation of I.R.C. § 465, it is not considered a passive activity deduction for the taxable year.[81] If any amount of the partner's distributive share of a partnership's loss is disallowed under I.R.C. § 704(d), a ratable portion of the partner's distributive share of each item of deduction or loss of the partnership is disallowed for the taxable year. The ratable portion of an item of deduction or loss is the amount of such item multiplied by a fraction, the numerator of which is the amount of the partner's distributive share of partnership loss that is disallowed for the taxable year, and the denominator of which is the sum of the partner's distributive share of all items of deduction and loss of the partnership for the taxable year.[82]

If an item of gross income or deduction is attributable to a transaction that is treated under I.R.C. § 707(a) as a transaction between a partnership and a partner acting in a non-partner capacity, such income or deduction is treated for purposes of the passive loss rule in a manner that is consistent with the treatment of the transaction under I.R.C. § 707(a).[83] Any payment to a partner for services or the use of capital described in I.R.C. § 707(c) is treated as a payment for services or a

---

[78] I.R.C. § 469(b).

[79] I.R.C. § 469(c)(2), (3), (7).

[80] I.R.C. § 469(e)(1)(A).

[81] Temp. Treas. Reg. § 1.469-2T(d)(6)(i).

[82] Temp. Treas. Reg. § 1.469-2T(d)(6)(ii).

[83] Temp. Treas. Reg. § 1.469-2T(e)(2)(i).

payment of interest, and not as a distributive share of partnership income.[84] If any payment is made to a retiring partner or a deceased partner's successor in interest under I.R.C. § 736(b), the gain or loss is treated as passive activity gross income or a passive activity deduction to the extent that the gain or loss would have been passive activity gross income or a passive activity deduction at the time the liquidation of the partner's interest commenced.[85] If a payment is made in liquidation of a retiring or deceased partner's partnership interest and the payment is described in I.R.C. § 736(a) and is attributable to unrealized receivables or goodwill of the partnership, the percentage of the income that is treated as passive activity gross income is limited to the amount that the retiring or deceased partner would have recognized if the unrealized receivables and goodwill had been sold at the time that the liquidation of the partner's partnership interest commenced.[86]

3. Material Participation

In general, the key to determining whether income or loss from a passive activity is passive is whether the taxpayer materially participates in the activity[87] (special rules apply to participation in rental activities and working interests in oil and gas property).[88] In the case of an activity conducted by a partnership, it is the participation of the partner, not the partnership, which is relevant.[89] Whether a partner materially participates in an activity conducted by a partnership is determined based upon the taxable year of the partnership, not the taxable year of the partner.[90]

I.R.C. § 469(h)(1) provides that a taxpayer is treated as materially participating in an activity only if the taxpayer is involved in the operation of the activity on a regular, continuous, and substantial basis. Temp. Treas. Reg. § 1.469-5T(a), however, provides that an individual is treated as materially participating in an activity if and only if one of seven tests are met. These tests are as follow:

(1) The individual participates in the activity more than 500 hours during the year.

(2) The individual's participation in the activity for the year constitutes substantially all of the participation in such activity of all individuals for such year.

(3) The individual participates in the activity for more than 100 hours during the taxable year and such participation for the year is not less than the participation in the activity of any other individual for such year.

---

[84] Treas. Reg. § 1.469-2(e)(2)(ii).

[85] Treas. Reg. § 1.469-2(e)(2)(iii)(A).

[86] Treas. Reg. § 1.469-2(e)(2)(3)(B).

[87] Passive activities do not include working interests in oil and gas properties. I.R.C. § 469(c)(3).

[88] I.R.C. § 469(c). Passive activities do not include working interests in oil and gas properties subject to certain requirements. I.R.C. § 469(c)(3). There is also an exception for real estate professionals, I.R.C. § 469(c)(7), and certain individuals subject to a $25,000 limitation. I.R.C. § 469(i).

[89] Temp. Treas. Reg. § 1.469-2T(e)(1).

[90] *Id.*

(4) The activity is a "significant participation activity" (within the meaning of Temp. Treas. Reg. § 1.469-5T(c)) for the year and the individual's aggregate participation in all significant participation activities during such year exceeds 500 hours.

(5) The individual materially participated in the activity for any five taxable years during the immediately preceding 10 taxable years.

(6) The activity is a personal service activity and the individual materially participated in the activity for any three taxable years preceding the taxable year in question.

(7) Based on all the facts and circumstances, the individual participates in the activity on a regular, continuous, and substantial basis during the year.

Notwithstanding the above, rental activities are passive except for rental real estate activities if more than half of the personal services performed by a taxpayer are in real property trades or businesses. Further, the taxpayer must perform more than 750 hours of personal services in real property trades or businesses and materially participate in those activities (as material participation is determined on an activity-by-activity basis, the 750-hour rule does not make this final requirement inevitable).[91]

I.R.C. § 469(h)(2) provides that except as provided in regulations, no interest in a limited partnership as a limited partner is treated as an interest with respect to which a taxpayer materially participates. The IRS originally took the position that a person would be treated as a limited partner if either: (i) the person's interest was so designated in the limited agreement or the certificate of limited partnership, or (ii) the liability of the person for obligations of the partnership is limited under state law to a determinable fixed amount. Following a series of losses in the courts with respect to interests in entities taxed as partnership but not limited partnerships under local law,[92] the IRS issues Proposed Regulations that take a different position with respect to the issue of when a person will be treated as a limited partner for purposes of I.R.C. § (h)(2).

Proposed Regulation § 1.469–5(e)(3)provides that for purposes of I.R.C. § 469(h)(2), an interest in an entity is treated as an interest in a limited partnership as a limited partner if: (i) the entity is treated as a partnersip for Federal income tax purpose, and (ii) the holder of the interest does not have rights to manage the entity at all times during the entity's taxable year under the law of the jurisdiction in which the entity is organized and under the gioverning agreement. It further provides that an individual will not be treated as holding an interest in the limited partnership as a limited partner if the individual also holds an interest in that partnership that is not an interest in a limited partnership as a limited partner (e.g., a general partner in a state law limited partnership). It is unclear whether the terms of an operating agreement can override state law. Thus, if the operating agreement of a member-managed LLC only authorizes certain membersto take

---

[91] I.R.C. § 469(c)(2), (7).

[92] See, e.g., Garnett v. Commissioner, 132 T.C. 368 (2009), and Thompson v. United States, 87 Fed. Cl. 728 (2009), *acq.* AOD 2010–002.

action on behalf of the LLC, an issue is raised as to whether the prohibition in the operating agreement with respect to remaining members results in them being treated as limited partners for purposes of I.R.C. § 469(h)(2).

A similar issue is raised as to when persons treated as partners for federal income tax purposes will be treated as limited partners for purposes of I.R.C. § 1402(a)(13). The Proposed Regulation under I.R.C. § 469(h)(2), however, is solely for purposes of I.R.C. § 469(h)(2), and may not be relied upon for purposes of I.R.C. § 1402(a)(13).

D. Disposition of Partnership Interest

I.R.C. § 469(g) provides that if during the taxable year a taxpayer disposes of the taxpayer's entire interest in any passive activity in a fully taxable transaction, the excess of: (i) any loss from such activity for such taxable year, over (ii) any net income or gains for such taxable year from all other passive activities, is treated as a loss which is not from a passive activity. The effect of this provision is that if a loss has been suspended by reason of the passive activity rule, the loss can be recognized when the taxpayer disposes of the interest in the activity. If, however, the person acquiring the activity is a related party within the meaning of I.R.C. § 267(b) or 707(b)(1), then the forgoing rule does not apply until the taxable year in which such interest is acquired by somebody who is not a related person. If the disposition is a result of the death of the taxpayer, then the general disposition rule only applies to the extent that the losses are greater than the excess of the basis of the property in the hands of the transferee over the basis of the property in the hands of the taxpayer immediately before death (i.e., the step-up in basis resulting from the taxpayer's death).[93] Any suspended losses up to the step-up in basis resulting from the death of the taxpayer are not allowed as a deduction for any taxable year.[94] If the disposition of the interest is by means of an installment sale, then a pro rata amount of the losses are deductible based upon the percentage of the income that is included in each year.[95]

Where the passive activity is conducted through a partnership and there is a sale, exchange, or other disposition of the partnership interest, a ratable portion of any gain or loss from the disposition is treated as gain or loss from the disposition of an interest in each trade or business, rental or investment activity in which the partnership owns an interest.[96] The ratable portion in the case of gain applicable to an activity is generally equal to the amount of gain recognized multiplied by a fraction, the numerator of which is the gain that would have been applicable to the partner had the partnership sold its entire interest in the activity for its fair market value, and the denominator of which is the amount of gain that would have been applicable to the partner had the partnership sold all of its activities in which gain would be recognized if sold for its fair market value.[97]

---

[93] I.R.C. § 469(g)(2)(A).

[94] I.R.C. § 469(g)(2)(B).

[95] I.R.C. § 469(g)(3).

[96] Temp. Treas. Reg. § 1.469-2T(e)(3)(ii)(A).

[97] Temp. Treas. Reg. § 1.469-2T(e)(3)(ii)(B)(1).

If the partner disposing of the partner's partnership interest has a basis adjustment under I.R.C. § 743(b), such adjustment is taken into account in computing the net gain or net loss that would have been allocated to such partner if the partnership had sold its entire interest in an activity.[98] If a partner receives a distribution in excess of the partner's basis for her partnership interest, since the gain is treated as a gain from the sale of a partnership interest, the rules dealing with a disposition of a partnership interest come into play.[99]

§ 4.08 TAXABLE YEAR OF PARTNERSHIP

A. Required Taxable Years

I.R.C. § 706(d)(1)(B) generally requires that a partnership have a taxable year which is determined by reference to the taxable year of its partners. There is a three-tier system for determining the partnership's taxable year on this basis. First, if there is a "majority interest taxable year," then that must be used by the partnership. If there is not a majority interest taxable year, then the partnership must use the taxable year of all of the "principal partners." If there is no taxable year of all of the principal partners, then except as provided in Regulations, the partnership must use the calendar year.

The term "majority interest taxable year" means the taxable year of one or more partners having an aggregate interest in partnership profits and capital of more than 50%.[100] A "principal partner" is a partner having an interest of 5% or more in partnership profits or capital. For purposes of determining a partner's interest in partnership profits, the partner's share of partnership profits for the current partnership taxable year is taken into account.[101] If the partnership does not expect that the partnership will have income for the current partnership taxable year, then a partner's interest in partnership profits is determined based upon the partner's percentage share of partnership net income for the first taxable year in which the partnership expects to have income.[102] Where the partners do not share income in straight percentages, the partnership is required to make a reasonable estimate of the amount and nature of its income for the taxable year to determine a partner's percentage share of partnership net income.[103]

For purposes of determining a partner's capital interest, a determination must be made of the assets the partner would be entitled to receive upon withdrawal from the partnership or upon liquidation of the partnership. If the partnership maintains capital accounts in accordance with Treas. Reg. § 1.704-1(b)(2)(iv), then the partnership is entitled to assume that a partner's interest in partnership capital is the ratio of the partner's capital account to all of the partners' capital accounts as

---

[98] Temp. Treas. Reg. § 1.469-2T(e)(3)(ii).

[99] Rev. Rul. 95-5, 1995-1 C.B. 100.

[100] I.R.C. § 706(b)(4)(A).

[101] Treas. Reg. § 1.706-1(b)(4)(ii)(A).

[102] *Id.*

[103] Treas. Reg. § 1.706-1(b)(4)(ii)(B).

of the first day of the partnership taxable year.[104]

In determining a partner's interest in partnership profits and capital, certain taxpayers may be disregarded. If the partnership has a tax-exempt partner, the interest of the tax-exempt partner may be disregarded if the tax-exempt partner was not subject to tax on any income attributable to its investment in the partnership during the immediately preceding taxable year. If the tax-exempt partner was not a partner during the partnership's immediately preceding taxable year, then this determination may be based upon the partnership's reasonable belief that the tax-exempt partner would not be subject to tax on any income attributable to such partner's investment in the partnership.[105]

Treas. Reg. § 1.706-1(b)(6)(i) provides that a foreign partner's interest in a partnership may be disregarded if none of the income of the partnership that was effectively connected with the conduct of a U.S. trade or business during the immediately preceding taxable year is allocable to the foreign partner. If the foreign partner was not a partner during the immediately preceding year, this determination may be made based upon the partnership's reasonable belief that no income effectively connected with the conduct of a U.S. trade or business will be allocated to such foreign partner. Even if income effectively connected with the conduct of a U.S. trade or business is allocable to a foreign partner, if such income may not be taxed under a U.S. income tax treaty, the interest of the foreign partner may still be disregarded.

As indicated above, I.R.C. § 706(b)(1)(B)(iii) requires that a partnership use a calendar year unless the Regulations provide otherwise. Treas. Reg. § 1.706-1(b)(2)(i)(c) requires that if there is no majority interest taxable year or no taxable year of all principal partners, then the taxable year which must be used is that which produces the least aggregate deferral of income. The aggregate deferral for a particular year is equal to the sum of the deferrals of each of the partners. The deferral for a partner is determined by multiplying the months of deferral that would be generated by the use of a particular taxable year and each partner's interest in partnership profits for that year. The partnership taxable year that produces the lowest sum when compared to the other partners' taxable years is the taxable year that results in the least aggregate deferral of income. If the calculation results in more than one taxable year qualifying as a taxable year with least aggregate deferral, the partnership may elect any of such taxable years, unless one of such years was the partnership's existing taxable year, in which case the partnership must maintain its existing taxable year.[106]

The following example, taken from Treas. Reg. § 1.706-1(b)(3)(iv), example 1, illustrates the application of the least aggregate deferral rule. A and B each have a 50% interest in partnership profits. A has a June 30 taxable year and B has a July 31 taxable year. The determination of the taxable year which produces the least aggregate deferral is made as follows:

---

[104] Treas. Reg. § 1.706-1(b)(4)(iii).

[105] Treas. Reg. § 1.706-1(b)(5).

[106] Treas. Reg. § 1.706-1(b)(3)(i).

Test 6/30	Year End	Interest in Partnership Profits	Months of Deferral for 6/30 Year End	Interest x Deferral
Partner A	6/30	.5	0	0
Partner B	7/31	.5	1	.5
Aggregate Deferral				.5

Test 7/31	Year End	Interest in Partnership Profits	Months of Deferral for 7/31 Year End	Interest x Deferral
Partner A	6/30	.5	11	5.5
Partner B	7/31	.5	0	0
Aggregate Deferral				5.5

Thus, June 30 is the year with the least aggregate deferral.

B. Business Purpose

I.R.C. § 706(b)(1)(C) provides that a partnership may have a taxable year other than the required taxable year determined in accordance with I.R.C. § 706(b)(1)(B) if it is established to the satisfaction of the IRS that there is a business purpose for such taxable year (which does not include the deferral of income to partners). The IRS has issued a Revenue Procedure providing guidance regarding when a partnership has established a business purpose for a taxable year.

Under Rev. Proc. 2002-38,[107] a partnership can establish a "natural business year" by satisfying the 25% gross receipts test set forth therein. The 25% gross receipts tests is met if the gross receipts from sales and services for the last two months of the desired business year are more than 25% of the gross receipts from sales and services for the 12-month period ending on that date or the most recent 12-month period ending on that date and for the two preceding 12-month periods. If such test is met, then the taxpayer may generally elect to use that year as a result of such year end being its natural business year.[108] To compute the 25% test, the taxpayer is required to use the method of accounting used to prepare its federal income tax return for the taxable year in question. If the taxpayer has a predecessor organization and is continuing the same business as its predecessor, the taxpayer must use the gross receipts of its predecessor for purposes of determining the 25% gross receipts test. If the taxpayer (including any predecessor) does not have a 47-month period of gross receipts, then it is unable to establish a natural business year under Rev. Proc. 2002-38.

Even if the taxpayer meets the 25% gross receipts test, the taxpayer must also establish that there is not another annual accounting period which also meets the

---

[107] 2002-1 C.B. (Vol. II) 1037.

[108] Rev. Proc. 2002-38, § 5.05(2)(a).

25% test and which produces a higher average of gross receipts than does the year requested by the taxpayer.[109]

In addition to the mathematical tests provided for in Rev. Proc. 2002-38, a partnership will be permitted to adopt a taxable year other than a required taxable year if the taxpayer can establish a business purpose for the taxable year based on all the relevant facts and circumstances.[110] The IRS has indicated that it will grant permission to adopt or change a taxable year under the facts and circumstances test only in rare and unusual circumstances.[111] Rev. Proc. 2002-39 indicates that reasons which will not qualify as a good business purpose include: (i) administrative and convenience reasons, (ii) the use of a particular year for regulatory or financial accounting purposes, (iii) hiring patterns, (iv) the use of price list, model years, or other items that change on an annual basis, (v) the use of a particular year by related entities, and (vi) the use of a particular year by competitors.[112]

Even if a partnership is unable to meet the 25% gross receipts test, it may still be able to meet the annual business cycle test or seasonal business test set forth in Rev. Proc. 2002-39.

C. § 444 Election

Under I.R.C. § 444, a partnership may elect to have a taxable year other than a required taxable year. I.R.C. § 444(b)(1) limits the choices of elected taxable year to one which does not provide a deferral period longer than three months (i.e., if the required taxable year is the calendar year, then only the last day of September, October, or November may be elected under I.R.C. § 444). The cost of making an election under I.R.C. § 444 is that the taxpayer is required to make the payments required by I.R.C. § 7519.[113] Although the manner of computing the payment required by I.R.C. § 7519 is rather complex, the effect of such payment is that the partnership is prepaying the tax applicable to the income deferred by reason of making the election under I.R.C. § 444.

The required payment is equal to the excess of: (i) the product of (A) the highest individual income tax rate plus 1%, multiplied by (B) the net base year income of the partnership, over (ii) the net required payment balance.[114] Pursuant to I.R.C. § 7519(d)(1), a partnership's net base year income is generally equal to the deferral ratio (the number of months of deferral which results from using the year elected under I.R.C. § 444 rather than the required year) multiplied by the partnership's net income for the base year (the taxable year of the partnership preceding the making of the election under I.R.C. § 444)[115] plus the excess of: (i) the deferral ratio multiplied by the aggregate amount of applicable payments during the base

---

[109] Rev. Proc. 2002-38, § 5.05(2)(b).

[110] Rev. Proc. 2002-39, § 5.02(1)(b).

[111] *Id.*

[112] *Id.*

[113] I.R.C. § 444(c)(1).

[114] I.R.C. § 7519(b).

[115] I.R.C. § 7519(e)(2)(A).

year, over (ii) the aggregate amount of applicable payments made during the deferral period of the base year. For illustrations of the computation of the required payments under I.R.C. § 7519, see Treas. Reg. § 1.7519-1T(b)(vi).

§ 4.09   READING, QUESTIONS AND PROBLEMS

A.   Reading

CODE:

I.R.C. §§ 108(d)(6), 108(e)(8)(B), 444, 447, 448, 464, 465, 469, 701, 702, 703, 704(d), 705, 706(b), 706(d), 724, 7519.

TREASURY REGULATIONS:

Treas. Reg. §§ 1.448-1T, 1.702-1, 1.704-1(d), 1.706-1(b).

Prop. Treas. Reg. § 1.465-67.

Prop. Treas. Reg. § 1.465-68.

CASES:

Fong v. Commissioner, 48 T.C.M. (CCH) 689 (1984), *aff'd*, 816 F.2d 684 (9th Cir. 1987).

United States v. Basye, 410 U.S. 441 (1973).

Polakof v. Commissioner, 820 F.2d 321 (9th Cir. 1987).

RULING AND OTHER INTERPRETATIONS:

Rev. Rul. 68-79, 1968-1 C.B. 216.

Rev. Proc. 2002-38, 2002-1 C.B. (Vol. II) 1037.

Rev. Proc. 2002-39, 2002-1 C.B. (Vol. II) 1046.

PLR 8405084 (Nov. 3, 1983).

TAM 9818003 (Dec. 24, 1997).

B.   Questions and Problems

1. During its first taxable year, the calendar year, Partnership ABCD has the following results:

Income

Gross Receipts — domestic inventory sales	$750,000	
Gross Receipts — foreign inventory sales	$500,000	
Total Gross Receipts		$1,250,000

Income

Cost of Goods Sold — domestic sales	$375,000	
Cost of Goods Sold — foreign sales	$250,000	
Total Cost of Goods Sold		$625,000
Gross Profit from Operations		$625,000
Interest Income	$10,000	
Municipal Bond Income (tax-exempt)	$2,000	
Domestic Dividends	$5,000	
Total Other Income		$17,000
Total Income		$642,000
Expenses		
Selling, General & Administrative	$250,000	
Section 179 Expenditures	$100,000	
Depreciation	$150,000	
Organization Expenses	$11,000	
Foreign Income Taxes	$50,000	
Charitable Contributions	$5,000	
Interest	$10,000	
Total Expenses		$576,000
Net Income		$66,000

A, B, and C have 10% profit and loss sharing ratios and D has a 70% profit and loss sharing ratio. A is a nonresident alien and all of the other partners are U.S. citizens.

   a. How will Partnership ABCD report its operations to its partners?

   b. Does it matter that D personally has $450,000 of I.R.C. § 179 expenditures?

2. Partnership DEF owns marketable securities with a value of $300,000, and a basis of $180,000 which it has owned for many years. DEF does not have an I.R.C. § 754 election in effect. On January 1 of the current year, D sells her one-third interest in DEF to G for $100,000. On February 1 of the current year, DEF sells all of its assets for $330,000 and liquidates. DEF recognizes a gain of $150,000.

   a. Is the gain from the sale of the marketable securities short-term or long-term as to G?

   b. What is G's basis for his partnership interest immediately before receiving the liquidating distribution?

3. Partnership GHI has assets with a book value of $2,100,000 and fair market value of $1,000,000, and liabilities of $1,500,000. The bank and GHI agree to a debt restructuring which has the effect of reducing the principal amount of the debt to $1,000,000. G, H, and I are all solvent. How much income is recognized by GHI?

4. Same as 3, except that the bank becomes a partner of GHI and is given a capital account credit of $500,000.

5. J Corp., K Corp., and L form a partnership. J Corp. has a 70% interest, and K Corp. and L both have 15% interests. J Corp.'s taxable year ends March 31, K Corp.'s taxable year ends September 30, and L uses the calendar year. What taxable year must partnership JKL adopt?

6. Same as 5, except that J Corp. and K Corp. each have a 30% interest and L has a 40% interest. What taxable year must partnership JKL adopt?

7. Partnership MNO owns vacant land which it has owned for a long period of time. M is a developer of residential subdivisions. MNO sells the land and realizes a profit. Is the gain capital gain or ordinary income as to M?

8. P is a partner of a partnership. P has a 25% profit interest and a 50% loss interest. P, along with the other three partners, contributed $10,000 to the partnership. The partnership obtained a $60,000 nonrecourse loan and purchased depreciable personal property for $100,000 which it leased. Without regard to depreciation, the partnership operated at a break even. The property was five-year property and the partnership used the straight line method of depreciation with the result that there was $20,000 of depreciation and a $20,000 loss each year, all of which was allocable to P. P is not active in the business. Assume that $15,000 of the nonrecourse debt was allocable to P.

   a. May P deduct the $20,000 loss in Year 1?

   b. If real property was involved rather than personal property, could P claim the $20,000 loss?

Chapter 5

OPERATION OF A PARTNERSHIP: ALLOCATION OF PARTNERSHIP INCOME AND LOSSES

§ 5.01 INTRODUCTION

As you have learned, a partnership is a flow-through entity. Income and deductions are passed through to the partners. A mechanism needs to exist, therefore, for determining what each partner's allocable share of partnership income and deductions are. I.R.C. § 704(b) and its Regulations generally allow partners a great deal of flexibility in this regard. The allocations do not necessarily need to be in proportion to the underlying ownership of the partnership interests (as is the case with S corporations).[1] Someone who is otherwise a 50% partner could be allocated 90% of depreciation deductions, for example. Or, all losses could initially be allocated to the "money partners," with subsequent income allocated to them to the same extent as losses were, and then income allocated 50% to the money partners and 50% to the promoters. (This is sometimes called a "flip"; flips are quite common.)

I.R.C. § 704(b) provides that a partner's "distributive share of income, gain, loss, and deduction, or credit . . . shall be determined in accordance with the partner's interest in the partnership . . . if" the partnership agreement does not provide for how a distributive share will be allocated *or* if the allocations do not have substantial economic effect. Thus, if an allocation *does* have substantial economic effect, it need not be in accordance with a partner's interest in the partnership. As we will learn, a partner's interest in the partnership is determined under a facts and circumstances test. The Regulations provide detailed and specific rules as to when allocations have substantial economic effect. These substantial economic effect rules provide a structure that is intended to be a safe harbor. If the partnership agreement complies with the rules, the partnership knows the transaction will be safe. Many practitioners will endeavor to comply with them if possible. It used to be that practitioners viewed compliance with the substantial economic effect rules as being virtually mandatory, but in recent years practitioners have been increasingly drafting agreements to come under the partners' "interest in the partnership" facts and circumstances test. Indeed, in large, complex deals, the latter approach is likely the norm. However, only those with a firm grasp of the safe harbor should consider planning outside the safe harbor.

---

[1] *See* I.R.C. § 1377(a); since partners can have varying interests in capital and profits, determining what the underlying ownership interest is may not be an easy task.

The partnership allocations rules have been called "a creation of prodigious complexity . . . essentially impenetrable to all but those with the time, talent, and determination to become thoroughly prepared experts on the subject."[2] Unfortunately, this is not an exaggeration. Trusting that you have the time, talent, and determination, we will proceed.

§ 5.02   CAPITAL ACCOUNTS

For an allocation to have substantial economic effect under the safe harbor, the capital accounts must be maintained in accordance with the rules in the Regulations.[3] As the name of the substantial economic effect test suggests, an allocation will meet the test if it has a genuine after-tax, economic effect on the partner to whom the allocation is made. The rules for maintaining the capital accounts help to fulfill this task. As the concern here is with the economic rather than tax impacts, the rules for keeping capital accounts are quite different from the rules for computing tax basis.

Under the Regulations, a partner's capital account is increased by:

1. The amount of money contributed to the partnership.

2. The fair market value of property contributed to the partnership (net of liabilities secured by the property that the partnership is considered to assume or take subject to under I.R.C. § 752).[4]

3. Allocations of partnership income and gain, including tax-exempt income.

A partner's capital account is decreased by:

1. The amount of money distributed to the partner.

2. The fair market value of property distributed to the partner (net of liabilities secured by the property that the partner is considered to assume or take subject to under I.R.C. § 752).

3. Allocations of expenditures of the partnership that can neither be capitalized nor deducted in computing taxable income.

4. Allocations of partnership loss and deduction.

Note that unlike the adjusted basis in the partnership interest, a partner's capital account does not include that partner's share of liabilities. If the partnership has liabilities, a partner's basis often will exceed his capital account balance.[5] Since,

---

[2] Lawrence Lokken, *Partnership Allocations*, 41 Tax L. Rev. 547 (1986).

[3] Treas. Reg. § 1.704-1(b)(2)(iv)(a).

[4] The fair market value assigned to property will be regarded as correct provided that: (1) such value is reasonably agreed to among the partners in arm's-length negotiations and (2) the partners have sufficiently adverse interests. *See* Treas. Reg. § 1.704-1(b)(2)(iv)(h).

[5] This is not inevitably the case, however. For example, if the partner contributes property to a partnership with a fair market value that greatly exceeds its basis, the capital account may exceed the tax basis of the partnership interest even after factoring in liabilities.

subject to the at risk and passive loss rules, a partner may receive loss allocations up to his basis in the partnership interest, a partner may have a positive tax basis and a negative capital account.

Many practitioners choose to comply with the capital account rules not by inserting a lengthy explanation into the partnership agreement, but instead by simply providing that the capital accounts will be maintained as specified in the relevant Regulation. This latter approach has the advantage that if the rules for keeping capital accounts change, there is no need to amend the partnership agreement.

The partnership normally keeps track both of a property's tax basis and its "book value." For example, if a partner contributes property with a tax basis of $7,000 and a fair market value of $10,000, the partnership's tax basis in that property under I.R.C. § 723 will be $7,000 (see Chapter 2). However, the partnership's book value (which one of the authors — uniquely — likes to call book basis) will be the full fair market value of $10,000. Book value, like capital accounts, focuses on the economic value of contributed property.If a partnership makes a distribution of property for which the fair market value differs from its book value, for capital account purposes the partnership recognizes the inherent gain or loss and allocates the gain or loss to the partners. This gain or loss may be recognized for capital account purposes only. There may not be any corresponding *taxable* gain or loss. For example, assume a partnership has two equal partners, A and B, and holds a property with a fair market value of $20,000 and a book value of $15,000 (ignore the tax basis and any possible tax consequences for now). It distributes the property to A. Recall that A's capital account will be reduced for the full fair market value of the property, that is, $20,000. To enable capital accounts to properly do their job, that is to reflect the economics of the partners' investments, the partners' capital accounts must be adjusted for the gain inherent in the distributed property. Accordingly, *for capital account purposes* (nothing need occur for tax purposes), the partnership recognizes the $5,000 of gain inherent in the property and allocates $2,500 of the gain to each partner's capital account. Thus, A's capital account will be increased by $2,500 and then decreased by $20,000.[6]

§ 5.03   SUBSTANTIAL ECONOMIC EFFECT RULES

A.   Introduction

As we mentioned above, the Regulations' substantial economic effect rules are a safe harbor. An allocation that has substantial economic effect will be allowed under I.R.C. § 704(b). There are two parts to the test. First, the allocation must have economic effect. The Regulations provide a largely mechanical test for determining whether or not an allocation has economic effect. Second, because it is possible to manipulate the economic effect test, the Regulations also provide that the economic effect of an allocation must be substantial. Generally, the economic effect of an allocation will be substantial if on an after tax, present value basis, a

---

[6] *See* Treas. Reg. § 1.704-1(b)(2)(iv)(e).

partner's economic investment in the partnership is either enhanced or diminished as a consequence of the allocation.

B. Economic Effect Rules

Partnerships have three options under the Regulations to meet the "economic effect" test, the "regular" economic effect test, the "alternate" economic effect test, and the "economic effect equivalence" test.

1. "Regular" Rules

The regular test has three parts:

1. The partnership must keep capital accounts in accordance with the rules described above.

2. When an interest of a partner is liquidated, the partner must be paid any positive balance in his capital account.

3. If a partner has a deficit balance in his capital account, he must pay the deficit to the partnership by the end of the tax year in which his partnership interest is liquidated (or, if later, 90 days after liquidation). This last rule is sometimes called a "deficit restoration obligation" or "DRO."[7]

Assume, for example, that on January 1 of Year 1, A and B invest $10,000 each in the AB partnership. The partnership purchases equipment for $20,000. The tax basis of the equipment is, of course, $20,000. In this case its book value is also $20,000.[8] Assume that depreciation deductions are $5,000 per year and the partnership has no debt.[9] Further assume the partnership breaks even on its operations except for depreciation deductions, and thus that the partnership operates at a $5,000 loss per year. The partnership agreement allocates all of the depreciation deductions to A. At the beginning of Year 1, A and B each have a capital account and a basis in their respective partnership interests of $10,000. As a result of the Year 1 allocation, A's capital account and basis will be reduced to $5,000 and B's will remain the same. If the capital accounts were not adjusted as described, the partnership would be failing to keep capital accounts in accordance with the Regulations and thus would fail the economic effect rules. The tax basis and book value of the equipment is reduced under I.R.C. § 1016 to $15,000. The Regulations generally assume that a property has a fair market value equal to its book value.[10] This can be important.

Assume at the beginning of Year 2 the equipment is sold and the partnership is liquidated. In order to comply with the economic effect rules, the partnership must

---

[7] Treas. Reg. § 1.704-1(b)(2)(ii)(a)–(c).

[8] If a book and tax basis vary, as would occur upon the contribution of property with a tax basis that is different from its fair market value, a number of important rules can apply, including those of I.R.C. § 704(c).

[9] We are making this number up and completely ignoring the actual rules of I.R.C. § 168, including the mid-year convention and I.R.C. § 179.

[10] Treas. Reg. § 1.704-1(b)(2)(iii)(c).

pay to each partner the balance in the capital accounts. We will assume that the equipment will have a fair market value equal to its book value, or $15,000. If that is indeed the case, the $15,000 proceeds from the sale would have to be distributed $5,000 to A and $10,000 to B. If, however, the partnership agreement provided that upon liquidation, all partnership funds must be distributed equally ($7,500 each), the allocation in Year 1 would not have had economic effect. This is because A would not have borne the economic burden of the depreciation allocation; in other words, the allocation would not fully have had an economic effect on her. For the allocation of the full amount of depreciation to A to have economic effect, A's capital account must be reduced by that amount and A must be paid no more than the balance in the capital account on its liquidation, or $5,000. If A is paid more than that ($7,500 in the modified example), she did not bear the full economic burden of the allocation. She only bore $2,500 of that burden and B (since he is getting $7,500 instead of the capital account balance of $10,000) actually bore the burden of the other $2,500. Consequently, if $7,500 is distributed to each partner, the Regulations would require that the allocation in Year 1 be changed and each partner would be allocated $2,500 of depreciation, giving each a capital account balance of $7,500 which would be distributed to each partner upon liquidation.[11] As you can see, the Regulations can trump the provision in the partnership agreement.

Now again assume that the partnership agreement provides that liquidation distributions will be made in accordance with capital account balances. Assume again that A and B each contribute $10,000 to the partnership and the partnership borrows $40,000 on a recourse basis with only interest due for the first five years of the note. Assume that under I.R.C. § 752 $20,000 of the liability is allocated to each partner. AB purchases equipment for $60,000. Assume the equipment generates depreciation deductions of $10,000 per year. A will therefore have a beginning tax basis in the partnership interest of $30,000 and a beginning capital account of $10,000. Now assume that in Year 1 the partnership breaks even except for depreciation deductions on the equipment and allocates the entire $10,000 of that depreciation to A. A's basis is reduced to $20,000 and her capital account is reduced to zero. Now assume that A's interest in the partnership is liquidated on January 1 of Year 2 with the partnership relieving A of any obligation on the partnership liabilities. In order to comply with the economic effect rules, on liquidation the partnership must pay the partner the amount of any positive balance in her capital account. In this example, however, the capital account is zero, and thus no payment need be made to A. Note that, generally, if the partnership is in compliance with the economic effect rules, after liquidation of a partner's interest, the partner's capital account will be zero. Can you see why? In the example, the partner's basis prior to liquidation is $20,000. No payment is made to her. What happens to A's $20,000 share of the liability? The answer is that I.R.C. § 752(d) provides that a partner's amount realized on the disposition of a partnership interest includes any liabilities of which the partner is relieved. Thus, A's amount realized includes the $20,000 of liability relief. As A's amount realized is $20,000 and A's basis in the partnership interest is $20,000, there is no tax gain or loss to A on the liquidation.

---

[11] Treas. Reg. § 1.704-1(b)(5), example 1(i).

Now let's take the example one step further. Assume that in Year 2 A remains a partner in the partnership. The partnership again breaks even on partnership operations except for depreciation, and again allocates $10,000 of depreciation to A. A's basis is reduced to $10,000 and A's capital is reduced to a negative ($10,000). If A's partnership interest is liquidated on January 1 of Year 3 with the partnership relieving A of any obligation on the partnership liabilities, A will be required to contribute $10,000 to the partnership to bring her capital account to zero.[12] Without this requirement, A in effect would be getting more out of the partnership than she put into it. She invested $10,000 initially plus was allocated a share of partnership liabilities. She received $20,000 in depreciation allocations and was relieved of any obligation on the partnership liabilities when her partnership interest was liquidated. To assure that the entire allocation of depreciation indeed has an "economic effect" on her, she needs to contribute $10,000 to the partnership. This will bring her capital account to zero. Her basis will be increased to $20,000. Under I.R.C. § 752(d), the amount realized will also be $20,000, for no gain or loss on the liquidation. If A had no obligation to restore a deficit capital account balance, the allocations to A would not have economic effect under the "regular" economic effect rules. How would the allocations in Years 1 and 2 then have to be made? The answer can actually be fairly complex, as we will shortly see, but under these facts the Year 2 depreciation allocation would have to be made to B, since it had an economic effect on him and not on A. Recall that B's capital account at the end of Year 2 was $10,000. After two years of depreciation, the equipment has a book value and presumed fair market value of $40,000. The debt is $40,000, so if the property were sold for $40,000, there are no proceeds left to pay B. If A had to contribute $10,000 to the partnership, her deficit capital account balance, that amount could have been paid to B. But if A has no such obligation, it means that B and not A bore the economic burden of the allocation of depreciation in Year 2, and under these facts the Year 2 depreciation allocation would have to be made to B.[13]

2. Alternate Economic Effect Rules

The difficulty with the regular economic effect rules is that partners are required to have an unlimited deficit restoration obligation. Especially for investors, that may not be wise. For example, assume the partners form a limited partnership and that all partners have unlimited deficit restoration obligations. An employee of the partnership, while conducting partnership business, runs over and kills a neurosurgeon with eight handicapped children. A large tort liability, in excess of insurance limits, results. The general partner is the only one liable under partnership law, and he contributes sufficient funds to the partnership to enable it to pay the liability, increasing the general partner's capital account. The payment results in a large tax loss to the partnership which (if the limited partners had deficit restoration obligations) may be primarily allocated to the limited partners. The allocation causes the limited partners to have substantial negative capital

---

[12] This requirement may exist for a general partnership under state law. For limited liability entities such as LLCs, the obligation to re-contribute a negative capital account would need to be contractually created. Contractually creating unlimited liability may be good tax planning in some circumstances, but it may not be consistent with business objectives.

[13] *See* Treas. Reg. § 1.704-1(b)(3)(iii).

accounts. Should they have to restore those deficit capital accounts (as might happen if the general partner decided to take this opportune moment to cause the partnership to liquidate), they would in effect be paying the tort liability, something that likely was not contemplated when they entered into the partnership agreement. The bottomless risk that an unlimited deficit obligation poses causes most advisors to recommend that their investor-clients not agree to such a provision.

The Regulations, recognizing this business reality, contain an alternative in Treas. Reg. § 1.704-1(b)(2)(ii)(d). Under this alternative, an allocation must meet the first two economic effect tests (keep capital accounts according to the rules and upon liquidation, pay to a partner any positive balance in his capital account). The next requirement is that the partnership agreement contain a qualified income offset provision (discussed below). If this alternative test is met, an allocation will be treated as having economic effect if allocation does not cause the partner to have a deficit capital account balance (taking certain adjustments into consideration) or increase an already-existing deficit capital account balance. As we discussed above, if a partner has a negative capital account balance, economically he has taken more out of the partnership than he has put into it, thus the requirement under the regular rules that he restore any deficit on liquidation of his interest. If the partner is not going to have a deficit restoration obligation, then it makes sense that a current allocation not be allowed to cause him to have a deficit capital account. Indeed, at one time that was almost all there was to the rule. The difficulty with keeping the rule that simple is that a capital account can become negative for reasons other than allocations. The partnership could, for example, make a distribution to a partner that would cause a deficit capital account balance. While the IRS can force a partnership to change the way it makes allocations, it cannot control to whom a partnership makes distributions.

The IRS needed a mechanism for eliminating the deficit capital account of a partner who has no obligation to restore it. That mechanism was to require the partnership to allocate income to the partner to offset any such deficit. Further, distributions are not the only events that the IRS cannot control that can cause a capital account to become negative. Certain provisions of Subchapter K can require allocations to a partner that might create a deficit capital account, so the IRS needed to account for these as well. Finally, it is obviously preferable to avoid the deficit capital account to begin with. To this end, the partnership is required to reduce the capital account for certain reasonably expected future events before determining whether or not the proposed allocation will create a deficit capital account. These adjustments are only for purposes of testing whether a current allocation will cause a partner to have a negative capital account. Once this testing has been done, the adjustments for future events are backed out of the capital accounts. They are not permanent adjustments to the capital account. For example, assume a partnership wants to allocate $8,000 of depreciation to a partner who does not have a deficit restoration obligation and falls within the alternate rules. The partner has a $15,000 balance in his capital account. Further assume that under the rules the partnership must reduce his capital account for testing purposes for a $10,000 distribution expected to be made in a future year. That would temporarily give the partner a $5,000 balance in his capital account, meaning that only $5,000 of the $8,000 of depreciation could be allocated to him. After that determination, the

$10,000 reduction for the future distribution is removed from the capital account, restoring it to $15,000, and then it is reduced for the $5,000 of depreciation that may be allocated to the partner.

The regulatory rule allowing allocations where a partner does not have an unlimited deficit restoration obligation is as follows:

(1) Requirements (1) and (2) of paragraph (b)(2)(ii)(b) of this section are satisfied (i.e., the requirement to keep capital accounts in accordance with the Regulations and pay to a partner on liquidation of his interest any positive capital account balance), and

(2) The partner to whom an allocation is made is not obligated to restore the deficit balance in his capital account to the partnership (in accordance with requirement (3) of paragraph (b)(2)(ii)(b) of this section), or is obligated to restore only a limited dollar amount of such deficit balance, and

(3) The partnership agreement contains a "qualified income offset,"

such allocation will be considered to have economic effect under this paragraph (b)(2)(ii)(d) to the extent such allocation does not cause or increase a deficit balance in such partner's capital account (in excess of any limited dollar amount of such deficit balance that such partner is obligated to restore) as of the end of the partnership taxable year to which such allocation relates.

In determining the extent to which the previous sentence is satisfied, such partner's capital account also shall be reduced for —

(4) Adjustments that, as of the end of such year, reasonably are expected to be made to such partner's capital account under paragraph (b)(2)(iv)(k) of this section for depletion allowances with respect to oil and gas properties of the partnership, and

(5) Allocations of loss and deduction that, as of the end of such year, reasonably are expected to be made to such partner pursuant to section 704(e)(2), section 706(d), and paragraph (b)(2)(ii) of 1.751-1, and

(6) Distributions that, as of the end of such year, reasonably are expected to be made to such partner to the extent they exceed offsetting increases to such partner's capital account that reasonably are expected to occur during (or prior to) the partnership taxable years in which such distributions reasonably are expected to be made.[14]

A partnership agreement contains a "qualified income offset" "if, and only if, it provides that a partner who unexpectedly receives an adjustment, allocation, or distribution described in (4), (5), or (6) above, will be allocated items of income and gain (consisting of a pro rata portion of each item of partnership income, including gross income, and gain for such year) in an amount and manner sufficient to

---

[14] Treas. Reg. § 1.704-1(b)(2)(ii)(d); I.R.C. § 704(e)(2) and I.R.C. § 706(d) are discussed below at §§ 5.08 and 5.09, respectively. I.R.C. § 751(b) (the Code section which the relevant Regulation addresses) is discussed in Chapter 7.

eliminate such deficit balance as quickly as possible."[15]

Thus, in the example discussed above, assuming there are no "reasonably expected" future events, if A has no deficit restoration obligation, the allocations to her will still be effective as long as they do not cause her to have a negative capital account.[16]

As the Regulations indicate, sometimes partners have limited deficit restoration obligations. They will agree to restore a deficit in their capital account up to a certain amount, but not beyond that. In this circumstance, the partnership will need to comply with the qualified income offset rules, and allocations can be made to a partner that create a negative capital account up to the fixed amount that partner is obligated to restore. Thus, if a partner has a $10,000 deficit restoration obligation, he could be given allocations that caused him to have up to a $10,000 negative capital account as long as the partnership otherwise complies with the qualified income offset rules.

3. Economic Effect Equivalence

The third alternative provided in the Regulations to meet the economic effect test is the "economic effect equivalence test." Allocations made to a partner that do not otherwise have economic effect under the rules discussed above can nevertheless be deemed to have economic effect under this test. The economic effect equivalence test is met provided that a liquidation of the partnership at the end of such year or at the end of each year would produce the same economic results to the partners as would occur if the formal economic effect test were met, regardless of the economic performance of the partnership.[17] For example, assume A and B contribute $75,000 and $25,000, respectively, to the AB partnership. Assume further that the partnership maintains no capital accounts and the partnership agreement provides that all income, gain, loss, deduction, and credit will be allocated 75% to G and 25% to H. G and H are ultimately liable (under a state law right of contribution) for 75% and 25%, respectively, of any debts of the partnership. Although the allocations do not satisfy the requirements of the economic effect rules discussed above, the allocations have economic effect under the economic effect equivalence test.[18]

C. Substantiality

1. General Rules

For all of their complexity, the economic effect rules are not enough to get the job done. They are, in effect, mechanical rules, and like all mechanical rules can be inappropriately manipulated. Accordingly, the Regulations provide that not only must the allocation have economic effect, that economic effect must be substantial. The Regulations provide four independent tests of whether the economic effect of

---

[15] Treas. Reg. § 1.704-1(b)(2)(ii)(d).

[16] The allocation could also not increase a negative capital account she already had for some reason.

[17] Treas. Reg. § 1.704-1(b)(2)(ii)(i).

[18] This example is based on Treas. Reg. § 1.704-1(b)(5), example 4(ii).

an allocation is substantial: the substantially affects dollar amounts test, the after-tax consequences test, the shifting tax consequences test, and the transitory allocations test.

Initially the Regulations provide that the economic effect of an allocation is substantial if there is a reasonable possibility that the allocation will substantially affect the dollar amounts to be received by the partners independent of tax consequences.[19] The Regulations then go on to provide that an allocation is *not* substantial if:

> (1) the after-tax economic consequences of at least one partner may, in present value terms, be enhanced compared to such consequences if the allocation were not contained in the partnership agreement, and

> (2) there is a strong likelihood that the after-tax economic consequences of no partner will, in present value terms, be substantially diminished compared to such consequences if the allocation were not contained in the partnership agreement.

Or, as one of the authors tells his students, the allocation is not substantial if, on a present-value, after-tax basis, someone is better off and no one is worse off than would be the case if the allocation were not present. Under these circumstances, it means that the allocation had a tax effect, but no economic effect (on a present value basis). For there to be an economic effect, if someone is better off, someone else has to be worse off. In determining whether a partner is better off or worse off, tax consequences that result from the interaction of the allocation with such partner's tax attributes that are unrelated to the partnership will be taken into account. This means that allocating substantial taxable income to a partner that has substantial net operating losses unrelated to the partnership that would otherwise expire would not necessarily increase the tax liability of the partner to whom the allocation was made, possibly rendering the economic effect of the allocation insubstantial.

In determining the effect of the after-tax consequences that result from an allocation as compared to the absence of the allocation, the comparison is made to the allocations that would be made in accordance with the partners' interests in the partnership.[20]

For example, assume taxpayers A and B are equal partners in the AB partnership. A expects to be in the 50% tax bracket over the next several years.[21] B, on the other hand, expects to be in the 15% tax bracket. Over the next several

---

[19] Treas. Reg. § 1.704-1(b)(2)(iii)(a).

[20] Treas. Reg. § 1.704-1(b)(2)(iii)(a). In addition, if the partner to whom an allocation is made is a pass-through entity or a member of a consolidated group, the partnership testing an allocation must look through the pass-through partner or member of the consolidated group to the owners of the pass-through partner and the consolidated group to test the after-tax consequences. A de minimis rule is provided that will allow partnerships to ignore partners holding less than 10% of the partnership for the purposes of testing the substantiality rules. Treas. Reg. § 1.704-1(b)(2)(iii)(d), (e). The IRS has proposed removing the de minimis rule.

[21] This example is based on Treas. Reg. § 1.704-1(b)(5), example 5 which uses this now fictitious 50% tax bracket. Even today it is possible for a taxpayer to approach this tax bracket if state and federal income taxes are combined and the taxpayer lives in a state with high income taxes.

years the partnership expects to earn approximately equal amounts of tax-exempt interest and taxable dividends. A and B agree that 80% of the tax-exempt income will be allocated to A and the balance of the tax-exempt income and all of the taxable dividends will be allocated to B. The partners can make this allocation without violating any of the economic effect rules. But according to the Regulations, the economic effect of the allocation will not be substantial, because on a present-value, after-tax basis, A's position is enhanced (compared to the situation she would be in if she had received half of each type of income) and B's position is not diminished (indeed his position is also enhanced).

Assume the partnership has $10,000 of tax-exempt income and $10,000 of taxable dividends. Under the allocation agreement, $8,000 of tax-exempt income is allocated to A. She owes no tax and so will net $8,000. The other $2,000 of tax-exempt income plus all of the taxable dividends are allocated to B. He will owe a tax of $1,500 on the taxable dividends, and so will net $10,500 ($12,000 − $1,500). Recall that you always have to contrast a given allocation with the alternative, that is, if the allocation were not present. Knowing that alternative is not always easy, but here it would be each partner receiving 50% of each type of income. If A received $5,000 of tax-exempt income and $5,000 of taxable dividends, his tax on the latter would be $2,500, for a net return of $7,500. So A's position is improved with the allocation. If B received $5,000 of tax-exempt income and $5,000 of taxable dividends, he would owe a tax on the dividends of $750, netting him $9,250. Thus, B's position is also enhanced. Since both partners improved their economic position as a result of the allocation, it means that all that was allocated were tax attributes, not economic attributes, and the economic effect of the allocation therefore cannot be substantial.[22]

2. Shifting and Transitory Allocations

The Regulations provide some additional fine-tuning to the substantiality rules for what the Regulations call "shifting" and "transitory" allocations. Generally, shifting allocations occur within a single tax year, and transitory allocations occur over a period of up to five years. In either case, the economic effect of an allocation will not be substantial if there is a strong likelihood that the capital accounts of the partners would be about the same as they would have been had the allocation not been made and the allocation results in a net reduction of the partners' tax liability.

Beginning with shifting allocations, assume our AB partnership now owns I.R.C. § 1231 property and capital assets and it expects to sell each type of property in the current tax year and incur a $50,000 I.R.C. § 1231 loss and a $50,000 capital loss. The partnership agreement complies with the economic effect rules. Partner A has ordinary income of $300,000 and no I.R.C. § 1231 gains. She can therefore fully use the I.R.C. § 1231 loss, but make only limited use of the capital loss.[23] Partner B has

---

[22] Some have criticized the regulatory example because A could have independently made the investments in tax-exempt securities and paid no tax, so why not allow it in a partnership?

[23] Under I.R.C. § 1231, if a taxpayer has losses in excess of gains from the sale of I.R.C. § 1231 property, the losses and gains are generally treated as ordinary losses. If I.R.C. § 1231 gains exceed I.R.C. § 1231 losses, the gains and losses are generally treated as long-term capital gains and losses. Under I.R.C. § 1211(b), capital losses are fully deductible from capital gains. Individuals may only deduct

$200,000 of ordinary income and $100,000 of I.R.C. § 1231 gains, meaning that he can fully use either type of loss and receive the same tax benefit. The partnership amends the partnership agreement and provides that for the current tax year only, all I.R.C. § 1231 losses will be allocated to A and all capital losses will be allocated to B. While the allocation will have economic effect, the economic effect will not be substantial because there is a strong likelihood that A and B will have the same capital account balances if the allocation were not contained in the partnership agreement (still a $50,000 loss each, consisting of equal parts of each type of loss), and the total taxes of A and B are reduced as a result of the allocation (A's taxes go down, B's taxes are unaffected).[24]

Transitory allocations operate in essentially the same way as shifting allocations, except they occur over a period of years. Under the Regulations, if there is a strong likelihood that: (1) an "original allocation" and a later "offsetting allocation" will leave the capital accounts approximately where they would have been had the allocations not occurred and (2) the tax liability of the partners will be reduced as a result of the allocations, then the economic effect of the allocations will not be substantial. The Regulations provide that if the offset happens and taxes are reduced, it will be presumed that there was a strong likelihood that this would happen unless the taxpayers can present facts and circumstances demonstrating otherwise. However, if there is a strong likelihood that the offsetting allocation will not be made "in large part" within five years of the original allocation, then the economic effect of the allocation will be substantial.[25]

For example, assume that our AB partnership has predictable, approximately equal amounts of income each year and A has an expiring net operating loss. To allow A to take greater advantage of the net operating loss, the partnership allocates all of its income in Year 1 to A. It allocates all of its income in Year 2 to B. Thereafter, it returns to allocating income equally between the partners. The partnership agreement complies with the economic effect rules. The economic effect of the allocation is insubstantial because there is a strong likelihood of the offset occurring and the partners' tax liability is less than it would have been without the allocation (the allocation lowers A's taxes and, except for time value of money considerations, is neutral as to B). Note that if the offset would occur more than five years after the original allocation (not that B would ever agree to that), the allocation would be allowed.[26]

3. Depreciation/Recapture Gain Chargebacks

It is quite common for partnership agreements to contain provisions that provide that gain on the sale of an asset equal to the prior depreciation deductions taken shall be allocated to the partners in the same manner as the depreciation itself was allocated. Such a provision is sometimes called a "gain chargeback." You might ask whether there is a transitory allocation issue, assuming the gain is recognized

---

$3,000 of capital losses in excess of capital gains from ordinary income.

[24] This example is based on Treas. Reg. § 1.704-1(b)(5), example 6.

[25] Treas. Reg. § 1.704-1(b)(2)(iii)(c).

[26] This example is based on Treas. Reg. § 1.704-1(b)(f), example 8(ii).

within five years of the depreciation deduction. The answer is no. There cannot be a strong likelihood of the offset occurring, since the Regulations assume, as we discussed early in this chapter, that a property has a fair market value equal to its book value.[27] Any gain is, given the presumption, a "surprise."

Gain chargebacks generally do not pose a problem in the case of depreciable real estate subject to straight-line depreciation as the character of the gain does not change even if it is attributable to the fact that depreciation deductions reduced the basis of the property.[28] There can be a substantiality issue when the gain is from the sale of equipment or other depreciable personal property. Generally, under I.R.C. § 1245, gain equal to the depreciation deductions taken is "recaptured" as ordinary income. Any gain beyond that amount typically falls within I.R.C. § 1231. The economic effect of the allocation of recapture income cannot be substantial as all that is being allocated is a tax attribute. In other words, whether you allocate $100 of I.R.C. § 1245 gain or $100 of I.R.C. § 1231 gain, the capital account goes up by the same amount. Thus, the only difference in the allocations is the tax effect, and as we have learned, an allocation of a tax attribute fails the substantiality test. Nonetheless, the Regulations permit allocations of depreciation recapture. Specifically, the Regulations provide that a partner's share of recapture gain is the lesser of:

- the partner's share of total gain from the disposition of the property, or

- the partner's share of depreciation with respect to the property.[29]

Thus, generally, the Regulations allocate depreciation recapture to the partners who were allocated the associated depreciation deductions.

Assume partnership AB purchases equipment for $10,000 and takes $6,000 of depreciation deductions. The depreciation deductions reduce the equipment's basis to $4,000.[30] All the depreciation deductions are properly allocated to A. Then the partnership sells the equipment for $7,000. On the sale, the partnership has $3,000 of gain, all of which would constitute I.R.C. § 1245 recapture. The partnership agreement contains a depreciation chargeback provision allocating gain equal to depreciation to the partners who were allocated the depreciation. The gain recognized by the partnership is less than the total depreciation taken. Under the partnership agreement, A is thus allocated all of the gain. This allocation is allowed by the Regulation discussed above. In this case, A's share of the gain is the "lesser figure," and all the gain allocated to A is recapture income. Now assume the partnership sold the equipment for $13,000. Under the partnership agreement, the first $6,000 of gain is allocated to A, and the remaining $3,000 of gain is allocated equally to A and B. The total gain allocated to A from the sale is thus $7,500. In this case, the lesser figure is the depreciation allocated to A or $6,000, and that amount

---

[27] Treas. Reg. § 1.704-1(b)(2)(iii)(c).

[28] Straight-line depreciation is typically the only type of depreciation allowed. I.R.C. § 168(b)(3). Even if there is character difference, there may be a capital gain tax rate differences on the gain from depreciated real property. *See* I.R.C. § 1(h)(6). *See also* I.R.C. § 1250; Treas. Reg. § 1.1250-1(f).

[29] Treas. Reg. § 1.1245-1(e)(2)(i). Special rules apply to depreciation recapture attributable to property contributed by a partner, *see* Treas. Reg. § 1.1245-1(e)(2)(ii).

[30] I.R.C. § 1016.

is recapture income. The balance of the $1,500 of gain allocated to A (and B) falls within I.R.C. § 1231.

4. Tax Credits

Allocations of tax credits and tax credit recapture are not reflected by adjustments to the partners' capital accounts. Therefore, their allocation cannot have economic effect. As we have discussed above, and will discuss below, if an allocation does not comply with the substantial economic effect safe harbor, it must be allocated in accordance with the "partners' interests in the partnership." The Regulations provide that if an allocation of a tax credit also gives rise to a valid allocation of partnership loss or deduction, then the credit may be allocated in the same proportion as the partners' respective shares of the loss or deduction.[31]

5. "q" Adjustments

For reasons too complex to address here, it is possible that the allocation system discussed above will not get the taxpayers to the "right" place, even if they try comply with it. Treas. Reg. § 1.704-1(b)(2)(iv)(q) provides that if guidance is lacking on how to properly maintain capital accounts, capital accounts should be made in a manner that: (1) maintains equality between the aggregate governing capital accounts of the partnership and the amount of partnership capital reflected on the partnership's balance sheet, as computed for book purposes, (2) is consistent with the underlying economic arrangement of the partners, and (3) is based, wherever practicable, on federal tax accounting principles. These adjustments are sometimes called "q" adjustments.

§ 5.04   PARTNER'S INTEREST IN THE PARTNERSHIP

A.   Introduction

The "partner's interest in the partnership" ("*PIP*") serves several functions in Subchapter K. It is used as the unit of property in which the partners have basis.[32] It represents the economic rights of partners the change of which signals a requirement that the distributive shares may also need to change.[33] Since 1976, PIP has also been the fallback manner in which the partners' distributive shares of partnership items have been determined.[34] Further, if property is reflected on the books of a partnership at a value that differs from the adjusted tax basis of such property, the tax items attributable to such differences must be allocated in

---

[31] Treas. Reg. § 1.704-1(b)(4)(ii). This rule does not apply to the "investment tax credit" to the extent it is still part of the Code, which (with limited exceptions) it is not.

[32] I.R.C. § 705.

[33] I.R.C. § 706(d)(1).

[34] The Regulations also cause the partners' interests in the partnership to be used as part of the test to determine whether a partnership allocation has substantial economic effect. Treas. Reg. § 1.704-1(b)(2)(iii)(a).

accordance with PIP.[35]

Many partnerships are designed to fail the substantial economic effect test for determining partnership allocations and, thus, rely upon the partners' interests in the partnership to determine the partners' distributive shares.

This chapter examines the various approaches to determining the partners' interests in the partnership.

B.   Partner's Interest in the Partnership, In General

PIP and the partner's interest in any particular item of partnership income, gain, or loss are generally determined by taking into account all facts and circumstances relating to the economic arrangement of the partners. References to a partner's interest in the partnership signify the manner in which the partners have agreed to share the economic benefit or burden (if any) corresponding to the income, gain, loss, deduction, or credit (or item thereof) that is allocated.[36]

This sharing arrangement may or may not correspond to the overall economic arrangement of the partners. For example, assume there is an unexpected downward adjustment to the capital account of a partner who does not have a deficit makeup obligation that, if allowed to stand, would cause the partner to have a negative capital account. As we discuss at § 5.03.B.2, it may be necessary to allocate a disproportionate amount of gross income of the partnership to the partner to bring that partner's capital account back up to zero. A partner who has a 50% overall interest in the partnership may, for example, have a 90% interest in a particular item of income or deduction as a consequence.

PIP may also vary in time. Where partners are allocated variable amounts of economic benefits, PIP for a particular year is determined taking into consideration the special allocations of economic consequences for such year.[37]

Any and all facts relating to the partners' underlying economic agreement will affect the determination of PIP. Treas. Reg. § 1.704-1(b)(3)(ii) provides that the following facts and circumstances are ordinarily taken into account for purposes of determining PIP or a partner's interest in any particular item of income, gain, or loss:

(i)   the partners' relative contributions to the partnership;

(ii)   the partners' interests in the economic profits and losses (if different than that in taxable income and loss);

(iii)   the interests of the partners in cash flow and other non-liquidating distributions; and

(iv)   the rights of the partners to distributions of capital upon liquidation.

---

[35] Treas. Reg. § 1.704-1(b)(4)(i). For these purposes, determining the "partners' interests in the partnership" requires applying the principles of I.R.C. § 704(c).

[36] Treas. Reg. § 1.704-1(b)(3)(i).

[37] Treas. Reg. § 1.704-1(b)(5), example 5.

Although PIP has been an important consideration in determining the partners' distributive shares for 30 years, there has been less than universal agreement as to the approach and reliability of PIP. This tension may be illustrated by contrasting the comments of the two major treatises on partnership taxation. Willis, Pennell, and Postlewaite conclude that "There is not a conflict between a partner's interest in the partnership and substantial economic effect. They both rely on the same overriding principle that the tax effects of partnership operations must conform to the economic effect of those operations."[38] On the other hand, McKee, Nelson, and Whitmire caution that "it is far from clear that identical results would in fact be achieved under both sets of rules, and drafters of partnership agreements who stray from the safe harbor do so at their peril."[39]

Part of the uncertainty relating to the determination of PIP is that the factors taken into consideration may have differing importance depending upon the facts and circumstances. A variety of approaches have developed.

C. Book-Value Liquidation as PIP

The Regulations provide a relatively clear rule for determining the partners' interests in the partnership in one circumstance. If capital accounts are maintained in accordance with the Regulations and the partnership liquidates in accordance with capital accounts, the partners' interests in the partnership with respect to an allocation that lacks economic effect will be determined by comparing the manner in which distributions (and contributions) would be made if all partnership property were sold at book value[40] and the partnership were liquidated immediately following the end of the taxable year to which the allocation related, adjusted for certain items specified in the Regulations.[41]

The book-value liquidation approach was applied by both parties in *Interhotel Company Ltd. v. Commissioner*,[42] with the twist that a minimum gain chargeback was applied to eliminate a negative capital account before the partners' interests in liquidation proceeds was determined.[43] Initially, the IRS maintained that under the facts of the case there would be no minimum gain chargeback. Prior to the hypothetical liquidation, one partner had a negative capital account, but no deficit restoration obligation, and another partner had a positive capital account. The IRS had allocated 100% of the income of the partnership to the partner with the positive capital account, arguing that only that partner would be entitled to proceeds in liquidation given that the partnership liquidated in accordance with

---

[38] WILLIS, PENNELL & POSTLEWAITE, PARTNERSHIP TAXATION ¶ 10.02[1] (WG&L 6th ed. 2007).

[39] McKEE, NELSON & WHITMIRE, FEDERAL TAXATION OF PARTNERSHIPS AND PARTNERS ¶ 10.02[3] (WG&L 3d ed. 1997).

[40] Example 15 of Treas. Reg. § 1.704-1(b)(5) applies this rule by using a hypothetical sale at adjusted tax basis rather than at book value. Although economically different results may be obtained by such an approach, the adjusted-basis liquidation approach has not been treated as a separate approach in this text.

[41] Treas. Reg. § 1.704-1(b)(3)(iii).

[42] T.C. Memo 2001-151.

[43] The court also included the amount of the minimum gain chargeback as liquidation proceeds.

capital accounts. Further, the hypothetical liquidation proceeds would have been insufficient to satisfy the positive capital account. Up to this point, the IRS had a strong argument, as allocating income to someone with a negative capital account but no obligation to restore it has no real substance, unless it would have created a positive capital account, which according to the IRS's initial calculations it would not have.[44] On the other hand, allocating income to the only partner with a positive capital account, and thus the only partner to be able to receive liquidation proceeds, has economic substance as it aligns the income with the partner who would ultimately be entitled to proceeds in liquidation. But, as the IRS conceded after the case was appealed and remanded, its allocation failed to take a minimum gain chargeback into account. After the IRS's concession that a minimum gain chargeback would be triggered in a hypothetical liquidation, the Tax Court first applied the minimum gain, which would have eliminated the negative capital account, and then permitted allocations to the partner with the erstwhile negative capital account that would have caused that partner's capital account to become positive. By giving the partner a (hypothetical) positive capital account, the allocations now had a real economic impact, as that positive balance would be distributable to that partner in liquidation. Using this approach, the court permitted 100% of the income to be allocated to the partner with the negative capital account for the relevant period.

The book-value liquidation may create unexpected results where partnership property is carried at a book value that is different from fair market value.

For example, if in Year 1 A and B each contribute $10,000 to LLC in order to acquire non-depreciable property RE, RE would initially have a basis and a book value of $20,000. In Year 2, at a time when RE is worth $30,000, LLC issues a profits interest to C in exchange for C's services that entitles C to share equally with each of A and B after $30,000 is paid to A and B collectively. LLC books up RE to $30,000, allocating the increase equally between A and B. If RE later appreciates in value to $39,000, the economic agreement among the parties would pay A and B $30,000 with the remaining $9,000 split three ways. However, a hypothetical liquidation after a sale at book value would suggest that C would receive nothing, because the book value of RE would still be $30,000 at the time of the sale absent a subsequent book-up event.[45]

Somewhat oddly, the Regulations provide that the book-value liquidation approach does not apply, however, if the resulting allocations would not be substantial.[46] This creates a bit of a quandary if PIP is included as part of the test for whether or not an allocation is in fact substantial. If PIP were determined

---

[44] It could also be permitted to have substantial economic effect under the alternative test for economic effect of Treas. Reg. § 1.704-1(b)(2)(ii)(d), but the partnership agreement did not comply with those rules.

[45] Although a liquidation of the partnership is itself a book-up event (Treas. Reg. § 1.704-1(b)(2)(iv)(f)(5)(ii)), Treas. Reg. § 1.704-1(b)(2)(iii)(c) provides that for the purposes of Treas. Reg. § 1.704-1(b)(3)(iii) (the PIP as book-value liquidation provision) book value is presumed to be fair market value.

[46] Treas. Reg. § 1.704-1(b)(3)(iii). The facts considered in *Interhotel Company Ltd.* included a 99-1/0-100 flip. The court concluded that the book-value liquidation resulted in substantial allocations without specifically addressing whether the allocations were transitory.

under the book-value liquidation approach and the allocations were tested against PIP for the purposes of the substantiality test, no partners' after-tax economic tax consequences would be enhanced compared to PIP, and so the allocation would always pass the after-tax benefit test, the shifting-tax consequences test, and the transitory benefit test. The reasoning, in other words, would be circular.

D.   Other Liquidation Models

Although the Regulations apply a book-value liquidation approach in specified circumstances, the courts have taken other approaches to establishing PIP based upon a liquidation model.

In *Estate of Tobias v. Commissioner*,[47] the Tax Court rejected the taxpayer's attempt to apply an overall percentage interest approach to determining PIP, finding instead that in a liquidation the taxpayer would be entitled under a state court ruling to a return of the taxpayer's disproportionately large capital contribution before the other partner was entitled to share in distributions. The court considered all four factors listed in the Regulations, but appeared to put emphasis on the rights in liquidation. Because the value of the assets of the partnership was less than the taxpayer's capital contributions, the state court had ordered all of the proceeds in liquidation to be distributed to the taxpayer. The Tax Court, relying in part upon the state court's determination of the rights of the parties in liquidation, found that the taxpayer's PIP in regard to partnership income was 100% for the years in question.

Applying the state law liquidation rights approach to the example in § 5.04.C (with the exception that liquidation is not in accordance with capital accounts), A and B would have a right to $18,000 each ($10,000 initial capital and, under the parties agreement, $5,000 from the Year 2 book-up, and $3,000 from the subsequent appreciation), and C would have a right to $3,000. The gain recognized by the partnership would be $19,000 ($39,000 less the basis of $20,000), but $10,000 should be allocated equally to A and B under the principles of I.R.C. § 704(c) as well as the parties' agreement.[48]

E.   Based on Capital Contributions

A somewhat different approach was taken in *PNRC Limited Partnership v. Commissioner*,[49] in which the Tax Court found that the PIP was best represented by the partners' relative capital contributions to the partnership. In the case in question, the general partner had initially contributed 71.4% of the capital to the partnership and the limited partner 28.6%. Two years later, the limited partner made an additional capital contribution to the partnership, reducing the general partner's percentage of total capital contributed to 38.6% and raising the limited partner's percentage to 61.4% (unadjusted for losses). Losses, however, were allocated 1% to the general partner and 99% to the limited partner. The

---

[47]   T.C. Memo 2001-37.

[48]   *See* Treas. Reg. § 1.704-3(a)(6)(i) and § 5.06.

[49]   T.C. Memo 1993-335.

partnership agreement allocated profits 60% to the general partner and 40% to the limited partner. The partnership only incurred losses for the years under review. Distributions in liquidation were to be made in accordance with the partners' profit percentages as opposed to capital account balances. The allocations thus lacked substantial economic effect. Ignoring the parties relative rights to profits and liquidation proceeds, the court concluded that the unadjusted capital contributions were most indicative of the partners' interests in the partnership, and required losses to be allocated in accordance with those varying contributions.

Applying this approach to the example above (with the exception that liquidation is not in accordance with capital accounts), since A and B made the only capital contributions to LLC, the result would appear to be that A and B would each have a 50% PIP.

F.   Avoiding Negative Capital Accounts as PIP

As discussed in § 5.03, if a partner does not have a deficit restoration obligation, but receives a downward adjustment to the capital account that gives the partner a negative capital account, it may be necessary to allocate a disproportionate amount of gross income of the partnership to such partner for such year so as to bring that partner's capital account back up to zero. The Regulations recognize that such an allocation may be consistent with PIP.[50] In *Vecchio v. Commissioner*,[51] the principle stated by the Regulations in a parenthetical was the focus of the court's analysis.

In *Vecchio*, the court considered a situation in which gain on the sale of property was disproportionately allocated to a partner with a negative capital account in an amount sufficient to restore the negative capital account to zero. The partnership agreement failed to comply with the economic effect rules, including not requiring that liquidation distributions be made in accordance with capital account balances, and not requiring that partners restore deficit capital account balances. The court thus concluded that the allocation lacked substantial economic effect. The court then considered whether the allocation was consistent with PIP.

The court noted that the Regulations anticipate that, in situations where prior deductions have created a negative capital account, gain may be allocated in a manner that produces the same results as an allocation that has substantial economic effect. The court viewed the fundamental principle underlying the requirement that an allocation have economic effect as being that the allocation must be consistent with the underlying economic arrangement of the partners.

Applying the rule that the partner to whom an allocation is made must receive the related economic benefit or bear the related economic burden,[52] the court reasoned that the partner receiving the disproportionate allocation on the sale should bear the economic "burden" of gain[53] necessary to bring its capital account

---

[50] Treas. Reg. § 1.704-1(b)(3)(i).

[51] 103 T.C. 170 (1994).

[52] Treas. Reg. § 1.704-1(b)(2)(ii)(a).

[53] Arguably, the court is merging economic and tax consequences here.

to zero to avoid the shifting of the economic burden of the prior losses that had been deducted by the partner to the other partners. Thus, the allocation to the partner of an amount sufficient to offset the prior deficit capital account was consistent with the partners' interests in the partnership.

In addition to considering the impact on the historic negative capital account on PIP, the court also considered the partners' rights to the proceeds on the sale of the property. The partner that received the disproportionate allocation and had the negative capital account was entitled to the first $766,100 of proceeds from the sale of the partnership real property. The court concluded that in order for the partners' capital accounts to reflect that right, gain in the year of the sale should be allocated first to the partner with the negative capital account in an amount necessary to bring the capital account up to zero and then in an amount equal to the partner's economic right to a preferential distribution on the sale.

Thus, the court applied a similar analysis to the prospective allocation of gain as the court had applied to the historic allocation of losses. To be consistent with PIP, the allocation should be in an amount that would bring the partner's capital account to zero after the contemplated transactions. In the case of a negative capital account, that meant bringing the capital account up to zero to offset historic losses. In the case of a right to a distribution of proceeds on sale, it meant bringing the capital account up to a point where the distribution of cash would not again drive the capital account negative.

Applying this approach to the example above (with the exception that liquidation is not in accordance with capital accounts), because the economic agreement was for $3,000 to be distributed to C, but C had a $0 capital account, the only way for C to not end up with a negative capital account would be for C to be allocated $3,000.

G. Overall Percentage

Other cases have looked to a partner's overall percentage interest in a partnership after finding that an allocation did not have substantial economic effect.

For example, in *Miller v. Commissioner*,[54] the partnership failed to adjust the capital accounts for special allocations to a partner or to liquidate in accordance with capital account balances. Instead, income and liquidation distributions were divided equally among the partners based on the partners' percentages of ownership. An effort to allocate all of the depreciation and all the tax items relating to one investment of the partnership to one partner for five years thus failed. The court reallocated the items in accordance with the partners' percentages of ownership interest.

Similarly, in *Hogan v. Commissioner*,[55] the partnership agreement failed to provide that the partnership would liquidate in accordance with capital account balances and that partners had an obligation to restore negative capital account balances. The Tax Court looked to the partners' understanding that they were, in

---

[54] T.C. Memo 1984-336.

[55] T.C. Memo 1990-295.

general, each one-third partners to justify reallocating losses that had been disproportionately deducted by one of the partners proportionately among all the partners. In two of the three years in question, the taxpayer had made disproportionately large contributions to the partnership to fund expenses of the partnership. Even taking these contributions into consideration, however, the taxpayer had not contributed two-thirds (the percentage of the losses deducted by the taxpayer) of the capital to the partnership. The court, noting testimony of the partners that they had come to no understanding as to how assets of the partnership would be distributed upon liquidation, concluded that losses of the partnership should be divided consistently with the partner's overall percentages.[56]

In a somewhat more sympathetic case, a taxpayer who had inherited a 25% interest in a furniture store claimed that she was a 25% partner in a partnership running the furniture store, but should not be taxable on the income from the furniture because she had not received any distributions from the furniture store and had apparently failed in an attempt to force the partnership into dissolution.[57] The court ignored the taxpayer's arguments that her PIP as to the operating income of the furniture store could not be 25% because she had not received distributions (and apparently could not force distributions) and relied upon her overall percentage interest.

Example 4(i) of Treas. Reg. § 1.704-1(b)(5) is consistent with the cases just discussed. The example notes that contributions were made in a 75/25 ratio and the partnership agreement indicated that all economic profits and losses of the partnership are to be shared in a 75/25 ratio. The example then reallocates partnership income, gain, loss, and deduction in the 75/25 split. Curiously, the example never specifically concludes that PIP is 75/25.

Although not absolutely clear from the cases, if the overall percentage is viewed as being the same as the residual percentage in a partnership with tiered allocations, the application of the approach to the example discussed above again results in an allocation that is consistent with the economic arrangement.

A, B, and C's residual sharing arrangement is that the gain over $30,000 would be split one-third, one-third, one-third. Thus, C's PIP as to $9,000 of gain (after the amount allocated under the principles of I.R.C. § 704(c) is excluded) should be one-third.

H. Interest in Net Profits

Although possibly more appropriately classified with the overall percentage cases, in *Mammoth Lakes Project v. Commissioner*,[58] the court allocated losses in a partnership consistently with the partners' percentage rights to the profits of the partnership. The taxpayer in the case had deducted 100% of the losses generated

---

[56] Interestingly, under the facts being considered the capital accounts of the partners were not in proportion to their overall percentages, so the decision of the court had the effect of allocating more losses to the taxpayer than his proportionate capital account would have justified.

[57] Brooks v. Commissioner, T.C. Memo 1995-400.

[58] T.C. Memo 1991-4.

by the partnership. The partnership agreement itself was silent on how losses should be allocated, but allocated 10% of net profits to the taxpayer. The only evidence offered pertaining to the allocation of losses by the taxpayer was a letter by a general partner, dated after the petition in the case was filed, which stated that it was the general partner's "understanding" that 100% of the losses were to be allocated to the taxpayer. The court did not find the letter persuasive because it was not contemporaneous with the agreement, and it was provided only in relation to an audit of petitioner's tax liability. As there was no evidence presented in the case as to any of the other factors that are normally considered in determining PIP, the court felt compelled to allocate losses the same as profits.

I.   Percentage of Assets and Percentage of Liabilities

Also similar to the overall percentage cases, is *Shumaker v. Commissioner*,[59] a case in which there was no partnership agreement and the taxpayers denied being partners. The court looked to the partners' ownership interests in the assets of the business and the manner in which they had agreed to share the liabilities of the business. Under the particular facts being considered, both the assets and the liabilities of the business were shared 50-50. This being the case, the court determined that the partners' interests in the partnership were 50-50.

J.   Income

As mentioned above, a partner's interest in the partnership may differ when applied to different partnership tax items. Except with respect to partnership items that cannot have economic effect (such as nonrecourse deductions of the partnership), the partners' interests in a given partnership item may or may not correspond to the overall economic arrangement of the partners. Thus, a partner who has a 50% overall interest in the partnership may have a 90% interest in a particular item of income or deduction.[60]

In example 5 of Treas. Reg. § 1.704-1(b)(5), an allocation of exempt interest in one manner, and taxable income in another manner, is first determined to lack substantial economic effect and then reallocated according to the partners' interests in the partnership. The example concludes:

> Since under the partnership agreement I will receive 36% (360/1,000) and J will receive 64% (640/1,000) of the partnership's total investment income in such year, under paragraph (b)(3) of this section the partnership's tax-exempt interest and taxable interest and dividends each will be reallocated 36 percent to I and 64 percent to J.

In the famous *TIFD III-E Inc. v. United States*[61] case (often called the "Castle Harbour case"), the District Court applied this rule to determine the partner's interest in the partnership's operating income separately from the partner's overall

---

[59]   T.C. Memo 1985-582.

[60]   Treas. Reg. § 1.704-1(b)(3)(i).

[61]   342 F. Supp. 2d 94 (Conn. Dist. Ct. 2004), *rev'd on other grounds*, 459 F.3d 220 (2d Cir. 2006), *on remand*, 660 F. Supp. 2d 367 (D.C. Conn. 2009), *rev'd*, 666 F.3d 836 (2d Cir. 2012).

interest in the partnership and the partner's ownership interest in the partnership. The court noted that example 5(ii) in Treas. Reg. § 1.704-1(b)(5) looks to the partnership agreement to determine the partners' interests in the partnership's total investment income. The court drew from this that the partner's interest in the partnership is determined exclusively by reference to the partnership agreement.[62] The court further reasoned:

> This example makes clear that (a) when the partnership agreement contains explicit allocation provisions, partner's interest in the partnership is determined by reference to the agreement, not by reference to ownership interest, and (b) this determination is not circular — it can lead to different allocations, particularly in cases where items are allocated based on their taxable characteristics.[63]

The court concluded that, under the particular facts it was considering, the partnership agreement's unambiguous assignment of 98% of the operating income to foreign banks (who were not subject to U.S. taxation on that income), with no further differentiation based on taxable characteristics (unlike example 5 of Treas. Reg. § 1.704-1(b)(5)), required that such partner's interest in operating income be determined to be 98%.

Applying this approach to the example with A, B, and C as partners of the LLC above (with the exception that liquidation is not in accordance with capital accounts), A, B, and C's profit-sharing arrangement is that the gain over $30,000 would be split one-third, one-third, one-third. Thus, C's PIP as to $9,000 of gain (after the amount allocated under the principles of I.R.C. § 704(c) is excluded) should be one-third.

K. Capital Account Impact

In Treas. Reg. § 1.704-1(b)(5), examples 6 and 7, the allocations had economic effect, but the economic effect was not considered to be substantial. The equal partners were allocated the same nominal amounts for the same capital account adjustment. But the amounts allocated had different tax consequences. Income or loss was allocated in a manner that optimized the tax benefits. The economic effects of the allocations were not substantial because there was a strong likelihood that the capital accounts of the partners would be the same as they would have been in the absence of the allocation. Thus, only tax consequences were being allocated. The examples first conclude that if the amounts specially allocated are offsetting, they would be allocated equally between the partners. The examples then continue and state that if the amounts specially allocated are not offsetting entirely, the amounts should be reallocated between the partners in proportion to the net decreases or increases in the partners' capital accounts that would occur if the allocations in the partnership agreement were recognized.

Because the particular partnerships being considered liquidated in accordance with the partners' positive capital accounts, these examples could be interpreted to

---

[62] *Id.* at 120.

[63] *Id.*

support an incremental liquidation rights approach to determining PIP. In other words, as to a particular item, PIP may be represented by the extent to which the item changes the partners' relative rights in liquidation.

Applying this approach to the example with A, B, and C as partners of the LLC above, the capital account impact of A, B, and C's profit-sharing arrangement is that the gain over $30,000 would be split one-third, one-third, one-third. Thus, C's PIP as to $9,000 of gain (after the amount allocated under the principles of I.R.C. § 704(c) is excluded) should be one-third.

L. Common Allocation Structures

1. Introduction

In an effort both to test and expand your understanding, we now provide examples of several common approaches to allocations and discuss issues related to the documentation and the qualification of the allocation. The following materials are more advanced and are best read after you have developed a thorough understanding of the substantial economic effect rules and PIP. As you will see, in many of the allocation structures discussed below, the partnership is choosing to allocate based on PIP rather than based on the substantial economic effect rules. In larger, more complex deals, using PIP rather than the substantial economic effect rules is likely the norm.

2. Percentage Interests

In the Percentage Interest Approach, the partnership agreement allocates items based upon percentages, often related to the relative initial capital contributions of the partners. If the partnership has been unitized (that is, divided into units representing fractional interests in the partnership), the percentage interests may be based upon the units held by a particular member as compared to the total number of units outstanding.

If the partnership has only a single class of interests, the allocation provisions of the agreement may be very simple. If the partnership has multiple classes, the allocation provisions may need to allocate first between classes and then among the members of a particular class.

a. Hypothetical Language

Section 1. All Net Profits and Net Losses of the Company in respect of a Fiscal Year shall be allocated to the Members in accordance with their Percentage Interests.

Section 2. Notwithstanding Section 1 hereof, Net Losses allocated pursuant to Section 1 to any Member for any Fiscal Year shall not exceed the maximum amount of Net Losses that may be allocated to such Member without causing such Member to have an Adjusted Capital Account Deficit at the end of such Fiscal Year. Any Net Losses in excess of the limitation in this Section 2 shall be specially allocated solely to the other Members to the maximum extent permitted by this Section 2. Thereafter, notwithstanding Section 1 hereof, subsequent Net Profits or items of income or gain shall be allocated to reverse any Net Losses specially allocated pursuant to the preceding sentence.

b. Discussion

The hypothetical language provided above illustrates one common approach to partnership allocations, although there are a great number of variations within the general approach.

One of the first things that should be noticed in Section 1 is that Net Profits and Net Losses appear to be defined terms. In modern practice, it is likely that Net Profits and Net Losses are defined in terms of book income and loss (income and loss calculated for the purposes of the capital account maintenance rules). Such an approach would be consistent with the current Regulation's general method of supporting substantial economic effect under I.R.C. § 704(b).

It is not uncommon to see versions of Section 1 in which Net Profits and Net Losses are not defined terms. Such approaches often would not include a Section 2. If the agreement includes a provision requiring capital accounts to be maintained according to the Regulations and a qualified income offset provision, it may still be that it is intended that Net Profits and Net Losses are intended to be book income and losses. If capital accounts are not maintained in accordance with the Regulations, it is probably best to interpret such provisions as an expression of what is intended to be the partners' interests in the partnership rather than a special allocation under I.R.C. § 704(b).

Older partnerships may define Net Profits and Net Losses in a manner that combines book income and loss and taxable income and loss within the definition. This approach is currently controversial, because allocations of taxable income and losses cannot have substantial economic effect. However, the approach may have the practical result that book income and loss is allocated in accordance with the provision and taxable income and loss would follow book income and loss. It is more common under current practice to have a separate provision expressing the intent of the partnership that taxable income and income would be allocated consistently with book income or losses, but it is not clear that a separate provision is required by the Regulations.

Partnership agreements drafted before 1986 may define Net Profits and Net Losses in terms of taxable income and loss. As mentioned above, under the current Regulations, allocations of taxable income and loss cannot have substantial economic effect. If the allocations reflected in the provision are not consistent with the partners' interests in the partnership, the provision may be ineffective.

Strictly speaking, Section 2 in the example above is not required by the Regulations, but you may remember that a qualified income offset provision only causes an allocation to have economic effect to the extent such allocation does not cause or increase a deficit balance in such partner's capital account (in excess of any limited dollar amount of such deficit balance that such partner is obligated to restore) as of the end of the partnership taxable year to which such allocation relates. Thus, if an allocation caused or increased a deficit balance, the allocation would have to be made in accordance with the partners' interests in the partnership. Thus, in a partnership in which it is important that all allocations have substantial economic effect, Section 2 adds support if the partners have capital accounts that are not in proportion to their Percentage Interests.

One shortcoming of the specific language used in the example is that it does not deal with the situation in which all partners have negative capital accounts. Allocations of losses in such a situation cannot have substantial economic effect and must be allocated in accordance with the partners' interests in the partnership, but it may be prudent to have some agreement in advance as to what the parties understanding of the partners' interests in the partnership may be.

3. Targeted Capital Account Approach

a.   Hypothetical Language

Section 1. Allocation of Net Profits and Net Loss. (a) After giving effect to the special allocations provided in Section 3, Net Profits or Net Losses for any Fiscal Year or other relevant period other than the Winding Up Year shall be allocated among the Partners so as to reduce, proportionately, the differences between their respective Targeted Capital Accounts and their respective Partially Adjusted Capital Accounts for such Fiscal Year or other period.

b.   Discussion

As with the Percentage Interest allocation provision, a Targeted Capital Account allocation provision is likely to rely upon the defined terms Net Profits and Net Losses. This means that the definitions of Net Profits and Net Losses in any agreement using such an approach should be carefully reviewed. Because the Targeted Capital Account Approach is less likely to be found in older partnership agreements, it is more likely that Net Profits and Net Losses will be based upon book income and loss. However, some agreements using this approach do not maintain capital accounts pursuant to the Regulations, in which case a variety of subtle, but sometimes significant modifications of the concepts may be found.

The focus of the Targeted Capital Account Approach is to drive the capital accounts so that they represent the economic relationship of the parties. When the partnership liquidates in accordance with capital accounts (one of the general requirements for economic effect), driving the capital accounts so that a liquidation does not result in an economic windfall to one of the parties may be consistent with the economic agreement of the parties.

If the intent is to cause the capital accounts to represent the agreed economic relationship of the parties, how "Targeted Capital Account" is defined may become critical. One might think that the Targeted Capital Account would be based upon the capital accounts that are maintained to support the economic effect of allocations, but they may not be. Targeted Capital Accounts may be formulaic: they may be based upon calculations including the unreturned capital of the investors and an agreed annual return to the investors (the "return on and return of capital approach"). Targeted Capital Accounts may also be mechanical: They may be based upon amounts that would be recorded in the capital accounts if the property of the partnership were sold and the partnership liquidated.

Two significant variations of this last approach exist which are worthy of specific mention: The sale at book value approach and the sale at fair market value approach. The sale at book value approach has the advantage of using a number that should already be available. The sale at book value approach does not take into consideration economic appreciation or depreciation that may have occurred since the last time the capital accounts were adjusted. Thus, the sale at book value approach is only a partial step toward driving the capital accounts to represent the economic relationship of the parties.

The sale at fair market value approach has the advantage that it may more closely reflect the economic relationship of the parties, but it has the disadvantage that the number that is used (fair market value) may not be readily available if the property of the partnership is not publicly traded. Many partnerships allow the general partner or the manager to assign a value to the partnership property for the purposes of driving the Targeted Capital Account allocations.

One other issue, that may either be viewed as an advantage or disadvantage, of the Targeted Capital Account Approach is that when a service partner receives a profits interest[64] in exchange for services, there is not normally any income recognition by the service partner on the issuance of the interest. In such a situation, the capital account of the service partner would normally start at zero. If the intent is that the service partner receives 20% of the value of the future appreciation of the property, the Targeted Capital Account Approach may (depending upon how it is drafted) force allocations of other income to the service partner to build the service partner's capital account up to the 20% level. Thus, the service partner may receive income before being entitled to receiving cash.[65]

4. Reverse Distribution Approach

a. Hypothetical Language

(a) *Allocation of Net Losses.* Net Losses shall be allocated among the Partners as follows:

    (i) First, to each Partner in proportion to the amounts by which cumulative Net Profits allocated to such Partner since the inception

---

[64] *See* discussion in Chapter 8. For the purposes of Rev. Proc. 93-27, 1993-2 C.B. 343, a profits interest is defined as an interest that would not give the holder a share of the proceeds if the partnership's assets were sold at fair market value and then the proceeds were distributed in a complete liquidation of the partnership at the time of the receipt of the partnership interest.

[65] Recently, some tax practitioners have raised the question of whether, if all the income is being forced to the service partner to build the service partner's capital account, does that cause the preferred return distributions to the investors to be guaranteed payments rather than partners' distributive shares? A balanced approach may be to allocate first consistently with the preferred return and then to build the service partner's capital account.

of the Partnership exceed cumulative Net Losses allocated to such Partner since the inception of the Partnership, until cumulative Net Losses allocated to such Partner since the inception of the Partnership are equal to cumulative Net Profits allocated to such Partner since the inception of the Partnership.

(ii)   Second, to the Class B Preferred Limited Partners in proportion to their then-current positive Capital Account balances, until such Capital Account balances are reduced to zero.

(iii)   Third, to the Class A Preferred Limited Partner until its Capital Account balance is reduced to zero.

(iv)   Fourth, among the Partners in proportion to the manner in which such Partners would receive cash from the Partnership if cash on hand at the end of the year were distributed to the Partners as provided in Section ___, and all assets on hand at the end of such year were sold for cash at their [Carrying] [Fair Market] Values and such cash were distributed to the Partners under Section ___.

(b)   *Allocation of Net Profits.* Net Profits shall be allocated among the Partners as follows:

(i)   First, to each Partner in proportion to the amounts by which cumulative Net Losses allocated to such Partner since the inception of the Partnership exceed cumulative Net Profits allocated to such Partner since the inception of the Partnership, until cumulative Net Profits allocated to such Partner since the inception of the Partnership is equal to cumulative Net Losses allocated to such Partner since the inception of the Partnership.

(ii)   Second, Net Profits shall be allocated pro rata (based upon the unreturned Capital Contributions of the Partners) among the Partners with unreturned Capital Contributions in such manner as to increase the Capital Account of such Partners until the Capital Accounts of such Partners equal the amount of unreturned Capital Contributions.

(iii)   Third, Net Profits shall be allocated among the Partners in such manner as shall cause the Capital Accounts of such Partners to equal, as nearly as possible, the amount such Partners would receive if cash on hand at the end of the year were distributed to the Partners as provided in Section ___, and all assets on hand at the end of such year were sold for cash at their [Carrying] Values and such cash were distributed to the Partners under Section ___.

b.   Discussion

The reverse distribution approach was often used in the period (before the passive loss rules were introduced) in which partnerships were used to generate tax losses for individual investors. It has been called by several other names, but the idea is that while profits are allocated consistently with cash flow (after giving effect to any preferences), losses are allocated in the order in which the partners are likely to absorb economic losses.

The second and third tiers of the allocation of losses in the example given probably represent a preference of one class over the other that should also be reflected in their economic rights. If the partnership liquidates in accordance with capital accounts, the allocation of losses first to the Class B partners would reduce the amount that Class B partners may receive on final liquidation (if the allocation of loss is not offset by an allocation of profits in tier one or two of the profit allocation).

Notice that the fourth tier of loss allocation only applies if the capital accounts of both Class A and Class B have been zeroed out. You may recall that a qualified income offset will only allow an allocation to have economic effect if the allocation does not cause the capital account to go negative (or become more negative) after giving effect to the partner's deficit restoration obligations (or deemed obligations under the Regulations). Thus, if the fourth tier only applies after the capital accounts have been zeroed out, the allocations under the fourth tier cannot have economic effect and must be made in accordance with the partners' interests in the partnership. As discussed above, there are a number of approaches to determining the partners' interests in the partnership. However, if the partnership maintains capital accounts consistently with the Regulations and liquidates in accordance with capital accounts, the Regulations require that the partners' interests in the partnership be determined under a deemed sale at book value followed by a liquidation.

The fourth tier of the allocation of losses suggests that the partnership is maintaining capital accounts in accordance with the Regulations and liquidating in accordance with capital accounts because it reflects the requirement for determining the partners' interests in the partnership in such a situation. The fourth tier probably represents the parties' intent to comply with the Regulation's safe harbor for allocations pursuant to partners' interests in the partnership when the partnership maintains capital accounts consistently with the Regulations and liquidates in accordance with capital accounts.

You will notice that the third tier of profit allocation is actually an incorporation of the Targeted Capital Account Approach. After the first two tiers, which are corrective in nature, it is necessary to make some allocation of profits. This can actually be done by incorporating any of the other three methods at this tier. In other words, the third tier may refer to percentage interest or cash flow instead of the deemed liquidation that is used in the sample language.

5. Cash Flow Approach

a. Hypothetical Language

Allocations of Profits and Losses from Operations. Subject to, and interpreted consistently with the Regulations, except as otherwise provided in this Section, all items of income, gain, profits, losses, credits and deductions of the Company with respect to any Fiscal Year shall be allocated to the

Members in proportion to the Cash Flow distributed to them, or if no Cash Flow is distributed in such Fiscal Year, in proportion to their Residual Percentage Interests.

b.   Discussion

Although at one time this was perhaps the most common approach to allocations, at the present time the approach is quite controversial in some circles under certain factual situations.

If all the sharing ratios of the partnership are consistent, this approach should work fine. However, if one of the partners has a preference to a return of capital or other cash flow preference, the approach has the effect of rebuilding the preference return partner's capital account back up for the cash flow distributed. If the partnership agreement provides for liquidation in accordance with capital accounts, building the preference return partner's capital back up could result in that partner receiving more than the partner was intended to receive on final dissolution.

For example, suppose Kora, Mellsande, and Allesandro form an LLC with Kora putting in cash of $100 and Mellsande and Allesandro receiving a profits interest for services. The economic deal is that Kora will receive a 7% annual return on her capital contribution, Kora will receive any excess cash flow first to the extent of her capital contribution and then the parties share equally. If in Year 1 the LLC has $10 of cash receipts and tax and book income, Kora is entitled to receive the entire $10 in cash. Under the sample language, the entire $10 of book income is allocated to Kora's capital account. Thus, her capital account goes down by the $10 distribution and back up by the $10 allocation. This sounds fine, except that Kora has already received $3 of her capital back. By building her capital account back up to the original $100, she will be entitled on liquidation to an additional $3 that the parties did not contemplate.

On the other side of the same coin, if one of the partners has received a profits interest, but is intended to have a back-end interest of a significant (e.g., one-third) percentage, the failure to build up the profits interest partner's capital account may, in some situations, shortchange the partner on liquidation, if liquidation is in accordance with capital accounts.

The results discussed above in regard to the Cash Flow Approach illustrate an irony of the I.R.C. § 704(b) Regulations. Although the capital accounts were originally designed to *reflect* the economic arrangement of the parties, when a partnership liquidates in accordance with capital accounts, the capital accounts may also *affect* the economic arrangement of the parties.

Allocating income according to the Cash Flow Approach in years in which the partnership does not have cash flow can have unexpected results depending upon the wording of the provision. If the provision is drafted to only refer to the percentage in respect of which cash flow is distributed in that year, income for years in which there is no cash flow has not been allocated in the partnership agreement and must be allocated in accordance with the partners' interests in the partnership. The suggested language falls back on the Percentage Interest

Approach when no cash flow is distributed. Alternatively, the Cash Flow Approach could fall back on the Targeted Capital Account Approach in years in which no cash is distributed.

§ 5.05   BOOK-TAX DISPARITIES — I.R.C. § 704(c) ALLOCATIONS

A.   Introduction

Under I.R.C. § 721, no gain or loss is recognized when a partner contributes property to the partnership. The partnership takes a carryover basis in the property under I.R.C. § 723 and the contributing partner takes a substituted basis in the property under I.R.C. § 722. Yet when the partners put their deal together, the primary focus is on the economics, not the tax basis. What is of primary importance is the fair market value of contributed property. This disjuncture between tax basis and economic value gave rise to a host of complex rules.

Example 1

A contributes Land #1 to the AB partnership in which A and B have equal interests. The land has a tax basis of $7,000 and a fair market value of $10,000. The partnership takes a tax basis in the property of $7,000, A's tax basis in her partnership interest is increased by that amount, and no gain or loss typically is recognized to A or the partnership under I.R.C. § 721(a). Note that there is $3,000 of tax gain inherent in the property. If the partnership now sells the property for $10,000, to whom should that gain be taxed? The gain arose on A's "watch," so it would make sense for the gain to be taxed to A and, indeed, I.R.C. § 704(c) so provides. But for I.R.C. § 704(c), on the sale of the property, half of the tax gain would be taxed to B instead of A. Permitting that violates assignment of income principles, though it should be noted that the shift need not be permanent.

Assume B contributed $10,000 to the partnership and thus has a $10,000 basis in his partnership interest. If $1,500 of the tax gain is taxed to B, B's tax basis increases to $11,500. If the fair market value of B's interest does not change, upon the sale or liquidation of B's interest, B would recognize a $1,500 tax loss offsetting the prior gain. But there could be a significant time lag between the gain and the loss, and there could be a character difference as well. If the land was a lot sold by the partnership in the ordinary course of its trade or business, the gain would be ordinary income, whereas B's loss would be a capital loss. I.R.C. § 704(c) also avoids these distortions.

In the absence of I.R.C. § 704(c), could the partnership have made a special allocation of the tax gain in A's land to B under section 704(b)? The answer is no. Recall that the land would be recorded on the books of the partnership at its fair market value of $10,000 (i.e., it has a book value of $10,000). If it were sold for $10,000, there would have been no book gain or loss to allocate, and the I.R.C. § 704(b) special allocation rules apply to *book* gains and losses, not to tax gains and losses. Tax gains and losses do not affect the capital accounts and therefore their allocation cannot have substantial economic effect. How is the tax gain handled?

I.R.C. § 704(c)(1)(A) provides that income, gain, loss, and deduction with respect to property contributed to the partnership by a partner is shared among the partners so as to take account of the variation between the basis of the property and its fair market value at the time of contribution. In the fact pattern we have been discussing, that means that $3,000 of the gain is taxed to A.

What if the property were sold for $12,000? The tax gain would be $12,000 − $7,000 = $5,000. The book gain would be $12,000 − $10,000 = $2,000. The $2,000 of book gain would be allocated equally to A and B or $1,000 each. Under I.R.C. § 704(c), the tax gain would be allocated $3,000 + $1,000 = $4,000 to A and $1,000 to B. Note that in this example, the tax gain equal to the book gain ($1,000 per partner) is allocated in the same manner as the book gain, and the tax gain in excess of the book gain ($3,000) is allocated to the contributing partner.[66] That makes sense. Generally, a partner should receive tax gain equal to his share of book gain. If tax gain exceeds the book gain, it means that the property had gain inherent in it on contribution to the partnership. That gain (here the $3,000) should be taxed to the contributing partner, and I.R.C. § 704(c) provides that it is.

Under the Regulations, I.R.C. § 704(c) property is contributed property that at the time of contribution has a book value that differs from its tax basis.[67] Note that if partners have contributed such property to the partnership, the partnership will have to keep two sets of books. One set will contain the book values of the partnership properties and the other will contain the tax values. The book items will be allocated based on the I.R.C. § 704(b) Regulations, commonly according to the substantial economic effect rules. These allocations generally reflect the economic sharing agreement of the parties. The tax items, when they differ from the book items, are allocated under the I.R.C. § 704(c) Regulations and generally must be determined so as to take account of the variation between the adjusted tax basis and the fair market value of the contributed property.[68] Thus, in Example 1 in which the property was sold for $12,000, the tax and book accounts would be:

	A		B	
	Tax	**Book**	**Tax**	**Book**
Formation	$7,000	$10,000	$10,000	$10,000
Gain	$4,000	$1,000	$1,000	$1,000
Balance	$11,000	$11,000	$11,000	$11,000

As we will see, I.R.C. § 704(c) and its Regulations are very complex, but this is the foundation. Be sure you understand it before proceeding further.[69] Note that after the sale, the book and tax accounts are equal. An objective of I.R.C. § 704(c)

---

[66] The Regulations achieve this result by allowing a partnership to apply the rules of I.R.C. § 704(c) with reference to the partners' distributive shares of the corresponding book items as determined under I.R.C. § 704(b). Treas. Reg. § 1.704-1(b)(1)(vi).

[67] Treas. Reg. § 1.704-3(a)(3)(i).

[68] Treas. Reg. § 1.704-1(b)(1)(vi).

[69] Treas. Reg. § 1.704-3(e) provides that a partnership can opt out of I.R.C. § 704(c) if there is only a "small disparity" between the book value of the property contributed by a partner in a single tax year and its tax basis. A small disparity exists if the book value of all properties contributed by one partner

is to eliminate the disparities between the book and tax accounts. As we shall see, however, it is not always possible to do so.

B.   I.R.C. § 704(c) Methods of Allocation

The Regulations permit partnerships to use any "reasonable" allocation method that takes into account the variation between the adjusted tax basis of property and its fair market value at the time of contribution.[70] The Regulations provide three allocation methods that are "generally" considered reasonable, but gives the IRS some wiggle room, stating that even one of these methods might not be reasonable.[71] The Regulations, however, also provide that the use of a given method is "not necessarily unreasonable merely because another method would result in a higher aggregate tax liability."[72] Thus, the fact that one method gives a better tax result than another will not, for that reason alone, disqualify it. For the most part, tax practitioners stick to one of the three methods, generally feeling free to use the method that gives the best tax results.[73] We give an example of an abusive use of the traditional method below.

1.   The Traditional Method

In general, the traditional method requires that when the partnership has income, gain, loss, or deduction attributable to I.R.C. § 704(c) property, it must make appropriate allocations to the partners to avoid shifting the tax consequences of the built-in gain or loss. Under this rule, if the partnership sells I.R.C. § 704(c) property and recognizes gain or loss, built-in gain or loss on the property is allocated to the contributing partner (subject to adjustments discussed below).

The traditional method used to be the only method of allocation allowed by the Regulations. It can lead to distortions. When other methods were added that can remove the distortions, the original approach was given the moniker "traditional method." Example 1 used a simple form of the traditional method. The tax gain or loss inherent in contributed property is allocated to the contributing partner. Any tax gain or loss in excess of that amount is allocated in the same manner as the partnership allocates the book gain or loss on the property.

The difficulty with the traditional method is that under some circumstances it cannot eliminate the disparity between the tax and book accounts.

Example 2

Assume the same facts as in Example 1 except that the land A contributed declines in value and is sold for $8,000. The partnership experiences a $2,000 economic loss, the amount by which the land dropped in value. But because the tax

---

during the partnership's tax year does not differ from its tax basis by more than 15% and the total gross disparity does not exceed $20,000.

[70] Treas. Reg. § 1.704-3(a)(1).

[71] *Id.*

[72] *Id.*

[73] *But see* PLR 9540034 (July 5, 1995); PLR 200530013 (Apr. 14. 2005).

basis of the property is $7,000, there is actually a tax gain of $1,000. Ideally, A should be given a $3,000 tax gain, and the partnership then given a $2,000 tax loss. That would be fair. A realized, but under I.R.C. § 721 did not recognize, $3,000 of gain when she contributed the land to the partnership. The partnership in fact suffered an economic loss of $2,000, and ideally it should be given a tax loss to match its economic loss. A would then have a net tax gain of $2,000 ($3,000 gain − $1,000 loss) and B would have a $1,000 tax loss. But under what has become known as the ceiling rule, if the traditional method is used, these tax gains and losses cannot be created. No partner can be allocated a tax gain or loss other than that which actually incurred. The partnership's tax basis in the land is $7,000. If it sells it for $8,000, it recognizes a $1,000 tax gain. That is its "ceiling." It cannot create a greater tax gain or create any tax losses.[74] Accordingly, the tax and book accounts would be:

| | A | | B | |
	Tax	Book	Tax	Book
Formation	$7,000	$10,000	$10,000	$10,000
Gain	$1,000	($1,000)	0	($1,000)
Balance	$8,000	$9,000	$10,000	$9,000

The tax and book accounts are now out of balance, and while the partnership operates, there is no way to bring them into balance under the traditional method. Only upon liquidation could the distortions be cured. If, after the sale of the land, the partnership distributed its $18,000 to the partners, each partner would be given the balance in the capital account, or $9,000. For tax purposes, A would recognize $1,000 of gain ($9,000 − $8,000) and B would recognize $1,000 of loss ($9,000 − $10,000). The distortions between the tax and book accounts would be eliminated. As we discussed above, however, the character of the gain and loss recognized on liquidation could be different from that associated with the land and the liquidation may occur many years after the disposition of the land. Finally, if a partner dies before liquidation, his heirs take a fair market value basis as of the date of death under I.R.C. § 1014, eliminating any tax gain or loss inherent in the partnership interest that existed before then. Thus, in the example above, if B dies before the partnership is liquidated, the one thing he can take with him is his unrecognized tax loss.

The distortions caused by the ceiling rule prompted the IRS to promulgate Regulations providing two optional alternatives. We discuss those below, but first let us look at an abusive use of the traditional method.

a. Abusive Use of Traditional Method

The Regulations contain the following example of the abusive use of the traditional method:[75] C and D form a partnership CD and agree that each will be allocated a 50% share of all partnership items and that CD will make allocations under section 704(c) using the traditional method. C contributes equipment with an

---

[74] *See* Treas. Reg. § 1.704-3(b)(1).

[75] *See* Treas. Reg. § 1.704-3(b)(2), example 2.

adjusted tax basis of $1,000 and a book value of $10,000, with a view to taking advantage of the fact that the equipment has only one year remaining on its cost recovery schedule although its remaining economic life is significantly longer. D contributes $10,000 of cash, which CD uses to buy securities. D has substantial net operating loss carryforwards that D anticipates will otherwise expire unused. Under section 1.704-1(b)(2)(iv)(g)(3), the partnership must allocate the $10,000 of book depreciation to the partners in the first year of the partnership. Thus, there is $10,000 of book depreciation and $1,000 of tax depreciation in the partnership's first year. CD sells the equipment during the second year for $10,000 and recognizes a $10,000 gain ($10,000, the amount realized, less the adjusted tax basis of $0).

At the beginning of the second year, both the book value and adjusted tax basis of the equipment are $0. Therefore, there is no remaining built-in gain. The $10,000 gain on the sale of the equipment in the second year is allocated $5,000 each to C and D. The interaction of the partnership's one-year write-off of the entire book value of the equipment and the use of the traditional method results in a shift of $4,000 of the precontribution gain in the equipment from C to D (D's $5,000 share of CD's $10,000 gain, less the $1,000 tax depreciation deduction previously allocated to D). (We discuss I.R.C. § 704(c) and depreciation, below.)

The traditional method is not reasonable under these circumstances because the contribution of property is made, and the traditional method is used, with a view to shifting a significant amount of taxable income to a partner with a low marginal tax rate and away from a partner with a high marginal tax rate.

The Regulations go on to provide that if the partnership agreement in effect for the year of contribution had provided that tax gain from the sale of the property (if any) would always be allocated first to C to offset the effect of the ceiling rule limitation, the allocation method would not be abusive.

2. Traditional Method with Curative Allocations

Under this method, a partnership may make reasonable curative allocations to reduce or eliminate disparities between book and tax items of noncontributing partners. A curative allocation is an allocation of income, gain, loss, or deduction for *tax* purposes. Recall that the objective is to bring the tax accounts in line with the book accounts, so it would only be appropriate to adjust the tax items. The curative allocation must be of an actually existing tax item incurred by the partnership (it can't make it up), cannot exceed the amount necessary to correct the distortion caused by the ceiling rule, and must generally be of the same character as the tax item limited by the ceiling rule.[76]

---

[76] *See* Treas. Reg. § 1.704-3(c); if depreciation deductions have been limited by the ceiling rule, the general limitation on character does not apply to income from the disposition of contributed property subject to the ceiling rule. For example, if allocations of depreciation deductions to a noncontributing partner have been limited by the ceiling rule, a curative allocation to the contributing partner of gain from the sale of that property can be considered reasonable. *See* Treas. Reg. § 1.704-3(c)(3)(iii)(B).

Example 3

Assume that in Example 2 the partnership invested the $10,000 B contributed in another parcel of land (Land #2) that it subsequently sold for a book and tax gain of $4,000. Assume both parcels are capital assets to the partnership with holding periods of more than one year and thus the character of the gain or loss on each is the same. The book gain would have to be allocated equally, but under the curative allocation method the tax gain could be allocated $3,000 to A and $1,000 to B. By being given less tax gain, B in effect receives a tax loss equal to his book loss on Land #1 and A is placed in the same position as if she had recognized her entire initial gain ($3,000) and then received a $1,000 tax loss equal to her book loss on Land #1. After the smoke clears, the book and tax accounts would be equal:

| | A | | B | |
	Tax	Book	Tax	Book
Formation	$7,000	$10,000	$10,000	$10,000
Sale Lane #1	$1,000	($1,000)		($1,000)
Sale Land #2	$3,000	$2,000	$1,000	$2,000
Balance	$11,000	$11,000	$11,000	$11,000

A partnership may make a curative allocation in one tax year to offset the effect of the ceiling rule for a prior tax year if the allocations are made over a "reasonable" period, and provided for in the partnership agreement for the year of the contribution.[77] The traditional method with curative allocations tends to be used less often than the traditional method or the remedial method (discussed next). The reason for this is that the curative method is neither as taxpayer-friendly to the contributor as the traditional method nor as likely to remedy book-tax disparities as the remedial method.[78]

3.   Remedial Method

The problem with the traditional method with curative allocations is that the partnership may not actually incur tax items that can properly offset other tax items limited by the ceiling rule. The Regulations respond by giving the partnership the option of using the remedial method. This method permits the partnership to create the offsetting tax item out of whole cloth. Again, the book accounts are unaffected. It is only tax items that can be adjusted.

Under the remedial method, the partnership first determines the partners' shares of book items under I.R.C. § 704(b). The partnership then allocates the corresponding tax items recognized by the partnership, if any, using the traditional method. If the ceiling rule causes the tax item to differ from the book items, the partnership creates a remedial item of income, gain, loss, or deduction equal to the full amount of the difference and allocates it to the noncontributing partner. The

---

[77]   Treas. Reg. § 1.704-3(c)(ii); the Regulations suggest that a property's economic life is a reasonable period.

[78]   *See* ARTHUR WILLIS, JOHN PENNELL & PHILIP POSTLEWAITE, PARTNERSHIP TAXATION ¶ 10.08[3][b] (6th ed.). ("PARTNERSHIP TAXATION").

partnership creates an offsetting remedial item in an identical amount and allocates it to the contributing partner.[79] The remedial allocations have the same tax attributes as the tax item limited by the ceiling rule. Thus, if the ceiling rule limited item is an item of long-term capital loss from the sale of a capital asset that was contributed to the partnership, the offset will be long-term capital gain.[80]

Example 4

The facts are the same as in Example 2 and Land #1 is a long-term capital asset to the partnership. The book accounts are unaffected. For tax purposes, the partnership would create $1,000 of long-term capital loss that it would allocate to B and would create $1,000 of offsetting long-term capital gain that it would allocate to A. This gives B a tax loss equal to his book loss. It places A in the same position as if she had recognized her entire initial gain ($3,000) and then received a $1,000 tax loss equal to her book loss. The tax and book accounts thus would be:

| | A | | B | |
	Tax	Book	Tax	Book
Formation	$7,000	$10,000	$10,000	$10,000
Sale Lane #1	$1,000	($1,000)		($1,000)
Remedial	$1,000		($1,000)	
Balance	$9,000	$9,000	$9,000	$9,000

4. Depreciation

The manner in which depreciation, amortization, and depletion are allocated among the partners is also governed by I.R.C. § 704(c)(1)(A). We will focus on depreciation deductions. Recall that the purpose of I.R.C. § 704(c)(1)(A) is to eliminate the disparities between book and tax accounts. Generally, a noncontributing partner should receive tax depreciation equal to that partner's share of book depreciation with the balance of the depreciation being allocated to the contributing partner. The rules are designed to help achieve that objective. This is most easily understood by way of an example.

Example 5(a)

In our ubiquitous AB partnership, in which A and B are equal partners, assume A contributes depreciable equipment with a tax basis of $6,000 and a book value of $10,000 and B contributes $10,000 cash. The equipment is depreciated using the straight-line method at the rate of 10% per year. Tax depreciation is $600 per year, and book depreciation is $1,000 per year. The book depreciation is allocated equally between the partners, or $500 each. The tax depreciation is allocated $500 to B. The balance of $100 is allocated to A.[81] The approach is logical. In a sense, B gave A $10,000 of "credit" for the equipment he contributed and should therefore receive,

---

[79] Treas. Reg. § 1.704-3(d)(1).

[80] *See* Treas. Reg. § 1.704-3(d)(3).

[81] This example is based on Treas. Reg. § 1.704-3(b), example 1.

if possible, his full share of the tax depreciation based on that amount; that is, tax depreciation equal to his share of book depreciation. This approach will also have the effect of eliminating the disparities between the tax and book accounts over time:

	A		B	
	Tax	Book	Tax	Book
Formation	$6,000	$10,000	$10,000	$10,000
Depreciation Years 1-10	($1,000)	($5,000)	($5,000)	($5,000)
Balance	$5,000	$5,000	$5,000	$5,000

Now assume the property is sold at the end of Year 2 for $9,000. Its tax basis at that time would be $4,800 ($6,000 − $1,200) and its book value would be $8,000 ($10,000 − $2,000). There would be tax gain of $4,200 ($9,000 − $4,800) and $1,000 of book gain ($9,000 − $8,000). How are the tax and book gain allocated? Book gain is allocated equally to the partners, or $500 each. Tax gain equal to book gain is allocated in the same manner as book gain, or $500 per partner. Tax gain in excess of book gain of $3,200 ($4,200 − $1,000) is entirely allocated to A, the contributing partner. Note that if the partnership sold the property immediately after it was acquired, the gain that would have been allocated to A is $4,000. After two years, the gain allocated to A is $800 less than that. Why did it go down? Because the tax and book accounts were "caught up" by two years of "preferential" allocations of the tax depreciation to B. Each year B received $400 more depreciation than A, or $800 over two years, hence there is less gain to be allocated to A under I.R.C. § 704(c)(1)(A).

Example 5(b)

The facts are the same as in Example 5(a), except the property that A contributes has a basis of $4,000. The tax depreciation is now $400 per year. The book depreciation remains $1,000 per year. The book depreciation is again allocated equally to the two partners, or $500 each. In this case, there is not sufficient tax depreciation to give B tax depreciation equal to his book depreciation. The ceiling rule has once again reared its ugly head. If the traditional method is being used, all of the tax depreciation is allocated to B, and a disparity will exist on the books of the partnership:

	A		B	
	Tax	Book	Tax	Book
Formation	$4,000	$10,000	$10,000	$10,000
Depreciation Years 1–10		($5,000)	($4,000)	($5,000)
Balance	$4,000	$5,000	$6,000	$5,000

If the partnership uses the remedial method, it can cure the disparity (though the cure can sometimes be complex).[82] If the partnership uses the traditional method

---

[82] *See* Treas. Reg. § 1.704-3(d), example 1. If the remedial method is used, book depreciation may

with curative allocations, it can also cure the disparity as long as it incurs another tax item that can be used as an offset.[83]

5. Other Considerations

The Regulations permit the partnership to select different methods for different properties.[84] The partnership may use any "reasonable" method, and a method is not necessarily unreasonable merely because another method will result in a higher tax liability. Indeed, the Regulations provide that a method other than one of the three listed above may be used, though only those three are described in the Regulations.[85] A method that would violate the anti-abuse rules (see Chapter 13) would, of course, not be considered to be reasonable, even if it is one of the three specified methods.

Which method the partnership and its partners will prefer will depend on a number of considerations, including the administrative burden of complying with the latter two methods. An important consideration will be the relative tax brackets of the partners. If they are all in approximately the same tax bracket, they generally will prefer a method that will give a tax consequence that is the same as the economic consequence. When choosing between the traditional method with curative allocations and the remedial method, an important consideration will be whether the partners can live with the "phantom income" that often results from the remedial method. In the traditional method with curative allocations, there is an actual taxable transaction that is being used to eliminate the disparities, which can often mean cash is being generated that can be used to pay any additional taxes. That cash might not be generated in the remedial method as no taxable transaction need take place.

If the partners are in different tax brackets, the analysis may change again. In Example 2, if A is in a high tax bracket and B is in a low tax bracket, and the partners are cooperative, they may prefer the traditional method, which gives A less total taxable gain.

Recall that, as we discussed in Chapter 2, I.R.C. § 724 can also apply. I.R.C. § 724 provides that any gain or loss recognized by a partnership on the disposition of contributed unrealized receivables, or contributed inventory items during the first five years the partnership holds them, is treated as ordinary income or loss.

C. I.R.C. § 704(c)(1)(C)

As we discussed above, losses inherent in contributed property are generally allocated to the contributing partner. Before the passage of the American Jobs Creation Act of 2004, however, it was possible for others to benefit from those losses. For example, a transferee of the contributing partner generally steps into

---

need to be computed using different periods for different portions of the book value. *See* Treas. Reg. § 1.704-3(d)(2).

[83] *See* Treas. Reg. § 1.704-3(c), example 1.

[84] Treas. Reg. § 1.704-3(a)(2).

[85] Treas. Reg. § 1.704-3(a)(1).

the shoes of that partner for I.R.C. § 704(c) purposes and thus previously could have been allocated any remaining I.R.C. § 704(c) losses. (See Chapter 6.) The losses could have been allocated to other partners in the case of a liquidation of the entire partnership, if the contributed property was distributed to another partner, or in the case of a liquidation of the interest of the contributing partner if the partnership continued to hold the contributed property. (See Chapter 7.) To address these issues Congress enacted I.R.C. § 704(c)(1)(C) in 2004. It provides that if contributed property has a built-in loss, that built-in loss is taken into account only in determining the amount of items allocated to the contributing partner. In determining the amount of items allocated to other partners, the basis of the contributed property in the hands of the partnership is treated as being equal to its fair market value on contribution.

§ 5.06   REVERSE I.R.C. § 704(c) ALLOCATIONS

An issue similar to the one that exists for contributed property arises if a partner enters a partnership after it has been in business for a while. The partnership may have assets that for book purposes are appreciated or depreciated. That appreciation and depreciation occurred before the new partner entered the partnership and logically should be allocated to the preexisting partners. That is indeed one option. The partnership could amend the partnership agreement to provide that the preexisting gains and losses will be allocated to the preexisting partners. Another option made available by the Regulations is to do what is called a "revaluation," often also called a "reverse I.R.C. § 704(c) allocation."[86] The book values of the assets and the partners' capital accounts are restated to fair market value as of the date the new partner enters the partnership. If that is done, depreciation, gain, and loss on the partnership property for book purposes will be different before and after the revaluation. That difference must be allocated following I.R.C. § 704(c) principles. For this purpose, it is as if a new partnership were formed, with the preexisting partners contributing the assets of the partnership and the new partner making his contribution, with I.R.C. § 704(c) then applied to get the gains, losses, depreciation, etc. to the right parties.

It is perhaps easiest to understand revaluations by way of an example. Assume that A and B again form the equal AB partnership.[87] A and B each contribute $10,000 and thus each have an initial capital account of $10,000. The $20,000 is invested in publicly traded securities. The securities appreciate in value to $50,000. At that time C makes a $25,000 contribution and becomes an equal one-third partner with A and B. The securities further appreciate to $59,000, and the partnership then sells them. Assume (not very realistically) that the partnership has no other activity and no other expenditures or income. The question is how to deal with the $39,000 of gain on the securities. $30,000 of that gain arose before C entered the partnership and properly belongs to A and B. The other $9,000 of gain occurred while C was a partner and belongs to all three partners. Since the $39,000 constitutes both book and tax gain, under I.R.C. § 704(b) the first $30,000 could be

---

[86]   Treas. Reg. § 1.704-1(b)(2)(iv)(f), (4)(i).

[87]   This example is based on Treas. Reg. § 1.704-1(b)(5), example 14.

allocated equally to A and B and the remaining $9,000 could be allocated equally to A, B, and C.

Alternatively, upon C's entry into the partnership, the partnership could do a reverse I.R.C. § 704(c) allocation and restate the capital accounts and book values of partnership property at fair market value. If that is done, A and B will each have a $25,000 capital account and the securities would have a book value of $50,000, while continuing to have a tax basis of $20,000. When the securities appreciate to $59,000 and are then sold, there will be $9,000 of book gain and $39,000 of tax gain. The book gain is allocated equally to the three partners. Under the Regulations, the tax gain must be allocated in accordance with I.R.C. § 704(c) principles. That is done by allocating tax gain equal to book gain ($9,000) equally to A, B, and C. The balance of the tax gain ($30,000) is allocated equally to A and B. Conceptually, it is as if the parties formed a partnership with A and B contributing securities with a tax basis of $20,000 and a fair market value of $50,000 and C contributing $25,000, the securities appreciating to $59,000, and then being sold.

Any of the I.R.C. § 704(c) allocation methods may be used in reverse I.R.C. § 704(c) allocations. To make matters more complex, the method used for a reverse I.R.C. § 704(c) allocation with regard to a particular property need not be the same as the method used for that property for "regular" I.R.C. § 704(c) allocation purposes.[88]

Revaluations are optional[89] and are allowed only under certain circumstances. The adjustments must be based on the fair market value of partnership property on the date of the adjustment and be principally made for a non-tax business purpose:

- in connection with the contribution of money or property in exchange for a new or increased partnership interest;

- in connection with the distribution of money or property in liquidation of part or all of a partnership interest;

- in connection with the issuance of a partnership interest in exchange for services performed by someone acting in a partner capacity or in anticipation of becoming a partner; or

- under generally accepted industry accounting practices, provided substantially all of the partnership's property, excluding money, consists of securities readily tradeable on an established securities market.[90]

Note that the partnership's tax bases in its assets and the partners' tax bases in their partnership interests are unaffected by a revaluation.

When would a partnership prefer a revaluation over an I.R.C. § 704(b) allocation? Revaluations are common in hedge and other investment funds holding marketable securities where partners may have the right to buy in and be bought out at some version of book value and there is a fair amount of partner turnover. By doing

---

[88] *See* Partnership Taxation at ¶ 10.08[3].

[89] Though the Proposed Regulations for noncompensatory options require revaluations in some circumstances. *See* Prop. Treas. Reg. § 1.704-1(b)(2)(iv)(s)(1).

[90] *See* Treas. Reg. § 1.704-1(b)(2)(iv)(f).

revaluations, the book values are kept current for these purposes. It has been noted that applying I.R.C. § 704(c) to revaluations results "in massive complexity for the sake of theoretical purity."[91]

What if in the example the partnership did none of the above? What if it did not do a revaluation and simply allocated the $39,000 of gain equally among the three partners? While there is technically nothing to stop this, the question arises as to why the partnership and the partners would agree to this (assuming they are properly informed, not always a given). Keep in mind that if A and B shift book gain to C, they lose the concomitant capital account increase, meaning less will be distributed to them on liquidation. Therefore, not only book and tax gain are being shifted to C, but economic value as well. Why would A and B do this? Well, it might be disguised compensation to C or it might be a gift to C and the IRS could restructure it in line with its true status.[92]

§ 5.07 ALLOCATIONS OF NONRECOURSE DEDUCTIONS

A. Introduction

A good grasp of how nonrecourse liabilities are allocated among the partners is necessary for an understanding of this area. Review Chapter 3, which discusses the allocation of nonrecourse liabilities, if necessary.

It is common for partnerships, particularly partnerships involved in the real estate industry, to use nonrecourse financing. The use of nonrecourse financing involves more than just tax planning. Avoiding personal liability is preferable for obvious reasons. Lenders would often, of course, prefer recourse lending, but commonly make nonrecourse loans to stay competitive in the lending market. Where enough equity is present, lenders may actually prefer nonrecourse loans as typically the interest rate on nonrecourse debt is higher than that on recourse debt. As you learned in Chapter 3, a partner's share of partnership nonrecourse liabilities increases his basis in the partnership interest. Subject to the at-risk rules of I.R.C. § 465 and the passive loss rules of I.R.C. § 469, a partner may deduct his share of partnership losses to the extent of his basis in the partnership interest.[93]

The use of nonrecourse financing, however, does pose a dilemma for partnership allocations. Recall that the cornerstone of the substantial economic effect rules is that allocations have a genuine economic effect on the partners. This poses a problem for deductions generated by nonrecourse debt ("nonrecourse deductions,"[94] a term we will define more precisely below), such as depreciation deductions for the part of a property's basis attributable to nonrecourse debt. The partners only have an economic risk to the extent of any cash or property invested. To the extent that basis and associated deductions are generated by nonrecourse debt, in truth only the lender is at risk. If the venture fails, the partners can walk

---

[91] PARTNERSHIP TAXATION at ¶ 10.08[3].

[92] *See* Treas. Reg. § 1.704-1(b)(5), example 14(iv); Treas. Reg. § 1.704-1(b)(1)(iv).

[93] I.R.C. § 704(d), which provides that losses in excess of basis may be carried forward indefinitely.

[94] Treas. Reg. § 1.704-2(b)(1).

away without any personal obligation on the debt. If the deductions generated by the nonrecourse deductions cause the partners to have negative capital accounts, a deficit restoration obligation may not be very meaningful. If all of the partners have negative capital accounts, which commonly eventually occurs when nonrecourse debt is used, there will be no one to enforce deficit restoration obligations.[95] Consequently, if property is purchased with nonrecourse debt, only allocations of deductions attributable to the equity invested by the partners can have economic effect.[96] Allocations of nonrecourse deductions (deemed to occur after the equity has been fully "used up" by depreciation and other deductions that reduce basis) cannot have economic effect.

Example 1

Assume in our AB partnership that A and B invest no funds in the partnership and the partnership borrows $200,000 on a nonrecourse basis and uses the proceeds to buy an apartment building for $200,000. No principal payments on the debt are due for five years. Capital accounts are not increased for a partner's share of loan proceeds, so the partners' beginning capital accounts are zero. If the property drops in value to $150,000, the partners could simply default on the loan and would not be obligated to make any payment to the lender. The lender bears the risk of loss on the decline in value of the property. Now assume that the AB partnership takes $20,000 in depreciation deductions on the property. If we assume that the partnership breaks even except for depreciation deductions, A and B will have negative capital accounts of $10,000 each and the partnership's basis in the property will be reduced to $180,000. In the unlikely event that A and B have deficit restoration obligations, it would not be meaningful as there would be no one to enforce it. Thus, neither A nor B have borne the economic burden of the allocation, and thus the allocations to them cannot have economic effect.

Since the allocation of nonrecourse deductions cannot have economic effect, the general rule of the Regulations is that they must be allocated in accordance with the partners' "interests in the partnership."[97] As we now know, that standard is quite vague. The use of nonrecourse debt is fairly common and there are legitimate nontax reasons for its use. It was thus incumbent on the IRS to come up with a more definite approach that would permit partners to allocate nonrecourse deductions, and indeed the Regulations provide a safe harbor. The cornerstone of the safe harbor is the fact that where there are nonrecourse deductions there is also "minimum gain." The Supreme Court held in *Commissioner v. Tufts*[98] that if a taxpayer sells or disposes of property encumbered by nonrecourse debt, the amount realized includes the amount of that debt. Thus, at a minimum, the taxpayer must recognize gain to the extent that the encumbering nonrecourse debt

---

[95] Unless the lender could make a claim under a third-party beneficiary theory, giving the lender such a claim would be something of a stretch, since the parties normally intend no personal obligation on the part of the partners, and enforcing a deficit restoration obligation would create that obligation.

[96] If recourse debt was also used, deductions attributable to the recourse debt can also have economic effect.

[97] Treas. Reg. § 1.704-1(b)(3).

[98] 461 U.S. 300 (1983).

exceeds the taxpayer's tax basis in the property. Indeed, on any taxable disposition of property subject to nonrecourse debt, this excess is the "minimum gain" that a taxpayer will have to recognize. While A and B may not be required to restore the deficits in their capital accounts, we may still be able to bring their capital accounts back to at least zero. This is done by allocating minimum gain to each partner in an amount at least sufficient to bring the capital account to zero. In Example 1, if the AB partnership defaults on the loan after the first year, the partnership and its two partners will have $20,000 of gain on the foreclosure ($200,000 debt minus $180,000 basis). Allocating that gain equally to A and B will bring their capital accounts back to zero. Thus, if allocations of nonrecourse deductions are made and the basis of the property is reduced below the amount of the debt, we can commonly be assured that at some point there will be compensating minimum gain. Generally, the Regulations allow allocations of nonrecourse deductions to a partner as long as an equal amount of minimum gain is allocated to that partner (this minimum gain is unrecognized but inherent in the property).[99] Further, partners may generally have negative capital accounts, even if they do not have deficit restoration obligations, to the extent of their shares of minimum gain. There can be a genuine economic impact to this minimum gain. If the only gain that is recognized is the amount of the minimum gain, no cash will be going to the taxpayer and he will have to reach into his pocket to pay the taxes on the minimum gain (income without cash is sometimes called "phantom income").

B. The Regulatory Safe Harbor

As we discussed above, since the allocation of deductions attributable to nonrecourse debt cannot have economic effect, the Regulations provide that they must be allocated in accordance with the partners' interests in the partnership.[100] The Regulations provide a complex safe harbor which contains a number of specialized terms. "Partnership minimum gain" is determined by computing for each partnership nonrecourse liability any *book* gain the partnership would realize if it disposed of the property subject to that liability for no consideration other than the full satisfaction of the liability; in other words, the amount by which the nonrecourse liabilities exceed the property's book value.[101] If A contributes property with a tax basis of $10,000, a fair market value of $20,000, and subject to a nonrecourse debt of $20,000, initially there would be no minimum gain as the nonrecourse debt does not exceed the $20,000 book value of the property. Indeed, it should be borne in mind that book value rules here. When we, for example, discuss depreciation in this context, book depreciation is meant. Of course, if property is acquired with cash, there will be no book/tax disparities (barring a revaluation).[102] I.R.C. § 704(c) governs book/tax disparities.

---

[99] Technically, the Regulations provide that if the allocation of nonrecourse deductions is in accordance with the regulatory rules, it will also be in accordance with the partner's interest in the partnership. Treas. Reg. § 1.704-2(b)(1).

[100] Treas. Reg. § 1.704-2(b)(1).

[101] Treas. Reg. § 1.704-2(d)(1), (3).

[102] Revaluations, however, generally cannot reduce minimum gain. *See* Treas. Reg. § 1.704-2(d)(4)(ii).

The amount of nonrecourse deductions for a partnership taxable year equals the net increase in partnership minimum gain during that year.[103] In Example 1, if the property was subject to $20,000 of depreciation deductions in the first year and there were no other expenses with regard to the property, the property's book value would have been reduced by $20,000, meaning that the increase in partnership minimum gain would also be $20,000. It went from zero to $20,000. Note that the partnership can have nonrecourse debt without generating nonrecourse deductions. Until there is minimum gain, any deductions are considered to come from the equity in the property. Nonrecourse deductions are created when the partnership generates minimum gain. Nonrecourse deductions and minimum gain are two sides of one coin. Nonrecourse deductions consist first of depreciation deductions with respect to property that is subject to nonrecourse debt and then, generally, pro rata portions of the partnership's other deductions and I.R.C. § 705(a)(2)(B) expenditures.[104]

The formal regulatory rules that have to be met in order for an allocation of nonrecourse deductions to be allowed under the safe harbor are:[105]

1. The partnership must comply with the economic effect test discussed above. Recall that part 3 of that test either requires a partner to have an unlimited deficit restoration obligation or meet the qualified income offset rules. Also, recall that under the qualified income offset rules a partner may have a deficit capital account to the extent of any "limited" deficit restoration obligation. Partnerships using nonrecourse debt commonly do not have deficit restoration obligations. Previously, the qualified income offset rules and the nonrecourse deduction rules were in mortal conflict. The nonrecourse deduction rules allow for deficit capital accounts notwithstanding the lack of a deficit restoration obligation, but the qualified income offset rules did not permit a deficit capital account absent such an obligation. The regulatory error was corrected, and the qualified income offset rules now provide that partners may have negative capital accounts to the extent of their shares of minimum gain. A partner's share of minimum gain is considered to be a "limited" deficit restoration obligation for purposes of the qualified income offset rules.[106]

2. Beginning in the first taxable year of the partnership in which there are nonrecourse deductions and thereafter throughout the full term of the partnership, the partnership agreement provides for allocations of nonrecourse deductions in a manner that is "reasonably consistent" with allocations of some other significant partnership item attributable to the property securing the nonrecourse liabilities that have substantial economic effect. (For example, assume depreciation deductions are exactly

---

[103] Treas. Reg. § 1.704-2(c)(1). This is reduced by any distributions of nonrecourse liabilities that are allocable to an increase in minimum gain, a subject we will discuss below. Increases in partnership minimum gain resulting from conversions, refinancing, and other changes to the debt instrument do not generate nonrecourse deductions.

[104] Treas. Reg. § 1.704-2(j)(1).

[105] Treas. Reg. § 1.704-2(e).

[106] Treas. Reg. § 1.704-2(g)(1).

equal to the nonrecourse deductions. Allocation of any other deductions generally would fall within the substantial economic effect rules.) In an example in the Regulations, allocations that have substantial economic effect are allocated initially 90% to the limited partner and 10% to the general partner until the items of income equal the items of loss, then shift to 50%-50%. The nonrecourse deductions may be allocated anywhere from 50%-50% to 90%-10%, but may not be allocated 99%-1%.[107] Of course, if nonrecourse deductions are allocated in the exact same manner as all other deductions (in this case starting at 90%-10% and shifting with the other items to 50%-50%), they are as "reasonably consistent" as is possible.

3. The partnership has a "minimum gain chargeback" provision, discussed below.

4. The partnership otherwise complies with the regulatory rules for allocations.

Eventually, minimum gain inherent in partnership property will be reduced. The partnership might sell the underlying property (meaning the associated minimum gain drops to zero) or it might pay down some or all of the nonrecourse debt. Of course, the key item that has been driving this whole allocation system is that there will be minimum gain available to offset the nonrecourse deductions. What does the partnership do when the minimum gain goes down? The Regulations provide that at that time there is a minimum gain chargeback, meaning that the partners must be allocated items of income and gain equal to their shares of the net decrease in minimum gain.[108] Of course, if the partnership sells the underlying property (or has it taken in foreclosure), finding the gain will not be a problem. The gain from the sale or foreclosure will be available for this purpose. Indeed, the Regulations provide that any minimum gain chargeback must consist first of gains recognized from the disposition of partnership property subject to partnership nonrecourse liabilities. But if there is no such disposition gain because, for example, the reduction in minimum gain resulted from paying down the debt, then the partnership must allocate a pro rata portion of the partnership's other items of income and gain to the partners to offset the drop in minimum gain. If insufficient income and gain is available in the year in which the drop in minimum gain occurs, the allocations continue in future years until the full offset has been made. This minimum gain chargeback allocation is made before any other I.R.C. § 704 allocations.[109]

What is a partner's share of partnership minimum gain? Generally, it is the sum of the nonrecourse deductions allocated to the partner, net of prior minimum gain chargebacks.[110]

---

[107] Treas. Reg. § 1.704-2(m), example 1(ii).

[108] Treas. Reg. § 1.704-2(f)(1).

[109] Treas. Reg. § 1.704-2(j).

[110] Treas. Reg. § 1.704-2(g)(1).

Example 2[111]

A and B form the AB limited partnership. Neither partner makes a capital contribution. Under the partnership agreement, the partners do not have a deficit restoration obligation, but the agreement contains a qualified income offset provision and otherwise complies with the substantial economic effect rules as well as the rules for allocating nonrecourse deductions. As a consequence, the partnership agreement meets the first test for allocating nonrecourse deductions. All losses are allocated 90% to A and 10% to B. All income is allocated first to restore previous losses and thereafter 50% to A and 50% to B. The partnership borrows $200,000 on a nonrecourse basis from a commercial lender and purchases an apartment building. Interest only is due on the note for the first five years. For its first three years, the partnership breaks even on its operations except for depreciation. Depreciation is $10,000 per year, so the partnership operates at a loss of $10,000 for each of its first three years. The basis of the apartment building is reduced by $10,000 per year under I.R.C. § 1016.

After three years, the partnership's basis in the building is reduced to $170,000. The debt remains at $200,000. Thus, there is $30,000 of minimum gain inherent in the property. Nonrecourse deductions exist to the extent of the increase in minimum gain, or $30,000 over the three years. The nonrecourse deductions must be allocated in a manner that is reasonably consistent with the allocations of items that have substantial economic effect. Note that the partnership is incurring other expenses, for example, interest on the debt. The interest expense does not contribute to the nonrecourse deductions as they come first out of cost recovery deductions attributable to the property securing the debt, and the nonrecourse deductions exactly equal to the depreciation deductions. Thus, the allocation of all other items of income and expense fall within the regular allocation rules. The allocation of the nonrecourse deductions must be reasonably consistent with these other allocations. Here they are exactly the same as everything is allocated the same way, thus the second part of the nonrecourse allocation rules is met.

After three years, A and B's capital accounts are as follows:

A	B
($27,000)	($3,000)

You might ask whether the partners can have negative capital accounts given that they do not have deficit restoration obligations. The answer here is yes. A partner is considered to have a deficit restoration obligation to the extent of that partner's share of minimum gain. Recall that under the qualified income offset rules a partner may have a negative capital account to the extent of any limited deficit restoration obligation as long as the partnership otherwise complies with the qualified income offset rules, as is the case here. The partners' shares of minimum gain are the same as the nonrecourse allocations made to them; that is, $27,000 for A and $3,000 for B. A partner's share of minimum gain is considered to be a limited

---

[111] This example is based on Treas. Reg. § 1.704-2(f)(7), example 1.

deficit restoration obligation.[112]

At the beginning of Year 4, the partnership sells the apartment building for $300,000. The total gain of the partnership on the sale is $300,000 − $170,000 = $130,000. Minimum gain drops to zero as the partnership no longer holds the property. Under the minimum gain chargeback rules, gain must be allocated to the partners in the same manner as nonrecourse deductions are allocated to the partners. Here there is gain available from the sale to do this, so the first $30,000 of gain from the sale is allocated $27,000 to A and $3,000 to B. Note this will eliminate the deficit capital accounts of each partner, a primary goal of the system. The one thing the IRS would not want to happen is for someone to be able to walk away from a negative capital account. Even if the partner has an unlimited deficit restoration obligation, as mentioned above, it may not be meaningful in this context as there is no one to enforce it. The minimum gain chargeback solves the problem by requiring an income allocation that offsets the negative capital account.

Continuing with Example 2, under the partnership agreement, income is first allocated in the same manner as losses were allocated. This occurred when we allocated the first $30,000 of gain to A and B as discussed. Under the partnership agreement, the balance of the $100,000 of gain is allocated equally between the partners. Thus the partners' capital accounts are as follows:

	A	B
Years 1-3	($27,000)	($3,000)
Min. Gain Chargeback	$27,000	$3,000
Other Gain	$50,000	$50,000
Balance	$50,000	$50,000

If the partnership were to now liquidate, it would be required to distribute $50,000 to each partner.[113]

If there is a reduction in partnership minimum gain that does not result from the sale of the underlying asset, as mentioned above, other items of income and gain must be allocated pro rata to the partners. In a general partnership, this may have no net effect since the partners will be allocated offsetting expenses. But in a limited partnership where the limited partners do not have a deficit restoration obligation, there could well be an adverse tax consequence. Likely, the limited partners would be allocated income sufficient to offset the minimum gain reduction, without perhaps receiving cash to pay the tax on that income. Any remaining income and expenses would be allocated to the general partner assuming, as would commonly be the case in this context, the general partner has an unlimited deficit

---

[112] Treas. Reg. § 1.704-2(g)(1).

[113] We kept this problem simple for pedagogical purposes, but when nonrecourse debt is used, the way the flip happens must be fine-tuned. In our Example 2, a distortion could have resulted if the flip occurred before the sale and minimum gain chargeback. The minimum gain chargeback would have had to flow mostly to A as he received most of the nonrecourse deductions, which would have been inconsistent with the overall economic structure had the flip already taken place. Generally, nonrecourse deductions should only be able to be offset by the minimum gain chargeback and should be "pulled out" of the general flip arrangement. See PARTNERSHIP TAXATION at ¶ 10.05 [7][d].

restoration obligation. An LLC might be a better option in this regard than a limited partnership. As none of the members would typically have a deficit restoration obligation, there would be no basis for disproportionately preferring one partner to another.

C.   Subsequent Nonrecourse Borrowing

Of course, a partnership might take out a nonrecourse loan other than for the purchase of a property. If the venture goes well and the property increases in value, the partnership might choose to borrow additional funds on a nonrecourse basis. If the funds are invested in the property, creating additional basis, the rules we discussed above would govern the tax consequences. But what if the funds create additional minimum gain but are invested in an unrelated project or distributed to the partners? The Regulations provide the additional guidance that is needed in this regard.

Recall that nonrecourse deductions generally equal the net increase in partnership minimum gain. The amount of partnership minimum gain is computed by taking all partnership nonrecourse debt into account, including debt arising from additional borrowings.[114] A partner's share of that minimum gain is based not only on the nonrecourse deductions allocated to that partner, but also distributions of proceeds of nonrecourse debt made to that partner.[115] Distributions would, of course, reduce a partner's capital account, potentially causing or increasing a deficit capital account. But since a partner's share of partnership minimum gain is increased for proceeds of nonrecourse debt distributed to that partner, that is normally not a problem. Recall that a partner's share of minimum gain is considered to be a deficit restoration obligation.[116] The partnership may use any reasonable method to determine whether the source of a distribution is, in fact, nonrecourse borrowing.[117]

D.   Partner Nonrecourse Deductions

As we learned in Chapter 3, when a partner or a related person has the economic risk of loss for a liability of the partnership, the liability is allocated to the partner in proportion to the extent to which the partner or the related partner bears the economic risk of loss.[118] Just as the liability is allocated among the partners that bear the economic risk of loss for the purposes of determining the partners' bases in their partnership interests under I.R.C. § 752, the deductions

---

[114] Treas. Reg. § 1.704-2(d)(1).

[115] Treas. Reg. § 1.704-2(g)(1). To avoid double counting, nonrecourse deductions equal the increase in partnership minimum gain reduced by the amount of nonrecourse debt proceeds that are distributed to the partners. Treas. Reg. § 1.704-2(c).

[116] Treas. Reg. § 1.704-2(g)(1).

[117] *See* Treas. Reg. §§ 1.704-2(h)(2), 1.704-2(h)(4), and 1.704-2(m), example (1)(vi), for rules that apply if the distribution in a given year is less than the minimum gain increase caused by the nonrecourse borrowing and how that interplays with nonrecourse deductions in this regard.

[118] Treas. Reg. § 1.752-2(a).

associated with such liabilities must be allocated to the partners that bear the economic risk of loss.

Although for purposes of I.R.C. § 752 such debt is treated as "recourse debt," for purposes of I.R.C. § 704 such debt is treated as "partner nonrecourse debt." Rules similar to the rules for allocating deductions attributable to partnership nonrecourse debt are required to be applied to partner nonrecourse debt.[119] Partner nonrecourse debt minimum gain is separately calculated from partnership minimum gain, and partner nonrecourse debt deductions are allocated to the partners according to their shares of increases in partner nonrecourse debt minimum gain. Also similar to the general rules for nonrecourse debt, if there is a reduction in a partner's share of partner nonrecourse minimum gain during a taxable year, the partnership is required to allocate to the partner that had the decrease items of income and gain equal to the amount of the decrease.

§ 5.08 GIFTED PARTNERSHIP INTERESTS

A. Introduction

As you know from your basic tax course, under the assignment of income doctrine (it really should be called the nonassignment of income doctrine), one person generally may not gift income to another. Instead, is it possible, for example, for a parent to give a partnership interest to a child and for the partnership to then allocate income attributable to the interest to the child? Under a substance over form argument you might think the answer is no, but often it is in fact yes. Congress preempted much of the area with I.R.C. § 704(e), though case law that predates the statute remains relevant in many cases.

B. Pre-I.R.C. § 704(e) Case Law

Prior to the enactment of I.R.C. § 704(e), cases addressed whether a donee of a partnership interest should be respected as a bona fide partner. In *Commissioner v. Tower*,[120] the Supreme Court concluded that the parties must have bona fide intent to create a partnership. If a party provided either "original capital" or "vital services" to the partnership, that would be indicative of an intent to become a member of the partnership. The Tax Court then held that in order for a partner to be respected as such, she must contribute either original capital or vital services.[121] The Supreme Court responded that no, that is not what it said, neither original capital nor vital services are required. The fact that participants are family members is not fatal, though it may justify further inquiry.[122] The real question is "whether, considering all the facts — the agreement, the conduct of the parties in execution of its provisions, their statements, the testimony of disinterested

---

[119] Treas. Reg. § 1.704-2(i).

[120] 327 U.S. 280 (1946).

[121] Culbertson v. Commissioner, T.C.M. (RIA) ¶ 47,168 (1947), *rev'd*, 168 F.2d 979 (5th Cir. 1948), *rev'd*, 337 U.S. 733 (1949); *see also* Monroe v. Commissioner, 7 T.C. 278 (1946).

[122] Commissioner v. Culbertson, 337 U.S. 733 (1949).

persons, the relationship of the parties, their respective abilities and capital contributions, the actual control of income and the purposes for which it is used, and any other facts throwing light on their true intent — the parties in good faith and acting with a business purpose intended to join together in the present conduct of the enterprise."[123]

C.   I.R.C. § 704(e)

Congress ultimately stepped in and enacted I.R.C. § 704(e). It provides that a person shall be recognized as a partner if she owns a capital interest in a partnership in which capital is a material income-producing factor, whether or not such interest was derived by purchase or gift from any other person.[124] Accordingly, I.R.C. § 704(e) trumps the assignment of income doctrine, at least as it was interpreted in the partnership context in early case law. Income may be allocated to a donee partner in a partnership in which capital is a material income-producing factor even if the partner contributed nothing to the partnership.

While I.R.C. § 704(e) is titled "Family partnerships," it is not, by its terms, limited to family partnerships, or limited to partnership interests acquired by gift. The title of a statute "cannot limit the plain meaning of the text."[125] I.R.C. § 704(e) has been applied in nonfamily contexts to partnership interests acquired in exchange for contributions; in one case it permitted a taxpayer to "win" (albeit temporarily) a case that it had previously lost on appeal.[126]

When is capital a material income-producing factor? While this can sometimes be difficult to ascertain, usually it is not, and generally means what you would expect. For example, a partnership that derives its income mainly from an apartment building will meet the test. A partnership that derives its income from the performance of services (e.g., a partnership of accountants or lawyers) will not. Note that when capital is not a material income-producing factor, I.R.C. § 704(e) does not apply, and we must rely on the *Tower/Culbertson* line of cases in determining whether a person's partnership status is to be respected.

There are other ways to game the system. One would be to underpay the donor partner for services she renders to the partnership. In response, I.R.C. § 704(e)(2) requires that the partnership pay the donor partner reasonable compensation for her services. It also effectively requires that the rate of return on the donee's capital not exceed the rate of return on the donor's capital.

I.R.C. § 704(e)(1) and (2) can apply even if one family member acquires the partnership interest from another family member by purchase. I.R.C. 704(e)(3) provides that under these circumstances the transferred partnership interest shall be considered to be gifted from the seller, "and the fair market value of the purchased interest shall be considered to be the donated capital." Thus, the

---

[123] *Id.* at 742.

[124] I.R.C. § 704(e)(1).

[125] Pennsylvania Department of Corrections v. Yeskey, 524 U.S. 206 (1998).

[126] *See* TIFD III-E Inc. v. United States, 660 F. Supp. 2d 367 (D. Conn. 2009), *rev'd* 666 F.3d 836 (2d. Cir. 2012).

assignment of income principles can potentially even apply to the purchase by one family member of another family member's partnership interest, unless capital is an income-producing factor. While I.R.C. § 704(e)(3) seems to provide an irrebuttable rule, the Regulations in fact provide exceptions.[127]

I.R.C. § 704(e) does not apply in the context of a services partnership in respect of which capital is not a material income-producing factor. For such partnerships, the early assignment of income cases are still relevant.

§ 5.09   CHANGES IN PARTNERSHIP INTERESTS DURING THE TAX YEAR

A.   General Rules

The interest that a partner has in the partnership is not locked in stone. A partner's percentage interest in the partnership can vary during a tax year if part of his or another partner's interest is sold or redeemed, if he or another partner contributes new capital to the partnership, or if new partners enter the partnership. The starting point is I.R.C. § 706(c)(2). It provides that the taxable year of a partnership closes with respect to a partner whose entire interest in the partnership terminates, whether it be by sale, death, or liquidation.[128] If, on the other hand, a partner disposes of part, but not all, of his interest in the partnership, whether by sale, entry of a new partner, redemption, gift, or otherwise, the partnership tax year does not close.

I.R.C. § 706(d)(1) provides that if a partner's interest changes during the tax year, each partner's distributive share of partnership income or loss is determined by taking into account the partners' varying interests in the partnership during the year. Of course, as you now know, I.R.C. § 704(b) permits the partnership to make allocations other than based on strict partnership ownership percentages. But what I.R.C. § 706(d) does not permit, and in this regard it trumps I.R.C. § 704(b), is for the partnership to make a retroactive allocation to a partner of deductions and losses that the partnership incurred prior to that person becoming a partner.[129]

The partnership has two options for allocating partnership items when the partners' interests change during the year: It can do an "interim closing of the books" or it can prorate the partnership items to the partners based on their varying interests in the partnership during the year.[130] For example, assume in the equal AB partnership, B sells half of his interest (one-quarter interest in the partnership) to C on October 1, so that after that date A has a one-half interest,

---

[127] *See* Treas. Reg. § 1.704-1(e)(4)(ii).

[128] I.R.C. § 706(c)(2)(A).

[129] *See* Staff of the Joint Committee on Taxation, *General Explanation of Tax Reform Act of 1976*, 94th Cong., 2d Sess. 91–94 (1976).

[130] *See* Treas. Reg. § 1.706-1(c)(2)(ii).

and B and C each have a one-quarter interest.[131] If the interim closing of the books method is used, the partnership would calculate what its income and expenses were for the first three-quarters of the year and allocate half of those amounts each to A and B. It would make the same calculation for the final quarter and allocate one-half to A and one-quarter each to B and C.

Closing the books in this fashion and determining exactly what was incurred when can be challenging. Accordingly, the partnership has the option of allocating items to the partners on a pro rata basis.[132] The pro rata method is based on the period of time a partner held a particular percentage interest in the partnership, without regard to when a partnership item was actually incurred. Continuing with the above example, under the pro rata method, A would be allocated half of all partnership items for the year. B would be allocated $1/2 \times 9/12$[133] of partnership items with respect to the portion of the year he was a one-half partner and $1/4 \times 3/12$ of partnership items with respect to the portion of the year he was a one-quarter partner. Finally, C would be allocated $1/4 \times 3/12$ of partnership items with respect to the portion of the year he was a partner.

Cash method partnerships could take advantage of the rules as discussed to this point. Assume in the above example that when C became a partner, the partnership is cash basis and has a $60,000 expense that it has incurred, but not paid. Under the pro rata method, C's share of that loss would be $1/4 \times 1/4 \times \$60,000$, or $7,500. If, however, the cash-method partnership used the interim closing of the books method, then paid the expense after C became a partner, C would be entitled to a full one-quarter share or $15,000, double what the result would be if the pro rata method were used.[134]

I.R.C. § 706(d)(2)(a) for the most part has stopped this ploy. Cash-method partnerships must now allocate listed "cash basis items" to the time during the taxable year to which these items are attributable, regardless of whether the partnership uses the interim closing of the books method or the pro rata method. The listed items are treated, therefore, as if the partnership were on the accrual method of accounting. The allocable cash basis items are interest, taxes, payments for services or for the use of property, and any other item specified in the Regulations (though to date the Regulations have not specified any). Thus, in the above example, if the $60,000 loss were for services and was attributable to a time before C became a partner, C could be allocated none of it. It would have to be allocated entirely to A and B. If, on the other hand, the $60,000 loss was not an allocable cash basis item (a judgment against the partnership, for example), it should still be possible to close the books and allocate an extra portion to C.

---

[131] *See* Partnership Taxation at ¶ 9.06[7]; this assumes the partnership is on a calendar year, as would typically be the case.

[132] Treas. Reg. § 1.706-1(c)(2)(ii).

[133] *i.e.*, 9 months divided by 12 months.

[134] The partnership successfully used this technique in *Richardson v. Commissioner*, 76 T.C. 512 (1981), *aff'd on other issues*, 693 F.2d 1189 (5th Cir. 1982).

B.   Additional Details/Proposed Regulations

Treas. Reg. § 1.706-1(c)(2)(ii) provides that, under the proration method, the partnership's income and losses may be prorated based on the portion of the taxable year that has elapsed prior to the date upon which the partners' interests varied, or "under any other method that is reasonable." These other reasonable methods have become known as conventions.

The IRS issued a news release[135] announcing that partnerships using the interim closing method were permitted to use a semi-monthly convention. Under a semi-monthly convention, partners entering during the first 15 days of the month are treated as entering on the first day of the month, and partners entering after the 15th day of the month (but before the end of the month) are treated as entering on the 16th day of the month (except to the extent that I.R.C. § 706(c)(2)(A) applied). The news release provided that, until Regulations were issued, partnerships that use the proration method were required to use a daily convention.

Proposed Regulations (the "706 Proposed Regulations")[136] have been issued that update and change the manner in which partnerships account for changes in interests of partners during the partnership taxable year. The 706 Proposed Regulations add a rule that for each partnership taxable year in which a partner's interest varies, the partnership must use the same method to take into account all changes in partnership interests occurring within that year (the "Consistency Rule").

Prop. Treas. Reg. 1.706-4(d) provides that by agreement among the partners, a partnership may use a proration method, rather than the interim closing of the books method, to take into account any variation in a partner's interest in the partnership during the taxable year. Under the proration method, except for extraordinary items,[137] the partnership allocates the distributive share of partnership items under I.R.C. § 702(a) among the partners in accordance with their pro rata shares of these same items for the entire taxable year. In determining a partner's pro rata share of partnership items, the partnership is required to take into account that partner's interest in such items during each segment of the taxable year.

In addition, Prop. Treas. Reg. § 1.706-4(d)(3) requires a partnership using the proration method to allocate extraordinary items among the partners in proportion to their interests at the beginning of the day on which they are taken into account. For this purpose, an extraordinary item is: (i) any item from the disposition or abandonment (other than in the ordinary course of business) of a capital asset as defined in I.R.C. § 1221 (determined without the application of any other rules of law); (ii) any item from the disposition or abandonment of property used in a trade or business (other than in the ordinary course of business) as defined in I.R.C. § 1231(b) (determined without the application of any holding period requirement);

---

[135] News Release 84–129 (Dec. 13, 1984).

[136] Prop. Treas. Reg. § 1.706-4.

[137] Defined in Prop. Treas. Reg. § 1.706-4(d)(3).

(iii) any item from the disposition or abandonment of an asset described in I.R.C. § 1221(1), (3), (4), or (5), if substantially all the assets in the same category from the same trade or business are disposed of or abandoned in one transaction (or series of related transactions); (iv) any item from assets disposed of in an applicable asset acquisition under I.R.C. § 1060(c); (v) any I.R.C. § 481(a) adjustment; (vi) any item from the discharge or retirement of indebtedness (for example, if a debtor partnership transfers a capital or profits interest in such partnership to a creditor in satisfaction of its recourse or nonrecourse indebtedness, any discharge of indebtedness income recognized under I.R.C. § 108(e)(8) must be allocated among the persons who were partners in the partnership immediately before the discharge); (vii) any item from the settlement of a tort or similar third-party liability; (viii) any credit, to the extent it arises from activities or items that are not ratably allocated (for example, the rehabilitation credit under I.R.C. § 47, which is based on placement in service); and (ix) any item which, in the opinion of the IRS, would, if ratably allocated, result in a substantial distortion of income in any consolidated return or separate return in which the item is included.

§ 5.10 READING, QUESTIONS AND PROBLEMS

A. I.R.C. § 704(b)

READING

CODE:

I.R.C. § 704(b).

TREASURY REGULATIONS:

Treas. Reg. §§ 1.704-1(b)(1)(i), (iii), (iv), -1(b)(2)(i)–(iii), (iv)(a)–(e), (h), (n), (p), (q), -1(b)(3), -1(b)(5), examples 1, 2, 3, 4, 5, 6, 7, 8, 15(i), 1.1245-1(e).

CASES:

TIFD III-E Inc. v. United States, 342 F. Supp. 2d 94 (D. Conn. 2004), *rev'd*, 459 F.3d 220 (2d Cir. 2006); *on remand*, 660 F. Supp. 2d 367 (D. Conn. 2009), *rev'd*, 666 F.3d 836 (2d Cir. 2012). Read all four cases.

RULINGS:

Rev. Rul. 97-38, 1997-2 C.B. 69.

Rev. Rul. 99-43, 1999-2 C.B. 506.

QUESTIONS AND PROBLEMS

1. A and B form a partnership on January 1 of Year 1. Each makes a cash contribution to the partnership of $80,000. The partnership purchases depreciable equipment for $160,000. The partnership agreement provides that all income and loss are allocated equally, except that all depreciation deductions are allocated to A.

Assume (Code provisions to the contrary notwithstanding) that the equipment generates depreciation deductions of $40,000 per year and that in all years the partnership breaks even except for depreciation deductions, and so incurs a loss each year of $40,000.

a. Generally describe what provisions the partnership agreement will have to contain in order for the allocations to A to be respected.

b. Assuming the partnership agreement contains all such provisions, compute capital accounts for A and B on formation and at the end of the first three years of partnership operations.

c. How would your answers to "a" and "b" change if A does not have a deficit restoration obligation?

d. Assume the same facts as in "c" except that in Year 2 it is reasonably expected that in Year 3 the partnership's equipment will appreciate in value by $20,000, and the partnership will borrow $20,000 against the equipment and distribute $10,000 to each partner in Year 3. How will your answer change? Would it make a difference if A had a *limited* deficit restoration obligation of $20,000?

e. Assume in "b" of the problem that the equipment is sold on January 1 of Year 3 for $180,000. State how the gain should be allocated and compute the partners' capital accounts immediately before the liquidation of the partnership. Does the gain allocation make sense? Do you have any alternative suggestions for how the gain might be allocated?

2. A and B form a partnership to drill for oil and gas. A contributes $10,000 and agrees to devote himself to the activities of the partnership on a full-time basis. B contributes $190,000 and promises to spend all of his time lounging by the pool. The partnership agreement provides that B shall be allocated 95%, and A 5% of partnership taxable income and loss until B has received allocations of taxable income equal to the sum of the prior allocations of taxable losses. Thereafter, A and B will share all taxable income and losses equally. Operating cash flow will be distributed equally between A and B. The partnership agreement provides that capital accounts will be maintained in accordance with the Regulations, and liquidating distributions will be made in accordance with capital account balances. The partnership agreement also gives both A and B an unlimited deficit restoration obligation. Address the tax consequences. Would your answer change if the partnership's only activity was to make a "triple-net" lease of property to a Fortune 500 corporation?

3. A and B are equal partners in AB partnership. The partnership agreement provides that capital accounts will be maintained in accordance with the Regulations and liquidating distributions will be made in accordance with capital account balances. The partnership agreement also gives both A and B an unlimited deficit restoration obligation. Generally, A and B are in the same marginal tax bracket. All income and losses are allocated equally to A and B. A has a net operating loss from another venture that will expire in the partnership's second tax year. The partnership agreement is amended at the beginning of the second tax year to provide that all of the partnership's net taxable income will be allocated to A for that

year. Thereafter, net taxable income for that year is to be allocated to B until B's allocation equals the allocation in the second tax year to A, after which the partnership will revert to 50-50 allocations. Describe the tax consequences.

4. A and B form the AB partnership to operate an international business. They make equal contributions to the partnership. The income of the business, as well as the sources of that income, is uncertain. The partnership agreement provides that capital accounts will be maintained in accordance with the Regulations and liquidating distributions will be made in accordance with capital account balances. The partnership agreement also gives both A and B an unlimited deficit restoration obligation. A is a U.S. citizen and B is a citizen and full-time resident of Germany, meaning that generally B is only taxable on income that is "U.S. source." The partnership conducts business in the United States and in Germany. The partnership agreement provides that B will be allocated all of the income, gain, loss, and deduction derived in Germany, and A is allocated the remaining income, gain, loss, and deduction. Describe the tax consequences. How would your answer change if the partnership agreement provided that all income, gain, loss, and deduction will be shared equally, but that B will be allocated all income, gain, loss, and deduction derived from his country in computing his equal share?

5. A and B come into your office. They have an agreement under which A will put $100,000 into a partnership with B. B will only put in services. The agreement is that A gets his money back and after that distributions are shared 80% for A and 20% for B. Describe how income and losses should be allocated.

6. Suzu, Kaneisha, and Vlad form an LLC that uses the Percentage Interest Approach. Kaneisha and Vlad put in $50 each (total $100), and Suzu contributes her services. The LLC uses the $100 to purchase non-depreciable property WhiteAcre. At the end of Year 1, WhiteAcre has an FMV of $109. The LLC has no other assets. The percentage interests agreed to by the parties are one-third each. Except in liquidation, cash flow will be distributed in accordance with percentage interests. The understanding of the parties is that they will share everything equally other than the return of Kaneisha and Vlad's capital. The LLC maintains capital accounts according to the Regulations, has a qualified income offset provision, and liquidates in accordance with capital accounts.

    a. If the LLC has $9 of net book income in Year 1, how is the income allocated?

    b. If the LLC has $9 of net book loss in Year 1, how is the loss allocated?

7. The same facts as Problem 6, except that the LLC uses the Targeted Capital Account Approach. For each of the following, please answer in respect of each of the return on and return of capital approach, the liquidation at book value approach and the liquidation at FMV approach.

    a. If the LLC has $9 of net book income in Year 1, how is the income allocated?

    b. If the LLC has $9 of net book loss in Year 1, how is the loss allocated?

8. The same facts as Problem 6, except that the LLC uses the Reverse Distribution Approach.

a. If the LLC has $9 of net book income in Year 1, how is the income allocated? If the LLC has $9 of net book loss in Year 2, how is the loss allocated?

b. If the LLC has $9 of net book loss in Year 1, how is the loss allocated? If the LLC has $9 of net book income in Year 2, how is the income allocated?

9. The same facts as Problem 6, except that the LLC uses the Cash Flow Approach.

a. If the LLC has $9 of net book income in Year 1, how is the income allocated?

b. If the LLC has $9 of net book loss in Year 1, how is the loss allocated?

10. Suzu, Kaneisha, and Vlad form an LLC that is treated as a partnership for federal income tax purposes. Kaneisha and Vlad put in $50 each (total $100), and Suzu contributes her services. The LLC uses the $100 to purchase non-depreciable property WhiteAcre. At the end of Year 1, WhiteAcre has an FMV of $109. The LLC has no other assets. The percentage interests agreed to by the parties are one-third each. Except in liquidation, cash flow will be distributed in accordance with percentage interests. On liquidation the unreturned capital is distributed first and then any remaining amounts are distributed in accordance with percentage interests. The understanding of the parties is that they will share everything equally other than the return of Kaneisha and Vlad's capital. The LLC maintains capital accounts according the Regulations, but does not include a deficit restoration provision or have a qualified income offset provision and does not liquidate in accordance with capital accounts.

a. On the first day of the LLC's taxable year, what is each of the member's interest in the partnership under:

(i) The Book-Value Liquidation Approach;

(ii) The FMV Liquidation Approach;

(iii) The Avoiding Negative Capital Account Approach;

(iv) The Overall Percentage Approach;

(v) The Interest in Net Profits Approach;

(vi) The Percentage of Assets and Percentage of Liabilities Approach;

(vii) The Income Approach; and

(viii) The Capital Account Impact Approach.

b. Are any of your answers different on the last day of the first taxable year?

11. How does the analysis in Problem 10 change if the LLC liquidates in accordance with capital accounts?

12. Do the members in Problem 10 have the same PIP in losses as they do in income? Does your answer change if the LLC liquidates in accordance with capital accounts?

13. Jarell, Loman, and Asha form a hedge fund as a Cayman Islands company that elects to be treated as a partnership for U.S. federal income tax purposes. Jarell and Loman each put in $50 making a total of $100 of initial assets. Asha is the fund manager and holds a profits interest which entitles her to share in 20% of the profits (both income and capital appreciation) in excess of the amount necessary to provide Jarell and Loman a 10% annual return on their investments. Annual distributions are made first to the 10% preference return, then split 20/40/40. Distributions in liquidation are paid first to Jarell and Loman to the extent of their unpaid preference and their unreturned capital contributions and then split 20/40/40. The hedge fund adjusts the capital accounts monthly to Asha's estimate of the fair market value of the assets.

For the first year of operations, the fund has the following results:

Month	Net Asset Value
January	100
February	101
March	102
April	101
May	104
June	105
July	106
August	105
September	107
October	109
November	111
December	112

a. With these facts, should PIP be determined monthly or annually? What facts might influence the answer?

b. On the last day of the LLC's taxable year (assuming for the purposes of this question PIP is determined for the entire year), what is each of the member's interest in the partnership under:

(i)   The Book-Value Liquidation Approach;

(ii)   The FMV Liquidation Approach;

(iii)   The Avoiding Negative Capital Account Approach;

(iv)   The Overall Percentage Approach;

(v)   The Interest in Net Profits Approach;

(vi)   The Percentage of Assets and Percentage of Liabilities Approach;

(vii)   The Income Approach; and

(viii)   The Capital Account Impact Approach.

c. Do the members have the same PIP in losses as they do in income? Does your answer change if PIP is determined on a monthly basis?

B.   I.R.C. § 704(c)

READING

CODE:

I.R.C. §§ 704(a), (c)(1)(A), (3), 724.

TREASURY REGULATIONS:

Treas. Reg. §§ 1.704-3(a)(1)–(5), (10), (b), (c), (d), (e)(1), 1.704-1(b)(1)(vi), -1(b)(2)(iv)(d)(1), (3), 1.7041(b)(2)(iv)(f), 1.704-1(b)(4)(i), -1(b)(5), examples 14(i)–(iv).

QUESTIONS AND PROBLEMS

14. A and B form the equal AB partnership. A contributes cash of $20,000. B contributes land with a basis of $9,000 and a fair market value of $20,000. The land is a capital asset to B and has been held for over one year. Describe the tax consequences under each of the three I.R.C. § 704(c) allocation methods if the partnership sells the land for either $21,000 or $19,000, assuming the partnership has adequate other income and deductions, if necessary.

15. A and B form the equal AB partnership on January 1 of Year 1. A contributes depreciable equipment with a tax basis of $6,000 and a fair market value of $20,000. B contributes cash of $20,000. Assume A's equipment is depreciated at the rate of 20% per year for book and tax purposes. Further assume that A's property generates $2,000 of net operating income each year. Calculate A and B's capital accounts for the first year of operations using the traditional method and the traditional method with curative allocations.

16. A and B form the equal AB partnership on January 1 of Year 1. A contributes equipment with a tax basis of $8,000 and a fair market value of $20,000. The equipment has been on a 10-year recovery period and has four years remaining. (Were the equipment newly acquired at the time of the contribution to the partnership, the recovery period would again be 10 years.) B contributes $20,000 which the partnership uses to buy land. The partnership's income equals expenses except for depreciation deductions. Assuming the partnership uses the remedial allocation method, describe how depreciation deductions will be allocated to A and B from the equipment. Ignore any applicable first year depreciation conventions. *See* Treas. Reg. § 1.704-3(d)(7), example 1.

C.   Nonrecourse Deductions

READING

TREASURY REGULATIONS:

Treas. Reg. § 1.704-2(b), (c), (d), (e), (f)(1)–(3), (6), (7), example 1, (g), (h), (i), (j), (m), examples 1(i)–(iv), (vi), (vii), (viii), 3(i).

QUESTIONS AND PROBLEMS

17. A and B form a limited partnership. A is a limited partner and B is the general partner. A contributes $360 and B contributes $40 to the partnership. The partnership agreement contains a minimum gain chargeback provision and complies with the qualified income offset rules of the I.R.C. § 704(b) Regulations. Neither partner has a deficit restoration obligation. The partnership agreement further provides that all losses will be allocated 90% to A and 10% to B and that all income will be allocated in the same manner until income allocations equal previous loss allocations. Thereafter income and losses will be allocated 50% to A and 50% to B. The partnership borrows $1,600 from an unrelated commercial lender on a nonrecourse basis and purchases depreciable real estate on leased land for $2,000. Only interest on the loan is due for the first five years that the debt is outstanding. The partnership breaks even in its first three years of operation except for depreciation deductions of $400 per year, and thus generates a loss each of its first three years of $400 (the depreciation rules in real life do not permit this rapid of a depreciation rate — we are ignoring the real world to make the problem more manageable; we are also ignoring first-year conventions).

a. Assume that on January 1 of Year 4, the partnership sells the property for $2,400. Assume that aside from this sale, the partnership breaks even on operations in Year 4. For Years 1–4, provide the partners' capital accounts and shares of minimum gain.

b. How would your answer change if instead of selling the property on January 1 of Year 4, the partnership borrows an additional $500 on a nonrecourse basis, securing it with a second mortgage on the property, and distributes the proceeds equally to A and B. For purposes of this question, assume the partnership breaks even in Year 4 except for depreciation deductions.

D. Family Allocations

READING

CODE:

I.R.C. § 704(e).

TREASURY REGULATIONS:

Treas. Reg. § 1.704-1(e).

CASES:

Commissioner v. Tower, 327 U.S. 280 (1946).

Commissioner v. Culbertson, 337 U.S. 733 (1949).

QUESTIONS AND PROBLEMS

18. Mother owns an apartment building that generates significant rental income. She gifts a 50% interest in the apartment building to Daughter, and they form a partnership. Mother manages the building and Daughter provides no services. The partnership agreement provides that each partner has a 50% interest in all items of income and deduction and each partner is entitled to 50% of any cash distributed and 50% of all liquidating distributions. Ignore gift tax considerations.

a. Describe the income tax consequences.

b. How would your answer in "a" change if Mother provides no services but receives 40% of all items of income and deduction, but 50% of any distributions.

E. Changes in Partnership Interests During the Tax Year

READING

CODE:

I.R.C. § 704(c)(2)(b), (d).

TREASURY REGULATIONS:

Treas. Reg. § 1.706-1(c)(1), (2), (4).

CASE:

Richardson v. Commissioner, 76 T.C. 512 (1981), *aff'd on other issues*, 693 F.2d 1189 (5th Cir. 1982).

QUESTIONS AND PROBLEMS

19. A and B are equal partners in the AB partnership. The partnership is on the calendar year and is in the construction business. As of July 1 of Year 1, the partnership has an unpaid $50,000 bill owed to a consulting company. To cover the loss and put the partnership on sounder financial footing, the partnership agrees to admit C as a partner on July 1 in exchange for a $50,000 contribution. Upon C's admission, A, B, and C each own a 33–1/3% interest in the partnership. Assume the partnership otherwise breaks even for the year and thus has a $50,000 loss for the year. It uses C's contribution to pay the loss generating a current deduction of $50,000. How will the $50,000 deduction be allocated among the partners if the partnership uses the "proration method" or alternatively "the closing of the books method?" Would your answer change if C's funds were used to pay a judgment against the partnership resulting from a car accident?

Chapter 6

DISPOSITIONS OF PARTNERSHIP INTERESTS

§ 6.01 INTRODUCTION

Chapter 6 will consider the issues relating to the sale by a partner of all or a portion of the partner's partnership interest. This will include consideration of the amount realized upon the sale, the partner's basis for the partner's partnership interest, particularly in situations in which a partner sells less than all of the partner's partnership interest, the partner's holding period for the partnership interest sold, the character of the gain or loss recognized (including the collapsible partnership rules relating to unrealized receivables and appreciated inventory), dispositions which do not qualify as sales or exchanges, and the special election which may be made by a partnership in the case of a purchase of a partnership interest. There will also be considered the termination of partnership rules which come into play in the case of certain sales or exchanges of partnership interest and the manner in which the income or loss of the partnership must be allocated as between the transferor and the transferee in the year of the sale.

§ 6.02 RECOGNITION OF GAIN OR LOSS

I.R.C. § 741 provides that in the case of a sale or exchange of a partnership interest, gain is recognized by the transferring partner. As in the case of all sales or exchanges, in order to be able to compute the gain or loss recognized by the transferring partner, it is necessary to know the amount realized and the partner's basis for the partnership interest transferred.[1]

A. Amount Realized

I.R.C. § 1001(b) provides the general rule that the amount realized from the sale or other disposition of property is equal to the sum of any money received plus the fair market value of any property other than money received. This general rule is applicable in the case of a sale of a partnership interest. If a partnership has no liabilities, then there are no unique issues with respect to the amount realized. Where, however, the partnership has liabilities, the provisions of I.R.C. § 752(d) must be taken into account.

As indicated in § 3.04.A, a partner is permitted to increase the basis of his partnership interest by his share of the liabilities of the partnership. If the liabilities of the partnership were not taken into account upon the sale by a partner

---

[1] I.R.C. § 1001(a).

of a partnership interest, the increase in the partner's basis for her partnership interest resulting from including her share of partnership liabilities in basis would artificially reduce the amount of gain, or increase the amount of loss, recognized by the partner upon the sale of the partnership interest. At § 3.03.G there is a discussion of the effect that the liabilities of the partnership have on the amount realized by a partner upon the sale of his partnership interest. As indicated therein, by virtue of I.R.C. § 752(d), the partner's share of the partnership's liabilities of which the partner is deemed relieved is treated as an amount realized from the sale or exchange of her partnership interest.

Where a partner disposes of the partner's entire partnership interest, the amount of the partnership's liabilities which the transferor is deemed relieved is simply the partner's share of the partnership's liabilities immediately prior to the disposition. Where, however, only a portion of a partner's partnership interest is disposed of, it is necessary to determine the extent to which there has been a decrease in the partner's share of the partnership's liabilities using all of the rules discussed in §§ 3.04.C and D.

It is possible that in certain circumstances there may not be any decrease in a partner's share of the partnership's liabilities by reason of the disposition of a portion of a partnership interest. For example, in the case of a limited partnership, if all of the partnership's liabilities were recourse liabilities and the general partner was both a general partner and a limited partner and sold a portion of her limited partner interest, by virtue of her still being the general partner of the partnership, there may be no reduction in her share of partnership liabilities. In such case, the amount realized would only be the cash and fair market value of property received by the selling partner. Another situation where this can occur is if a partner has guaranteed the indebtedness of the partnership or where the partner or related party was the lender to the partnership.

B. Basis

Where a partner disposes of his entire interest in the partnership, the partner's entire basis is used to determine whether the taxpayer has recognized a gain or loss. Where a partner disposes of only a portion of her partnership interest, however, more difficult rules come into play. The IRS has held that a partner has a single basis for a partnership interest, even if the partner is both a general partner and a limited partner.[2] Presumably, this rule would also apply if a partner had different classes of partnership interests (e.g., Class A Units and Class B Units, or Common Interests and Preferred Interests).

Treas. Reg. § 1.61-6(a) provides that when a taxpayer sells a part of a larger property, the basis of the entire property is apportioned among the several parts. Consistent with that Regulation, Rev. Rul. 84-53 provides that when a partner disposes of a portion of a partnership interest, the basis of the transferred portion is generally equal to the amount which bears the same relationship to the partner's basis in the partnership as the fair market value of the transferred portion bears to the entire fair market value of the interest. Where a partner's basis includes the

---

[2] Rev. Rul. 84-53, 1984-1 C.B. 159.

partner's share of partnership liabilities, however, additional rules come into play. If the partner's share of all of the partnership's liabilities does not exceed the partner's adjusted basis for his partnership interest, the liabilities included in basis are subtracted and the remaining basis is allocated to the transferred portion in the manner set forth above. There is then added to that amount the share of the partnership's liabilities which the partner is deemed relieved under I.R.C. § 752(d). If, on the other hand, the partner's share of the partnership's liabilities exceeds the partner's basis for her partnership interest, then the basis applicable to the portion sold is equal to the partner's adjusted basis for her partnership interest multiplied by a fraction, a numerator of which is the amount of the partnership's liabilities which the partner is deemed relieved under I.R.C. § 752(d), and the denominator of which is the partner's share of all the partnership's liabilities. Rev. Rul. 84-53 contains four situations in which it illustrates the rules set forth above. It should be noted that if a partner only owned a single class of interests, it is not necessary to determine the fair market value of the interest sold and the entire interest, but rather the percentage of the entire interest sold may be used.

§ 6.03   CHARACTER OF GAIN OR LOSS

A.   General Rule

I.R.C. § 741 provides that upon a sale or exchange of a partnership interest, the gain or loss is treated as gain or loss from the sale or exchange of a capital asset, except as otherwise provided in I.R.C. § 751. Thus, assuming that a disposition of a partnership interest constitutes a sale or exchange, the gain or loss recognized will be capital gain or capital loss.

B.   Unrealized Receivables and Inventory Items

1.   Ordinary Income Recognition

I.R.C. § 751(a) provides that the amount received by a partner upon a disposition of all or portion of a partnership interest which is attributable to: (i) unrealized receivables of the partnership, or (ii) inventory items of the partnership, is treated as an amount realized from the sale or exchange of property other than a capital asset. Thus, amounts so treated will result in ordinary income or ordinary loss (and almost always ordinary income).

I.R.C. § 741 generally may be thought of as an entity approach to partnerships, whereas I.R.C. § 751(a) may be thought of as the aggregate approach, but only to the extent that the partnership has unrealized receivables or inventory items. The key, therefore, is determining whether an item is an unrealized receivable or an inventory item.

2.   Unrealized Receivables

I.R.C. § 751(c) provides that the term "unrealized receivables" "includes, to the extent not previously includible in income under the method of accounting used by the partnership, any rights (contractual or otherwise) to payment for: (1) goods delivered, or to be delivered, to the extent the proceeds therefrom would be treated as amounts received from the sale or exchange of property other than a capital asset, or (2) services rendered, or to be rendered." In addition, however, I.R.C. § 751(c) also includes for purposes of I.R.C. § 741, (i) mining property (as defined in I.R.C. § 617(f)(2)), (ii) stock in a DISC, (iii) section 1245 property, (iv) stock in certain foreign corporations, (v) section 1250 property, (vi) farm land described in I.R.C. § 1252(a), (vii) franchises, trademarks, or tradenames, and (viii) oil, gas, or geothermal property, but only to the extent of the amount that would be treated as ordinary income under I.R.C. §§ 617(d)(1), 995(c), 1245(a), 1248(a), 1250(a), 1252(a), 1253(a), or 1254(a) if the property had been sold for its fair market value.

The first category of unrealized receivables, goods delivered or to be delivered, generally applies to the sale of inventory or property held for sale in the ordinary course of business where the cash method is used. Because taxpayers having inventory will generally be required to use the accrual method, most accounts receivable will not qualify as unrealized receivables. If the partnership holds an installment obligation from the sale of depreciable property or real property used in a trade or business held for less than one year, such installment obligation will be an unrealized receivable because the property will not meet the definition of property used in a trade or business for purposes of I.R.C. § 1231(b).

The services rendered, or to be rendered, portion of the definition of an unrealized receivable principally has applicability to cash method service businesses. The cases, however, have given this provision wider applicability. Thus, contracts to manage a business,[3] and exclusive distribution agreements[4] have been held to be unrealized receivables in situations in which the contracts were not cancelable by the party for whom the services will be rendered. Where the contracts are terminable by the party for whom the services are to be rendered, the issue is less clear.

The third type of unrealized receivables, which are basically those properties upon whose sale ordinary income would be recognized under specific recapture provisions of the Code, are designed to put the selling partner in the same place the selling partner would be if the partner had directly sold the assets of the partnership.

3. Inventory Items

I.R.C. § 751(d) defines the term "inventory items" to mean: (i) property described in I.R.C. § 1221(a)(1), (ii) any other property the sale or exchange of which would be considered property other than a capital asset or property described in I.R.C. § 1231, and (iii) any other property which if held by the selling partner would be considered property of the type described in (i) or (ii) above. In many instances, it would appear that the definition of inventory items includes items which are also unrealized receivables. For example, most of the recapture-type items which are part of the definition of unrealized receivables would also fall within

---

[3] United States v. Woolsey, 326 F.2d 287 (5th Cir. 1963); Ledoux v. Commissioner, 77 T.C. 293 (1981), aff'd per curiam, 695 F.2d 1320 (11th Cir. 1983).

[4] Roth v. Commissioner, 321 F.2d 607 (9th Cir. 1963).

the class of property described in clause (ii) above.

Clause (iii) above significantly broadens the scope of the term inventory item. It is likely most applicable to situations in which the partnership is not a dealer with respect to its property, but a partner might be a dealer with respect to such property.

§ 6.04 HOLDING PERIOD

Assuming that some portion of the gain or loss recognized upon the sale or exchange of a partnership interest is treated as a gain or loss from a sale of a capital asset, it is then necessary to determine whether the gain or loss is a long-term gain or loss or a short-term gain or loss. I.R.C. § 1222, in effect, provides that a gain or loss from the sale or exchange of a capital asset is a short-term capital gain or loss if the asset has not been held for more than one year, whereas it is a long-term capital gain or loss if the asset has been held for more than one year. This general rule is applicable to sales or exchanges of partnership interests.

As indicated in § 6.02.B, the IRS has taken the position that a partner has a single basis for the partner's partnership interest. Notwithstanding this rule, Treas. Reg. § 1.1223-3(a) provides that a partner will have a divided holding period if: (i) the partner acquired portions of the partnership interest at different times or (ii) the partner contributed property at the same time, but the nature of the property contributed results in different holding. These rules are discussed in detail in § 2.07. Thus, it is possible that a sale of a partnership interest will result in both long-term capital gain or loss and short-term capital gain or loss.

§ 6.05 INSTALLMENT SALES

A partnership interest is personal property which may be sold on the installment method provided for in I.R.C. § 453(a).[5] I.R.C. § 453(b)(1) defines the term "installment sale" to mean a disposition of property where at least one payment is to be received after the close of the taxable year in which the disposition occurs.

I.R.C. § 453(b)(2) prohibits the installment reporting of sales of inventory or property held for sale in the ordinary course of business. While it is clear that I.R.C. § 751(a) would treat the gain from the sale of a partnership interest attributable to such items as ordinary income, there is still the question of whether a partner may report gain from the sale of a partnership interest on the installment method where the assets of the partnership consist, in whole or in part, of inventory or property held for sale in the ordinary course of business. The IRS has stated its position that there cannot be an installment sale of a partnership interest with respect to that portion of the gain which would be treated as ordinary income because inventory items were involved.[6]

---

[5] Rev. Rul. 76-483, 1976-2 C.B. 131.

[6] Rev. Rul. 89-108, 1989-2 C.B. 100.

Although the gain from the sale of property may be reported on the installment method, the "recapture income" must be reported in the year of the disposition.[7] The term "recapture income" means the amount that would be treated as ordinary income under I.R.C. § 1245 or 1250 if all payments to be received on the installment obligation were received in the taxable year of disposition, and I.R.C. § 453(i) specifically indicates that this applies with respect to I.R.C. § 751 as it relates to I.R.C. §§ 1245 and 1250. Thus, if a partner makes an installment sale of a partnership interest and had the partnership sold its assets for their fair market value there would have been depreciation recapture under I.R.C. § 1245 or 1250, that gain must be reported in the year of sale.

§ 6.06 DISPOSITIONS OTHER THAN SALES OR EXCHANGES

A. Gifts and Charitable Contributions

As indicated above, I.R.C. § 752(d), by its terms, is only applicable to a sale or exchange of a partnership interest. There is a question, therefore, as to whether I.R.C. § 752(d) is applicable to a disposition of a partnership interest which does not constitute a sale or exchange, such as gifts and charitable contributions. The IRS takes the position that I.R.C. § 752(d) is applicable to these situations.[8] Since a gift or charitable contribution in which no consideration is received by the transferor is not, by itself, a sale or exchange, it is arguable that I.R.C. § 752(d) does not apply to the transaction. In such case, I.R.C. § 752(b) would apply to the transaction if there were a decrease in the donor partner's share of the partnership's liabilities. While it would make no difference in the amount of liabilities of which the donor partner would be deemed relieved whether I.R.C. § 752(d) or (b) were the operative section, the consequences of that deemed relief of liability could change depending upon which section was applicable.

As indicated above, it is clearly the IRS's position that I.R.C. § 752(d) applies to all dispositions of partnership interests whether or not they would be categorized as sales or exchanges before applicability of I.R.C. § 752(b). Given the IRS's position and the consequences flowing therefrom, it will be assumed for the balance of this Chapter 6 that such is the correct approach.

In Rev. Rul. 75-194,[9] the IRS set forth the tax consequences of a charitable contribution of a limited partner interest. In that Ruling, the partner's share of the value of the partnership's assets was greater than the partner's share of the liabilities of the partnership, but because of prior partnership losses allocated to the partner, the partner's adjusted basis for his partnership interest was less than his share of the partnership's liabilities. The Ruling holds that the partner is entitled to a charitable contribution equal to the value of the partnership interest contributed. It further held, however, that by virtue of the provisions of I.R.C.

---

[7] I.R.C. § 453(i)(1).

[8] Treas. Reg. § 1.1001-2(a)(4)(v); Treas. Reg. § 1.1001-2(c), example 4.

[9] 1975-1 C.B. 80.

§§ 752(d) and 1011(b), there was an amount realized by the contributing partner. Thus, there was a bargain sale of the partnership interest on which gain or loss was to be recognized.

Under I.R.C. § 1011(b), where a charitable deduction is allowed by reason of a bargain sale to charity, the adjusted basis for determining the gain from the sale must be apportioned between the contributed property and the sold property based upon the ratio of the amount realized to the fair market value of the property contributed. The effect of the interaction of I.R.C. §§ 752(d) and 1011(b), and the IRS's interpretation as set forth in Rev. Rul. 75-194, is illustrated in Treas. Reg. § 1.1001-2(c), example 4. In that example, the contributing partner's basis for the partnership interest being sold under I.R.C. § 1011(b) was $3,000 and the partner's share of the partnership's liabilities was $9,000, resulting in a gain realized of $6,000.

In the case of a gift, other than a charitable gift, I.R.C. § 1011(b) is not relevant. The same rules regarding the applicability of I.R.C. § 752(d), however, continue to come into play. Therefore, if a partner with a negative capital account were to make a gift of the partner's entire partnership interest, the transaction should be treated as a sale to the extent the amount deemed realized under I.R.C. § 752(d) exceeds the gifting partner's basis for the partnership interest.

In Rev. Rul. 60-352,[10] the IRS considered the effect of a gift of a partnership interest where the partnership held an installment receivable which was being reported on the installment method. Although the facts in this Ruling do not explicitly so state, it must be assumed that the partnership in question did not have any liabilities because no mention was made of I.R.C. § 752(d). In fact, the Ruling states that the partnership interest was transferred without receipt of consideration, which would be contrary to the IRS's position had there been liabilities in the partnership. The Ruling provides that the sale of a partnership interest is generally treated as the sale of a capital asset rather than as a sale of the partner's undivided interest in the assets owned by the partnership, but this does not necessarily mean that you could not look through the partnership in certain circumstances. The Ruling ultimately held that the donation of the partnership interest to the charity constitutes both a transfer of a capital asset as well as a disposition of the installment obligation under what is now I.R.C. § 453B. To the extent that the transaction is treated as a disposition of the installment obligation, the gain must be recognized by the transferring partner.

Because I.R.C. § 751(a) is only applicable when something is received by the transferor partner in exchange for all or a portion of the transferor's partnership interest, in the rare circumstance in which the partnership has no liabilities, or the transferring partner has no share of the partnership's liabilities, I.R.C. § 751(a) would not be applicable (such as in the case of a gift or charitable contribution of such partnership interest). In that unusual context, the position stated in Rev. Rul. 60-352 would be relevant. In most other circumstances, the provisions of I.R.C. § 751(a) would be applicable to the transaction, as discussed above, since the installment obligation would constitute an unrealized receivable. The amount of

---

[10] 1960-2 C.B. 208.

gain recognized, however, may be different depending upon whether you apply the reasoning of Rev. Rul. 60-352 or the provisions of I.R.C. § 751(a) in situations in which less than all of the partner's partnership interest is gifted or donated.

B. Death of a Partner

If an individual were to die owning real property encumbered by a mortgage, no deemed sale of the property would be deemed to have occurred in which gain or loss would be recognized. The same should be true upon the death of a partner owning a partnership interest, even if the partnership has liabilities and the deceased partner had a negative capital account. In this context, I.R.C. § 752(b) should not be applicable to treat the transaction as a sale or exchange.

The basis of a partnership interest acquired from a decedent is equal to the fair market value of the partnership interest on the date of death (or alternative valuation date if elected), increased by the successor's share of partnership liabilities as of the date of death, reduced to the extent that any of such value is attributable to items constituting income in respect of a decedent under I.R.C. § 691.[11] Thus, the death of a partner has the effect of eliminating permanently any gain which otherwise would be recognized by a partner having a negative capital account upon a disposition of the partnership interest.

As indicated above, Rev. Rul. 60-352 generally treats the transfer of a partnership interest as a disposition of any installment obligations held by the partnership. It would not appear that a similar rule should apply in the case of the death of a partner. As indicated above, the successor to a deceased partner's partnership interest is required to reduce the basis for the partnership interest received by the portion of the value that is attributable to items which constitute income in respect of a decedent under I.R.C. § 691. Since an installment receivable is an item which is characterized as income in respect of a decedent under I.R.C. § 691, the reduction in basis has the effect of preserving the recognition of the installment gain.

C. Exchanges of Partnership Interest

While the exchange of property held for investment or use in a trade or business for like-kind property is a tax-free transaction under I.R.C. § 1031(a)(1), it is clear that an exchange of one partnership interest for another partnership interest, even if the assets of the partnerships would meet the like-kind requirement, does not qualify under I.R.C. § 1031(a)(1).[12] Where, however, the partnership has in effect a valid election under I.R.C. § 761(a) to be excluded from the application of Subchapter K of the Code, then a partnership interest is treated as an interest in each of the assets of the partnership, and not as an interest in the partnership.[13] Thus, in such circumstances, a partnership interest may be exchanged for another partnership interest when an effective election under I.R.C. § 761(a) is in effect, or

---

[11] Treas. Reg. § 1.742-1.

[12] I.R.C. § 1031(a)(2)(D).

[13] I.R.C. § 1031(a).

property which is like-kind to the assets of the partnership whose interest is being transferred.

D. Abandonment and Worthlessness

Generally, when a taxpayer abandons property, the taxpayer is entitled to an ordinary loss in an amount equal to the tax basis for the property abandoned.[14] This is true even if the property abandoned is a capital asset. The reason this is the case is that there is no sale or exchange in the case of an abandonment or worthlessness of an asset, and in order for a capital gain or capital loss to result, there must be a sale or exchange.[15] It is then necessary to determine whether this general rule is equally applicable to partnerships.

If the abandoning partner does not have a share of the partnership's liabilities, either because the partnership has no liabilities or because the partner does not have a share of the partnership's liabilities, then the rule stated above with respect to property generally is equally applicable to partnerships.[16] Where, however, the abandoning taxpayer has a share of partnership liabilities, different rules apply.

If a partner abandons a partnership interest, or claims that her partnership interest is worthless, and the partner has a share of partnership liabilities, the act of abandonment will result in the rules of I.R.C. § 752 coming into play. The transaction can be viewed as a sale or exchange to the extent of the partner's share of liabilities (i.e., I.R.C. § 752(d) is applicable), in which case there is a sale or exchange, and if the partnership interest was held as a capital asset, the loss would be a capital loss. Alternatively, the transaction can be viewed as a distribution by the partnership to the abandoning partner pursuant to the provisions of I.R.C. § 752(b).[17]

What happens if a taxpayer abandons his partnership interest, but the taxpayer nevertheless remains liable for a partnership liability (e.g., because of a guaranty given by the abandoning partner or because the partner was a general partner and the partnership had recourse liabilities)? At least one court has held that in these circumstances the abandoning partner does not realize his share of partnership liabilities.[18]

Precisely what is required in order for a partner to abandon her partnership interest is unclear. The courts seem to require some overt act to manifest the intention of the partner to abandon the partnership interest. The Tax Court has stated, "for an abandonment to be effective for purposes of [I.R.C.] section 165(a), the abandoning party must manifest an intent to abandon by some overt act or statement reasonably calculated to give a third party notice of the abandonment."[19] In that case, a partner announced at a partners' meeting that he would no longer

---

[14] Rev. Rul. 57-503, 1957-2 C.B. 139.

[15] I.R.C. § 1222.

[16] Rev. Rul. 93-80, 1993-2 C.B. 239. *See also* Gannon v. Commissioner, 16 T.C. 1134 (1951).

[17] *See* O'Brien v. Commissioner, 77 T.C. 113 (1981); Stilwell v. Commissioner, 46 T.C. 247 (1966).

[18] Weiss v. Commissioner, 956 F.2d 242 (11th Cir. 1992).

[19] Echols v. Commissioner, 93 T.C. 553, 557 (1989), *rev'd*, 935 F.2d 703 (5th Cir. 1991).

make contributions to the partnership and that he would convey his partnership interest to anyone who would assume his portion of the debt payments. The Tax Court found that this was not sufficient to constitute an abandonment, while the Fifth Circuit held that it was. In *Citron v. Commissioner*,[20] the limited partner told the general partner that the limited partner would not contribute additional funds to the partnership and wanted nothing further to do with the partnership. This was held to constitute a sufficient manifestation of his intention to abandon his partnership interest by an overt act.

In Rev. Rul. 93-80,[21] the IRS concluded that a loss incurred as a result of the abandonment or worthlessness of a partnership interest where the partnership had debt at the time of the abandonment or worthlessness would be treated under I.R.C. § 751(b), rather than I.R.C. § 751(a). One of the results of such treatment, which is discussed in greater detail in Chapter 7, is that in order for a partner to have ordinary income treatment, the inventory would need to be substantially appreciated. "Substantially appreciated" in this context means having a fair market value in excess of 120% of the adjusted basis of the inventory.

Thus, in the situations in which a partner is most likely to abandon a partnership interest — when the value of partnership property is low — Rev. Rul. 93-80 may not permit ordinary loss treatment on an abandonment if the partnership has debt.

E.   Conversion to Corporation

If a taxpayer transfers property to a corporation and the transferors in the aggregate own at least 80% of the stock of the transferee corporation, under I.R.C. § 351(a), no gain or loss is recognized by the taxpayer upon the receipt of the stock of the corporation. The question presents itself, therefore, whether the same rule is applicable if a partnership interest is transferred to a corporation.

A partnership interest would be treated as property for purposes of I.R.C. § 351(a). As is always the case whenever there is a disposition of a partnership interest, the liabilities of the partnership must be taken into account under I.R.C. § 752. Under I.R.C. § 357(a), if a transfer would be tax-free under I.R.C. § 351(a), but as part of the consideration for the property transferred, the corporation assumes the liability of the transferor, or acquires the property subject to a liability, the assumption of the liability or taking of the property subject to the liability is not treated as money or other property for purposes of I.R.C. § 351(a). Under I.R.C. § 357(c), however, if in a transaction to which I.R.C. § 351 applies the amount of liabilities assumed and to which the transferred property is subject exceeds the basis of the property transferred, then the excess is treated as a gain from the sale or exchange of property.

By virtue of the provisions of I.R.C. § 752(d), if a taxpayer transfers her partnership interest to a corporation in a transaction to which I.R.C. § 351 applies, then the liabilities which the taxpayer is deemed relieved is subject to the rules of I.R.C. § 357. Thus, if the liabilities which the taxpayer is deemed relieved are less

---

[20] 97 T.C. 200 (1991).

[21] 1993-2 C.B. 239.

than the taxpayer's basis for her partnership interest, then no gain or loss will be recognized by virtue of the liabilities, whereas if the liabilities which the taxpayer is deemed relieved exceed the taxpayer's basis for her partnership interest, then gain or loss will be recognized.[22] If, however, the principal purpose of a taxpayer with respect to the assumption of the liability or the taking of the property subject to the liability, was to avoid federal income tax or not for a bona fide purpose, then all of the liabilities involved are treated as boot.[23]

Rev. Rul. 84-111[24] describes three methods pursuant to which a partnership may be converted to a corporation:

1. The assets of the partnership may be contributed to a newly formed corporation in exchange for stock of the corporation, and then the partnership is terminated by distributing all of the stock of the corporation (the "Assets-Over Form");

2. The assets of the partnership may be distributed out to the partners in liquidation of the partnership, and the partners then contribute the assets to a newly formed corporation in exchange for stock in the corporation; and

3. The partners of the partnership contribute all of their partnership interests to a newly formed corporation in exchange for stock in the corporation.

The Ruling assumes that the steps chosen for the particular structure actually occur. As the Ruling discusses, the alternatives must be analyzed based upon the general rules for contributions of assets under I.R.C. § 351 and partnership distributions.

With the introduction of the check-the-box Regulations and the state law development of between-entity mergers and formless conversion statutes, a method needed to be developed for dealing with partnership-to-corporate conversions that did not actually take some or all of the steps described in the alternatives in Rev. Rul. 84-111.

The check-the-box Regulations themselves contemplate that a partnership may file Form 8832 and elect to be treated as a corporation even though the entity continues as a partnership or LLC for state law purposes. If a partnership makes such an election, the partnership is deemed to use the Assets-Over Form described above.[25] The contribution is deemed to occur at the end of the day before the effective date of the election, and the first day of the taxable year of the corporation is the effective date of the election.[26]

Of course, a partnership may convert for state law purposes without filing an election under the check-the-box Regulations. Rev. Rul. 2004-59[27] provides that if a partnership converts to a corporation for state law purposes using a method that

---

[22] Rev. Rul. 84-111, 1984-2 C.B. 88; Rev. Rul. 81-38, 1981-1 C.B. 386; Rev. Rul. 80-323, 1980-2 C.B. 124.

[23] I.R.C. § 357(b).

[24] 1984-2 C.B. 88.

[25] Treas. Reg. § 301.7701-3(g)(1)(i).

[26] Treas. Reg. § 301.7701-3(g)(3)(i).

[27] 2004-1 C.B. 1050.

does not require an actual transfer of assets or interests, such as a cross-entity merger statute or an elective conversion statute, the partnership will also be deemed to use the Assets-Over Form. Unlike the check-the-box Regulations, Rev. Rul. 2004-59 does not specify the times at which the deemed transactions are deemed to occur. In regard to a conversion to an S corporation, the IRS has clarified the timing issue in Rev. Rul. 2009-15.[28] In Rev. Rul. 2009-15, the IRS ruled that a partnership that converts to a corporation under a formless conversion statute may elect to be treated as an S corporation effective as of the day the state law conversion became effective. Thus, the deemed contribution of assets by the partnership and the deemed liquidation of the partnership are deemed to occur immediately before the start of the day on which the state law conversion was effective.

F.   Transfers to Other Partnerships

As discussed in more detail at § 2.02, no gain or loss is recognized if a person transfers property to a partnership in exchange for a partnership interest. A partnership interest would constitute property for this purpose, with the result that the general rule of I.R.C. § 721(a) applies. Again, however, it is necessary to consider the effect of the liabilities of the partnership whose interest was transferred, as well as the liabilities of the partnership to which the partnership interest is transferred.

Treas. Reg. § 1.752-1(f) provides that if, as a result of a single transaction, a partner incurs both an increase in the partner's share of partnership liabilities and a decrease in the partner's share of partnership liabilities, only the net decrease is treated as a distribution from the partnership and only a net increase is treated as a contribution to the partnership. That Regulation further provides that in the case of the merger or consolidation of two partnerships, liabilities are netted. Thus, if a partner transfers a partnership interest to another partnership, it is necessary to determine the partner's share of the transferee partnership's liabilities (which includes its share of the liabilities of the partnership whose interest was transferred) to determine whether there is a deemed net distribution to the contributing partner.

For example, assume that A is a 25% partner of partnership ABCD, that A's basis for A's partnership interest is $10,000 and that A's share of the $60,000 of liabilities of ABCD is $15,000. If A were to transfer A's partnership interest in ABCD to a newly formed partnership AZ, of which A was a 50% partner, A's share of the liabilities ABCD would now be $7,500 and there would have been a decrease in A's share of ABCD's liabilities of $7,500. Since this is less than A's basis for his partnership interest in ABCD, no gain or loss would be recognized by A on the transfer.[29] If the partnership interest is contributed to an existing partnership, a question is presented as to whether the contributing partner's share of the liabilities of the transferee partnership can be taken into account in the netting

---

[28]   2009-1 C.B. 1035.

[29]   *See* Rev. Rul. 79-205, 1979-2 C.B. 255; Rev. Rul. 77-309, 1977-2 C.B. 216; Rev. Rul. 87-120, 1987-2 C.B. 161.

process. It appears that they could be taken into account.

§ 6.07   OPTIONAL ADJUSTMENT TO BASIS OF PARTNERSHIP PROPERTY

As we have discussed, the Code sometimes treats the partnership as an aggregate of its partners and sometimes treats the partnership as an entity apart from its partners. In many instances, treating a partnership as an aggregate is beneficial to the partners and provides flexibility that is not available in the case of corporations. One example of this is the ability to adjust the basis of partnership property when there is a sale or exchange of a partnership interest.

Under the general rule, if a partner purchases a partnership interest from another partner, the purchase price of that partnership interest has no effect on the partnership's basis in its assets.[30] This can produce an inequitable result for the purchasing partner. To illustrate, if a partnership's sole assets are marketable securities with a basis of $200,000 and a fair market value of $1 million, and A purchases a 50% interest in that partnership for $500,000, the partnership's basis for the marketable securities remains $200,000. If the partnership then were to sell one-half of its assets for $500,000, the partnership recognizes a $400,000 gain, $200,000 of which is allocated to the purchasing partner. As to A, however, there has been no appreciation since A acquired her interest in the partnership. Nevertheless, she will be subject to tax on her $200,000 share of the partnership's gain. It should be noted that the exact same inequity would be produced if what was acquired by A was a 50% interest in an S corporation, rather than a partnership. Note further that if the partnership holds I.R.C. § 751 assets instead of marketable securities, A recognizes ordinary income. The gain A recognizes will increase A's basis in her partnership interest, creating an inherent loss, but that loss may not be recognized for some time, creating a timing distortion, and if the partnership holds I.R.C. § 751 assets, there is also a character distortion as the partnership interest is a capital asset under I.R.C. § 741 and the loss thus a capital loss. To correct these distortions, I.R.C. § 743(b) was enacted. It should be noted that there is no comparable provision in the case of an S corporation, even though the same inequity exists.

A.   I.R.C. § 743(b)

The optional adjustment to the basis of partnership property provided by I.R.C. § 743(b) is only available in the case of a sale or exchange of a partnership interest or upon the death of a partner. Thus, the provisions of I.R.C. § 743(b) do not apply to partnership interests acquired directly from a partnership or acquired by gift.[31] In order for I.R.C. § 743(b) to be applicable, the partnership must have in effect an election under I.R.C. § 754. In fact, if an election has already been made under

---

[30]   I.R.C. § 743(a).

[31]   In many instances, this same inequity resulting from a purchase of a partnership interest will not result in the case of a contribution to a partnership, either because the existing partners will be subject to tax on the appreciation by virtue of a revaluation of the partnership assets and the making of reverse section 704(c) allocations or because of a special allocation of the pre-contribution gain to the existing partners.

I.R.C. § 754, an adjustment is mandatory under I.R.C. § 743(b). This is true even if the adjustment results in a reduction in the basis of assets, rather than an increase. Therefore, an adjustment under I.R.C. § 743(b) is only optional if the partnership has not yet made an I.R.C. § 754 election.

Even if the partnership has not made a section 754 election, if the partnership has a substantial built-in loss in its assets immediately after the transfer, the partnership is required to adjust the basis of its properties.[32] Exceptions to this rule are provided in I.R.C. § 743(e) and (f) in the case of investment partnerships and securitization partnerships.

I.R.C. § 743(d)(1) provides that a partnership has a substantial built-in loss if the partnership's adjusted basis for its property exceeds by more than $250,000 the fair market value of the partnership's property. I.R.C. § 743(d)(2) authorizes the IRS to issue Regulations to carry out the purposes of I.R.C. § 743(d)(1), which may include aggregating related partnerships or disregarding property acquired by a partnership in an attempt to avoid this rule.

B. Making the I.R.C. § 754 Election

I.R.C. § 754 provides that if a partnership files an election under that section, then the basis of partnership property shall be adjusted as provided in I.R.C. § 734 (in the case of a distribution of property) and I.R.C. § 743 (in the case of a transfer of a partnership interest). I.R.C. § 754 further provides that once an election is made, it applies to all distributions of property by the partnership and all transfers of partnership interests during the taxable year in which the election is made, as well as for all subsequent taxable years. While an election under I.R.C. § 754 may be revoked, it may only be revoked with the consent of the IRS.

Treas. Reg. § 1.754-1(b) provides that an election under I.R.C. § 754 is to be made in a written statement filed with the partnership return for the taxable year in which the distribution or transfer occurs. For the election to be valid, the return must be timely filed (including extensions). The IRS has provided in a Revenue Procedure, however, that an election filed within 12 months of the original due date for the election will be treated as timely if all affected taxpayers report their income consistently with the election for the election year and each subsequent year.[33]

Once an election has been made under I.R.C. § 754, it must apply with respect to all distributions and all sales of partnership interests. It is not possible to make an election only with respect to distributions of partnership property, or only with respect to sales of partnership interests. Adjustments under I.R.C. § 734(b) are discussed at § 7.07.

If a partnership wishes to revoke an election under I.R.C. § 754, it must file with the IRS an application setting forth the grounds on which the revocation is desired. The application has to be filed not later than 30 days after the close of the partnership taxable year with respect to which the revocation is intended to

---

[32] I.R.C. § 743(a), (d).

[33] Rev. Proc. 92-85, § 4.01, 1992-2 C.B. 490, *as amended by* Rev. Proc. 93-28, 1993-2 C.B. 344.

apply.[34] The Regulations give as examples of situations which might result in a favorable response to an application for revocation: (i) a change in the nature of the partnership's business, (ii) a substantial increase in the assets of the partnership, (iii) a change in the character of partnership assets, or (iv) an increased frequency of retirements or shifts of partnership interests which would result in an administrative burden to the partnership. The Regulations make clear, however, that an application for revocation will not be approved where the revocation is intended primarily to avoid stepping down the basis of partnership assets.[35]

C.   Effect of I.R.C. § 743(b)

I.R.C. § 743(b) provides that in the case of a transfer of a partnership interest when an election under I.R.C. § 754 is in effect, (i) the partnership shall increase the adjusted basis of its assets by the excess of the basis of the transferee partner for his partnership interest over his proportionate share of the adjusted basis of the partnership's assets, or (ii) decrease the adjusted basis of the partnership's assets by the excess of the transferee partner's proportionate share of the adjusted basis of the partnership's assets over the basis of the transferee partner's basis for his interest in the partnership. Notwithstanding the language of I.R.C. § 743(b), it would now be more accurate to state that the purchasing partner is given an I.R.C. § 743(b) adjustment with respect to the partnership assets, rather than a special basis in those assets, as we discuss below. The I.R.C. § 743(b) adjustment is made solely with respect to the transferee partner, and not the other partners. Further, this is purely a tax adjustment, and does not affect capital accounts.

The effect of an adjustment under I.R.C. § 743 generally is a matter of timing and the character of income realized by the transferee partner.

To illustrate the effect of I.R.C. § 743(b), returning to the example in § 6.07.A, if no section 754 election were in effect, the transferee partner has $200,000 of gain at the time of the sale of one-half of the securities. The $200,000 of gain would increase the transferee's basis for his partnership interest by $200,000. When the transferee sells his partnership interest, or when the partnership interest is liquidated, this $200,000 increase in basis will ultimately result in less income or loss in an equal amount. If, on the other hand, a section 754 election were in effect, then no income would be recognized by the transferee partner upon the sale of one-half of the marketable securities, nor would a loss be available upon the subsequent sale of the partnership interest or liquidation of the partnership. Thus, in this case, there has been solely a timing difference.

Instead of the partnership having marketable securities as its assets, assume that the partnership was in the equipment leasing business and had personal property as its assets. Upon the sale of the partnership interest, the personal property would have an increased basis as to A of $400,000. A would be entitled to depreciate this additional basis and claim ordinary deductions as a result thereof.[36]

---

[34] Treas. Reg. § 1.754-1(c)(1).

[35] *Id.*

[36] Treas. Reg. § 1.743-1(j)(4).

If instead of personal property, the partnership owned real property, the transferee partner would be entitled to additional depreciation deductions and upon the liquidation of the assets of the partnership, or the sale of the partnership interest, at worst the transferee would have capital gains subject to tax at the preferential rate applicable to capital gains. In this instance, there has been an actual change in the character of the deductions and income.

Lastly, if the partnership owned personal property on which it had claimed depreciation, the effect of I.R.C. § 743(b) would be to eliminate the depreciation recapture with respect to the depreciation claimed by the partnership prior to the purchase of the interest by the transferee. Again, this could have a character effect. If the effect of I.R.C. § 743(b) was to allow additional depreciation to the transferee and the transferee died while owning the partnership interest and before the property was sold, there might be a permanent difference depending upon whether a section 754 election was in effect.

As indicated above, I.R.C. § 743(b) can have the effect of stepping down the basis of the partnership's assets as to the transferee. This occurs where either the sales price of the partnership interest is less than the transferee partner's share of the partnership's basis, or where the value of the partnership interest upon the death of a partner is less than the successor's share of the partnership's basis for its assets. In many situations, if a person dies owning a partnership interest, the estate will attempt to claim various discounts (such as marketability or lack of control) to reduce the value of the partnership interest for estate tax purposes. If the effect of such discounts is to reduce the value of the partnership interest below the successor's share of the partnership's basis for its assets, then if a § 754 election is in effect with respect to the partnership, there will be a step-down in the assets of the partnership as to the successor. Obviously, in this situation, it would not make sense for the partnership to make a § 754 election. If, however, the partnership has previously made the § 754 election, then the provisions of I.R.C. § 743(b) would automatically apply and a step-down in basis results. Furthermore, a partnership (other than certain investment partnerships) is required to adjust the basis of assets as if it had made a § 754 election if the step down in basis would exceed $250,000.[37]

Having to keep track of I.R.C. § 743(b) and (as we will discuss in the next chapter) I.R.C. § 734(b) adjustments can pose a substantial administrative burden on the partnership, particularly if they arise with some frequency. Historically, that has caused partnerships often to resist making I.R.C. § 754 elections. However, because of the mandatory step downs, these elections are becoming more common.

D.   Computation of Transferee's Proportionate Share of I.R.C. § 743(b) Adjustment

In order to determine the adjustment which will result from a transfer of a partnership interest when a section 754 election is in effect, it is necessary to determine the transferee partner's proportionate share of the adjusted basis of the partnership's assets. I.R.C. § 743(b) provides that a partner's proportionate share

---

[37] I.R.C. § 743(a), (d); *see* I.R.C. § 743(e), (f).

of the adjusted basis of partnership property is determined in accordance with his interest in partnership capital, taking into account the provisions of I.R.C. § 704(c) in the case of contributed property. Treas. Reg. § 1.743-1(d)(1) provides that a transferee's share of the adjusted basis of partnership property is equal to the transferee's interest in the partnership's "previously taxed capital" plus the transferee's share of partnership liabilities. A transferee partner's share of the previously taxed capital is equal to: (i) the amount of cash which the transferee would receive in liquidation if the partnership sold all of its assets for their fair market value (a hypothetical sale), increased by (ii) the amount of tax loss that would be allocated to the transferee from the hypothetical sale, and decreased by (iii) the amount of tax gain that would be allocated to the transferee from the hypothetical sale.

Treas. Reg. § 1.743-1(d)(3), example 1, illustrates the above provisions. In that example, the partnership owns assets having a fair market value of $76,000, which have a basis of $55,000 and the partnership has liabilities of $10,000. A partner sells her one-third interest in the partnership to a transferee for $22,000. The transferee's basis for her partnership interest is $25,333 ($22,000 + ($10,000/3)). The transferee's share of the previously taxed capital is $15,000 (the $22,000 of cash which she would have received in liquidation following the hypothetical sale minus the $7,000 of gain which would have been allocated to her in the hypothetical sale). The transferee's share of the adjusted basis of the partnership property is thus $18,333 (the $15,000 of previously taxed capital plus her $3,333 share of the partnership's liabilities). This results in a basis adjustment under I.R.C. § 743(b) of $7,000 (the difference between the $25,333 purchase price ($22,000 plus $3,333 of liabilities) and the $18,333 share of partnership basis).

The formula provided for in the Regulations is complex, and its provisions only have to be followed in situations in which the partnership either has non pro rata allocations, adjustments under I.R.C. § 704(c) or reverse section 704(c) allocations (resulting from prior revaluations). In simpler situations, the basis adjustment would simply be the excess of the purchase price (including liabilities, here $25,333) over the transferee partner's one-third interest in the adjusted basis of the partnership's assets ($55,000/3).

E. Allocation of Basis Adjustment Among Partnership Assets

If a partnership has a single asset, it is obvious that any adjustment available under I.R.C. § 743(b) will be allocated to that asset. In most cases, however, partnerships do not have a single asset. Therefore, it becomes necessary to determine how the adjustment under I.R.C. § 743(b) is to be allocated among the various assets of the partnership.

I.R.C. § 755(a) generally provides that the adjustment to be made under I.R.C. § 743(b) shall be made in such fashion as will result in having the effect of reducing the difference between the fair market value and the adjusted basis of partnership properties. I.R.C. § 755(b) provides that in applying the allocation rules provided for in I.R.C. § 755(a), increases or decreases allocable to: (i) capital assets and property described in I.R.C. § 1231(b), and (ii) other property, shall be allocated to partnership property of a like character, except that the basis of any partnership assets shall not be reduced below zero. The rules of I.R.C. § 755 are not at all clear as to how the allocation is to be made. The Regulations, however, go into great detail as to the manner in which the allocation is to be made.

The first issue which must be determined is whether I.R.C. § 743(b) applies in a situation in which the amount paid by the transferee partner is equal to the transferee partner's share of the partnership's basis. Despite the language of I.R.C. § 743(b), the Regulations take the position that an allocation may nevertheless be required. This would occur in a situation in which some partnership assets have fair market values in excess of their bases, and others have fair market values less than their bases, netting to zero.[38]

The allocation of the basis adjustment between the classes of property, and among the items of property within each class, are made based upon the amount of gain or loss the transferee partner would have allocated to him with respect to the transferred interest if immediately after the transfer all of the partnership's property was disposed of in a fully taxable transaction for cash in an amount equal to the fair market value of the property.[39] The amount of basis adjustment that is allocated to the ordinary income class of property is equal to the total amount of gain or loss that would be allocated to the transferee from the sale of all of the ordinary income property in the hypothetical sale referred to above. The amount of the basis adjustment that is allocable to the capital gain property is equal to the total amount of the basis adjustment under I.R.C. § 743(b), less the amount of the basis adjustment allocated to the ordinary income class of property.[40] There is also a special rule which provides that in no event may the amount of any decrease in basis allocable to capital gain property exceed the partnership's basis for the capital gain property. In such circumstances, the decrease in basis is allocated to the capital gain property to the extent of the partnership's basis for the capital gain property, and any excess is applied to reduce the basis of ordinary income property.[41] Allocations to particular property within a class are generally made on a similar basis.[42] Note that within a given class, there may be upward and downward adjustments if the class contains assets with fair market values in excess of their bases and others with fair market values less than their bases. The point of the adjustment is, as of the date of the purchase, to eliminate any net gain or loss from partnership assets to the purchasing partner. In determining the amount of gain or loss that would be allocated to the transferring partner, allocations under I.R.C. § 704(c) must be taken into account, as must reverse section 704(c) allocations.[43]

The Regulations provide for coordination between I.R.C. §§ 755 and 1060. If there is a basis adjustment under I.R.C. § 743(b) and the assets of the partnership

---

[38] Treas. Reg. § 1.755-1(b)(1)(i).

[39] Treas. Reg. § 1.755-1(b)(1)(ii).

[40] Treas. Reg. § 1.755-1(b)(2)(i).

[41] *Id.*

[42] Treas. Reg. § 1.755-1(b)(3).

[43] Treas. Reg. § 1.755-1(b)(1)(ii); Treas. Reg. § 1.755-1(b)(2)(ii), example 1.

constitute a trade or business (within the meaning of Treas. Reg. § 1.1060-1(d)(2)), then the partnership is required to use the residual method to assign values to the partnership's section 197 intangibles.[44] Under this method, it is first necessary to determine the value of the assets other than section 197 intangibles and the amount in excess of the value of such non-section 197 intangibles is allocated to section 197 intangibles.[45] The Regulations provide that in determining the value of partnership property other than section 197 intangibles, the provisions of I.R.C. § 7701(g) must be taken into account.[46] Under I.R.C. § 7701(g), in determining the amount of gain or loss with respect to any property, the property is treated as having a fair market value which is not less than the amount of any nonrecourse indebtedness to which the property is subject.

If, as a result of applying the residual method, any portion of the basis adjustment is to be allocated to section 197 intangibles, the value allocated to section 197 intangibles must be divided into two classes: (i) section 197 intangibles other than goodwill and going concern value, and (ii) goodwill and going concern value.[47] After an appropriate amount of value is allocated to the section 197 intangibles other than goodwill and going concern value, any remaining value is then allocated to the goodwill and going concern value.[48]

F. Additional Aspects of Adjustment

1. Transfer of Partnership Interest

I.R.C. § 743(b) provides that any increase or decrease in basis resulting from its application is to constitute an adjustment to the basis of partnership property only with respect to the transferee. If a transferee which has had a basis adjustment under I.R.C. § 743(b) subsequently transfers all or a portion of the partnership interest with respect to which the special basis adjustment applies, the new transferee's basis adjustment is determined without regard to the prior transferee's basis adjustment.[49] If the transfer is by gift, however, then the donee stands in the shoes of the donor with respect to the basis adjustment.[50]

2. Distribution of Partnership Property

If there is distributed to a partner of a partnership an asset with respect to which such partner has a special basis adjustment, then such basis adjustment is taken into account for purposes of I.R.C. § 732.[51] If a partner receives a partnership asset with respect to which there is a special basis adjustment as to another partner, such

---

[44] Treas. Reg. § 1.755-1(a)(2).

[45] *Id.*

[46] Treas. Reg. § 1.755-1(a)(3).

[47] Treas. Reg. § 1.755-1(a)(5).

[48] Treas. Reg. § 1.755-1(a)(5)(iii).

[49] Treas. Reg. § 1.743-1(f).

[50] *Id.*

[51] Treas. Reg. § 1.743-1(g)(1).

special basis adjustment is not taken into account by the distributee partner for purposes of I.R.C. § 732.[52] In such circumstances, the partner having the special basis adjustment with respect to the property distributed reallocates the basis adjustment among the remaining items of partnership property in accordance with the rules of Treas. Reg. § 1.755-1(c).[53]

3.   Contribution of Property to Lower-Tier Partnership

If a partnership contributes property to another partnership in a transaction to which I.R.C. § 721(a) applies with respect to which a partner of the transferring partnership has a special basis adjustment, then the basis adjustment is treated as contributed to the lower-tier partnership regardless of whether the lower-tier partnership has an election under I.R.C. § 754 in effect.[54] Nevertheless, the upper-tier partnership's special basis with respect to the partnership interest in the lower-tier partnership must be allocated solely to the transferee partner having the special basis adjustment.

4.   Contribution of Property to Corporation

If a partnership contributes an asset to a corporation in a transaction to which I.R.C. § 351 applies with respect to which a partner of the transferring partnership has a special basis adjustment, the corporation's basis for such property generally includes the basis adjustment.[55] If any gain is recognized by the transferee partnership in such transaction, the transferee partnership determines the amount of gain *without* regard to the basis adjustment, but when allocating the gain to the transferee partner having the basis adjustment, the basis adjustment is taken into account.[56] The partnership's basis in the stock of the transferee corporation is determined *without* regard to the special basis adjustment, but the transferee partner's basis for such stock includes the basis adjustment.[57]

5.   Computation of Income and Expenses

If a special basis adjustment is in effect with respect to a partnership, the partnership first computes its items of income, deduction, gain or loss at the partnership level without regard to the special basis adjustment, and then allocates those items among the partners in accordance with the provisions of I.R.C. § 704. The partnership then adjusts the transferee partner's distributive share of such items so as to take into account the special basis with respect to the transferee partner. These adjustments must be taken into account on Schedules K and K-1 of the partnership's Form 1065, but do not affect the transferee's capital account.[58] The transferee's share of gain or loss from the sale of property with respect to

---

[52] Treas. Reg. § 1.743-1(g)(2).

[53] *Id.*

[54] Treas. Reg. § 1.743-1(h)(1).

[55] Treas. Reg. § 1.743-1(h)(2)(i).

[56] Treas. Reg. § 1.743-1(h)(2)(ii).

[57] Treas. Reg. § 1.743-1(h)(2)(iii).

[58] Treas. Reg. § 1.743-1(j)(2).

which there is a special basis adjustment is equal to the amount of the transferee's share of the partnership's gain or loss with respect to the assets sold, decreased by a positive basis adjustment and increased by any negative basis adjustment.[59] Thus, if there were a positive I.R.C. § 743(b) basis adjustment to a given property of $5,000, and the transferee's share of gain pre-adjustment is $7,000, she has "net gain" from the property of $2,000. Conversely, if the transferee's share of gain pre-adjustment is $2,000, she has a "net loss" from the property of $3,000.

6. Special Basis Adjustment and Depreciable Property

If a property with respect to which a special basis adjustment is in effect is depreciable property, and the adjustment is positive, as noted above, the adjustment gives the transferee partner additional depreciation deductions. The adjustment is treated as if it were newly purchased property placed in service when the transfer occurs.[60] The special basis adjustment may be depreciated using any applicable recovery period and method. No change, however, is made with respect to the portion of the basis of the asset for which there is no increase.[61]

To illustrate, assume that partnership AB has a single asset which is depreciable personal property having a recovery period of five years. The asset was originally purchased for $5,000 with the result that there is $1,000 of depreciation available each year, one half of which is allocated to each of A and B. At the end of Year 4, A sells her partnership interest to C for $1,500, reflecting that the asset owned by partnership AB is worth $3,000. C would have a basis adjustment with respect to the asset of $1,000 ($1,500 − $500). During Year 5, C's share of the depreciation deduction with respect to the partnership's basis for the asset would be $500. In addition, C would be entitled to depreciate the $1,000 basis adjustment over five years. If the straight line method were used, C would have an additional depreciation deduction in each of Years 5 through 9 of $200.

If a special basis adjustment with respect to depreciable property is negative, the special basis adjustment that is recovered with respect to a year first decreases the transferee partner's distributive share of the depreciation for that item of property. If the amount of the basis adjustment recovered in that year exceeds the transferee's distributive share of the depreciation for that item, then the transferee's distributive share of depreciation of other items of partnership property is decreased. If the amount recovered in any year exceeds the transferee partner's distributive share of all of the partnership's depreciation for that year, then the transferee is required to recognize income to the extent of such excess.[62] The portion of the decrease which is recovered in any year is based upon the remaining useful life of the property to which the basis is allocated.[63]

So far, none of the authors have had the courage to put an I.R.C. § 743(b)/ depreciation combo question on an exam.

---

[59] Treas. Reg. § 1.743-1(j)(3).

[60] Treas. Reg. § 1.743-1(j)(4)(i)(B)(1).

[61] *Id.*

[62] Treas. Reg. § 1.743-1(j)(4)(ii)(A).

[63] Treas. Reg. § 1.743-1(j)(4)(ii)(B).

7.   Return Filing Requirements

If a partnership is required to adjust the bases of partnership property under I.R.C. § 743(b), the partnership must attach a statement to the partnership return for the year of the transfer, setting forth the name and taxpayer identification number of the transferee, the amount of the adjustment and the allocation of the adjustment among the partnership's assets.[64] If the partnership has a section 754 election in effect, a transferee of a partnership interest is required to notify the partnership of the sale or exchange within 30 days of the sale or exchange. The notice must be signed under penalties of perjury and include: (i) the name and address of the transferee, (ii) the name and address of the transferor (if ascertainable), (iii) the taxpayer identification number of the transferee and of the transferor (if ascertainable), (iv) the relationship between the transferor and transferee, if any, (v) the date of the transfer, and (vi) the amount paid for the partnership interest.[65] In the case of the death of a partner where the partnership has a section 754 election in effect, the transferee must notify the partnership, in writing, within one year of the death of the deceased partner. This written notice must be signed under penalties of perjury and include: (i) the names and addresses of the deceased partner and the transferee, (ii) the taxpayer identification numbers of the deceased partner and the transferee, (iii) the relationship between the transferor and the transferee, if any, (iv) the deceased partner's date of death, (v) the date on which the transferee became the owner of the partnership interest, (vi) the fair market value of the partnership interest on the applicable valuation date for purposes of I.R.C. § 1014, and (vii) the manner in which the fair market value of the partnership interest was determined.[66]

§ 6.08   ALLOCATION OF INCOME AND LOSS

I.R.C. § 706(a) provides that a partner is required to include the partner's distributive share of the income, gain, loss, deduction, or credit of the partnership for the taxable year of the partnership ending within or with the taxable year of the partner. In determining the partnership items of income, gain, loss, and deduction for the taxable year in which a partner transfers all or a portion of his partnership interest, it is necessary to know when the partnership's taxable year closes.

A.   Closing of Partnership Taxable Year

I.R.C. § 706(c)(1) sets forth the general rule that except as provided in I.R.C. § 706(c)(2) or the termination of the partnership, the taxable year of the partnership is not closed as the result of the death of a partner, the entry of a new partner, the liquidation of a partner's interest in the partnership or the sale or exchange of a partner's interest in the partnership. This is true, whether or not any of such transactions result in the partnership being dissolved or liquidated for state

---

[64]   Treas. Reg. § 1.743-1(k)(1).

[65]   Treas. Reg. § 1.743-1(k)(2)(i).

[66]   Treas. Reg. § 1.743-1(k)(2)(ii).

law purposes.[67] I.R.C. § 706(c)(2) provides, however, special rules with respect to dispositions of partnership interests.

B. Sale of Entire Interest

I.R.C. § 706(c)(2)(A) provides that the taxable year of the partnership closes with respect to a partner whose entire interest in the partnership terminates. The closing of the partnership's taxable year is only with respect to the partner disposing of her interest, not the other partners. It does not matter whether the partner's interest terminates because of sale or exchange, death, liquidation, or any other event. I.R.C. § 706(c)(2)(B), however, provides that the partnership's taxable year does not close with respect to a partner who sells or exchanges less than his entire interest in the partnership.

I.R.C. § 706(d)(1) sets forth the general rule that if there is any change in a partner's partnership interest during the year, each partner's distributive share of the items of income, gain, loss, deduction, or credit of the partnership for that taxable year is determined by taking into account the varying interests of the partners during the year. Treas. Reg. § 1.706-1(c)(2)(ii) provides that in the case of a sale or exchange of a partner's entire partnership interest, the partner includes in her taxable income for her taxable year within or with which her partnership interest in the partnership ends, her distributive share of the items of income, gain, loss, deduction, or credit, and any guaranteed payments under I.R.C. § 707(c) (discussed in Chapter 8), for her partnership taxable year ending with the date of such sale or exchange. That Regulation further provides that in order to avoid an interim closing of the partnership's books, the terminating partner's distributive share of such items may, if agreed to by the partners,[68] be estimated by taking into account her pro rata share of the amount of such items that would have been included in her taxable income had she remained a partner until the end of the partnership's taxable year. If such alternative method is used, the transferee includes in her taxable income a pro rata share of the amount of the items that would have been included in her income had she been a partner from the beginning of the taxable year. The pro rata portions that are included in the transferor and transferee partners' income must be determined in the same fashion.

C. Methods of Allocation

Treas. Reg. § 1.706-1(c)(2)(ii) permits the allocation to be made on any reasonable basis. It specifically indicates that an allocation based upon time would be appropriate. The Regulation gives no further guidance as to what is reasonable. Where there is an unusual item of income during the taxable year of the disposition, such as a sale of assets other than in the ordinary course of business, it may be appropriate to allocate most items on a time basis, but allocate the gain or loss from the sale of assets based upon when they actually occur.

---

[67] Treas. Reg. § 1.706-1(c)(1).

[68] The Regulation does not indicate whether this agreement must be unanimous or whether the general voting rules applicable to the partners is sufficient.

D. Sale of Less Than Entire Interest

As indicated above, the partnership's taxable year does not close when a partner disposes of less than his entire interest in the partnership. Nevertheless, under I.R.C. § 706(d)(1), it is still necessary to determine the transferor's and transferee's shares of the income of the partnership for the year of the sale by taking into account their varying interests in the partnership during the taxable year. Presumably, this will involve the same interim closing of the books or prorated methods described above in the case of the sale or exchange of an entire partnership interest.

E. Anti-Abuse Rule

I.R.C. § 706(d)(2) contains special rules designed to prevent the artificial shifting of deductions of partnerships using the cash method of accounting. This provision applies to "allocable cash basis items." The term "allocable cash basis item" means, in the case of a partnership using the cash receipts and disbursements method of accounting, deductions for interest, taxes, payments for services, payments for the use of property, and any other items determined by the IRS to be appropriate.[69]

I.R.C. § 706(d)(2)(A) provides that if during any taxable year of a partnership there is a change in any partner's interest in the partnership, then each partner's distributive share of any allocable cash basis item is determined by assigning the appropriate portion of such item to each day in the period to which it is attributable and by allocating the portion assigned to any day among the partners in proportion to their interest in the partnership on that day. Thus, if a cash method partnership borrowed money on January 1 of the year and it provided for interest only, payable on December 31 of each year, a purchase of a 50% partner's entire partnership interest on December 30 would not enable the purchasing partner to deduct one-half of all of the interest paid on December 31.

§ 6.09 TERMINATION OF PARTNERSHIPS

I.R.C. § 708(a) provides that a partnership is considered to continue until it is terminated. Under I.R.C. § 708(b)(1), a partnership is terminated if: (i) no part of any business, financial operation, or venture of the partnership continues to be carried on by any of its partners, or (ii) within a 12-month period there is a sale or exchange of 50% or more of the total interest in partnership capital and profits.[70] It is the latter provision which is relevant in the case of transfers of partnership interests.

---

[69] I.R.C. 706(d)(2)(B).

[70] For special rules with respect to the termination of a partnership in the case of mergers or divisions, see § 9.02.

A. What Transactions Are Taken into Account

Not all transfers of partnership interests are necessarily taken into account in determining whether the required 50% change has occurred. A sale from one partner to an existing partner is taken into account.[71] A transfer of a partnership interest by gift, bequest, inheritance, or liquidation of a partnership interest is not treated as a sale or exchange for purposes of I.R.C. § 708(b)(1)(B).[72] Likewise, a contribution of property to a partnership is not treated as a sale or exchange.[73]

If a sale or exchange of an interest in an upper-tier partnership results in a termination of the upper-tier partnership, the upper-tier partnership is treated as exchanging its interest in the capital and profits of the lower-tier partnership. If, however, the sale or exchange of an interest in the upper-tier partnership does not result in a termination of the upper-tier partnership, then such sale or exchange is *not* treated as a sale or exchange of a proportionate part of the upper-tier partnership's interest in the capital and profits of the lower-tier partnership.[74]

A question is raised as to whether a sale or exchange for purposes of I.R.C. § 708(b)(1)(B) has occurred where a partnership interest is transferred in a transaction which does not result in the recognition of gain. The IRS has generally taken the position that as long as there is an exchange, the fact that the exchange qualifies for tax-free treatment does not prevent the transaction from being treated as an exchange for purposes of I.R.C. § 708(d)(1)(B). It has been held that a transfer of a 50% interest in capital and profits by a partner to a corporation in a transaction which was tax-free pursuant to I.R.C. § 351 qualified as an exchange for purposes of I.R.C. § 708(b)(1)(B).[75]

In Private Rulings, the IRS has held that the transfer of a partnership interest to another partnership is an exchange for purposes of I.R.C. § 708(b)(1)(B).[76] Where a partnership interest is owned by a corporation which participates in a tax-free reorganization within the meaning of I.R.C. § 368(a) in which the assets of the corporate partner are transferred to another party to the reorganization, the IRS has held that the transfer of the partnership interest is an exchange to which I.R.C. § 708(d)(1)(B) applies.[77]

I.R.C. § 761(e) provides that for purposes of I.R.C. § 708, any distribution of an interest in a partnership is treated as an exchange. It would appear clear that a distribution of a partnership interest by a corporation to its shareholders should be treated as an exchange for purposes of I.R.C. § 708(b)(1)(B), because such a transaction would be treated as a sale of the partnership interest at the corporate

---

[71] Treas. Reg. § 1.708-1(b)(2).

[72] *Id.*

[73] *Id.*

[74] *Id.*

[75] Evans v. Commissioner, 54 T.C. 40 (1970), *aff'd*, 447 F.2d 547 (7th Cir. 1971); *see also* Rev. Rul. 81-38, 1981-1 C.B. 386.

[76] PLR 8116041 (Jan. 21, 1981); PLR 8229034 (Apr. 20, 1982).

[77] Rev. Rul. 87-110, 1987-2 C.B. 159. The Revenue Ruling carved out an exception for those reorganizations which are described in I.R.C. § 368(a)(1)(F).

level.[78] That a distribution by a partnership to its partners would be treated as an exchange for purposes of I.R.C. § 708(b)(1)(B) is not as intuitive. If the partnership distributed an interest in a lower-tier partnership pro rata to its partners, the partners are now merely holding directly that which they previously owned indirectly, and such transaction would not appear to be an appropriate transaction to be taken into account for purposes of I.R.C. § 708(b)(1)(B).

It is easier to see that a distribution by an upper-tier partnership of an interest in a lower-tier partnership to one of its partners should be treated as a distribution (at least to the extent the transferee partner receives a greater percentage interest in the lower-tier partnership than he indirectly owned previously). In such circumstances, the IRS has held that the distribution constitutes an exchange for purposes of I.R.C. § 708(b)(1)(B) of the entire partnership interest distributed, not merely the excess over the amount indirectly owned by the transferee partner.[79]

If a partnership has terminated under I.R.C. § 708(b)(1)(B), the deemed distribution by the old partnership of the partnership interest in the new partnership pursuant to Treas. Reg. § 1.708-1(d)(1)(iv) is not treated as a sale or exchange of an interest in the new partnership.[80]

B. Computing Capital and Profits

As indicated above, in order for there to be a termination of a partnership under I.R.C. § 708(b)(1)(B), there must be a sale or exchange of 50% or more of both the capital interests and the profits interests. The Regulations made clear that a sale of a 30% interest in partnership capital and a 60% interest in partnership profits does not result in a termination of the partnership.[81] The Regulations also make clear that a sale by partner A of a 30% interest in a partnership to D, followed by the sale by D of her 30% interest in the partnership to E, would not be treated as a sale of more than a 50% interest in partnership capital and profits because the same 30% interest was transferred.[82]

The Regulations do not indicate how to determine a partner's capital interest. For example, if partnership AB is comprised of A, a service partner, who has made no capital contribution to the partnership, and B, who has contributed all of the capital to the partnership, and B transfers 60% of his interest in the partnership to C, is this necessarily a transfer of a 50% interest in partnership capital? Suppose the partnership agreement provided that gain from the sale of AB's assets were to be allocated 70% to A and 30% to B, and at the time of the transfer by B of his 60% interest in AB, the assets of AB have significantly increased so that on a sale of the assets of AB at fair market value and a subsequent liquidation, A would receive more money than B.

---

[78] *See* I.R.C. §§ 311(d)(1), 336(a).

[79] Rev. Rul. 92-15, 1992-1 C.B. 215.

[80] Treas. Reg. § 1.761-1(e).

[81] Treas. Reg. § 1.708-1(b)(2).

[82] *Id.*

There would appear to be two methods for determining a partner's capital interest for purposes of I.R.C. § 708(b)(1)(B). The first would be to assume that all assets are worth their book value and simply look to the capital accounts of the partners. This would be consistent with the rules set forth in Treas. Reg. § 1.704-1(b)(3)(iii)(D) for purposes of determining a partner's interest in the partnership. Alternatively, a partner's percentage interest in capital may be the percentage of the assets of the partnership which a partner would receive if the partnership sold all of its assets for their fair market value. This would be consistent with the rule for determining a partner's interest in capital for purposes of I.R.C. § 704(e).[83]

Determining a partner's interest in partnership profits is a simple case if under the partnership agreement a partner has a fixed interest in partnership profits. Where, as is often the case, a partner's interest varies over time, or varies depending upon whether it is an ordinary transaction or a capital transaction, how to determine profit interests is not clear. Is the determination based upon the income or loss of the partnership through the date of the sale? If so, what happens if there has been a loss through the date of sale? What happens if the pro rata method is to be used in determining the income allocated to the selling partner (so it is impossible to determine the allocation of profits for the year until the year ends)?

C. The Twelve-Month Rule

Since there must be a sale or exchange of a 50% interest in both capital and profits during a 12-month period, a natural question is presented as to whether a sale can be structured so that less than 50% is sold within the 12-month period, and the balance is sold following the expiration of the 12-month period. In Private Rulings, the IRS has approved transactions of this type.[84]

The issue becomes more complicated if the transaction involves the sale of a 49% interest in the partnership and the purchaser has either an option or an obligation to purchase an additional 1% after the expiration of 12 months from the date of the initial purchase. Under these circumstances, a question will be raised as to whether the option is a true option, or whether the future sale was really consummated at the time of the first sale.

D. Effect of Partnership Termination

1. Transactions Deemed to Occur

Treas. Reg. § 1.708-1(b)(4) provides that if a partnership is terminated pursuant to I.R.C. § 708(b)(1)(B) as a result of a sale or exchange, the partnership is deemed to have contributed all of its assets and liabilities to a new partnership in exchange for the interests in the new partnership and to immediately thereafter distribute those interests in the new partnership to the purchasing partner and the other remaining partners, in proportion to their respective interests in the terminated

---

[83] Treas. Reg. § 1.704-1(e)(1)(v).

[84] *See* PLR 8517022 (Jan. 25, 1985); PLR 7952057 (Sept. 25, 1979).

partnership, in liquidation of the terminated partnership. As a result of these deemed transactions, the new partnership's basis for its assets is unchanged, as are the capital accounts of the partners.[85] Even though the assets of the old partnership may have been appreciated, no new section 704(c) gain is created as a result of the deemed transfer by the old partnership of its assets to the new partnership.[86] In order for the purchasing partner to obtain the benefit of a step-up in basis of the partnership's assets under I.R.C. § 743(b), the old partnership must have a section 754 election in effect (which can be made on the final return of the old partnership).[87]

2. Employer Identification Number

The new partnership retains the taxpayer identification number of the old partnership.[88]

3. Elections

Since the Regulations treat the old partnership as having transferred its assets to a new partnership, the new partnership should be able to make all new tax elections, although this is not specifically stated. If the old partnership had a section 754 election in effect, if this is desired by the new partnership, prudence dictates that the new partnership make a new section 754 election.

4. I.R.C. §§ 704(c)(1)(B) and 737

A termination of a partnership under I.R.C. § 708(b)(1)(B) will not trigger gain recognition under either I.R.C. § 704(c)(1)(B) or 737.[89]

5. Depreciation and Amortization

The principal issue which occurs with respect to a termination of a partnership under I.R.C. § 708(b)(1)(B) relates to depreciation. Under I.R.C. § 168(i)(7)(A), if depreciable property is transferred to a partnership in a transaction to which I.R.C. § 721 applies, the transferee partnership steps in the shoes of the transferor with respect to depreciation. The provisions of I.R.C. § 168(i)(7)(A), however, do not apply in the case of a termination of a partnership under I.R.C. § 708(b)(1)(B). Thus, the new partnership is treated as having newly acquired the assets of the old partnership and must depreciate the basis of those assets using the appropriate life under the modified accelerated cost recovery system.

To illustrate, assume that the old partnership held commercial real property with a remaining basis of $390,000 and that it had 10 years remaining in its depreciable life. Thus, the partnership would claim $39,000 of depreciation deductions in each of the next 10 years. Upon a termination of that partnership under I.R.C.

---

[85] Treas. Reg. § 1.708-1(b)(4), example (ii); Treas. Reg. § 1.704-1(b)(2)(iv)(l).

[86] Treas. Reg. § 1.708-1(b)(4), example (iii); Treas. Reg. § 1.704-3(a)(3)(i).

[87] Treas. Reg. § 1.708-1(b)(5).

[88] Treas. Reg. § 1.708-1(b)(4), example (ii); Treas. Reg. § 301.6109-1(d)(2)(iii).

[89] Treas. Reg. §§ 1.704-4(c)(3), 1.737-2(a).

§ 708(b)(1)(B), the new partnership would have a basis for the real property of $390,000, but be required to depreciate that basis over 39 years, resulting in a depreciation deduction of only $10,000 per year. Thus, the termination of the partnership under I.R.C. § 708(b)(1)(B) has resulted in reducing the depreciation deduction of the partnership by $29,000 per year for 10 years.

I.R.C. § 709(b)(1) provides for the amortization of organization expenses if the partnership has properly elected to do so. I.R.C. § 709(b)(2)(B) provides that if a partnership is liquidated before the organization expenses have been fully amortized, the unamortized expenses may be deducted to the extent provided under I.R.C. § 165. The question presented, therefore, is whether a deemed liquidation under I.R.C. § 708(b)(1)(B) constitutes a liquidation which would permit the claiming of a deduction for the unamortized organization expenses. Although there does not appear to be any authority directly in point, it would appear that the deduction should be available.

I.R.C. § 197 allows the amortization of certain intangible costs incurred by a taxpayer. I.R.C. § 197(f)(2) provides for a step-in the shoes rule in the case of transactions described in I.R.C. §§ 721 and 731. Unlike the situation with depreciation generally, however, the step-in the shoes rule in the case of intangibles applies in the case of a termination of a partnership under I.R.C. § 708(b)(1)(B).

§ 6.10 READING, QUESTIONS AND PROBLEMS

A. Reading

CODE:

I.R.C. §§ 357, 706, 708, 741, 743(b), 743(d), 751(a), 751(c), 751(d), 752(d), 754, 755, 761(e).

TREASURY REGULATIONS:

Treas. Reg. §§ 1.704-4(c)(3), 1.706-1, 1.708-1, 1.737-2(a), 1.742-1, 1.743-1, 1.755-1, 1.761-1(c), 1.1001-2, 1.1011-2(b), 1.1223-3.

CASES:

United States v. Woolsey, 326 F.2d 287 (5th Cir. 1963).

Roth v. Commissioner, 321 F.2d 607 (9th Cir. 1963).

O'Brien v. Commissioner, 77 T.C. 113 (1981).

Echols v. Commissioner, 93 T.C. 553 (1989), *rev'd*, 935 F.2d 703 (5th Cir. 1991).

Citron v. Commissioner, 97 T.C. 200 (1991).

Evans v. Commissioner, 54 T.C. 40 (1970).

RULING AND OTHER INTERPRETATIONS:

  Rev. Rul. 60-352, 1960-2 C.B. 208.

  Rev. Rul. 75-194, 1975-1 C.B. 80.

  Rev. Rul. 79-205, 1979-2 C.B. 255.

  Rev. Rul. 81-38, 1981-1 C.B. 386.

  Rev. Rul. 84-53, 1984-1 C.B. 159.

  Rev. Rul. 84-111, 1984-2 C.B. 88.

  Rev. Rul. 87-110, 1987-2 C.B. 159.

  Rev. Rul. 89-108, 1989-2 C.B. 100.

  Rev. Rul. 92-15, 1992-1 C.B. 215.

  Rev. Rul. 93-80, 1993-2 C.B. 239.

  PLR 8116041 (Jan. 21, 1981).

B. Questions and Problems

1. A is a one-third partner in partnership ABC. A sells his one-third interest in ABC to D on January 1 of the current year for $200,000. ABC is a cash-method, calendar-year partnership. ABC does not have a section 754 election in effect. The balance sheet of ABC is as follows:

Assets	Basis	FMV
Cash	$10,000	$10,000
Account Receivable	0	$50,000
Inventory	$30,000	$40,000
Furniture, fixture and equipment	$150,000	$200,000
Goodwill	$210,000	$400,000
	$400,000	$700,000
Liabilities	$100,000	$100,000
Capital — A	$100,000	$200,000
Capital — B	$100,000	$200,000
Capital — C	$100,000	$200,000
	$400,000	$700,000

$150,000 of depreciation was taken on the furniture, fixtures, and equipment, and thus the original basis was $300,000. Assume for the sake of the problem that the outside basis of the partners in their partnership interests (without taking into consideration their allocable share of debt under I.R.C. § 752) is equal to their capital as shown on the balance sheet.

  a.   What is A's amount realized?

  b.   How much gain is recognized by A?

c.   What is the character of A's gain?

d.   What is D's basis for her partnership interest?

2. Same as 1, except A sells one-half of his one-third interest for $100,000.

3. Same as 1, except the sale occurs on June 30 of the current year and ABC has income of $200,000 for the year of sale, none of which is distributed.

a.   How much of the income for the year is allocated to A?

b.   What effect does the income for the year have on the gain recognized by A?

4. Same as 1, except A, B, and C each contributed $15,000 to the capital of ABC on January 15 of the immediately preceding year and an additional $15,000 each on June 30 of the immediately preceding year.

5. Same as 1, except that instead of A selling his interest in ABC, he contributes his one-third interest in ABC to a public charity.

6. Same as 1, except that A dies on January 1 of the current year. What is A's estate's basis for the ABC partnership interest?

7. Same as 1, except that A sells his one-third partnership interest in ABC to D for $20,000 plus D's $180,000 promissory note.

8. Same as 1, except that ABC has a section 754 election in effect.

a.   How much of a step-up in basis is available?

b.   How is the step-up in basis allocated to ABC's assets?

9. Same as 8, except that instead of A contributing only cash to ABC, A contributed property (which is included in Furniture, Fixture, and Equipment) which at the time of the contribution had an adjusted tax basis of $5,000 and a fair market value of $15,000. Assume that at the time D purchases A's interest, that property has a fair market value of $13,000, an adjusted tax basis of $3,000, and a book value of $10,000. Thus, the remaining Furniture, Fixture, and Equipment has a fair market value of $187,000 and an adjusted tax basis of $147,000.

10. Same as 1, except that, in addition, on June 30 of the current year B sells her one-third interest in ABC to E for $200,000.

11. Same as 10, except that it is D who sells her one-third interest in ABC to E.

Chapter 7

PARTNERSHIP DISTRIBUTIONS

§ 7.01 INTRODUCTION

Subchapter K prefers not to tax distributions from a partnership to a partner, just as it prefers not to tax contributions by a partner to a partnership. It will only do so when necessary to prevent a negative basis, the conversion of ordinary income into capital gain, and abuse. Sometimes the rule of nontaxation seems to be overwhelmed by the exceptions, and the exceptions are often quite complex. If, however, you keep track of the general rule as we proceed with this chapter, it will help you understand the material that follows.

In Chapter 6 we discussed the distortions in inside and outside bases that can arise when a partner sells her partnership interest.[1] I.R.C. § 743(b) usually provides an optional adjustment that can address this issue. Distributions can cause similar distortions between inside and outside bases. I.R.C. § 734(b) again usually provides optional adjustments to reduce or eliminate the distortion. We will discuss these as well.

Finally, we will look at I.R.C. § 736, which in principle is designed to address how to treat the retirement of a partner from the partnership where payments are made over time. As we shall see, the reach of I.R.C. § 736 is far broader, however.

§ 7.02 NONLIQUIDATING DISTRIBUTIONS OF MONEY

Under I.R.C. § 731(a), a partner generally recognizes no gain or loss on the receipt of money from a partnership. The partner's basis in the partnership interest is reduced by the amount of money distributed under I.R.C. § 733, but not below zero. Recall that a partner's basis is increased by the amount of money and basis of property he contributes to the partnership as well as by his share of partnership income.[2] To the extent that any distribution, from a tax perspective, at least, represents a return of capital or a return of income that was previously allocated to him, not taxing the distribution makes sense. If the money distributed to a partner exceeds that partner's basis in the partnership interest, the distribution exceeds his tax investment in the partnership. Since the partner cannot have a negative basis, the only answer is to tax the partner on the amount by which the distribution exceeds basis, and I.R.C. § 731(a)(1) so provides.

---

[1] Recall, that a partner's basis in her partnership interest is called the "outside basis," and the partnership's basis in its assets is called the "inside basis."

[2] I.R.C. §§ 722, 705(a)(1).

Under I.R.C. § 731(a), the gain is characterized as gain from the sale of the partnership interest, typically capital gain. Generally, I.R.C. § 731(a)(1) looks at the basis of the partner at the time the distribution is made. The Regulations, however, provide that distributions which are draws against a partner's share of income are considered to be made on the last day of the partnership tax year, when the partner's outside basis is increased by his share of any partnership income.[3] To insure draw status, it may be advisable for the partnership agreement to contain a provision requiring repayment of any amount distributed that ultimately exceeds the partner's share of partnership income.[4] The draw "exception" largely swallows the rule in real life as most partnerships consider current distributions to be draws against income.

A money distribution may include situations other than handing over small, unmarked bills. The amount of the reduction in a partner's share of partnership liabilities is treated as a distribution of money to the partner.[5] Such a distribution is treated as if it were a draw against income and is thus considered to be made on the last day of the partnership tax year.[6] The distribution rules only apply to bona fide distributions. A loan to a partner, for example, is not a distribution and is governed by I.R.C. § 707(a).[7] If a loan is cancelled, however, the partner is considered to have received a distribution of the money at the time of the cancellation.[8]

§ 7.03   NONLIQUIDATING DISTRIBUTIONS OF PROPERTY

A.   General Rules

In line with the general bias against gain recognition, I.R.C. § 732(a) and (b), respectively, provide that neither the distributee partner nor the partnership recognizes a gain or loss on the distribution of property to a partner.[9] The distributee partner takes a carryover basis in the property under I.R.C. § 732. The gain or loss inherent in the distributed property is thus preserved and the gain or loss awaits recognition at a later date when the partner disposes of the property in a taxable transaction. I.R.C. § 733 requires the partner to reduce his basis in her partnership interest by the carryover basis taken in the distributed property. This makes sense. To the extent the partner received property with a basis tax-free, he should give up a concomitant part of his basis in the partnership interest. If cash is distributed in the same transaction, the partner's outside basis is first reduced for the cash, then for the carryover basis in the distributed property.

---

[3] Treas. Reg. § 1.731-1(a)(1)(ii); I.R.C. § 706(a).

[4] *See* McKee, Nelson & Whitmire, Federal Taxation of Partnerships and Partners ¶ 19.03[2] ("Federal Taxation of Partnerships and Partners"); *contra* Partnership Taxation at ¶ 13.02[1][b].

[5] I.R.C. § 752(b).

[6] Rev. Rul. 94-4, 1994-1 C.B. 196.

[7] Treas. Reg. § 1.731-1(c)(2).

[8] *Id.*

[9] There are a number of exceptions, including those for marketable securities and I.R.C. § 751 assets discussed below and those contained in I.R.C. §§ 704(c)(1)(B) and 737 discussed in Chapter 13.

If a partnership distributes property encumbered by a liability to a partner, the partner's share of partnership liabilities goes down, but his personal liabilities go up. Assume, for example, that the AB partnership with two equal partners holds a property with a basis of $1,000, subject to a $500 liability. The property is distributed to B in a nonliquidating distribution. Both A's and B's share of partnership liabilities would go down, and A and B would each have a deemed distribution of $250 under I.R.C. § 752(b). Since B is taking on the full liability, however, he will be deemed to make a contribution to the partnership under I.R.C. § 752(a) of $500. The liability decrease and increase simultaneously offset one another, for a deemed net contribution under I.R.C. § 752(a) by B of $250 with a concomitant increase in the basis of B's partnership interest.[10]

Not every time that a partnership conveys property to a partner will that conveyance necessarily be a distribution. In some circumstances, the conveyance may be a sale. I.R.C. § 707(a) (discussed in detail in Chapter 8) provides that if a partner engages in a transaction with a partnership other than in his capacity as a member of the partnership, the transaction is treated as if occurring between the partnership and someone who is not a partner.

In Rev. Rul. 2007-40,[11] a partnership was obligated to make a guaranteed payment to a partner of the type described in I.R.C. § 707(c). In lieu of distributing cash in satisfaction of the guaranteed payment, the partnership distributed real property having a fair market value equal to the guaranteed payment. Generally, if a partnership makes a distribution of property to a partner, no gain or loss is recognized under I.R.C. § 731(b). On the other hand, if a taxpayer conveys property to another in satisfaction of an obligation, or in exchange for the performance of services, the taxpayer must recognize gain or loss measured by the difference between the basis of the property conveyed and the fair market value of the property. Rev. Rul. 2007-40 holds that the conveyance of the real property to the partner was not a distribution, but rather was a sale of the real property under the general rules.

In Chief Counsel Advice 200650014 (Dec 15, 2006), the taxpayer's interest in a partnership was to be liquidated. To accomplish the liquidation, the partnership formed a single member LLC (treated as a disregarded entity) that purchased a house which it then transferred to the partner in exchange for his partnership interest. The taxpayer treated the transaction as a liquidating distribution in which neither he nor the partnership had any gain or loss pursuant to I.R.C. § 731. The IRS concluded, however, that I.R.C. § 731 did not apply because the house was acquired solely for the purpose of the distribution, and was not related to the partnership's business. It also stated that the partnership was never the owner of the house for tax purposes. Lastly, the IRS stated that there was no economic substance to the transaction.

---

[10] Rev. Rul. 79-205, 1979-2 C.B. 255.

[11] 2007-1 C.B. 1426.

B. Outside Basis Less Than Inside Basis

Sometimes, however, the partner does not have enough outside basis in his partnership interest to go around. If the outside basis is less than the basis of the distributed property, reducing the outside basis by the full amount of the partnership's inside basis in the distributed asset would give the partner a negative outside basis. The one consistent rule in tax is that one cannot have a negative basis. To resolve this problem, I.R.C. § 732(a)(2) provides that if the outside basis (after first reducing it for any cash distributed in the same transaction) is less than the inside basis of the distributed asset, then the partner's basis in the distributed asset is limited to the available outside basis. Under I.R.C. § 733, the outside basis is then reduced to zero.

For example, assume the partnership distributes property to a partner with a fair market value of $100 and a basis of $50. The partner has an outside basis of $40. Under these rules, the partner's basis in the distributed property is limited to $40 and her basis in the partnership interest is reduced to zero. Note that on the sale of the property, the partner will necessarily recognize more gain than the partnership would have recognized.

What happens if the partnership distributes several properties to a partner and the partner's outside basis is insufficient to give her a full carryover basis in the distributed properties? The maximum basis the partner is allowed in all of the properties is limited to the outside basis. How is it allocated amongst the distributed properties? I.R.C. § 732(c) provides the applicable rules. These rules are somewhat complex. The outside basis is first allocated to unrealized receivables and inventory to the extent possible. Note that this limits the extent to which the distributee partner may have more ordinary income to recognize than the partnership would have had.[12] If the outside basis of the partner is insufficient to give the partner a full carryover basis in those assets, then the basis of the assets must be reduced to equal the available outside basis. Any decrease in the basis of the distributed assets is first allocated to properties with built-in loss (i.e., a basis in excess of fair market value) in proportion to the respective built-in losses, but not in an amount in excess of any property's built-in loss. If an additional decrease in basis in the distributed properties is necessary, it is allocated among the distributed properties in proportion to their respective bases.[13]

If there is sufficient outside basis to give the distributee partner a full carryover basis in the inventory and unrealized receivables, then the balance of the basis is again allocated to any other distributed assets. Again, the basis decrease to those assets is first allocated to assets with built-in loss in proportion to the built-in losses (but not in excess of any built-in loss) and any remaining decrease is allocated in proportion to the respective bases of the other distributed assets.[14]

---

[12] I.R.C. § 735, discussed below, generally provides that the character of the assets to the partner will be the same as they were to the partnership.

[13] I.R.C. § 732(c)(3).

[14] *Id.*

For example, assume partner A has an outside basis of $9,000 and the partnership distributed to A inventory with a basis to the partnership of $5,000 and a fair market value of $9,000, and two parcels of land (both capital assets) each with a basis to the partnership of $3,000 and a fair market value of $500. A's outside basis of $9,000 is first allocated to the inventory, giving A a carryover basis in the inventory of $5,000 and reducing his outside basis to $4,000 ($9,000 − $5,000). A's remaining outside basis of $4,000 is insufficient to give him a carryover basis in the two parcels of land which together have a basis of $6,000. The bases of the two parcels thus must be reduced by $2,000. The relative depreciation in each parcel is the same, $2,500, so the basis of each parcel is reduced by 50% of the total $2,000 reduction, or $1,000 each. Thus, A's basis in each parcel is $3,000 − $1,000 = $2,000.

C. Marketable Securities

As we have seen, a distribution of money is only tax free to the extent of a partner's outside basis. Any distribution of money in excess of the basis causes the partner to recognize gain. A distribution of property, on the other hand, can be tax free irrespective of the partner's outside basis. If marketable securities were treated like any other non-cash property, a partnership might be inclined to distribute them instead of money in situations where a money distribution would cause the partner to recognize gain. For that reason, I.R.C. § 731(c) generally treats a distribution of marketable securities as a distribution of money to the extent of their fair market value at the time of the distribution. Marketable securities are primarily financial instruments and foreign currencies that are actively traded, including interests in common trust funds and mutual funds.[15] The partner's basis in the marketable security will be a carryover basis under I.R.C. § 732 increased by any gain recognized to the partner on the distribution,[16] though for purposes of reducing the distributee's basis under I.R.C. § 733, the gain is ignored.[17] If different marketable securities are distributed in the same transaction and gain is recognized, the basis increase in the securities is allocated in proportion to the built-in gain in the securities (i.e., the amount by which the fair market value exceeds basis).[18]

Assume, for example, that A and B form the AB partnership as equal partners. A contributes an asset with a fair market value of $1,000 and an adjusted basis of $300, and B contributes $1,000 of cash. AB subsequently purchases Marketable Security Y for $200 that appreciated in value to $500 and then distributes it to A in a current distribution. AB holds no other marketable securities. Under I.R.C. § 722, A's basis in his partnership interest is $300. The distribution of the security is treated as a distribution of money in the amount of $500. Ignoring (for the sake of simplicity) I.R.C. § 731(c)(3)(B), A recognizes a gain of $200 under I.R.C. § 731(a)(1). A's basis in the security is initially a carryover basis of $200 under

---

[15] This is a partial list, see I.R.C. § 732(c)(2) for the full definition.

[16] I.R.C. § 732(c)(4). The gain will normally be capital gain, as it would be with a distribution of money, unless the marketable securities constitute unrealized receivables or inventory items, in which case the gain will be ordinary income. I.R.C. § 731(c)(6).

[17] I.R.C. § 731(c)(5).

[18] I.R.C. § 731(c)(4)(B).

I.R.C. § 732(a)(1), but then increased for the $200 of gain recognized under I.R.C. § 731(c)(4)(A), giving A a basis in the security of $400. A's basis in the partnership interest, after factoring in I.R.C. § 731(c)(5), is $300 − $200, or $100.[19]

I.R.C. § 731(c)(3)(A), in conjunction with the Regulations contains a number of exceptions. A distribution of a marketable security to a partner who contributed it will not ordinarily be treated as a distribution of money. The same is generally true if the marketable securities distributed were acquired by the partnership in a nonrecognition transaction if two conditions are met: (1) the marketable securities constituted less than 20% of the value of all the assets exchanged by the partnership in the nonrecognition transaction; and (2) the marketable securities are distributed within five years of either the date the partnership acquired them or the date the security became marketable.[20] Another exception is provided under certain circumstances if the security was not marketable when acquired by the partnership.[21] Finally, there is also an exception for a distribution by an investment partnership if the distributee partner did not contribute any property to the partnership other than money or securities.[22]

Under I.R.C. § 731(c)(3)(B), the fair market value of marketable securities distributed generally is reduced by the excess of:

1. the distributee partner's share of the net gain that would have been recognized if all of the marketable securities held by the partnership were sold over

2. the distributee partner's share of that gain for the marketable securities held by the partnership immediately after the distribution.[23]

Assume, for example, that A and B form partnership AB as equal partners. AB subsequently distributes security X to A in a current distribution. Immediately before the distribution, AB held the following securities:

	FMV	Basis	Gain (Loss)
Security X	100	70	30
Security Y	100	80	20
Security Z	100	110	(10)

If AB had sold the securities for their fair market values immediately before the distribution, AB would have recognized $40 of net gain. A's distributive share would have been $20. If AB had sold Securities Y and Z immediately after the distribution of Security X to A, the partnership would have recognized $10 of net gain. A's distributive share of that would have been $5. Thus, the distribution resulted in a $15 reduction in A's distributive share of the net gain in AB's securities ($20 before − $5 after). Under I.R.C. § 731(c)(3)(B), the amount of the distribution of Security

---

[19] This example is based on Treas. Reg. § 1.731-2(j), example 1.

[20] Treas. Reg. § 1.731-2(d)(1)(ii).

[21] Treas. Reg. § 1.731-2(d)(1)(iii).

[22] I.R.C. § 731(c)(3)(A)(iii), (c)(3)(C).

[23] *See* Treas. Reg. § 1.731-2(b).

X that is treated as a distribution of money is reduced to $85 ($100 − $15).[24]

§ 7.04 CAPITAL ACCOUNTS

Recall that capital accounts are designed to measure the economic value of a partner's partnership interest. (See Chapter 5.) At the time property is distributed to a partner, there may be inherent in it both book and tax gain or loss. As we have seen, the tax gain or loss is generally not recognized on the distribution. The capital accounts would be distorted if they were reduced for the fair market value of distributed property (as the Regulations require), but not adjusted for the book gain or loss inherent in distributed property. Consequently, the Regulations also require that book gain or loss be recognized on the distribution of property (which is allocated under the allocation formula in the partnership agreement).[25] For example, assume A and B are equal partners in the AB partnership and the partnership distributes $10,000 to A and land (which is a capital asset to the partnership) to B. The land has a fair market value of $10,000 and a book and tax basis of $6,000. None of the tax gain is recognized. The $4,000 of book gain, however, is recognized for book purposes, and the capital accounts of A and B are increased for half of the book gain or $2,000 each. B's capital account is reduced by the fair market value of the distributed land, or $10,000.

§ 7.05 I.R.C. § 732(d)

I.R.C. § 732(d) applies to partners who receive distributions of property from the partnership, but acquired their partnership interests by sale, exchange, or inheritance[26] from another partner when an I.R.C. § 754 election is *not* in effect. (See Chapter 6.) The distribution must occur within two years of the transfer of the partnership interest to the distributee partner. In determining the basis of the distributed assets, the distributee partner receives the basis adjustment provided in I.R.C. § 743(b) notwithstanding the lack of an I.R.C. § 754 election. This adjustment applies only for the purpose of determining the basis of distributed property and not (as would be the case with an actual I.R.C. § 754 election) for purposes of partnership depreciation, depletion, or gain or loss on disposition.[27] The transferee partner, not the partnership as is the case with I.R.C. § 754, must make an election to use I.R.C. § 732(d).[28]

The I.R.C. § 732(d) option may be particularly valuable when the partnership is about to sell ordinary income property that would be eligible for an I.R.C. § 743(b) adjustment had an I.R.C. § 754 election been made. If the partnership distributes to the transferee partner his share of that ordinary income property within two

---

[24] This example is based on Treas. Reg. § 1.731-2(j), example 2.

[25] Treas. Reg. § 1.704-1(b)(2)(iv)(e)(1).

[26] I.R.C. § 732(d) provides that the partner is given an often modified version of the I.R.C. § 743(b) adjustment. The I.R.C. § 743(b) adjustment in turn applies when the partner acquired the partnership interest by sale, exchange, or purchase. *See* PARTNERSHIP TAXATION at ¶ 13.03[6][a].

[27] Treas. Reg. § 1.732-1(d)(1)(vi).

[28] Treas. Reg. § 1.732-1(d)(1)(iii).

years of when the partnership interest was acquired, then when that partner sells the property he can avoid, or at least reduce, the ordinary income realized due to the I.R.C. § 743(b) adjustment.[29] Of course, this assumes the transferee partner has sufficient outside basis to be able to take meaningful advantage of the I.R.C. § 743(b) adjustment.[30]

The Code and Regulations require an I.R.C. § 743(b) adjustment under some circumstances. The Regulations require the distributee partner to apply the special basis rule contained in I.R.C. § 732(d) to any distribution of property made by the partnership to him at any time (not just within two years of acquiring the interest) if at the time of the acquisition of the transferred interest:

1. The fair market value of all partnership property (other than money) exceeded 110% of its adjusted basis to the partnership.

2. An allocation of basis under I.R.C. § 732(c) upon a liquidation of his interest immediately after the transfer of the interest would have resulted in a shift of basis from property not subject to an allowance for depreciation, depletion, or amortization, to property subject to such an allowance; and

3. An I.R.C. § 743(b) basis adjustment would change the basis to the transferee partner of the property actually distributed.[31]

The point here is to prevent the distributee from obtaining tax benefits that might arise as the result of shifting basis from, for example, nondepreciable property to depreciable property via a distribution. The likelihood of this Regulation applying is somewhat reduced by I.R.C. § 197, which allows the amortization of intangible assets that were often not amortizable before its promulgation.

§ 7.06 THE SALE OF DISTRIBUTED PROPERTY

As we discussed in Chapter 4, partnership income is normally characterized at the partnership level. As we discussed in Chapter 2, I.R.C. § 724 provides an exception under which unrealized receivables, inventory, and capital loss property that were contributed to the partnership by a partner are characterized by reference to their status in the hands of the contributing partner. I.R.C. § 735 is the analogue of I.R.C. § 724 for distributions. Under I.R.C. § 735(a)(1) and (2), when a distributee partner sells distributed unrealized receivables or inventory, he generally recognizes ordinary gain or loss. Unrealized receivables stay tainted forever; inventory loses its taint after five years and is then characterized based on how the distributee holds it. Neither the partner nor the partnership can end run I.R.C. § 735 by swapping the distributed unrealized receivables or inventory for other property in a nonrecognition transaction. I.R.C. § 735(c)(2) provides that the provisions of I.R.C. § 735 will apply to the property received in the exchange. The Code, however, excepts from this rule C corporation stock received in an exchange

---

[29] *See* PARTNERSHIP TAXATION ¶ 13.03[6][a].

[30] *See* I.R.C. § 732(a)(2).

[31] Treas. Reg. § 1.732-1(d)(4).

under I.R.C. § 351, apparently figuring that the burden of corporate double taxation outweighs the need to continue the ordinary income taint.

I.R.C. § 735 defines unrealized receivables by reference to I.R.C. § 751(c). While the definition of unrealized receivables in I.R.C. § 751(c) can include I.R.C. § 1245 recapture property,[32] it does not do so for I.R.C. § 735 purposes. The "recomputed basis" rules of I.R.C. § 1245, however, will keep the recapture taint attached to the property. Thus, when the partner sells a distributed property, I.R.C. § 1245 will apply to the sale.[33]

I.R.C. § 735(b) generally gives the distributee partner a tacked holding period in the distributed property, though there is of course no tacking for purposes of the five-year taint that applies to inventory.

§ 7.07   I.R.C. § 734(B) ADJUSTMENTS

A.   Introduction

Under I.R.C. § 734(a), the distribution of property to a partner does not affect the inside basis of partnership property. This can lead to distortions. Consider the equal ABC partnership with the following balance sheet:

P/S Assets	Adj. Basis	F.M.V.	Partners	Adj. Basis	F.M.V.
Cash	$12,000	$12,000	A	$6,000	$12,000
Land	$6,000	$24,000	B	$6,000	$12,000
			C	$6,000	$12,000
Total	$18,000	$36,000		$18,000	$36,000

Assume the land is a capital asset and that the partnership distributes $12,000 of cash to C in liquidation of C's interest. Under I.R.C. § 731(a)(1), C will recognize $6,000 of gain on the distribution. This is appropriate enough since that is the gain inherent in her interest. But look at the problem that creates for A and B. Before the liquidation of C's interest, their shares of the $18,000 of gain inherent in the land were $6,000 each. After the distribution, their shares of that gain become $9,000 each. If and when recognized, that gain will increase their bases in the partnership interest to $15,000, notwithstanding the fact that the fair market value of the interest remains at $12,000. Assuming no change in the figures, on a subsequent sale or liquidation of their partnership interests, A and B will recognize a $3,000 loss which, when offset against the $9,000 of gain, will give them the same $6,000 of gain C recognized. But the sale or liquidation could be years away, and if A or B dies in the interim, he will take the losses with him.

---

[32] Generally, I.R.C. § 1245 provides that if a taxpayer sells depreciable personal property at a gain, he recognizes ordinary income on the sale to the extent of any depreciation taken on the property. Any additional gain is normally governed by I.R.C. § 1231, which would generally characterize the additional gain as long-term capital gain if total I.R.C. § 1231 gains exceed total I.R.C. § 1231 losses.

[33] I.R.C. § 1245(b)(3), (6).

In a manner that is reminiscent of the I.R.C. § 743(b) adjustment discussed in Chapter 6, if an I.R.C. § 754 election is in effect, I.R.C. § 734(b) provides an adjustment that can solve the problem. In our example, the basis of the land would be increased by the gain C recognized on the distribution, or $6,000. That would give the partnership a basis in the land of $12,000, and A's and B's shares of the remaining gain would return to being $6,000 each.

B.   The Devil Is in the Details

I.R.C. § 754 and its Regulations provide for the election, I.R.C. § 734(b) and its Regulations provide the amount of the adjustment, and I.R.C. § 755 and its Regulations provide for how the adjustment is allocated to the partnership assets. While I.R.C. § 743(b) adjustments only benefit the buying partner, I.R.C. § 734(b) adjustments benefit all of the continuing partners as the basis adjustments apply to partnership property and do not belong to a particular partner.

There are four ways for an I.R.C. § 734(b) adjustment to arise:[34]

1. When a distributee partner recognizes a gain on a distribution under I.R.C. § 731(a)(1).[35] The amount of the adjustment is the amount of the gain.

2. When a distributee partner recognizes a loss on a distribution under I.R.C. § 731(a)(2). This can only happen in liquidation of a partner's interest, discussed below. The amount of the adjustment is the amount of the loss.

3. When a distributee partner takes a lesser basis under I.R.C. § 732(a)(2) in distributed property than that which the partnership had. As discussed above, this will occur when the distributee partner has insufficient outside basis to give her a full carryover basis in the distributed property. The amount of the adjustment is the difference between the basis the partnership had in the property and the basis the distributee partner took in the property. For example, assume the partnership's basis in distributed property was $10,000 and the distributee's outside basis in the partnership interest is $8,000. The adjustment is $2,000.

4. When a distributee partner takes a greater basis under I.R.C. § 732(b) in distributed property than that which the partnership had. This again can only happen in liquidation of a partner's interest, discussed below. For example, if the partnership's basis in distributed property was $6,000 but the distributee's basis is $9,000, the adjustment is $3,000.

How the adjustments are allocated to partnership property is provided in I.R.C. § 755 and its Regulations. As was the case for I.R.C. § 743(b) adjustments, the partnership's assets are divided into two categories: (1) the capital asset and I.R.C. § 1231 property class and (2) the ordinary income class. If the adjustment results

---

[34] Treas. Reg. § 1.735-1(b).

[35] Note that in each of the four cases the partnership must have made a bona fide distribution and not, for example, a disguised sale under I.R.C. § 707(a)(2)(A).

from the distributee partner recognizing a gain or loss, the capital asset and I.R.C. § 1231 property class of assets is adjusted.[36] Under I.R.C. § 734(b)(1)(A) and (B), gain gives an upward adjustment, loss yields a downward adjustment. Note that any gain or loss recognized by a partner will normally be a capital gain or loss. If the relevant I.R.C. § 734(b) adjustment could be allocated to the ordinary income class, the taxpayers would be able to arbitrage tax rates. Capital gains to the distributee would reduce ordinary income to the remaining partners.[37] To prevent that, the Regulations require that the adjustment be allocated to the capital asset and I.R.C. § 1231 property class.

If the adjustment results from the distributee partner taking a different basis in distributed property than that which the partnership had, the class of assets adjusted is the same as the class to which the distributed property belongs.[38] Thus, if a capital asset is distributed and the distributee partner takes a different basis in that asset than that which the partnership had, the capital and I.R.C. § 1231 property class is adjusted. Under I.R.C. § 734(b)(1)(B) and (2)(B), if the distributee takes a lesser basis, it is an upward adjustment; if the distributee takes a greater basis, it is a downward adjustment.

An upward adjustment is allocated in up to two steps. Step 1: The adjustment is allocated to appreciated assets within a class in proportion to the appreciation inherent in each asset, but under this step the amount allocated to a property cannot exceed the appreciation inherent in that property. Step 2: If the first step does not fully use the available I.R.C. § 734(b) adjustment, any remaining upward adjustment is allocated to *all* of the assets in the class in proportion to their fair market values.[39]

A downward adjustment is allocated in up to three steps. Step 1: The adjustment is allocated to depreciated assets within a class in proportion to the depreciation inherent in each asset, but under this step the amount allocated to a property cannot exceed the depreciation inherent in that property. Step 2: If the first step does not fully use the available I.R.C. § 734(b) adjustment, any remaining downward adjustment is allocated to *all* of the assets in the class in proportion to their adjusted bases.[40] The basis of a property cannot, of course, be reduced below zero, which leads to Step 3: Any unused adjustment remaining after Step 2 is held in abeyance until assets with basis are added to that class. Thus, if the downward adjustment held in abeyance is to the ordinary income class, assets will have to be acquired in *that* class that have basis which can then be adjusted downward.[41]

First return to the example presented at the start of this section and make sure you understand how the I.R.C. § 734(b) adjustment works with those facts. Then take a look at an expanded version of that example:

---

[36] Treas. Reg. § 1.755-1(c)(1)(ii).

[37] *See* Partnership Taxation at ¶ 13.05[8].

[38] Treas. Reg. § 1.755-1(c)(1)(i).

[39] Treas. Reg. § 1.755-1(c)(2)(i).

[40] Treas. Reg. § 1.755-1(c)(2)(ii).

[41] Treas. Reg. § 1.755-1(c)(3), (4).

P/S Assets	Adj. Basis	F.M.V.	Partners	Adj. Basis	F.M.V.
Cash	$18,000	$18,000	A	$10,000	$18,000
Land	$6,000	$24,000	B	$10,000	$18,000
Land #2	$6,000	$12,000	C	$10,000	$18,000
Total	$30,000	$54,000		$30,000	$54,000

Again, both parcels of land are capital assets. $18,000 is distributed to C in liquidation of her interest.[42] C has gain under I.R.C. § 731(a)(1) of $8,000. An I.R.C. § 754 election is in effect. Since there is a gain, there is an $8,000 upward adjustment to the capital asset and I.R.C. § 1231 property class, the only class of assets that exists in this example. There is a total of $24,000 of gain inherent in the two parcels of land, $18,000 in land #1 and $6,000 in land #2. Land #1 thus has 75% of the total gain (18,000/24,000) and land #2 has 25% (6,000/24,000). Therefore 75% of the $8,000 upward adjustment, or $6,000, is allocated to land #1 and 25% of $8,000, or $2,000, is allocated to land #2. The partnership's ending balance sheet thus would be:

P/S Assets	Adj. Basis	F.M.V.	Partners	Adj. Basis	F.M.V.
			A	$10,000	$18,000
Land	$12,000	$24,000	B	$10,000	$18,000
Land #2	$8,000	$12,000			
Total	$20,000	$36,000		$20,000	$36,000

I.R.C. § 734(b) can interact with both I.R.C. § 732(d) (discussed above) and I.R.C. § 743(b) (discussed in Chapter 6). Assume that E buys A's interest in the ABC partnership and no I.R.C. § 754 election is in effect. Within two years of the purchase, the partnership makes an I.R.C. § 754 election and distributes property to E that reduces E's interest in the partnership from one-third to one-quarter. Assume E's outside basis in the partnership interest is $10,000. The partnership's "regular" basis in the distributed property is $8,000, but the basis in that property for I.R.C. § 732(d) purposes is $12,000. It is that latter basis that is used for determining whether I.R.C. § 734(b) applies.[43] Since for these purposes the partnership's inside basis of $12,000 exceeds E's outside basis of $10,000, there is an upward I.R.C. § 734(b) adjustment of $2,000 that applies to the same class of property as the class to which the distributed property belonged.

Assume the same facts set forth above except that an I.R.C. § 754 election was in effect before E's purchase and at the time of the distribution.[44] Assume after making the I.R.C. § 743(b) adjustment, with regard to E, the property's basis is

---

[42] Note that while in our example we are liquidating C's interest, in part to simplify the math, I.R.C. § 734(b) also applies when a partner's interest in the partnership is merely reduced.

[43] *See* I.R.C. § 734(b)(1)(B), (2)(B).

[44] To create the higher I.R.C. § 743(b) adjustment in the distributed property, E's outside basis must exceed E's share of the inside basis. So why is E's outside basis now less than the basis of the partnership property after accounting for I.R.C. § 743(b)? Perhaps E's outside basis was reduced in the interim by cash distributions or partnership losses.

$12,000. The answer would be the same as when I.R.C. § 732(d) applied.[45]

C. Mandatory "As If" I.R.C. § 754 Elections

As we note above, I.R.C. § 754 elections can result in downward adjustments as well as upward adjustments. Downward adjustments are much less fun. Assume, for example, that A, B, and C form a partnership. In Year 1, A and B each contribute $300,000 and C contributes $600,000. The partnership purchases two parcels of land. Both are capital assets. The partnership pays $400,000 for Parcel #1 and $800,000 for Parcel #2. In Year 2 Parcel #2 drops in value to $400,000. In Year 2 the partnership distributes Parcel #1 to C in liquidation of his interest. Under the liquidation rules, discussed in detail below, C's basis in Parcel #1 is $600,000, her entire outside basis.[46] If the values do not change, C will recognize a $200,000 capital loss when she sells this parcel. As we discussed above, if an I.R.C. § 754 election is in effect, the partnership must reduce its basis in Parcel #2 by $200,000, the excess of C's basis in Parcel #1 over the basis it had to the partnership. That would give the partnership a basis of $600,000 in Parcel #2. Assuming no value changes, the partnership would then recognize a $200,000 capital loss on the sale of Parcel #2 ($400,000 − $600,000). But if an I.R.C. § 754 election is not in effect, there is no basis adjustment, and the partnership will recognize a $400,000 loss on the sale of Parcel #2 ($400,000 − $800,000), effectively duplicating C's loss on the sale of Parcel #1.

Congress was unenthusiastic about this duplication (though gains can also be duplicated if no I.R.C. § 754 election is in effect — though it is more likely to be in effect if the partnership is sane, or at least well-advised). As a consequence, the American Jobs Creation Act of 2004 amended I.R.C. § 734(b) to mandate a downward basis adjustment, even if no I.R.C. § 754 election is in effect, if there is a "substantial basis reduction." New I.R.C. § 734(d) provides that a substantial basis reduction exists if the downward adjustments provided in I.R.C. § 734(b)(2) exceed $250,000.[47] As we discussed above, I.R.C. § 734(b)(2) provides for a downward basis adjustment if a distributee partner recognizes a loss on distribution or takes a greater basis in distributed partnership property than that which the partnership had, both of which can only happen in liquidation. Normally, an I.R.C. § 754 election must be in effect for the I.R.C. § 734(b)(2) adjustments to be applicable, but the amendments to the code trigger the adjustments when an I.R.C. § 754 election is not in effect if the adjustment exceeds $250,000. In the above example, this new rule would not apply as the basis adjustment would have only been $200,000, but had it exceeded $250,000, the partnership would have had to reduce the basis of Parcel #2 even if an I.R.C. § 754 election were not in effect.[48]

---

[45] For an article discussing some of the problems with I.R.C. § 734(b), see Howard Abrams, *The Section 734(b) Basis Adjustment Needs Repair*, 57 Tax Law. 343 (2004).

[46] I.R.C. § 732(b).

[47] There is an exception for "securitization partnerships." *See* I.R.C. § 734(e).

[48] There is a corresponding rule in I.R.C. § 743, discussed in Chapter 6. *See* Jeffery Rosenberg, *AJCA Imposes New Burdens for Partnership Basis Adjustments Under Sections 734 and 743*, 101 J. Tax'n 334 (2004).

§ 7.08 SHIFTS IN ORDINARY INCOME PROPERTY

A. Introduction

Congress would not have been wise to stop with the rules we have discussed so far, for if it did, it would be easy for a distributee partner to avoid ordinary income recognition, at least if her other partners were cooperative. For example, assume that a partner in that partnership with a $10,000 basis in her partnership interest receives $15,000 of cash in complete liquidation of the partnership interest. Based on the rules we have discussed so far, the partner would typically recognize *capital* gain of $5,000 on the distribution under I.R.C. § 731(a)(1). It would usually be capital gain because I.R.C. § 731(a) provides that any gain or loss recognized is considered to be gain or loss from the sale or exchange of the distributee's partnership interest, and the partnership interest is usually a capital asset to the distributee.

But what if the partnership held ordinary income assets such as receivables and inventory? Without other Code provisions, the distributee partner could avoid recognizing her share of any ordinary income she would have recognized had she stayed a partner and the partnership had collected the receivables or sold the inventory. Or saying the same thing in other words, she would have converted ordinary income into capital gain. Congress hates that and enacted I.R.C. § 751(b) in response. In Chapter 6 we discussed I.R.C. § 751(a), which performs a similar function in the case of a sale of a partnership interest. Effectively, I.R.C. § 751(b) trumps the other rules of I.R.C. §§ 731 and 732 and requires ordinary income (and possibly other gain) recognition on the part of the partner and/or the partnership if a distribution shifts the partners' interests in certain ordinary income property.

B. Unrealized Receivables and Substantially Appreciated Inventory

I.R.C. § 751(b) will apply if the partnership holds unrealized receivables or substantially appreciated inventory.[49] To simplify our lives, we will sometimes call unrealized receivables and inventory "I.R.C. § 751 property." You should know that tax professionals also sometimes refer to these assets as "hot assets." We will sometimes call any other property "I.R.C. § 741 property." We covered I.R.C. § 751 property in detail in Chapter 6, but some additional rules apply to inventory.

Inventory is an I.R.C. § 751(b) asset only if it is "substantially appreciated," meaning that it has a fair market value in excess of 120% of its adjusted basis.[50] It would conceivably be possible to manipulate this test by buying inventory for quick resale. The basis and fair market value would be about the same. When added to the "genuine" inventory, it would increase the basis of the inventory proportionately more than the fair market value, and it might help the partnership avoid the substantial appreciation test. To help thwart such efforts, I.R.C.

---

[49] Note that for I.R.C. § 751(a) purposes, the inventory does not need to be substantially appreciated.

[50] I.R.C. § 751(b)(3)(A); special basis adjustments of a partner are ignored for these purposes. Treas. Reg. § 1.751-1(d)(1).

§ 751(b)(3)(B) contains an anti-stuffing rule, which provides that any property acquired for the principal purpose of avoiding the application of I.R.C. § 751(b) will not be counted as inventory.

Under I.R.C. § 751(d)(2), inventory includes any property that would not constitute a capital or I.R.C. § 1231 asset. As a consequence, unrealized receivables usually also meet the definition for inventory. This is important because it makes it far easier for inventory to meet the substantial appreciation test for partnerships on the cash method of accounting. The typical unrealized receivable will have a basis of zero. It would thus add nothing to basis, but increase the overall fair market value of inventory items, making it more likely that the fair market value of the inventory will exceed 120% of their adjusted basis. Of course, for I.R.C. § 751(b) purposes, you cannot count an asset more than once. Thus, while unrealized receivables can count as inventory for purposes of the substantial appreciation test, they go back to their regular status for purposes of implementing I.R.C. § 751(b).[51]

Assume a partnership has the following balance sheet:

P/S Assets	Adj. Basis	F.M.V.	Partners	Adj. Basis	F.M.V.
Cash	$30,000	$30,000	A	$16,000	$26,600
Inventory	$18,000	$19,800	B	$16,000	$26,600
Acct. Rec.	0	$30,000	C	$16,000	$26,600
Total	$48,000	$79,800		$48,000	$79,800

Note that the "true" inventory by itself is not substantially appreciated. The fair market value of $19,800 is only 110% of the $18,000 basis. But when the accounts receivable are added in, the inventory becomes substantially appreciated. The combined fair market value of $49,800 is more than double the combined basis of $18,000.

If a partnership is on the accrual method of accounting, on the other hand, counting the accounts receivable as inventory might actually prevent the inventory from being substantially appreciated. For example:

P/S Assets	Adj. Basis	F.M.V.	Partners	Adj. Basis	F.M.V.
Cash	$21,000	$21,000	A	$21,000	$22,000
Inventory	$2,000	$5,000	B	$21,000	$22,000
Acct. Rec.	$40,000	$40,000	C	$21,000	$22,000
Total	$63,000	$66,000		$63,000	$66,000

In this example, the fair market value of the inventory is more than double its basis, but when the accounts receivable are added in, the fair market value of $45,000 is less than 120% of the basis of $42,000.

---

[51] *See* Treas. Reg. § 1.751-1(g), example 2.

C.   The Nuts and Bolts

We gave brief examples earlier illustrating why Congress put I.R.C. § 751(b) into the Code. Now let's take a more detailed look. Assume that A, B, and C are equal partners in the ABC partnership. The partnership has the following balance sheet:

P/S Assets	Adj. Basis	F.M.V.	Partners	Adj. Basis	F.M.V.
Cash	$30,000	$30,000	A	$21,000	$30,000
Inventory	$21,000	$30,000	B	$21,000	$30,000
Cap. Asset	$12,000	$30,000	C	$21,000	$30,000
Total	$63,000	$90,000		$63,000	$90,000

Assume that partner C receives the inventory in liquidation of his interest. It is of no particular significance that it is a liquidating as opposed to an operating distribution; we have made it a liquidating distribution in order to make the numbers easier to follow. Note that the inventory is substantially appreciated. The fair market value of $30,000 exceeds 120% of the basis of $18,000 (120% of $18,000 is $21,600). Also, assume that the capital asset has been held for more than one year. If I.R.C. § 751(b) did not exist, C would receive the inventory with a basis of $18,000 and a fair market value of $30,000 and his basis in his partnership interest would be reduced to zero.[52] There is $12,000 of gain inherent in the inventory in C's hands. There is $24,000 of gain inherent in the capital asset the partnership continues to hold, or $12,000 each for A and B. Thus, all the partners have the same *amount* of gain that they had before C's interest was liquidated. But the *character* of the gain has changed. If the partnership had sold all of its assets before C's interest was liquidated, each partner would have had $4,000 of ordinary income and $8,000 of long-term capital gain. If the partnership sells all of its assets and C sells the inventory after C's interest is liquidated, A and B each have $12,000 of long-term capital gain and C has $12,000 of ordinary income.[53] A and B have shifted their shares of the ordinary income that was inherent in the inventory to C; that is, A and B have converted ordinary income into capital gains. I.R.C. § 751(b) stops this, though as we will see, it does not always do so perfectly. While it prevents partners from converting ordinary income into capital gains, it does not always prevent partners from shifting ordinary income among themselves.[54]

The mechanics of I.R.C. § 751(b) are complex. The starting point of I.R.C. § 751(b) is that each partner has, in effect, an undivided interest in the assets that constitute I.R.C. § 751 property and I.R.C. § 741 property. If an interest in one class is swapped for an interest in the other class, a taxable event has occurred. Note that partners (or LLC members) are generally not considered to have an ownership interest in partnership (or LLC) property for state law purposes.[55]

---

[52] I.R.C. §§ 731(a), 732(b), (c)(1)(A).

[53] I.R.C. § 735(a)(2).

[54] *See* Monte Jackel & Avery Stok, *Blissful Ignorance: Section 751(b) Uncharted Territory*, 98 TAX NOTES 1557 (2003).

[55] *See* Revised Uniform Partnership Act ("RUPA") § 203.

I.R.C. § 751(b) creates a fiction to avoid ordinary income shifting. From the perspective of I.R.C. § 751(b), C held a one-third interest in the partnership assets consisting of:

Assets	Adjusted Basis	F.M.V.
Cash	$10,000	$10,000
Inventory	$7,000	$10,000
Capital Asset	$4,000	$10,000
Total	$21,000	$30,000

C effectively exchanged his interest in the cash and the capital asset (the I.R.C. § 741 assets) for the "extra" two-thirds of the inventory (the I.R.C. § 751(b) asset). I.R.C. § 751(b) requires C and the partnership (now A and B) to treat what is an exchange in substance as an exchange for tax purposes.[56]

The partnership is deemed to have made a phantom distribution of the I.R.C. § 741 assets to C. The partners may actually choose which I.R.C. § 741 assets are deemed to have been distributed to C. The partners could, for example, choose just the cash or just the capital asset. If there is no specific agreement, as we will assume here, C is deemed to receive a pro rata share of each I.R.C. § 741 asset.[57] Thus, the partnership is deemed to have made a phantom distribution to C of one-third of the cash and the capital asset. The "regular" distribution rules apply to this phantom distribution. C will thus first reduce his $18,000 basis for the $10,000 of cash deemed received, leaving him with a basis of $8,000 in the partnership interest. C will then reduce his basis by the partnership's $2,000 basis in the capital asset and take a full carryover basis in that asset, leaving C with a $6,000 basis in his partnership interest. Under I.R.C. § 731, C recognizes no gain or loss.

C now enters into a phantom, taxable exchange with the partnership, as follows:

C		Partnership
Cash $10,000 and		Inventory
Capital Asset	For	F.M.V. $20,000
F.M.V. $10,000		Basis $14,000
Basis $4,000		

C will recognize $6,000 of capital gain on the capital asset and the partnership will recognize $8,000 of ordinary income on the inventory.[58] Logically enough, the Regulations require that the partnership's ordinary income be allocated to A and B.[59] Note that at this point A and B have recognized the pro rata shares of the ordinary income inherent in the inventory and each will increase his basis in his partnership interest by the $4,000 of income recognized.[60] C will take a fair market

---

[56] Treas. Reg. § 1.751-1(b)(2)(i).

[57] Treas. Reg. § 1.751-1(g), example 4(c).

[58] I.R.C. § 1001(a), (c).

[59] Treas. Reg. § 1.751-1(b)(2)(ii), (b)(3)(ii).

[60] I.R.C. § 705(a)(1)(A).

basis of $20,000 in two-thirds of the inventory, and the partnership will take a fair market value basis of $10,000 in one-third of the capital asset.[61]

After the phantom exchange, the balance sheet of the partnership is as follows:

Assets	Adj. Basis	F.M.V.	Partners	Adj. Basis	F.M.V.
Cash	$30,000	$30,000	A	$24,000	$30,000
Inventory	$7,000	$10,000	B	$24,000	$30,000
Cap. Asset	$18,000	$30,000	C	$7,000	$10,000
Total	$55,000	$70,000		$55,000	$70,000

The regular operating rules are now back in effect, and the final one-third of the inventory is deemed distributed to C. C takes a basis of $7,000 in the one-third of the inventory, his partnership interest basis is reduced to zero, and he recognizes no gain on the distribution.[62] C thus now holds the inventory with a total basis of $27,000 (fair market value basis of $20,000 in two-thirds of the inventory plus $7,000 under I.R.C. § 732(b) for the final one-third of the inventory considered distributed). Assuming its value does not change, when C sells the inventory for $30,000, he recognizes $3,000 of ordinary income. This is what his share of ordinary income inherent in the inventory was to begin with when the partnership held it, and all is right with the world.

The balance sheet of the partnership after completion of the transaction is as follows:

Assets	Adj. Basis	F.M.V.	Partners	Adj. Basis	F.M.V.
Cash	$30,000	$30,000	A	$24,000	$30,000
Cap. Asset	$18,000	$30,000	B	$24,000	$30,000
Total	$48,000	$60,000		$48,000	$60,000

Note that in order for I.R.C. § 751(b) to apply, an interest in the I.R.C. § 751 property must be swapped for an interest in the I.R.C. § 741 property. If C had simply received a distribution with a value of $30,000 consisting of his proportionate one-third share of I.R.C. § 751(b) property plus cash and/or a portion of the capital asset to make up the difference, no deemed swap would have occurred, and I.R.C. § 751(b) would not have applied. Further, I.R.C. § 751(b) will not apply to a distribution of property that the distributee contributed to the partnership.[63] I.R.C. § 751(b) also will not apply to I.R.C. § 736(a) payments[64]

---

[61] I.R.C. § 1012.

[62] I.R.C. §§ 731(a)(1), 732(b), and 733(2). Technically, because it is a liquidating distribution, C does not take a carryover basis in the one-third of the inventory, as would be the case if it had been an operating distribution. Instead, his basis in his partnership interest of $6,000 becomes the basis in this part of the inventory. Note that if it had been an operating distribution, C's carryover basis would have been the same $6,000. Further, a partner is never permitted to take a greater basis than that which the partnership had in inventory and unrealized receivables, regardless of the type of distribution involved. I.R.C. § 732(c)(1).

[63] I.R.C. § 751(b)(2)(A).

[64] I.R.C. § 751(b)(2)(B).

(discussed below), draws or advances that a partner receives against his distributive share of partnership income, or to gifts, payments for services, or use of capital.[65]

Now let's look at an example involving a nonliquidating distribution.[66] Assume the ABC Partnership has the following balance sheet:

Assets	Adj. Basis	F.M.V.	Partners	Adj. Basis	F.M.V.
Cash	$24,000	$24,000	A	$12,000	$24,000
Equipment	0	$24,000	B	$12,000	$24,000
Cap. Asset	$12,000	$24,000	C	$12,000	$24,000
Total	$36,000	$72,000		$36,000	$72,000

Assume all of the gain inherent in the equipment is I.R.C. § 1245 recapture and thus is treated as an unrealized receivable. Assume the partnership distributes $12,000 of cash to C and C becomes a one-fifth partner.

To ascertain whether C has "exchanged" his interest in I.R.C. § 751 property for additional I.R.C. § 741 property, we can either compare his interest in I.R.C. § 751 property before and after the distribution, or his interest in I.R.C. § 741 property before and after the distribution. Either approach will yield the same result.

C's indirect interest in I.R.C. § 751 property:

Before the Distribution	1/3 of recapture of $24,000 =	$8,000
After the Distribution	1/5 of recapture of $24,000 =	$4,800
C's share dropped by		($3,200)

Similarly, C's indirect interest in I.R.C. § 741 property:

Before the Distribution	1/3 of combined value of cash and capital asset or 1/3 of $48,000 =	$16,000
After the Distribution	1/5 of combined value of partnership cash and capital asset, or 1/5 of $36,000 = $7,200 plus distributed cash of $12,000 =	$19,200
C's share increased by		$3,200

Accordingly, C must receive a phantom distribution of $3,200 of the "recapture unrealized receivable" which he will be deemed to exchange with the partnership

---

[65] Treas. Reg. § 1.751-1(b)(i)(ii).

[66] *See* Treas. Reg. § 1.751-1(g), example 6. For a discussion of some special problems that can arise with nonliquidating distributions, see FEDERAL TAXATION OF PARTNERSHIPS AND PARTNERS at ¶ 21.03[8].

for $3,200 of cash that was actually received. Since under I.R.C. § 732, C's carryover basis in the recapture unrealized receivable is zero, C will have $3,200 of ordinary income on the transaction and the partnership will have a basis step-up in the equipment of the same amount. Then, under the regular distribution rules, C receives the balance of the cash of $8,800, reducing his basis in the partnership interest to $3,200. Thus, the partnership's balance sheet is as follows:

Assets	Adj. Basis	F.M.V.	Partners	Adj. Basis	F.M.V.
Cash	$12,000	$12,000	A	$12,000	$24,000
Equipment	$3,200	$24,000	B	$12,000	$24,000
Cap. Asset	$12,000	$24,000	C	$3,200	$12,000
Total	$27,200	$60,000		$27,200	$60,000

D. Associated Issues

In the example just above, assume that C purchased his interest in the partnership from X for $60,000 and that at the time of the purchase and since then the value of the partnership assets and their bases to the partnership are unchanged. Assume further that no I.R.C. § 754 election is in effect and more than two years has elapsed since C's purchase. C would in effect have paid $24,000 of the purchase price for an indirect one-third interest in the equipment. Nonetheless, C will have to recognize the same amount of ordinary income as in the example above because no I.R.C. § 754 election was made. If the distribution to C took place within two years of C's purchase of the interest, then I.R.C. § 732(d), discussed above, would provide relief and for purposes of the distribution give C the equivalent of an I.R.C. § 754 election.[67]

In Rev. Rul. 77-412,[68] the IRS ruled that I.R.C. § 751(b) applies to the liquidation of a two-person partnership, even though the partnership ceased to exist with the liquidating distributions. Under the Ruling "the distribution is treated as a sale or exchange of such properties between the distributee partner and the partnership (as constituted after the distribution), even though after the distribution the partnership consists of a single individual." The Ruling notes that it does not make any difference which partner is considered to be the distributee partner and which partner is considered to be "the partnership" for purposes of making the I.R.C. § 751(b) exchange. While this was true under the facts of the Ruling, it will necessarily be true with partnerships with more than two members which make disproportionate distributions of I.R.C. § 751 property.

Liability shifts can also create I.R.C. § 751(b) issues. Assume a partnership with liabilities and I.R.C. § 751 property distributes cash to a partner in liquidation of that partner's partnership interest. The total amount of cash considered to be distributed for purposes of doing the I.R.C. § 751(b) calculation would include both the money actually distributed and the money deemed distributed under I.R.C.

---

[67] *See* Treas. Reg. § 1.751-1(b)(2)(iii), (b)(3)(iii).

[68] 1977-2 C.B. 223.

§ 752(b) as a result of the distributee partner's reduction in his share of partnership liabilities.

I.R.C. §§ 751(b)/752(b) issues can also arise when a partner enters the partnership. In Revenue Ruling 84-102,[69] a partnership had liabilities and unrealized receivables. When the new partner entered the partnership, he was allocated a share of the existing partnership liabilities under I.R.C. § 752(a) and concomitantly, the other partners' shares of partnership liabilities were reduced, resulting in a deemed distribution of money under I.R.C. § 752(b). Since the new partner also was considered to share in the existing unrealized receivables, all the elements necessary to trigger I.R.C. § 751(b) were in place. The existing partners' shares of the unrealized receivables changed, and they were deemed to receive a distribution of money. Consequently, the IRS ruled that I.R.C. § 751(b) applied to the existing partners. The IRS also ruled that I.R.C. § 751(b) did not apply to the entering partner as there was no actual or constructive distribution of property to him. The consequences of the Revenue Ruling can be avoided if the partnership does not allocate existing liabilities or a share of the unrealized receivables to the incoming partner. The latter could be achieved by a revaluation or an appropriate allocation provision (see Chapter 5).

Note that unlike I.R.C. § 751(a), which focuses on giving a selling partner his share of the gain or loss inherent in each hot asset of the partnership, I.R.C. § 751(b) focuses on whether the partner received his proportionate share of I.R.C. § 751 property based on the overall fair market values. This can permit some gain shifting. Assume, for example, that the one-third interest of partner A in the ABC partnership is liquidated. The partnership has $30,000 of I.R.C. § 751 property, including $15,000 of unrealized receivables with a zero basis and $15,000 of substantially appreciated inventory with a significant basis. Assume there is more gain inherent in the unrealized receivables than in the inventory and that the partnership wishes to distribute to A his one-third share of I.R.C. § 751 property. In doing so, the partnership can choose $10,000 of higher gain unrealized receivables or $10,000 of lower gain inventory or a combination of both. A tax advisor to A would want the type of assets to be distributed to be specified in any agreement to liquidate A's interest.[70]

§ 7.09 LIQUIDATIONS OF PARTNERSHIPS AND PARTNERSHIP INTERESTS

A. Introduction

We will cover two topics, the complete liquidation of a partnership and the liquidation of a partner's interest where the partnership, as such, continues. There are a number of variations on this theme. Many of the rules we have discussed so far will apply and, in some cases, fully resolve the tax issues. But some additional

---

[69] 1984-2 C.B. 119.

[70] The IRS has indicated that it is considering extensive changes to the I.R.C. § 751(b) rules. One possible change would make the I.R.C. § 751(b) rules similar to the I.R.C. § 751(a) rules and prevent this type of income shifting. 2006-1 C.B. 498, Notice 2006-14 (Feb. 21, 2006).

rules are necessary to address differences between the partner's outside basis and the basis of distributed property.

B. Liquidations of the Partnership or of a Partnership Interest

State law on partnership termination is not controlling for federal tax purposes.[71] I.R.C. § 708(b)(1)(A) provides that a partnership terminates "if no part of any business, financial operation, or venture of the partnership continues to be carried on by any of its partners in a partnership." Note that this definition is met if one partner buys the interests of the other partners and continues the partnership business as the partnership form is no longer used.[72] On the other hand, the death of one partner in a two-person partnership will not terminate the partnership if the estate or other successor of the deceased partner continues to share in profits or losses of the partnership business.[73] If the surviving partner purchases the interest of the deceased partner, the partnership would, of course, terminate.

If a partnership terminates, its tax year closes for all of the partners.[74] Any successor partnership would thus be a new partnership permitting (or requiring) fresh elections. Similarly, if the interest of a particular partner terminates, the tax year closes with regard to that partner; the relevant share of income and expense arising from the beginning of the partnership tax year up to when it closes is allocated to that partner.[75]

If a partnership terminates or if the interest of an individual partner is liquidated, the rules we have discussed generally govern with a few additions. As we discussed above, if a partner's outside basis is less than the partnership's inside basis in distributed property, under I.R.C. § 732(a)(2), the partner's basis in that property is limited to the outside basis. But what if the converse is the case and the partner's outside basis exceeds the partnership's basis in the distributed property?

I.R.C. § 732 provides that a distributee partner cannot take a greater basis in distributed inventory and unrealized receivables than that which the partnership had. To permit the partner to take a greater basis in these assets would enable the distributee partner to avoid ordinary income. Under I.R.C. § 731(a)(2), if the only assets that are distributed to a partner are cash, unrealized receivables, and inventory, and the partner's outside basis exceeds the amount of distributed cash and the carryover basis in the unrealized receivables and inventory, the partner recognizes a loss to the extent of any unused basis. The loss is considered to arise

---

[71] *See* the Revised Uniform Partnership Act ("RUPA") § 801 for events causing dissolution and winding up of a state law partnership. RUPA § 802 provides that a partnership is terminated after it has been wound up. This may or may not coincide with the tax definition. *See also* Fuchs v. Commissioner, 80 T.C. 506 (1983).

[72] Treas. Reg. § 1.708-1(b)(1); *see also* Harbor Cove Marina Partners Partnership v. Commissioner, 123 T.C. 64 (2004).

[73] Treas. Reg. § 1.708-1(b)(1)(i).

[74] I.R.C. § 706(c)(1).

[75] I.R.C. § 706(c)(2)(A); *see* § 5.09.

from the sale or exchange of the partnership interest and is, therefore, normally a capital loss.

For example, assume that A is a one-third partner in the ABC partnership. The partnership uses the calendar year for reporting and makes a liquidating distribution to A on January 1 (making it unnecessary to allocate any income or expense from the current year to A). The partnership distributes to A in complete liquidation of his interest $10,000 of cash and inventory with a basis of $4,000 and a fair market value of $15,000. A's outside basis in his partnership interest is $20,000. After reducing A's basis for the cash and a carryover basis in the inventory, A has $6,000 of basis left over. A recognizes a $6,000 loss from the sale or exchange of the partnership interest as a consequence. Note that the fair market value of the assets and cash A receives is $25,000 which exceeds her basis of $20,000. Economically, therefore, A has a gain on the transaction. Nonetheless, A recognizes a loss to preserve the ordinary income in the inventory. When A disposes of the inventory, she will recognize $11,000 of ordinary income. Offset that against the $6,000 loss, and it nets to the $5,000 economic gain A had on the liquidation and all is right with the world. Also note that if A does not receive his proportional share of I.R.C. § 751 property, I.R.C. § 751(b) will apply.

Recall that fundamental to all of Subchapter K is the preference for avoiding gain or loss on contributions of property to a partnership and distributions of property to a partner. In the above example, Congress could not avoid loss recognition. There was $6,000 of unused basis, and Congress could not give A a greater basis in I.R.C. § 751 property than that which the partnership had and still maintain one of the holier principles in the world of tax, preserving ordinary income. However, if A receives any other assets, we can simply shift any unused basis to those assets, even if it means that A takes a greater basis in those assets than that which the partnership had. Assume in the above example that A's partnership interest is more valuable and that in addition to the cash and inventory, the partnership also distributes land to A and that the land is a capital asset to the partnership. The land has basis to the partnership of $2,000 and a fair market value of $10,000. After reducing her basis for the cash and the inventory, A has $6,000 of basis in the partnership interest left. That $6,000 is allocated to the land, giving A greater basis in the land than that which the partnership had.

If a partnership distributes several assets to a partner (excluding I.R.C. § 751 property) and the partner's outside basis exceeds the partnership's aggregate bases in the distributed properties, the Code provides rules for allocating the "extra" basis among the distributed properties. It is first allocated in proportion to the relative appreciation inherent in the distributed properties. If the extra basis exceeds the inherent appreciation, any remaining amount is allocated based on the relative fair market values of the distributed assets. In the above example, assume that instead of one parcel of land, A receives two parcels each with a basis of $1,000 and a fair market value of $6,000. A has $6,000 of available basis. A carryover basis in each asset would use $2,000 of that $6,000. The extra $4,000 must be allocated based on the relative appreciation in the assets. In this example, each asset has the same amount of appreciation, or $5,000. Accordingly, half of the extra $4,000 of basis is allocated to each asset, or $2,000 each. Thus, A's basis in each parcel of land is $3,000.

Recall from Chapter 5 that a partner is ordinarily paid the balance of his capital account on the liquidation of his partnership interest. As we discussed above, for the capital accounts to perform their function properly, the Regulations provide that they must be adjusted for any book gain or loss inherent in distributed property, notwithstanding the fact that tax gain or loss might not be recognized.[76]

C. I.R.C. § 736 Payments

1. Introduction

I.R.C. § 736 applies when a partner retires from the partnership and the partnership continues.[77] It is in some ways a curious provision. Subchapter K could probably live without I.R.C. § 736 and instead merge its key provisions into I.R.C. § 751(b). But to date Congress has not seen fit to do that, and as a consequence, you will have to learn to juggle the two Code sections. I.R.C. § 736 does serve a useful function. If payments made to a retiring partner are either guaranteed payments (discussed in Chapter 8) or a distributive share of partnership income, they reduce the income of the other partners. If payments are for the partner's share of partnership property, they generally are thought of as nondeductible distributions. Which category a particular payment fits into obviously has a great deal of tax significance. I.R.C. § 736 gives a substantial measure of certainty to this area, though questions remain.

A primary focus of I.R.C. § 736 is the tax treatment of payments of money to a retiring partner over time, but it can also apply when a retiring partner's interest is fully liquidated with a single payment. Further, while the clear implication of the statute is that payments will be made with money, there is nothing in the statute to prevent payments being made with property other than money.[78] Making payments with property can create a number of theoretical problems.[79] Further, as I.R.C. § 736 applies to "payments," it suggests that the partner is being "paid" (typically with money) for his interest in something (typically partnership property). Therefore, if a partner only receives a pro rata distribution of the assets of the partnership, it does not seem that I.R.C. § 736 should apply.

I.R.C. § 736 divides the world into I.R.C. § 736(a) payments and I.R.C. § 736(b) payments. I.R.C. § 736(b) applies to payments for the retiring partner's interest in partnership property. I.R.C. § 736(a) applies to all other payments. I.R.C. § 736(a) and (b) merely classify payments. Other Code provisions that we have covered in this and other Chapters govern the tax treatment of those payments.

---

[76] Treas. Reg. § 1.704-1(b)(2)(iv)(e)(1).

[77] It can also apply to payments made to the successor-in-interest of a deceased partner. I.R.C. § 736(a).

[78] *See* PARTNERSHIP TAXATION at ¶ 15.06[1], [2].

[79] *See* PARTNERSHIP TAXATION at ¶ 15.06.

2.   I.R.C. § 736(a) Payments

I.R.C. § 736(a) covers all payments not within I.R.C. § 736(b). I.R.C. § 736(a) does not apply to all partnerships in the same way. I.R.C. § 736 has different rules for partnerships in which "capital is an income producing factor" and for *general* partners in partnerships in which capital *is not* a material income-producing factor.[80] According to the legislative history, capital is not an income-producing factor where substantially all of the gross income of the business consists of fees, commissions, or other compensation for personal services. Note that under this definition the practice of his or her profession by a lawyer, accountant, doctor, or architect will not be treated as a trade or business in which capital is a material income-producing factor even though the professional may have a substantial capital investment in professional plant or equipment if that investment is merely incidental to the performance of the services.[81] We will call these "services partnerships."

In a services partnership, I.R.C. § 736(a) applies to payments to withdrawing general partners for:

1. Partnership unrealized receivables to the extent their fair market value exceeds any basis the partnership has in them (unrealized receivables do not include recapture for these purposes),[82] and

2. "Unstated goodwill" to the extent the fair market value exceeds the partnership's basis. Unstated goodwill exists where part of the value of the partnership indeed includes goodwill, but the partnership agreement does not provide for payments for goodwill. Thus the goodwill is unstated.[83]

In any kind of partnership (services or nonservices), I.R.C. § 736(a) applies to the portion of the payment that exceeds the partner's share of the fair market value of all partnership property (including goodwill), sometimes known as "premium payments."[84] Note that premium payments are the only item included in I.R.C. § 736(a) if capital is a material income-producing factor. Premium payments are also the only item included in I.R.C. § 736(a) for services partnerships making payments to *non*general partners (i.e., limited partners).

3.   I.R.C. § 736(b) Payments

I.R.C. § 736(b) applies to all payments for a partner's interest in partnership property. Thus, in a *non*services partnership, I.R.C. § 736(b) will apply to all payments to a retiring partner except premium payments. In a services partnership, I.R.C. § 736(b) will apply to payments attributable to any basis the partnership has in unrealized receivables and goodwill as well, in the case of payments to a general partner, to payments for goodwill in excess of that basis if goodwill is

---

[80]   *See* I.R.C. § 736(b)(2), (3).

[81]   H.R. No. 103-11, 103rd Cong., 1st Sess. 345 (1993).

[82]   I.R.C. § 751(c) flush language.

[83]   *See* I.R.C. § 736(b)(2)(B).

[84]   Treas. Reg. § 1.736-1(a)(3).

stated.[85] Thus, services partnerships making payments to general partners have the option of having I.R.C. § 736(b) cover the appreciation in goodwill or not by their choice to include a relevant provision in the partnership agreement, or not. As the tax consequences of I.R.C. § 736(a) and (b) are different, this provides for a planning opportunity depending on the tax circumstances of the partners.

A question that is unanswered by the Code and Regulations is what constitutes goodwill. Items that might be included are customer lists, insurance agency listings, formulas, know-how, going concern value (i.e., the fact that a business is up and running), the value of the company's name, to name but a few.[86]

The distribution rules discussed earlier in this chapter apply to I.R.C. § 736(b) payments. Thus, the relevant Code sections are I.R.C. §§ 731, 741, and 751(b). For example, if cash is distributed to a retiring partner that falls within I.R.C. § 736(b), under I.R.C. § 731(a)(1) the partner will recognize gain to the extent the cash distributed exceeds the partner's basis in the partnership interest. I.R.C. § 751(b) will apply to payments for substantially appreciated inventory and to payments for unrealized receivables that are not covered by I.R.C. § 736(a). Where capital *is* an income-producing factor, that would include *all* unrealized receivables. Where capital is *not* an income-producing factor, I.R.C. § 751(b) would, for example, apply to unrealized receivables in the form of I.R.C. § 1245 recapture.

4. Allocating and Taxing I.R.C. § 736 Payments

I.R.C. § 736 applies whether a retiring partner receives a single payment for his partnership interest or is paid for it over time. If a partner receives a single payment in liquidation of his partnership interest, the payment is allocated between the I.R.C. § 736(a) and (b) payments pursuant to the rules discussed above. If a partner receives payments over a period of years, the parties may agree on how a payment in a given year is allocated provided that the aggregate amount allocated to property under I.R.C. § 736(b) does not exceed the fair market value of such property at the date of the retirement.[87] Barring that, the Regulations provide a formula for allocating the payment; this varies depending on whether the payments are fixed in amount or not. If the partnership pays the retiring partner a fixed amount over a fixed number of years, the following formula is used to allocate a portion of each annual payment to I.R.C. § 736(b):[88]

$$\text{I.R.C. § 736(b) amount} = \text{Total Payment Fixed for Year} \times \frac{\text{Total Fixed Agreed 736(b) Payments}}{\text{Total I.R.C. § 736(a) and (b) Fixed Agreed Payments}}$$

The balance, if any, of the amount received in the same taxable year falls within I.R.C. § 736(a). If the payments are not fixed because, for example, the retiring

---

[85] Treas. Reg. § 1.736-1(b)(2), (3).

[86] *See* PARTNERSHIP TAXATION at ¶ 15.03[2].

[87] Treas. Reg. § 1.736-1(b)(5)(iii).

[88] Treas. Reg. § 1.736-1(b)(5)(i).

partner is paid a percentage of partnership profits each year, the partnership's payments are first considered to be I.R.C. § 736(b) payments. Once the I.R.C. § 736(b) amount has been fully paid, payments are then considered to be I.R.C. § 736(a) payments.[89]

If the payments are fixed, I.R.C. § 736(a) payments are treated as guaranteed payment under I.R.C. § 707(c),[90] with the proviso that they are generally deductible to the partnership and considered ordinary income to the retiring partner.[91] Following the general rules for guaranteed payments (discussed in Chapter 8), it is income to a recipient for his tax year with or within which ends the partnership tax year in which the guaranteed payment may be deducted, whether or not it is paid.[92] When the payments are not fixed, the portion falling within I.R.C. § 736(a) is treated as a distributive share under I.R.C. § 702. For example, if a partner is allocated a 10% share of partnership income and the partnership incurs ordinary income and capital gains, then the portion of the payments falling within I.R.C. § 736(a) will be partly ordinary income and partly capital gains.[93] These I.R.C. § 736(a) payments are again income to the retiring partner for his tax year with or within which ends the partnership tax year to which the allocable share is attributable, again regardless of whether or not it is paid.[94]

Note that if the partnership can fit a payment within I.R.C. § 736(a), it gets a deduction or its equivalent and the withdrawing partner has income. As the subsequent discussion will show, if the payment falls within I.R.C. § 736(b), the partnership effectively has to capitalize it and the withdrawing partner normally recovers basis or has capital gain (subject to the application of I.R.C. § 751(b)). Thus, from both the partner's and the partnership's perspectives, how a payment is classified can be highly important.

I.R.C. § 736(a) used to apply to all partnerships in the way it currently applies to general partners in services partnerships. Congress changed it because of a perceived abuse.[95] Assume A operates a nonservices business as a sole proprietor and the business has significant goodwill. B wants to buy the business. To optimize the tax consequences from B's perspective, the parties often would engage in the following planning transaction. A and B would form a partnership. A would contribute the business and B would contribute cash. A would then withdraw from the partnership with the partnership paying A for her interest with the cash. There would be no provision made for goodwill. B (as the partnership) now has a current deduction for payments made for goodwill (in excess of any basis).[96] If B had bought the partnership directly, the payments for goodwill would have had to have been

---

[89] Treas. Reg. § 1.736-1(b)(5)(ii).

[90] I.R.C. § 736(a)(2).

[91] Treas. Reg. § 1.736-1(a)(4).

[92] *See* Chapter 8.

[93] Treas. Reg. § 1.736-1(a)(3), (4).

[94] *See* Chapter 4.

[95] H.R. Rep. No. 103-11, 103d Cong., 1st Sess. 344 (1993).

[96] Even though the partnership will cease to be a partnership as a matter of law once A's interest is purchased, it should be viewed as a partnership for I.R.C. § 736 purposes until payment is complete. *See,*

capitalized and amortized over 15 years under I.R.C. § 197.

I.R.C. § 736(b) payments, on the other hand, fall within the distribution rules and are taken into account when actually paid.[97] Under the general rule, whether or not the payments are fixed, the partner first recovers her basis in the partnership interest. Any payment in excess of that basis is treated as gain from the sale or exchange of a partnership interest, typically capital gain.[98] Under this method, any loss recognition is postponed until the final payment is received.[99] There is an alternative in which the total I.R.C. § 736(b) payments are fixed. The retiring partner may elect to prorate the partnership interest basis over the payments being made, and recognize gain or loss as each payment is made.[100]

As we discussed above, I.R.C. § 751(b) can apply to restructure a distribution if there is a shift in partners' interests in unrealized receivables and substantially appreciated inventory. To the extent unrealized receivables are covered by I.R.C. § 736(a), they are not subject to I.R.C. § 751(b). I.R.C. § 751(b) continues to apply to substantially appreciated inventory and to unrealized receivables not covered by I.R.C. § 736(a) (and thus instead covered by I.R.C. § 736(b)). I.R.C. § 736(a) does not cover unrealized receivables at all for partnerships in which capital *is* a material income-producing factor or for services partnerships making payments to *non*-general partners. Just to keep life interesting, I.R.C. § 736(a) also does not apply to certain types of "special" unrealized receivables, such as recapture, in the case of services partnerships making payments to general partners.

If there is a single I.R.C. § 736 payment, particularly if it is in cash, there is no great (additional) challenge; one simply applies I.R.C. § 751(b) to the payments falling within I.R.C. § 736(b). But in situations where payments are made over time, how does I.R.C. § 751(b) apply? The answer is not clear, but likely the parties would calculate the I.R.C. § 751(b) impact assuming a single payment and then allocate the ordinary income or loss over all of the payments that are made. This assumes that the payments are fixed. If they are not, things get even murkier. Since I.R.C. § 736(a) payments (along with their typically ordinary income consequence) are considered to be made after the I.R.C. § 736(b) payments have been completed, there is an argument that the I.R.C. § 751(b) ordinary income treatment also should only come after the I.R.C. § 736(b) payments have been completed.[101]

---

e.g., Rev. Rul. 77-137, 1977-1 C.B. 178; Rev. Rul. 77-332, 1977-2 C.B. 483; Partnership Taxation at ¶ 15.01[3].

[97] I.R.C. § 736(b)(1).

[98] I.R.C. § 731(a)(1); Treas. Reg. § 1.736-1(b)(6), (7), example 1.

[99] Treas. Reg. § 1.731-1(a)(2).

[100] Treas. Reg. § 1.736-1(b)(6).

[101] *See* Partnership Taxation at ¶ 15.05[2].

Liquidating Distributions § 736

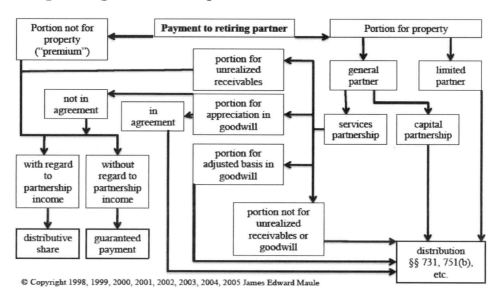

© Copyright 1998, 1999, 2000, 2001, 2002, 2003, 2004, 2005 James Edward Maule

The above flow chart, prepared by Professor James Maule at Villanova Law School, summarizes I.R.C. § 736.

§ 7.10 READING, QUESTIONS AND PROBLEMS

A. Nonliquidating Distributions

READING

CODE:

> I.R.C. §§ 731, 732(a), (c)(1), (3), (d), 733, 735, 1245(b)(6).

TREASURY REGULATIONS:

> Treas. Reg. §§ 1.731-1(a)(1), (3), (c), -2, 1.732-1(a), (c), (d), 1.733-1, 1.735-1, 1.1245(f)(2), (3), 1.704-1(b)(2)(iv)(e)(1).

RULINGS:

> Rev. Rul. 94-4, 1994-1 C.B. 196.

> Rev. Rul. 79-205, 1979-2 C.B. 255.

QUESTIONS AND PROBLEMS

1. A and B are 50-50 partners in the AB partnership. The partnership is in the manufacturing business. A's basis in her partnership interest is $2,000 and B's basis in his partnership interest is $7,000. At the time of the distribution, the partnership

has cash of $50,000 and four items of inventory each with a basis of $2,000 and a fair market value of $4,000. Each of the following questions is in the alternative, meaning that in answering each question, you should ignore the other questions. What are the tax consequences if:

a. On June 1 of the current year, the partnership distributes to each partner cash of $4,000 and one item of inventory.

b. How would your answer to "a" change if the inventory were distributed on June 1 and the cash on July 1?

c. How would your answer for A in "b" change if the cash distributed were a draw against income, and each partner's net income for the year was $30,000.

d. Assume B is a medical doctor and that is his sole occupation. What are the tax consequences to B if one year after the distribution he sells the inventory for $5,000? What if B gifts the inventory to his nephew N and N sells if for $5,000? How would your answer change if instead of inventory, the partnership distributed equipment with a basis of $2,000 and a fair market value of $4,000. The partnership took $2,000 of depreciation on the equipment and B sells it for $5,000.

e. Describe the tax consequences if the partnership distributes two items of inventory to A and two items of inventory to B.

f. Now assume that C buys B's interest on January 1 of the current year and pays B $33,000 at a time when no I.R.C. § 754 election is in effect. At that time, the partnership holds the same assets, cash of $50,000 and four items of inventory, each with a basis of $2,000 and a fair market value of $4,000. In the current year, the partnership distributes to C cash of $4,000 and one item of inventory with a fair market value of $4,000. Describe the tax consequences to C and the options available to her. Assume I.R.C. § 704(c) does not apply to any partnership assets. If the partnership also held (but did not distribute) depreciable property, are there any special benefits available to C?

2. A and B are equal partners in the AB partnership. The partnership is in the business of producing widgets. The partnership distributes a U.S. treasury bond to A. Immediately before the distribution, the partnership held the following securities:

Security	F.M.V.	Adjusted Basis
U.S Treasury Bond	$200	$140
Microsoft Stock	$200	$160
Exxon Stock	$200	$220

Describe the tax consequences of the distribution.

B. I.R.C. § 734(b)

READING

CODE:

I.R.C. §§ 731(b), 734, 754, 755, 1245(b)(3).

TREASURY REGULATIONS:

Treas. Reg. §§ 1.734-1, 1.755-1(a), (c).

QUESTIONS AND PROBLEMS

3. A, B, and C are equal partners in the ABC partnership, which has following balance sheet:

Assets	Adj. Basis	F.M.V.	Partners	Adj. Basis	F.M.V.
Cash	$40,000	$40,000	A	$20,000	$40,000
Land #1	$30,000	$40,000	B	$45,000	$40,000
Land #2	$40,000	$40,000	C	$45,000	$40,000
Total	$110,000	$120,000		$110,000	$120,000

Assume both parcels of land are capital assets. The cash is distributed to A in liquidation of her interest. Assume the partnership has an I.R.C. § 754 election in effect. Describe all tax consequences and reconstruct the balance sheet of the partnership after the transaction.

C. I.R.C. § 751(b)

READING

CODE:

I.R.C. §§ 731(d), 732(e), 751(b).

TREASURY REGULATIONS:

Treas. Reg. § 1.751-1(b)–(e), (g), example 2.

CASES:

Roth v. Commissioner, 321 F.2d 607 (9th Cir. 1963).

Ledoux v. Commissioner, 77 T.C. 293 (1981), *aff'd per curiam*, 695 F.2d 1320 (11th Cir. 1983).

RULINGS:

Rev. Rul. 77-412, 1977-2 C.B. 223.

Rev. Rul. 84-102, 1984-2 C.B. 119.

D.   Liquidations

READING

CODE:

I.R.C. §§ 708(a), (b)(1), 731(a)(2), 732(c)(2), 761(d), (e)(1), 736.

TREASURY REGULATIONS:

Treas. Reg. §§ 1.708-1(a), (b), 1.731-1(a)(2), 1.732-2(b), (c), 1.736-1.

CASES:

McCauslen v. Commissioner, 45 T.C. 588 (1966).

Harbor Cove Marina Partners Partnership v. Commissioner, 123 T.C. 64 (2004).

Evans v. Commissioner, 54 T.C. 40 (1970), *aff'd*, 447 F.2d 547 (7th Cir. 1971).

Oehlschlager v. Commissioner, T.C.M. (RIA) ¶ 88,210 (1998).

RULINGS:

Rev. Rul. 99-6, 1999-1 C.B. 432.

Rev. Rul. 95-37, 1995-1 C.B. 130.

Rev. Rul. 93-80, 1993-2 C.B. 239.

Rev. Rul. 87-110, 1987-2 C.B. 159.

QUESTIONS AND PROBLEMS FOR I.R.C. § 751(B) AND LIQUIDATIONS

4. A, B, and D are equal general partners in the ABD Partnership, which manufactures internal guidance systems for NASA rockets, and has the following balance sheet:

Assets	Adj. Basis	F.M.V.	Partners	Adj. Basis	F.M.V.
Cash	$21,000	$21,000	A	$17,000	$30,000
Acc. Rec.	$0	$30,000	B	$17,000	$30,000
Inventory	$27,000	$30,000	D	$30,000	$30,000
Land	$3,000	$9,000			
Total	$51,000	$90,000		$64,000	$90,000

D's outside basis in his partnership interest is different from the other partners' outside bases due to the fact that he purchased his interest several years ago from then partner C. At that time, the partnership did not have an I.R.C. § 754 election in effect.

The partnership distributes the inventory to D in liquidation of his interest. Describe the tax consequences.

5. A, B, and C are equal general partners in the ABC Medical Practice, which has the following balance sheet:

Assets	Adj. Basis	F.M.V.	Partners	Adj. Basis	F.M.V.
Cash	$60,000	$60,000	A	$21,000	$30,000
Acc. Rec.	$0	$21,000	B	$21,000	$30,000
Goodwill	$3,000	$9,000	C	$21,000	$30,000
Total	$63,000	$90,000		$63,000	$90,000

a. A decides to open a T-shirt shop in Guadalajara and wants to leave the partnership. The other partners never much liked A anyway, thought he was a lousy doctor, and are happy to be rid of him. The partnership agrees to pay A $11,000 per year for three years for his partnership interest. Describe the tax consequences assuming the partnership agreement makes no provision for goodwill.

b. You saw this one coming, what if the partnership agreement provides for payments for goodwill?

c. Returning to the facts of "a," what if the payment were $12,000 per year, with the additional provision that the payments drop by $1,000 per year if A engages in competitive activities within the geographic area in which the partnership currently does business.

d. Returning again to the facts of "a," what if instead the partnership agrees to pay A 20% of partnership profits for three years and that turns out to be $11,000 per year?

Chapter 8

TRANSACTIONS BETWEEN PARTNER AND PARTNERSHIP; ISSUANCE OF A PARTNERSHIP INTEREST FOR SERVICES

§ 8.01 INTRODUCTION

Chapter 8 will focus on I.R.C. § 707(a) partner-partnership transactions, guaranteed payments under I.R.C. § 707(c), the special rules relating to controlled partnerships under I.R.C. §§ 267 and 707(b), and the tax consequences of the issuance of partnership interests for services.

§ 8.02 THE DIFFERENT ROLES OF PARTNERS IN TRANSACTIONS WITH A PARTNERSHIP

In general, transactions between partners and partnerships fall into one of three categories for federal income tax purposes. The three categories are: (i) all payments to a partner in the partner's capacity as a partner other than guaranteed payments to a partner for the use of capital or for services, (ii) guaranteed payments to a partner for the use of capital or for services rendered in the partner's capacity as a partner, and (iii) transactions with a partner other than in the partner's capacity as a partner. I.R.C. §§ 702, 703, 704, and 731 are applicable to the first category of transactions. I.R.C. § 707(c) is applicable to the second category. I.R.C. § 707(a) is applicable to the third category. Which category a particular transaction, relationship, or arrangement falls into may affect the timing, character and, potentially, amount of income in respect of which a partner is subject to tax.

§ 8.03 PAYMENTS TO A PARTNER AS A PARTNER OTHER THAN GUARANTEED PAYMENTS

Payments (other than guaranteed payments) to a partner in the partner's capacity as a partner are generally distributions of partnership income or returns of capital.

The determination of a partner's allocable share of partnership income was discussed in Chapter 5. The treatment of distributions to partners in respect of their partnership interests was discussed in Chapter 7. The issues and treatment discussed in these units are a backdrop to the issues discussed below in regard to guaranteed payments and payments to partners other than in their capacity as partners. Allocations of income and distributions to a partner are in many ways the starting point of the analysis and the residual category to which the analysis defaults if a payment is shown to be neither a guaranteed payment nor a payment to a partner other than in the partner's capacity as a partner.

This chapter will not include a detailed discussion of allocations of income to partners or distributions to partners, but only highlight the differences in treatment as issues are discussed. Still, it is important to keep in mind that treatment as an allocation of income and a distribution in respect of partnership interests is often the result that the taxpayer wishes to achieve. One of the primary characteristics of treatment as an allocation of income is that the character of the income is determined at the partnership level.[1] For example, a partner who renders services to a partnership may receive an allocation of capital gain if the partnership recognizes capital gain, rather than being limited to recognizing ordinary income for a payment in exchange for services. Congress has built sections into the Code to prevent taxpayers from abusing this rule,[2] but these provisions are included in the Code as exceptions from the general rule rather than eliminations of the general rule.

§ 8.04   GUARANTEED PAYMENTS

Like allocations of income and distributions in respect of partnership interests, guaranteed payments are made to a partner in a partner's capacity as a partner. A taxpayer cannot receive a guaranteed payment if the taxpayer is not also a partner. However, I.R.C. § 707(c), which governs the treatment of guaranteed payments, provides that to the extent determined without regard to the income of the partnership, payments to a partner for services or the use of capital will be considered as having been made to one who is not a member of the partnership, but only for purposes of I.R.C. § 61(a) (which relates to items of gross income generally) and, subject to I.R.C. § 263 (which relates to requirements for capitalization of certain expenses), for purposes of I.R.C. § 162(a) (which allows the deduction of certain ordinary and necessary business expenses). Thus, guaranteed payments differ in treatment from allocations of income and distributions in respect of partnership interests in that, for some purposes, guaranteed payments are treated as being made to a non-partner, but, for other purposes, guaranteed payments are treated as being made to a partner.

The leading case interpreting guaranteed payments is *Pratt v. Commissioner*[3]. In *Pratt*, the general partners of a real estate limited partnership received a fee of 5% of the gross rentals received by the partnership in consideration for management services provided to the partnership by the general partner. The taxpayers in *Pratt* contended that the management fees should either be treated as guaranteed payments or payments to a partner other than in the partner's capacity as a partner. Both the Tax Court and the Court of Appeals for the Fifth Circuit held that the management fees were not payments to a partner other than in the partner's

---

[1] *See, e.g.*, Podell v. Commissioner, 55 T.C. 429 (1970) (income from the sale of property which was inventory to the partnership, but would have been a capital asset in the hands of the partner treated as ordinary income).

[2] I.R.C. §§ 724, 751.

[3] 64 T.C. 203 (1975), *aff'd in part, rev'd in part*, 550 F.2d 1023 (5th Cir. 1977).

capacity as a partner because, in the court's view, the general partners were acting in their capacities as partners performing basic duties of the partnership business pursuant to the partnership agreement.

Once the determination is made that a distribution is made to a partner in the partner's capacity as a partner, the question of the characterization of payments to a partner becomes limited to whether the distributions were guaranteed payments or allocations and distributions of partnership income under I.R.C. §§ 702, 703, 704, and 731. Guaranteed payments only include amounts that are paid without regard to the income of the partnership. In *Pratt*, the Tax Court held that the management fees were not guaranteed payments because they were computed as a percentage of gross rental income received by the partnership. The court reasoned that the gross rental income was "income" of the partnership and, thus, the requirement that a guaranteed payment be determined without regard to the income of the partnership was not satisfied. However, in Rev. Rul. 81-300,[4] the IRS ruled that the fees based upon gross income of a partnership should not be treated as being determined with regard to partnership income, and so, under Rev. Rul. 81-300, the payment in *Pratt* would have been treated as a guaranteed payment.

The IRS has also indicated that guaranteed payments may not be discretionary. In PLR 8642003,[5] when a partnership did not provide for payments to partners as compensation for the services provided by the partners to the partnership, the IRS concluded that the payments were discretionary and, thus, not "guaranteed" payments but were, instead, distributions of partnership income.

If a payment to a partner is a guaranteed payment, the payment is treated as ordinary income to the recipient partner without regard to the character of the income of the partnership.[6] In addition, the payment is taken into income by the partner based upon the accounting method of the partnership rather than the accounting method of the partner.[7] In general, so long as the payment meets the requirements of an ordinary and necessary business expense, a guaranteed payment would result in a deduction to the partnership in the year the services are performed for an accrual basis partnership or the year in which payment is made for a cash basis partnership. In other words, if a payment is for services and the services are performed in 2006 for an accrual basis partnership, the partner will take the payment into income in 2006 even if the payment is made in 2007 — without regard to whether the partner is a cash basis or an accrual basis taxpayer.

A payment that would otherwise be deductible by the partnership may be required instead to be capitalized under I.R.C. § 263.

---

[4] 1981-2 C.B. 143.

[5] June 30, 1986.

[6] Treas. Reg. § 1.707-1(c).

[7] *Id.*

§ 8.05   PAYMENTS TO A PARTNER OTHER THAN IN THEIR CAPACITY AS A PARTNER

A partner may have more than one relationship with a partnership. In other words, some of the actions of the partner may be in the partner's capacity as a partner and some of the actions may be in some other capacity, not as a partner.

For example, in Rev. Rul. 81-301,[8] a general partner was an investment adviser to the partnership of which the adviser was a general partner. The adviser performed substantially the same services for other persons as an independent contractor or agent. The adviser was responsible for the adviser's own expenses and could be removed as the investment adviser for the partnership on 60 days' notice. The IRS concluded that because of the factors just listed, the adviser was acting as an investment adviser for the partnership, not in its partner capacity, but rather in the capacity of a person who is not a partner.

I.R.C. § 707(a) provides that if a partner engages in a transaction with a partnership other than in the capacity of a member of such partnership, the transaction will, except as otherwise provided, be considered as occurring between the partnership and one who is not a partner.

Partnerships can be tempted to convert capital expenditures into ordinary deductions using partnership allocations. Assume, for example, that an attorney is a partner in a real estate partnership. He advises the partnership on the acquisition of a new apartment building. His normal fee for this service is $10,000. If the partnership pays him the $10,000 and treats it as an I.R.C. § 707(a) payment, the amount is capitalized into the cost of the property, an unappealing result. More appealing would be for the partnership to allocate an extra $10,000 of the partnership's income to the attorney/partner. The tax consequence to the attorney is the same, assuming ordinary income is allocated. But the partnership, by having less income to allocate, is given the equivalent of a deduction. Thus, if allowed, by using partnership allocations, the partnership can turn a capital item into an ordinary deduction.

Needless to say, Congress was unenthusiastic about this result. To deal with this and similar abuses, it enacted I.R.C. § 707(a)(2)(A). I.R.C. § 707(a)(2)(A) provides that if a partner performs services for a partner or transfers property to a partnership and there is a related direct or indirect allocation and distribution to such partner, and the performance of services and the allocation and distribution, when viewed together, are properly characterized as occurring between the partnership and a person acting other than in his capacity as a partner, that is how it will be treated. Thus, in the above example, the purported allocation/distribution to the attorney/partner will be treated as a payment to a nonpartner and required to be capitalized.[9]

The legislative history behind I.R.C. § 707 provides some guidance in determining whether a partner is receiving a distribution in the partner's capacity as a

---

[8]   1981-2 C.B. 144.

[9]   It is unlikely that I.R.C. § 707(a)(2)(A) would apply to a disguised sale of property to the partnership. *See* § 13.04.E.

partner.[10]

According to the Senate Finance Committee Report, the first and generally the most important factor is whether the payment is subject to an appreciable risk as to amount.[11] Equity owners of all sorts generally make profits based upon the success of the business venture, while third parties generally receive payments which are not subject to this risk. An allocation and related distribution provided for a partner which subjects the partner to significant entrepreneurial risk as to both the amount and the fact of payment generally should be recognized as an allocation of a partner's distributive share and a partnership distribution. In contrast, a distribution provided for a service partner which involves limited risk as to amount and payment should generally be treated as a fee under I.R.C. § 707(a).

The second factor indicated by the Senate Finance Committee Report is whether the partner status of the recipient is transitory. If a so-called partner has claimed partnership status for only a short period, it suggests that a payment to the transitory partner is a fee or is in return for property.[12]

The third factor in the Senate Finance Committee Report is whether a distribution to a partner is close in time to the partner's performance of services for, or transfers of property to, the partnership.[13] A distribution close in time to the performance of services or the transfer of property is more likely to be related to the services or property.

The fourth factor from the Senate Finance Committee Report is whether the recipient of a distribution became a partner primarily to obtain tax benefits for himself or the partnership, such as the avoidance of capitalization requirements, which would not have been available if the recipient had rendered services to the partnership in a third-party capacity.[14] Although ordinary and necessary business expenses are generally deductible in the year paid or accrued,[15] in a variety of circumstances a taxpayer is required to add otherwise deductible expenses to the basis of an asset and amortize or depreciate the expenses as part of the asset's basis.[16] Although an allocation of income is, strictly speaking, not a deduction to the partnership, it has a very similar effect in that it removes the allocated income from the other partners' taxable income.[17] Thus, an allocation of income that is respected in circumstances where an expense would be required to be capitalized has the result of accelerating the tax benefit of the expense.

The fifth factor from the Senate Finance Committee Report is whether the value of the recipient's interest in partnership profits is generally small in relation to the

---

[10] S. Rep. No. 169, vol. 1, 98th Cong., 2d Sess. 227 (Apr. 2, 1984).

[11] *Id.*

[12] *Id.*

[13] *Id.*

[14] *Id.* at 228.

[15] *See* I.R.C. § 162.

[16] *See* I.R.C. §§ 263, 263A.

[17] *See* Chapter 5.

allocation in question.[18] In other words, if a partner had a very small continuing interest, but for a period of time (probably contemporaneous with the period during which services are being provided) the partner has a disproportionately large interest, this factor would suggest that a distribution based on the disproportionately large interest was being paid to the partner other than in the partner's capacity as a partner.

The sixth factor from the Senate Finance Committee Report is whether the partnership maintains capital accounts under the rules of Treas. Reg. § 1.704-1(b)(2)(iv)[19] and otherwise economically respects the capital accounts so that allocations which are disguised payments for capital may be economically unfeasible and therefore less likely to occur.[20] From the Regulations promulgated under I.R.C. § 707(a)(2), discussed below, one could conclude, however, that the Treasury is less optimistic than the Senate Finance Committee appears to have been about the effectiveness of the capital account maintenance rules in preventing disguised sales.

The Senate Finance Committee Report also provided the following example: An office building to be constructed by a partnership is projected to generate at least $100,000 per year indefinitely from high-credit tenants. The architect for the partnership, who usually charges $40,000 for her services, contributes cash for a 25% interest in the partnership and receives both a 25% distributive share of net income for the life of the partnership, and a disproportionate allocation of $20,000 of partnership gross income for the first two years of partnership operations after lease-up. The projections indicate that there will be sufficient cash-flow to pay $20,000 to the architect in each of the first two years, and the agreement requires such a distribution. The report concludes that the $20,000 disproportionate gross income allocation and partnership distribution should be treated as a fee under I.R.C. § 707(a), rather than as a distributive share. The report indicated that the factors which contribute to this conclusion are: (i) the allocation is fixed in amount and there is a substantial probability that there will be sufficient income and cash to make the allocation/distribution; (ii) the allocation is disproportionate to the architect's general interest in the partnership; (iii) the distribution is fairly close in time to the services provided; and (iv) it is not unreasonable to conclude from all the facts and circumstances that the architect became a partner primarily for tax-motivated reasons. If, on the other hand, the project were a "spec building," and the architect assumed significant entrepreneurial risk that the partnership would be unable to lease the building, the disproportionate allocation might, depending on all the facts and circumstances, properly be treated as an allocation of the architect's distributive share and a partnership distribution.[21]

The Senate Finance Committee Report indicates that it was the intent of the Committee that provisions introduced in I.R.C. § 707 would lead to the conclusions

---

[18] S. Rep. No. 169, vol. 1, 98th Cong., 2d Sess. 228 (Apr. 2, 1984).

[19] *See* Chapter 5.

[20] S. Rep. No. 169, vol. 1, 98th Cong., 2d Sess. 228 (Apr. 2, 1984).

[21] *Id.* at 228–29.

contained in Rev. Rul. 81-300[22] and Rev. Rul. 81-301,[23] except that the transaction described in Rev. Rul. 81-300 (which was based upon the *Pratt* decision) would be treated as a transaction described in I.R.C. § 707(a).[24]

§ 8.06 DISGUISED SALES

A. The Disguised Sale of Assets

In addition to a service partner potentially entering into a relationship with the partnership other than in the service partner's capacity as a partner, a partner contributing property to a partnership may more properly be treated as selling the property to the partnership if a distribution to the contributing partner is associated with the contribution.

Because the general rule is that property may be contributed to a partnership without gain recognition[25] and also distributed from a partnership without gain recognition,[26] partnerships have provided a tempting arena for taxpayers to attempt to structure otherwise taxable sales as nonrecognition transactions. One of the most successful of such attempts was described in the case of *Otey v. Commissioner.*[27] In *Otey*, the taxpayer contributed property to a partnership, after which the partnership borrowed against the property contributed, distributing a portion of the proceeds of the loan to the taxpayer. The Tax Court respected the form of the transaction as a contribution to capital followed by a current distribution with the result that the taxpayer had no current gain. Although there were cases before and after *Otey* that came to similar results, the provisions in the Code designed to stop disguised sales through the use of partnership structures, I.R.C. §§ 704(c), 707(a), and 737, are often called the anti-*Otey* provisions.

For example, the legislative history of I.R.C. § 707(a)(2)(B) mentions the *Otey* decision and indicates that the provision was adopted as a result of Congress's concern that taxpayers were deferring or avoiding tax on sales of partnership property, including sales of partnership interests, by characterizing sales as contributions of property, including money, followed or preceded by a related partnership distribution.[28] The Senate Finance Committee Report indicates that Congress was concerned about court decisions such as *Otey* that allowed tax-free treatment in cases which were economically indistinguishable from sales of property to a partnership or another partner.[29] Congress believed that these transactions should be treated for tax purposes in a manner consistent with their underlying economic substance.

---

[22] 1981-2 C.B. 143.

[23] 1981-2 C.B. 144.

[24] *Id.* at 230.

[25] *See* Chapter 2.

[26] *See* Chapter 7.

[27] 70 T.C. 312 (1978).

[28] S. Rep. No. 169, vol. 1, 98th Cong., 2d Sess. 225 (Apr. 2, 1984).

[29] *Id.*

I.R.C. § 707(a)(2)(B) provides that if: (i) there is a direct or indirect transfer of money or other property by a partner to a partnership, (ii) there is a related direct or indirect transfer of money or other property by the partnership to such partner (or another partner), and (iii) the transfers described in clauses (i) and (ii), when viewed together, are properly characterized as a sale or exchange of property, such transfers shall be treated either as occurring between the partnership and one who is not a partner, or as a transaction between two or more partners acting other than in their capacity as members of the partnership.

In general, a transfer of property by a partner to a partnership and a transfer of money or other consideration by the partnership to the partner constitute a sale of the property only if based on all the facts and circumstances: (i) the transfer of money or other consideration would not have been made but for the transfer of property, and (ii) in cases in which the transfers are not made simultaneously, the subsequent transfer is not dependent on the entrepreneurial risks of the partnership operations.[30] The facts and circumstances that are taken into consideration in making the determination include:

i.   whether the timing and amount of a subsequent transfer are determinable with reasonable certainty at the time of an earlier transfer;

ii. whether the transferor has a legally enforceable right to the subsequent transfer;

iii. whether the partner's right to receive the transfer of money or other consideration is secured;

iv. whether any person has made or is legally obligated to make contributions to the partnership in order to enable the partnership to make the transfer;

v.   whether any person has loaned the partnership the money or other consideration to enable the partnership to make the transfer;

vi. whether the partnership holds liquid assets, beyond those required by the reasonable needs of the business, that are expected to be available to make the transfer;

vii. whether partnership distributions, allocations, or control of partnership operations are designed to effect an exchange of the burdens and benefits of ownership of property;

viii. whether the transfer by the partnership to the partner is disproportionately large in relationship to the partner's general and continuing interest in partnership profits; and

ix. whether the recipient partner has an obligation to return or repay the distribution.[31]

To address the difficult factual determination of whether a transfer from the partnership is related to a transfer to the partnership, Treas. Reg. § 1.707-3(c)

---

[30] Treas. Reg. § 1.707-2(b)(1).

[31] Treas. Reg. § 1.707-2(b)(2).

provides that if within a two-year period a partner transfers property to a partnership and the partnership transfers money or other consideration to the partner (without regard to the order of the transfers), the transfers are presumed to be a sale of the property to the partnership unless the facts and circumstances clearly establish that the transfers do not constitute a sale.

If a taxpayer takes the position that a pair of transfers that would otherwise be presumed to be a sale is, under all the facts and circumstances, not a sale, the taxpayer is required to disclose the transfers to the IRS, unless the transfer from the partnership is a guaranteed payment, a reasonable preferred return, or an operating cash flow distribution.[32] Operating cash flow distribution means, for these purposes, a distribution of cash based upon the partnership's taxable income adjusted for certain non-taxable or non-cash items in percentages equal to the lesser of a partner's interests in overall partnership profits for that year or the partners' interests in overall partnership profits for the life of the partnership, unless the distribution is subject to a separate characterization rule.[33] If a transfer of money or other consideration is made to a partner by a partnership and the recipient partner made a transfer to the partnership more than two years before or after the transfer to the partnership, the transfers are presumed not to be a sale of the property to the partnership unless the facts and circumstances clearly establish that the transfers constitute a sale.[34]

The Regulations illustrate these rules with the following example:

> A transfers property X to partnership AB on April 9, 1992, in exchange for an interest in the partnership. At the time of the transfer, property X has a fair market value of $4,000,000 and an adjusted tax basis of $1,200,000. Immediately after the transfer, the partnership transfers $3,000,000 in cash to A. Assume that, under this section, the partnership's transfer of cash to A is treated as part of a sale of property X to the partnership. Because the amount of cash A receives on April 9, 1992, does not equal the fair market value of the property, A is considered to have sold a portion of property X with a value of $3,000,000 to the partnership in exchange for the cash. Accordingly, A must recognize $2,100,000 of gain ($3,000,000 amount realized less $900,000 adjusted tax basis ($1,200,000 multiplied by $3,000,000/$4,000,000)). Assuming A receives no other transfers that are treated as consideration for the sale of the property under this section, A is considered to have contributed to the partnership, in A's capacity as a partner, $1,000,000 of the fair market value of the property with an adjusted tax basis of $300,000.[35]

In other words, when the consideration given in the deemed sale is less than the fair market value of the property contributed, the transaction is divided into two transactions: a sale of the portion of the property contributed represented by the

---

[32] Treas. Reg. § 1.707-3(c). Proposed Regulations would extend the period during which disclosure is required to seven years. Prop. Treas. Reg. § 1.707-5(a)(8).

[33] Treas. Reg. § 1.704-4(b)(2).

[34] Treas. Reg. § 1.707-3(d).

[35] Treas. Reg. § 1.707-3(f), example 1.

relationship of the consideration given by the partnership to the fair market value of the entire property, and second, a contribution of the remaining portion of the fair market value of the property contributed, with the carryover basis also based upon the same proportion of the basis of the property contributed.

Special safe harbors are provided for reasonable guaranteed payments for capital and reasonable preferred returns. In this context, a guaranteed payment means any payment to a partner by a partnership for the use of capital and that is determined without regard to partnership income.[36] A guaranteed payment for these purposes does not include payments designed to liquidate all or part of the partner's interest in partnership property.[37] A preferred return in this context means a preferential distribution of partnership cash flow to a partner with respect to capital contributed to the partnership by the partner that will be matched, to the extent available, by an allocation of income or gain.[38] A preferred return or a guaranteed payment is viewed as reasonable for the purposes of the deemed sale rules only if: (i) the payment is reasonable in amount, (ii) the payment is pursuant to a written provision in the partnership agreement, and (iii) the payment is made after the provision providing for the payment is added to the partnership agreement.[39] A preferred return or guaranteed payment is reasonable in amount if the sum of any preferred return and any guaranteed payment does not exceed the product of the partner's unreturned capital at the beginning of the year (or the partner's weighted average capital balance for the year) multiplied by a rate that does not exceed 150% of the highest applicable federal rate,[40] at the appropriate compounding period or periods, in effect at any time from the time that the right to the payment is established, through the end of the taxable year.[41]

Exceptions are also provided for operating cash flow distributions and reimbursement of preformation expenditures.[42] A distribution meets the operating cash flow exception, to the extent it is not otherwise characterized by the parties, if they do not exceed the product of the net cash flow of the partnership from operations for the year multiplied by the lesser of: (i) the partner's percentage interest in overall partnership profits for that year or (ii) the partner's percentage interest in overall partnership profits for the life of the partnership.[43] Preformation expenditures are limited to the amounts incurred during the two years prior to the transfer by the partner to the partnership and are incurred by the partner in regard to organization and syndication costs or property contributed to the partnership by the partner (subject to a limitation of 20% of the fair market value of the property

---

[36] Treas. Reg. § 1.707-4(a)(1)(i).

[37] *Id.*

[38] Treas. Reg. § 1.707-4(a)(2).

[39] Treas. Reg. § 1.707-4(a)(3)(i).

[40] The applicable federal rate is a rate that is published monthly by the Treasury pursuant to I.R.C. § 1274(d) based upon the term of the obligation and the compounding period.

[41] Treas. Reg. § 1.707-4(a)(3)(ii).

[42] Treas. Reg. § 1.707-4(b), (d).

[43] Treas. Reg. § 1.707-4(b)(2).

contributed).[44]

If a partnership assumes or takes property subject to a qualified liability of a partner, the partnership is treated as transferring consideration to the partner only to the extent provided in Treas. Reg. § 1.707-5(a)(5).[45] Treas. Reg. § 1.707-5(a)(5) provides that if a transfer of property by a partner to a partnership is not otherwise treated as part of a sale, the partnership's assumption of or taking subject to a qualified liability in connection with a transfer of property is not treated as part of a sale. On the other hand, if a transfer subject to a qualified liability is treated as part of a sale without regard to the partnership's assumption of or taking subject to a qualified liability, the assumption of or taking subject to the qualified liability is treated as consideration in a sale to the extent of the lesser of:

i. the amount of consideration that the partnership would be treated as transferring if the liability were not a qualified liability, or

ii. the amount obtained by multiplying the amount of the qualified liability by the partner's net equity percentage[46] with respect to the property contributed by the partner.

For these purposes, a "qualified liability" means a liability assumed or taken subject to by a partnership in connection with a transfer of property to the partnership by a partner that: (i) was incurred by the partner more than two years prior to the transfer and that has continually encumbered the transferred property, (ii) was not incurred in anticipation of the transfer, but was incurred within the two-year period prior to the transfer, and that has continually encumbered the transferred property, (iii) is allocable under the rules of Treas. Reg. § 1.163-8T to capital expenditures with respect to the property, or (iv) is incurred in the ordinary course of the trade or business in which the property transferred to the partnership was used or held, but only if all the assets related to that trade or business are transferred other than assets that are not material to a continuation of the trade or business.[47] If, within a two-year period, a partner incurs a liability and transfers property to a partnership, and in connection with the transfer the partnership assumes or takes the property subject to the liability, the liability is presumed to be incurred in anticipation of the transfer unless the facts and circumstances clearly establish that the liability was not incurred in anticipation of the transfer.[48]

By contrast, if the partnership assumes or takes property subject to a liability of the partner other than a qualified liability, the partnership is treated as transferring

---

[44] Treas. Reg. § 1.707-4(d).

[45] Treas. Reg. § 1.707-5(a)(1).

[46] A partner's net equity percentage with respect to a property equals the percentage determined by dividing: (i) the aggregate consideration provided by the partnership to the partner that is treated as proceeds realized on the sale of the transferred property by (ii) the excess of the fair market value of the property over any qualified liability encumbering or properly allocable to the property. Treas. Reg. § 1.707-5(a)(5)(ii).

[47] Treas. Reg. § 1.707-5(a)(6).

[48] Treas. Reg. § 1.707-5(a)(7)(i). If a partner treats a liability incurred within two years of the transfer as not being in anticipation of the transfer, the partner must disclose the treatment. Treas. Reg. § 1.707-5(a)(7)(ii).

consideration to the partner to the extent that the amount of the liability exceeds the partner's share of that liability immediately after the partnership assumes or takes subject to the liability.[49] In general, a partner's share of a liability after the partnership assumes or takes subject to the liability for the purposes of the disguised sale rules is the partner's share of the liability determined under Treas. Reg. § 1.752, with the exception that a partner's share of partnership liabilities is reduced by any amount of liabilities to the extent that it is anticipated that the transferring partner's share of liabilities will be subsequently reduced and the subsequent reduction is part of a plan to minimize the impact of the disguised sale rules.[50]

Treas. Reg. § 1.704-2(h)(1) also provides that, in certain circumstances, a distribution funded by a nonrecourse liability will increase a partner's share of minimum gain, which under Treas. Reg. § 1.752-3(a)(1) would increase the partner's share of partnership liabilities. As you will remember from Chapter 3, Treas. Reg. § 1.752-1(f) provides that increases and decreases in a partner's share of partnership liabilities are netted if they result from a single transaction. Similarly, if a partner transfers property to a partnership and the partnership incurs a liability that is allocable in whole or in part to a transfer of money or other consideration to the partner within 90 days of the partnership incurring the liability, the transfer of money or other consideration to the partner is taken into consideration under the disguised sale rules only to the extent that the money or other consideration exceeds the partner's allocable share of the partnership liability.[51]

B. The Disguised Sale of Partnership Interests

One of the distinctions that hopefully is now apparent between the sale of a portion of a partnership interest and a distribution from a partnership to a partner reducing (but not liquidating) the partner's interest in the partnership is the manner in which gain is calculated. As discussed in Chapter 7, I.R.C. § 731 generally provides that a partner does not recognize gain on a distribution except to the extent that the money distributed exceeds the recipient partner's basis immediately before the distribution. As discussed in Chapter 6, if a partner disposes of a portion of the partner's partnership interest, the partner must allocate the partner's basis between the portion retained and the portion transferred. Thus, a partner is able to use the partner's entire basis to absorb distributions from a partnership, but only a portion of the partner's basis when a portion of a partner's interest is sold.

Other differences also may occur. For example, a transferee succeeds to a proportionate share of the transferor's capital account and I.R.C. § 704(c)(1)(A) built-in gain amount. A new partner by contribution would start with a clean slate.

---

[49] Treas. Reg. § 1.707-5(a)(1).

[50] Treas. Reg. § 1.707-5(a)(2), (3).

[51] Treas. Reg. § 1.707-5(b). Rules similar to those set forth in Treas. Reg. § 1.707-3 apply in determining whether a transfer of property by a partnership to a partner and one or more transfers of money or other consideration by that partner to the partnership are treated as a sale of property, in whole or part, to the partner. Treas. Reg. § 1.707-6.

Whenever economically similar transactions are treated differently by the Code, taxpayers will have a tendency to structure the transaction in a manner that produces the least tax.

For example, A and B own partnership AB in which each partner owns a 50% interest. A and B each have a basis in their respective partnership interests of $30. C wants to join the partnership and is willing to pay $30 for a one-third interest in the partnership. If C buys one third of each of A and B's interests in the partnership, each of A and B will have gain of $5 ($15 paid to each less $10 (one-third of basis)). If A and B were successfully able to structure the transaction as a contribution by C to AB followed by a distribution to A and B, neither A nor B would have gain recognition ($30 basis less $15 distribution).

Although the Proposed Regulations dealing with the disguised sale of partnership interests had been promulgated, those Proposed Regulations have now been withdrawn. In the absence of Regulations addressing the issues, the authority related to disguised sales of partnership interests is relatively sparse.

One case that has addressed the issue of a disguised sale of a partnership interest is *Jupiter Corp. v. United States*.[52] In *Jupiter Corp.*, a partnership that had been formed in 1962 admitted new partners in 1966, with the new partners contributing capital to the partnership. The contribution to capital was distributed to the pre-existing partners in proportion to their prior percentage interests. The court looked to the intent of the parties and found that neither the old partners nor the new partners would have agreed to a purchase of a partnership interest from the old partners. In addition, the economic interest that the new partners held was different from that held by the old partners. The court held that the transaction was not a camouflaged sale of a partnership interest.

Similarly, in *Communications Satellite Corp. v. United States*,[53] the admission of new partners and the contemporaneous distribution of cash to the pre-existing partners were held not to be a disguised sale of partnership interests. In making its determination, the court looked particularly to the lack of financial negotiations between the pre-existing partners and the incoming partners and the lack of control of the pre-existing partners over the admission of the new partners.

On the other hand, in *Crenshaw v. United States*,[54] the court viewed: (i) a distribution of a partnership asset, (ii) a like-kind exchange with a related party of the distributed asset, (iii) a sale of the distributed asset by the related party, and (iv) a contribution of the distributed property back to the partnership by the buyer, as a sale of a partnership interest under the step-transaction doctrine.

Relying largely on the legislative history to I.R.C. § 707, the IRS has issued two technical advice memoranda that conclude that transactions constitute disguised sales of partnership interests.[55] In PLR 200301004, the IRS acknowledged that the facts being considered were similar to those in *Communications Satellite Corp.*,

---

[52] 2 Cl. Ct. 58 (1983).

[53] 625 F.2d 997 (Cl. Ct. 1980).

[54] 450 F.2d 472 (5th Cir. 1971).

[55] TAM 200301004 (Aug. 27, 2002); TAM 200037005 (May 18, 2000).

but indicated that the legislative history allowed the IRS to reach a contrary conclusion.

§ 8.07 LIMITATIONS ON RECOGNITION OF LOSSES AND RECHARACTERIZATION OF GAINS IN RELATED PARTY TRANSACTIONS

A. Limitations on Recognition of Losses

Although I.R.C. § 707(a) provides that in the circumstances described above a transaction between a partner and a partnership may be treated as a transaction between the partnership and a person who is not a partner, I.R.C. § 707(b)(1) provides that no deduction shall be allowed for losses from sales or exchanges of property (other than an interest in the partnership) between a partnership and a person owning, directly or indirectly, more than 50% of the capital interest or the profits interest in the partnership or between two partnerships in which the same persons own, directly or indirectly, more than 50% of the capital interests or profits interests.

For example, if the ABC partnership sold its property at a loss to the BCD partnership, and each partnership was owned one-third by each of its partners, the loss recognized by the ABC partnership would not be deductible by ABC. Instead, the disallowed loss is treated as a reduction of gain on subsequent sale by BCD.[56]

For the purposes of I.R.C. § 707(b), the constructive ownership rules of I.R.C. § 267(c) apply except that there is no attribution among partners solely because they are partners.[57] Under such attribution rules: (i) stock owned, directly or indirectly, by or for a corporation, partnership, estate, or trust is considered owned proportionately by or for its shareholders, partners, or beneficiaries and (ii) an individual is considered to own the stock owned, directly or indirectly, by or for the individual's family. The family of an individual for these purposes includes the individual's siblings, spouse, ancestors, and lineal descendants. Stock owned constructively by reason of attribution from a corporation, partnership, estate, or trust is considered owned by the person to whom the ownership is attributed for further application of the constructive ownership rules as well.

In the sale by ABC to BCD, above, if BCD was instead CDE, with E being B's parent, the result would be the same. In addition to the loss disallowance rules under I.R.C. § 707(b)(1), I.R.C. § 267(a) disallows recognition of losses and requires the matching of certain items of income and expense where the losses or the income and expense items result from transactions between related persons within the meaning of I.R.C. § 267(b). I.R.C. § 267(b) does not treat a partnership as "related" to its partners. However, Treas. Reg. § 1.267(b)-1(b) provides that a transaction occurring between a partnership and a person other than a partner shall be treated as occurring between the person and the partners individually. This would mean that if a person undertook a transaction with a partnership, and

---

[56] I.R.C. § 267(d).

[57] I.R.C. § 707(b)(3).

some or all of the partners of the partnership were related to the person undertaking the transaction, I.R.C. § 267(a) may apply to limit the recognition of any loss otherwise recognizable in the transaction.

Also, I.R.C. § 267(e) provides that the rule of I.R.C. § 267(a)(2) requiring matching of income and expense is applicable to certain transactions involving partnerships. In the case of any amount paid or incurred by, to, or on behalf of, a partnership: (i) the entity, (ii) any person owning a capital or profits interest in such entity, (iii) any person who owns any capital or profits interest of a partnership in which the entity owns any capital or profits interest, and (iv) any person related to any person described in (ii) or (iii) (within the meaning of I.R.C. § 267(b) or I.R.C. § 707(b)(1)), are treated as persons specified in I.R.C. § 267(b). Thus, payments between such persons are not deductible until the recipient includes the payment in income.

B.   Recharacterization of Gains

Separately from the limitations on the ability of persons related to a partnership to recognize losses or take deductions with respect to transactions with the partnership, when gain is recognized in certain transactions between a person related to a partnership and the partnership, the gain is recharacterized as ordinary income.

I.R.C. § 707(b)(2)(B) provides that in the case of a sale or exchange, directly or indirectly, of property which in the hands of the transferee is property other than a capital asset (as defined in I.R.C. § 1221), any recognized gain shall be considered as gain from the sale or exchange of property other than a capital asset, if the sale or exchange is between partnerships in which the same persons own, directly or indirectly, more than 50% of the capital or profits interests in each partnership or between a partnership and a person owning, directly or indirectly, more than 50% of the capital interests, or profits interests, in such partnership.

As with the rules on loss disallowance, in determining ownership for the purposes of I.R.C. § 707(b)(2)(B), the rules for the constructive ownership of stock provided in I.R.C. § 267(c)(1), (2), (4), and (5) are applied.

§ 8.08A   ISSUANCE OF A PARTNERSHIP INTEREST IN EXCHANGE FOR SERVICES

A.   Potential Income to Partner and Gain to Partnership

In general, a service recipient recognizes gain on the transfer of appreciated property to a service provider in payment for the performance of services to the extent of the amount the value of the services received exceeds the service recipient's basis in the property transferred.[58] The service recipient is treated as having sold the property transferred.[59] The service provider has income equal to

---

[58] Treas. Reg. § 1.83-6(b).

[59] United States v. General Shoe Corp., 282 F.2d 9 (6th Cir. 1960).

the fair market value of the property received (and takes a fair market value basis in the property).[60]

When the service recipient is issuing equity in itself to the service provider, this general approach creates an issue because the service recipient will generally have a zero basis in its own equity.

In the case of a corporation transferring its own stock to a service provider, I.R.C. § 1032 prevents the corporation from recognizing any gain or loss on the issuance of the stock.[61] As discussed in Chapter 2, the Code section for partnerships that is similar to I.R.C. § 1032 is I.R.C. § 721.

In the case of partnerships, it is necessary to distinguish between two types of interests: profits interests and capital interests. Profits interests, as used here, mean a right to share in future profits only. Thus, if a partnership was liquidated immediately after a service provider was given a profits interest, the service provider would receive nothing in the liquidation. A capital interest, on the other hand, gives the service provider a right to the existing capital of the partnership. If capital accounts are kept in accordance with the Regulations discussed in Chapter 5, a partner receiving a capital interest starts with a positive capital account. If the partnership were liquidated immediately after a service provider was given a capital interest, the service provider would receive a distribution in the liquidation.

In contrast to the treatment under I.R.C. § 1032, the Regulations under I.R.C. § 721 provide:

> To the extent that any of the partners gives up any part of his right to be repaid his contributions (as distinguished from a share in partnership profits) in favor of another partner as compensation for services (or in satisfaction of an obligation), section 721 does not apply.[62]

As I.R.C. § 721 does not apply, a partner who receives a capital interest in the partnership in exchange for services should fall under the regular income tax rules and have income equal to the fair market value of the interest received. Her basis in the partnership interest would also be that same fair market value. Further, partnerships arguably are subject to income recognition on the issuance of their own interests in exchange for services under the current Regulations because the partnership is paying compensation with a partnership interest in which the partnership has a zero basis.

The general issue as to the potential of gain recognition by the partnership as a service recipient is further augmented because the Regulations treat the issuance of a partnership interest in exchange for services as a guaranteed payment.[63] In 2007, the IRS issued a public ruling that the transfer of property in satisfaction of a guaranteed payment results in an exchange under I.R.C. § 1001.[64]

---

[60] *See, e.g.*, International Freighting Corporation, Inc. v. Commissioner, 135 F.2d 310 (2d Cir. 1943).

[61] Treas. Reg. § 1.1032-1(a).

[62] Treas. Reg. § 1.721-1(b).

[63] Treas. Reg. § 1.721-1(b)(2).

[64] Rev. Rul. 2007-40, 2007-1 C.B. 1426.

Thus, whether the issue is approached from authorities focused on compensation or Subchapter K, absent the application of other authority, a partnership may be required to recognize gain equal to the value of the services received on the issuance of a partnership interest in exchange for services.

B.   Receipt of Profits Interests by Service Partners

I.R.C. § 83 requires that, in general, if property is issued in connection with the performance of services, the excess of the value of the property over the amount paid for the property is included in the gross income of the service provider in the first year the rights of the recipient of the property are transferable or not subject to a substantial risk of forfeiture.[65] Special rules are provided for an election to recognize income in respect of property subject to a substantial risk of forfeiture in the year the property is transferred rather than the year of vesting.[66]

The question of how service providers should be taxed upon the receipt of partnership profits interests issued in payment for services was subject to substantial controversy. If a partnership profits interest issued for services was shown to have clear value through a sale of the partnership interest shortly after the issuance, the partnership interest was treated as taxable to the service provider in the amount of the interest's value.[67] On the other hand, a service partner was not taxable on the receipt of a profits interest where the interest had only speculative value at the time of its issuance.[68]

A variety of theories were addressed by both taxpayers and the IRS, with varying degrees of success.

In *Hale v. Commissioner*,[69] a pre-I.R.C. § 83 case, the court concluded that the income recognized on the assignment of a profits interest should be given ordinary income treatment, although the partnership interest itself was a capital asset. The court also observed in a footnote that the mere receipt of a partnership interest in future profits of the partnership does not create a current tax liability.[70] For many years, that footnote was the sole authority for the position that the value of a profits interest was not income to the service provider.

In *Diamond v. Commissioner*,[71] also a pre-I.R.C. § 83 case, the court found that the taxpayer had taxable ordinary income treated as compensation for services on the receipt of a profits interest where the profits interest had clearly determinable

---

[65] I.R.C. § 83(a). The rights of a person in property are subject to a substantial risk of forfeiture if such person's rights to full enjoyment of such property are conditioned upon the future performance of substantial services by any individual. I.R.C. § 83(c)(1).

[66] I.R.C. § 83(b).

[67] Diamond v. Commissioner, 56 T.C. 530 (1971), *aff'd*, 492 F.2d 286 (7th Cir. 1974).

[68] Campbell v. Commissioner, 943 F.2d 815 (8th Cir. 1991). A general discussion of the issues surrounding the issuance of a capital interest for services may be found in Frost, *Receipt of Capital and Profits Interests Continues to Have Uncertain Tax Consequences*, 75 J. Tax'n 38 (1991).

[69] T.C. Memo 1965-274.

[70] *Id.* at 65–1646 n.3.

[71] 492 F.2d 286 (7th Cir. 1974).

fair market value because of a sale of the interest within a month after the interest was originally issued.

In other cases, the court has concluded, or the IRS has conceded, that receipt of a profits interest by a service partner creates no tax liability, primarily because it could not be reliably valued.[72] Similarly, in *Campbell v. Commissioner*,[73] the Eighth Circuit found that a profits interest had only speculative, if any, value and, therefore, was not taxable.

Much of the uncertainty and litigation over the treatment of profits interests was resolved by the IRS through the promulgation of Rev. Proc. 93-27.[74] Under Rev. Proc. 93-27, if a person receives a profits interest for the provision of services to or for the benefit of a partnership in a partner capacity or in anticipation of being a partner, the IRS will not treat the receipt of such an interest as a taxable event for the partner or the partnership.

Under Rev. Proc. 93-27, a profits interest is defined as an interest that would not give the holder a share of the proceeds if the partnership's assets were sold at fair market value and then the proceeds were distributed in a complete liquidation of the partnership at the time of the receipt of the partnership interest. Rev. Proc. 93-27 does not apply, however, if: (i) the profits interest relates to a substantially certain and predicable stream of income from partnership assets; (ii) the partner disposes of the profits interest within two years of receipt; or (iii) the profits interest is a limited partnership interest in a "publicly traded partnership" within the meaning of I.R.C. § 7704(b).

Rev. Proc. 93-27 was further clarified in Rev. Proc. 2001-43.[75] Rev. Proc. 2001-43 provides that if a partnership grants a nonvested interest to a service provider, the time for testing whether the interest qualifies as a profits interest is, under certain circumstances, at the time the interest is granted (rather than at the time of vesting). To qualify for such treatment: (i) the service provider must be treated as a partner from the time of grant; (ii) neither the partnership nor the other partners may deduct any amount in respect of the vesting of the interest; and (iii) the interest otherwise must qualify as a profits interest under Rev. Proc. 93-27.

Thus, as to a profits interest under Rev. Proc. 93-27, neither the recipient partner nor the partnership will recognize income on the issuance of the interest in exchange for services if the requirements of Rev. Proc. 93-27 and Rev. Proc. 2001-43 are satisfied. As to a capital interest, which under Rev. Proc. 93-27 is any interest other than a profits interest, the general rules would appear to still apply.

---

[72] *See* National Oil Co. v. Commissioner, 52 T.C.M. (CCH) 1223, 1228 (1986) (Commissioner conceded that if taxpayer received only profits interest, no taxable event had occurred); Kenroy, Inc. v. Commissioner, 47 T.C.M. (CCH) 1749, 1756–59 (1984) (profits interest had no fair market value, thus no tax liability upon receipt).

[73] 943 F.2d 815 (8th Cir. 1991).

[74] 1993-2 C.B. 343. *See* Paravano, *IRS Adopts "Capacity" Approach for Treatment of Receipt of a Partnership Profits Interest*, 94 TNT 4-57 (Jan. 3, 1994).

[75] 2001-2 C.B. 191. *See* Mincey, Sloan & Banoff, *Rev. Proc. 2001-43, Section 83(b), and Unvested Profits Interests — the Final Facet of* Diamond?, 95 J. Tax'n 205 (Oct. 2001).

§ 8.08B   COMPENSATORY INTEREST PROPOSED REGULATIONS

On May 24, 2005, the Treasury and I.R.S. released proposed regulations (the *"Compensatory Interest Proposed Regulations"*) concerning the issuance of equity and equity related interests in partnerships in exchange for services.[76] The Compensatory Interest Proposed Regulations provide that the transfer of partnership equity in connection with the performance of services is subject to I.R.C. § 83. The Compensatory Interest Proposed Regulations also provide that no gain or loss is recognized by a partnership on the transfer or vesting of an interest in the transferring partnership in connection with the performance of services for the transferring partnership. The Compensatory Interest Proposed Regulations provide a default rule that the gross income of the recipient of the interest will include an amount based upon the fair market value of the interest at the time of the transfer or vesting. However, the Treasury also issued Notice 2005-43[77] together with the Compensatory Interest Proposed Regulations, which describes a proposed revenue procedure that would, subject to some limitations, permit the amount included in the gross income of the recipient of the interest to be based upon the liquidation value of the interest issued.

A.   Background

I.R.C. § 83 requires that, in general, if property is issued in connection with the performance of services, the excess of the value of the property over the amount paid for the property is included in the gross income of the service provider in the first year the rights of the recipient of the property are transferable or not subject to a substantial risk of forfeiture.[78] Special rules are provided for an election to recognize income in respect of property subject to a substantial risk of forfeiture in the year the property is transferred rather than the year of vesting[79] and for the general treatment of the income in respect of options without a readily ascertainable fair market value[80] as being at the time of exercise rather the time of transfer or vesting.[81]

---

[76] REG-105346-03, 70 Fed. Reg. 29675 (May 24, 2005) (the *"Compensatory Interest Proposed Regulations"*).

[77] 2005-24 I.R.B. 1221.

[78] I.R.C. § 83(a).

[79] I.R.C. § 83(b). The rights of a person in property are subject to a substantial risk of forfeiture if such person's rights to full enjoyment of such property are conditioned upon the future performance of substantial services by any individual. I.R.C. § 83(c)(1).

[80] The value of an option is ordinarily not treated as having a readily ascertainable value unless the option is actively traded on an established market. Treas. Reg. § 1.83-7(b)(1). If the option is not actively traded, it does not have a readily ascertainable fair market value unless its fair market value can otherwise be measured with reasonable accuracy. Treas. Reg. § 1.83-7(b)(2).

[81] I.R.C. § 83(e)(3).

B. Explanation of Provisions of the Compensatory Interest Proposed Regulations

The Compensatory Interest Proposed Regulations provide that a partnership interest is property within the meaning of I.R.C. § 83 and that the transfer of a partnership interest in connection with the performance of services is subject to I.R.C. § 83.[82]

The Compensatory Interest Proposed Regulations apply I.R.C. § 83 equally to partnership capital interests and partnership profits interests. However, a right to receive allocations and distributions from a partnership that is treated under I.R.C. § 707(a)(2)(A) as being more properly treated as a disguised payment of compensation to the service provider is not a partnership interest under the Proposed Regulations.[83]

I.R.C. § 83(b) allows a person who receives property subject to a substantial risk of forfeiture in connection with the performance of services to elect to include in gross income the difference between: (i) the fair market value of the property at the time of transfer (determined without regard to a restriction other than one that by its terms will never lapse); and (ii) the amount paid for such property. Under I.R.C. § 83(b)(2), the election under I.R.C. § 83(b) must be made within 30 days of the date of the transfer of the property to the service provider.

Except as otherwise provided in Treas. Reg. § 1.83-6(a)(3),[84] because I.R.C. § 83(h) provides that any deduction allowable to the person for whom the services are provided will be in an amount equal to the amount included in the service provider's income and in the taxable year of the person for whom the services are provided in which or with which ends the taxable year in which the amount is included in the gross income of the service provider, the I.R.C. § 83(b) election will also affect the amount and timing of the service recipient's deduction.

The Compensatory Interest Proposed Regulations provide that the I.R.C. § 83 timing rules override the timing rules in Subchapter K to the extent that they are inconsistent.[85] Accordingly, under the Compensatory Interest Proposed Regulations, if a partnership transfers a partnership interest to a partner in connection with the performance of services, the timing and the amount of the related income inclusion and deduction are determined by I.R.C. § 83 and the regulations thereunder.[86]

---

[82] Prop. Treas. Reg. § 1.83-3(e) is amended by the Proposed Regulations to explicitly provide that "property" includes a partnership interest.

[83] *See* S. Rep. No. 98-169, vol. 1, 98 Cong., 2d Sess. 226 (Apr. 2, 1984).

[84] Treas. Reg. § 1.83-6(a)(3) provides two exceptions. First, when property is substantially vested upon transfer, an otherwise allowable deduction is allowed to the service recipient in accordance with its method of accounting (in conformity with I.R.C. §§ 446 and 461). Also, in the case of a transfer to an employee benefit plan described in Treas. Reg. § 1.162-10(a) or a transfer to an employees' trust or annuity plan described in I.R.C. § 404(a)(5), section 83(h) does not apply.

[85] Prop. Treas. Reg. § 1.707-1(c).

[86] The Treasury Department and the Service have requested comments on alternative approaches to resolving the timing inconsistency between I.R.C. § 83 and I.R.C. § 707(c).

Consistent with the current treatment of S corporation shareholders, the Compensatory Interest Proposed Regulations provide that if a partnership interest that was transferred in connection with the performance of services is subject to a substantial risk of forfeiture, and if an election under I.R.C. § 83(b) is not made, then the holder of the partnership interest is not treated as a partner for federal tax purposes until the interest becomes substantially vested. Under such an approach, the testing point for the amount of income included in the income of the service provider is at the time the interest becomes substantially vested. If the partnership interest has appreciated in value between the time of grant and the time of vesting, the service provider may include a greater amount in income than the service provider might otherwise have included in income had an I.R.C. § 83(b) election been timely made — depending upon the value of the interest when it vests compared to the service provider's allocable share of income over the period of vesting and the fair market value at the time of grant.

If an election under I.R.C. § 83(b) has been made with respect to a substantially nonvested interest, the holder of the nonvested interest may be allocated partnership items that may later be forfeited. Under the Proposed Regulations, for this reason, allocations of partnership items while the interest is substantially nonvested cannot have economic effect.[87] Under the Proposed Regulations, such allocations will be deemed to be in accordance with the partners' interests in the partnership if: (i) the partnership agreement requires that the partnership make forfeiture allocations (described below) if the interest for which the I.R.C. § 83(b) election is made is later forfeited and (ii) all material allocations and capital account adjustments under the partnership agreement not pertaining to substantially nonvested partnership interests for which an I.R.C. § 83(b) election has been made are recognized under I.R.C. § 704(b).[88] This safe harbor does not apply if, at the time of the I.R.C. § 83(b) election, there is a plan that a substantially nonvested interest will be forfeited.[89] All of the facts and circumstances (including the tax status of the holder of the substantially nonvested interest) will be considered in determining whether there is a plan that the interest will be forfeited. In such a case, the partners' distributive shares of partnership items shall be determined in accordance with the partners' interests in the partnership under Treas. Reg. § 1.704-1(b)(3).[90]

§ 8.08C CURRENT LEGISLATIVE PROPOSALS

Several recent legislative proposals would change the way in which the issuance of a partnership interest in exchange for services would be taxed.[91] One such bill, H.R. 1935, would amend I.R.C. § 83 to treat the fair market value of a partnership

---

[87] Prop. Treas. Reg. § 1.704-1(b)(4)(xii).

[88] Prop. Treas. Reg. § 1.704-1(b)(4)(xii)(b).

[89] Prop. Treas. Reg. § 1.704-1(b)(4)(xii)(e).

[90] *Id.*

[91] *See, e.g.*, H.R. 1935, 11th Cong., 1st Sess. (Apr. 2, 2009). Howard E. Abrams has predicted that the current form of the proposal will ultimately be abandoned by Congress because of the technical flaws in the proposal. Howard E. Abrams, *Carried Interests: The Past Is Prologue* at 9 (Jan. 19, 2008), *available at* SSRN: http://ssrn.com/abstract=1085582.

interest issued in connection with the performance of services as the liquidation value of the partnership interest unless the recipient partner elected not to have the provision apply. Such a provision would expand the treatment now provided by Rev. Proc. 93-27[92] to types of partnership interests excluded by Rev. Proc. 93-27.

Currently proposed legislation would also add a new I.R.C. § 710 that would provide that, in the case of an investment services partnership interest, net income with respect to such interest will be treated as ordinary income for the performance of services, and net loss with respect to such interest (to the extent not disallowed) will be treated as ordinary loss.[93] In addition, any gain realized on the disposition of an investment services partnership interest would be treated as ordinary income for the performance of services.[94]

An "investment services partnership interest" means any interest in a partnership which is held by any person if such person provides (directly or indirectly) a substantial quantity of any of the following services to the partnership: (i) advising the partnership as to the value of any specified asset; (ii) advising the partnership as to the advisability of investing in, purchasing, or selling any specified asset; (iii) arranging financing with respect to acquiring specified assets; or (iv) any activity in support of the forgoing services.[95] "Specified asset" means, in this context, securities, real estate, interests in partnerships, commodities, or options or derivative contracts with respect to securities, real estate, or commodities.

The bill provides an exception to the general recharacterization treatment for a portion of the investment services partnership interest that is acquired for invested capital.

As of the time of this writing, the adoption of the proposals remains unclear. However, the president has incorporated a similar proposal in his budget.

§ 8.09   COMPARISON WITH S CORPORATIONS

Partially because S corporations are subject to I.R.C. § 311(b), which requires gain recognition if a corporation distributes appreciated property to its shareholders, and because I.R.C. § 351, which provides for nonrecognition of gain on a contribution to a corporation, is more restrictive than I.R.C. § 721, which provides for nonrecognition of gain on a contribution to a partnership, there has not been as extensive congressional or regulatory focus on the use of S corporations to facilitate disguised sales.

There is no equivalent to I.R.C. § 707(a) in the provisions of the Code dealing with corporations. On the other hand, the treatment of nonqualified preferred stock as boot (causing gain recognition) and the general denial of nonrecognition

---

[92]   1993-2 C.B. 343.

[93]   Prop. I.R.C. § 710(a)(1). The designation "Prop." has been used to indicate a portion of the bill that would change or add a current Code provision.

[94]   Prop. I.R.C. § 710(b)(1).

[95]   Prop. I.R.C. § 710(c)(1).

treatment on contributions to investment companies in I.R.C. § 351 do relate to the same fundamental issues.

The equivalent of guaranteed payments in an S corporation context would be the executive compensation of shareholders.

Although S corporations are not subject to the rules of I.R.C. § 707(b), I.R.C. § 267 applies equally to both S corporations and partnerships.

§ 8.10   READING, QUESTIONS AND PROBLEMS

A.   Reading

CODE:

I.R.C. §§ 707, 267

TREASURY REGULATIONS:

Treas. Reg. §§ 1.707-1, 1.707-3, 1.707-4, 1.707-5, 1.707-6, 1.707-8

Prop. Treas. Reg. § 1.707-7

CASES:

Pratt v. Commissioner, 64 T.C. 203 (1975), *aff'd in part, rev'd in part*, 550 F.2d 1023 (5th Cir. 1977).

RULINGS AND OTHER INTERPRETATIONS:

Rev. Rul. 81-300, 1981-2 C.B. 143.

Rev. Rul. 81-301, 1981-2 C.B. 144.

B.   Questions and Problems

1. The taxpayers are the general partners in a limited partnership formed to purchase, develop, and operate a shopping center. The partnership agreement specifies the taxpayers' shares of the profit and loss of the partnership. The general partners have a 10% interest in each item of partnership income, gain, loss, deduction, or credit. In addition, the partnership agreement provides that the general partners must contribute their time, managerial abilities, and best efforts to the partnership and that in return for their managerial services each will receive a fee of 5% of the gross rentals received by the partnership. These amounts will be paid to the general partners in all events.

Pursuant to the partnership agreement, the taxpayers carried out their duties as general partners and provided the management services required in the operation of the shopping centers. The management fee of 5% of gross rentals was reasonable in amount for the services rendered.

How would these facts be analyzed under the *Pratt* decision, Rev. Rul. 81-300, and the legislative history to I.R.C. § 707(a)?

2. *ABC* is a limited partnership and is registered with the Securities and Exchange Commission as a management company pursuant to the Investment Company Act of 1940, as amended. Under the partnership agreement, *ABC*'s assets must consist only of municipal bonds, certain readily marketable temporary investments, and cash. The agreement provides for two classes of general partners: (1) "director general partners" (directors) who are individuals and (2) one "adviser general partner" (adviser) that is a corporate investment adviser registered as such in accordance with the Investment Advisors Act of 1940, 15 U.S.C.A., section 80b-5 (1971).

Under the partnership agreement, the directors are compensated and have complete and exclusive control over the management, conduct, and operation of *ABC*'s activities. The directors are authorized to appoint agents and employees to perform duties on behalf of *ABC* and these agents may be, but need not be, general partners. Under the partnership agreement, the adviser has no rights, powers, or authority as a general partner, except that, subject to the supervision of the directors, the adviser is authorized to manage the investment and reinvestment of *ABC*'s assets. The adviser is responsible for payment of any expenses incurred in the performance of its investment advisory duties, including those for office space and facilities, equipment, and any of its personnel used to service and administer *ABC*'s investments. The adviser is not personally liable to the other partners for any losses incurred in the investment and reinvestment of *ABC*'s assets.

The nature of the adviser's services are substantially the same as those it renders as an independent contractor or agent for persons other than *ABC*, and, under the agreement, the adviser is not precluded from engaging in such transactions with others.

Each general partner, including the adviser general partner, is required to contribute sufficient cash to *ABC* to acquire at least a 1% interest in the partnership. The agreement requires an allocation of 10% of *ABC*'s daily gross income to the adviser. After reduction by the compensation allocable to the directors and the adviser, *ABC*'s items of income, gain, loss, deduction, and credit are divided according to the percentage interests held by each partner.

The adviser's right to 10% of *ABC*'s daily gross income for managing *ABC*'s investment must be approved at least annually by a majority vote of the directors or a majority vote of all the partnership interests. Furthermore, the directors may remove the adviser as investment manager at any time on 60 days' written notice to the adviser. The adviser can terminate its investment manager status by giving 60 days' written notice to the directors. The agreement provides that the adviser will no longer be a general partner after removal or withdrawal as investment manager, but will continue to participate as a limited partner in the income, gains, losses, deductions, and credits attributable to the percentage interest that it holds.

How would these facts be analyzed under the *Pratt* decision, Rev. Rul. 81-301, and the legislative history to I.R.C. § 707(a)?

3. C transfers undeveloped land to the CD partnership in exchange for an interest in the partnership. The partnership intends to construct a building on the land. At the time the land is transferred to the partnership, it is unencumbered and has an adjusted tax basis of $500,000 and a fair market value of $1,000,000. The partnership agreement provides that upon completing construction of the building the partnership will distribute $900,000 to C.

    a. If the distribution to C occurs within two years of the transfer to CD, how will the transfer be characterized?

    b. What facts would establish that the transaction should not be presumed to be a sale?

    c. If the distribution to C occurs more than two years after the transfer to CD, how will the transfer be characterized?

    d. What facts would establish that the transaction should be presumed to be a sale?

4. A and B each owns a 50% interest in partnership AB. AB holds Blackacre, real property with a fair market value of $400x. AB has no liabilities. On May 25, 2008, C transfers $100x in cash to AB in exchange for an interest in AB. Simultaneously, AB transfers $100x in cash to A.

    a. How is the transaction characterized under the Proposed Regulations?

    b. What facts would establish that a different treatment would be appropriate?

5. A and B each owns a 50% interest in partnership AB. AB holds, among other things, Whiteacre, real property with a fair market value of $1,000x and a tax basis of $700x, along with other assets. AB has no liabilities. On January 1, 2008, C transfers investment property, with a fair market value of $1,500x and a tax basis of $300x, to AB. Simultaneously with that transfer, AB transfers Whiteacre to B.

    a. How is the transaction characterized under the Proposed Regulations?

    b. What facts would establish that a different treatment would be appropriate?

6. GP is a cash-basis general partnership organized in the current year under the laws of Y. LP is an accrual-basis limited partnership organized in the current year under the laws of X. The partners of GP are A (20%), B (25%), C (30%), and E (25%). B is a corporation wholly owned by A.

    LP was owned by F (33⅓%), G (33–⅓%), and a corporation (33⅓%) wholly owned by F. G is a general partnership organized under the laws of Y; its partners are A (33⅓%), C (33⅓%), and E (33⅓%). F is a general partnership organized under the laws of Y; its partners are A, B, C, D, and E (20% each). D is a corporation wholly owned by a corporation wholly owned by C.

    On December 22 of the current year, GP transferred a land sale contract to LP in exchange for its interest-bearing nonrecourse promissory note secured by a mortgage on the underlying property.

a. At the time of the sale of a land sale contract, was GP related to LP for the purposes of I.R.C. § 707 or I.R.C. § 267?

b. If the property were sold at a loss, would any portion of the loss be deferred? What portion?

Chapter 9

BUSINESS COMBINATIONS: PARTNERSHIP MERGERS AND DIVISIONS

§ 9.01   INTRODUCTION

Chapter 9 will focus on the consequences of partnership mergers and divisions under I.R.C. § 708(b) and the Regulations thereunder.

§ 9.02   PARTNERSHIP MERGERS

A.   General Rules

I.R.C. § 708(b)(2)(A) provides that in the case of a merger or consolidation of two or more partnerships, the resulting partnership is, for purposes of I.R.C. § 708, considered the continuation of any merging or consolidating partnership whose members own an interest of more than 50% in the capital and profits of the resulting partnership. Treas. Reg. § 1.708-1(c)(2) provides that if the resulting partnership could otherwise be considered a continuation of more than one of the merging partnerships, the resulting partnership is solely the continuation of the partnership that is credited with the contribution of assets having the greatest fair market value (net of liabilities) to the resulting partnership. Any other merging or consolidating partnerships are considered to be terminated.[1] If the members of none of the merging partnerships own more than a 50% interest in the capital and profits of the resulting partnership, all of the merged partnerships are considered terminated, and a new partnership results.[2] The taxable years of the merging partnerships that are considered terminated are closed under I.R.C. § 706(c), ending upon the date of the merger or consolidation.[3]

The resulting partnership's taxable year does not close, and the partnership files a return for the taxable year of the merging or consolidating partnership that it is considered to be continuing.[4] The resulting partnership retains the taxpayer identification number of the partnership that is continuing.[5]

---

[1] Treas. Reg. § 1.708-1(c)(1).

[2] *Id.*

[3] Treas. Reg. § 1.708-1(c)(2).

[4] *Id.*

[5] *Id.*

Example 1. Partnership AB, in whose capital and profits A and B each own a 50-percent interest, and partnership CD, in whose capital and profits C and D each own a 50-percent interest, merge on September 30, and form partnership ABCD. Partners A, B, C, and D are on a calendar year, and partnership AB and partnership CD also are on a calendar year. After the merger, the partners have capital and profits interests as follows: A, 30 percent; B, 30 percent; C, 20 percent; and D, 20 percent. Since A and B together own an interest of more than 50 percent in the capital and profits of partnership ABCD, partnership ABCD is considered a continuation of partnership AB and continues to file returns on a calendar year basis. Since C and D own an interest of less than 50 percent in the capital and profits of partnership ABCD, the taxable year of partnership CD closes as of September 30, the date of the merger, and partnership CD is terminated as of that date. Partnership ABCD is required to file a return for the taxable year January 1 to December 31, indicating that, until September 30, it was partnership AB. Partnership CD is required to file a return for its final taxable year, January 1 through September 30.[6]

The determination of which of the partnerships continues for tax purposes is made without regard to which partnership is treated as continuing for state law purposes.

Example 2. (i) Partnership X, in whose capital and profits A owns a 40-percent interest and B owns a 60-percent interest, and partnership Y, in whose capital and profits B owns a 60-percent interest and C owns a 40-percent interest, merge on September 30. The fair market value of the partnership X assets (net of liabilities) is $100X, and the fair market value of the partnership Y assets (net of liabilities) is $200X. The merger is accomplished under state law by partnership Y contributing its assets and liabilities to partnership X in exchange for interests in partnership X, with partnership Y then liquidating, distributing interests in partnership X to B and C.

(ii) B, a partner in both partnerships prior to the merger, owns a greater than 50-percent interest in the resulting partnership following the merger. Accordingly, because the fair market value of partnership Y's assets (net of liabilities) was greater than that of partnership X's, under Treas. Reg. § 1.708-1(c)(1), partnership X will be considered to terminate in the merger. As a result, even though, for state law purposes, the transaction was undertaken with partnership Y contributing its assets and liabilities to partnership X and distributing interests in partnership X to its partners, pursuant to Treas. Reg. § 1.708-1(c)(3)(i), for Federal income tax purposes, the transaction will be treated as if partnership X contributed its assets to partnership Y in exchange for interests in partnership Y and then liquidated, distributing interests in partnership Y to A and B.[7]

---

[6] Treas. Reg. § 1.708-1(c)(5), example 1.

[7] Treas. Reg. § 1.708-1(c)(5), example 2.

If this example applied only the rule of I.R.C. § 708(b)(2)(A), which provides that the resulting partnership is considered the continuation of any merging or consolidating partnership whose members own an interest of more than 50% in the capital and profits of the resulting partnership, the resulting partnership would be viewed as a continuation of both partnerships X and Y, because B, a member of each of X and Y, owns more than 50% of the capital and profits of the resulting partnership. However, under the tie-breaker rule, the resulting partnership is treated as a continuation of partnership Y for tax purposes, because partnership Y contributed the greatest portion of the fair market value of the assets of the resulting partnership.[8] The result of applying the tie-breaker rule in this situation is that a different partnership continues for tax purposes than continues for state law purposes.

B.   Form of a Merger

Generally, there are two ways in which the form of a partnership merger may be characterized for tax purposes, as the Assets-Over Form or as the Assets-Up Form. In the Assets-Over Form, any merged or consolidated partnership that is treated as terminated is first treated as contributing its assets and liabilities to the resulting partnership in exchange for interests in the resulting partnership.[9] Immediately after the contribution, the terminated partnership is treated as distributing interests in the resulting partnership to its partners in liquidation of the terminating partnership. In the Assets-Up Form, the terminating partnership distributes its assets and liabilities to its partners who then contribute the assets and liabilities to the resulting partnership.[10]

If two or more partnerships merge or consolidate into one partnership under the applicable local jurisdictional law without undertaking a form for the merger or consolidation, or undertake a form for the merger or consolidation that is not the Assets-Up Form (described below), then the Assets-Over Form is deemed to apply. This means, for example, that a merger of two partnerships under a state law pursuant to which the merger is accomplished merely by filing articles or a certificate of merger is deemed to be undertaken in the Assets-Over Form.

> *Example 3.* The facts are the same as in Example 2, except that partnership X is engaged in a trade or business and has, as one of its assets, goodwill. In addition, the merger is accomplished under state law by having partnership X convey an undivided 40-percent interest in each of its assets to A and an undivided 60-percent interest in each of its assets to B, with A and B then contributing their interests in such assets to partnership Y. Partnership Y also assumes all of the liabilities of partnership X.[11]

In this example, because partnership X followed the Assets-Up Form for state law purposes, the choice of the form of the partnership merger will be respected so

---

[8] Treas. Reg. § 1.708-1(c)(2).

[9] Treas. Reg. § 1.708-1(c)(3)(i).

[10] Treas. Reg. § 1.708-1(c)(3)(ii).

[11] Treas. Reg. § 1.708-1(c)(5), example 3.

that partnership X will be treated as following the Assets-Up Form for federal income tax purposes. However, if partnership X had chosen a form other than the Assets-Up Form or Assets-Over Form, the choice of the form would not be respected.

> *Example 4.* Partnership X and partnership Y merge when the partners of partnership X transfer their partnership X interests to partnership Y in exchange for partnership Y interests. Immediately thereafter, partnership X liquidates into partnership Y. The resulting partnership is considered a continuation of partnership Y, and partnership X is considered terminated.[12]

The partnerships in this example attempted to use what is sometimes called an "interests over" form[13] — the partners contribute their partnership interest to the partnership that continues for state law purposes. However, the partnerships are treated as undertaking the Assets-Over Form for tax purposes because the "interests over" form is not one of the permitted forms for partnership mergers under the Regulations. Accordingly, for federal income tax purposes, partnership X is deemed to contribute its assets and liabilities to partnership Y in exchange for interests in partnership Y. Immediately thereafter, partnership X is deemed to have distributed the interests in partnership Y to its partners in liquidation of their interests in partnership X.

While a partnership merger may be accomplished by using any number of transactional structures, the result is a single transaction that combines two partnerships. In the two alternatives permitted by the Regulations, each partner must participate (or will be deemed to participate) in the partnership merger in the same manner (with the exception of those partners who are subject to the buy-out rule). Therefore, if the partners wish for a partnership merger to be characterized under the Assets-Up Form, the terminated partnership must undertake the steps of the Assets-Up Form for all of its assets when it distributes the assets to its partners. Otherwise, the transaction will be characterized under the Assets-Over Form. However, where more than two partnerships are combined, each combination will be viewed as a separate merger so that the characterization of a merger of one partnership into the resulting partnership under the Assets-Over Form will not prevent a simultaneous merger of another partnership into the same resulting partnership from being characterized under the Assets-Up Form.

Most partnership mergers are characterized under the Assets-Over Form, because of the greater simplicity in undertaking the form. However, sometimes the Assets-Up Form is viewed as advantageous because of the way in which the basis of the property is calculated in a liquidating distribution. As you learned in Chapter 7, I.R.C. § 732(b) requires that the basis of property (other than money) distributed by a partnership in liquidation of the partner's interest will be equal to the partner's

---

[12] Treas. Reg. § 1.708-1(c)(5), example 4.

[13] The "interests over" form is one of the three permitted structures for converting a partnership to a corporation. *See* Rev. Rul. 84-111, 1984-2 C.B. 88. *See* Eric. B. Sloan, Richard M. Lipton, Deborah Harrington & Marc Frediani, *New Prop. Regs. Provide Expanded Guidance on Partnership Mergers and Divisions — Part 1*, 93 J. Tax'n 198 (2000).

basis in the partnership interest reduced by the amount of any money distributed in the same transaction. This means that if a partner's basis in her partnership interest were greater than her proportionate share of the partnership's bases in its assets, the partner could obtain a step-up in the bases of the assets distributed to her and re-contributed if the partnership merged using an Assets-Up Form.

Consider the ABC partnership, which holds three properties of equal value: Whiteacre, Blackacre, and Redacre. C's total proportionate share of the inside bases of the three properties is $300, but her basis in her partnership interest is $500. If ABC were to merge with DEF in a transaction in which ABC was the terminated partnership and the Assets-Over Form were used, the bases of the three properties would carry over without change. However, if the Assets-Up Form were used, C's proportionate share of the bases of the three properties would be increased to $500.

If a partnership merger is part of a larger series of transactions, the Regulations give the IRS authority to disregard the form if the substance of the larger series of transactions is inconsistent with following the form.[14]

C.   Built-In Gain Resulting from the Merger

If a merger or consolidation is treated as using the Assets-Over Form, the normal rules under I.R.C. § 721, relating to the contribution of assets to a partnership in exchange for a partnership interest, would apply to the deemed contribution by any terminating partnerships. In the Assets-Up Form, I.R.C. § 721 would apply to the contribution by the partners of any assets of the terminating partnership to the continuing partnership. I.R.C. §§ 731 and 736 would similarly apply to the deemed or actual distribution of the partnership interests or assets of the terminating partnership to its partners (depending upon whether the transaction is characterized under the Assets-Over Form or Assets-Up Form).

In general, I.R.C. § 704(c)(1)(B) provides that if any property contributed to a partnership is distributed to a partner, other than the contributing partner, within seven years of the contribution, the contributing partner will recognize gain or loss in an amount equal to the remaining gain allocable to the contributing partner from the built-in gain in the property at the time of contribution. Similarly, I.R.C. § 737 provides that a partner who contributed property with built-in gain and who receives a distribution (other than the property originally contributed) from a partnership within seven years of the contribution may recognize gain on the distribution. However, Treas. Reg. § 1.704-4(c)(4) provides that I.R.C. § 704(c)(1)(B) does not apply to a transfer by a partnership of all of its assets and liabilities to a second partnership in an exchange described in I.R.C. § 721, followed by a distribution of the interest in the transferee partnership in a liquidation of the contributing partnership. Instead, a subsequent distribution of I.R.C. § 704(c) property by the continuing partnership is subject to I.R.C. § 704(c)(1)(B) to the same extent that a distribution by the transferor partnership would have been subject to I.R.C. § 704(c)(1)(B).[15] Similarly, Treas. Reg. § 1.737-2(b)(1) provides

---

[14]   Treas. Reg. § 1.708-1(c)(6)(i).

[15]   Treas. Reg. § 1.704-4(c)(4).

that I.R.C. § 737 does not apply under the same conditions as described in Treas. Reg. § 1.704-4(c)(4).

Neither section provides relief from the application of the seven-year holding period if the Assets-Up Form is used.

In spite of the apparent exception from the seven-year holding period provided in Treas. Reg. § 1.704-4(c)(4) and Treas. Reg. § 1.737-2(b)(1) for the Assets-Over Form, the Treasury took the position in Rev. Rul. 2004-43[16] that both I.R.C. § 704(c)(1)(B) and I.R.C. § 737 would still apply to the built-in gain or loss that existed in the assets of a continuing partnership that were deemed to be contributed by the terminating partnership to the continuing partnership. Under this interpretation, although gain recognition under I.R.C. § 704(c)(1)(B) and I.R.C. § 737 are not triggered by the deemed contribution and distribution resulting from the merger or consolidation, the merger or consolidation itself begins a new seven-year holding period during which the built-in gain in existence at the time of the merger or consolidation could be recognized by the partners of a partnership that is treated as terminating in a merger or consolidation.

Rev. Rul. 2004-43[17] illustrated its conclusions with the following example:

> *Example 5.* On January 1, 2004, A contributed Asset 1, with a basis of $200x and a fair market value of $300x to partnership AB in exchange for a 50 percent interest. On the same date, B contributed $300x of cash to AB in exchange for a 50 percent interest. Also on January 1, 2004, C contributed Asset 2, with a basis of $100x and a fair market value of $200x to partnership CD in exchange for a 50 percent interest. D contributed $200x of cash to CD in exchange for a 50 percent interest.

> On January 1, 2006, AB and CD undertake an assets-over partnership merger in which AB is the continuing partnership and CD is the terminating partnership. At the time of the merger, AB's only assets are Asset 1, with a fair market value of $900x, and $300x in cash, and CD's only assets are Asset 2, with a fair market value of $600x and $200x in cash. After the merger, the partners have capital and profits interests in AB as follows: A, 30 percent; B, 30 percent; C, 20 percent; and D, 20 percent.

> On January 1, 2012, which is eight years after the initial contributions and six years after the merger, AB has the same assets that it had immediately after the merger. Each asset has the same value that it had at the time of the merger. On this date, AB distributes Asset 2 to A in liquidation of A's interest in AB.

In this example, on the date of the partnership merger, CD contributes cash and Asset 2 to AB in exchange for an interest in AB. Immediately thereafter, CD distributes, in liquidation, interests in AB to C and D. Under Treas. Reg.

---

[16] 2004-1 C.B. 842, *revoked by* Rev. Rul. 2005-10, 2005-1 C.B. 492. Although Rev. Rul. 2005-10 revoked Rev. Rul. 2004-43, the Treasury has proposed Regulations implementing the principles of Rev. Rul. 2004-43. *See* Prop. Treas. Reg. §§ 1.704-4(c)(4), 1.737-2(b).

[17] 2004-1 C.B. 842, *revoked by* Rev. Rul. 2005-10, 2005-1 C.B. 492. We include Rev. Rul. 2004-43 in the text, as its principles were followed by the Proposed Regulations discussed below.

§ 1.704-4(c)(4) and Treas. Reg. § 1.737 2(b)(1), the transaction considered in the example would appear to meet the exception from the application of I.R.C. § 704(c)(1)(B) and I.R.C. § 737. However, Rev. Rul. 2004-43 applies an I.R.C. § 704(c)(1)(B) analysis as if the exceptions in Treas. Reg. § 1.704-4(c)(4) and Treas. Reg. § 1.737-2(b)(1) did not apply.

As Rev. Rul. 2004-43 continues its analysis, Asset 2 has a basis of $100x and a fair market value of $600x upon contribution. Of the $500x of built-in gain in Asset 2, $100x is preexisting I.R.C. § 704(c) gain attributable to C's contribution of Asset 2 to CD, and $400x is additional I.R.C. § 704(c) gain created as a result of the merger. Rev. Rul. 2004-43 concludes, applying Treas. Reg. § 1.704-3(a)(7), that as the transferees of CD's partnership interest in AB, C and D each succeed to one-half of CD's $400x of I.R.C. § 704(c) gain in Asset 2 (each $200x). Thus, C's share of I.R.C. § 704(c) gain is $300x, and D's share of I.R.C. § 704(c) gain is $200x.

The distribution of Asset 2 to A occurs more than seven years after the contribution of Asset 2 to CD. Therefore, I.R.C. § 704(c)(1)(B) does not apply to the $100x of preexisting 704(c) gain attributable to that contribution. However, the distribution of Asset 2 to A occurs within seven years of the contribution of Asset 2 by CD to AB. According to Rev. Rul. 2004-43, the contribution of Asset 2 by CD to AB creates I.R.C. § 704(c) gain of $400x subject to the seven-year holding period. As the transferees of CD's partnership interest in AB, C and D each succeed to one-half of the $400x of 704(c) gain created by the merger. Under the analysis of Rev. Rul. 2004-43, I.R.C. § 704(c)(1)(B) applies to that I.R.C. § 704(c) gain because of the distribution of Asset 2 to A within seven years of the merger, causing C and D each to recognize $200x of gain.

It should be particularly noted that in this example, D, who originally contributed only cash, and who received nothing in the distribution from AB, has been required to recognize $200x of gain on the distribution of Asset 2 to A. This gain is solely attributable to the start of another I.R.C. § 704(c)(1)(B) seven-year period at the time of the merger of the two partnerships.

Proposed Regulations that implement the principles articulated in Rev. Rul. 2004-43 have now been issued. Prop. Treas. Reg. §§ 1.704-4(c)(4) and 1.737-2(b) provide that in an assets-over merger, I.R.C. §§ 704(c)(1)(B) and 737 do not apply to the transfer by a partnership (the transferor partnership) of all of its assets and liabilities to another partnership (the transferee partnership), followed by a distribution of the interests in the transferee partnership in liquidation of the transferor partnership as part of the same plan or arrangement. The Proposed Regulations, however, provide that I.R.C. § 704(c)(1)(B) applies to a subsequent distribution by the transferee partnership of I.R.C. § 704(c) property contributed in the assets-over merger by the transferor partnership to the transferee partnership. The Proposed Regulations also provide that I.R.C. § 737 applies when a partner of the transferor partnership receives a subsequent distribution of property (other than money) from the transferee partnership.

D. Buy-Out Rule

The Regulations contain a special buy-out rule that allows a resulting partnership in a merger to fund the purchase of one or more partners' interests in a terminating partnership without triggering the disguised sale rules, which otherwise could cause all of the partners in the terminating partnership to recognize gain or loss as a result of the purchase. Specifically, the Regulations provide that if the merger agreement (or similar document) specifies that the resulting partnership is purchasing the exiting partner's interest in the terminating partnership and also specifies the amount paid for the interest, the transaction will be treated as a sale of the exiting partner's interest to the resulting partnership.[18] The partner who is being bought out must also consent to the treatment.

Example 5 in Treas. Reg. § 1.708-1(c)(4) indicates that the partner who is being bought out is treated as if his interest was purchased immediately prior to the merger. Thus, the resulting partnership, and the partners (determined prior to the merger) of the partnership that is treated as continuing, would succeed to the withdrawing partner's capital account and built-in gain.[19] Although not discussed in the Regulations, it follows from treating the buyout as a sale to the resulting partnership occurring immediately prior to the merger that, if exiting partners sell 50% or more of the total interest in the terminating partnership's capital and profits as part of a merger, then a partnership termination under I.R.C. § 708(b)(1)(B) will occur immediately before the merger.

§ 9.03 PARTNERSHIP DIVISIONS

A. General Rules

I.R.C. § 708(b)(2)(B) provides that, in the case of a division of a partnership into two or more partnerships, all the resulting partnerships the members of which had an interest of more than 50% in the capital and profits of the preexisting partnership are considered a continuation of the preexisting partnership. Treas. Reg. § 1.708-1(b)(2)(ii) provides that any other resulting partnership is not considered a continuation of the preexisting partnership but is considered a new partnership. If the members of none of the resulting partnerships owned an interest of more than 50% in the capital and profits of the preexisting partnership, the preexisting partnership is terminated.[20] If members of a preexisting partnership do not become members of a resulting partnership that is considered a continuation of the preexisting partnership, such members' interests are considered liquidated as of the date of the division.[21]

---

[18] Treas. Reg. § 1.708-1(c)(4).

[19] Treas. Reg. § 1.708-1(c)(5), example 5(iii).

[20] Treas. Reg. § 1.708-1(d)(1).

[21] *Id.*

As with partnership mergers, the divided partnership in a partnership division is treated as transferring all or a portion of its assets and liabilities to one or more resulting partnerships either in the Assets-Over Form or the Assets-Up Form.[22] A "divided partnership," for the purposes of this discussion, means the continuing partnership that is treated as transferring assets and liabilities to the recipient partnership or partnerships.[23] If a partnership divides into two or more partnerships and only one of the resulting partnerships is a continuation of the prior partnership, then the partnership that is a continuation of the prior partnership is the divided partnership. If more than one resulting partnership is a continuation of the prior partnership, the resulting partnership that, in form, transferred the assets and liabilities of the prior partnership will be treated as the divided partnership (if it is also treated as a continuation of the prior partnership). If a preexisting partnership divides and more than one resulting partnership is a continuing partnership (but the rule in the preceding sentence does not apply), then the continuing resulting partnership with assets having the greatest fair market value (net of liabilities) will be treated as the divided partnership.[24]

The divided partnership that is regarded as continuing is required to file a return for the taxable year of the partnership that has been divided.[25] The divided partnership will also retain the employer identification number of the preexisting partnership. All other resulting partnerships that are regarded as continuing and all new partnerships (i.e., resulting partnerships that are not considered continuing) will file separate returns for the taxable year beginning on the day after the date of the division with new employer identification numbers for each partnership.[26]

All resulting partnerships that are continuing partnerships are subject to preexisting elections that were made by the preexisting partnership.[27] However, a post-division election that is made by a resulting partnership will not bind any of the other resulting partnerships.

> *Example 6.* Partnership ABCD owns three parcels of property: property X, with a value of $500; property Y, with a value of $300; and property Z, with a value of $200. A and B each own a 40-percent interest in the capital and profits of partnership ABCD, and C and D each own a 10 percent interest in the capital and profits of partnership ABCD. On November 1, partnership ABCD divides into three partnerships (AB1, AB2, and CD) by contributing property X to a newly formed partnership (AB1) and distributing all interests in such partnership to A and B as equal partners, and by contributing property Z to a newly formed partnership (CD) and distributing all interests in such partnership to C and D as equal partners in exchange for all of their interests in partnership ABCD. While partnership

---

[22] Treas. Reg. § 1.708-1(d)(3).

[23] Treas. Reg. § 1.708-1(d)(4)(i).

[24] *Id.*

[25] Treas. Reg. § 1.708-1(d)(2)(i).

[26] *Id.*

[27] Treas. Reg. § 1.708-1(d)(2)(ii).

ABCD does not transfer property Y, C and D cease to be partners in the partnership. Accordingly, after the division, the partnership holding property Y is referred to as partnership AB2.[28]

In this example, partnerships AB1 and AB2 are both continuations of partnership ABCD (because A and B own more than 50% of the capital and profits of the preexisting partnership), while partnership CD is considered a new partnership formed at the beginning of the day on November 2. For each of the divisions, partnership ABCD will be treated as following the Assets-Over Form, with partnership ABCD contributing property X to partnership AB1 and property Z to partnership CD, and distributing the interests in such partnerships to the designated partners. ABCD will also be treated as contributing property Y to partnership AB2 for tax purposes even though no transfer occurs for state law purposes. Because property X has a greater fair market value than property Y, partnership AB1 will be viewed as the divided partnership.

The Regulations do not define what constitutes a partnership division. However, the Regulations do clarify that to have a division, at least two members of the preexisting partnership must be members of each resulting partnership that exists after the transaction.[29]

B.   Form of a Division

In partnership divisions, a preexisting partnership generally transfers certain assets and liabilities to a resulting partnership in exchange for interests in the resulting partnership, and immediately thereafter, the preexisting partnership distributes the resulting partnership interests to partners who are designated to receive interests in the resulting partnership (the *"Assets-Over Form"*).[30] Alternatively, the preexisting partnership may distribute certain assets and liabilities to some or all of its partners who then contribute the assets and liabilities to a resulting partnership in exchange for interests in the resulting partnership (the *"Assets-Up Form"*).[31] As with partnership mergers, the default rule for partnership divisions is the Assets-Over Form, so that if a transaction does not follow the formal steps of the Assets-Up Form, the transaction will be characterized under the Assets-Over Form regardless of whether that form is followed.[32] Also, as with mergers, the Assets-Up Form will be respected for divisions where the assets are conveyed to the partners under the laws of the applicable jurisdiction and then reconveyed to the resulting partnership.[33]

The rules for divisions also parallel the rules for mergers in that a division resulting in a single new partnership cannot be treated both in the Assets-Over Form and the Assets-Up Form. If a partnership attempted to combine the two

---

[28]   Treas. Reg. § 1.708-1(d)(5), example 4.

[29]   Treas. Reg. § 1.708-1(d)(4)(iv).

[30]   Treas. Reg. § 1.708-1(d)(i)(A).

[31]   Treas. Reg. § 1.708-1(d)(ii)(A).

[32]   Treas. Reg. § 1.708-1(d)(3)(i).

[33]   Treas. Reg. § 1.708-1(d)(ii)(A).

forms so that the choice of form was not clear, the Assets-Over Form would be applied. However, where a single partnership is divided in a transaction that involves a transfer of assets (either actual or deemed) to multiple partnerships, the transfer to each resulting partnership should be viewed separately. If a partnership division is part of a larger series of transactions, the Regulations give the IRS authority to disregard the form if the substance of the larger series of transactions is inconsistent with following the form.[34]

C.   Built-In Gain in Divisions

The preamble to the Regulations under I.R.C. § 708 dealing with partnership divisions indicates that the IRS and Treasury agree that, in general, a partnership division should not create new I.R.C. § 704(c) property or I.R.C. § 737 net precontribution gain.[35] However, the preamble also indicates that the Treasury was not certain that this result is necessarily appropriate where a division is non-pro rata as to the partners, where some property is extracted from or added to the partnerships in connection with the division, or where new partners are added to the ownership group in connection with the division.

§ 9.04   THE EFFECT ON THE PARTNERS AND THE PARTNERSHIP

Whether a merger or division of a partnership is structured as an Assets-Up Transaction or an Assets-Over Transaction, two steps occur: there is a transfer of property to a partnership and a distribution of property from the partnership to the partners. Although the sequence and nature of the property distributed varies between the two structures, the partners receive their property as a distribution from the partnership and will have their bases determined in the property received under I.R.C. § 732, which generally provides that the bases to the partners in the property received will be the same as the bases were to the partnership immediately before the distribution. If the distribution was made other than in liquidation of the partner's partnership interest, the partner would reduce her basis in the partnership interest by the basis of the property received.[36]

In each case, a contribution is made to a resulting partnership, and the basis of the partnership interest received in exchange for the contribution will generally be determined under I.R.C. § 722, which generally provides that the basis in the partnership interest will equal the basis of the property contributed to the resulting partnership in the transaction. Similarly, the partnership would generally have a basis in the property contributed equal to the basis in the contributed property in the hands of the party that contributed that property.[37] The holding period of the resulting partnerships will include the holding periods of the contributors of the

---

[34] Treas. Reg. § 1.708-1(d)(6).

[35] T.D. 8925, 66 Fed. Reg. 715 (Jan. 4, 2001).

[36] I.R.C. § 733.

[37] I.R.C. § 723.

property, assuming no gain is recognized on the transaction.[38]

The result of these rules in the context of a merger is that the partners of the terminating partnerships will generally have bases in their partnership interests in the continuing partnership equal to their bases in their partnership interests in the terminating partnership (assuming no gain is recognized in the transaction).

However, the form, and thus the sequence, of the transaction chosen may create a difference in the bases of the assets held by the resulting partnerships when there is a difference between the bases of the assets held by a terminating partnership and the aggregate bases of the partners' partnership interests in the terminating partnership. I.R.C. § 732(b) provides that the basis of property other than money distributed to a partner in liquidation of the partner's interest will be equal to the adjusted basis of such partner's interest in the partnership reduced by any money distributed in the same transaction. This means that if partnership ABC merges into partnership DEF using an Assets-Up Form, because the property of ABC is first distributed to partners A, B, and C in liquidation of their partnership interests prior to contribution to DEF, DEF will have a basis in the former property of ABC equal to the aggregate bases of A, B, and C in their partnership interests (rather than the basis that such property had in the hands of ABC). In contrast, if the Assets-Over Form is used, the continuing partnership has the same basis in the assets as the terminating partnership had in the assets. The same type of difference between inside and outside bases can result in similar differences between the Assets-Over Form and Assets-Up Form in partnership divisions.

§ 9.05 COMPARISON WITH S CORPORATIONS

Except for the issue of continued qualification of S corporation status, the rules for mergers and divisions of S corporations are generally the same as those for C corporations. A detailed discussion of such rules is beyond the scope of this text, but the following discussion summarizes the basic rules.

A. Mergers and Acquisitions

The rules for mergers and acquisitions of corporations are a combination of common law rules, statutory provisions, and regulatory provisions. Three major common law doctrines have developed that are reflected in part in the regulations. The continuity of proprietary interest doctrine requires that the target's shareholders retain a continuing proprietary interest in the acquiring corporation.[39] The continuity of business enterprise doctrine requires that the acquiring corporation must either continue the target's historic business or continue to use a significant portion of the target's historic business assets in a business.[40] The business purpose doctrine requires a reorganization to be

---

[38] I.R.C. § 1223(2); Treas. Reg. § 1.723-1.

[39] Rev. Proc. 77-37, 1977-2 C.B. 568. Current Regulations approve transactions in which at least 40% of the consideration received by the shareholders of the acquired company to be in stock of the acquiring company (or, where permitted, its parent). Treas. Reg. § 1.368-1(e)(v), example 1.

[40] Treas. Reg. § 1.368-1(d)(2)(i).

motivated by a bona fide corporate business purpose apart from tax avoidance.[41]

The most basic type of merger structure is simply a merger or consolidation of two corporations under local law, called an "A reorganization."[42] One of the most important qualification requirements is that the shareholders of the target corporation ("T") maintain continuity of proprietary interest by owning stock in the acquiring corporation ("P"). For advance ruling purposes, the Service requires that at least 50% of the consideration paid by P to the T shareholders must consist of P stock, which need not be common or voting stock.[43] Redemptions and related party acquisitions of stock occurring after a merger may be considered in applying the continuity of interest test.

Alternatively, a reorganization may be structured as a stock for stock acquisition, called a "B reorganization." A B reorganization is P's acquisition of T's stock *solely* in exchange for P voting stock where P has control (i.e., 80%) of T immediately after the acquisition.[44] No consideration other than stock may be used in a B reorganization.

A third alternative for corporations is a stock for assets acquisition, called a "C reorganization." A C reorganization is P's acquisition of substantially all of T's assets solely in exchange for P voting stock followed by the liquidation of T.[45] In applying the solely for voting stock requirement, P's assumption of T's liabilities is disregarded. Under a boot relaxation rule, P's use of consideration other than voting stock is permitted provided that P acquires at least 80% of the value of all of T's assets solely for voting stock. For purposes of this rule, liabilities assumed by P are treated as cash consideration. Under the case law, if P previously acquired more than 20% of T's stock and then acquires all of T's assets solely in exchange for P voting stock, the asset acquisition may not qualify as a C reorganization.

If a transaction qualifies as a reorganization, the corporate participants to the reorganization and the target shareholders generally do not recognize gain or loss on an exchange of their T stock solely for P stock, or an exchange of T securities solely for P securities.[46]

B. Corporate Divisions

In general, a distribution of appreciated property by a corporation to its shareholders is taxable to the corporation as if it sold the property distributed for cash.[47] Such distributions may also be taxable to the shareholders.[48]

---

[41] Gregory v. Helvering, 293 U.S. 465 (1935).

[42] I.R.C. § 368(a)(1)(A).

[43] The qualified consideration does not include certain types of nonqualified preferred stock. I.R.C. §§ 354(a)(2)(C), 351(g)(2).

[44] I.R.C. § 368(a)(1)(B).

[45] I.R.C. § 368(a)(1)(C).

[46] I.R.C. §§ 354, 361, 1032.

[47] I.R.C. § 311(b).

[48] I.R.C. § 301.

However, if a corporation distributes solely stock or securities of a controlled corporation to shareholders with respect to the distributing corporation's stock or to security holders in exchange for the distributing corporation's stock or securities, the distribution may qualify for special tax-free treatment.[49] Control in this situation means 80% of the total combined voting power of all classes of stock entitled to vote and at least 80% of the total number of shares of all other classes. The distribution must not be a device for distributing the earnings and profits of the distributing corporation. The distributing corporation and the controlled corporation must each be engaged immediately after the spin-off in the active conduct of a trade or business. All of the stock of the controlled subsidiary must be distributed or, at a minimum, enough of the stock to constitute control. Other additional technical rules may apply.

§ 9.06   READING, QUESTIONS AND PROBLEMS

A.   Reading

CODE:

I.R.C. § 708.

TREASURY REGULATIONS:

Treas. Reg. § 1.708-1(c), (d).

Prop. Treas. Reg. §§ 1.704-4(c)(4), 1.737-2(b).

B.   Questions and Problems

1. Partnership AB, in whose capital and profits A and B each own a 50% interest, and partnership CD, in whose capital and profits C and D each own a 50% interest, merge on September 30, and form partnership ABCD. Partners A, B, C, and D are on a calendar year, and partnership AB and partnership CD also are on a calendar year. After the merger, the partners have capital and profits interests as follows: A, 30%; B, 30%; C, 20%; and D, 20%.

a. Which partnership is treated as continuing?

b. How is the other partnership treated?

c. For what taxable year is the continuing partnership required to file its first return?

d. For what taxable year is the other partnership required to file its return?

2. A, B, and C are partners in partnership X. D, E, and F are partners in Partnership Y. Partnership X and partnership Y merge, and the resulting partnership is considered a continuation of partnership Y. Partnership X is considered terminated. Under state law, partnerships X and Y undertake the Assets-Over

---

[49] I.R.C. § 355.

Form to accomplish the partnership merger. C does not want to become a partner in partnership Y, and partnership X does not have the resources to buy C's interest before the merger. C, partnership X, and partnership Y enter into an agreement specifying that partnership Y will purchase C's interest in partnership X for $150 before the merger, and as part of the agreement, C consents to treat the transaction in a manner that is consistent with the agreement. As part of the merger, partnership X receives from partnership Y $150 that will be distributed to C immediately before the merger, and interests in partnership Y in exchange for partnership X's assets and liabilities.

a. How will C be treated in the transaction?

b. Who inherits C's tax characteristics in regard to the partnership interest?

c. How is the terminating partnership treated in the transaction?

3. A, B, and C are equal partners in partnership ABC. ABC holds no I.R.C. § 704(c) property. D and E are equal partners in partnership DE. B and C want to exchange their interests in ABC for all of the interests in DE. However, rather than exchanging partnership interests, DE merges with ABC by undertaking the Assets-Up Form, with D and E receiving title to the DE assets and then contributing the assets to ABC in exchange for interests in ABC. As part of a prearranged transaction, the assets acquired from DE are contributed to a new partnership, and the interests in the new partnership are distributed to B and C in complete liquidation of their interests in ABC.

How will the transaction be characterized?

4. Partnership ABCD is in the real estate and insurance businesses. A owns a 40% interest, and B, C, and D each owns a 20% interest, in the capital and profits of the partnership. The partnership and the partners report their income on a calendar year. On November 1, they separate the real estate and insurance businesses and form two partnerships. Partnership AB takes over the real estate business, and partnership CD takes over the insurance business.

a. Which partnership is the continuing partnership?

b. For what taxable year does the continuing partnership file its return?

c. For what taxable year will the other partnership file its first return?

5. Partnership ABCD owns properties W, X, Y, and Z, and divides into partnership AB and partnership CD. Partnership AB is considered a continuation of partnership ABCD and partnership CD is considered a new partnership. Partnership ABCD distributes property Y to C and titles property Y in C's name. Partnership ABCD distributes property Z to D and titles property Z in D's name. C and D then contribute properties Y and Z, respectively, to partnership CD in exchange for interests in partnership CD. Properties W and X remain in partnership AB.

What form will this division be treated as using?

6. The facts are the same as in Problem 5, except partnership ABCD distributes property Y to C and titles property Y in C's name. C then contributes property Y to

partnership CD. Simultaneously, partnership ABCD contributes property Z to partnership CD in exchange for an interest in partnership CD. Immediately thereafter, partnership ABCD distributes the interest in partnership CD to D in liquidation of D's interest in partnership ABCD.

What form will this division be treated as using?

7. Partnership ABCD owns three parcels of property: property X, with a value of $500; property Y, with a value of $300; and property Z, with a value of $200. A and B each own a 40% interest in the capital and profits of partnership ABCD, and C and D each own a 10% interest in the capital and profits of partnership ABCD. On November 1, partnership ABCD divides into three partnerships (AB1, AB2, and CD) by contributing property X to a newly formed partnership (AB1) and distributing all interests in such partnership to A and B as equal partners, and by contributing property Z to a newly formed partnership (CD) and distributing all interests in such partnership to C and D as equal partners in exchange for all of their interests in partnership ABCD. While partnership ABCD does not transfer property Y, C and D cease to be partners in the partnership. Accordingly, after the division, the partnership holding property Y is referred to as partnership AB2.

a. What partnership(s) is/are continuing partnerships?

b. What partnership is the divided partnership?

c. What form will each division be treated as using?

8. Partnership ABCDE owns Blackacre, Whiteacre, and Redacre, and divides into partnership AB, partnership CD, and partnership DE. Partnership ABCDE is considered terminated (and, thus, none of the resulting partnerships are a continuation of the preexisting partnership) because none of the members of the new partnerships (partnership AB, partnership CD, and partnership DE) owned an interest of more than 50% in the capital and profits of partnership ABCDE. Partnership ABCDE distributes Blackacre to A and B and titles Blackacre in the names of A and B. A and B then contribute Blackacre to partnership AB in exchange for interests in partnership AB. Partnership ABCDE distributes Whiteacre to C and D and titles Whiteacre in the names of C and D. C and D then contribute Whiteacre to partnership CD in exchange for interests in partnership CD. Partnership ABCDE does not liquidate under state law so that, in form, the assets in new partnership DE are not considered to have been transferred under state law.

What form will each division be treated as using?

Chapter 10

PARTNERSHIP OPTIONS

§ 10.01 INTRODUCTION[1]

It has become increasingly common for partnerships to issue options. There is a dearth of authority on the federal tax treatment of options to acquire interests in partnerships. In this context, there are two main categories of options, "compensatory options" and "noncompensatory options." Compensatory options, unsurprisingly, are options to acquire partnership interests where the option is received in exchange for services. Noncompensatory options cover the rest of the waterfront.[2] The simplest version of the latter would be partnership analog to "normal" options found outside the partnership context: The option holder pays an "option premium" to acquire an option to purchase a partnership interest sometime in the future for a fixed price. The IRS has promulgated proposed regulations for both types of options. The proposed regulations for noncompensatory options were promulgated in 2003,[3] those for compensatory options in 2005. We will take a non-detailed look at those proposed regulations and associated issues.

§ 10.02 BACKGROUND FOR NONCOMPENSATORY OPTIONS

Assuming an option is recognized as an option for federal income tax purposes, the basic principles that apply to the taxation of the issuance and exercise of noncompensatory options have been clear for some time. They are contained in I.R.C. § 1234 and various pronouncements of the courts and the IRS:[4]

---

[1] Portions of this chapter are derived from Professor Schwidetzky's article *The Proposed Regulations on Noncompensatory Options: A Light at the End of the Tunnel*, 21 J. TAX'N OF INVESTMENTS 155 (2004). As Professor Schwidetzky noted in the article, he is indebted to the "Options Group," composed of members of the Partnerships, Real Estate, and Employee Benefits Committees of the ABA Section of Taxation. The Options Group, of which three of the authors were members, submitted extensive recommendations to the IRS on the taxation of partnership options both before and after the IRS promulgated Proposed Regulations. Paul Carman headed the group when it commented on the Proposed Regulations. The resulting recommendations are entitled "Comments in Response to REG-1003580-02" (hereinafter "ABA Comments").

[2] *See* Prop. Treas. Reg. § 1.721-2(d).

[3] 68 Fed. Reg. 2930, Proposed Rules, Department of the Treasury Internal Revenue Service (IRS), 26 C.F.R. pt. 1, [REG-103580-02] RIN 1545-BA53, Noncompensatory Partnership Options, Wednesday, January 22, 2003 (hereinafter "Proposed Regulations"). They are privately published at 2003 Tax Notes Today 14-13.

[4] Palmer v. Commissioner, 302 U.S. 63 (1937); Rev. Rul. 58-234, 1958-1 C.B. 279 (as clarified in Rev. Rul. 68-151, 1968-1 C.B. 363); Rev. Rul. 78-182, 1978-1 C.B. 265; *see* ABA Comments at IIID1.

i. Option contracts are generally treated as open transactions[5] until exercise or expiration.

ii. There is no federal income tax consequence on account of either the receipt or the payment of the option premium by either the issuer or the option holder until the option is exercised or terminated.[6]

iii. Under I.R.C. § 1234(a), if the option goes unexercised, the option holder is treated as having a loss from the sale or exchange of property which has the same character as the property to which the option relates. Thus, if the option relates to a capital asset, the loss will be a long-term or short-term capital loss depending on how long the option holder has held the option. Regardless of how long the option is outstanding, the option issuer's gain on the lapse is short-term capital gain under I.R.C. § 1234(b).

iv. Upon exercise, both the issuer and the option holder use the total of the option premium and the exercise price to determine the amount realized on the sale and the cost basis of the property acquired, respectively.

v. The exercise of an option at a time when the value of the relevant property had risen above the exercise price of the option does not cause the option holder to have income. The Proposed Regulations depart from this principle in a limited way, as we will discuss.

If the option holder disposes of the option before exercise, it is treated like any other disposition of property. Gain or loss is recognized under I.R.C. § 1001 unless an exclusionary rule applies. The character of the gain or loss is a function of the character of the property to which the option relates in the hands of the option holder.[7]

When an entity issues interests in itself, it can raise tax issues in addition to those discussed above. Normally, when a taxpayer satisfies an obligation with appreciated property, the taxpayer recognizes gain to the extent of the excess of the fair market value of the property over the basis of the property transferred.[8] Until the IRS issued the Proposed Regulations, there was no guidance in the partnership context, but there has been guidance for some time with regard to corporations. I.R.C. § 1032(a) provides that a corporation recognizes no gain or loss on the lapse or acquisition of an option to buy or sell its stock. The actual exercise of the option is not taxable to the corporation either, as I.R.C. § 1032(a) also provides that a corporation recognizes no gain or loss on the receipt of money or other property for its stock. The treatment of the option holder is covered by the regular rules discussed above.

---

[5] "An open transaction" generally means that no tax consequences apply while it is "open." In this context, there are usually no tax consequences until the option is exercised or lapses, thereby closing the open transaction.

[6] This assumes the premium is paid in cash. If property is transferred in exchange for the option, I.R.C. § 1001 would require gain or loss recognition on the property transfer.

[7] I.R.C. § 1234(a)(1).

[8] United States v. Davis, 370 U.S. 65 (1962). Similarly, the exercise of an option is normally a taxable event to the seller of the referenced property. *See* Converse v. Earle, 43 A.F.T.R. 1308 (D. Or. 1951).

Partnerships are very different tax (and nontax) creatures than corporations, and when they issue options they raise different tax issues. Most of the issues that arise relate to the fact that unlike C corporations, partnerships are not taxable entities, and income is taxed to and losses are deducted by the partners. Appreciation in partnership property and undistributed income typically inures in part to the benefit of the option holder. How should the partnership keep track of that benefit? Since the economics of a partner's investment in the partnership are generally measured by the partner's capital account, a corollary question is how should capital accounts be kept when an option is outstanding? If a new partner acquires a partnership interest while an option is outstanding, how should the existence of the option be taken into account? There are times when an option holder should be treated as a partner. If there were no anti-abuse rules, taxpayers could give option holders so many rights that they would have all the economic benefits of being a partner without actually being treated as a partner. High bracket taxpayers would buy options, avoid taxable ordinary income on the partnership earnings, through the option economically benefit from undistributed earnings, and then sell the option at a long-term capital gain and receive preferential tax rates. The Proposed Regulations address these and other issues.

Another piece of the puzzle is I.R.C. § 721. As you now know, it provides that no gain or loss is recognized to a partnership or its partners in the case of a contribution of property to the partnership in exchange for a partnership interest. A major question is when and how I.R.C. § 721 applies in the options context. To the extent it does apply, the transaction becomes nontaxable, the tax equivalent of the promised land. In the typical, nonabusive case, the Proposed Regulations sensibly take the view that an option holder is not a partner. Accordingly, the issuance of the option is not within the purview of I.R.C. § 721 (though the issuance of an option usually is still nontaxable). I.R.C. § 721 usually literally applies to the exercise of the option, however, inasmuch as then a partnership interest is being received for cash or property.

A final issue involves the potential for capital account shifts between the partners. Indeed, there may be no single issue more important than this one. When an option holder exercises an appreciated option, it may be necessary to shift capital from the continuing partners to the option holder/partner to give her the appropriate interest in the partnership. The form of this would be a transfer of a portion of the capital account balances from the continuing partners to the option holder/partner. The fear has been that this "capital shift" could be seen as a taxable transfer of partnership property by the continuing partners to the option holder/partner to the extent of the transfer. If the continuing partners transferred 5% of partnership capital to the option holder/partner, could they have made a taxable disposition of 5% of the partnership assets and have to recognize the associated gain or loss? If so, it would obviously inhibit option (and other) transactions, at least where gain would be recognized. No case ever held that such a capital shift was a taxable transaction to the continuing partners, but academics and practitioners have spilt a lot of ink speculating on this possibility. The Proposed Regulations generally put the fear to rest in the partnership options context. A capital shift is not treated as a taxable transfer of the underlying partnership property, though there can be an income tax effect to the option holder/partner, as we will discuss.[9]

§ 10.03 SCOPE OF PROPOSED REGULATIONS ON NONCOMPENSATORY OPTIONS

The Proposed Regulations on noncompensatory options only cover noncompensatory options issued by partnerships.[10] In addition to "standard" options, the Proposed Regulations also apply to warrants, convertible debt, and convertible preferred equity, though we will focus on traditional options. The final regulations will be prospective from the date they are promulgated.[11] The Proposed Regulations are technically of no formal, legal effect; they do give taxpayers a sense of where the IRS stands and that can be useful in planning.[12]

§ 10.04 ISSUANCE, LAPSE AND STRAIGHTFORWARD EXERCISE OF NONCOMPENSATORY OPTIONS

In line with the existing nonpartnership authority, it is apparent from the Proposed Regulations that the issuance of the option usually is treated as an open transaction for the issuer (while outside the scope of I.R.C. § 721). The option holder is seen as having made a capital expenditure to acquire an option that is neither taxable to the partnership nor deductible to the holder. The Proposed Regulations never explicitly state this, however, though there is language in the Preamble and in an example to this effect.[13]

The Proposed Regulations note that under general rules of taxation, if the holder exchanges property for the option, there has been a taxable disposition of the property. Gain or loss is recognized.

The Proposed Regulations provide limited coverage of the tax treatment of a lapse of an option. The regulations themselves merely state the obvious: That a lapse is outside the scope of I.R.C. § 721.[14] It would have to be outside the scope of I.R.C. § 721 inasmuch as the erstwhile option holder has not contributed property to the partnership in exchange for an interest in the partnership. The Preamble then observes that, consistent with general tax principles, the lapse of a noncompensatory option generally results in the recognition of income by the partnership and the recognition of loss by the former option holder. Under the general principles of I.R.C. § 1234, there should be short-term capital gain to the partner-

---

[9] *See* McDougal v. Commissioner, 62 T.C. 720 (1974), where a transfer was taxable where the court deemed the sequence to be the transfer of property to a service provider followed by the formation of the partnership.

[10] Prop. Treas. Reg. § 1.721-2(d); the Proposed Regulations do not apply to any interest on convertible debt that has been accrued by the partnership (including original issue discount). *Id.*

[11] Prop. Treas. Reg. § 1.721-2(g).

[12] But proposed Regulations are "substantial authority" that can avoid the application of accuracy related penalties under I.R.C. § 6662. Treas. Reg. § 1.6662-4(d)(3)(iii).

[13] Preamble; Prop. Treas. Reg. § 1.721-2(b), (f) example.

[14] Prop. Treas. Reg. § 1.721-2(c).

ship in the amount equal to the option premium and a (typically capital) loss of the same amount to the option holder.

The Proposed Regulations generally apply I.R.C. § 721 to the exercise of the option, making it a nontaxable transaction to the partners and the partnership. The option holder is viewed as contributing money or property in the form of the exercise price and option privilege to the partnership and receiving a partnership interest in exchange. Thus, if in the exercise of the option the option holder transfers property to the partnership, no gain or loss is recognized to the option holder or the partnership. The partnership takes a carryover basis in any contributed property under I.R.C. § 723. The option holder takes a substituted basis in the partnership interest under I.R.C. § 722.

The Proposed Regulations contain some highly important rules for computing capital accounts. An option holder, not being a partner, has no capital account.[15] The option holder becomes a partner upon exercise of the option, the option holder's initial capital account is equal to the option premium and option exercise price paid, including the fair market value of any contributed property. Typically, the value of the partnership interest received will be different from the total amount paid by the option holder. Of course, what commonly induces an option holder to exercise an option is the belief that what she is receiving is worth more than what she is paying. If true, this would mean that the option privilege itself would have value inherent in it. Since the option exercise is a nontaxable event, the gain is not recognized on exercise (neither would be the loss in the less likely event the option holder exercises the option even though the exercise price exceeds the value of the option). In principle, the option privilege is an asset with built-in gain or loss that should be allocated to the option holder under I.R.C. § 704(c). The difficulty is that the option privilege is not in fact contributed to the partnership, but rather disappears on exercise. Accordingly, the value of the option privilege itself does not increase the capital account. To get to the right result, the Proposed Regulations generally substitute gain or loss inherent in the partnership's assets for gain or loss inherent in the option privilege. This is done by first requiring the partnership to revalue its property immediately after the exercise of the option. Allowable revaluations have to date been optional. Under the Proposed Regulations, however, revaluations in this context are mandatory.[16] As we discussed in Chapter 5, a "revaluation" restates the property and the capital accounts of the partners at fair market value. The tax basis in the property is unaffected and there is no tax consequence to the revaluation. Revaluations are only allowed in certain circumstances, including on contributions in exchange for a partnership interest or distributions in exchange for a partnership interest. Under the "regular" rules, once a revaluation is made, I.R.C. § 704(c) principles have to be followed in allocating the tax gain or loss. Any tax gain or loss inherent in the assets at the time of the revaluation must be allocated to the continuing partners based on the shares they would have received had the partnership properties been sold at the time of the revaluation.[17]

---

[15] This assumes the option holder does not also hold a partnership interest. It also assumes the recharacterization rules we discuss below do not apply.

[16] Prop. Treas. Reg. § 1.704-1(b)(2)(iv)(s)(1).

[17] Treas. Reg. § 1.704-1(b)(2)(iv)(f).

Under the Proposed Regulations, any unrealized gain or loss from the revaluation is first allocated to the option holder to the extent necessary to reflect the holder's right to share in partnership capital under the partnership agreement. Thereafter, the gain or loss is allocated to the historic partners to reflect the manner in which they would be allocated among them if there were a taxable disposition of the partnership property.[18] I.R.C. § 704(c) principles are then used to make sure that tax gain or loss tracks the book gain or loss. This is perhaps easiest to understand by way of an example.

EXAMPLE 1

In Year 1, Jacob and Ginger each contribute cash of $10,000 to LLC, a newly formed LLC (that is, a tax partnership) in exchange for 100 Units in LLC. Under the LLC agreement, each Unit is entitled to participate equally in the profits and losses of LLC. LLC uses the cash contributions to purchase a non-depreciable property, Property A, for $20,000. Also in Year 1, at a time when Property A is still valued at $20,000, LLC issues an option to Lolly. The option allows Lolly to buy 100 Units in LLC in Year 2 for an exercise price of $15,000. Lolly pays $1,000 to the LLC for the issuance of the option. In Year 2, Lolly exercises the option, contributing the $15,000 exercise price to LLC. At the time the option is exercised, the value of Property A is $35,000.[19]

| | Assets | | | Liabilities and Capital | |
	Basis	FMV		Basis	FMV
Prop. A	$20,000	$35,000	Jacob	$10,000	$17,000
Cash Prem.	$1,000	$1,000	Ginger	$10,000	$17,000
Exer. Price	$15,000	$15,000	Lolly	$16,000	$17,000
Totals	$36,000	$51,000		$36,000	$51,000

Lolly's tax basis in the partnership interest is $16,000, the total amount she invested. Lolly's capital account initially is credited with that same $16,000, which includes the amount paid for the option ($1,000) and the exercise price of the option ($15,000). Under the LLC agreement, however, Lolly is entitled to LLC capital corresponding to 100 Units of LLC (1/3 of LLC's capital). Immediately after the exercise of the option, LLC's assets are cash of $16,000 and Property A, which has a value of $35,000. Thus, the total value of LLC's assets is $51,000. Lolly is entitled to LLC capital equal to one-third of this value, or $17,000.

Thus, Lolly is entitled to $1,000 more LLC capital than her capital contributions to LLC. Under the Proposed Regulations, LLC must increase Lolly's capital account from $16,000 to $17,000 by, first, revaluing LLC property and allocating the first $1,000 of book gain to Lolly. The net "book" gain inherent in LLC's assets (Property A) is $15,000 ($35,000 value less $20,000 basis). The first $1,000 of this gain must be allocated to Lolly, and the remaining $14,000 of this gain is allocated equally to Jacob and Ginger. These capital account adjustments have no immediate tax impact. Note that all of the partners, including Lolly, are allocated their fair

---

[18] Prop. Treas. Reg. § 1.704-1(b)(2)(iv)(s)(1), (2).

[19] This example is based on Prop. Treas. Reg. § 1.704-1(b)(5), example 20.

shares of the book gain. Some of the book gain is allocable to Lolly because it economically belonged to her due to the increase in the value of her option privilege.

After the smoke clears, the tax and book accounts are as follows:

	Jacob		Ginger		Lolly	
	Tax	Book	Tax	Book	Tax	Book
Beg. Cap.	$10,000	$10,000	$10,000	$10,000	$16,000	$16,000
Reval		$7,000		$7,000		$1,000
Total	$10,000	$17,000	$10,000	$17,000	$16,000	$17,000

The disparity between the tax and book accounts must be allocated in accordance with I.R.C. § 704(c) principles.[20] In this context, this means that of the $15,000 of tax gain, $7,000 each must be allocated to Jacob and Ginger and $1,000 must be allocated to Lolly, i.e., the tax gain effectively earned by them.

§ 10.05 COMPLICATIONS ON THE EXERCISE OF NONCOMPENSATORY OPTIONS

A. New Partner Enters While Option Outstanding

The Proposed Regulations provide rules for doing the revaluation math if a new partner enters the partnership while an option is outstanding.[21] The fair market value of partnership property is adjusted for any outstanding options. There are two components to the adjustment.

The first component: The fair market value of partnership property is reduced by the option premium paid to the partnership.[22] This reduction occurs because the value of the option premium in a sense belongs to the option holder, and he will be able to increase his capital account by the amount of the premium if he exercises the option.

The second component: If the fair market value of the outstanding option exceeds the premium payable by the option holder, then the fair market value of partnership property is reduced by the excess value to the extent of unrealized income or gain in partnership property that has not previously been reflected in the capital accounts. The reduction is allocated only to properties with unrealized appreciation in proportion to their respective amounts of unrealized appreciation. This adjustment insures that gain economically attributable to the option holder is not allocated to the partners. If the option premium payable by the option holder exceeds the fair market value of the option, then the value of partnership property is

---

[20] *See* Treas. Reg. § 1.704-1(b)(2)(iv)(s)(1), (2).

[21] Logically these rules should apply even if a new partner is not entering the partnership, but the partnership interests change due to additional capital contributions from some of the existing partners while an option is outstanding.

[22] Prop. Treas. Reg. § 1.704-1(b)(2)(iv)(f)(1).

increased by that excess to the extent of the unrealized deduction or loss in partnership property not previously reflected in the capital accounts. The increase is allocated only to properties with unrealized depreciation in proportion to their respective amounts of unrealized depreciation.[23] This adjustment insures that a loss economically attributable to the option holder is not allocated to the partners. If the option ultimately lapses, as would be likely where the value of what is to be received is less than the option exercise price, I.R.C. § 1234 will trigger short-term capital gain to the partnership in the amount of the option premium and a corresponding loss to the option holder. At that point, the adjustments discussed above would no longer be appropriate. The Proposed Regulations do not address this issue, but presumably the partnership would have to await a subsequent revaluation to get the numbers right again.

EXAMPLE 2

In Year 1, Jacob and Ginger each contribute cash of $10,000 to LLC, a newly formed LLC that is a tax partnership, in exchange for 100 Units in LLC. LLC uses the cash to purchase two nondepreciable properties, Property A and Property B, for $10,000 each. Also in Year 1, at a time when Property A and Property B are still valued at $10,000 each, LLC issues an option to Lolly for $1,000. The option allows Lolly to buy 100 Units in LLC for an exercise price of $15,000 in Year 2.[24]

Prior to the exercise of Lolly's option, Matt contributes $17,000 to LLC for 100 Units in LLC. At the time of Matt's contribution, Property A has a value of $30,000 and a basis of $10,000, Property B has a value of $5,000 and a basis of $10,000, and the fair market value of Lolly's option is $2,000.[25] Upon Matt's admission to the partnership, the capital accounts of Jacob and Ginger (which were $10,000 each prior to Matt's admission) are revalued, thus reflecting their shares of the unrealized appreciation in the partnership's assets.

Under the Proposed Regulations, the fair market value of partnership property ($36,000) must be reduced by the option premium paid by Lolly to the partnership to acquire the option ($1,000) and the excess of the fair market value of the option as of the date of the adjustment over the option premium paid by Lolly to acquire the option ($1,000), but only to the extent of the unrealized appreciation in LLC property ($15,000). Therefore, the revaluation adjustments must be based on a value of $34,000 ($36,000 − $2,000). Accordingly, Jacob and Ginger's capital accounts must be increased to $17,000. The second $1,000 reduction is attributable to the "profit" inherent in the option premium ("the second component") and is allocated entirely to Property A, the only asset having unrealized appreciation. Therefore, the book value of Property A is $29,000 ($30,000 − $1,000).[26]

---

[23]   Prop. Treas. Reg. § 1.704-1(b)(2)(iv)(f)(1), (h)(2).

[24]   This example is based on Prop. Treas. Reg. § 1.704-1(b)(5), example 22.

[25]   Example 22 in the Proposed Regulations simply gives this as a fact. This will be discussed in more detail below.

[26]   The $19,000 of built-in gain in Property A and the $5,000 of built-in loss in Property B must be allocated equally between Jacob and Ginger in accordance with I.R.C. § 704(c) principles. Treas. Reg. § 1.704-1(b)(1)(iv)(f)(4).

	Tax Basis	FMV	Option Adjustment	Book
Property A	$10,000	$30,000	($1,000)	$29,000
Property B	$10,000	$5,000		$5,000
Cash	$1,000	$1,000		$1,000
Subtotal	$21,000	$36,000	($1,000)	$35,000
Matt's cash contribution	$17,000	$17,000	0	$17,000
Total	$38,000	$53,000	($1,000)	$52,000

Asset

	Tax	FMV
Jacob	$10,000	$17,000
Ginger	$10,000	$17,000
Matt	$17,000	$17,000
Lolly's Option	$1,000	$2,000
Total	$38,000	$53,000

Liabilities and Capital

After Matt becomes a member, and when the property values are unchanged, Lolly exercises the option. On the exercise of the option, Lolly's capital account is credited with the amount paid for the option ($1,000) and the exercise price of the option ($15,000). Under the LLC agreement, however, Lolly is entitled to LLC capital corresponding to 100 Units of LLC (1/4 of LLC's capital). Immediately after the exercise of the option, LLC's assets are worth $68,000 ($15,000 contributed by Lolly, plus the value of LLC assets prior to the exercise of the option, $53,000). Lolly is entitled to LLC capital equal to one-fourth of this value, or $17,000. As discussed above, the Proposed Regulations require a revaluation and capital account adjustments at this stage.

The LLC must increase Lolly's capital account from $16,000 to $17,000 by first revaluing LLC property and allocating the first $1,000 of book gain to Lolly. The net increase in the value of LLC properties since the previous revaluation is $1,000 (the difference between the actual value of Property A, $30,000, and the book value of Property A, $29,000). The entire $1,000 of book gain is allocated to Lolly.[27]

	Jacob		Ginger	
	Tax	Book	Tax	Book
Cap. post Matt	$10,000	$17,000	$10,000	$17,000
Cap. post Lolly exer.	$10,000	$17,000	$10,000	$17,000
End Cap.	$10,000	$17,000	$10,000	$17,000

---

[27] Again, I.R.C. § 704(c) principles must be followed in allocating tax gain and loss. Treas. Reg. § 1.704-1(b)(2)(iv)(f)(4).

| | Matt | | Lolly | |
	Tax	Book	Tax	Book
Cap. post Matt	$17,000	$17,000	$16,000	$16,000
Cap. post Lolly exer.	$17,000	$17,000	$16,000	$1,000
End Cap.	$17,000	$17,000	$16,000	$17,000

Obviously, these rules are highly complex. They accomplish one very useful objective. They hold out of the capital account adjustments the appreciation (and, less important, depreciation) attributable to the outstanding option, as well as the option premium itself. If this were not done, the capital accounts of the continuing partners and entering partners would tend to be overstated upon a revaluation, assuming the partnership property had appreciated while the option was outstanding. That is because some of the increased value of the property would really "belong" to the option holder who would be allocated it as soon as the option was exercised. Moreover, the more appreciation there would be, the more likely it would be that the option would be exercised, making it increasingly pointless to allocate the appreciation to anyone other than the option holder. Further, if the option is ignored in these circumstances, and upon a revaluation (while the option is outstanding) all of the value is allocated to the new and existing partners, when the option is exercised and a revaluation is again done, a portion of the capital accounts of the existing partners would have to be allocated to the option holder/partner. Yet economically, the relevant gain belonged to the option holder all along. The Proposed Regulations solve this problem by pulling the appreciation attributable to the option holder — as well as the option premium — out of the revaluation equation (though the issue arises again for curative allocations, as we discuss below).

There is one practical problem with the approach of the Proposed Regulations. When doing a revaluation, both the Proposed Regulations and the existing regulations[28] require the partnership to restate the book values of the partnership properties at their fair market at the time of the revaluation. The capital accounts of the partners are in turn also restated to their fair market values, and the balance of the capital accounts is what partners would generally receive if the partnership were liquidated.[29] The practical problem is that the values of the partnership properties in real life in most instances will not be knowable with precision without going to the often great expense of an appraisal. In most cases, that will not be an economically viable option.

Partnerships, when doing revaluations, commonly do not attempt to independently determine the fair market values of the partnership properties. Rather, they "reverse engineer" the value of the partnership properties based on the value of the cash and/or property contributed by the new partner and the percentage interest that partner will have in the partnership. Thus, if an entering partner pays $10,000 for a 10% interest, it is assumed that the partnership

---

[28] *See* Treas. Reg. § 1.704-1(b)(2)(iv)(f).

[29] *See* Treas. Reg. § 1.704-1(b)(2)(iv)(b).

property (inclusive of the $10,000) is worth $100,000. Thus, ultimately the revaluation is not based on the value of the partnership property but on the value of the partnership interest being acquired.[30]

Typically, a reverse-engineered revaluation will yield values of partnership properties that are less than the amount for which they could be sold and capital accounts that are less than the liquidation value of the partnership interest. This is because an incoming partner will often discount what he will pay for the partnership interest to take into account economic realities. These realities could include the facts that the interest is not marketable, that it represents a minority interest in the enterprise, and therefore does not have control, and/or other relevant discounting considerations.[31] Thus, in the example above, where the entering partner paid $10,000 for a 10% partnership interest, the actual value of the partnership property on a sale might be $120,000, but the entering partner might have discounted the value by 20% to take into account the lack of marketability and the fact that he is receiving a minority interest. In that circumstance, the revaluation based on reverse engineering will generate capital accounts that will be lower than what the partners would receive on a liquidation of the partnership and book values of partnership properties that will be lower than the amount the partnership could receive on their sale.

It would be best if both the existing and Proposed Regulations were amended to take this real-world approach into account. If it is not done and a partnership (perhaps foolishly given the low risk of audit) wanted to comply literally with the Regulations, the results would be anomalous. In the example, upon the revaluation the entering partner arguably could be given a capital account of $12,000 notwithstanding the fact he only paid $10,000, which in addition to being aesthetically unpleasing, will cause a lot of confusion. Taxpayers will wonder why their capital accounts are different from their contribution, and many legal and accounting advisors will not understand the rules and make the capital account $10,000 regardless. Further, there is no real harm done by formally permitting the real-world approach, as everything will come out in the wash on an actual liquidation. The Regulations require the partnership to recognize any book gain or loss inherent in the assets at that time.[32] Without regulatory authorization, however, a less than wise IRS auditor might claim the partnership is not keeping capital accounts properly and launch a full-blown attack on an otherwise allowable allocation regime.[33] Further, it would create disjunctures with other rules. If the new partner gifts the interest, the gift will have a value of $10,000, not the $12,000

---

[30] *See* ABA Comments, *supra* note 1, at IVD2; this approach is most workable where a straight percentage is acquired. However, often a partner does not acquire a "10% interest," but instead acquires an interest that varies depending on partnership performance.

[31] There is ample case law supporting the use of discounts. *See, e.g.*, Gross v. Commissioner, 272 F.3d 333 (6th Cir. 2001); Church v. United States, 268 F.3d 1063 (5th Cir. 2001); *but see* Estate of Strangi v. Commissioner, 115 T.C. 478 (2000), *aff'd in part and rev'd in part*, 293 F.3d 279 (5th Cir. 2002), *on remand*, T.C. Memo 2003-145, *aff'd*, 417 F.3d 468 (5th Cir. 2005). Sometimes a premium is paid for "going concern value."

[32] Treas. Reg. § 1.704-1(b)(2)(iv)(e)(1). This rule also requires book gain or loss to be recognized on a nonliquidating distribution of property.

[33] In order to meet the "substantial economic effect" safe harbor for allocations of income and loss

in the capital account. The same is true with regard to the amount realized on a sale.

The Proposed Regulations are internally inconsistent and do not base capital accounts on liquidation values in one important respect. As we discuss in the above examples, in calculating the capital accounts of the partners in the case of a new partner entering the partnership while an option is outstanding, an adjustment is made for the "fair market value" of the outstanding option.[34] That fair market value is presumably the value an independent third party would pay for the option, not the "liquidation profit" that would be generated if the option were exercised and the partnership were immediately liquidated.[35] Using the actual fair market value of the option can create unnecessary problems with the corrective allocations rules (that we discuss immediately below). By using the fair market value rather than liquidation profit to value the outstanding option, the Proposed Regulations will tend to overstate the capital accounts of the existing partners. This is because the fair market value of the option will likely be less than the liquidation profit due to economic realities associated with minority interests, lack of marketability, and other factors, considerations the Proposed Regulations otherwise ignore. When the option is exercised, if the continuing partners have overstated capital accounts, the option holder/partner will need a larger capital account than would otherwise be the case, increasing the chance that a corrective allocation will be necessary.

B.   Corrective Allocations

In some cases, the built-in gain or loss in the option will exceed the unrealized appreciation or depreciation in the partnership's assets. As a consequence, a disparity will remain after all of the unrealized appreciation or depreciation in the partnership's assets have been allocated to the option holder after the revaluation. In this case, the Proposed Regulations still shift capital between the historic partners and the option holder so that the option holder has the economically correct capital account balance. In a controversial move, the Proposed Regulations require the partnership to make corrective allocations of gross income or loss to the partners so as to take into account this disparity.[36] This can mean, for example, that the option holder can incur taxable income on exercise of the option. Allocations under the partnership agreement will not be considered to have substantial economic effect unless the agreement complies with these rules.

EXAMPLE 3

Assume the same facts as in Example 1, except that, in Year 1, LLC sells Property A for $40,000, recognizing gain of $20,000. LLC does not distribute the sale proceeds to its partners and it has no other earnings in Year 1. With the proceeds ($40,000), LLC purchases Property B, a nondepreciable property. Also

---

among the partners, capital accounts must be maintained as provided in the Regulations. Treas. Reg. § 1.704-1(b)(2)(ii)(b), (b)(2)(iv)(b). *See* Chapter 5.

[34]   Prop. Treas. Reg. § 1.704-1(b)(2)(iv)(f)(1), (h)(2).

[35]   In Prop. Treas. Reg. § 1.704-1(b)(5), example 22, the Proposed Regulations assume the fair market value of the option is equal to the liquidation profit, but in real life that will not necessarily be the case.

[36]   Prop. Treas. Reg. § 1.704-1(b)(2)(iv)(s)(3).

assume that Lolly exercises the option at the beginning of Year 2 and that, at the time Lolly exercises the option, the value of Property B is $41,000. In Year 2, LLC has gross income of $3,000 and deductions of $1,500.[37]

| | Assets | | | Liabilities and Capital | |
	Basis	FMV		Basis	FMV
Property B	$40,000	$41,000	Jacob	$20,000	$19,000
Cash	$16,000	$16,000	Ginger	$20,000	$19,000
			Lolly	$16,000	$19,000
Total	$56,000	$57,000		$56,000	$57,000

Lolly's capital account is credited with the amount paid for the option ($1,000) and the exercise price of the option ($15,000). Under the LLC agreement, however, Lolly is entitled to LLC capital corresponding to 100 Units of LLC (one-third of LLC's capital). Immediately after the exercise of the option, LLC's assets are $16,000 cash and Property B, which has a value of $41,000. Thus, the total value of LLC's assets is $57,000. Lolly is entitled to LLC capital equal to one-third of this amount, or $19,000. Lolly is thus entitled to $3,000 more LLC capital than her capital contributions to LLC.

Under the Proposed Regulations, LLC must increase Lolly's capital account from $16,000 to $19,000. First, LLC revalues its property, allocating the $1,000 of book gain from the revaluation to Lolly. This brings Lolly's capital account to $17,000. There being no other book gain available, LLC must now reallocate $2,000 of capital from Jacob and Ginger to Lolly to bring Lolly's capital account to $19,000 (the "capital account reallocation"). As Jacob and Ginger have equal shares, each of their capital accounts is reduced by one-half of the $2,000 reduction, or $1,000 each.

Beginning in the year in which the option is exercised, LLC must make corrective allocations so as to take into account the capital account reallocation. In Year 2, LLC has gross income of $3,000 and deductions of $1,500. The book gross income of $3,000 is shared equally by Jacob, Ginger, and Lolly. For tax purposes, however, LLC must allocate all of its gross income ($3,000) to Lolly. Her normal share would have been one-third or $1,000. The extra $2,000 of income "offsets" the $2,000 of Jacob and Ginger's capital allocated to Lolly's capital account. According to the Proposed Regulations, LLC's book and tax deductions ($1,500) are allocated equally among Jacob, Ginger, and Lolly.[38]

---

[37] This example is based on Prop. Treas. Reg. § 1.704-1(b)(5), example 21.

[38] Note that there are still book/tax disparities meaning that future tax items from Property B must still be allocated in accordance with I.R.C. § 704(c) principles.

	Jacob		Ginger		Lolly	
	Tax	Book	Tax	Book	Tax	Book
Cap. acct. post exer.	$20,000	$20,000	$20,000	$20,000	$16,000	$16,000
Re-valuation						$1,000
Cap. acct. after reval.	$20,000	$20,000	$20,000	$20,000	$16,000	$17,000
Realloc.		($1,000)		($1,000)		$2,000
Cap. acct. after realloc.	$20,000	$19,000	$20,000	$19,000	$16,000	$19,000
Inc. alloca.		$1,000		$1,000	$3,000	$1,000
Ded. alloca.	($500)	($500)	($500)	($500)	($500)	($500)
Cap. acct. end Year 2	$19,500	$19,500	$19,500	$19,500	$18,500	$19,500

§ 10.06   OPTION HOLDER TREATED AS PARTNER

Generally, the Proposed Regulations treat an option as such and not as a partnership interest. Accordingly, the Proposed Regulations do not normally require the partnership to take an outstanding option into account when making partnership allocations of income and loss. There are exceptions, however, and they are necessary. If every option were blindly respected, it would be easy for high-bracket taxpayers to avoid partnership income while effectively owning an interest in the partnership. Rather than acquire a partnership interest, they would buy an option. The terms of the option and the partnership agreement could be written so they fully benefit from partnership profits. The terms might provide that the partnership may not make distributions or, more likely, only make limited distributions to cover partner tax liabilities. Since the profits will mostly stay in partnership solution, the option will increase in value, giving the option holder the benefit of partnership income without being taxed on it. Down the road, the option holder could even sell the option at a capital gain, which typically would only be taxed at a 15% rate rather than ordinary income rates of up to 35% on a partner's share of operating profits.[39] Further, had the option holder sold a partnership interest instead of the option, I.R.C. § 751 would have required him to recognize ordinary income to the extent of ordinary income inherent in partnership receiv-

---

[39] I.R.C. § 1(h), (i)(2).

ables and inventory.[40] Even before the Proposed Regulations, the IRS has ruled, and the courts have held, that under the right facts options can be viewed as ownership interests.[41] The Proposed Regulations would have fallen far short if they had not addressed this issue.

The Proposed Regulations treat an option holder as a partner if two tests are met. The option holder's rights must be substantially similar to the rights afforded a partner ("substantially similar test").[42] Additionally, as of the date that the option is issued, transferred, or modified, there must be a strong likelihood that the failure to treat the option holder as a partner would result in a substantial reduction in the present value of the partners' and the option holder's aggregate tax liabilities ("strong likelihood test").[43]

If an option is "reasonably certain" to be exercised, then the holder of the option ordinarily has rights that are "substantially similar" to the rights afforded to a partner.[44] The Proposed Regulations list a series of factors that are relevant in determining whether or not an option is reasonably certain to be exercised:

i. The fair market value of the partnership interest that is the subject of the option;

ii. The exercise price of the option;

iii. The term of the option;

iv. The volatility, or riskiness, of the partnership interest that is the subject of the option;

v. The fact that the option premium and, if the option is exercised, the option exercise price, will become assets of the partnership;

vi. Anticipated distributions by the partnership during the term of the option;

vii. Any other special option features, such as an exercise price that declines over time or declines contingent on the happening of specific events;

viii. The existence of related options, including reciprocal options; and

ix. Any other arrangements (express or implied) affecting the likelihood that the option will be exercised.[45]

---

[40] That said, a well-advised purchaser of the option is likely to discount the price paid for the option for the associated I.R.C. § 751 tax liabilities she will be assuming on exercise of the option. Note that an I.R.C. § 754 election could not solve this problem if the option is respected as an option since there has been no sale or exchange of a partnership interest.

[41] Kwait v. Commissioner, T.C.M. (RIA) ¶ 89,382 (1989); Penn-Dixie Steel Corp. v. Commissioner, 69 T.C. 837 (1978); Rev. Rul. 82-150, 1982-2 C.B. 110; *also see* Griffin Paper Corp. v. Commissioner, T.C.M. (RIA) ¶ 97,409 (1997), *aff'd*, 180 F.3d 272 (11th Cir. 1999).

[42] Prop. Treas. Reg. § 1.761-3(a).

[43] We borrow these descriptive terms from the ABA Comments, *supra* note 1, at IVE1. *See* Treas. Reg. § 1.761-3(a).

[44] Prop. Treas. Reg. § 1.761-3(c)(1).

[45] Prop. Treas. Reg. § 1.761-3(c)(2).

The Proposed Regulations give some examples of when the rights given to an option holder do or do not cross the line to partner status. In one example, an option holder pays $8 for a seven-year option to acquire a 10% partnership interest for $17. The relevant partnership interest is worth $16 at the time the option is issued. The business of the partnership is a risky one. Given the length of the term of the option and the fact that it is barely out of the money, the option holder is economically not very differently situated from a partner with a profits interest in the partnership. Under the facts, however, the option holder does not have the same risk of loss as a partner. Further, the riskiness of the business means that the value of a 10% interest in seven years is not reasonably predictable. For these reasons, the Proposed Regulations conclude that the option holder is not treated as a partner.[46]

In another example, a partnership owns rental property. The property is 95% rented to good quality corporate tenants on triple-net leases and is expected to remain so rented for 20 years. Occupancy rates are high in the relevant geographic area and it is expected to stay that way for 10 years. The option holder pays $6.50 for a seven-year option to acquire a 10% interest in the partnership for $17. The value of a 10% interest at the time of issuance of the option is $16.50. Net cash flow is reasonably expected to be $10 per year for the next seven years. Finally, no distributions are allowed to be made to the partners during that time. Under these assumptions, some of which require an unusually good crystal ball, the value of the option can be expected to go up in value over the seven-year option term (as no distributions are being made), and the value of the option can be expected to be greater than the option exercise price — and of course it can be expected that the option will be exercised. Under these circumstances, the Proposed Regulations conclude that the option holder has rights substantially similar to the rights afforded a partner. If there is also a strong likelihood that failure to treat the option holder as a partner would result in a substantial reduction in the partners' and the option holder's aggregate tax liabilities (because, for example, the option holder is in a high tax bracket and the partners in low tax brackets), the option holder will be treated as a partner.[47]

Options that are deep in the money[48] raise similar issues. In one example in the Proposed Regulations, a limited partnership business is engaged in a risky Internet start-up venture. (Is there any other kind?) The option holder pays $14 for an 10-year option to acquire a 5% interest for $6. A 5% interest has a fair market value of $15 at the time the option is issued. Given the riskiness of the venture, it is not certain that the option will be exercised, but what the option holder has paid as a premium, $14, almost equals what the corresponding partnership interest currently is worth, $15. Thus, if the business goes south, the option holder stands to lose almost as much as a partner. The option holder will also be able to participate in the success of the partnership. According to the Proposed Regulations, the option holder has similar economic benefits and detriments of a partner and, therefore, has rights similar to that afforded a partner. If there is a strong likelihood that the

---

[46] Prop. Treas. Reg. § 1.761-3(d)(2), example 1.

[47] Prop. Treas. Reg. § 1.761-3(d)(2), example 2.

[48] Meaning the exercise price is well below the value of the partnership interest that will be acquired with the option.

failure to treat the option holder as a partner would result in a substantial reduction in the partners' and the option holder's aggregate tax liabilities, the Proposed Regulations conclude that the option holder will be treated as a partner.[49]

If the option holder is considered to be a partner, she is allocated her allocable share of partnership income or loss based on her interest in the partnership. Computing her interest in the partnership is the hard part. The Regulations do not provide a lot of guidance in this regard beyond noting that an option holder may have contributed less than other partners, making her economic interest in the partnership smaller.[50] Many different factors might go into calculating the allocable share, including the amount of the option premium paid, future rights to current profits if they cannot be currently distributed and rights on liquidation, if any.

There are other complexities that can arise when an option holder is required to be treated as a partner. The biggest problems will occur when the partnership does not treat an option holder as a partner when it should have. Any audit that would detect the mistake may come years after the fact. In the interim, the other partners may have been allocated too much income, while the option holder will have been allocated none. That will all have to be undone, assuming the statute of limitations has not expired on the personal tax returns of the partners. The problem gets worse if, for example, the option holder is a tax-exempt organization with a strong aversion to partner status and its associated unrelated business taxable income.[51] If any partners have come or gone during the period an option holder that should have been treated as partner but was not, the complexities of setting it all right reach Kafkaesque proportions.

Those same problems exist in reverse if the option holder is treated as a partner only to discover he was not one. Another complication in this regard is if the option holder/partner who is considered a partner allows the option to lapse. Now what? Presumably it would be treated as an abandonment of the partnership interest, generating possible debt shifts and deemed cash distributions under I.R.C. §§ 752 and 731, basis adjustments under I.R.C. § 734 if an I.R.C. § 754 election is in effect, and hot asset problems under I.R.C. § 751.[52]

One of the most problematic areas in the rules is the fact that the option is tested to determine whether or not it constitutes a partnership interest not only when the option is issued, but also when it is transferred or modified. It is not clear when a transaction qualifies as a modification or transfer. Modifications to the terms of options are not uncommon. It is important that the final Regulations make clear what is a modification that triggers a recharacterization review and what is not, so that taxpayers have adequate guidance.

---

[49] Prop. Treas. Reg. § 1.761-3(d)(2), example 3.

[50] The partnership agreement itself may be silent on the manner in which allocations are made to the option holder causing the allocations to the option holder to be made in accordance with the partners' interests in the partnership. I.R.C. § 704(b).

[51] This income is taxed to the tax-exempt organization at regular tax rates. *See* I.R.C. §§ 511, 512.

[52] *See* ABA Comments at IVE1.

§ 10.07 COMPENSATORY OPTIONS

Unlike the Proposed Regulations with respect to noncompensatory options, the Proposed Regulations issued with respect to the issuance of partnership interests in exchange for services are virtually devoid of provisions dealing with compensatory options.

A. Issuance of a Compensatory Option

Prop. Treas. Reg. § 1.83-3(e) provides that the term "property" includes a partnership interest. Treas. Reg. § 1.83-7(a) provides that if a compensatory option is granted to an employee or an independent contractor and if I.R.C. § 421[53] does not apply to such option, then I.R.C. § 83(a) and (b) apply to the grant of the option if the option has a readily ascertainable fair market value at the time the option is granted. If the option does not have a readily ascertainable fair market value, then I.R.C. § 83(a) and (b) apply at the time the option is exercised or otherwise disposed of by the optionee.

Treas. Reg. § 1.83-7(b) provides rules for determining when an option has a readily ascertainable fair market value. In effect, this Regulation makes it virtually impossible for an option to have a readily ascertainable fair market value unless it is similar to an option which is traded on an established market. Since this is virtually never the case for compensatory options, no income is recognized by the optionee upon the receipt of a compensatory option.

B. Exercise of Compensatory Option

Assuming that the compensatory option does not have a readily ascertainable fair market value (which, as indicated above, is virtually always the case), then income will be recognized by the optionee upon the exercise of the option in an amount equal to the excess of the fair market value of the partnership interest acquired over the exercise price.[54] This assumes that the partnership interest received is not subject to a substantial risk of forfeiture within the meaning of I.R.C. § 83(c)(1). If the partnership has a liquidation value election in effect, then the fair market value of the partnership interest received will be deemed to be its liquidation value.[55]

C. Repurchase or Sale of Option

If the partnership repurchases the compensatory option, the optionee should have compensation income in an amount equal to the purchase price. Treas. Reg. § 1.83-7(a) provides that if the option does not have a readily ascertainable fair market value, I.R.C. § 83(a) applies at the time the option is exercised or otherwise disposed of by the optionee. If the option is sold or otherwise disposed of in an

---

[53] This section refers to incentive stock options and employee stock purchase plans. *See* I.R.C. §§ 422, 423.

[54] I.R.C. § 83(a).

[55] *See* § 8.08.

arm's-length transaction, I.R.C. § 83(a) applies to the cash or other property received in the same manner as I.R.C. § 83(a) would have applied to the transfer of property pursuant to the exercise of the option.

The partnership should be entitled to a compensation deduction in an amount equal to the income recognized by the optionee (unless the compensation has to be capitalized).[56] If instead of repurchasing the option, the optionee sells the option to an independent third party, the results should be the same as in the case of a repurchase of the option.

D.　Effect of Outstanding Option

As indicated at § 10.04.A, the Proposed Regulations with respect to noncompensatory options contain detailed rules for performing a revaluation when a new partner enters the partnership while a noncompensatory option is outstanding. The preamble to the Compensatory Partnership Interest Proposed Regulations indicate that a similar rule was not provided in the case of compensatory options. The preamble indicates that this is because the obligation to issue a partnership interest in satisfaction of an option is a liability that should be taken into account in determining the fair market value of the partnership for purposes of making the revaluation. This is based on Treas. Reg. § 1.752-7, which has the effect of treating the outstanding option as a section 1.752-7 liability.[57]

E.　Recharacterization Rule

As indicated at § 10.05, the Proposed Regulations dealing with noncompensatory options contain detailed rules with respect to treating the holder of an option as a partner. The preamble to the Proposed Regulations dealing with compensatory transfers of partnership interests indicate that the Proposed Regulations for compensatory options do not have a similar rule because constructive transfers of property subject to I.R.C. § 83 may occur under circumstances other than those described in the Proposed Regulations with respect to noncompensatory options. It remains to be seen whether the final Regulations for compensatory options will have their own recharacterization rules, or whether the issue will be left to general principles of income tax law.

The issue can be illustrated by a simple example. Assume that a partnership has issued Units, each of which has a fair market value of $10. The employee with responsibility for managing the partnership is granted an option to purchase 100 Units at an exercise price of $0.01 per Unit. If the option is treated as an option, since it does not have a readily ascertainable fair market value within the meaning of Treas. Reg. § 1.83-7(b), no income would be recognized by the employee, even though the option is deep-in-the-money and the employee is making most of the decisions for the partnership. In contrast, if the partnership had issued 100 Units to the employee, the employee would have had $1,000 of compensation income and the partnership would have been entitled to a $1,000 deduction. With the exception

---

[56]　I.R.C. § 83(h).

[57]　*See* § 3.04.H.

of the obligation to pay $0.10 for the Units, the employee seems to be in the same position as if the partnership interest was actually issued to him rather than an option to acquire a partnership interest.

§ 10.08   READING, QUESTIONS AND PROBLEMS

A.   Reading

Notice of Proposed Rulemaking [REG — 103580-02], 68 Fed. Reg. 2930 (Jan. 22, 2003).

Notice of Proposed Rulemaking [REG — 105346-03], 70 Fed. Reg. 29,675 (May 24, 2005).

B.   Questions and Problems

1. Brent, Angeni, and Carolina form an LLC treated as a partnership for federal income tax purposes with each holding a one-third interest. Each member contributes $30, and the LLC purchases WhiteAcre for $90. At a time when WhiteAcre has a value of $120, the LLC sells an option to Daria for $5 to purchase a one-fourth interest in WhiteAcre for $40. Please describe the tax consequences to the LLC and its members on the issuance and exercise of the option.

2. Same facts as Problem 1, except that the LLC sells Daria an option to acquire a one-fourth interest in the LLC. Please describe the tax consequences to the LLC and its members on the issuance and exercise of the option. If the answer is not clear, please describe the alternative approaches.

3. How would your answers to Problem 2 change if the members had elected to treat the LLC as an S corporation?

4. Same facts as Problem 2, except that the LLC grants Daria the option without consideration in exchange for her services. Please describe the tax consequences to the LLC and its members on the issuance and exercise of the option. If the answer is not clear, please describe the alternative approaches.

5. How would your answers to Problem 4 change if the members had elected to treat the LLC as an S corporation?

Chapter 11

I.R.C. § 197 INTANGIBLES AMORTIZATION

§ 11.01 INTRODUCTION

Chapter 11 will focus on partnership problems relating to I.R.C. § 197 amortization of intangible assets, including sales of partnership interests, distributions to partners, and contributions of property to partnerships.

§ 11.02 SUMMARY OF I.R.C. § 197

Taxpayers are permitted to amortize the adjusted basis of certain types of intangibles over a 15-year period. These types of intangibles are generally referred to as I.R.C. § 197 intangibles.[1] I.R.C. § 197 intangibles include goodwill, going concern value, workforce in place, business books and records, operating systems, other information systems, patents, copyrights, any franchise, trademark, or trade name.[2] Such types of intangibles are generally amortizable over 15 years if they were acquired after I.R.C. § 197 was enacted[3] and held in connection with the conduct of a trade or business or an activity for the production of income, the management, conservation, or maintenance of property held for the production of income or in connection with the determination, collection, or refund of any tax.[4] For most types of property, amortizable I.R.C. § 197 intangibles exclude property that is created by the taxpayer, except if such property is acquired in connection with the acquisition of assets constituting a trade or business or a substantial portion thereof.[5]

An I.R.C. § 197 intangible is created by the taxpayer to the extent that the taxpayer makes payments or otherwise incurs costs for its creation, production, development, or improvement, whether the actual work is performed by the taxpayer or by another person under a contract with the taxpayer entered into before the creation, production, development, or improvement of the intangible.[6]

---

[1] I.R.C. § 197(a).

[2] I.R.C. § 197(d)(1). I.R.C. § 197 intangibles also include formulas, processes, designs, patterns, know-how, formats, customer based intangibles, supplier based intangibles, licenses, permits, other rights granted by a governmental unit or an agency or instrumentality, and covenants not to compete entered into in connection with an acquisition of an interest in a trade or business. Treas. Reg. § 1.197-2(a)(5).

[3] I.R.C. § 197 was enacted on August 10, 1993.

[4] I.R.C. § 197(c)(1) applying definitions from I.R.C. § 212.

[5] I.R.C. § 197(c)(2).

[6] Treas. Reg. § 1.197-2(d)(2)(ii)(A).

For purposes of I.R.C. § 197, a group of assets constitutes a trade or business if their use would constitute a trade or business under I.R.C. § 1060 (that is, if goodwill or going concern value could, under any circumstances, attach to the assets).[7] In addition, a group of assets is treated as a trade or business if they include, with certain exceptions, any franchise, trademark, or trade name.[8]

I.R.C. § 197 also contains anti-churning rules intended to prevent taxpayers from converting goodwill, going concern value, and similar assets previously held or used into amortizable I.R.C. § 197 intangibles through transactions such as transfers to related parties.

§ 11.03 GENERAL RULES APPLICABLE TO PARTNERSHIPS UNDER I.R.C. § 197

Partnerships are generally treated as taxpayers for the purposes of I.R.C. § 197. However, the rules under I.R.C. § 197 reflect a tension between the entity and the aggregate theories of partnership taxation discussed in Chapter 1. This tension is described more specifically in connection with the anti-churning rules, discussed below.

A. Contributions

If an I.R.C. § 197 intangible is transferred to a partnership in a transaction described in I.R.C. § 721, the transfer is disregarded in determining: (i) whether, with respect to so much of the intangible's basis in the hands of the partnership as does not exceed its basis in the hands of the contributing partner, the intangible is an amortizable I.R.C. § 197 intangible and (ii) the amount of the deduction under I.R.C. § 197 with respect to such basis.[9]

As discussed in Chapter 2, I.R.C. § 721 generally provides that no gain or loss will be recognized to a partnership or to any of its partners in the case of a contribution of property to the partnership in exchange for an interest in the partnership.[10] I.R.C. § 723 also provides that the basis of property contributed to a partnership by a partner will be the adjusted basis of such property in the hands of the contributing partner at the time of the contribution increased by the amount (if any) of gain recognized to the contributing partner at such time. As a result of the combination of the application of I.R.C. § 721 and I.R.C. § 723, if an I.R.C. § 197 intangible is contributed to a partnership in exchange for an interest, the partnership's treatment of the I.R.C. § 197 intangible generally will be based on the treatment of the I.R.C. § 197 intangible in the hands of the contributing partner.

---

[7] Treas. Reg. § 1.197-2(e)(1). *See* Treas. Reg. § 1.1060-1(b)(2).

[8] Treas. Reg. § 1.197-2(d)(2)(i).

[9] Treas. Reg. § 1.197-2(g)(2)(ii)(A).

[10] I.R.C. § 721(a). This nonrecognition treatment is subject to some limitations, such as the exception provided in I.R.C. § 721(b) for transfers to partnerships that would be treated as investment companies if the partnership were incorporated.

If the I.R.C. § 197 intangible contributed to the partnership was an amortizable I.R.C. § 197 intangible in the hands of the contributing partner, the partnership will continue to amortize its adjusted basis, to the extent it does not exceed the contributing partner's adjusted basis, ratably over the remainder of the contributing partner's 15-year amortization period. Similarly, if the intangible was not an amortizable I.R.C. § 197 intangible in the hands of the contributing partner, the partnership's adjusted basis cannot be amortized under I.R.C. § 197, to the extent it does not exceed the partner's adjusted basis. In either event, the intangible is treated with respect to so much of its adjusted basis in the hands of the partnership as exceeds its adjusted basis in the hands of the contributing partner in the same manner for purposes of I.R.C. § 197 as an intangible acquired from the contributing partner in a transaction that is not described in I.R.C. § 721.[11]

B.   Distributions

A rule similar to the one for contributions also applies for distributions of property from a partnership.

As discussed in Chapter 7, I.R.C. § 731 generally provides that in the case of a distribution by a partnership to a partner, no gain will be recognized to such partner except to the extent that any money distributed exceed the adjusted basis of such partner's interest in the partnership immediately before the distribution.[12] I.R.C. § 732 also provides that the basis of property (other than money) distributed by a partnership to a partner other than in liquidation of the partner's interest will, subject to a limitation of the recipient partner's basis in such partner's partnership interest, be its adjusted basis to the partnership immediately before such distribution.[13] As a result of the combination of the application of I.R.C. § 731 and I.R.C. § 732, if an I.R.C. § 197 intangible is distributed by a partnership other than in liquidation of a partnership interest and the basis of the distributed property is less than the recipient partner's basis in the partnership interest, the transfer is disregarded in determining: (i) whether, with respect to so much of the intangible's basis in the hands of the recipient partner as does not exceed its basis in the hands of the partnership, the intangible is an amortizable I.R.C. § 197 intangible and (ii) the amount of the deduction under I.R.C. § 197 with respect to such basis,[14] and the recipient partner's treatment of the I.R.C. § 197 intangible generally will be based on the treatment of the I.R.C. § 197 intangible in the hands of the partnership.

If the I.R.C. § 197 intangible distributed by the partnership was an amortizable I.R.C. § 197 intangible in the hands of the partnership, the recipient partner will continue to amortize its adjusted basis, to the extent it does not exceed the partnership's adjusted basis, ratably over the remainder of the partnership's 15-year amortization period. Similarly, if the intangible was not an amortizable I.R.C.

---

[11]   Treas. Reg. § 1.197-2(g)(2)(ii)(B).

[12]   I.R.C. § 731(a)(1).

[13]   I.R.C. § 732(a)(1).

[14]   Treas. Reg. § 1.197-2(g)(2)(ii)(A).

§ 197 intangible in the hands of the partnership, the recipient partner's adjusted basis, to the extent it does not exceed the partnership's adjusted basis, cannot be amortized under I.R.C. § 197. In either event, the intangible is treated, with respect to so much of its adjusted basis in the hands of the recipient partner as exceeds its adjusted basis in the hands of the partnership, in the same manner for purposes of I.R.C. § 197 as an intangible acquired from the partnership in a transaction that is not described in I.R.C. § 731.[15]

C. Terminations

The rules limiting the treatment of I.R.C. § 197 intangibles acquired in nonrecognition transactions apply to a termination of a partnership under I.R.C. § 708, whether by cessation of the business in partnership form or by the sale or exchange of 50% or more of the total interests in partnership capital and profits within a 12-month period.[16]

You will recall from Chapter 6, that in a termination resulting from a sale or exchange of the partnership interests, the terminating partnership is deemed to contribute all of its assets and liabilities to a new partnership in exchange for an interest in the new partnership; and, immediately thereafter the terminating partnership is deemed to distribute interests in the new partnership to the purchasing partner and the remaining partners in proportion to their respective interests in the terminating partnership in liquidation of the terminating partnership.[17] In applying the rule relating to transfers of I.R.C. § 197 intangibles acquired in a nonrecognition transaction to a partnership that is terminated by a transfer of interests, the terminating partnership is the transferor and the new partnership is the transferee.[18] Thus, the rules described above in regard to contributions would apply, treating the terminating partnership as the contributing partner.

If the partnership is terminated by reason of cessation of business in partnership form, the terminating partnership is generally treated as the transferor and the distributee partner is treated as the transferee.[19] Thus, the treatment described above in regard to distributions would generally apply.

D. Basis Adjustments

Under circumstances described in Chapters 6 and 7, property distributed from a partnership and property held by a partnership after a distribution of property, after a sale or exchange of a partnership interest, on the death of a partner or when the partnership has a substantial built in loss may have its adjusted basis adjusted to an amount more or less than that of the adjusted basis of such property

---

[15] Treas. Reg. § 1.197-2(g)(2)(ii)(B).

[16] Treas. Reg. § 1.197-2(g)(2)(iv)(A).

[17] Treas. Reg. § 1.708-1(b)(4).

[18] Treas. Reg. § 1.197-2(g)(2)(iv)(B).

[19] Treas. Reg. § 1.197-2(g)(2)(iv)(C).

in the hands of the partnership before such transaction.[20] Any increase in the adjusted basis of an I.R.C. § 197 intangible as a result of such adjustments is treated as a separate I.R.C. § 197 intangible. For the purposes of determining the amortization period under I.R.C. § 197 with respect to the basis increase, the intangible is generally treated as having been acquired at the time of the transaction that causes the basis increase.[21]

E.   Allocations in Regard to Built-In Gain

If the intangible was an amortizable I.R.C. § 197 intangible in the hands of the contributing partner, a partnership may make allocations of amortization deductions with respect to the built-in gain of the intangible to all of its partners under any of the permissible methods described in Chapter 5.[22]

If the intangible was not an amortizable I.R.C. § 197 intangible in the hands of the contributing partner, in general, the intangible is not amortizable under I.R.C. § 197 by the partnership. However, if a partner contributes an I.R.C. § 197 intangible to a partnership and the partnership adopts the remedial allocation method, described in Chapter 5, for making I.R.C. § 704(c) allocations of amortization deductions, the partnership generally may make remedial allocations of amortization deductions with respect to the contributed I.R.C. § 197 intangible.[23]

To illustrate this, consider the following example:

On January 1, L and M, who are unrelated, form partnership LM and agree that each will be allocated a 50% share of all partnership items. The partnership agreement provides that LM will make allocations in regard to built-in gain using the remedial allocation method. L contributes an I.R.C. § 197 intangible with an adjusted tax basis of $4,000 and a fair market value of $10,000. The property was not an amortizable § 197 intangible in L's hands. M contributes $10,000 that the partnership uses to purchase a nonamortizable asset. Except for the amortization deductions, LM's expenses equal its income in each year of the 15 years commencing with the year the partnership is formed.

Without any remedial allocations, no amortization deductions under I.R.C. § 197 would be allowed for tax purposes. The partnership has a carry-over basis and steps into the shoes of L. The I.R.C. § 197 property was nonamortizable to L and so it is nonamortizable to the partnership.

---

[20]   I.R.C. §§ 732(b), 732(d), 734(b), 743(b).

[21]   Treas. Reg. § 1.197-2(g)(3). If the partnership elects the remedial allocation method described in Chapter 5 with respect to property whose basis is adjusted by reason of a sale or exchange of a partnership interest or the death of a partner, the portion of any increase in the basis that is attributable to built-in gain at the time of the contribution of the property to the partnership is recovered over the remaining recovery period for the partnership's excess book value in the property. Treas. Reg. § 1.743-1(j)(4)(i)(B)(2).

[22]   Treas. Reg. § 1.197-2(g)(4)(i).

[23]   Treas. Reg. § 1.197-2(g)(4)(ii).

With remedial allocations, with regard to the $10,000 difference between the amortizable book value of the property when it was contributed and its zero eligible amortizable tax basis to the partnership, M would be entitled to a $333 per year amortization deduction over the 15-year amortization period equal to the $333 per year that M would have been entitled to had the partnership purchased an amortizable I.R.C. § 197 intangible from an unrelated party for $10,000. To balance the $333 per year amortization deduction allowed to M, a remedial allocation of $333 per year of taxable income is allocated to L over the 15-year amortization period.

In other words, because the contributed property was nonamortizable in the hands of the contributing partner, the other partner is permitted an amortization deduction only if the contributing partner is charged with notional taxable income to create a net zero at the partnership level.

§ 11.04 ANTI-CHURNING RULES APPLICABLE TO PARTNERSHIPS UNDER I.R.C. § 197

A. General Rules

The anti-churning rules under I.R.C. § 197 provide that amortizable I.R.C. § 197 intangibles do not include goodwill and going concern value ("*I.R.C. § 197(f)(9) intangibles*") if the taxpayer acquired the intangible after July 25, 1991, and: (i) the intangible was held or used at any time during the transition period by the taxpayer or a related person, (ii) the intangible was acquired from a person who held the intangible at any time during the transition period, and the user of the intangible does not change as a result of the transaction, or (iii) the taxpayer grants the right to use the intangible to a person (or a person related to such person) who held or used such intangible at any time during the transition period (property satisfying (i), (ii), or (iii) being *Transition Period Property*").[24] A person is "related" to another person for these purposes if a person bears a relationship to such other person described in I.R.C. § 267(b) or I.R.C. § 707(b)(1) (except that "20 percent" is used rather than "50 percent" when applying such sections) or the related person and such other person are engaged in trades or businesses under common control (within the meaning of I.R.C. § 41(f)(1)(A) and (B)).[25]

I.R.C. § 197 provides that a relationship is tested for purposes of the anti-churning rules both immediately before and immediately after the acquisition.[26] The Regulations further provide that, in the case of intangibles acquired in a series of related transactions, testing is made immediately before the first transaction

---

[24] I.R.C. § 197(f)(9)(A). The third rule would only apply if the transaction in which the taxpayer grants the right and the transaction in which the taxpayer acquired the intangible are part of a series of related transactions. Treas. Reg. § 1.197-2(h)(2)(iii). The transition period is the period beginning on July 25, 1991, and ending on August 10, 1993, unless an election is made to make the transition period July 25, 1991. Treas. Reg. § 1.197-2(h)(4).

[25] I.R.C. § 197(f)(9)(C)(i).

[26] I.R.C. § 197(f)(9)(C)(ii).

and immediately after the last transaction.[27]

As mentioned above, the anti-churning rules reflect the tension between characterizing a partnership as an entity and an aggregate that is found in many parts of the Code. In general, a partnership is treated as an entity separate from its partners in characterizing related party transfers.[28] However, in determining whether the anti-churning rules apply to any increase in the basis of an I.R.C. § 197(f)(9) intangible in connection with an adjustment to the basis of property distributed from a partnership, property held by a partnership after a distribution of property, and property held by a partnership after a sale or exchange of a partnership interest, on the death of a partner or when the partnership has a substantial built-in loss, the determinations are made at the partner level and each partner is treated as having owned and used the partner's proportionate share of partnership property.[29] In determining whether the anti-churning rules apply to any other transaction, the determinations are made at the partnership level unless the IRS determines that the partner level is more appropriate.

I.R.C. § 197(f)(9)(E) provides that, in applying the anti-churning rules for basis adjustments under I.R.C. §§ 732, 734, and 743, determinations are made at the partner level, and each partner is treated as having owned and used such partner's proportionate share of the partnership's assets. With respect to basis adjustments under I.R.C. §§ 732(b) and 734(b), this rule requires taxpayers and the IRS to analyze transactions that actually involve a distribution of property from the partnership to a partner as deemed transactions involving transfers of property directly among the partners. In applying the anti-churning rules to basis adjustments under I.R.C. § 732(b), the distributee partner is deemed to acquire the distributed intangible directly from the continuing partners of the distributing partnership. Similarly, in applying the anti-churning rules to basis adjustments under I.R.C. § 734(b), the continuing partners are deemed to acquire interests in the intangible that remains in the partnership from the partner who received a distribution (giving rise to the I.R.C. § 734(b) basis adjustment) of property other than the intangible.

Consistent with this view of the transactions, Treas. Reg. § 1.197-2(g)(3) provides that the increase in the basis of a distributed I.R.C. § 197(f)(9) intangible under I.R.C. § 732(b) or the increase in the partnership's basis of an undistributed I.R.C. § 197(f)(9) intangible under I.R.C. § 734(b) is treated as a new intangible acquired as a result of the distribution. The rules for determining whether such basis adjustments are subject to the anti-churning rules under I.R.C. § 197(f)(9) operate by reference to the facts surrounding each partner's acquisition of its interest in the partnership, the relation of the distributee partner and the continuing partners, and the portion of the intangible that is allocable to such partners. Although the specific rules are not phrased in terms of analyzing a deemed transfer of a portion of an intangible between the distributee partner and the continuing partners, the effect of the rules is to analyze such a deemed

---

[27] Treas. Reg. § 1.197-2(h)(6)(ii)(B).

[28] *See, e.g.*, I.R.C. § 707(b)(1) (specifically referenced in I.R.C. § 197(f)(9)(C)(i)(I)).

[29] Treas. Reg. § 1.197-2(h)(12)(i).

transfer. Accordingly, in order for a basis adjustment to an I.R.C. § 197(f)(9) intangible under I.R.C. § 732(b) or 734(b) to be amortizable, the deemed transfer (as a result of the basis adjustment) must be to an unrelated partner.

Under an exception to the related party transaction rules, the anti-churning rules do not apply to transactions that qualify for the "gain recognition exception," except to the extent of the acquiring taxpayer's basis in the intangible exceeds the gain recognized by the transferor.[30] To qualify for the gain recognition exception:

> a. the acquiring taxpayer must acquire the intangible from a person who would not be related to the acquiring taxpayer if 50% were used instead of 20% in the application of the tests of I.R.C. § 267(b) or I.R.C. § 707(b)(1); and

> b. the transferor must elect to recognize gain on the disposition of the intangible and agrees to pay tax on the gain at the highest marginal rate for the relevant taxable year.[31]

B. Contributions

The anti-churning rules do not have a special rule for contributions of property. The determination of whether the property is subject to the anti-churning rules is, therefore, determined by whether or not the partnership is related to the contributing partner.[32] Because whether the contributing partner and the partnership are related is determined immediately before and after the acquisition by the partnership of the I.R.C. § 197 intangible, if the contributing partner receives more than 20% of the interests in the partnership (or is otherwise related to the partnership) the property could be subject to the anti-churning rules if the property is Transition Period Property.[33]

The Regulations generally permit a partnership to make curative or remedial allocations to its noncontributing partners of amortization relating to an asset that was amortizable (or a zero-basis intangible that otherwise would have been amortizable) in the hands of the contributor. The Regulations provide that the anti-churning rules do not apply to curative or remedial allocations of amortization with respect to an I.R.C. § 197 intangible if the intangible was an amortizable I.R.C. § 197 intangible in the hands of the contributing partner.[34] Thus, curative or remedial allocations of the amortization attributable to the built-in gain existing at the time of the contribution could be made in respect of I.R.C. § 197 intangibles that would otherwise be subject to the anti-churning rules.

For assets that were I.R.C. § 197(f)(9) intangibles (and thus nonamortizable) in the hands of the contributor, however, the partnership may make deductible amortization allocations to the noncontributing partners under the remedial

---

[30] Treas. Reg. § 1.197-2(h)(9)(ii).

[31] Treas. Reg. § 1.197-2(h)(9)(i).

[32] Treas. Reg. § 1.197-2(h)(12).

[33] *See* Treas. Reg. § 1.197-2(h)(6), (10).

[34] Treas. Reg. § 1.197-2(h)(12)(vii)(A).

method only. The Regulations permit remedial allocations because, under I.R.C. § 704(c), remedial allocations treat the amortizable portion of contributed property like newly purchased property with a new holding period. This result, which is similar to the result obtained for basis increases under I.R.C. § 743, does not follow under the curative method because curative allocations are not determined as if the applicable property were newly purchased property.

However, the partners related to the contributing partner may not receive remedial allocations of amortization under I.R.C. § 704(c) if the contributing partner or a related person (other than the partnership) becomes or remains a direct user of the contributed intangible.[35] Partnerships may use any reasonable method to determine amortization of the asset for book purposes, provided that the method does not contravene the purposes of I.R.C. § 197 (including the anti-churning rules). A method will be viewed as contravening the purposes of I.R.C. § 197 if the effect of the book adjustments is such that any portion of the tax deduction is allocated directly or indirectly to a partner subject to the anti-churning rules.

Rev. Rul. 2004-49[36] considers the situation in which a new partner joins a partnership, contributing cash to the partnership for the new partner's proportionate share. The partnership revalues the assets of the partnership for capital account purposes, creating a book-tax difference to which the principles of I.R.C. § 704(c) would apply.[37] Rev. Rul. 2004-49 concludes that if a partnership revalues an I.R.C. § 197 intangible that was amortizable in the hands of the partnership prior to the revaluation, the partnership may make reverse I.R.C. § 704(c) allocations (including curative and remedial allocations) of amortization to take into account the built-in gain or loss from the revaluation of the intangible. If the revalued I.R.C. § 197 intangible was not amortizable in the hands of the partnership prior to the revaluation and the new partner is not related to the historic partners, the partnership may make remedial (but not traditional or curative) allocations of amortization to take into account the built-in gain or loss from the revaluation of the intangible subject to the prohibition on allocating any amortization to the historic partners and partners related to them.[38]

C.   Distributions

As discussed in Chapter 7, the basis of property (other than money) distributed from a partnership other than in liquidation of a partner's interest in the partnership will generally be such property's adjusted basis to the partnership immediately before the distribution.[39] However, if property is distributed in

---

[35] Treas. Reg. § 1.197-2(h)(12)(vii)(B).

[36] 2004-1 C.B. 939.

[37] *See* Treas. Reg. § 1.704-3(a)(6).

[38] Certain problems may arise in maintaining capital accounts where a partnership elects to make remedial allocations, and the anti-churning rules apply with respect to one or more partners resulting in the prohibition of the allocation of a proportionate share of amortization to such partners. These problems also arise in the context of I.R.C. § 734(b) adjustments.

[39] I.R.C. § 732(a).

liquidation of a partner's interest in the partnership or within two years of acquiring an interest by purchase under certain circumstances, the basis of the property received may be higher in the hands of the recipient partner than in the hands of the partnership.[40] For purposes of determining whether the anti-churning rules apply to such basis increase, the distributee partner is viewed as having received the partnership property directly from the other partners.[41]

To determine how the anti-churning rules apply to the distributed property, it first is necessary to determine whether the portion of an intangible that a partner is deemed to acquire as a result of the distribution was subject to the anti-churning rules immediately prior to the deemed transfer. Even if the intangible is an I.R.C. § 197(f)(9) intangible with respect to the partnership, for purposes of analyzing a deemed transfer, the partner's share of the intangible is treated as not being subject to the anti-churning rules if the intangible was held by the partnership at the time that the partner (or predecessor partner) acquired the partnership interest, and the partner (or predecessor partner) would have been able to amortize the intangible had the partner (or predecessor partner) directly acquired the intangible under the same circumstances that the partner (or predecessor partner) acquired the partnership interest. If a partner's share of the intangible is treated as not being subject to the anti-churning rules for this purpose, then the anti-churning rules would not apply to the portion of the basis adjustment that is attributable to the deemed transfer.

If the partner's share of the intangible was treated as being subject to the anti-churning rules immediately prior to the deemed transfer, it is necessary, as a further step, to determine whether the deemed transferor and transferee are related. If the partners are not related, the anti-churning rules would not apply to the basis adjustment resulting from the deemed transfer.

To determine whether such a basis increase on a liquidation of a partnership interest is subject to the anti-churning rules, the Regulations assume a hypothetical sale of the intangible immediately before the distribution.[42] The anti-churning rules do not apply to any increase in the basis of the intangible in an amount equal to the gain that would have been attributable to partners other than the distributee partner or persons related to the distributee partner.[43] The anti-churning rules also may not apply to the amount of basis increase of the intangible equal the amount of gain that would have been attributable to the distributee partner and related persons if the intangible was acquired by the partnership before August 10, 1993, the distributee partner or the related persons acquired the interest after August 10, 1993, and a person or persons unrelated to the distributee partner held the interest after August 10, 1993.[44] If the partnership acquired the I.R.C. § 197(f)(9) intangible after August 10, 1993, and the intangible was not

---

[40] *See* I.R.C. § 732(b), (d).

[41] I.R.C. § 197(f)(9)(E).

[42] Treas. Reg. § 1.197-2(h)(12)(ii)(D).

[43] Treas. Reg. § 1.197-2(h)(12)(ii)(A)(1).

[44] Treas. Reg. § 1.197-2(h)(12)(ii)(A)(2). The transaction whereby the interest was acquired by the unrelated person also cannot be part of a series of transactions in which the distributee partner or persons related to the distributee partner acquired the interest.

amortizable in the hands of the partnership, rules similar to those in the previous sentence apply. The main exception is that the trigger date is the date the partnership acquired the intangible rather than August 10, 1993.

The anti-churning rules do not apply to an increase in the basis of an I.R.C. § 197(f)(9) intangible resulting from a distribution within two years after the acquisition of the interest in the partnership under I.R.C. § 732(d), if had an I.R.C. § 754 election been in effect at the time of the acquisition of the interest in the partnership the distributee partner would have been able to amortize the basis adjustment made pursuant to I.R.C. § 743(b).[45]

D.   Adjustments to Basis of Partnership Property

If an I.R.C. § 754 election is in effect at the time of a distribution or the basis of the distributed property in the hands of the distributee partner is over $250,000 more than the basis of the property in the hands of the partnership,[46] the basis of property held by the partnership after the distribution may be subject to adjustment under I.R.C. § 734. The anti-churning rules of I.R.C. § 197 do not apply to a continuing partner's share of an increase in the basis of an I.R.C. § 197(f)(9) intangible as a result of such an adjustment under the same conditions that apply to a basis increase to distributed property.[47] However, a continuing partner's share of the basis increase is calculated differently. Instead of a hypothetical sale, the total basis increase in the intangible is multiplied by the percentage represented by the partner's post-distributed capital account divided by all of the post-distribution capital accounts of the partners.[48]

> *Example.* (i) On January 1, 2001, A, B, and C form a partnership (ABC) in which each partner shares equally in capital and income, gain, loss, and deductions. On that date, A contributes an I.R.C. § 197(f)(9) intangible with a zero basis and a value of $150, and B and C each contribute $150 cash. A and B are related, but neither A nor B is related to C. ABC does not adopt the remedial allocation method for making I.R.C. § 704(c) allocations of amortization expenses with respect to the intangible. On December 1, 2004, when the value of the intangible has increased to $600, ABC distributes $300 to B in complete redemption of B's interest in the partnership. ABC has an election under I.R.C. § 754 in effect for the taxable year that includes December 1, 2004. (Assume that, at the time of the distribution, the basis of A's partnership interest remains zero, and the basis of each of B's and C's partnership interest remains $150.)
>
> (ii) Immediately prior to the distribution, the assets of the partnership are revalued pursuant to Treas. Reg. § 1.704-1(b)(2)(iv)(f), so that the I.R.C. § 197(f)(9) intangible is reflected on the books of the partnership at a value

---

[45] Treas. Reg. § 1.197-2(h)(12)(iii).

[46] As adjusted by I.R.C. § 732(d).

[47] Treas. Reg. § 1.197-2(h)(12)(iv)(B).

[48] Treas. Reg. § 1.197-2(h)(12)(iv)(D)(1). If the partnership does not maintain capital accounts, then the relevant percentage is the partner's overall percentage in the partnership as determined under Treas. Reg. § 1.704-1(b)(3).

of $600. B recognizes $150 of gain under I.R.C. § 731(a)(1) upon the distribution of $300 in redemption of B's partnership interest. As a result, the adjusted basis of the intangible held by ABC increases by $150 under I.R.C. § 734(b). A does not satisfy any of the tests set forth under Treas. Reg. § 1.197-2(h)(12)(iv)(B) and thus is not an eligible partner. C is not related to B and thus is an eligible partner under Treas. Reg. § 1.197-2(h)(12)(iv)(B)(1). The capital accounts of A and C are equal immediately after the distribution, so each partner's share of the basis increase is equal to $75. Because A is not an eligible partner, the anti-churning rules apply to A's share of the basis increase. The anti-churning rules do not apply to C's share of the basis increase.

(iii) For book purposes, ABC determines the amortization of the asset as follows: First, the intangible that is subject to adjustment under I.R.C. § 734(b) will be divided into three assets: the first, with a basis and value of $75 will be amortizable for both book and tax purposes; the second, with a basis and value of $75 will be amortizable for book, but not tax purposes; and a third asset with a basis of zero and a value of $450 will not be amortizable for book or tax purposes. Any subsequent revaluation of the intangible pursuant to § 1.704-1(b)(2)(iv)(f) will be made solely with respect to the third asset (which is not amortizable for book purposes). The book and tax attributes from the first asset (i.e., book and tax amortization) will be specially allocated to C. The book and tax attributes from the second asset (i.e., book amortization and non-amortizable tax basis) will be specially allocated to A. Upon disposition of the intangible, each partner's share of gain or loss will be determined first by allocating among the partners an amount realized equal to the book value of the intangible attributable to such partner, with any remaining amount realized being allocated in accordance with the partnership agreement. Each partner then will compare its share of the amount realized with its remaining basis in the intangible to arrive at the gain or loss to be allocated to such partner.[49]

I.R.C. § 743(b) provides for an optional adjustment to the basis of partnership property following certain transfers of partnership interests. The amount of the basis adjustment is the difference between the transferee's basis in the partnership interest and the transferee's share of the partnership's basis in the partnership's assets. Once the amount of the basis adjustment is determined, it is allocated among the partnership's individual assets pursuant to I.R.C. § 755.

Under the Regulations, a partnership is required to assign values to its assets as follows. First, the partnership must determine the values of each of its assets other than I.R.C. § 197 intangibles under all the facts and circumstances, taking into account I.R.C. § 7701(g).[50] The partnership then must determine the gross value of all partnership assets (partnership gross value). Last, the partnership is required to use the residual method to assign values to the partnership's I.R.C. § 197

---

[49] This is example 31 from Treas. Reg. § 1.197-2. The Treasury concludes in the example that the method of amortization illustrated in the example is reasonable.

[50] The fair market value of a property is treated as being not less than the amount of any nonrecourse indebtedness to which the property is subject.

intangibles.[51] For purposes of the Regulations, "I.R.C. § 197 intangibles" includes all I.R.C. § 197 intangibles, as well as any goodwill or going concern value that would not qualify as an I.R.C. § 197 intangible.

If the aggregate value of partnership property other than I.R.C. § 197 intangibles is equal to or greater than partnership gross value, then all I.R.C. § 197 intangibles are deemed to have a value of zero. In all other cases, the aggregate value of the partnership's I.R.C. § 197 intangibles (the residual I.R.C. § 197 intangibles value) is deemed to equal the excess of partnership gross value over the aggregate value of partnership property other than I.R.C. § 197 intangibles. The residual I.R.C. § 197 intangibles value must be allocated, first, among I.R.C. § 197 intangibles other than goodwill and going concern value. Any remaining value is assigned to goodwill and going concern value.[52]

If a partnership interest is transferred in a taxable transaction, the transferee's basis in its partnership interest provides a frame of reference for determining partnership gross value. In these transactions, the Regulations generally provide that partnership gross value is the amount that, if assigned to all partnership property, would result in a liquidating distribution to the transferee partner equal to that partner's basis (reduced by the amount, if any, of such basis that is attributable to partnership liabilities) in the transferred partnership interest immediately following the relevant transfer.[53]

The anti-churning rules do not apply to an increase in the basis of an I.R.C. § 197 intangible under I.R.C. § 743(b) if the person acquiring the partnership interest is not related to the person transferring the partnership interest. In addition, the anti-churning rules of I.R.C. § 197 do not apply to a partner's share of an increase in the basis of an I.R.C. § 197(f)(9) intangible as a result of an adjustment under I.R.C. § 743(b) under similar conditions as those under which the basis increase to distributed property would be eligible for an exception to the anti-churning rules.[54] If a partner acquires an interest in a partnership from an unrelated partner after August 10, 1993, and after the partnership has acquired the I.R.C. § 197(f)(9) intangible, the partner will be treated as holding a portion of the intangible that is not subject to the anti-churning rules. Under I.R.C. § 743(b), only the purchasing partner shares in the basis adjustment.

> *Example.* (i) A and B are partners with equal shares in the capital and profits of general partnership P. P's only asset is an amortizable I.R.C. § 197 intangible, which P had acquired on January 1, 1995. On January 1, 2000, the asset had a fair market value of $100 and a basis to P of $50. On that date, A sells his entire partnership interest in P to C, who is unrelated

---

[51] Treas. Reg. § 1.755-1(a)(2).

[52] Treas. Reg. § 1.755-1(a)(5).

[53] Treas. Reg. § 1.755-1(a)(4)(i)(A). In certain circumstances involving basis adjustments under I.R.C. § 743(b), such as where income or loss with respect to particular I.R.C. § 197 intangibles is allocated differently among partners, partnership gross value may vary depending on the fair market values of particular I.R.C. § 197 intangibles held by the partnership. In these situations, the Regulations require the partnership to use a reasonable method, consistent with the purposes of the Regulations, to determine partnership gross value. Treas. Reg. § 1.755-1(a)(4)(i)(B).

[54] Treas. Reg. § 1.197-2(h)(12)(v).

to A, for $50. At the time of the sale, the basis of each of A and B in their respective partnership interests is $25.

(ii) The sale causes a termination of P under I.R.C. § 708(b)(1)(B). Under I.R.C. § 708, the transaction is treated as if P transfers its sole asset to a new partnership in exchange for the assumption of its liabilities and the receipt of all of the interests in the new partnership. Immediately thereafter, P is treated as if it is liquidated, with B and C each receiving their proportionate share of the interests in the new partnership. The contribution by P of its asset to the new partnership is governed by I.R.C. § 721, and the liquidating distributions by P of the interests in the new partnership are governed by I.R.C. § 731. C does not realize a basis adjustment under I.R.C. § 743 with respect to the amortizable I.R.C. § 197 intangible unless P had an I.R.C. § 754 election in effect for its taxable year in which the transfer of the partnership interest to C occurred or the taxable year in which the deemed liquidation of P occurred.

(iii) Under I.R.C. § 197, if P had an I.R.C. § 754 election in effect, C is treated as if the new partnership had acquired two assets from P immediately preceding its termination. Even though the adjusted basis of the new partnership in the two assets is determined solely under I.R.C. § 723, because the transfer of assets is a transaction described in I.R.C. § 721, the application of I.R.C. §§ 743(b) and 754 to P immediately before its termination causes P to be treated as if it held two assets for purposes of I.R.C. § 197. B's and C's proportionate share of the new partnership's adjusted basis is $25 each in one asset, which continues to be amortized over the 10 years remaining in the original 15-year amortization period. For the other asset, C's proportionate share of the new partnership's adjusted basis is $25 (the amount of the basis increase resulting from the application of I.R.C. § 743 to the sale or exchange by A of the interest in P), which is amortized over a new 15-year period beginning in January 2000.[55]

However, if the transaction is structured so that, under general principles of tax law, the transaction is not properly characterized as a sale of a partnership interest, then I.R.C. § 197 will apply to the transaction as recast to reflect its true economic substance.[56]

E.   Partner's Use of Partnership Property

The Regulations provide that where, for purposes of the anti-churning rules, a partner is treated as holding its proportionate share of partnership property under I.R.C. § 197(f)(9)(E), the continued or subsequent use (by license or otherwise) of an intangible by a partner could cause the anti-churning rules to apply with respect to that partner's share of the intangible in situations where a basis step-up under I.R.C. § 732(d) or 743(b) otherwise would be amortizable. The IRS has indicated that this rule is necessary in order to prevent the circumvention of I.R.C. § 197(f)(9)(A) through the use of a partnership.

---

[55] This is example 16 of Treas. Reg. § 1.197-2.

[56] Treas. Reg. § 1.197-2(j).

Treas. Reg. § 1.197-2(h)(12)(vi) makes clear that the proscribed use must be by an anti-churning partner or related person other than the partnership. Attributed use of the intangible from the partnership to a partner will not cause this rule to apply.

§ 11.05 COMPARISON WITH S CORPORATIONS

The rules related to the acquisition of properties with a carryover basis and the anti-churning rules apply both to S corporations and to partnerships. However, there is no provision similar to I.R.C. § 197(h)(9)(E), which requires the application of the anti-churning rules to adjustments to partnership bases of assets resulting from the application of I.R.C. § 732, 734, or 743, to S corporations. Thus, when property is distributed by an S corporation, the determination of whether the property is subject to the anti-churning rules would generally be made at the corporate level rather than at the level of the continuing shareholders. When shares in an S corporation are sold, there is no election available to treat the transferee shareholder's basis in the stock as such shareholder's basis in the underlying assets of the S corporation — without the recognition of gain by the other shareholders.

S corporations may, upon the taxable acquisition of at least 80% of the shares of the corporation by another corporation, elect to treat the stock purchase as an asset purchase, but the election would require gain on a deemed sale of assets to be recognized by all the historic shareholders of the S corporation.[57]

§ 11.06 READING, QUESTIONS AND PROBLEMS

A. Reading

CODE:

I.R.C. §§ 197, 732, 734, 743, 755.

TREASURY REGULATIONS:

Treas. Reg. §§ 1.197-2, 1.755-1.

B. Questions and Problems

1. On January 1 of Year 1 (on a date after the transition period), A and B, who are unrelated, form partnership AB and agree that each will be allocated a 50% share of all partnership items. The partnership agreement provides that AB will make allocations in regard to built-in gain using the remedial allocation method. A contributes an I.R.C. § 197 intangible with an adjusted tax basis of $10,000 and a fair market value of $10,000. The property was not an amortizable I.R.C. § 197 intangible in A's hands. B contributes $10,000, which the partnership uses to purchase a nonamortizable asset. Except for the amortization deductions, AB's

---

[57] I.R.C. § 338(h)(10).

expenses equal its income in each year of the 15 years commencing with the year the partnership is formed.

a. May AB amortize the property without electing remedial allocations?

b. If AB elects to use remedial allocations, how are the resulting allocations divided between A and B?

2. On January 1 of Year 3, C, who is unrelated to both A and B, purchases A's interest in the partnership for $20,000.

a. What is allocated to C if the partnership does not have an I.R.C. § 754 election in effect?

b. What is allocated to C if the partnership does have an I.R.C. § 754 election in effect?

c. Do the allocations to B change?

3. On January 1 of Year 4, the exclusive European and Asian rights (which B and C agree are worth half of the worldwide rights in regard to the I.R.C. § 197 intangible) to use the I.R.C. § 197 property are distributed to C in complete redemption of C's interest in partnership AB.

a. What is C's basis in the European and Asian rights? Does it matter whether there was an I.R.C. § 754 election in effect when C purchased C's interest in AB?

b. What is B's basis in the interest in the remaining rights in the I.R.C. § 197 intangible? Does it matter whether there was an I.R.C. § 754 election in effect when C purchased C's interest in AB? Does it matter whether there is an I.R.C. § 754 election in effect when the European and Asian rights are distributed to C?

4. Same facts as Question 2, except that C is related to A. How do the answers change? What would be the result if A elects to apply the gain recognition exception?

5. Same facts as Question 2, except that at the beginning of Year 4, C sells C's entire interest in AB to D, who is related to A, for $25,000.

a. What is allocated to D if the partnership does not have an I.R.C. § 754 election in effect?

b. What is allocated to D if the partnership does have an I.R.C. § 754 election in effect?

c. Do the allocations to B change?

Chapter 12

FOREIGN PARTNERSHIPS, FOREIGN PARTNERS, AND PARTNERSHIPS WITH TAX-EXEMPT ENTITIES

§ 12.01 INTRODUCTION

Chapter 12 will focus on the problems created by the interrelationship of the rules applicable to entities taxed under Subchapter K with the U.S. rules relating to international taxation. Because the two areas are closely related, Chapter 12 will also cover the tax issues that arise in connection with partnerships that include tax-exempt entities. In addition, Chapter 12 will discuss the limitations placed upon the deductibility of losses (and the eligibility for like-kind exchange treatment) of certain partnerships with tax exempt or foreign partners.

§ 12.02 FOREIGN PARTNERSHIPS

A. Classification

As discussed in Chapter 1, the classification of non-U.S. entities must start with the question of whether or not the entity is a business entity. The question is somewhat complicated because the system of classification of entities in other countries is often different from that of the United States. The check-the-box Regulations provide a list of non-U.S. entities that will be treated as corporations and are not eligible to elect to be treated otherwise.[1] Thus, to discuss foreign partnerships from a U.S. tax perspective, one must first start with an entity that is not a *per se* corporation under the check-the-box Regulations.

If a non-U.S. business entity is not *per se* classified as a corporation under the check-the-box Regulations, an analysis is applied that is very similar to that applied to domestic unincorporated business entities, except that the starting place is generally a default classification of the entity as a corporation (assuming the entity shields its owners from liability).[2] In other words, a non-U.S. entity that is not a *per se* corporation may elect to be either a disregarded business entity or a partnership for U.S. tax purposes, depending upon whether the entity has one owner or more than one owner. If the entity shields its members from liability and

---

[1] Treas. Reg. § 301.7701-2. For example, all Canadian companies are *per se* corporations, unless the liability of at least one member is not limited.

[2] Treas. Reg. §§ 301.7701-2, -3.

no election is made, the entity will be treated as a corporation for U.S. federal income tax purposes.

If the liability of any owner of the entity is not limited, the default classification of the entity is either as a disregarded entity, if the entity has only one owner, or as a partnership, if the entity has more than one owner.[3] Like domestic disregarded business entities and partnerships, such non-U.S. entities may elect to be treated as corporations for U.S. tax purposes, if such treatment is desired.[4]

For non-U.S. entities with U.S. taxpayers as owners, the availability of an election to choose between treatment as a corporation and treatment as a partnership has a different meaning in the context of a foreign partnership than it does in regard to a domestic partnership. In the context of a domestic partnership, the choice is generally between the flow-through treatment of Subchapter K and the entity level tax treatment of Subchapter C. In the context of a foreign partnership, the choice may be between the flow-through treatment of Subchapter K, the quasi-flow-through treatment of Subchapter F or the elective flow-through treatment provided for qualified electing funds under I.R.C. § 1295. For the purposes of this Chapter, we shall assume the choice has been made to elect to treat the foreign business entity as a partnership for U.S. tax purposes.

For these purposes, a "foreign" partnership is a partnership that is not created or organized in the United States or under the laws of the United States or any state thereof.[5] A business entity that is created or organized both in the United States and in a foreign jurisdiction is a domestic entity.[6]

> *Example*: P is an entity with more than one owner organized under the laws of Country A as an unlimited company. It is also an entity that is organized as a general partnership under the laws of State B. P has been classified as a partnership for federal tax purposes under the check-the-box Regulations.

P in this example is treated as a U.S. partnership for U.S. federal tax purposes.[7]

If an entity is created or organized in more than one jurisdiction and Treas. Reg. § 301.7701-2 would classify the entity as a corporation as a result of its formation in any one of the jurisdictions in which it is created or organized, the entity is treated as a corporation for U.S. tax purposes.[8]

---

[3] Treas. Reg. § 301.7701-3(b)(2).

[4] Treas. Reg. § 301.7701-3(a).

[5] I.R.C. § 7701(a)(5).

[6] Treas. Reg. § 301.7701-5(a).

[7] Treas. Reg. § 301.7701-5(b), example 2.

[8] Treas. Reg. § 301.7701-2(b)(9).

B. Foreign Tax Credit Rules in Regard to Foreign Partnerships

1. Generally

The United States employs a worldwide tax system under which U.S. individuals and domestic corporations generally are taxed on all income, whether derived in the United States or abroad; the foreign tax credit provided under I.R.C. § 901 allows some relief from double taxation. Subject to certain limitations, a U.S. taxpayer is allowed to claim a credit against its U.S. income tax liability for the foreign income taxes that it pays or accrues. A "foreign income tax" is any income, war profits, or excess profits tax paid or accrued to any foreign country or to any U.S. possession. A "foreign income tax" includes any tax paid in lieu of such a tax within the meaning of I.R.C. § 903. A domestic corporation that owns at least 10% of the voting stock of a foreign corporation (a *"section 902 corporation"*) is allowed a deemed-paid credit for foreign income taxes paid by the foreign corporation that the domestic corporation is deemed to have paid when the foreign corporation's earnings are distributed[9] or included in the domestic corporation's income under the provisions of subpart F.[10]

Although partnerships cannot benefit directly from the foreign tax credit, the Regulations provide that a U.S. citizen, a resident alien, or a domestic corporation may claim a share of a partnership's taxes that are attributable to such person.[11] I.R.C. § 702(a)(6) provides that each partner (including individuals or corporations) of a partnership must take into account separately its distributive share of the partnership's foreign taxes paid or accrued. In addition, under I.R.C. § 703(b)(3), the election under I.R.C. § 901 (whether to take a credit in respect of the foreign taxes) is made by each partner separately. In Rev. Rul. 71-141,[12] the IRS held that a foreign corporation's stock held indirectly by two domestic corporations through their interests in a domestic general partnership is attributed to such domestic corporations for purposes of determining the domestic corporations' eligibility to claim a deemed-paid foreign tax credit with respect to the foreign taxes paid by such foreign corporation. Accordingly, a general partner of a domestic general partnership is permitted to claim deemed paid foreign tax credits with respect to a dividend distribution from the foreign corporation to the partnership.

In addition, I.R.C. § 902(c)(7) now explicitly provides that a domestic corporation is entitled to claim deemed-paid foreign tax credits with respect to a foreign corporation that is held indirectly through a foreign or domestic partnership,

---

[9] I.R.C. § 902.

[10] I.R.C. § 960. Subpart F is the portion of the Code dealing with the conditions under which U.S. shareholders are required to currently include income recognized by a controlled foreign corporation. A controlled foreign corporation is a foreign corporation if more than 50% of (i) the total combined voting power of all classes of stock of such corporation entitled to vote, or (ii) the total value of the stock of such corporation, is owned or is considered as owned by United States shareholders on any day during the taxable year of such foreign corporation. I.R.C. § 957. Controlled foreign corporations are sometimes referred to as *"CFCs."*

[11] Treas. Reg. § 1.901-1(a).

[12] 1971-1 C.B. 211.

provided that the domestic corporation owns (indirectly through the partnership) 10% or more of the foreign corporation's voting stock.

Allocations of creditable foreign taxes do not have substantial economic effect within the meaning of the Regulations under I.R.C. § 704(b),[13] and, accordingly, such expenditures must be allocated in accordance with the partners' interests in the partnership.[14] An allocation of a creditable foreign tax expenditure ("*CFTE*") will be deemed to be in accordance with the partners' interests in the partnership if: (i) the CFTE is allocated (whether or not pursuant to an express provision in the partnership agreement) and reported on the partnership return in proportion to the distributive shares of income to which the CFTE relates; and (ii) allocations of all other partnership items that, in the aggregate, have a material effect on the amount of CFTEs so allocated to a partner are valid.

Under the so-called "technical taxpayer" rule of Treas. Reg. § 1.901-2(f)(1), the person by whom tax is considered to have been paid for purposes of I.R.C. §§ 901 and 903 is the person on whom foreign law imposes legal liability for the tax. This focus on legal liability applies even if another person, such as a withholding agent, actually remits the tax.[15] It also applies even if another person bears the economic burden of the tax, for example through a gross-up clause.[16]

Treas. Reg. § 1.901-2(f)(3) extends the technical taxpayer rule to situations in which more than one person is liable for a foreign income tax under the foreign law. That Regulation provides that if foreign income tax is imposed on the combined income of two or more related persons (such as a corporation and one or more of its subsidiaries) and they are jointly and severally liable for the tax under foreign law, the foreign law is considered to impose legal liability on each such person for the amount of the foreign income tax that is attributable to its portion of the base of the tax, regardless of which person actually pays the tax.

In 2007, the U.S. Court of Appeals for the Federal Circuit held that a U.S. company that wholly owned a foreign hybrid entity (a Luxembourg company treated as a disregarded entity for U.S. tax purposes, but as a corporation for Luxembourg tax purposes) was entitled to claim a direct foreign tax credit under I.R.C. § 901 for Luxembourg taxes paid by the hybrid entity on behalf of a consolidated group of companies of which it was the parent.[17] The other Luxembourg entities that were part of the consolidated group were operating companies treated as corporations for U.S. tax purposes. The income earned by those companies was not subpart F income, and the U.S. company consequently had no current income inclusions from those other group members, because the Luxembourg parent company was disregarded for U.S. tax purposes. The Luxembourg taxes paid by the hybrid entity thus were available for credit against U.S. income

---

[13] Foreign taxes taken as credits do not reduce capital accounts.

[14] Treas. Reg. § 1.704-1(b)(4)(viii)(a).

[15] *See* Norwest Corp. v. Commissioner, 69 F.3d 1404 (8th Cir. 1995); Continental Illinois Corp. v. Commissioner, 998 F.2d 513 (7th Cir. 1993); Nissho Iwai American Corp. v. Commissioner, 89 T.C. 765 (1987); Gleason Works v. Commissioner, 58 T.C. 464 (1972).

[16] Treas. Reg. § 1.901-2(f)(2)(i); *cf.* Continental Illinois Corp. v. Commissioner, 998 F.2d at 516.

[17] Guardian Industries Corp. v. United States, 477 F.3d 1368 (Fed. Cir. 2007).

tax imposed on other foreign source income derived by the U.S. company.

2.　Foreign Tax Credit Splitter Transactions

In reaction in part to the *Guardian Industries* case, Congress added I.R.C. § 909 to the Code in 2010. I.R.C. § 909 adopts a matching rule to prevent the separation of creditable foreign taxes from the associated foreign income.

In general, I.R.C. § 909 provides that when there is a foreign tax credit splitting event with respect to a foreign income tax paid or accrued by the taxpayer, the foreign income tax is not taken into account for federal tax purposes before the taxable year in which the related income is taken into account by the taxpayer. In addition, if there is a foreign tax credit splitting event with respect to a foreign income tax paid or accrued by a section 902 corporation, that tax is not taken into account for purposes of I.R.C. § 902 or 960, or for purposes of determining earnings and profits under I.R.C. § 964(a), before the taxable year in which the related income is taken into account for federal income tax purposes by the section 902 corporation, or a domestic corporation that meets the ownership requirements of I.R.C. § 902(a) or (b) with respect to the section 902 corporation. Thus, such tax is not added to the section 902 corporation's foreign tax pool, and its earnings and profits are not reduced by such tax.

For purposes of the provision, there is a "foreign tax credit splitting event" with respect to a foreign income tax if the related income is (or will be) taken into account for U.S. federal income tax purposes by a covered person.[18] "Related income" means, with respect to any portion of any foreign income tax, the income (or, as appropriate, earnings and profits), calculated under U.S. tax principles, to which such portion of foreign income tax relates. The legislative history to I.R.C. § 909 indicates that it is not intended that differences in the timing of when income is taken into account for U.S. and foreign tax purposes (e.g., as a result of differences in the U.S. and foreign tax accounting rules) should create a foreign tax credit splitting event in cases in which the same person pays the foreign tax and takes into account the related income, but in different taxable periods.

In the case of a partnership, I.R.C. § 909's matching rule is applied at the partner level, and, except as otherwise provided by the Treasury, a similar rule applies in the case of any S corporation or trust. Notice 2010-92[19] provides that for post-2010 taxable years, there will not be a foreign tax credit splitting event with respect to a foreign income tax paid or accrued by a partner with respect to its distributive share of the related income of a partnership that is a covered person with respect to the partner to the extent the related income is taken into account by the partner.

---

[18] With respect to any person who pays or accrues a foreign income tax (the "payor"), a "covered person" is: (1) any entity in which the payor holds, directly or indirectly, at least a 10% ownership interest (determined by vote or value); (2) any person that holds, directly or indirectly, at least a 10% ownership interest (determined by vote or value) in the payor; (3) any person that bears a relationship to the payor described in I.R.C. § 267(b) or 707(b) (including by application of the constructive ownership rules of I.R.C. § 267(c)); and (4) any other person specified by the Treasury. Accordingly, the Treasury may issue Regulations that treat an unrelated counterparty as a covered person in certain transactions deemed abusive.

[19] 2010-2 C.B. 916 (Dec. 6, 2010).

Notice 2010-92 also provides that future guidance will provide that allocations described in Treas. Reg. § 1.704-1(b)(4)(viii)(d)(3) (discussed below) will result in a foreign tax credit splitting event in post-2010 taxable years to the extent such allocations result in foreign income taxes being allocated to a different partner than the related income.

Current Treas. Reg. § 1.704-1(b)(4)(viii)(d)(3) provides that the foreign tax imposed on payments received by one branch of a partnership from another branch of the partnership ("inter-branch payments") is allocated to the creditable foreign tax expenditure ("*CFTE*") category that includes the items attributable to the relevant activities of the recipient branch. In cases where the partnership agreement results in more than one CFTE category with respect to activities of the recipient branch, the tax is allocated to the CFTE category that includes the items attributable to the activity to which the inter-branch payment relates. However, foreign taxes paid or accrued by a partner with respect to a distributive share of partnership income, and foreign taxes deemed paid under I.R.C. § 902 or 960 by a corporate partner with respect to stock owned, directly or indirectly, by or for a partnership, are not taxes paid or accrued by a partnership and, therefore, are not CFTEs subject to the rules of Treas. Reg. § 1.704-1(b)(4)(viii)(d)(3).

In general, I.R.C. § 909 is effective with respect to foreign income taxes paid or accrued by U.S. taxpayers and section 902 corporations in taxable years beginning after December 31, 2010.[20]

C.   Controlled Foreign Corporations as Partners in Foreign Partnerships

U.S. shareholders of a foreign corporation of which more than 50% of the total combined voting power of all classes of stock, or more than 50% of the total value of the stock, of the corporation is held or is considered as held by U.S. shareholders (a "*CFC*") are generally required to include in their gross income their pro rata share of certain types of income of the foreign corporation in the year such income is earned, whether or not such income is distributed to the U.S. shareholder.[21] A "U.S. shareholder" for these purposes is a shareholder that owns or is considered as owning 10% or more of the total combined voting power of all classes of stock of the relevant foreign corporation.[22] The income required to be included in the U.S. shareholder's income includes (among other things) insurance income, certain types of passive income (called foreign personal holding company income), foreign base company service income, and foreign base company sales income.[23]

---

[20]   In some instances, earnings and profits accrued before 2011 will need to be taken into consideration in determining whether there is a foreign tax credit splitting event. 2010-2 C.B. 916, Notice 2010-92, provides an exclusive list of arrangements that will be treated as giving rise to foreign tax credit splitting events for purposes of applying I.R.C. § 909 to pre-2011 taxes and directions on how to identify pre-2011 split taxes and related income with respect to each such arrangement.

[21]   I.R.C. § 951.

[22]   I.R.C. § 951(b).

[23]   I.R.C. § 952.

Foreign personal holding company income includes (among other things) dividends, interest, royalties, rents, and annuities and the excess of gains over losses from the sale or exchange of property: (i) which gives rise to dividends, interest, royalties, rents, and annuities, (ii) which is an interest in a trust, partnership, or REMIC, or (iii) which does not give rise to any income.[24] In the case of any sale by a CFC of an interest in a partnership with respect to which such corporation is a 25% owner of an interest in the capital or profits of the partnership, such corporation is treated as selling the proportionate share of the assets of the partnership attributable to such interest.[25]

"Foreign base company services income" means income derived in connection with the performance of technical, managerial, engineering, architectural, scientific, skilled, industrial, commercial, or like services which are performed on behalf of any related person, and are performed outside the country in which the CFC is organized.[26]

"Foreign base company sales income" means income derived in connection with: (a) (i) the purchase of personal property from a related person and its sale to any person, (ii) the sale of personal property to any person on behalf of a related person, (iii) the purchase of personal property from any person and its sale to a related person, or (iv) the purchase of personal property from any person on behalf of a related person, if (b) (i) the property so purchased or sold was not manufactured in the country in which the CFC is organized, and (ii) the property is purchased or sold for use, consumption, or disposition outside of the country in which the CFC is organized.[27]

In some circumstances, branches of CFCs may be treated as separate corporations. If a CFC conducts sales or purchasing activity outside its country of organization through a branch, and the use of a branch for such operations has substantially the same effect as the use of a separate corporation, the branch is treated as if it were a separate corporation.[28]

Although, as just noted, the CFC rules may treat a branch as a separate entity in some circumstances, in other situations the CFC rules apply an aggregate theory of partnerships. A CFC's distributive share of any item of partnership income must be included in the income of a U.S. shareholder if the income would have been required to be included in the U.S. shareholder's income if the income had been received directly by the CFC.[29] Similarly, to determine whether an entity is a related person and whether an activity occurred within or outside the country under the laws of which the CFC is created or organized, the determination is made by reference to the CFC and not by reference to a partnership in which the

---

[24] I.R.C. § 954(c)(1).

[25] I.R.C. § 954(c)(4)(A).

[26] I.R.C. § 954(e).

[27] I.R.C. § 954(d)(1).

[28] I.R.C. § 954(d)(2).

[29] In other words, the test is applied as if the CFC owned the right to income directly rather than through the partnership. Treas. Reg. § 1.952-1(g)(1).

CFC is a partner.[30] Also, a sale to or purchase from a partnership by a CFC will be treated as a transaction with a related entity if the CFC purchases the property from or sells the property to a person that is related to the CFC other than the partnership. A transaction will also be treated as being made with a related entity in the case where the partnership purchases personal property from (or sells personal property on behalf of) the CFC and the branch rule of I.R.C. § 954(d)(2) applies to treat the income of the CFC from selling personal property that the CFC has manufactured to the partnership (or a third party) as foreign base company income.[31]

> *Example*: CFC, a CFC organized in Country A, is an 80 percent partner in MJK Partnership, a Country B partnership. CFC purchased goods from J Corp, a Country C corporation that is a related person with respect to CFC. CFC sold the goods to MJK Partnership. In turn, MJK Partnership sold the goods to P Corp, a Country D corporation that is unrelated to CFC. P Corp sold the goods to unrelated customers in Country D. The goods were manufactured in Country C by persons unrelated to J Corp. CFC's distributive share of the income of MJK Partnership from the sale of goods to P Corp will be treated as income from the sale of goods purchased from a related person for purposes of I.R.C. § 954(d)(1) because CFC purchased the goods from J Corp, a related person. Because the goods were both manufactured and sold for use outside of Country A, CFC's distributive share of the income attributable to the sale of the goods is foreign base company sales income. Further, CFC's income from the sale of the goods to MJK Partnership will also be foreign base company sales income.[32]

In contrast with the applications of the aggregate theory of partnerships just described, in some places the CFC rules apply a hybrid entity-aggregate theory. In determining whether property sold by a partnership is considered to be manufactured, produced, or constructed by the CFC, the exclusion from foreign base company sales income for manufacturing, producing, or constructing personal property applies to exclude the income from foreign base company sales income if the CFC had earned the income directly, taking into account only the activities of, and property owned by, the partnership.[33]

> *Example*: CFC, a CFC organized under the laws of Country A, is an 80 percent partner in Partnership X, a partnership organized under the laws of Country B. Partnership X performs activities in Country B that would constitute the manufacture of Product O, if performed directly by CFC. Partnership X, through its sales offices in Country B, then sells Product O to Corp D, a corporation that is a related person with respect to CFC, within the meaning of I.R.C. § 954(d)(3), for use within Country B. CFC's distributive share of Partnership X's sales income is not foreign base

---

[30]   Treas. Reg. § 1.954-1(g)(1).

[31]   Treas. Reg. § 1.954-1(g)(2).

[32]   Treas. Reg. § 1.954-1(g)(3), example 3.

[33]   Treas. Reg. § 1.954-3(a)(6).

company sales income because the manufacturing exception of Treas. Reg. § 1.954-3(a)(4) would have applied to exclude the income from foreign base company sales income if CFC had earned the income directly.[34]

If a CFC has investments in U.S. property at the end of any quarter, a proportionate part of any earnings and profits of the CFC that are not otherwise required to be included in the U.S. shareholders' income may be required to be included in the income of the U.S. shareholders up to such shareholders' pro rata shares of such investment.[35] For the purposes of determining whether a CFC has an investment in U.S. property, if a CFC is a partner in a partnership that owns property that would be U.S. property if owned directly by the CFC, the CFC is treated as holding an interest in the property equal to its interest in the partnership and such interest is treated as an interest in U.S. property.[36]

S, a wholly owned Country *X* subsidiary of *P*, a domestic corporation, is a CFC. *S* reports its income on a calendar year basis. *S* is not engaged in any United States business activity and does not earn any income that is effectively connected with a United States trade or business. *PRS*, an entity classified as a partnership for United States Federal tax purposes, is organized under the laws of Country *X*. *S* owns a 25 percent interest in the capital and profits of *PRS*, which it purchased in 1987. The remaining 75 percent interest in *PRS* is owned by an unrelated Country *X* corporation. In 1988, *PRS* purchased undeveloped land in the United States. The land is not subject to any mortgages or other liabilities.

For purposes of I.R.C. § 956, *S* is considered to hold on the last day of its 1988 taxable year, a 25 percent interest in the undeveloped land that is owned by *PRS* on such date. The amount taken into account, for purposes of I.R.C. § 956, with respect to *S*'s 25 percent interest in the undeveloped land will be 25 percent of *PRS*'s adjusted basis in the land, limited by *S*'s total basis in *PRS*. The result would be the same if *PRS* were a domestic partnership.[37]

The Treasury has also proposed regulations that would treat the non-subpart F income of a CFC as subpart F income under certain circumstances if a hybrid branch payment is made that reduces a foreign tax and falls within a category of foreign personal holding company income.[38] A hybrid branch payment means the gross amount of any payment (including an accrual) that under the tax laws of any foreign jurisdiction to which the payor is subject is regarded as a payment between two separate entities, but is regarded under U.S. income tax rules as not income to the recipient because the payment is treated as being made between two parts of a single entity.[39] The rules relating to hybrid branches may also apply to payments

---

[34] Treas. Reg. § 1.954-3(a)(6)(ii).

[35] I.R.C. § 956(a).

[36] Treas. Reg. § 1.956-2(a)(3); Rev. Rul. 90-112, 1990-2 C.B. 186.

[37] Rev. Rul. 90-112, 1990-2 C.B. 186.

[38] Prop. Treas. Reg. § 1.954-9(a).

[39] Prop. Treas. Reg. § 1.954-9(a)(6).

between a partnership and a hybrid branch under certain circumstances.[40]

D. U.S. Source of Income Rules in Regard to Foreign Partnerships

I.R.C. § 861 generally defines payments of interest by noncorporate residents to be from U.S. sources.[41] Residents, for these purposes, generally include a foreign partnership that at any time during its taxable year is engaged in a trade or business in the United States.[42] However, in the case of a foreign partnership that is predominantly engaged in the active conduct of a trade or business outside of the United States, any interest paid by such partnership that is not paid by a trade or business engaged in by the partnership in the United States, and is not allocable to income which is effectively connected (or treated as effectively connected) with the conduct of a trade or business in the United States, is not treated as being from U.S. sources.[43]

Historically, the amount of U.S. withholding on payments to foreign partnerships, after the application of the hybrid entity rules discussed below, turned on the delivery of a U.S. Form W-8IMY by the partnership and U.S. Forms W-8BEN by the partners.

In 2010, Congress added new I.R.C. §§ 1471 through 1474 (the "FATCA rules") which add an alternative system of withholding on payments to foreign partnerships. The FATCA rules may impose a 30% withholding tax on withholdable payments made to non-U.S. persons (including foreign partnerships). Withholdable payments include interest, dividends, and the gross proceeds from the sale of stock and bonds of U.S. issuers.

If the foreign partnership is a financial institution or otherwise is in the business of investing in stocks or securities, the FATCA rules require the fund to enter into an agreement with the IRS to disclose information about the U.S. investors and any non-U.S. entities that have substantial U.S. owners in order to avoid the 30% withholding tax. If the foreign partnership is not a financial institution and not in the business of investing in stocks or securities, the FATCA rules require the disclosure of any U.S. owners to the payor of a withholding payment.

If the foreign partnership is entitled to treaty benefits, the foreign partnership may file a claim for refund for the tax paid over the amount permitted under the treaty. If the foreign partnership is not entitled to treaty benefits, the tax may be lost if the partnership meets the definition of a financial institution.[44]

The FATCA are discussed in greater detail in § 12.08, below.

---

[40] Prop. Treas. Reg. § 1.954-9(a)(2)(ii).

[41] I.R.C. § 861(a).

[42] Treas. Reg. § 1.861-2(a)(2).

[43] I.R.C. § 861(a)(1)(C).

[44] I.R.C. § 1474(b)(2)(A)(ii).

E. The Hybrid Entity Rules

The U.S. tax imposed on payments to foreign persons of items of income received by an entity that is fiscally transparent under the laws of the United States and/or any other jurisdiction is eligible for a reduction of U.S. tax under the terms of a U.S. income tax treaty only if the item of income is derived by a resident of the applicable treaty jurisdiction.[45] For these purposes, an entity is treated as being fiscally transparent if a holder of an equity interest in the entity is required to take into account the income of the entity on a current basis (whether or not the income is distributed) and the character and source of the income is determined as if the income were realized directly by the interest holder from the source of the income to the entity.[46] An item of income may be derived by either the entity receiving the item of income or by the interest holders in the entity, or both. An item of income is considered to be derived by the entity only if the entity is not fiscally transparent under the laws of the entity's jurisdiction. An item of income paid to the entity is considered to be derived by the interest holder in the entity only if the interest holder is not fiscally transparent in its jurisdiction, and the entity is fiscally transparent in the interest holder's jurisdiction.

An income tax treaty may not apply to reduce the amount of U.S. federal income tax on U.S.-source payments received by a domestic reverse hybrid entity. A domestic reverse hybrid entity is a domestic entity that is treated as not fiscally transparent for U.S. tax purposes and as fiscally transparent under the laws of the interest holder's jurisdiction, with respect to the item of income received by the domestic entity.[47] The foreign interest holders of a domestic reverse hybrid entity are not entitled to the benefits of a reduction of U.S. income tax under an income tax treaty on items of income received from U.S. sources by such entity.

For example, if A and B, both residents of Canada, formed a Delaware limited partnership AB and AB elected to be taxed as a corporation in the United States, AB would not be fiscally transparent for U.S. tax purposes, but would be fiscally transparent for Canadian tax purposes. A and B would not be eligible for treaty benefits on payments to AB.

Similarly, subject to some exceptions, an item of income paid by a domestic reverse hybrid entity to an interest holder in such entity has the character of such item of income under U.S. law and is considered to be derived by the interest holder, provided the interest holder is not fiscally transparent in its jurisdiction with respect to the item of income. In determining whether the interest holder is fiscally transparent with respect to the item of income, the determination is to be made based on the treatment that would have resulted had the item of income been paid by an entity that is not fiscally transparent under the laws of the interest holder's jurisdiction with respect to any item of income.

---

[45] Treas. Reg. § 1.894-1(d)(1).

[46] Treas. Reg. § 1.894-1(d)(3).

[47] Treas. Reg. § 1.894-1(d)(2).

§ 12.03   U.S. PARTNERSHIPS WITH FOREIGN PARTNERS

A.   General Rules Relating to U.S. Taxation of Foreign Persons

The United States taxes the income of nonresident foreign persons if the income is fixed, determinable, annual or periodic ("*FDAP Income*") from U.S. sources, or is effectively connected with the conduct of a trade or business in the United States.[48] FDAP Income includes, among other things, interest, dividends, rents, salaries, wages, premiums, annuities, compensations, remunerations, and emoluments. Capital gains of nonresident foreign individuals (other than from the disposition of a U.S. real property interests) are taxed in the United States only if the person is in the United States for 183 days or more or the gains are effectively connected with a U.S. trade or business.[49]

U.S.-source FDAP Income is generally subject to tax at a rate of 30% of the gross amount of the payment.[50] However, the amount of the tax is subject to change by any applicable tax treaty, and a number of items have independent exceptions that may cause FDAP Income to be excluded from U.S. tax. For example, although interest earned by a foreign person is nominally subject to a 30% tax, interest (other than effectively connected interest) is generally excluded from U.S. tax by the exceptions for portfolio debt investments. Interest that is effectively connected to a U.S. trade or business is subject to tax at the regular graduated tax rates.[51]

In contrast, foreign persons engaged in a U.S. trade or business are generally taxable on the taxable income (as opposed to gross income) effectively connected with the U.S. trade or business at the graduated rates provided in sections 1 and 11. Tax treaties may also exclude from U.S. tax income of a foreign person that is effectively connected to a U.S. trade or business, but the treaty exclusions would generally only apply if the foreign person does not have a permanent establishment in the United States, such as an office or other fixed place of business.[52] If a foreign person is a partner in a partnership that is engaged in a U.S. trade or business, the foreign person will also be viewed as being engaged in a U.S. trade or business.[53]

For example: P is a service partnership that is organized under the laws of Delaware. P has offices in Germany and the United States. Its U.S. office is a permanent establishment for purposes of the applicable treaty. P is comprised of two partners: A, a nonresident alien individual who is a resident of Germany under Article 4 of the Treaty, and B, a U.S. resident. A performs services solely at P's office in Germany and B performs services solely at P's office in the United States.

---

[48] I.R.C. §§ 871, 881, 882.

[49] I.R.C. § 871(a)(2).

[50] I.R.C. §§ 871(a), 881(a).

[51] I.R.C. §§ 871(h), 881(c).

[52] For these purposes, the permanent establishment of a partnership in the United States is attributable to foreign partners. Donroy, Ltd. v. United States, 301 F.2d 200 (9th Cir. 1962).

[53] I.R.C. § 875.

A and B agree to divide the profits of the partnership equally.

A is treated as having a permanent establishment regularly available to him in the United States and is subject to U.S. net income taxation on his allocable share of income from P to the extent that such income is attributable to P's fixed base in the United States, without regard to whether A performs services in the United States.[54]

The effecting of stock or securities transactions through a resident broker, commission agent, custodian, or other independent agent does not generally cause a taxpayer to be treated as engaging in a trade or business in the United States.[55] Similarly, trading in stocks or securities by a taxpayer for the taxpayer's own account is not generally engaging in a trade or business in the United States.[56] The latter statement is true also if the taxpayer is a partner in a partnership that effectuates trades for its own account.[57]

However, whether foreign investors in a U.S. real estate partnership are viewed as engaged in a U.S. trade or business may be not entirely clear during the life of the partnership.[58] Where real estate is leased, but not on a net lease basis,[59] some courts have been able to infer trade or business activity. One court found that the activity of being a lessor (other than on a net lease) necessarily:

> involved alterations and repairs commensurate with the value and the number of buildings cared for and such transactions as were necessary to constitute a recognized form of business. The management of real estate on such a scale for income producing purposes required regular and continuous activity of the kind of which is commonly concerned with the employment of labor; the purchase of materials; the making of contracts; and many other things which come within the definition of business.[60]

However, the rule that a lease (other than a net lease) will constitute a U.S. trade or business has not been applied uniformly. For example, in *Herbert v. Commissioner*,[61] the court found that an elderly English woman was not engaged in a U.S. trade or business in spite of the fact that the lease of the U.S. property that she owned obligated her to make major repairs, and pay insurance, taxes, and interest. The court cited *Pinchot*, but relied primarily on a prior case dealing with another

---

[54] Rev. Rul. 2004-3, 2004-1 C.B. 486.

[55] I.R.C. § 864(b)(2)(A)(i). This exclusion does not apply if the taxpayer has an office or other fixed place of business in the United States through which, or by direction of which, the transactions are effected. I.R.C. § 864(b)(2)(C).

[56] I.R.C. § 864(b)(2)(A)(ii). This exception does not apply in the case of a dealer in stocks or securities.

[57] Treas. Reg. § 1.864-2(c)(2)(ii).

[58] On the ultimate sale or disposition of the U.S. real property interests held by the venture, I.R.C. § 897 will statutorily cause any gain to be treated as if it were effectively connected with a U.S. trade or business.

[59] A net lease is a lease in which the tenant is responsible for some or all of the expenses of maintaining and operating the property, usually including taxes, interest, insurance, and maintenance.

[60] Pinchot v. Commissioner, 113 F.2d 718, 719 (2d Cir. 1940).

[61] 30 T.C. 26 (1958).

elderly English woman who (in regard to a net lease) had been found not to be engaged in a U.S. trade or business.[62]

In regard to net leases, a more general rule of not treating the lessor as engaged in a U.S. trade or business has developed. In Rev. Rul. 73-522,[63] where a foreign taxpayer owned rental property situated in the United States that was subject to long-term net leases, and the taxpayer was in the United States for only one week, the taxpayer was not engaged in a trade or business in the United States.

U.S. partnerships must generally withhold on FDAP Income from U.S. sources under I.R.C. §§ 1441, 1442, and 1443.[64] Withholding in respect of dispositions of U.S. real property interests is generally governed by I.R.C. § 1445.[65] Income that is effectively connected with a U.S. trade or business is, on the other hand, subject to withholding by the partnership under I.R.C. § 1446.

B. Withholding Obligations in Regard to FDAP Income

U.S. partnerships are required to withhold 30% of the gross amount of a nonresident foreign partner's distributive share of fixed or determinable annual or periodic income, whether or not such income is distributed,[66] unless the partner qualifies for a specific exception in the Code or the Regulations. Such withholding is not required in respect of income to the extent such income is exempt from withholding or subject to reduced withholding because of a treaty.[67]

As to the withholding obligation on interest payments, the Code provides for a broad exception from withholding if the recipient of the interest is not a bank, a controlled foreign corporation related to the borrower or a 10% shareholder of the borrower.[68] The IRS and Treasury have clarified that for the purposes of the 10% shareholder rule, if the debt is held by a partnership, the 10% shareholder exclusion is tested at the level of the partner rather than the level of the partnership.[69] This means that a partnership that was widely held could theoretically own 100% of the stock of a borrower from the partnership and still qualify for the portfolio interest exception.

It is currently unclear how the FATCA rules will apply to U.S. partnerships with foreign partners (see the discussion of FATCA at § 12.08). Notice 2010-60[70] has

---

[62] Neill v. Commissioner, 46 B.T.A. 197 (1942).

[63] 1973-2 C.B. 226.

[64] Treas. Reg. § 1.1441-5.

[65] The withholding obligations under I.R.C. § 1445 are not discussed in this chapter because the Regulations under I.R.C. § 1446 provide that satisfaction of the rules under such Regulations satisfy the obligations under I.R.C. § 1445. A disposition of a partnership interest by a foreign partner may still be subject to withholding under I.R.C. § 1445, because no I.R.C. § 1446 withholding would occur on such a transaction. *See* I.R.C. § 897(g).

[66] Treas. Reg. § 1.1441-5(b)(2).

[67] Treas. Reg. § 1.1441-6.

[68] I.R.C. §§ 871(h), 881(c).

[69] Treas. Reg. § 1.871-14(g)(3).

[70] 2010-2 C.B. 329.

indicated that U.S. partnerships that meet the definitions of a financial institution under I.R.C. § 1471 will be required to determine whether to treat entities to which it makes withholdable payments as U.S. persons, participating foreign financial institutions, deemed-compliant foreign financial institutions, non-participating foreign financial institutions, entities described in I.R.C. § 1471(f), excepted non-financial foreign entities, or other non-financial foreign entities, but the rules in the notice apply directly to foreign financial institutions. It is, thus, possible that final Regulations may require U.S. partnerships to undertake the same type of due diligence as to the nature of their partners as is required by the Code in regard to foreign financial institutions.

C. Withholding in Regard to Income Effectively Connected with a U.S. Trade or Business

As mentioned above, I.R.C. § 1446, in general, requires a partnership that has income that is effectively connected with a U.S. trade or business to withhold on the portion of such income that is allocable to any foreign partner. The withholding obligation applies to any income that is treated as effectively connected income, including partnership income subject to a partner's election under I.R.C. § 871(d) or I.R.C. § 882(d) to treat real property income as effectively connected with a U.S. trade or business, or income from the disposition of interests in U.S. real property.[71] A foreign partner's allocable share of partnership effectively connected income does not include income or gain that is excluded from U.S. tax by reason of a provision of the Code.[72] Similarly, withholding under I.R.C. § 1446 does not apply to income or gain that is exempt from U.S. tax by operation of any U.S. income tax treaty or other reciprocal agreement. In calculating a foreign partner's share of effectively connected income for purposes of determining the withholding obligation of the partnership, certain deductions, losses, and credits ordinarily allowable are not included or are required to be recalculated.[73]

The Code provides that the withholding on effectively connected income of foreign partners will be applied at the highest rate specified in I.R.C. § 1 or I.R.C. § 11, as applicable.[74] The Regulations interpret this requirement to generally permit the partnership to apply the highest rate of tax applicable to a particular type of income or gain.[75] The partnership is required to pay such withholding on a quarterly basis,[76] and the payment of the tax is treated as an advance against the

---

[71] Treas. Reg. § 1.1446-2(b)(2)(ii); *see* I.R.C. § 897. A partner that makes an election under I.R.C. § 871(d) or I.R.C. § 882(d) is required to furnish the partnership a statement that the election has been made. Treas. Reg. § 1.1446-2(b)(2)(ii).

[72] Treas. Reg. § 1.1446-2(b)(2)(iii).

[73] Treas. Reg. § 1.1446-2(b)(3), (4). Oil and gas depletion allowances are required to be recalculated. Charitable deductions, net operating losses, capital loss carryovers, personal exemptions, and partnership credits are not included in the calculation of the withholding obligation.

[74] I.R.C. § 1446(b).

[75] Treas. Reg. § 1.1446-3(a)(2). A partnership is only allowed to take into consideration rates that depend upon the corporate or noncorporate status of the recipient if the partnership has documentation establishing such status.

[76] Treas. Reg. § 1.1446-3(b)(1).

foreign partner's share of partnership profits.[77]

Although I.R.C. § 1445 normally applies to withholding on the amount realized from dispositions of U.S. real property, the Regulations provide that a U.S. partnership that satisfies its withholding obligations under I.R.C. § 1446 will be deemed to have also satisfied its obligations under I.R.C. § 1445.[78]

In general, where a partnership (a "*lower tier partnership*") that has effectively connected income has a partner that is itself treated as a partnership for U.S. tax purposes (an "*upper tier partnership*"), the lower tier partnership is not required to withhold tax with respect to the upper tier partnership's allocable share of net income if the upper tier partnership is domestic, regardless of whether the upper tier domestic partnership's partners are foreign.[79] If the upper tier partnership is foreign, the lower tier partnership generally computes its withholding obligation based upon documentation provided to it relating to the identity and nationality of the partners of the upper tier partnership.[80] Such look-through rules do not apply, however, if the upper tier partnership is publicly traded.[81]

As discussed above, a partnership normally only takes into account certain specified partnership level deductions and losses in calculating partnership's effectively connected taxable income.[82] Under certain circumstances, partnership may also consider partner level deductions and losses in computing its I.R.C. § 1446 tax obligation.[83] A partnership may only consider such partner level deductions and losses if: (i) a foreign partner has submitted valid documentation as to the partner's identity and nationality; and (ii) the foreign partner submits a certificate to the partnership that sets forth the deductions and losses that such partner reasonably expects to be available for the partner's taxable year to reduce the partner's U.S. income tax liability on the partner's allocable share of effectively connected income or gain from the partnership. A foreign partner must submit a separate certificate for each partnership taxable year.

The foreign partner against whose share the tax has been withheld is entitled to apply the withholding tax as a credit against the partner's other U.S. income tax liabilities.[84]

D.   Branch Profits Tax

As mentioned above, foreign corporations are subject to U.S. tax on income that is effectively connected with the conduct of a U.S. trade or business. In addition, foreign corporations engaged in a U.S. trade or business may be subject to a

---

[77] Treas. Reg. § 1.1446-3(d)(2)(v).

[78] Treas. Reg. § 1.1446-3(c)(2)(i).

[79] Treas. Reg. § 1.1446-5(a).

[80] Treas. Reg. § 1.1446-5(c).

[81] Treas. Reg. § 1.1446-5(d)(1).

[82] Treas. Reg. § 1.1446-2(b).

[83] Treas. Reg. § 1.1446-6(a). This procedure is not available to publicly traded partnerships. Treas. Reg. § 1.1446-6(b)(1).

[84] I.R.C. § 1446(d)(1).

second tax, a "branch profits tax" under I.R.C. § 884. Generally, the branch profits tax is a tax imposed on a foreign corporation's post-1987 U.S. business profits that are not reinvested in U.S. branch operations. The tax is imposed at 30% of a calculated "dividend equivalent amount."[85] In effect, the branch profits tax is a substitute for a tax on dividends that would be imposed if the U.S. branch were a separately incorporated domestic subsidiary. A U.S. tax treaty may apply to reduce the rate of the branch profits tax applied to qualified residents of the country whose treaty is applied.[86]

The dividend equivalent amount is based in part upon increases and decreases in a foreign corporation's U.S. assets over U.S. liabilities. A foreign corporation's ownership of an interest in a domestic partnership is treated as a U.S. asset for the purposes of calculating the branch profits tax.[87] Calculation of the branch profits tax requires, among other things, a determination of the partnership's items of income, gain, loss, and deduction.[88]

E. Disposition of Interests in U.S. Partnerships by Non-U.S. Persons

In general, the disposition of a partnership interest results in gain or loss treated as gain or loss from the sale or exchange of a capital asset, except as provided in I.R.C. § 751, relating to unrealized receivables and inventory items.[89] Gain or loss recognized by a nonresident, foreign person is generally not subject to tax in the United States, unless the gain is effectively connected with a U.S. trade or business.[90]

A foreign partner's gain or loss from the disposition of an interest in a partnership that is engaged in a trade or business through a fixed place of business in the United States will be effectively connected income, gain or loss to the extent such gain or loss is attributable to effectively connected income property of the partnership.[91] The gain or loss attributable to the effectively connected income property of the partnership is an amount that bears the same ratio to the gain or loss realized by the foreign partner from the disposition of its partnership interest as the foreign partner's distributive share of partnership net effectively connected income gain or loss would have borne to the foreign partner's distributive share of partnership net gain or loss if the partnership had itself disposed of all of its assets at fair market value at the time the foreign partner disposes of its partnership

---

[85] I.R.C. § 884(a).

[86] I.R.C. § 884(e). However, a foreign corporation is exempt from the branch profits tax for the taxable year in which it completely terminates its U.S. trade or business. Treas. Reg. § 1.884-2T(a).

[87] Treas. Reg. § 1.884-1(d)(3)(i).

[88] Treas. Reg. § 1.884-1(d)(6)(iii).

[89] I.R.C. § 741.

[90] I.R.C. §§ 871, 881. This rule is subject to some exceptions. For example, non-U.S. individuals who are present in the United States for 183 days or more are subject to U.S. tax on U.S. source gains.

[91] Rev. Rul. 91-32, 1991-1 C.B. 107. The rule established by Rev. Rul. 91-32 does not apply to effectively connected property that is a U.S. real property interest. Dispositions of partnerships that hold U.S. real property interests are governed by I.R.C. § 897(g). *Id.*

interest. In computing the foreign partner's distributive share of net gain or loss of the partnership, net effectively connected income gain or loss, and net non-effectively connected gain or loss are computed independently of one another. Thus, net non-effectively connected loss will not offset effectively connected gain, and net effectively connected loss will not offset net non-effectively connected gain.

If the consideration received on the disposition of a partnership interest is attributable to a U.S. real property interest, the consideration may be considered as an amount received in exchange for the U.S. real property interest.[92] Regulations provide that if 50% or more of the value of an interest in a partnership is attributable to U.S. real property interests, the partnership interest may be treated as being entirely a U.S. real property interest.[93]

§ 12.04   PARTNERSHIPS WITH TAX-EXEMPT ENTITIES

Exempt organizations, like foreign taxpayers, are very sensitive to being determined to be engaged in a trade or business as that can cause the associated income to be taxable or cause the exempt organization to lose its exempt status. Exempt organizations, like foreign taxpayers, have significant categories of income that are not subject to tax. For this reason, it is not uncommon for investment structures to combine foreign taxpayers and exempt organizations, but there are also significant differences in the U.S. tax treatments of the two groups of investors that raise issues when the two are combined.

A.   Impact on the Organization's Exempt Status

Where exempt organizations enter into joint ventures with for-profit organizations to conduct active trades or businesses rather than just collect investment income, the structure and operation of the joint venture may impact both the taxability of the income derived by the charity from the joint venture and the charity's tax-exempt status. The creation of unrelated business taxable income is discussed in greater detail below. The charity's tax-exempt status is implicated because to maintain its status the charity must not only be organized, but must also be operated exclusively for charitable purposes.[94] If an activity of the organization is substantial, an activity may destroy the exempt status of the organization even if the organization is undertaking other activities with valid charitable purposes.[95]

The fact that a charity undertakes a trade or business does not itself cause a loss of the charity's exempt status, if the trade or business furthers the exempt purpose of the charity.[96] Since *Plumstead Theatre Society v. Commissioner*,[97] the IRS has

---

[92] I.R.C. § 897(g).

[93] Treas. Reg. § 1.897-7T. This rule only applies if the percentage of gross assets of the partnership that are comprised of U.S. real property interests and cash equals or exceeds 90%.

[94] I.R.C. § 501(c)(3); Treas. Reg. § 1.501(c)(3)-1(c)(1).

[95] *See* Better Bus. Bureau, Inc. v. United States, 326 U.S. 279, 283 (1945).

[96] *See* Federation Pharmacy Servs., Inc. v. Commissioner, 72 T.C. 687, 691 (1979), *aff'd*, 625 F.2d 804 (8th Cir. 1980).

[97] 74 T.C. 1324 (1980), *aff'd*, 675 F.2d 244 (9th Cir. 1982).

permitted joint ventures between charities and for-profit entities, in limited situations, without causing the exempt status of the charity to be jeopardized.

Where the operations of the joint venture in reality comprise the total operations of the charity, the IRS will allow the creation of the joint venture to not terminate the charity's tax-exempt status if: (i) the charity controls the governing body of the joint venture without regard to the percentage of the joint venture held by the charity, (ii) any management company and the joint venture executives are independent of the for-profit joint venturer, and (iii) the members of the joint venture's governing body have a legally enforceable duty to promote charitable purposes that takes precedence over the duty of such persons to operate the venture for the benefit of the owners.[98] The standards applied by the IRS have continued to be controversial, and the final resolution of the standards by the courts is uncertain at this time.[99]

The IRS has applied somewhat more liberal standards where the operations of the joint venture are insubstantial in comparison to the total operations of the charity.[100] Where the activity is insubstantial, the charity's participation in the joint venture, taken alone, will not affect the charity's tax-exempt status.[101]

B. Unrelated Business Taxable Income

Like foreign taxpayers, exempt organizations that are determined to be engaged in a trade or business may be subject to U.S. tax without regard to their normally exempt status.

Tax-exempt organizations are, in general, taxable on unrelated business taxable income ("*UBTI*").[102] If a trade or business that would generate UBTI to an exempt organization is conducted by a partnership, an exempt organization that is a partner in the partnership includes its share of the UBTI of the partnership whether or not such UBTI is distributed.[103] UBTI starts with gross income from any unrelated trade or business that is regularly carried on.[104] From this gross income, some types of income are subtracted. Deductions directly related to the unrelated trade or business may also be subtracted.[105]

An activity does not constitute an unrelated trade or business if the activity relates to the organization's exempt purpose. An activity relates to an

---

[98] Rev. Rul. 98-15, 1998-1 C.B. 718.

[99] *See* Redlands Surgical Services v. Commissioner, 113 T.C. 47 (1999), *aff'd*, 242 F.3d 904 (9th Cir. 2001); St. David's Health Care System v. United States, 349 F.3d 232 (5th Cir. 2003).

[100] Rev. Rul. 2004-51, 2004-1 C.B. 974.

[101] *Id.* In addition, the IRS ruled that if the activities of the joint venture contribute importantly to the accomplishment of the charity's exempt purpose, the income will not be subject to unrelated business income tax.

[102] I.R.C. § 511(a).

[103] I.R.C. § 512(c).

[104] Unrelated trade or business income also includes unrelated debt-financed income, discussed below.

[105] Calculated with certain modifications. I.R.C. § 512(a)(1).

organization's exempt purpose when the activity makes an important contribution to achieving the exempt purpose. A trade or business does not relate to an exempt purpose solely because the organization needs money for its exempt purpose.[106]

Entering an unrelated business with another exempt organization will not make the business a related activity. For example, renting to an exempt organization will not always relate to the landlord's exempt purpose. It will relate only if the tenant uses the property in an activity related to the landlord's exempt purpose.[107]

An activity in which almost all the work is done without pay is not an unrelated trade or business.[108] An activity primarily for the convenience of members, students, patients, officers, or employees is not an unrelated trade or business.[109] Selling donated goods is not an unrelated trade or business.[110] "Trade or business" does not include the distribution of low-cost items as part of asking for contributions.[111]

"Trade or business" includes most activities carried on for the production of income. It includes the sale of goods and the performance of services.[112] An activity may still be a trade or business even if it does not make a profit.[113] However, if an organization does not intend to make a profit from an activity and the activity is run at a loss, the activity is not a trade or business.[114]

A business is still a business even if it is part of a larger activity.[115] For example, selling advertising is a business even though an exempt organization publishes the advertising with material related to the exempt purpose of the organization.[116]

In general, an activity is "regularly carried on" by an exempt organization if its frequency and length are like the activities of for-profit groups in the same business.[117] If an exempt organization periodically engages in an activity, without the competitive and promotional efforts typical of for-profit groups, the activity will not be "regularly carried on."[118]

UBTI generally excludes: (i) dividends, interest, certain security loan payments, and annuities; (ii) royalties based upon income; (iii) most rents from real property; (iv) capital gains; and (v) some types of research income.

---

[106] I.R.C. § 513(a).

[107] Rev. Rul. 58-547, 1958-2 C.B. 275.

[108] Treas. Reg. § 1.513-1(e)(1).

[109] Treas. Reg. § 1.513-1(e)(2).

[110] Treas. Reg. § 1.513-1(e)(3).

[111] Treas. Reg. § 1.513-1(b).

[112] *Id.*

[113] *Id.*

[114] Iowa State University of Science and Technology v. United States, 500 F.2d 508 (Ct. Cl. 1974); Rev. Rul. 81-69, 1981-1 C.B. 351.

[115] Treas. Reg. § 1.513-1(b).

[116] *Id.*

[117] Treas. Reg. § 1.513-1(c)(1).

[118] Treas. Reg. § 1.513-1(c)(2)(ii).

In general, I.R.C. § 512(b)(3) excludes from UBTI rents from real property. However, Treas. Reg. § 1.512(b)-1(c)(5) provides that payments for the use of space where services are also rendered to the occupant do not constitute rent from real property. The Regulation clarifies, though, that services are considered rendered to the occupant if they are primarily for his convenience and are other than those usually or customarily rendered in connection with the rental of space. The supplying of maid service, for example, constitutes a service provided for the convenience of the occupant that is not customary. On the other hand, furnishing heat and light, cleaning public areas, collecting trash are not considered services rendered to the occupant because they are customarily rendered in connection with the rental of space.[119]

The Regulation also provides that payments for the use or occupancy of offices in any office building are generally rent from real property.[120] Also, rent from real property may not depend upon the income derived by any person from the property.[121]

C. Debt-Financed Income

Debt-financed income is an area in which the treatment of exempt organizations diverges significantly from the treatment of foreign taxpayers. Foreign taxpayers have no special treatment of debt-financed income. Exempt organizations, on the other hand, are taxable on otherwise excludable income if the income is unrelated debt-financed income. Unrelated debt-financed income includes income from property subject to acquisition indebtedness.[122] Acquisition indebtedness includes: (i) indebtedness incurred before the acquisition of the property if such indebtedness would not have been incurred but for such acquisition and (ii) indebtedness incurred after the acquisition of the property if such indebtedness would not have been incurred but for such acquisition and the indebtedness was reasonably foreseeable at the time of such acquisition.[123]

Excluded from unrelated debt-financed income is income from property used in the exempt purpose of the organization.[124] If an organization acquires real property for the principal purpose of using the land (within 10 years of the acquisition) in a manner substantially related to the exempt purpose of the organization and the property is in the neighborhood of other property owned by the organization and used in a manner related to its exempt purpose, the real property acquired for future use shall not be treated as debt-financed property so long as the organization does not abandon its intent to use the property in a manner related to its exempt purpose.[125] However, this exception will apply after

---

[119] Treas. Reg. § 1.512(b)-1(c)(5).

[120] *Id.*

[121] Treas. Reg. § 1.512(b)-1(c)(2)(iii)(b).

[122] I.R.C. § 514(a).

[123] I.R.C. § 514(c).

[124] I.R.C. § 514(b).

[125] I.R.C. § 514(b)(3)(A). Churches have a 15-year period rather than a 10-year period and are not required to meet the neighborhood test.

the fifth year only if the organization establishes to the satisfaction of the IRS that it is reasonably certain that the land will be used in a manner related to the organization's exempt purpose before the expiration of the tenth year. If the exception is inapplicable because either: (i) the land was not in the neighborhood of other land owned by the organization, or (ii) the organization was unable to establish to the satisfaction of the IRS that it was reasonably certain that the land would be used in a manner related to the organization's exempt purpose, but (iii) the land is converted to a use related to the exempt purpose of the organization within the 10-year period, then (iv) the land will not be treated as debt-financed property during the 10-year period (even prior to the conversion).[126]

The 10-year related use exception does not apply to structures that are on the land when acquired unless the intended use of the land requires that the structure be demolished.[127] The exception also does not apply to structures erected on the property after it is acquired. The exception also does not apply to a "business lease."

Certain exempt organizations (schools, trusts of qualified pension and profit-sharing plans, and certain title holding companies) will not be considered to have acquisition indebtedness in regard to indebtedness incurred to acquire or improve any real property if: (i) the property is acquired for a fixed price, (ii) the timing and amounts of payments are not contingent upon the income of the property, (iii) the property is not leased to a related party, (iv) the property is not acquired from certain related parties, and (v) the financing of the purchase was not provided by a related party.[128]

If certain conditions are met, debt allocated to an exempt organization of the type described in the preceding paragraph by a partnership that holds real estate will also be excluded from "acquisition indebtedness."[129] To qualify for this exclusion, the partnership must meet all the tests in the preceding paragraph and: (i) all partners must be exempt organizations, (ii) all allocations must be consistent over the life of the partnership, or (iii) the allocations of income to any exempt organization must not be greater than the allocations of loss to such exempt organization for any year of the partnership and each allocation with respect to the partnership has substantial economic effect within the meaning of I.R.C. § 704(b)(2).[130] In determining an exempt organization's share of allocations of income, certain chargebacks, reasonable preferred returns, and reasonable guaranteed payments are disregarded.[131]

---

[126] I.R.C. § 514(b)(3)(B); Treas. Reg. § 1.514(b)-1(d)(2). From a practical perspective, the organization in this case would generally treat the income from property as debt-financed income until the conversion and then seek a refund of the taxes paid after the actual use condition is satisfied. *See* Treas. Reg. § 1.514(b)-1(d)(4).

[127] I.R.C. § 514(b)(3)(C).

[128] I.R.C. § 514(c)(9)(B).

[129] I.R.C. § 514(c)(9)(B)(vi).

[130] I.R.C. § 514(c)(9)(E). The Regulations interpret "substantial economic effect" to include, for these purposes, allocations that are deemed to be in accordance with the partners' interests in the partnership. Treas. Reg. § 1.514(c)-2(b)(1)(ii).

[131] Treas. Reg. § 1.514(c)-2(d), (e).

§ 12.05   LIMITATIONS ON DEDUCTIONS ALLOCABLE TO PROPERTY USED BY TAX-EXEMPT ENTITIES

A.   General Rule on Limitation on Losses

I.R.C. § 470 expands the loss limitation approach in I.R.C. § 469 to tax-exempt use losses. Under I.R.C. § 470(a), a taxable entity is not permitted to deduct any loss from tax-exempt use property in excess of the taxpayer's gross income from the property for that taxable year. Under I.R.C. § 470(b), any such excess non-deductible tax-exempt use loss with respect to any tax-exempt use property is suspended and treated as a deduction with respect to such property in the next taxable year. A taxable partner may use a suspended tax-exempt use loss when the taxpayer disposes of its entire interest in the tax-exempt use property (under rules similar to those in I.R.C. § 469(g)).[132] Thus, if a partnership has any tax-exempt use property, the portion of any loss that is a suspended tax-exempt use loss will generally not be deductible by a taxable partner until the property is sold.

A tax-exempt use loss is defined as the amount by which the sum of the aggregate deductions (other than interest) directly allocable to a tax-exempt use property plus the aggregate deductions for interest properly allocable to such property exceed the aggregate income from such property.[133] "Tax-exempt use property" is generally defined for purposes of I.R.C. § 470 by reference to I.R.C. § 168(h), which provides (in I.R.C. § 168(h)(1)(A)) that tax-exempt use property means that portion of any tangible property (other than nonresidential real property) leased to a tax-exempt or foreign entity.

In the case of nonresidential real property, I.R.C. § 168(h)(1)(B)(i) provides that tax-exempt use property means the portion of the property leased to a tax-exempt or foreign entity in a "disqualified lease." A disqualified lease is defined in I.R.C. § 168(h)(1)(B)(ii) as any lease of the property to a tax-exempt entity, but only if: (i) part or all of the property was financed (directly or indirectly) by tax-exempt debt, (ii) under such lease there is a fixed or determinable purchase or sale option, (iii) the lease has a term in excess of 20 years, or (iv) there is a sale-leaseback with respect to the property. There are a number of exceptions in I.R.C. § 168(h)(1), including an exception where the property is used in an unrelated trade or business of the tax-exempt entity. Also, under I.R.C. § 168(h)(1)(B)(iii), nonresidential real property is not treated as tax-exempt use property unless more than 35% of the property is leased to tax-exempt entities.

Although I.R.C. § 470 generally defines "tax-exempt use property" by reference to I.R.C. § 168(h), it makes several important exceptions as well. First, the exceptions in I.R.C. § 168(h) for short-term leases and leases of high technology equipment do not apply for purposes of I.R.C. § 470.[134] Second, for purposes of applying I.R.C. § 470, any I.R.C. § 197 intangible, or any property described in

---

[132]   I.R.C. § 470(e)(2). I.R.C. § 470 generally applies to leases of tax-exempt use property entered into after March 12, 2004.

[133]   I.R.C. § 470(c)(1).

[134]   I.R.C. § 470(c)(2)(A).

I.R.C. § 167(f)(1)(B) (computer software) or I.R.C. § 167(f)(2) (intangible assets that are separately acquired), is treated as if it were tangible property, so that the utilization of such property by a tax-exempt entity could give rise to a lease.[135] However, I.R.C. § 470 does not apply to property which is treated as tax-exempt use property solely because the property is owned by a partnership that has tax-exempt partners.[136]

B. Special Application to Partnerships

Included in the cross-reference to I.R.C. § 168(h) in the definition of "tax-exempt use property" in I.R.C. § 470 are the provisions of I.R.C. § 168(h)(6), which particularly apply to partnerships with tax-exempt or foreign partners. I.R.C. § 168(h)(6) provides that if: (i) any property which would otherwise not be tax-exempt use property is owned by a partnership which has both a tax-exempt or foreign entity and a person who is not a tax-exempt or foreign entity as partners, and (ii) any allocation to the tax-exempt or foreign entity of partnership items is not a "qualified allocation," an amount equal to such tax-exempt entity's proportionate share of such property is treated as tax-exempt use property. A qualified allocation is any allocation to a tax-exempt entity which has substantial economic effect and which is consistent with such entity being allocated the same distributive share of each item of income, gain, loss, deduction, credit and basis, and such share remains the same during the entire period the entity is a partner in the partnership.[137] The proportionate share of the tax-exempt entity is such entity's largest proportionate share of income or gain of the partnership (excluding gain allocated under I.R.C. § 704(c)), and if allocations vary during the period in which the tax-exempt entity is a partner, only the highest share is taken into account.[138] Similar rules apply in the case of any pass-through entity other than a partnership and to tiered partnerships.

A "qualified allocation" requires a pro rata allocation that never varies — a preferred return, incentive allocations, or any type of carried interest would not be consistent with a "qualified allocation." As you learned in Chapter 5, the requirement that qualified allocations have substantial economic effect could also be interpreted to exclude allocations of nonrecourse deductions, because such deductions do not have economic effect.[139] Regulations under I.R.C. § 514(c)(9) interpret "substantial economic effect" to include allocations that are deemed to be in accordance with the partners' interests in the partnership (and, thus, permit allocations of nonrecourse deductions),[140] but Regulations under I.R.C. § 168(h) do not explicitly include allocations that are deemed to be in accordance with the partners' interests in the partnership within the meaning of allocations that have

---

[135] I.R.C. § 470(c)(2)(B).

[136] I.R.C. § 470(c)(2).

[137] I.R.C. § 168(h)(6)(B).

[138] I.R.C. § 168(h)(6)(C).

[139] Treas. Reg. § 1.704-2(b)(1).

[140] Treas. Reg. § 1.514(c)-2(b)(1)(ii).

"substantial economic effect."[141]

C. Exceptions

"Tax-exempt use property" does not include property which would otherwise be tax-exempt use property solely by reason of the application of I.R.C. § 168(h)(6) (discussed above) if a low-income housing credit or a rehabilitation credit is allowable with respect to such property.[142]

There is also an exception in I.R.C. § 470(d) for certain leases which meet very narrow requirements:

> (1) The tax-exempt lessee may not have more than an "allowable amount" of funds subject to either (i) any arrangement described in I.R.C. § 470(d)(1)(B) or (ii) any arrangement under which a reasonable person would conclude, based on the facts and circumstances, that funds were set aside or expected to be set aside. I.R.C. § 470(d)(1)(B) refers to a defeasance arrangement, a loan by the lessee to the lessor or any lender, a deposit arrangement, a letter of credit collateralized with cash or cash equivalents, a payment undertaking agreement, prepaid rent, a sinking fund arrangement, a guaranteed investment contract, financial guaranty insurance, and any similar arrangement. An "allowable amount" of funds is generally equal to 20 percent of the lessor's adjusted basis in the property at the time the lease is entered into, although a higher percentage could be allowed by regulation.[143] If the lessee has the option to purchase property for a fixed price or for other than the fair market value of the property (determined at the time of exercise), the allowable amount at the time such option may be exercised may not exceed 50 percent of the price at which such option may be exercised;[144]

> (2) The taxpayer must make and maintain a substantial equity investment in the leased property. For this purpose, the taxpayer generally does not make or maintain a substantial equity investment unless (x) at the time the lease is entered into, the taxpayer initially makes an unconditional at-risk equity investment in the property of at least 20 percent of the taxpayer's adjusted basis in the leased property at that time, and (y) the taxpayer maintains such equity investment throughout the lease term;[145]

---

[141] Treas. Reg. § 1.168(j)-1T, A-22. The Regulations do allow allocations required under I.R.C. § 704(c) to be disregarded for these purposes.

[142] I.R.C. § 470(c).

[143] I.R.C. § 470(d)(1)(C)(i). This amount is reduced to zero with respect to any arrangement which involves (i) a loan from the lessee to the lessor or a lender, (ii) any deposit received, letter of credit issued, or payment undertaking entered into by a lender otherwise involved in the transaction, or (iii) in the case of a transaction which involves a lender, any credit support made available to the lessor in which any such lender does not have a claim that is senior to the lessor.

[144] I.R.C. § 470(d)(1)(C)(iii).

[145] This requirement does not apply to leases with a term of five years or less.

(3) At all times during the lease term, the fair market value of the property at the end of the lease term is reasonably expected to equal at least 20 percent of its initial value;[146]

(4) There is no arrangement under which the lessee bears (i) any portion of the loss that would occur if the fair market value of the leased property were 25 percent less than its reasonably expected fair market value at the time the lease is terminated, or (ii) more than 50 percent of the loss that would occur if the fair market value of the leased property at the time the lease is terminated were zero;[147] and

(5) If the property has a class life of more than seven years (other than fixed-wing aircraft) and if the lessee has the option to purchase the property, the purchase price must be equal to the fair market value of the property at the time of exercise of the purchase option.

D.   Application to Like-Kind Exchanges and Condemnations

There are several special rules under I.R.C. § 470 that further broaden its potential impact on taxpayers in general and partnerships in particular. First, I.R.C. §§ 1031(a) and 1033(a) will not apply if the exchanged or converted property is tax-exempt use property subject to a lease which was entered into before March 13, 2004, and which would not have met the requirements for an exempt lease under I.R.C. § 470(d) had such requirements been in effect.[148] Furthermore, I.R.C. §§ 1031(a) and 1033(a) will not apply to an exchange if the replacement property is tax-exempt use property subject to a lease which is not an exempt lease under I.R.C. § 470(d).[149] Thus, every acquirer of leased replacement property will need to determine whether there is any tax-exempt or foreign user of the property. In addition, an acquirer of leased replacement property will generally need to determine if the seller is a partnership or other pass-through entity that has an exempt or foreign person as an owner. If the seller has an exempt or foreign user or an exempt or foreign owner, the seller will generally also need to verify that the lease satisfies the requirements of I.R.C. § 470(d).

§ 12.06   COMPARISON WITH S CORPORATIONS

Foreign corporations and nonresident foreign individuals are not eligible to be S corporation shareholders.[150] Organizations that are exempt from U.S. tax under I.R.C. § 501(a) may be S corporation shareholders, but, for the majority of them, all items of income, loss, or deduction from the S corporation and any gain or loss on the disposition of the stock of the S corporation must be taken into account as

---

[146] I.R.C. § 470(d)(2)(A)(ii).

[147] I.R.C. § 470(d)(3). The IRS is granted authority to issue Regulations under which this requirement is not met if the lessee bears more than a minimal risk of loss.

[148] I.R.C. § 470(e)(4)(A)(i).

[149] I.R.C. § 470(e)(4)(A)(ii).

[150] I.R.C. § 1361. There is a narrow exception to this in the case of a foreign corporation that is exempt from U.S. taxation under I.R.C. § 501(a).

unrelated business taxable income of the exempt organization.[151] Thus, for both foreign taxpayers and exempt organizations, an entity treated as a partnership is generally a preferable investment vehicle to an S corporation.

§ 12.07   COVERED ASSET ACQUISITIONS

In general, certain elections or transactions can result in the creation of additional asset basis eligible for cost recovery for U.S. tax purposes without a corresponding increase in the basis of such assets for foreign tax purposes. These include: (i) a qualifying stock purchase of a foreign corporation or domestic corporation with foreign assets for which an I.R.C. § 338 election is made; (ii) an acquisition of an interest in a partnership holding foreign assets for which an I.R.C. § 754 election is in effect; and (iii) certain other transactions involving an entity classification ("*check-the-box*") election in which a foreign entity is treated as a corporation for foreign tax purposes and as a partnership or disregarded entity for U.S. tax purposes.[152]

As we have previously discussed, a partnership does not generally adjust the basis of partnership property following the transfer of a partnership interest unless the partnership has made a one-time election under I.R.C. § 754 for such purposes.[153] If an election is in effect (or if such adjustments are otherwise required), adjustments to the basis of partnership property are made with respect to the transferee partner to account for the difference between the transferee partner's proportionate share of the adjusted basis of the partnership property and the transferee's basis in its partnership interest. Because an I.R.C. § 754 election has relevance only for U.S. tax purposes, to the extent that the underlying assets of the partnership include assets generating income subject to foreign tax, the basis adjustments made to these assets may also result in permanent differences between: (i) the foreign taxable income upon which foreign income tax is levied, and (ii) the U.S. taxable income (or earnings and profits, depending upon the context) upon which U.S. tax is levied (whether currently or upon repatriation) and with respect to which a foreign tax credit may be allowed for any foreign income taxes paid.

Similar permanent differences between foreign taxable income and U.S. taxable income (or earnings and profits) may also be achieved as a result of making a check-the-box election. Since a check-the-box election generally has no effect for foreign tax purposes, a sale of a wholly owned foreign corporation for which an election to be disregarded is in effect will be respected as the sale of the stock of the corporation for foreign tax purposes, but treated as the sale of branch assets for U.S. tax purposes. If the purchaser is a U.S. taxpayer or a foreign entity owned by a U.S. taxpayer, the U.S. taxpayer may have additional asset basis eligible for cost recovery for U.S. tax purposes without a corresponding increase in the tax basis of such assets for foreign tax purposes. In this case, there would be a permanent

---

[151]   I.R.C. § 512(e).

[152]   Treas. Reg. § 301.7701-1 *et seq.*

[153]   I.R.C. § 743(a). *But see* I.R.C. § 743(d) (requiring a reduction to the basis of partnership property in certain cases where there is a substantial built-in loss).

difference between U.S. and foreign income, as described above.

When differences are created between U.S. and foreign income, I.R.C. § 901(m) denies a foreign tax credit for the disqualified portion of any foreign income tax paid or accrued in connection with a covered asset acquisition.

A "covered asset acquisition" means: (i) a qualified stock purchase (as defined in I.R.C. § 338(d)(3)); (ii) any transaction that is treated as the acquisition of assets for U.S. tax purposes and as the acquisition of stock (or is disregarded) for purposes of the foreign income taxes of the relevant jurisdiction; (iii) any acquisition of an interest in a partnership that has an election in effect under I.R.C. § 754; and (iv) to the extent provided by the IRS, any other similar transaction.

The disqualified portion of any foreign income taxes paid or accrued with respect to any covered asset acquisition, for any taxable year, is the ratio (expressed as a percentage) of: (i) the aggregate basis differences allocable to such taxable year with respect to all relevant foreign assets, divided by (ii) the income on which the foreign income tax is determined. For this purpose, the income on which the foreign income tax is determined is the income as determined under the law of the relevant jurisdiction. If the taxpayer fails to substantiate such income, then such income is determined by dividing the amount of such foreign income tax by the highest marginal tax rate applicable to such income in the relevant jurisdiction.

For purposes of determining the aggregate basis difference allocable to a taxable year, the term "basis difference" means, with respect to any relevant foreign asset, the excess of: (i) the adjusted basis of such asset immediately after the covered asset acquisition, over (ii) the adjusted basis of such asset immediately before the covered asset acquisition.[154] Thus, it is the tax basis for U.S. tax purposes that is relevant, and not the basis as determined under the law of the relevant foreign jurisdiction.

In general, the amount of the basis difference allocable to a taxable year with respect to any relevant foreign asset is determined using the applicable cost recovery method under U.S. tax rules. If there is a disposition of any relevant foreign asset before its cost has been entirely recovered or of any relevant foreign asset that is not eligible for cost recovery (e.g., land), the basis difference allocated to the taxable year of the disposition is the excess of the basis difference with respect to such asset over the aggregate basis difference with respect to such asset that has been allocated under I.R.C. § 901(m) to all prior taxable years. Thus, any remaining basis difference is captured in the year of the sale, and there is no remaining basis difference to be allocated to any subsequent tax years.

An asset is a "relevant foreign asset" with respect to any covered asset acquisition, whether the entity acquired is domestic or foreign, only if any income, deduction, gain, or loss attributable to the asset (including goodwill, going concern value, and any other intangible asset) is taken into account in determining foreign income tax in the relevant jurisdiction. For this purpose, the term "foreign income

---

[154] A built-in loss in a relevant foreign asset (i.e., in cases in which the fair market value of the asset is less than its adjusted basis immediately before the asset acquisition) is taken into account in determining the aggregate basis difference; however, a built-in loss cannot reduce the aggregate basis difference allocable to a taxable year below zero.

tax" means any income, war profits, or excess profits tax paid or accrued to any foreign country or to any possession of the United States, including any tax paid in lieu of such a tax within the meaning of I.R.C. § 903.

§ 12.08 FATCA

In addition to the regular rules relating to withholding on payments to non-U.S. persons under I.R.C. §§ 1441–1446, the United States has a second-tier withholding system designed to force non-U.S. persons to disclose the identities of U.S. persons having economic relations with the payee.

I.R.C. §§ 1471 and 1472 impose a 30% withholding tax on withholdable payments to non-U.S. persons if the non-U.S. person does not comply with U.S. disclosure requirements. In general, a withholdable payment includes: (i) any payment of interest (including original issue discount), dividends, rents, salaries, wages, premiums, annuities, compensations, remunerations, emoluments, and other fixed or determinable annual or periodic gains, profits, and income if such payment is from U.S. sources, and (ii) any gross proceeds from the sale or other disposition of any property of a type that can produce interest or dividends from U.S. sources.[155]

Withholdable payments do not include any item of income that is effectively connected with a U.S. trade or business that is taken into account under I.R.C. § 871(b) or 882, dealing with income that is effectively connected income with a U.S. trade or business.[156]

Gross proceeds from the sale of stocks and securities may be withholdable payments without regard to whether U.S. source rules would characterize any gain or loss generated by the sale as U.S.-source income or loss. For example, U.S. source rules would generally treat the income from the sale of U.S. stock and securities by a non-U.S. person as not being U.S.-source income.[157] However, the distribution of the gross proceeds of the sale of stock and securities may be a withholdable payment even though the income would not be U.S. source. The distribution of proceeds from the sale of stocks or securities may be a withholdable payment even if there is no income. In other words, the withholding may apply even if a loss is recognized.

As mentioned above, I.R.C. § 1471 will impose 30% withholding on withholdable payments to non-U.S. financial institutions[158] if the financial institution does not agree to comply with certain U.S. due diligence and reporting requirements. In general, each financial institution will need to determine and disclose information

---

[155] I.R.C. § 1473(1)(A).

[156] I.R.C. § 1473(1)(B).

[157] I.R.C. § 865(a)(2).

[158] A financial institution is any entity that (i) accepts deposits in the ordinary course of a banking or similar business, (ii) as a substantial portion of its business, holds financial assets for the account of others, or (iii) is engaged (or holds itself out as being engaged) primarily in the business of investing, reinvesting, or trading in securities, partnership interests, commodities, or any interest (including a futures or forward contract or option) in such securities, partnership interests, or commodities. A financial institution would include a hedge fund or a private equity fund.

concerning the identity and amounts of depository accounts, custodial accounts, and equity or debt investments (other than interests which are regularly traded on an established securities market) in the financial institution of specified U.S. persons[159] or U.S.-owned non-U.S. entities.[160]

Withholding is generally not required if an agreement is in effect between the non-U.S. financial institution and the U.S. Treasury under which the institution agrees to collect and disclose taxpayer information about its depositors, shareholders, and investors.[161]

I.R.C. § 1472 requires a withholding agent to deduct and withhold a tax equal to 30% of any withholdable payment made to a non-financial non-U.S. entity if the beneficial owner of such payment is a non-financial non-U.S. entity that does not meet specified disclosure requirements.[162]

A non-financial non-U.S. entity is any non-U.S. entity that is not a financial institution under the new rules. A non-financial non-U.S. entity meets the requirements of I.R.C. § 1472 if the payee or the beneficial owner of the payment either provides the withholding agent with a certification that the non-US entity does not have a substantial U.S. owner or provides the withholding agent with the name, address, and taxpayer identification number of each substantial U.S. owner.[163] Additionally, the withholding agent must not know or have reason to know that the certification or information provided regarding substantial U.S. owners is incorrect, and the withholding agent must report the name, address, and taxpayer identification number of each substantial U.S. owner to the U.S. Treasury.

I.R.C. § 1472 does not apply to any payment beneficially owned by a publicly traded corporation or a member of an expanded affiliated group of a publicly traded corporation (defined without the inclusion of partnerships or other non-corporate entities).[164] In addition, I.R.C. § 1472 does not apply to any payment beneficially owned by any: (i) entity that is organized under the laws of a possession of the United States and that is wholly owned by one or more bona fide residents of the possession, (ii) non-U.S. government, political subdivision of a non-U.S. government, or wholly owned agency or instrumentality of any non-U.S. government or political subdivision of a non-U.S. government, (iii) international organization or any wholly owned agency or instrumentality of an international organization, (iv) non-U.S. central bank of issue, or (v) any other class of persons identified by the IRS for purposes of I.R.C. § 1472, or to any class of payments identified by the IRS

---

[159] A specified U.S. person is any person other than a publicly traded corporation, an affiliate of a publicly traded corporation, an exempt organization or retirement plan, the United States, a state or any political subdivision thereof, a bank, a real estate investment trust, a common trust fund, and certain other exempt trusts.

[160] A U.S.-owned non-U.S. entity is any non-U.S. entity which has one or more substantial U.S. owners. A substantial U.S. owner is a specified U.S. person that directly or indirectly owns more than 10% of the stock of a corporation, 10% of the profits or capital of a partnership, or 10% of the beneficial interests of a trust.

[161] I.R.C. § 1471(b)(1).

[162] I.R.C. § 1472.

[163] I.R.C. § 1472(b).

[164] I.R.C. § 1472(c)(1)(A), (B).

as posing a low risk of U.S. tax evasion.[165]

I.R.C. §§ 1471 and 1472 on their face would generally apply to payments made after December 31, 2012, but no withholding is required in respect of obligations outstanding on March 18, 2012. However, Notice 2011-53[166] delayed the application of I.R.C. §§ 1471 and 1472 until January 1, 2014, in regard to U.S.-source FDAP payments.[167] FATCA withholding will begin in regard to gross proceeds from the sale or other disposition of any property of a type that can produce interest or dividends from sources within the United States on January 1, 2015. Foreign financial institutions will be treated as participating foreign financial institutions (and not subject to the withholding) if they have registered as participating foreign financial institutions and entered into agreements with the IRS by June 30, 2013. The withholding obligations of participating foreign financial institutions in regard to pass-through payments will begin no earlier than January 1, 2015.

§ 12.09   READING, QUESTIONS AND PROBLEMS

A.   Reading

CODE:

> I.R.C. §§ 470, 512, 514, 861, 871, 881, 897, 951, 954, 1441, 1445, 1446, 901, 902, 909, 1471, 1473, 1474.

TREASURY REGULATIONS:

> Treas. Reg. §§ 1.513-1, 1.514(c)-2, 1.884-1, 1.897-7T, 1.952-1(g), 1.954-1(g), 1.954-3(a)(6), 1.956-2(a)(3), 1.1441-5, 1.1446-2, -3, -5, 301.7701-2, 3, -5T, 1.901-2(f).

B.   Questions and Problems

1. NSULC is a Nova Scotia unlimited liability company.

> a. If NSULC has more than one member, what is NSULC's initial classification for U.S. tax purposes?

> b. If NSULC has only one member, what is NSULC's initial classification for U.S. tax purposes?

> c. May NSULC elect to change its classification for U.S. tax purposes?

2. Investment Trust is an Ontario investment trust. Assume that under Ontario law, investors in registered investment trusts have limited liability. Investment Trust

---

[165] I.R.C. § 1472(c)(1)(C), (D), (E), (F), (G).

[166] 2011-32 C.B. 124.

[167] "FDAP payments" include any payments of interest (including original issue discount), dividends, rents, salaries, wages, premiums, annuities, compensations, remunerations, emoluments, and other fixed or determinable annual or periodic gains, profits, and income if such payment is from sources within the United States.

explicitly has the power to vary the investment of the certificate holders.

a. If Investment Trust has more than one member, what is Investment Trust's initial classification for U.S. tax purposes?

b. If Investment Trust has only one member, what is Investment Trust's initial classification for U.S. tax purposes?

c. May Investment Trust elect to change its classification for U.S. tax purposes?

3. A, a country X corporation, and B, a country Y corporation, form KG, a Kommanditgesellschaft in Germany to sell personal property manufactured by A. Assume, for purposes of answering the question, that at least one partner in a Kommanditgesellschaft must have unlimited liability. A and B are both owned 100% by C, a U.S. corporation.

a. What is KG's initial classification for U.S. tax purposes?

b. May KG elect to change its classification for U.S. tax purposes?

c. In determining C's U.S. foreign tax credits, may C take the taxes imposed upon the operations of KG into consideration?

d. Assuming KG is a transparent entity in Germany, will a payment to KG from a U.S. person be eligible to claim benefits of the U.S.-German tax treaty?

e. Assuming KG does not elect to change its classification for U.S. tax purposes, will the income on the sales of personal property by KG be foreign base company sales income?

f. Assuming KG elects to change its classification for U.S. tax purposes, will the income on the sales of personal property by KG be foreign base company sales income?

4. LP is an investment partnership formed in Delaware with its principal office in Nevada. LP's only activity is to trade in stocks and securities for its own account. LP is not a dealer in stocks or securities. Among the partners in LP are F, a U.K. resident, and EXP, an organization generally exempt from tax under I.R.C. § 501(c)(3).

a. Solely taking the activities of LP into consideration, is F engaged in a U.S. trade or business?

b. Would LP be obligated to withhold on F's distributive share of income?

c. Does EXP have unrelated trade or business income?

d. If LP normally maintains a 1:1 debt-equity ratio in all of its investments, does your answer to c. change?

5. LP is a real estate investment partnership formed in Delaware with its principal office in Nevada. LP's only activity is to triple net lease an office building in Las Vegas to a master tenant who subleases portions of the building to the operating tenants. LP provides no services related to the lease. LP's rights under the lease

are not dependent upon the income or receipts of any person. Among the partners in LP are F, a U.K. resident, and EXP, an organization generally exempt from tax under I.R.C. § 501(c)(3).

a. If F does not make the election under I.R.C. § 871(d), is F engaged in a U.S. trade or business? What are LP's withholding obligations?

b. If F makes the election under I.R.C. § 871(d), is F engaged in a U.S. trade or business? What are L.P.'s withholding obligations?

c. Does EXP have unrelated trade or business income?

d. If LP normally maintains a 1:1 debt-equity ratio in all of its investments, does your answer to c. change?

e. What provisions would EXP require to be added to the partnership agreement to change the answer to d.?

6. Partnership ABC operates a widget export business. In general, all income and expenses are allocated one-third, one-third, one-third, but foreign tax credits are allocated 5% to A, 5% to B, and 90% to C. Will the allocation of foreign tax credits have substantial economic effect? How are the credits likely to be reallocated?

7. Partnership ABC operates a widget export business. It runs its distribution business through a Luxembourg holding company that is treated as a disregarded entity for U.S. tax purposes. The Luxembourg holding company has several subsidiaries (one for each jurisdiction in which operations are maintained) with which it consolidates for Luxembourg tax purposes. The subsidiaries are treated as corporations separate from the holding company for U.S. tax purposes. Foreign taxes are imposed upon the subsidiaries, but the holding company pays the taxes as parent of the consolidated group. The holding company has no income for Luxembourg tax purposes. May ABC allocate the foreign taxes paid by the holding company among its partners as the taxes are paid?

8. ABC operates a widget export business. In Year 1, ABC purchased the stock of WidgetKnockOff Co., one of its competitors in jurisdiction X. WidgetKnockOff Co. had elected to be a disregarded entity for U.S. tax purposes. The purchase price paid by ABC was in excess of the basis of the assets of WidgetKnockOff Co. In Year 2, ABC sold the assets of WidgetKnockOff Co. in a transaction subject to tax in jurisdiction X. What portion, if any, of the tax imposed by jurisdiction X will be creditable in the United States?

9. ABC manufactures and sells widgets in the Unites States. A and B are U.S. domestic individuals, but C is a non-U.S. entity that is primarily engaged in the business of manufacturing and selling widgets around the world. C's stock is not publicly traded. ABC makes annual allocations and distributions of the partner's allocable shares of income. C also loaned $100x to ABC on April 1, 2012, to support the capitalization of ABC. ABC pays C $5x of interest annually. What portions of the allocations, distributions, and payments to C will be subject to FATCA withholding? What must C do to avoid the withholding?

Chapter 13

ANTI-ABUSE PROVISIONS

§ 13.01   INTRODUCTION

As you have seen from the prior chapters, Subchapter K gives partnerships and its partners a great deal of flexibility in structuring their transactions for tax purposes. In many transactions, a partnership can avoid taxation where a corporation could not. Both the Congress and the IRS have felt that the flexibility afforded partnerships can sometimes be too much of a good thing. Congress has enacted a number of statutes and the IRS has promulgated Regulations designed to reign in taxpayers' more aggressive tendencies. Further, a number of judicial doctrines are relevant to the application of Subchapter K. These provisions, beginning with the latter, are the focus of this chapter.

§ 13.02   JUDICIAL DOCTRINES

A.   Introduction

To begin at the beginning, no taxpayer is required to pay more taxes than he owes and can arrange his tax affairs so as to minimize taxes. In the famous words of Judge Learned Hand:

> [A] transaction, otherwise within an exception of the tax law, does not lose its immunity, because it is actuated by a desire to avoid, or, if one choose, to evade taxation. Any one may so arrange his affairs that his taxes shall be as low as possible; he is not bound to choose that pattern which will best pay the Treasury; there is not even a patriotic duty to increase one's taxes.[1]

Still, there is a limit on the extent to which the courts will allow taxpayers to run with the ball. When a literal application of the law overly strains the courts' sense of tax justice, they will often step in and apply one or more of a variety of judicial doctrines to set things right. These doctrines have different names, but the purpose is always the same: Not to let overly clever taxpayers (or, more likely, their overly clever tax advisers) let a literal application of the tax law or the external form of the transaction trump reason. Indeed, commonly the various doctrines can be applied

---

[1] Helvering v. Gregory, 69 F.2d 809, 810 (2d Cir. 1934), *aff'd sub nom.* Gregory v. Helvering, 293 U.S. 465 (1935); as the lingo of tax law has developed since this case, the term "tax evasion" has come to be associated with criminal conduct, so the reader may want to substitute "avoidance" for "evasion" in Judge Hand's opinion. It is also noteworthy that the taxpayer actually lost in this case.

interchangeably and yield the same result.[2] Of course, no one can exactly pinpoint the line that cannot be crossed, and what might seem to be properly arranging one's affairs to lower taxes to one judge might seem grossly over the line to another judge or appellate court, and vice versa. Further, even if a particular taxpayer's hands are reasonably clean, courts may still rule against him if they fear that other taxpayers might take inappropriate advantage of the structure he used.[3] Consequently, it is very difficult to provide ready touchstones for when the judicial doctrines will apply. Finally, courts often combine the doctrines discussed below. Thus a court might conclude that a transaction lacks substance *and* a business purpose.

B. Substance Over Form

From the earliest days of the tax law, the courts have held that there is a limit on the extent to which form can control substance. Particularly when the taxpayer controls the relevant aspects of the form of the transaction, or when the transaction only involves related parties, the courts will commonly feel free to ignore the form and look at the substance of the transactions. In the words of the Supreme Court:

> We recognize the importance of regarding matters of substance and disregarding form in applying the provisions of the Sixteenth Amendment and income tax laws enacted thereunder.[4]

This doctrine is also sometimes called the "sham transaction" doctrine.

That does not mean form never counts. Often form absolutely controls. If a taxpayer has two identical assets, one with an inherent loss and one with an inherent gain, he has complete control over which one to sell and whether or not to recognize a gain or a loss. If, however, the loss sale is to a relative or friend, who sells the property back shortly after buying it, the courts may step in even where the legislature has not.[5]

The court applied the substance over form doctrine in *Norton v. Commissioner.*[6] There the taxpayer placed business and personal assets in three domestic trusts and moved income and expenses among them and a foreign trust in an effort to avoid taxable income.[7] The taxpayer effectively had complete control over what went on in the domestic trusts and it was apparent that the foreign trust was operated in a cooperative manner. The court ignored the trusts under the substance over form doctrine and treated their income as directly earned by the taxpayer.

Courts commonly intervene where the economic profit from a transaction is primarily based on the tax savings. For example, in *Winn-Dixie Stores, Inc. v.*

---

[2] *See* ASA Investerings Partnership v. United States, 201 F.3d 505, 512 n.4 (D.C. Cir. 2000), *cert. denied*, 531 U.S. 871 (2000): "Because of the ultimate unity of the tests . . . ."

[3] BORIS BITTKER & MARTIN MCMAHON, JR., FEDERAL INCOME TAXATION OF INDIVIDUALS ¶ 1.3[2] ("FEDERAL INCOME TAXATION").

[4] United States v. Phellis, 257 U.S. 156, 168 (1921).

[5] Often in this context, the legislature has stepped in. *See* I.R.C. § 267.

[6] T.C. Memo 2002-137.

[7] It is not uncommon to see similar structures used by "tax protestors."

Commissioner,[8] Winn-Dixie embarked on a broad based, company-owned life-insurance program whose sole purpose, as shown by contemporary memoranda, was to give Winn-Dixie interest deductions. Under the program, Winn-Dixie purchased whole life insurance policies on almost all of its full-time employees, who numbered in the tens of thousands. Winn-Dixie was the sole beneficiary of the policies. Winn-Dixie would borrow against those policies' account values at an interest rate of more than 11%. The high interest rate and the administrative fees that came with the program outweighed the net cash surrender value and benefits paid on the policies, with the result that in pre-tax terms Winn-Dixie lost money on the program. The deductibility of the interest and fees post-tax, however, yielded a benefit projected to reach into the billions of dollars over 60 years. Winn-Dixie participated until 1997, when a change in tax law jeopardized this tax arbitrage, and it eased its way out.[9] The court affirmed the Tax Court's application of the sham transaction doctrine as the structure was not expected to generate a pre-tax profit and thus was purely a tax savings maneuver.

If, on the other hand, the form reflects the substance, the fact that there was also a desire to obtain tax benefits will not usually cause a problem. Thus, for example, in *Winn Dixie*, if the company had only insured key employees, and the insurance had served the needs of the business to protect against financial disruption that might occur on a key employee's death, the structure should have passed muster. The fact that there also would have been tax benefits from borrowing against the policies, that in part motivated the transaction, should not change the result.

Transactions that are at arm's length are more likely to survive scrutiny than transactions between related parties, though it should be noted that the Code often has something to say about related party transactions. For example, I.R.C. § 267 often denies losses on sales between related parties.

Usually, the substance over form doctrine may only be used by the government. A taxpayer normally is bound by the form he uses (and the associated tax consequences).[10]

---

[8] 254 F.3d 1313 (11th Cir. 2001).

[9] *Id.* at 1314. *See* I.R.C. § 264(e)(2), which lowered the interest rate that could be used beginning on January 1, 1996.

[10] *See* Commissioner v. Danielson, 378 F.2d 771, 775 (3d Cir. 1967), holding that a taxpayer may only "challenge the tax consequences of his agreement as construed by the Commissioner only by adducing proof which in an action between the parties to the agreement would be admissible to alter that construction or to show its unenforceability because of mistake, undue influence, fraud, duress, etc." Some circuit courts and the Tax Court somewhat more liberally permit a taxpayer to disavow the form of an agreement if the taxpayer provides "strong proof" that the parties intended a different arrangement. *See* Coleman v. Commissioner, 87 T.C. 178 (1986); Kreider v. Commissioner, 762 F.2d 580 (7th Cir. 1985). The burden in the former courts will usually be impossible to overcome, in the latter courts it will merely be highly difficult. The moral? For planning purposes assume the taxpayer will be stuck with the form he chooses.

C. Business Purpose

The business purpose doctrine originated in the Second Circuit in the case of *Helvering v. Gregory*.[11] There taxpayers attempted to use the tax-free corporate reorganization provisions to avoid a taxable dividend. The court held that the transaction did not qualify as a reorganization as it was not part of the conduct of the business of the relevant organizations, the sole motivation being tax savings. Judge Learned Hand, who authored the Second Circuit's opinion in *Helvering v. Gregory*, later summarized the business purpose doctrine as follows:

> The doctrine of *Gregory v. Helvering* . . . means that in construing words of a tax statute which describe commercial or industrial transactions we are to understand them to refer to transactions entered upon for commercial or industrial purposes and not to include transactions entered upon for no other motive but to escape taxation.[12]

Again, there is no bright line and the application of the business purpose doctrine will depend upon the facts of each case. As one court noted:

> [T]he "business purpose" doctrine is hazardous. It is uniformly recognized that taxpayers are entitled to structure their transactions in such a way as to minimize tax. When the business purpose doctrine is violated, such structuring is deemed to have gotten out of hand, to have been carried to such extreme lengths that the business purpose is no more than a façade. But there is no absolutely clear line between the two. Yet the doctrine seems essential. A tax system of rather high rates gives a multitude of clever individuals in the private sector powerful incentives to game the system. Even the smartest drafters of legislation and Regulations cannot be expected to anticipate every device.[13]

In *Lynch v. United States*,[14] a corporation declared a dividend in kind of boxes of apples. Instead of actually distributing the apples, however, the shareholders agreed that the corporation should sell the apples and distribute the proceeds to them. The corporation then sold the apples in the ordinary course of its business. The court, citing the business purpose doctrine, held that the dividend should be ignored and the gain on the sale of the apples be taxed directly to the corporation. On the other hand, in *Peter Pan Seafoods, Inc. v. United States*,[15] the taxpayer corporation had executed two mortgage notes. Six years later it appeared they could be purchased at a substantial discount, but if the corporation had done so directly, the discount would have constituted cancellation of indebtedness income.[16] Instead, more than 85% of the shareholders of the taxpayer corporation plus outsiders formed another corporation to acquire the notes. The funds to acquire the notes came in large part from a loan from the taxpayer corporation, but a significant

---

[11] 69 F.2d 809 (2d Cir. 1934), *aff'd sub nom.* Gregory v. Helvering, 293 U.S. 465 (1935).

[12] Commissioner v. Transport Trading & Terminal Corp., 176 F.2d 570, 572 (2d Cir. 1949).

[13] ASA Investerings Partnership v. Commissioner, 201 F.3d 505, 513 (D.C. Cir. 2000).

[14] 192 F.2d 718 (9th Cir. 1951).

[15] 417 F.2d 670 (9th Cir. 1969).

[16] *See* United States v. Kirby Lumber, 284 U.S. 1 (1931); I.R.C. § 108.

amount was contributed by the new corporation's shareholders and obtained from a bank loan.

The IRS had successfully argued at the trial level that there was no business purpose for the second corporation and the transactions into which it entered. The primary motivation, it claimed, was tax avoidance. But the appellate court reversed, holding that there was sufficient economic substance to the structure to allow it to be respected. The court noted that in actuality the taxpayer corporation did not purchase the notes. The second corporation did. The existence of tax benefits to the taxpayer did not negate the fact that there were real economic effects to the structure, not least of which was the possibility that the new corporation and its shareholders could make a substantial profit. As we discussed above and as this case demonstrates, planning for tax benefits is not fatal if accompanied by a sufficient pre-tax profit motive.

D.   Step Transaction Doctrine

Under the step transaction doctrine, interrelated steps are collapsed and treated as part of a single transaction. The doctrine has three variations, the "binding commitment" test, the "interdependence" test, and the "end result" test.[17] The binding commitment test will apply if the parties are legally required to take each of the steps. In *Gordon v. Commissioner*,[18] it was actually the taxpayer who was endeavoring to have the doctrine applied. The case involved a "spin-off" of a subsidiary corporation that would have been tax-free if the requirements of I.R.C. § 355 had been met. That section requires an amount of stock equal to control (generally 80% of the stock) of the subsidiary be distributed. Initially, the amount distributed did not constitute control. The court noted that there may have been an intention at the time of the earlier distribution to distribute an additional amount in the future that, combined, would have constituted control (and indeed it was distributed). But since at the time of the initial distribution the distributing corporation was under no binding obligation to make the subsequent distribution, the step transaction doctrine was not applied.

The interdependence test looks to whether the various steps taken were so interrelated that it would have been pointless to have taken any single step without taking the others. In *McDonald's Restaurants v. Commissioner*,[19] the hamburger giant was the taxpayer. It issued stock to acquire the interests of franchise holders. The question was whether that issuance should be stepped together with a subsequent registration of the stock and sale of the stock by the erstwhile franchise holders. If not stepped together, the first step could be seen as a tax-free reorganization under I.R.C. § 368. That treatment would not have been beneficial for McDonald's as it meant a lower basis in the acquired assets and thus lower depreciation deductions. The court held, however, that the transactions should be stepped together and the first step was thus not a tax-free reorganization.[20] In the

---

[17] *See* McDonald's Restaurants v. Commissioner, 688 F.2d 520 (7th Cir. 1982).

[18] 391 U.S. 83 (1968).

[19] 688 F.2d 520 (7th Cir. 1982).

[20] When stepped together, the reorganization lacked "continuity of interest," a necessary component

court's view, the franchise holders would not have entered into the transaction without the assurance that the stock they received would be registered so that they could sell it (which they promptly did).[21]

Finally, the end result test combines the various steps together if the intention is to reach a particular "end result." In *Kornfield v. United States,*[22] the taxpayer created a revocable trust that held bonds. He engaged in a series of transactions in an attempt to separate a life estate from the remainder interest, with the hope of creating the equivalent of amortization deductions on bonds. Bonds are normally not amortizable. The court applied the end result test to disallow the scheme.[23]

E.   Failure to Form a Valid Partnership for Tax Purposes

Several recent cases have concluded that a taxpayer's tax avoidance motives prevented the taxpayer from forming a valid partnership for tax purposes. These cases are sometimes referred to as the *"ACM"* decisions after the first such decision.[24] The facts of these cases are highly complex. We will very briefly summarize the facts in *ASA Investerings Partnership v. Commissioner,*[25] which is representative of the other cases. In this case, the taxpayer was trying to shelter substantial gains the taxpayer had from an unrelated transaction. In a strategy proposed by Merrill Lynch & Co.,[26] the taxpayer formed a partnership with a foreign entity, initially with the foreign entity holding the substantial majority of the interests in the partnership. The foreign entity was ultimately controlled by a large foreign lending institution. The partnership bought debt instruments and sold them on the installment basis. The partnership took advantage of the installment sale rules of I.R.C. § 453 that apply when the sale price is contingent. It sold the debt instrument partly for a fixed amount and partly for a contingent amount. Under the rules of I.R.C. § 453, this initially created a substantial gain. That gain was allocated to the foreign partner, who as a nonresident alien was not subject to U.S. tax on the gain. Subsequently, the ownership of the partnership was adjusted so that the taxpayer owned the substantial majority of the partnership interests. When the transaction was brought to closure, the rules of I.R.C. § 453 generated a large loss, which was mostly allocated to the taxpayer, sheltering the large gain on the unrelated transaction. Overall the transactions were approximately a wash, but because of the timing of the gain and loss and the

to a tax-free reorganization. McDonald's Restaurants v. Commissioner, *supra.*

[21] Indeed, the court held that any of the three forms of the step transaction doctrine could have been applied.

[22] 137 F.3d 1231 (10th Cir. 1998).

[23] The court also noted that the interdependence test could have been applied as well.

[24] *See generally* ACM Partnership v. Commissioner, T.C. Memo 1997-115, *aff'd,* 157 F.3d 231 (3d Cir. 1998); Lipton, *The Tax Court Upsets New Corporate Tax Shelter — Lessons from the* Colgate *Case,* 86 J. Tax'n 331 (1997); Lipton, *Brush Up Your Planning — More Lessons from the* Colgate *Case,* 90 J. Tax'n 89 (1999); Boca Investerings Partnership v. United States, 167 F. Supp. 2d 298 (D.C. 2001), *rev'd,* 314 F.3d 625 (D.C. Cir. 2003), *cert. denied,* 540 U.S. 826 (2003); *see also* Saba Partnership v. Commissioner, 273 F.3d 1135 (D.C. Cir. 2001). We discuss some of these cases in Chapter 1.

[25] 201 F.3d 505 (D.C. Cir. 2000), *cert. denied,* 531 U.S. 871 (2000).

[26] Merrill Lynch's fee for proposing and fostering the transaction in one case was $7,000,000; ASA Investerings Partnership v. Commissioner, 201 F.3d 505 (D.C. Cir. 2000).

partnership ownership interest changes, the transactions generated a large paper loss for the taxpayer. The D.C. Circuit noted that the transaction could have been attacked as a sham transaction.[27] Instead, though, the court affirmed the Tax Court's conclusion that the parties had failed to form a valid partnership for tax purposes under the principles of *Commissioner v. Culbertson*[28] that we discussed in Chapter 1. The appellate court concluded that the partnership could not be respected as it was formed for no significant reason other than tax avoidance.

A result similar to that which occurred in *ASA Investerings Partnership* occurred in *TIFD III-E Inc. v. United States*,[29] also known as the Castle Harbour case. Although the District Court had originally found that the banks that invested in the venture had nearly unlimited upside potential and were, therefore, partners, the Second Circuit found that as a practical reality the interest of the banks was limited and guaranteed and was, thus, "in the nature of" debt. The appellate court concluded that the banks did not hold a partnership interest in the venture.[30]

F. Codification of the Economic Substance Doctrine

The President signed the Health Care and Education Reconciliation Act of 2010 ("*HCERA*") on March 30, 2010. One of the most significant tax changes included in HCERA is the codification of the economic substance doctrine in new I.R.C. § 7701(o).

The common law-based economic substance doctrine is sometimes applied to deny tax benefits for transactions that would otherwise potentially qualify for such benefits under the literal language of the Code. Under the codified version, any transaction to which the economic substance doctrine is relevant will be treated as having economic substance only if: (i) the transaction changes in a meaningful way (apart from federal income tax effects) the taxpayer's economic position, *and* (ii) the taxpayer has a substantial purpose (apart from federal income tax effects) for entering into the transaction. For the purposes of the first requirement, a profit potential for the transaction is taken into account only if the present value of pre-tax profit from the transaction is substantial in relation to the present value of the expected net tax benefits from the transaction if the transaction were respected.

Fees and other expenses, including foreign taxes to the extent provided by Regulations, will be taken into account in determining pre-tax profit. State and local tax benefits are treated in the same manner as federal tax benefits. Accounting benefits are disregarded if the origin of the accounting benefit is a reduction in federal tax.

The new provisions are only intended to apply to transactions entered into in connection with a trade or business or for the production of income.

---

[27] *Id.*

[28] 337 U.S. 733 (1949).

[29] 459 F.3d 220 (2d Cir. 2006), *on remand*, 660 F. Supp. 2d 367 (D. Conn. 2009), *rev'd* 666 F.3d 836 (2d Cir. 2012).

[30] On remand, the trial court again held for the taxpayer and was again reversed on appeal.

The new provision expresses an intent not to change the determination of whether the economic substance doctrine is relevant to a transaction.

The report of the Staff of the Joint Committee indicates that if the realization of the tax benefits of a transaction is consistent with the Congressional purpose or plan that the tax benefits were designed by Congress to effectuate, it is not intended that such tax benefits be disallowed under the new provision. Thus, for example, the report of the Staff of the Joint Committee indicates that it is not intended that a tax credit (e.g., I.R.C. § 42 (low-income housing credit), I.R.C. § 45 (production tax credit), I.R.C. § 45D (new markets tax credit), I.R.C. § 47 (rehabilitation credit), I.R.C. § 48 (energy credit), etc.) be disallowed in a transaction pursuant to which, in form and substance, a taxpayer makes the type of investment or undertakes the type of activity that the credit was intended to encourage.

According to the legislative history, the provision is not intended to alter the tax treatment of certain basic business transactions that, under longstanding judicial and administrative practice, are respected, merely because the choice between meaningful economic alternatives is largely or entirely based on comparative tax advantages. Among these basic transactions are: (1) the choice between capitalizing a business enterprise with debt or equity; (2) a U.S. person's choice between utilizing a foreign corporation or a domestic corporation to make a foreign investment; (3) the choice to enter into a transaction or series of transactions that constitute a corporate organization or reorganization under Subchapter C of the Code; and (4) the choice to utilize a related party entity in a transaction, provided that the arm's-length standard of I.R.C. § 482 and other applicable concepts are satisfied. Leasing transactions, like all other types of transactions, will continue to be analyzed in light of all the facts and circumstances. As under present law, whether a particular transaction meets the requirements for specific treatment under any of these provisions is a question of facts and circumstances.

The amendment, which is immediately effective, also increases penalties for transactions without economic substance in some circumstances. A new 20% strict liability penalty is added for understatements due to the failure of a transaction to satisfy the economic substance doctrine, which is increased to 40% if the transaction is not disclosed. There is no reasonable cause defense to the penalty.

§ 13.03 ANTI-ABUSE REGULATIONS

The IRS often has had to play catch-up to crafty tax planners and in 1994 it decided it needed a more powerful weapon and promulgated the anti-abuse Regulations of Treas. Reg. § 1.701-2. These Regulations essentially permit the IRS to ignore the structure of a transaction that might technically comply with partnership tax law if the transaction is deemed to be abusive under these Regulations.

Specifically, the Regulations provide that three requirements are implicit in the intent of Subchapter K:

1. The partnership must be bona fide and each partnership transaction or series of related transactions must be entered into for a substantial business purpose.

2. The form of each partnership transaction must be respected under substance over form principles.

3. The application of a given Code provision and the ultimate tax results, taking into account all the relevant facts and circumstances, must be clearly contemplated by that provision.[31]

The Regulations go on to provide that if a partnership is used in a transaction the principal purpose of which is to reduce the present value of the partners' aggregate federal tax liability in a manner that is inconsistent with the intent of Subchapter K, the IRS is authorized to recast the transaction for federal tax purposes as appropriate to achieve tax results that are consistent with the intent of Subchapter K. The Regulations specifically note that literal compliance with the rules of Subchapter K will not save the day. The intent test must also be met. The Regulations give the IRS very broad authority to restructure the transaction, including disregarding the partnership, not treating a purported partner as a partner, adjusting the partnership's method of accounting, and reallocating income and loss.

The anti-abuse Regulations have met with substantial criticism from tax professionals, partly because of their ambiguous nature and partly because transactions in compliance with the tax law can run afoul of the Regulations, injecting much uncertainty into the planning process. It is also true, however, that Subchapter K was often used abusively to inappropriately reduce taxes. Of course, as we discussed above, there are judicial doctrines available to the IRS with which to attack such transactions, including substance over form, step transaction, and business purpose. Some view the Regulations as an attempt to codify these doctrines, although the IRS appears to believe the Regulations give it an additional weapon.[32]

The Regulations contain a nonexclusive list of facts and circumstances that could be relevant in determining whether a partnership was formed or availed of with a principal purpose to reduce substantially the present value of the partners' aggregate tax liabilities in a manner inconsistent with the intent of Subchapter K. The weight given a factor can vary depending on the totality of the circumstances, and the presence or absence of a factor is neither fatal nor a guarantee of safety. Ultimately, it comes down to whether the transaction meets the "smell test," but since you may be new to tax and not yet have had the chance to fully develop your olfactory senses, the following list of the facts and circumstances can be helpful in getting a sense of the area:

1. The present value of the partners' aggregate federal tax liability is substantially less than if the partners had owned the partnership's assets and conducted the partnership's activities directly.

---

[31] Treas. Reg. § 1.702-2(a).

[32] *See* PARTNERSHIP TAXATION at ¶ 1.03[6].

2. The present value of the partners' aggregate federal tax liability is substantially less than would be the case if purportedly separate transactions designed to achieve a particular end result are integrated and treated as steps in a single transaction. For example, this analysis may indicate that it was contemplated that a partner who was necessary to achieve the intended tax results and whose interest in the partnership was liquidated or disposed of (in whole or in part) would be a partner only temporarily in order to provide the claimed tax benefits to the remaining partners.

3. One or more partners who are necessary to achieve the claimed tax results either have a nominal interest in the partnership, are substantially protected from any risk of loss from the partnership's activities (through distribution preferences, indemnity or loss guaranty agreements, or other arrangements), or have little or no participation in the profits from the partnership's activities other than a preferred return that is in the nature of a payment for the use of capital.

4. Substantially all of the partners (measured by number or interests in the partnership) are related (directly or indirectly) to one another.

5. Partnership items are allocated in compliance with the literal language of Treas. Reg. §§ 1.704-1 and 1.704-2, but with results that are inconsistent with the purpose of I.R.C. § 704(b) and those Regulations. In this regard, particular scrutiny will be paid to partnerships in which income or gain is specially allocated to one or more partners that may be legally or effectively exempt from federal taxation (for example, a foreign person, an exempt organization, an insolvent taxpayer, or a taxpayer with unused federal tax attributes such as net operating losses, capital losses, or foreign tax credits).

6. The benefits and burdens of ownership of property nominally contributed to the partnership are in substantial part retained (directly or indirectly) by the contributing partner (or a related party).

7. The benefits and burdens of ownership of partnership property are in substantial part shifted (directly or indirectly) to the distributee partner before or after the property is actually distributed to the distributee partner (or a related party).[33]

The examples in the Regulations endeavor to provide taxpayers with a greater sense of what does and does not cross the line. The Regulations contain 11 examples. Eight pass muster and often involve transactions that have been commonly used by tax professionals. One such example gives its blessing to a partnership between an S corporation and a nonresident alien.[34] A nonresident alien cannot be a shareholder of an S corporation.[35] There might have been an argument that a nonresident alien was essentially end-running this prohibition by forming a partnership with an S corporation. For that reason, there might have

---

[33] Treas. Reg. § 1.701-2(c).

[34] Treas. Reg. § 1.701-2(d), example 2.

[35] I.R.C. § 1361(b)(1)(c).

been an argument that the structure violated the anti-abuse Regulations. But the example finds this commonly used approach unobjectionable.

The examples that are deemed to run afoul of the anti-abuse Regulations are undisputedly abusive. Let's review one of them, example 8. A owns land with a basis of $100 and a fair market value of $60, and thus with an inherent $40 loss. A would like to sell the land to B. A and B devise a plan, a principal purpose of which is to permit the duplication, for a substantial period, of the tax benefit of A's built-in loss in the land. To effect this plan, A, C (A's brother), and W (C's wife) form partnership PRS, to which A contributes the land, and C and W each contribute $30. All partnership items are shared in proportion to the partners' respective contributions to PRS. PRS invests the $60 of cash in an investment asset (that is not a marketable security within the meaning of I.R.C. § 731(c)). PRS also leases the land to B under a three-year lease pursuant to which B has the option to purchase the land from PRS upon the expiration of the lease for an amount equal to its fair market value at that time. All lease proceeds received are immediately distributed to the partners. (If they were retained, they would affect the overall value of the partnership.) In year 3, at a time when the values of the partnership's assets have not materially changed, PRS agrees with A to liquidate A's interest in exchange for the investment asset held by PRS. Under I.R.C. § 732(b), A's basis in the asset distributed equals $100, A's basis in A's partnership interest immediately before the distribution. The fair market value of the asset is still $60. Shortly thereafter, A sells the investment asset to X, an unrelated party, recognizing a $40 loss. This is the first recognition of the loss. Effectively, A recognized the loss he had on the land via the sale of the investment asset.

PRS does not make an election under I.R.C. § 754. As a consequence, PRS's basis in the land contributed by A remains $100, its fair market value remains at $60, and thus it continues to have a $40 loss inherent in it. At the end of year 3, pursuant to the lease option, PRS sells the land to B for $60. Thus, PRS recognizes a $40 loss on the sale, which is allocated equally between C and W. C's and W's bases in their partnership interests are reduced to $10 each pursuant to I.R.C. § 705. Their respective interests continue to be worth $30 each, the amount they originally contributed, thus the loss they have inherent in their interests is artificial and duplicates A's loss. If the value of the partnership holdings remain unchanged, upon liquidation of PRS (or their interests therein), C and W will each recognize $20 of gain, offsetting the earlier $40 loss. But if PRS continues in existence, the gain recognition can be deferred indefinitely, permanently if C and W die. Under these facts, the Regulations unsurprisingly conclude that the transaction runs afoul of the anti-abuse Regulations and would not be respected. The IRS does not say how it would recast the transaction. One possibility would be to treat A as if he sold the land on a deferred basis to B at the outset and simply ignore the partnership for tax purposes.

Note that while it would be clearly inappropriate to permit the loss to be duplicated, B is taking some risk as he has to wait three years to buy the land and when he does, it must be purchased at the then fair market value. Given the overall abusive nature of the transaction, that might not be sufficient grounds to allow the transaction to stand, but at least one person has to take a real risk in the transaction. How much more risk and how much less abuse is necessary to pass muster? A complaint practitioners have is that no one knows when you cross the line. Then again, that same issue exists under the judicial doctrines discussed above. One helpful assist for practitioners is that it will not be easy for an auditing agent of the IRS to use the anti-abuse Regulations as an inappropriate bargaining chip. National office approval must be obtained before asserting that a transaction falls within the anti-abuse Regulations.

§ 13.04   MIXING BOWL TRANSACTIONS

A.   Introduction

A number of Code sections address what have become known as "mixing bowl" transactions. Congressional scrutiny of the area was prompted in part by a well-publicized transaction involving two corporations, the May Company and PruSimon.[36] May Company had a subsidiary that operated a real estate business that PruSimon wanted to acquire. Had PruSimon simply purchased the stock of the subsidiary, May Company would have had a substantial gain as the subsidiary stock was highly appreciated.

To avoid taxable gain, in 1989 May Company and PruSimon formed an equal partnership. May Company contributed the stock of the real estate subsidiary, and PruSimon contributed $550 million. Using the contributed cash, the partnership purchased the stock of May Company on the open market.[37] Thus, after the purchase the partnership held two assets, the stock of the erstwhile real estate subsidiary and the stock of May Company itself. For financial accounting (but not tax) purposes, the transaction is treated as a redemption of half of the acquired May Company stock for half of the stock of the real estate subsidiary, inasmuch as May Company owns half of the partnership that owns its stock and the stock of the real estate subsidiary. Had it been a redemption for tax purposes, May Company would have had to recognize gain on the one-half of appreciated real estate stock deemed used to redeem the parent May Company stock.[38] By using a partnership, May Company was arguably able to avoid the gain while economically achieving the same result. Similarly, PruSimon is in the same economic place it would have been had it purchased one-half of the stock of the subsidiary. As we will discuss below, to avoid I.R.C. § 707(a)(2)(B), May Company likely would for some time have had to accept the risk that went along with an indirect economic interest in one-half of the real estate subsidiary stock. The partnership could not, for example, have safely given PruSimon effective control over, and the risk associated with, the real estate subsidiary under the partnership agreement. However, after two years, the partnership most likely could have brought the transaction to closure by distributing the May Company stock to May Company and the real estate

---

[36] *See* Scott Schmedel, *A Special Summary and Forecast of Federal and State Tax Developments*, WALL ST. J., Feb. 1, 1989.

[37] Technically, the partnership purchased the stock from May Company, which had purchased it in a self-tender.

[38] I.R.C. § 311(b) provides that a corporation must recognize the gain inherent in appreciated property when it distributes it to a shareholder.

subsidiary stock to PruSimon, distributions that again could be tax-free under the law that applied at the time.[39]

Keen observers might ask whether a problem for PruSimon was that it was paying the full fair market value for the real estate subsidiary, but on the eventual distribution could only have taken a carryover basis in the stock under I.R.C. § 732, that is, the same basis May Company and thus the partnership had? This need not necessarily be the case. If the stock is distributed to PruSimon in liquidation of the partnership, under I.R.C. § 732(b), PruSimon takes the same basis in the stock it had in its partnership interest, that is, the full $550 million.[40]

Upon hearing of the May Company transaction, the IRS promptly issued a notice under its corporate taxation regulatory authority stating that in the future such transactions would be treated for tax purposes in the same manner they were treated for financial accounting purposes.[41] That was followed with Proposed Regulations that, if finalized, would have fully implemented this objective.[42]

Congress also entered the fray. It decided that the IRS needed more weapons than substance over form and other judicial doctrines. Congress had previously enacted I.R.C. § 707(a)(2)(B). It added I.R.C. §§ 704(c)(1)(B), 737, and 732(f).

B.   I.R.C. § 707(a)(2)(B)

I.R.C. § 707(a)(2)(B) was enacted in 1984 and applies to a "disguised sale" of property between the partnership and a partner. For a full discussion, see section 8.06.

I.R.C. § 707(a)(2)(B) has a somewhat limited application. While it was on the books at the time the May Company transactions took place, as long as the parties were willing to wait two years before bringing the transaction to closure, I.R.C. § 707(a)(2)(B) posed little risk. Likely, the partnership could not have shifted the risk of the real estate subsidiary to PruSimon under the partnership agreement during the two years. Such an agreement would likely be a fact and circumstance that could be used to overcome the two-year presumption and would indicate that a sale between PruSimon and May Company took place on the distribution. (Indeed, it might suggest a sale took place on formation of the partnership. Can you see why?) Thus, May Company likely took the market risk as to one-half of the real estate subsidiary stock during the two years. The tax savings and the probable economic prospects of the real estate subsidiary apparently made that a risk worth taking.

As I.R.C. § 707(a)(2)(B) does not slam the door on mixing bowl transactions, Congress chose to enact several other Code provisions. We discuss these next.

---

[39] *See* I.R.C. § 731(a) and Chapter 7; *also see* Lee Shepard, *May Department Stores and the Use of Partnerships to Avoid Asset Gain Recognition*, 45 TAX NOTES 23 (1989).

[40] As adjusted during the time the partnership was in existence. *See* Chapter 7.

[41] 1989-1 C.B. 679, Notice 89-37.

[42] *See* Prop. Treas. Reg. § 1.337(d)-3, commonly known as the "May Company Regulations."

C. I.R.C. § 704(c)(1)(B)

As you learned in Chapter 5, I.R.C. § 704(c)(1)(A) requires gain or loss inherent in contributed property to be allocated to the contributing partner, subject to the adjustments it provides. Prior to the enactment of I.R.C. § 704(c)(1)(B), however, there was no tax impact to the contributing partner if the property he contributed was distributed to another partner. The partnership took a carryover basis in the property under I.R.C. § 723 and that basis in the property then generally carried over to the distributee under I.R.C. § 732. Thus, the gain or loss inherent in the property could be shifted to another partner, possibly one in a lower tax bracket. Moreover, if the distribution was in liquidation and the distributee had a high basis in her partnership interest, the gain or loss in the distributed property could disappear as the outside basis of the partner is shifted to the distributed asset under I.R.C. § 732(b). The partnership would not be required to adjust the inside bases of its assets to account for this unless an I.R.C. § 754 election were in effect.[43]

I.R.C. § 704(c)(1)(B) applies if property contributed by one partner is distributed to another partner within seven years of the original contribution. In that event, the contributing partner recognizes the gain or loss he would have recognized under I.R.C. § 704(c)(1)(A) had the contributed property been sold for its fair market value to the distributee. The character of the gain or loss is the same as the character that would have resulted had the property actually been sold to the distributee.[44] For example, assume A contributes land to a partnership with a fair market value of $10,000 and a basis of $6,000 and B contributes cash of $10,000. Further assume that three years later, when the land has appreciated in value to $15,000, it is distributed to B when B's basis in his partnership interest is $10,000. Under I.R.C. § 704(c)(1)(B), A will recognize $4,000 of gain, the gain he would have recognized under I.R.C. § 704(c)(1)(A) had the property been sold at its fair market value.[45] Note that while there is $9,000 of gain inherent in the distributed property, not all of that gain has to be recognized, only the portion to which I.R.C. § 704(c)(1)(A) would have applied.

I.R.C. § 704(c)(1)(B)(iii) provides that "appropriate adjustments" are made to the basis of the contributed property and the contributing partner's basis in the partnership interest. The Regulations provide that the contributing partner's partnership interest basis is increased for gain and reduced for any loss resulting from the distribution. The partnership's basis in the contributed property is also increased for any gain and reduced for any loss, and this is deemed to occur immediately before the distribution of the property.[46] Thus, continuing with the above example, since A recognized $4,000 of gain, A's basis in the partnership

---

[43] *See* Chapter 7.

[44] The fact that it is deemed sold to the distributee can have unexpected consequences. For example, if the distributee owns more than 50% of the partnership, and the asset is not a capital asset to him, the gain will be ordinary income under I.R.C. § 707(b)(2) even if the asset was a capital asset to the contributing partner and the partnership. I.R.C. § 707(b)(1) could deny a loss.

[45] Note that the I.R.C. § 704(c)(1)(A) method used, whether it be the traditional, traditional with curative allocations, or remedial method, will determine the amount of gain or loss that is allocated.

[46] Treas. Reg. § 1.704-4(e)(1), (2).

interest and, immediately before the distribution, the partnership's basis in the land, is increased by $4,000 to $10,000. When the land is distributed to B, he takes it with a $10,000 carryover basis, and his basis in the partnership interest is reduced to zero.[47] The I.R.C. § 704(c)(1)(B) "taint" attaches to the partnership interest. Thus, if all or a portion of A's partnership interest is transferred, a proportionate share of the I.R.C. § 704(c)(1)(B) gain or loss goes with it.[48]

Note that there has to be both a contribution of property and its subsequent distribution. If property is, for example, purchased or sold by the partnership, including a disguised sale under I.R.C. § 707(a)(2)(B), I.R.C. § 704(c)(1)(B) does not apply. I.R.C. § 704(c)(1)(B) also provides that it does not apply if property is distributed to the partner who contributed it.

The Regulations provide a number of exceptions to the application of I.R.C. § 704(c)(1)(B). It does not apply in the case of an I.R.C. § 708 termination, though the relevant property is subject to I.R.C. § 704(c)(1)(B) in the hands of the new partnership to the same extent it would have been in the old partnership. Thus, if the old partnership held the property for four years, the new partnership would have to hold the property for three years before I.R.C. § 704(c)(1)(B) would cease to apply. I.R.C. § 704(c)(1)(B) also does not apply in the case of partnership mergers, but as with I.R.C. § 708, continues to apply to the property in the hands of the transferee partnership.[49] It also does not apply in the case of the incorporation of a partnership, unless the property of the partnership is distributed to the partners and they transfer it to the corporation.[50] There is a complex exception for undivided interests.[51] There is another complex exception that can apply in liquidations.[52] It also does not apply to a distribution that is treated as a sale or exchange of unrealized receivables or substantially appreciated

---

[47] *See* I.R.C. §§ 732(a)(1), 733.

[48] Treas. Reg. § 1.704-4(d)(2). *See* Partnership Taxation at ¶ 10.08[5][b][v] for some interesting planning opportunities in this regard.

[49] Treas. Reg. § 1.704-4(c)(3). *See* Prop. Treas. Reg. §§ 1.704-4(c)(4) and 1.737-2(b), providing that in a merger I.R.C. § 704(c)(1)(B) applies to the appreciation that accrued in the assets of the nonsurviving partnership while the partnership held those assets.

[50] This assumes the erstwhile partnership is liquidated, *see* Treas. Reg. § 1.704-4(c)(5).

[51] I.R.C. § 704(c)(1)(B) does not apply to a distribution of an undivided interest in property to the extent that the undivided interest does not exceed the undivided interest, if any, contributed by the distributee partner in the same property. The portion of the undivided interest in property retained by the partnership after the distribution, if any, that is treated as contributed by the distributee partner, is reduced to the extent of the undivided interest distributed to the distributee partner. Treas. Reg. § 1.704-4(c)(2). For example, if two partners contribute undivided interests in property to the partnership, the distribution of an undivided interest to one partner does not trigger gain recognition to the other partner, provided what the distributee partner received does not exceed what he contributed to the partnership. *See* Partnership Taxation at ¶ 10.08[5][b][v].

[52] I.R.C. § 704(c)(1)(B) does not apply to a distribution of an interest in I.R.C. § 704(c) property to a partner other than the contributing partner in a liquidation of the partnership if (i) the contributing partner receives an interest in the I.R.C. § 704(c) property contributed by that partner (and no other property); and (ii) the built-in gain or loss in the interest distributed to the contributing partner, determined immediately after the distribution, is equal to or greater than the built-in gain or loss on the property that would have been allocated to the contributing partner under section 704(c)(1)(A). Treas. Reg. § 1.704-4(c)(2).

inventory under I.R.C. § 751(b) or a distribution that is treated as a guaranteed payment under I.R.C. § 736(a).[53]

Generally, if the partnership disposes of the I.R.C. § 704(c)(1)(B) property in a nonrecognition transaction, such as a like-kind exchange under I.R.C. § 1031, I.R.C. § 704(c)(1)(B) is not triggered, but applies to the replacement property to the same extent.[54] If the I.R.C. § 704(c)(1)(B) property is distributed to a noncontributing partner, to the extent I.R.C. § 1031 like-kind property is distributed to the contributing partner within the I.R.C. § 1031 times frame, I.R.C. § 704(c)(1)(B) is again not triggered.[55] Finally, the Regulations contain an anti-abuse rule that permits the IRS to recast the transaction if the rules of I.R.C. § 704(c)(1)(B) are literally met, but the principal purpose of the transaction is to achieve a tax result inconsistent with the purpose of I.R.C. § 704(c)(1)(B).[56]

D. I.R.C. § 737

Congress remained concerned with transactions directly between the contributing partner and the partnership. While I.R.C. § 707(a)(2)(B) could apply, Congress believed its scope was too narrow. Consequently, it enacted I.R.C. § 737. I.R.C. § 737 requires the contributing partner to recognize gain (but not loss) if he contributes *appreciated* property to the partnership and within seven years receives a current or liquidating distribution of property other than money from the partnership.[57] The amount of gain that is recognized is the lesser of:

1. The fair market value of the distributed property less the partner's outside basis just before the distribution (the basis is first reduced by any money received as part of the same distribution), or

2. The "net precontribution gain."

The net precontribution gain is the net gain that would have been recognized by the distributee partner under I.R.C. § 704(c)(1)(B) if all property held by the partnership which had been contributed to the partnership by that partner within seven years of the distribution had been distributed to another partner. This latter amount is the same as the net I.R.C. § 704(c)(1)(A) gain allocable to the partner.

The character of the gain the distributee partner recognizes is determined by reference to the character of the net precontribution gain inherent in the contributed property *to the partnership.*[58] The gain increases the partner's outside basis immediately before the property distribution.[59] The gain also generally increases the inside basis of the property the partner contributed to the

---

[53] Treas. Reg. § 1.704-4(a)(2).

[54] *See* Treas. Reg. § 1.704-4(d)(1), (2).

[55] *See* Treas. Reg. § 1.704-4(d)(3).

[56] *See* Treas. Reg. § 1.704-4(f).

[57] Marketable securities can be treated as money. I.R.C. §§ 737(e), 731(c).

[58] *See* Treas. Reg. § 1.737-1(d).

[59] I.R.C. § 737(c)(1); Treas. Reg. § 1.737-3(a).

partnership.[60] The distributee takes the normal I.R.C. § 732 basis in the distributed property.[61]

I.R.C. § 737 is perhaps most easily understood by way of an example. Assume A contributes land #1 to a partnership with a fair market value of $10,000 and an adjusted basis of $6,000. B contributes cash of $3,000 and land #2 with an adjusted basis and fair market value of $7,000. Within seven years, land #2 is distributed to A in an operating distribution and the facts and the values otherwise remain unchanged. Under I.R.C. § 737, A's gain is the lesser of:

1. $1,000, the fair market value of the distributed land of $7,000 less A's outside basis of $6,000, or

2. $4,000, A's net precontribution gain.

Thus, in this case A recognizes $1,000 of gain. A increases his outside basis to $7,000 for the gain and this is done immediately before the distribution. A then takes a $7,000 adjusted basis in the distributed property under I.R.C. § 732(a)(1), and his adjusted basis in the partnership is reduced to zero under I.R.C. § 733.[62] Finally, the partnership increases its adjusted basis in land #1 that A contributed by $1,000 to $7,000. If A contributes multiple properties at different times to the partnership, allocating the basis increase among partnership properties can become quite complex.[63] If the increase in basis is made to depreciable property, the increase is recovered using any applicable recovery method that applies to newly purchased property.[64]

I.R.C. §§ 737 and 704(c)(1)(B) can apply simultaneously. This will occur, for example, if one partner contributes appreciated property to the partnership, bringing I.R.C. § 737 into play, and a second partner contributes appreciated or depreciated property to the partnership, bringing I.R.C. § 704(c)(1)(B) into play. If the property contributed by the second partner is distributed to the first partner, both Code sections will apply assuming the contributions and distribution occur within the seven-year time frame. I.R.C. § 704(c)(1)(B) is applied (with the concomitant partnership interest basis adjustment) before I.R.C. § 737 is applied.[65]

There are exceptions to the application of I.R.C. § 737. They are similar to the exceptions applicable to I.R.C. § 704(c)(1)(B). Under I.R.C. § 737(d), if any portion of the property distributed consists of property which had been contributed by a distributee partner to the partnership, that property is not taken into account in determining whether the fair market value of the distributed property exceeds the

---

[60] *See* Treas. Reg. § 1.737-3(c) for a fairly involved set of rules in this regard.

[61] Treas. Reg. § 1.737-3(b).

[62] *See* Chapter 7. Note that the basis increase to A's interest only occurs for purposes of determining his basis in the distributed property and not for purposes of determining his gain or loss on the I.R.C. § 737 transaction.

[63] *See* Treas. Reg. § 1.737-3(c). If an I.R.C. § 754 election is in effect, any I.R.C. § 734(b) adjustments are made after the I.R.C. § 737 adjustments.

[64] Treas. Reg. § 1.737-3(d).

[65] Treas. Reg. § 1.737-3(e), example 2.

outside basis or in determining the amount of the net precontribution gain.[66] There must be both a contribution of property and a subsequent distribution to the contributing partner. If property is, for example, purchased or sold by the partnership, including a disguised sale under I.R.C. § 707(a)(2)(B), I.R.C. § 737 would not apply. I.R.C. § 737 does not apply to the extent I.R.C. § 751(b) applies to the distribution. It also does not apply to a distribution that is treated as a guaranteed payment under I.R.C. § 736(a).[67]

I.R.C. § 737 will not apply in the case of an I.R.C. § 708 termination, but I.R.C. § 737 will apply to a subsequent distribution of property by the new partnership to a partner who was also a partner in the terminated partnership to the same extent it would have applied to the old partnership.[68] Thus, if the old partnership held the property for four years, the new partnership would have to hold the property for three years before I.R.C. § 737 would cease to apply. I.R.C. § 737 also does not apply in the case of partnership mergers but, as with I.R.C. § 704(c)(1)(B), continues to apply to the property in the hands of the transferee partnership.[69] It also does not apply in the case of the incorporation of a partnership, unless the property of the partnership is distributed to the partners and they transfer it to the corporation.[70] There is a complex exception for undivided interests.[71]

Generally, if the partnership disposes of the contributed appreciated property in a nonrecognition transaction, such as a like-kind exchange under I.R.C. § 1031, I.R.C. § 737 is not triggered, but applies to the replacement property to the same extent.[72] Finally, the I.R.C. § 737 Regulations also contain an anti-abuse rule that permits the IRS to recast a transaction if the principal purpose of the transaction

---

[66] Under Treas. Reg. § 1.737-2(b)(2), if both previously contributed and other property are distributed in the same distribution, the previously contributed property is considered to be distributed first in a separate distribution. Any resulting basis reduction increases the possibility of I.R.C. § 737 gain. If the property distributed consists of an interest in an entity, the exception does not apply to the extent that the value of such interest is attributable to property contributed to such entity after such interest had been contributed to the partnership. For example, assume A contributes corporate stock to the partnership and the partnership than contributed property to the corporation, increasing the corporation's value. I.R.C. § 737 still applies to the increased value of the stock. *See* I.R.C. § 737(d). Query: What happens if the property contributed to the partnership is improved and that improved property is then distributed back to the contributing partner. *See* PARTNERSHIP TAXATION at ¶ 10.08[5][c][iv].

[67] Treas. Reg. § 1.737-1(a)(2), *see* Chapter 7.

[68] Treas. Reg. § 1.737-2(a); *see* Prop. Treas. Reg. §§ 1.704-4(c)(4) and 1.737-2(b), providing that in merger I.R.C. § 737 applies to the appreciation that accrued in the assets of the nonsurviving partnership while the partnership held them.

[69] Treas. Reg. § 1.737-2(b)(1); I.R.C. § 737 will also not apply in the case of certain divisive transactions. *See* Treas. Reg. § 1.737-2(b)(2).

[70] Treas. Reg. § 1.737-2(c). This assumes the erstwhile partnership is liquidated.

[71] I.R.C. § 737 does not apply to the distribution of an undivided interest in property to the extent that the undivided interest does not exceed the undivided interest, if any, contributed by the distributee partner in the same property. The portion of the undivided interest in property retained by the partnership after the distribution, if any, that is treated as contributed by the distributee partner, is reduced to the extent of the undivided interest distributed to the distributee partner. Treas. Reg. § 1.737-2(d)(4).

[72] *See* Treas. Reg. § 1.737-2(d)(3).

is to achieve a tax result inconsistent with the purpose of I.R.C. § 737.[73]

E. I.R.C. § 707(a)(2)(A)

We discussed this Code section in detail in Chapter 8. While it is not likely to apply to a mixing bowl transaction, it is possible. Recall that I.R.C. § 707(a)(2)(A) can apply when there is a transfer of property to the partnership and a related *allocation* and distribution to the partner, and the transaction is properly characterized as one occurring between the partnership and a partner acting other than in his capacity as a partner. As we discussed in Chapter 8, except for I.R.C. § 707(a)(2)(A), a partnership might be tempted to use allocations to convert a capital expense into an immediately deductible item. It is unlikely, however, that in the I.R.C. § 707(a)(2)(A) context there would be disguised sale. If capital accounts are kept normally, they are increased for the fair market value of contributed property.[74] I.R.C. § 707(a)(2)(A) also requires that there be an allocation to the contributing partner. If income equal to the fair market value of the contributed property were also allocated to the contributing partner, while there would be an income tax effect to the partner, his capital account would in effect be increased twice for the same property. It would be increased by the fair market value once on contribution, and by that same amount again on the allocation. If the partnership keeps capital accounts in accordance with the I.R.C. § 704(b) Regulations,[75] a partner is entitled to receive the balance of his capital account on liquidation. The other partners would normally object to the partner receiving two such bites of the apple.

For example, A contributes equipment with a fair market value of $10,000 and an adjusted basis of $4,000 to the equal ABC partnership. B and C each contribute $10,000. Following the capital account rules in the Regulations,[76] the capital account of each partner is increased by $10,000. If the partnership now also allocates the first $10,000 of income to A for the contributed equipment (and the rest of the income and deductions are allocated equally), A's capital account will be increased by $20,000 for a $10,000 property. Assuming B and C are independent third parties, they will not agree to that. However, if capital accounts are not kept in accordance with the Regulations, I.R.C. § 707(a)(2)(A) becomes more relevant. Thus if A's capital account is only increased by $100 for the contributed property, it would not cause the partners any great pain to allocate $10,000 of income disproportionately to A. I.R.C. § 707(a)(2)(A) would prevent this attempt to convert a capital acquisition expenditure into an immediate deduction.

F. I.R.C. § 732(f)

This Code section was enacted to combat the use of Subchapter K to circumvent certain corporate tax provisions. It is a complex Code section, and we will only cover it briefly here.

---

[73] *See* Treas. Reg. § 1.737-4.

[74] *See* Chapter 5.

[75] *See* § 5.02.

[76] Treas. Reg. § 1.704-1(b)(2)(iv)(b).

If an 80% controlled subsidiary is liquidated into a parent corporation, I.R.C. §§ 332(a), 337, and 334 generally provide that no gain or loss is recognized to the parent or subsidiary, and the parent takes a carryover basis in the assets of the subsidiary. If the partnership distributes to a corporate partner stock in another corporation and the corporate partner thereafter controls what is now its subsidiary, the common rule under I.R.C. § 732(a)(1) is that the corporation takes a carryover basis in the subsidiary's stock and the basis of the subsidiary's assets is unaffected. This gave rise to a possible planning opportunity for a corporate partner with a low basis in its partnership interest.

Assume the partnership directly owns the assets of a business. It wants to distribute those assets to a corporate partner, but the basis of the assets exceeds the corporate partner's basis in its partnership interest. The partnership could place the assets in a corporation tax free under I.R.C. § 351, taking the same basis in the stock it receives as it had in the assets under I.R.C. § 358. The newly formed corporation takes a carryover basis in the contributed assets under I.R.C. § 362. The partnership then distributes the stock to the corporate partner. The corporate partner's basis in the distributed stock would be limited to its outside basis in the partnership interest under I.R.C. § 732(a)(2), but the assets inside what is now the corporate partner's subsidiary would be unaffected. Later, the subsidiary could be liquidated tax-free, and the parent would take a full carryover basis in the assets. I.R.C. § 732(f) closes the door on this tax maneuver and provides that the basis in the subsidiary's assets are reduced to the same extent the basis of the stock the partnership held was reduced in the hands of the corporate partner. Generally, after the stock distribution, the corporate partner must own 80% or more of the subsidiary's stock for I.R.C. § 732(f) to apply.[77]

§ 13.05 READING, QUESTIONS AND PROBLEMS

A. Reading

CODE:

I.R.C. §§ 707(a)(2)(B), 704(c)(1)(B), 737, (skim 731(c)), 707(a)(2)(A), 732(f).

TREASURY REGULATIONS:

Treas. Reg. §§ 1.701-2, 1.707-3, -4, -5, -6, 1.737, 1.732-3, 1.1502-34.

Skim Prop. Treas. Reg. § 1.337(d)-3.

CASES:

Helvering v. Gregory, 69 F.2d 809 (2d Cir. 1934), *aff'd sub nom. Gregory v. Helvering*, 293 U.S. 465 (1935).

United States v. Phellis, 257 U.S. 156 (1921).

Norton v. Commissioner, T.C. Memo 2002-137.

---

[77] *See* I.R.C. § 732(f)(1)(B), (f)(5); Treas. Reg. §§ 1.732-3, 1.1502-34.

Winn-Dixie Stores, Inc. v. Commissioner, 254 F.3d 1313 (11th Cir. 2001).

ASA Investerings Partnership v. Commissioner, 201 F.3d 505 (D.C. Cir. 2000).

Lynch v. United States, 192 F.2d 718 (9th Cir. 1951).

B.   Questions and Problems

1. A, a foreign corporation, B, a domestic corporation, and C, a promoter, form the ABC partnership. A contributes $18,000 in exchange for a 90% interest, B contributes $1,980 in exchange for a 9.9% interest, and C contributes $20 in exchange for a 0.1% interest. ABC buys offshore equipment for $20,000 and validly leases the equipment offshore for a term representing most of its projected useful life. Shortly thereafter, ABC sells the rights to receive income under the lease to a third party for $18,000 and allocates the resulting $18,000 of income $16,200 to A, $1,782 to B, and $18 to C. Then ABC distributes $18,000 to A in complete liquidation of its interest. ABC then restates the partners' capital accounts (as permitted by I.R.C. § 1.704-1(b)(2)(iv)(f)) to reflect its assets consisting of offshore equipment worth $2,000 and $18,000 of cash. ABC then purchases real property by borrowing the $16,000 purchase price on a recourse basis. ABC then sells the offshore equipment for $2,000 and allocates the $18,000 tax loss $17,820 to B and $180 to Z. Address the tax consequences.

2. Sam, Mary, and Gail operate the SMG partnership. It manufactures automobile transmissions. Before the following transactions, each partner has a basis of $5,000 in the partnership interest attributable to a prior contribution of cash. Sam contributes land with a fair market value of $10,000 and a basis of $4,000 to the partnership in year 1. In that same year, Gail contributes equipment with a basis and fair market value of $10,000. In year 4, the partnership distributes the land to Gail. Its basis and fair market value have not changed. The partnership breaks even throughout this period, and no other contributions or distributions are made.

    a. Describe the tax consequences.

    b. How would your answer change if the land is not a capital asset to Gail and Mary is her daughter?

3. A, B, and C form the ABC partnership as equal partners. A contributes Blackacre, a parcel of land, with a basis of $15,000 and a fair market value of $30,000. B contributes Greenacre, also a parcel of land, with a basis and fair market value of $20,000 and $10,000 of cash. C contributes cash of $30,000. For the first three years of its existence, the partnership breaks even on its activities. No other contributions are made, and no distributions are made except that in year 3 the partnership distributes Greenacre to A.

    a. Describe the tax consequences.

    b. How would your answer change if B's basis in Greenacre were $10,000?

Chapter 14

FAMILY PARTNERSHIPS[1]

§ 14.01 INCOME TAX ISSUES ON THE PARTNERSHIP'S FORMATION

Entities are formed by families for a variety of reasons. As indicated in the preamble, the family is one of the basic units of business. The history (and definition) of a family business has been subject to some debate. Some have argued that the family business arose fairly late in the industrial revolution.[2] On the other hand, family farms may well date back to the beginning of agriculture. Family units as the basis for hunting and gathering "partnerships" may go back even further.

In addition to running a family business, some of the traditional reasons for forming an entity for the family were to provide a unified voting block for family held stock (similar to a voting trust), to provide a larger investment base to save money on investment advice and other fees, and to provide a mechanism for joint ownership of family assets.

Family partnerships and LLCs are still formed for all of these reasons. But somewhere along the way, the estate planners realized that the estate tax value of an asset held inside a partnership may be lower than if the asset were held directly.[3] While we will mostly speak of family limited partnerships, keep in mind that LLCs are often also used for family planning purposes, and indeed in some states are the preferable vehicle.

The use of family limited partnerships and LLCs as estate planning tools introduced two significant factual issues, each with significant tax consequences to the partners on the formation and termination of the partnership. First, it became much more likely that a significant portion of the assets of the partnership would be comprised of stock or other investment assets, not just of a family controlled corporation, but of a variety of issuers. Second, in contrast to the trend in partnerships generally after the introduction of the check-the-box Regulations,[4]

---

[1] The issues addressed in this chapter were previously addressed in Paul Carman, *Unwinding the Family Limited Partnership: Income Tax Impact of Scratching the Pre-Seven-Year Itch*, 98 J. TAX'N 163 (Mar. 2002). *See also* Robert Held & Paul Carman, *Handling Family Limited Partnerships and LLCs*, ILL. EST. ADMIN. 2009, IICLE (2009).

[2] ANDREA COLLI, THE HISTORY OF FAMILY BUSINESS, 1850–2000 (Cambridge University Press 2003).

[3] *See, e.g.*, Samuel Weiner & Stephen Leipzig, *Family Limited Partnerships and Leverage the Annual Exclusion and Unified Credit*, 82 J. TAX'N 164 (Mar. 1995).

[4] Treas. Reg. §§ 301.7701-1, -2, -3. Prior to the check-the-box Regulations, the previous Regulations used the existence of a limited life as one of the characteristics that distinguished a partnership from an

family limited partnerships formed for estate planning purposes often either explicitly or implicitly would be assumed to terminate within a reasonable period of time after the older generation died.

Chapter 2 describes the rules relating to the formation of a partnership and the transfer of property to a partnership. The repeal of *General Utilities*[5] and the ability of partnerships to move assets in and out of the partnership on a tax-free basis have caused many taxpayers to turn to partnerships when the asset structure or the life of the enterprise are fluid. It is generally assumed by taxpayers forming a partnership, including family members forming a family limited partnership or LLC, that the initial contribution of property to the partnership is eligible for tax-free treatment under I.R.C. § 721. Thus, it is generally assumed by taxpayers that assets will be contributed to a partnership on a tax-free basis, and the partnership will have a carryover basis in the assets. The rules regarding such contributions were introduced in Chapter 2.

However, because it is quite likely that a family limited partnership may be unwound after the death of the older generation, the rules relating to the distribution of appreciated assets from partnerships are also quite important. As with the formation of partnerships, taxpayers generally assume that the distribution of appreciated assets from a partnership may be done on a tax-free basis. The rules relating to the distribution of assets were introduced in Chapter 7.

The rules related to contributions and distributions are related. Many of the issues on the final distribution of the assets are substantially modified if the initial contribution is taxable.[6] We will start by reviewing the rules relating to contributions.

In general, I.R.C. § 721(a) provides that gain or loss is not recognized by a partner on a contribution of property to a partnership in exchange for an interest in the partnership. If, however, a partnership would be treated as an investment company for the purposes of I.R.C. § 351 if the partnership were a corporation, under I.R.C. § 721(b), gain (but not loss) may be recognized by a partner on contribution of property to a partnership in exchange for a partnership interest. For the purposes of I.R.C. § 351, a transfer is treated as a transfer to an investment company if:

1. The transfer results in diversification of the transferor's interests.

2. The transferee is (a) a regulated investment company (a "*RIC*"), (b) a real estate investment trust (a "*REIT*"), or (c) a corporation more than 80% of the value of whose assets is held for investment and include certain defined investment assets ("portfolio assets").[7]

---

association taxable as a corporation. Under the check-the-box Regulations, partnerships are often perpetual.

[5] 296 U.S. 200 (1935). Under the *General Utilities* doctrine, a corporation could distribute appreciated assets under certain circumstances without recognizing gain. Changes to the Code made in 1986 largely repealed the vestiges of the doctrine.

[6] Similarly, if the property contributed to the partnership has a fair market value equal to its basis at the time of the contribution, many of the issues will be reduced or modified.

[7] Treas. Reg. § 1.351-1(c)(1). Under I.R.C. § 351(e)(1), the portfolio assets taken into consideration

Family limited partnerships are often structured to avoid gain recognition on the initial formation of the partnership. The manner in which they are structured to avoid this initial issue will affect the consequences of a subsequent unwinding of the partnership.

A. Diversification

A transfer results in diversification of the transferor's interests if two or more persons transfer non-identical assets to the entity in the exchange.[8] If two or more persons transfer identical assets to a newly organized entity, the transfer will generally be treated as not resulting in diversification (the "identical asset exception").[9]

One of the traditional uses of a family limited partnership applies the identical asset exception: the use of the partnership to create a unified voting block for stock in a closely held corporation.

For example, suppose Anna, who founded a corporation, Brilliant Ideas, Inc., dies and leaves some of the stock in Brilliant Ideas to her daughter, Edna, and her grandchildren, Bill, age 25, Charlotte, age 30, and Dudley, age 45. If Edna, who has been CEO of the business for the last 10 years, only has one-third of the stock of the company, and non-family members hold 20%, who the grandchildren vote with could determine whether Edna would still have control of the business. If Bill, Charlotte, Dudley, and Edna all contribute their stock in Brilliant Ideas, Inc. to Brilliant Holdings, LLC, no diversification is obtained (assuming the stock is the only asset contributed), and although stock is specifically identified as taken into consideration in I.R.C. § 351(e)(1), the transfer is not treated as a transfer to an investment company for the purposes of I.R.C. § 721(b) because no diversification is obtained.[10]

---

are: (1) all stock and securities; (2) money; (3) stocks and other equity interests in a corporation, evidences of indebtedness, options, forward or futures contracts, national principal contracts, and derivatives; (4) any foreign currency; (5) any interest in a REIT, a common trust fund, a RIC, a publicly traded partnership (as defined in I.R.C. § 7704(b)), or any other equity interest (other than in a corporation) which pursuant to its terms or any other arrangement is readily convertible into, or exchangeable for, any asset described in any preceding clause, this clause, or clause (6) or (9); (6) except to the extent provided in Regulations, any interest in a precious metal, unless such metal is used or held in the active conduct of a trade or business after the contribution; (7) except as otherwise provided in Regulations, interests in any entity if substantially all of the assets of such entity consist (directly or indirectly) of any assets described in any preceding clause or clause (9); (8) to the extent provided in Regulations, any interest in any entity not described in clause (6), but only to the extent of the value of such interest that is attributable to assets listed in clauses (1) through (6) or clause (9); or (9) any other asset specified in Regulations.

[8] Treas. Reg. § 1.351-1(c)(5). It is common in a family limited partnership situation for a husband and wife who own non-identical assets to equalize their assets (transfer a one-half interest in each asset to the other spouse) prior to contributing the assets to a family limited partnership if another exception to gain recognition is not available.

[9] *Id.*

[10] The legislative history to I.R.C. § 351(e) specifically notes that although Congress intended to expand the list of property taken into consideration for purposes of identifying a transfer to an investment company, Congress did not intend to change the requirement in the Regulations that the transfer must create diversification before the transfer is treated as a transfer to an investment company.

Cash, like other property, is taken into consideration for the purposes of the diversification test. In Rev. Rul. 87-9,[11] publicly traded stock was transferred to a newly formed corporation in exchange for 89% of the Newco stock. Cash was contributed in exchange for the remainder of the stock. Diversification was not obtained by the stock alone, because all of the stock contributed was of the same corporation. The IRS ruled, however, that the contribution of cash could not be ignored and did cause diversification for the purposes of the investment company exception. Thus, everyone who contributed stock to Newco recognized gain on that contribution to the extent that the value of the stock received in the exchange exceeded the basis of the stock contributed.

The determination of whether a transfer to a partnership is a transfer to an investment company for the purposes of I.R.C. § 721(b) is ordinarily made by reference to the circumstances in existence immediately after the contribution. However, where the circumstances change pursuant to a plan in existence at the time of the contribution, the determination of whether the contribution to a partnership is a contribution to an investment company is made by reference to the circumstances in existence after the planned change occurs.[12]

As stated above, the test as to whether a contribution is being made to an investment company is a two-part test. For the purposes of I.R.C. § 351, a transfer is treated as a transfer to an investment company if:

1. The transfer results in diversification of the transferor's interests.

2. The transferee is (a) a RIC, (b) a REIT, or (c) a corporation more than 80% of the value of whose assets are portfolio assets.[13]

The structure of the Regulations would appear to apply both tests after the execution of a plan in existence at the time of the contribution.[14]

Thus, although cash is taken into consideration for purposes of the diversification test, if the cash is being contributed to the partnership to acquire identical (or fungible) property, no diversification will be obtained (if such assets are, in fact, acquired pursuant to the plan).

For example, if Edna contributed her stock in Brilliant Ideas, Inc. to Brilliant Holdings, LLC, but Bill, Charlotte and Dudley contributed cash, if at the time of the contribution, the purpose of the contribution of cash was to enable Brilliant Holdings, LLC to acquire additional stock in Brilliant Ideas (and such stock is purchased using all of the contributed cash), no diversification is obtained.

H.R. Rep. 105-148, 105th Cong., at 447, 1997 U.S.C.C. & A.N. 841 (1997).

[11] 1987-1 C.B. 133.

[12] Treas. Reg. § 1.351-1(c)(2).

[13] Treas. Reg. § 1.351-1(c)(1).

[14] The general explanation of the legislation adding I.R.C. § 351(e)(1) only provides an example of the application of the 80% test after the execution of a plan in existence at the time of the contribution. However, the general explanation notes that it was the intent of Congress not to change the rule in the Regulations that the determination of whether a transfer is made to an investment company is made taking into consideration plans in existence at the time of the contribution. *See* JOINT COMMITTEE ON TAXATION, GENERAL EXPLANATION OF TAX LEGISLATION ENACTED IN 1997, at 184 (1997).

If the non-identical assets involved in an exchange constitute an insignificant portion of the total value of assets transferred, the non-identical nature of the assets is ignored for the purposes of determining whether a transfer is to be treated as a transfer to an investment company. As indicated above, 11% is more than an insignificant portion. The Regulations provide an example in which 0.99% is viewed as an insignificant portion.[15] In the example, two stockholders contribute a total of $20,000 in publicly traded stock, and a third stockholder contributes $200 in cash. The example concludes that the contribution of the third stockholder should be ignored for purposes of determining whether diversification has occurred.

A transfer of stock or securities to a partnership does not result in diversification if each transferor transfers a diversified portfolio of stock and securities (the "*diversified portfolio exception*").[16] For these purposes, a portfolio will be considered diversified if not more than 25% of the value of each portfolio is invested in any one issuer and not more than 50% of the value of each portfolio is invested in the stock and securities of five or fewer issuers. Government securities are included in the denominator for the purposes of the test (i.e., included in determining the total value of the portfolio), but are not treated as securities of an issuer.

The theory behind the diversified portfolio exception would seem to be that if a portfolio is already diversified, any incremental diversification by adding another diversified portfolio is not significant.

B. Investment Companies

As noted above, even if diversification is obtained, I.R.C. § 721(b) does not require gain recognition unless the transferee is (a) a RIC, (b) a REIT, or (c) a partnership more than 80% of the value of whose assets is comprised of portfolio assets.[17] RICs and REITs are both required to be taxed as corporations other than in the context of the special Code provisions designed for them,[18] so I.R.C. § 721 would not be applicable to a contribution to a RIC or a REIT in any event. However, the third type of investment company, a partnership with more than 80% portfolio assets, is relevant in the context of I.R.C. § 721(b).

A transfer is not treated as being to an investment company if less than 80% of the value of the transferee (generally determined at the time of the transfer) is represented by portfolio assets (the "*80% exception*"). Family limited partnerships often attempt to meet the 80% exception if the identical asset exception or the diversified portfolio exception is not available.

If Edna contributed her stock with a value of $75 to Brilliant Holdings, LLC, but Bill, Charlotte, and Dudley contributed undivided interests in WhiteAcre, a parcel of undeveloped land with a value of $25, the partners would have obtained

---

[15] Treas. Reg. § 1.351-1(c)(7), example 1. In at least one Private Letter Ruling, the IRS ruled that a non-identical transfer of less than 5% of the total assets was insignificant. *See* PLR 200006008 (Feb. 14, 2000).

[16] Treas. Reg. § 1.351-1(c)(6).

[17] Treas. Reg. § 1.351-1(c)(1).

[18] *See* I.R.C. §§ 851(a), 856(a)(3).

diversification but the transfer is not subject to I.R.C. § 721(b) because less than 80% of the assets are portfolio assets and, thus, the transfer is treated as not being to an investment company.

§ 14.02   WHO ARE THE PARTNERS OF FAMILY LIMITED PARTNERSHIPS?

As noted in § 5.08, the question of whether certain individuals were partners in a family partnership resulted in extensive litigation.[19] In reaction to the continuing litigation, the statute and the Regulations were clarified to provide rules as to who is treated as a partner in a partnership in which capital is a material income-producing factor.

I.R.C. § 704(e)(1)[20] provides that a person should be recognized as a partner for purposes of federal income taxes if the person owns a capital interest in a partnership in which capital is a material income-producing factor, whether or not such interest was derived by purchase or gift from any other person. Treas. Reg. § 1.704-1(e)(1)(iii) provides that a donee or purchaser of a capital interest in a partnership is not recognized as a partner under the principles of I.R.C. § 704(e)(1) unless such interest is acquired in a bona fide transaction, not a mere sham for tax avoidance or evasion purposes, and the donee or purchaser is the real owner of such interest. To be recognized, a transfer must vest dominion and control of the partnership interest in the transferee. The existence of such dominion and control in the donee is to be determined from all the facts and circumstances. A transfer is not recognized if the transferor retains such incidents of ownership that the transferee has not acquired full and complete ownership of the partnership interest. The Regulations also indicate that transactions between members of a family will be closely scrutinized, and the circumstances, not only at the time of the purported transfer but also during the periods preceding and following it, will be taken into consideration in determining whether the purported gift or sale should be recognized.

Treas. Reg. § 1.704-1(e)(1)(iv) provides, in part, that for purposes of I.R.C. § 704(e)(1), capital is a material income-producing factor if a substantial portion of the gross income of the business is attributable to the employment of capital in the business conducted by the partnership. Capital is ordinarily a material income-producing factor if the operation of the business requires substantial inventories or a substantial investment in plant, machinery, or other equipment. In general, capital is not a material income-producing factor where the income of the business consists principally of fees, commissions, or other compensation for personal services performed by members or employees of the partnership.[21]

---

[19] *See also* Paul Carman & Colleen Kushner, *The Uncertain Certainty of Being a Partner: Partner Classification for Tax Purposes*, 109 J. Tax'n 165 (Sept. 2008).

[20] The subsection heading of I.R.C. § 704(e) is "Family Partnerships," but the rules of the section and the underlying Regulations are applicable to partnerships generally. While the language of the section heading may be used as an interpretative aid, it will not be so employed as to limit the meaning and purpose of the text. Maguire v. Commissioner, 313 U.S. 1 (1941).

[21] However, goodwill may be a significant income-producing capital factor. *See* Bateman v. United

Treas. Reg. § 1.704-1(e)(1)(i) begins with the statement that the production of income by a partnership is attributable to the capital or services, or both, contributed by the partners. In *Carriage Square, Inc. v. Commissioner*,[22] the partners contributed a small amount of capital and then the partnership borrowed the funds to do its business (with a guarantee by a non-partner). The court concluded that capital was not a material income-producing factor of the partnership because the capital used was not provided by the partners.

Treas. Reg. § 1.704-1(e)(1)(v) provides that for purposes of I.R.C. § 704(e), a capital interest in a partnership means an interest in the assets of the partnership, which is distributable to the owner of the capital interest upon his withdrawal from the partnership or upon liquidation of the partnership. The mere right to participate in the earnings and profits of a partnership is not a capital interest in the partnership.

Whether a person claiming to be a partner who is a donee of a capital interest in a partnership is the real owner of such capital interest, and whether the donee has dominion and control over such interest, must be determined from all the facts and circumstances of the particular case.[23] Isolated facts are not determinative; the reality of the donee's ownership must be determined in the light of the transaction as a whole. The execution of legally sufficient and irrevocable deeds or other instruments of gift under state law is a factor to be taken into account, but is not determinative of ownership by the donee for the purposes of I.R.C. § 704(e). The reality of the transfer and of the donee's ownership of the property attributed to the donee are to be determined from the conduct of the parties with respect to the claimed gift and not by any mechanical or formal test.

Treas. Reg. § 1.704-1(e)(2)(ii) lists a series of factors to be considered in determining whether a partner is, in fact, the real owner of a capital interest in a partnership. The factors to be considered, which are illustrative rather than exhaustive, break down into five categories: retained controls (including retention of control of assets essential to the business), indirect controls, participation in management, income distributions, and conduct of partnership business. The first two factors indicate lack of ownership, while the last three factors indicate ownership.

Retention of control by the donor of the distribution of amounts of income or restrictions on the distributions of amounts of income (other than amounts retained in the partnership annually with the consent of the partners, including the donee partner, for the reasonable needs of the business) would be a factor indicating that the donor may be more appropriately treated as having dominion and control.[24] If there is a partnership agreement providing for a managing partner or partners, then amounts of income may be retained in the partnership without the acquies-

---

States, 490 F.2d 549 (9th Cir. 1973) (a brokerage firm may rely upon I.R.C. § 704(e) where goodwill is a significant income-producing factor).

[22] 69 T.C. 119 (1977).

[23] Treas. Reg. § 1:704-1(e)(2)(i).

[24] Treas. Reg. § 1.704-1(e)(2)(ii)(a).

cence of all the partners if such amounts are retained for the reasonable needs of the business.

If the donor limits the right of the donee to liquidate or sell the donor's interest in the partnership at the donor's discretion without financial detriment, such a limitation would be a factor indicating that the donor may be more appropriately treated as having dominion and control.[25]

If the donor retains control of assets essential to the business, such controls would be a factor indicating that the donor may be more appropriately treated as having dominion and control.[26] For example, if the donor of a partnership interest owned the real property upon which the partnership had its manufacturing facility, and the lease was terminable at will by the donor without penalty, the donor has essentially retained the ability to take control of the assets of the partnership at any time.

If the donor retains management powers inconsistent with normal relationships among partners, such powers would be a factor indicating that the donor may be more appropriately treated as having dominion and control.[27] Retention by the donor of control of business management or of voting control, such as is common in ordinary business relationships, is not by itself inconsistent with normal relationships among partners, provided the donee is free to liquidate the donee's partnership interest at the donee's discretion without financial detriment. The donee will not be considered free to liquidate the donor's partnership interest unless the donee is independent of the donor and has such maturity and understanding of donor's rights as to be capable of deciding to exercise, and capable of exercising, the donee's right to withdraw the donee's capital interest from the partnership.

Substantial participation by the donee in the control and management of the business (including participation in the major policy decisions affecting the business) is strong evidence of a donee partner's exercise of dominion and control over his interest.[28] Such participation presupposes sufficient maturity and experience on the part of the donee to deal with the business problems of the partnership.

In determining the reality of the donee's ownership of a capital interest in a partnership, whether the donee is actually treated as a partner in the operation of the business must be taken into consideration. Whether or not the donee has been held out publicly as a partner in the conduct of the business, in relations with customers, or with creditors or other sources of financing, is of primary significance.

While I.R.C. § 704(e) sets forth certain rules for establishing the ownership of interests in a family partnership and the allocation of partnership income, the common thought projected throughout the Regulations implementing I.R.C. § 704(e) is that each case must be decided on its own particular facts and surrounding circumstances.

---

[25] Treas. Reg. § 1.704-1(e)(2)(ii)(b).

[26] Treas. Reg. § 1.704-1(e)(2)(ii)(c).

[27] Treas. Reg. § 1.704-1(e)(2)(ii)(c).

[28] Treas. Reg. § 1.704-1(e)(2)(iv).

In *United States v. Ramos*,[29] an alleged family partnership was found to be invalid under I.R.C. § 704(e) where the taxpayer-parents retained the complete interests in the operating assets of a ranch, and the children contributed neither property nor services (other than bookkeeping services) for which compensation was paid. The failure of the parents to transfer title to the property to the partnership was one of the most important factors in the court's decision not to recognize the partnership. Although capital was a material income-producing factor to the business, the children received no interest in the capital of the business.

The recognition of an assignee's interest in a limited partnership will depend, as in the case of other donated interests, on whether the transfer of property is real and on whether the donee has acquired dominion and control over the interest purportedly transferred to him. To be recognized for federal income tax purposes, a limited partnership must be organized and conducted in accordance with the requirements of the applicable state limited partnership law.[30] The absence of services and participation in management by a donee in a limited partnership is immaterial if the limited partnership meets all the other requirements of Treas. Reg. § 1.704-1(e).

Thus, the question of whether the assignee obtains dominion and control of the assigned partnership interest is crucial to the determination of the tax consequences of the assignment. The courts have recognized the dominion and control test as being the deciding factor in attributing the earning of partnership income or loss to a particular individual in partnerships in which capital is a material income-producing factor.[31] In *Pflugradt*, the court states:

> To be recognized for tax purposes, a transfer of a partnership interest must vest dominion and control in the transferee. . . . [This] includes not only control with respect to the partnership business, which in this case is non-existent because the general partner had sole control of the business, but also control of the interest as a property right.

The Seventh Circuit subsequently decided another case applying the test of ownership of a capital interest to the assignment of a general partnership interest. *Evans v. Commissioner*[32] relies on Treas. Reg. § 1.704-1(e) to conclude that the assignee of a general partnership interest, and not the assigning general partner himself, was the "partner" for purposes of reporting partnership distributive shares. In *Evans*, the taxpayer sold his entire beneficial interest in a partnership to his closely held corporation, without the knowledge or consent of his equal partner in the business. The taxpayer continued to perform the same work for the

---

[29] 393 F.2d 618 (9th Cir. 1968), *cert. denied*, 393 U.S. 983 (1968).

[30] Treas. Reg. 1.704-1(e)(2)(ix). It should be noted that this statement out of context would appear to conflict with Treas. Reg. 301.7701-1(a)(1), which provides that the recognition of an entity for federal income tax purposes is not a question of local law. One way of reconciling the two provisions would be to read the provision in Treas. Reg. § 1.704-1(e)(2)(ix) to be introduced by the phrase "For the purposes of this paragraph," but other methods of reconciliation may also apply.

[31] *See, e.g.*, Pflugradt v. United States, 310 F.2d 412 (7th Cir. 1962), where the court refused to recognize certain purported transfers of limited partnership interests to minor children (whose ages ranged from one to three and one-half years).

[32] 447 F.2d 547 (7th Cir. 1971), *aff'g* 54 T.C. 40 (1970).

partnership as before, but the court found that this was done in his capacity as an officer and director of the assignee corporation, not as a partner. As a fiduciary of the corporation, the taxpayer would have been required to exercise his remaining partnership powers in the interest of the corporation. Under these unique facts, the court held that the corporation (the assignee) and not the taxpayer (the assignor) was taxable on the partnership distributive share.

While all the facts and circumstances must be taken into consideration, note that the rights of the parties may be designed to intentionally meet the five factors of Treas. Reg. § 1.704-1(e)(2).

§ 14.03   INCOME TAX ISSUES FOR VACATION/RENTAL HOMES

The discussion above on family limited partnerships focuses on partnerships that are intended to be used as family investment vehicles in stocks, other securities, and businesses. One other frequent use of a family limited partnership is to hold title to either a home or a vacation home. If the property is a vacation home, the property is often held out for rent to third parties as well as made available for use for family members.

Where a dwelling unit is used both for rental use and for personal use, the Code provides very particular limitations on the deductions attributable to the dwelling unit. In any case where a taxpayer who is an individual uses a dwelling unit for personal purposes on any day during the taxable year, the amount deductible with respect to the rental of the unit (or portion thereof) may not exceed an amount which bears the same relationship to such expenses as the number of days during each year that the unit (or portion thereof) is rented at fair rental bears to the total number of days during such year that the unit (or portion thereof) is used for both rental and personal uses.[33]

I.R.C. § 280A(c)(5) limits the deduction of expenses incurred in the rental use of a residence that may be allowed under I.R.C. § 280A(c)(3) to an amount not in excess of the gross income derived from the rental use for the taxable year over the sum of: (i) the deductions allocable to the rental use that are otherwise allowable regardless of such rental use (such as mortgage interest and real estate taxes); plus (ii) any deductions that are allocable to the rental activity in which the rental use of the residence occurs, but that are not allocable to the rental use of the residence itself. Thus, a taxpayer may not normally offset a net rental loss incurred from, and attributable to, the rental use of the taxpayer's residence or vacation home against unrelated income.

A taxpayer will not be treated as using a dwelling unit for personal purposes by reason of a rental arrangement under which the dwelling unit is rented to any person at a fair rental value for use as such person's principal residence.[34] This means that the rental of a dwelling unit to a member of the taxpayer's family or the family of a co-owner of the dwelling unit does not constitute the personal use of the

---

[33] I.R.C. § 280A(e).

[34] I.R.C. § 280A(d)(3)(A).

dwelling unit by the taxpayer if the dwelling unit is rented at a fair rental for use as the family member's principal residence. Of course, if the taxpayer continues to use the dwelling unit, the taxpayer's own use will be considered personal use by the taxpayer without regard to the rental agreement.

In the case of a vacation home owned by a partnership, the number of days of personal use of the vacation home is determined by reference to the total number of days of personal use by the partners.[35] However, if two or more partners use the vacation home during the same day, the day would constitute only one day of personal use.

I.R.C. § 208A(f)(1)(B) provides that the term "dwelling unit" does not include that portion of a unit that is used exclusively as a hotel, motel, inn, or similar establishment. The IRS has issued Proposed Regulations that state that this exception applies only if the portion of the unit is regularly available for occupancy by paying customers and only if no person with an interest in the property is deemed to have used it as a residence during the taxable year.

§ 14.04 INCOME TAX ISSUES ON UNWINDING

As mentioned above, family limited partnerships formed for estate planning purposes often are either explicitly or implicitly designed to terminate within a reasonable period after the older generation dies. The family has two basic choices for unwinding the partnership — the sale of the property followed by a distribution of the cash proceeds or a distribution of the property in kind. In Chapter 7 we discussed partnership distributions generally.

A. Sale of the Assets

Partnerships formed for estate planning purposes often start with a one or more appreciated properties that were held by one or more of the partners prior to the formation of the partnership. On a sale of property that was appreciated upon contribution to the partnership, I.R.C. § 704(c) generally requires the gain inherent in the property on contribution to be allocated to the contributing partner.[36] If a partnership interest is included in the estate of one of the partners, the pre-contribution gain as to that partner may be eliminated in whole or in part if an I.R.C. § 754 election has been made.[37]

It is common during the life of a family limited partnership for gifts of partnership interests to be made to one or more members of a younger generation. Successors, such as donees of gifts, are treated as also receiving a proportionate part of the precontribution gain that had been attributable to the donor of the

---

[35] S. Rep. No. 94-938, 94th Cong., 2d Sess. 153–54 (1976).

[36] Unless the precontribution gain already had been taken into consideration through allocations in the course of the partnership's operations; *see* Treas. Reg. § 1.704-3 and § 5.05.

[37] *See* § 6.07. It should be noted that if the estate takes a discounted value for the partnership interest for estate tax purposes, the I.R.C. § 754 election will only cause the basis to step-up to the discounted value.

gift.[38] In a partnership in which all the partners have precontribution gain, the gain recognized on a sale of the assets is allocated among the partners proportionately to their precontribution gain. Any gain in excess of the precontribution gain is generally allocated pursuant to the partnership agreement.

Under I.R.C. § 731, the distribution of cash resulting from the sale is taxable to the extent the cash distributed exceeds the recipient partner's basis in her partnership interest.

B. Distribution in Kind

Although I.R.C. § 731 generally provides that distributions of property other than cash will not result in the recognition of gain or loss, a number of exceptions have crept in the Code over the years so that a distribution in kind may result in unexpected gain recognition.

If property is contributed by a partner and then distributed to another partner within seven years, the contributing partner will generally recognize gain at the time of the distribution.[39] If, however, property is distributed to the partner who contributed that property, no gain recognition is required under I.R.C. § 704(c) (the *"I.R.C. § 704(c) previously contributed property exception"*). For these purposes, the donee of a contributing partner is treated as a contributing partner to the extent of the precontribution gain allocated to the donee.[40]

For example, if Felicia contributed WhiteAcre to an LLC at a time when the fair market value was $100 and the basis $40, the built-in gain for I.R.C. § 704(c) purposes would be $60. If within seven years of the contribution the property is distributed to another partner, Gordon, Felicia will recognize the built-in gain remaining that is attributable to WhiteAcre, unless Gordon is treated as a successor to Felicia and has succeeded to Felicia's built-in gain account in respect of WhiteAcre.

Similar to I.R.C. § 704(c), I.R.C. § 737 generally provides that if a partner contributes appreciated property to a partnership and the contributing partner receives a distribution of other property (other than cash) within seven years of the contribution, the partner will recognize the lesser of (i) the excess of the fair market value of the property distributed over the contributing partner's tax basis in its partnership interest immediately before the distribution (reduced by the amount of money included in the distribution), or (ii) the precontribution gain in the property contributed by the partner.[41]

---

[38] Treas. Reg. § 1.704-3(a)(7).

[39] *See* § 13.04; I.R.C. § 704(c)(1)(B).

[40] Treas. Reg. § 1.704-4(d)(2).

[41] *See generally* Crnkovich & Swirsky, *Multiple Recognition Rules Complicate Partner-Partnership Transactions*, 79 J. Tax'n 50 (July 1993). For more on the rules of I.R.C. § 737, see Cuff, *The Anti-Abuse Rule and the Basis Rules of the Final Section 737 Regulations*, 14 J. Partnership Tax'n 28 (Spring 1997), and *Final Section 737 Regulations Explain Contribution and Distribution Transactions*, 13 J. Partnership Tax'n 303 (Winter 1997).

Like the Regulations under I.R.C. § 704(c), the Regulations under I.R.C. § 737 provide that the successor of a partner succeeds also to the transferor's precontribution gain for the purposes of I.R.C. § 737[42] and a distribution of contributed property to the contributing partner will not cause the gain recognition provided for in I.R.C. § 737 (the *"I.R.C. § 737 previously contributed property exception"*).[43] The latter exception, however, does not provide that a distribution to a successor of a contributing partner of property contributed by the transferor is treated as a distribution of contributed property to the contributing partner.[44] Thus, the answer is unclear.

A further exception to the general rule under I.R.C. § 731 that gain is not recognized to a partner on the distribution of property other than money to the partner is the treatment of marketable securities. Marketable securities generally are treated as money under I.R.C. § 731 for the purposes of determining the gain on a distribution. However, marketable securities are not treated as money if: (i) the security distributed was contributed by the distributee partner (the *"I.R.C. § 731 previously contributed property exception"*), (ii) the security was acquired by a partnership in certain nonrecognition transactions,[45] (iii) the security was not a marketable security when acquired by the partnership,[46] or (iv) the partnership is an investment partnership and the distribution is to an eligible partner (the *"investment partnership exception"*).

A partnership is an investment partnership for the purposes of the investment partnership exception in I.R.C. § 731 if (i) the partnership has never been engaged in a trade or business and (ii) substantially all[47] of the assets (by value) of the partnership have always consisted of money, stocks, notes, bonds, debentures or other evidences of indebtedness, interest rate currency or equity notional principal contracts, foreign currencies, interests in or derivatives of financial instruments, or other assets specified by the IRS.[48] An eligible partner is a partner who did not

---

[42] Treas. Reg. § 1.737-1(c)(2)(iii).

[43] Treas. Reg. § 1.737-2(d)(1).

[44] Treas. Reg. § 1.737-1(c)(2)(iii) includes a cross reference to Treas. Reg. § 1.704-4(d)(2) (where the Regulations provide that the successor is also treated as having contributed property for the purposes of I.R.C. § 704(c)).

[45] To qualify under this exception, the value of any marketable securities and money exchanged by the partnership in the nonrecognition transaction must be less than 20% of the value of all the assets exchanged by the partnership in the nonrecognition transaction, and the partnership must distribute the security within five years of either the date the security was acquired by the partnership or, if later, the date the security became marketable. Treas. Reg. § 1.731-2(d)(1)(ii).

[46] To qualify under this exception, the entity that issued the security must have had no outstanding marketable securities at the time the security was acquired by the partnership, the security must have been held by the partnership for at least six months before the date the security became marketable, and the partnership must distribute the security within five years of the date the security became marketable. Treas. Reg. § 1.731-2(d)(1)(iii).

[47] "Substantially all" probably means, for these purposes, 90% or more. *See* Treas. Reg. § 1.731-2(c)(3)(i). However, the cross reference in Treas. Reg. § 1.731-2(c)(3)(i) is to I.R.C. § 731(c)(2)(B)(v) (treating interests in an entity as an interest in marketable securities), rather than to I.R.C. § 731(c)(3)(C)(i) (the definition of an investment partnership).

[48] These assets are herein generally referred to as "marketable securities."

contribute any property to the partnership other than property listed in clause (ii) of the immediately preceding sentence.

If, at the time of the formation of a partnership, a family limited partnership qualifies for either the identical asset exception or the diversified portfolio exception to gain recognition on the transfer of assets to the partnership (in respect of transfers to potential investment companies) described above, the partnership may qualify as an investment partnership for purposes of I.R.C. § 731 and a distribution of marketable securities may not be treated as money under the investment partnership exception, described above. If, however, the partnership used the less-than-80% exception to escape gain recognition on the transfer of assets to the partnership, the partnership is unlikely to be an investment partnership for the purposes of I.R.C. § 731 and distributions of marketable securities will be treated as distributions of money unless another exception applies.

Some distributions of marketable securities may not be treated as distributions of money under the I.R.C. § 731 previously contributed property exception. If the distribution is a simple unwinding during the life of the contributing partners with the assets simply being returned to the contributing partners, this exception would be quite useful. However, like I.R.C. § 737, but unlike I.R.C. § 704(c), the I.R.C. § 731 previously contributed property exception does not provide that the donee of a partnership interest is to be treated as the contributor of the securities actually contributed by the donor of the partnership interest. Again, for this reason, the answer is not clear.

Another reduction in the amount of marketable securities treated as cash comes from I.R.C. § 731(c)(3)(B). That section provides that the amount treated as a distribution of money under I.R.C. § 731(c)(1) is reduced (but not below zero) by an amount equal to the excess (if any) of the distributee partner's share of net gain that would be recognized if the partnership sold all of its marketable securities[49] held immediately before the distribution over the distributee partner's share of net gain that would be recognized if the partnership sold all of its marketable securities held immediately after the distribution.

---

[49] For these purposes, all marketable securities held by the partnership are treated as if they were of the same class and issuer as the marketable securities that are distributed. *See* Treas. Reg. § 1.731-2(b)(1).

§ 14.05   AN INTRODUCTION TO THE ESTATE AND GIFT TAX CONSEQUENCES

A.   Background

Family limited partnerships, LLCs, and limited liability limited partnerships are commonly formed to avoid estate and gift taxes.[50] Again, we will primarily focus on family limited partnerships, but recall that the other vehicles are sometimes preferable depending upon state law. The gift and estate tax savings come from the ability to reduce the value of the gifted or devised property with minority-interest and lack-of-marketability discounts. A minority-interest discount is based on the fact that a donee's minority interest in the entity means that he lacks control and that the interest is worth less for that reason. The lack-of-marketability discount is based on the fact that the donee has no ready way to sell or liquidate the interest and that the interest is worth less for that reason. A property that, if owned by donors directly, is worth $100,000, can be gifted or devised through interests in a family limited partnership at a value of perhaps only $65,000. Discounts commonly run between 30% and 60%.[51] If properly gifted, the family limited partnership interests are also excluded from the donor's estate when he dies. Further, any income associated with the gifted family limited partnership interests is taxed to the donees and that income is also removed from the donor's estate.[52]

In a typical structure, the donors (commonly parents or grandparents) form a limited partnership, and contribute the relevant assets to it. As we will discuss below, it is preferable, but not necessarily obligatory, for the donors not to control the family limited partnership. If they do retain control, they will hold the general partnership interests in the case of a limited partnership and the managerial interest in the case of an LLC. Formation of the family limited partnership normally will be tax-free, and the family limited partnership will typically take a carryover basis in the assets it receives.[53] The donors forming the family limited partnership generally will take the same basis in the family limited partnership interests that they had in the underlying property.[54] Over time they will make gifts of the family limited partnership interests to the donees (commonly the children, grandchildren, or trusts for their benefit). It is generally not advisable to gift the family limited partnership interests within a short amount of time of the contribution of the property to the family limited partnership, as that runs the risk that the IRS may try to collapse the transactions together and claim there has been a gift of the underlying property. In making their annual gifts donors will

---

[50] The following materials are in large part reprinted from Mark Sargent and Walter Schwidetzky, Limited Liability Company Handbook with the permission of Thomson Reuters. Further reproduction of any kind is strictly prohibited.

[51] *See* Martha Britton Eller, *Which Estates Are Affected by the Estate Tax?: An Examination of the Filing Population for Year-of-Death 2001*, 25 Stat. Inc. Bull. 185, 197 (Summer 2005).

[52] I.R.C. § 1(g) generally taxes income of children of the donor under the age of 14 at the highest marginal rate the donor would have paid had he received the income.

[53] I.R.C. §§ 721, 722.

[54] I.R.C. § 723.

want to take advantage of the I.R.C. § 2503(b) annual exclusion, which may permit the first $13,000 of discounted value gifted by a donor to each donee each year to be excluded from gift tax.[55] Thus, two parents can gift $26,000 per year per donee without gift tax consequence. Further, spouses may split gifts, so that a $26,000 gift by one spouse is treated as if each spouse made a $13,000 gift.[56] As we will discuss, however, the $13,000 exclusion is often not available. If the donors gift amounts in excess of the $13,000 exclusion, or if they make gifts but the $13,000 exclusion is not available, the donors must file a gift tax return. An actual gift tax is only due, however, if the total gifts exceed both the $13,000 annual exclusion (if available) and the lifetime gift tax exemption. The lifetime gift tax exemption is currently $5 million.[57] The maximum gift tax rate is 35%.[58]

The use of family limited partnerships can also reduce a decedent's estate taxes. If the decedent holds interests in family limited partnerships rather than holding the underlying assets, the value of the decedent's estate can be less than if the decedent held the underlying assets directly due to discounts for lack of marketability and minority interests. Estates are generally only taxable to the extent they exceed the estate tax exemption of $5,000,000, reduced by any use the decedent made of the lifetime gift tax exemption.[59] The estate tax exemption can be increased by any unused exemption of a predeceased spouse.[60] The maximum estate tax rate is 35%.[61]

B. Marketable Securities

While the question is not definitively resolved, it seems increasingly unlikely that a family limited partnership that primarily holds marketable securities will be allowed discounts. At the outset, we should note that the Code itself acknowledges the existence of investment partnerships. It defines them as partnerships (including family limited partnerships classified as partnerships) that have never engaged in a trade or business and which primarily hold cash, stocks, bonds, notes, etc.[62] Many practitioners do form family limited partnerships that only hold marketable securities and take the discounts. But such family limited partnerships often receive heightened scrutiny from the IRS. Several cases have permitted discounts for family limited partnerships holding primarily marketable securities, but they typically did not involve a discussion of I.R.C. § 2036, which eventually became the dominant issue. Given the manner in which courts are applying I.R.C. § 2036 to family limited partnerships, it will be difficult for a family limited partnership holding only marketable securities to be an effective tax planning

---

[55] I.R.C. § 2503(b) provides that the annual exclusion is $10,000, but is adjusted for inflation after 1998. The current inflation adjusted figure is $13,000.

[56] I.R.C. § 2513. All gifts for that year must be split. Treas. Reg. § 25.2513-2.

[57] I.R.C. § 2505.

[58] I.R.C. § 2502.

[59] I.R.C. § 2010(c)(3).

[60] I.R.C. § 2010(c)(2), (c)(4).

[61] I.R.C. § 2001(c).

[62] I.R.C. § 731(c)(3)(C)(i).

device. We discuss I.R.C. § 2036 and these cases below. The gift tax return form requires taxpayers to disclose any discounts that are taken, and approval from the IRS's national office may be required for any settlement.

Having the family limited partnership hold both traditional business assets and marketable securities may make it easier to survive scrutiny. For example, *Church v. United States*[63] involved a limited partnership that held both marketable securities as well as a sizeable working ranch. The court permitted substantial discounts. Family limited partnerships using this structure can also readily meet the business purpose test.

C.　Near-Death (and Not So Near-Death) Family Limited Partnerships

A fairly common, last-minute effort to reduce estate taxes involves the following scenario. Family members create an LLC or limited partnership shortly before a parent's death, when it is apparent that the parent does not have long to live. In one case, a limited partnership was created within two days of the parent's death and after the parent had been removed from life support. A substantial portion of the parents' assets are transferred to the family limited partnerships in exchange for family limited partnership interests, and the family limited partnerships interests are included in the parents' estates at a substantial discount from the fair market value of the contributed assets. Typically, the children create the family limited partnerships on behalf of the parent using either a power of attorney granted them by the parent or their powers as trustees of a trust created for the benefit of the parent.[64]

These arrangements have (unsurprisingly) come under attack by the IRS. As the number of litigated cases increased, they began to include family limited partnerships not formed particularly closely to the time of death of the donor or formed at a time when the donor was believed to be in good health. Many of these transactions have been held to afoul of I.R.C. § 2036 with the typical (though not uniform) result that the assets of the family limited partnerships (rather than the ownership interests in the family limited partnerships) were included in the decedent's estate. Accordingly, the benefits of discounting were lost.

D.　Judicial Responses

Perhaps the first important case in this area is *Estate of Strangi v. Commissioner*,[65] a case with many lives. It involved a self-made millionaire who lived and died in Waco, Texas. He was a widower with children from his first marriage and stepchildren from his second marriage. A son-in-law, a lawyer,

---

[63] 85 A.F.T.R.2d 804 (W.D. Tex. 2000), *aff'd*, 268 F.3d 1063 (5th Cir. 2001).

[64] *See, e.g.*, TAM 9719006 (Jan. 14, 1997); TAM 9723009 (Feb. 24, 1997); TAM 9725002 (Mar. 3, 1997); TAM 9730004 (Apr. 3, 1997); TAM 9735003 (May 8, 1997); TAM 9736004 (June 6, 1997).

[65] Estate of Strangi v. Commissioner, 115 T.C. 478 (2000), *aff'd in part, rev'd in part*, 293 F.3d 279 (5th Cir. 2002) (aka *Strangi* 2), focusing on I.R.C. § 2036, T.C. Memo 2003-145 (aka Strangi 3), *aff'd*, 417 F.3d 468 (5th Cir. 2005) (aka Strangi 4).

prepared many of the estate planning documents and held the decedent's general power of attorney.

In August, 1994, the son-in-law formed a Texas limited partnership, SFLP, and its Texas corporate general partner, Stranco, Inc. At the time Strangi was suffering from terminal cancer and had a brain disorder. The son-in-law handled all of the details of the formation and executed the documents in Strangi's name as his attorney-in-fact. The son-in-law assigned to SFLP Strangi's interest in certain real estate, securities, accrued interest and dividends, insurance policies, and annuities with a combined fair market value of $9,876,929 in exchange for a 99% interest in the partnership. Seventy-five percent of the value was attributable to cash and securities. Strangi acquired a 47% interest in Stranco for $49,350, and his four children acquired the remaining 53% for $55,650. Stranco contributed $100,333 to the limited partnership in exchange for a 1% partnership interest. Since the children had control of Stranco, they technically also had control of the limited partnership. All of these transactions were completed by August, 1994. In October of that year, Strangi died. By 1998, SFLP had distributed around $2.5 million to each of the Strangi children.

When filing the estate tax return, Strangi's estate took minority-interest and lack-of-marketability discounts on the value of the SFLP interests it held. At trial, the IRS argued that the existence of SFLP should be disregarded for lack of a business purpose and economic substance. The estate argued that by creating another layer through which creditors would have to bore, SFLP helped insulate Strangi from an anticipated tort claim from a caregiver and helped insulate the estate from a will contest from disinherited stepchildren. The estate also maintained that SFLP provided a joint investment vehicle for managing Strangi's assets. The court largely rejected the estate's arguments, stating that there was no realistic prospect of either a tort claim or a will contest. The court noted that Strangi ended up with 99.47% of SFLP, directly or indirectly, and that the three of the four Strangi children were not meaningfully involved in the affairs of SFLP prior to the division of the partnership's Merrill Lynch account about two years after Strangi died. This division had given the children control over their respective shares of that account. The court, therefore, concluded that a joint investment motive was not apparent either. Further, SFLP conducted no active business. Actual control was exercised by the son-in-law, via the power of attorney, meaning that technically Strangi remained in control. The Tax Court, however, refused to disregard the entities that were created. It also held that the IRS had raised I.R.C. § 2036 too late in the proceedings and did not consider it. In the first trial, the Tax Court allowed the taxpayer significant discounts.

The Fifth Circuit reversed, holding that it was improper not to have considered I.R.C. § 2036 and directing the Tax Court to do so. On remand, the Tax Court held that 99% of the net asset value of SFLP and 47% of the net asset value of Stranco (these percentages equal the percentages Strangi owned in the two entities) were included in the decedent's estate under both I.R.C. § 2036(a)(1) and (2). As the assets were included and not the ownership interests in the entities, the estate lost the benefits of the discounts.

I.R.C. § 2036(a)(1) provides that the estate of a decedent includes transferred property if the decedent retained possession or enjoyment of the property or the right to income from the property. I.R.C. § 2036(a)(2) provides that the estate includes all assets that the decedent has transferred while retaining the right to designate who shall possess or enjoy the associated property or income. In holding that I.R.C. § 2036(a)(1) required inclusion, the court emphasized that the decedent retained the same relationship to the assets he had before SFLP and Stranco were formed.[66] In holding that I.R.C. § 2036(a)(2) also required inclusion, the court emphasized that the decedent's attorney-in-fact, the son-in-law, was in a position to make distribution decisions. The court also noted that the decedent could act together with other Stranco shareholders essentially to revoke the SFLP arrangement and thereby to bring about or accelerate the present enjoyment of partnership assets.[67] The *Strangi* decisions have, for the most part, sounded the death knell for near-death family limited partnerships designed to save estate taxes as the decedent breathed his last. No case since then has sanctioned *Strangi*-type planning, though *Kimbell v. United States*,[68] discussed below, gets close to the line.

In the cases that have come out since *Strangi*, the focus has often been on an exception to I.R.C. § 2036. That exception provides that I.R.C. § 2036 does not apply if the transfer is a bona fide sale for an adequate and full consideration in money or money's worth ("§ 2036 exception").[69] The Tax Court in *Estate of Stone v. Commissioner*[70] held that the § 2036 exception applied to an exchange of property for interests in several family limited partnerships where legitimate negotiations took place between all of the parties (all of whom were represented by counsel), and the transfer was motivated by investment and business concerns.

In that case, the primary source of the family's wealth was a sports apparel manufacturing business which the family limited partnerships did not manage. Bitter litigation had arisen between the children about the management of the company, however, and there were strong rivalries among the children as to who succeeded to which of the parents' assets. The decedent and his wife were no longer interested in managing their own assets, which were substantial and diverse, and wanted help with their management. Forming the family limited partnerships resolved the litigation among the children and provided the parents with the help they wanted in managing their assets, help they may have genuinely needed. The children were actively involved in the family limited partnerships.

The court specifically found that the transfers by the decedent and his wife were not gifts to their children, who were the other partners in the partnership, and that there were legitimate, nontax reasons for the transfers. Further, the decedent retained substantial assets for the support of him and his wife, and he and his wife

---

[66] *See* Estate of Reichardt v. Commissioner, 114 T.C. 144 (2000).

[67] The *Strangi* case was again appealed. This time the Fifth Circuit affirmed the Tax Court. Strangi v. Commissioner, 417 F.3d 468 (5th Cir. 2005), reh'g granted, 429 F.3d 1154 (5th Cir. 2005).

[68] 371 F.3d 257 (5th Cir. 2004).

[69] *See also* Estate of Harper v. Commissioner, T.C. Memo 2002-121; Estate of Reichardt v. Commissioner, 114 T.C. 144 (2000).

[70] Estate of Stone v. Commissioner, T.C. Memo 2003-309.

were in good health during most of the negotiations. The fact that the decedent died shortly after the family limited partnerships were funded did not change the outcome. In the family limited partnership world, facts such as those in *Stone* are, to say the least, out of the ordinary.

A rather more typical case is the Fifth Circuit's decision in *Kimbell v. United States*.[71] While the facts were in some respects reminiscent of those in *Strangi*, there were important differences. The family limited partnership held business interests (in the form of oil and gas working interests) as well as investments, and the decedent retained sufficient assets for her support. Here the crucial entities were formed about two months before the decedent died at the age of 96. Unlike in *Estate of Stone*, there was no suggestion of legitimate negotiations between the parties. The decedent had years earlier formed a revocable living trust to hold the bulk of her assets. This trust could have helped her avoid probate, but would not have reduced estate taxes as the assets of a revocable trust are included in the decedent's estate under I.R.C. § 2038.

About two months before her death, doubtless under direction from her son, the decedent, her son, and her son's wife formed two other entities. The most important of these was a family limited partnership to which the trust contributed $2.5 million, primarily in cash, oil and gas working interests and royalty interests, securities, and notes. In exchange, the trust received a 99% limited partnership interest. Because it was a revocable trust, the transfer by the trust was seen as a transfer by the decedent. An LLC, of which her son was the sole manager, became the general partner of the family limited partnership. A likely important fact was that the decedent retained $450,000 in assets for her own support. When the estate filed its federal estate tax return, it took a 49% discount on the value of the decedent's interest in the family limited partnership. On cross summary judgment motions, the district court held for the IRS. The Fifth Circuit reversed and held that the § 2036 exception applied.[72] This exception can be seen as having two parts: (i) there must be a bona fide sale and (ii) the bona fide sale must be for an adequate and full consideration in money or money's worth.

The Fifth Circuit focused on the second part of the test first, holding that there is adequate and full consideration if the transfer does not deplete the estate. Arguably an estate is not depleted when assets are transferred to a family limited partnership and the estate receives family limited partnership interests in exchange for the assets, as long as the interests received are proportional to the assets transferred. The court noted that the inquiry is an objective one, and the answer need not change because family members are involved in the transaction. Having a tax savings motive is not fatal. The court held that, unlike in *Estate of Stone*, the absence of negotiations between the parties was not a compelling factor in the determination of whether or not the § 2036 exception applied. The court did observe, however, that transactions involving family members may receive heightened scrutiny to insure that they are undertaken in good faith, not a sham or a disguised gift, and have a business purpose; a transaction motivated solely by tax

---

[71] 371 F.3d 257 (5th Cir. 2004).

[72] *See also* Church v. United States, 85 A.F.T.R.2d 804 (W.D. Tex. 2000), *aff'd*, 268 F.3d 1063 (5th Cir. 2001).

planning with no business or corporate purpose is nothing more than a contrivance without substance that is rightly ignored for purposes of the tax computation.

In the court's view, the fact that in *Kimbell* the family limited partnership interest was discounted for valuation purposes did not prevent a finding that the consideration was adequate, provided that the interest received was proportionate to the property transferred. The court noted that investors who acquire partnership interests do so knowing they cannot sell them for 100 cents on the dollar and with the expectation of realizing benefits of management expertise, security, preservation of assets, capital appreciation and avoidance of personal liability. The court concluded that the partnership interest credited to the decedent was proportionate to her contribution and that there was thus adequate and full consideration. There is tension between this opinion of the Fifth Circuit and the views of the Tax Court. The Tax Court has held that an arm's length bargain cannot exist in a transaction where the decedent stands on both sides of it.[73] The Tax Court has held that the adequate and full consideration part of the § 2036 exception is not met where:

> Without any change whatsoever in the underlying pool of assets or prospect for profit, as, for example, where others make contributions of property or services in the interest of a true joint ownership or enterprise, there exists nothing but a circuitous recycling of value. We are satisfied that such instances of pure recycling do not rise to the level of a payment of consideration. To hold otherwise would open section 2036 to a myriad of abuses engendered by unilateral paper transformations.[74]

The Fifth Circuit briefly took note of the Tax Court's second decision in *Strangi*, implicitly approving of the holding. The Fifth Circuit emphasized the Tax Court's conclusion that the partnership patently failed to qualify as the sort of functioning business enterprise that could potentially inject intangibles that would lift the situation beyond mere recycling. While this perhaps points out the value of having the family limited partnership conduct a business, it does not resolve the tension. The latter language notwithstanding, the Fifth Circuit would seem to permit recycling where the Tax Court would not. (As we discussed above, the Fifth Circuit subsequently affirmed the holding in *Strangi*.)

Moving on to the bona fide sale part of the § 2036 exception, the Fifth Circuit held that there was evidence that the transaction was entered into for substantial business and other non-tax reasons. The court noted the following:

> (1) the taxpayer retained sufficient assets for her own support and there was no commingling of partnership and personal assets;

> (2) partnership formalities were satisfied and the assets to be contributed were actually assigned to the partnership;

> (3) there was a need for the active management of the oil and gas properties, which included working interests;

---

[73] Estate of Harper v. Commissioner, T.C. Memo 2002-121.

[74] *Id.*

(4) greater creditor protection was available to a limited partnership than to the trust structure the taxpayer had been using;

(5) the decedent wanted the operation of the oil and gas properties to continue beyond her lifetime;

(6) the structure permitted the avoidance of the costs of recording transfers of oil and gas properties as they are transferred from one generation to the next;

(7) holding the assets in an entity preserved the property as separate property of decedent's descendants, in the event, for example, of a divorce;

(8) the structure provided for management of the assets if something should happen to decedent's son; and

(9) the structure provided a means to avoid intrafamily litigation by providing for disputes to be resolved through mediation or arbitration.

Most of these tests could be met by most family limited partnerships. The ones that stand out as perhaps being particularly important are that the decedent kept sufficient assets for her own support and that some of the assets required active management.

The Third Circuit weighed in against the taxpayer in *Estate of Thompson v. Commissioner*.[75] The decedent, while in his nineties, transferred assets, mostly securities, to a family limited partnership. He owned 49% of the corporate general partner. The estate took the usual discounts for lack of marketability and minority interest. The Third Circuit affirmed the Tax Court and held that I.R.C. § 2036(a)(1) included the full value of the transferred assets in the estate. The decedent did not retain sufficient assets to support himself.[76] While the decedent lacked technical control since others owned the majority of the stock of the corporate general partner, he sought and received assurances that he could make withdrawals as needed, implying an understanding that he would be the primary beneficiary of the assets of the family limited partnership. Further, the family limited partnership engaged in minimal business activities outside the family, and thus the valuation discount provided the primary benefit for converting marketable assets into illiquid family limited partnership interests. The court rejected the argument that the transfers fell within the § 2036 exception because of the lack of significant business operations and the fact that the family limited partnership did not provide the decedent with any potential non-tax benefit. In the court's view, if there is no discernable purpose or benefit for the transfer other than estate tax savings, the sale is not bona fide within the meaning of the § 2036 exception; while this test does not necessarily demand a transaction between a transferor and an unrelated third party, intrafamily transfers are subjected to heightened scrutiny. *Estate of Thompson* is distinguishable from *Kimbell* in that the assets transferred were arguably

---

[75] 382 F.3d 367 (3d Cir. 2004).

[76] This same issue arose in the following cases, the taxpayer losing in each instance: Estate of Bigelow v. Commissioner, T.C. Memo 2005-65; Estate of Korby v. Commissioner, T.C. Memo 2005-102; Estate of Korby, T.C Memo 2005-103 (the two *Korby* cases involve spouses that died within five months of each other).

more passive in nature, the decedent did not retain sufficient assets for his support, and there was an implied agreement he would be the primary beneficiary of the family limited partnership. The *Estate of Thompson* court decision strongly suggests, but never quite says, that the family limited partnership would have to operate a business to pass muster.

The cases discussed to this point have all involved family limited partnerships that were formed toward the end of the decedent's expected life, though in *Estate of Thompson* the decedent lived for two years after the family limited partnerships were formed. While the language of the cases could surely apply more broadly, many practitioners took solace from the fact that longer standing family limited partnerships remained unscathed. However, the facts and the broadness of the Tax Court decision in *Estate of Bongard v. Commissioner*[77] took away much of that solace and raised fundamental questions about the efficacy of family limited partnerships as an estate planning tool in many circumstances. The majority of the Tax Court judges adopted a two-part test.

In sum, the court concluded that in order to fall within the section 2036 exception, there must be meaningful nontax reasons for forming the family limited partnership, and the transferors must receive family limited partnership interests proportionate to the value of the property transferred. The case did not involve a last-minute family limited partnership as the decedent formed it about two years before he unexpectedly died while on a hunting trip in Austria. He was 58 when he died and appeared to be in good health at the time the family limited partnership was formed.

The corporate and estate planning structures used were complex, and we will focus on the essentials. In 1980, Wayne Bongard formed, and at all times controlled, Empak, a corporation which conducted a number of highly successful businesses and that was the primary source of the taxpayer's wealth. In 1986, Bongard contributed shares of Empak stock to the ISA Trust for the benefit of his children and a daughter of his wife. The trustees of the trust were Bongard's son, his attorney, and a close advisor. Bongard wanted to eventually make a private or public offering of Empak stock and believed that investors would be more likely to invest in Empak if the Bongard family ownership were placed in a holding company. To this end, in 1996 Bongard and the ISA Trust established the WCB Holdings, LLC. They contributed their Empak stock to the LLC. Bongard held the controlling interest in the LLC.

In December 1996, Bongard and the ISA Trust formed the Bongard Family Limited Partnership (BFLP) and contributed nonvoting membership units in WCB Holdings, LLC to it. The ISA Trust was the general partner. Later, as part of a post-nuptial agreement, Bongard gave a 7.72% interest in BFLP to his wife. The estate claimed that BFLP was formed as a means of giving assets to Bongard's family members without deterring them from working hard and becoming educated. Further objectives claimed by the estate included providing a method for

---

[77] 124 T.C. 95 (2005). Subsequent Tax Court cases essentially follow the reasoning of *Estate of Bongard*: Estate of Korby v. Commissioner, T.C. Memo 2005-102 (husband); Estate of Korby v. Commissioner, T.C. Memo 2005-103 (wife); Estate of Bigelow v. Commissioner, T.C. Memo 2005-65.

protecting Bongard's estate from frivolous law suits and creditors, tutelage with respect to managing the family's assets, and, of course, the transfer tax benefits. BFLP did not perform any activities and never acted to diversify its assets or make any distributions. BFLP was not intended to be a last-minute tax savings device and indeed was two years old before Bongard's unexpected death.

The IRS argued that both the assets of WCB Holdings, LLC and BFLP should be included in the estate under I.R.C. § 2036. Bongard's estate reported that it owed an estate tax of about $17 million. The IRS claimed an estate tax deficiency of more than $52 million (the estate's Empak stock was valued at $141.6 million).

The court concluded that the § 2036 exception applied to the formation of WCB Holdings, LLC. In reviewing the bona fide sale part of the test, the court noted that significant nontax considerations were involved. The formation of WCB Holdings, LLC was part of a plan to increase the liquidity of Empak and make it more attractive to potential investors. The LLC's funds were not commingled with those of Bongard, the members' capital accounts were properly credited and maintained, and all distributions that were made were pro rata, indicating to the court that there was a true pooling of assets. In reviewing the full and adequate consideration part of the test, the court noted that Bongard and the ISA trust each received an interest proportionate to what they contributed. In something of an overlap with the bona fide sale part of the test, the court again pointed out that capital accounts of the partners were properly maintained and that there were legitimate and significant nontax business reasons for engaging in the transaction. The court rejected the IRS's argument that Bongard should have received a control premium as Bongard stayed in effective control.

BFLP, on the other hand, was a different story. The court observed that on formation Bongard received a 99% limited partnership interest in BFLP. The court did not say, but implied, that there was no genuine pooling of assets. Further, BFLP did not perform management functions for the assets it received, engage in any businesslike transactions, or attempt to diversify its assets. The court concluded that Bongard did not receive any benefit beyond the transfer tax savings; there was a mere recycling of his assets. In response to the estate's argument that BFLP was formed, in part, to continue Bongard's gift giving, the court noted that he did not make any gifts of BFLP interests. The only transfer was of a 7.72% interest to his wife as part of a post-nuptial agreement.[78] The court also rejected that BFLP served to protect Bongard from creditors, as WCB Holdings, LLC already served that purpose. Given the noted factors, the court concluded that the transfer to BFLP did not satisfy the § 2036 exception.

That actually was not the end of the discussion, inasmuch as for the general rule of I.R.C. § 2036 to apply, Bongard must either have kept possession or enjoyment, or the ability to determine (alone or with others) who would possess or enjoy the transferred property. In the court's view, Bongard controlled, via his interests in Empak and WCB Holdings, LLC, whether or not BFLP could transform its interest in WCB Holdings, LLC into a liquid asset and engage in any kind of asset

---

[78] Query if the result in the case would have been different if Bongard had had a program of regularly gifting interests.

management. This ability indicated to the court (doubtless accurately) that there was an implied agreement of the parties that decedent retained the right to control the units transferred to BFLP. Further, the court concluded that the estate's argument that the general partner's state law fiduciary duties to the limited partners prevents a finding of an implied agreement was overcome by the lack of activity following BFLP's formation and BFLP's failure to perform any meaningful functions as an entity.[79]

It was a profitable trial for the IRS. The Tax Court's decision has been estimated to be worth $66.9 million in estate taxes.[80]

The First Circuit chimed in with *Abraham v. Commissioner*.[81] It is less controversial and in many respects reminiscent of *Estate of Thompson*. The decedent, Mrs. Abraham, had suffered from Alzheimer's disease and a guardian had been appointed for her. Litigation ensued between several of her children over the amount needed for the decedent's protection. A court-approved settlement was reached between the children and the guardian under which three commercial properties were placed in three separate family limited partnerships. Mrs. Abraham died about two years later. The court concluded that it was understood that the support of Mrs. Abraham would be the first claim against the funds of the family limited partnerships even though the family limited partnership agreements might not have technically required that outcome. As our discussion above shows, this type of understanding triggers I.R.C. § 2036 and in this instance required the inclusion of the family limited partnerships' assets in Mrs. Abraham's estate.

Estate of Korby v. Commissioner,[82] an Eighth Circuit decision, involved a variation on a strategy that had already been rejected by other courts. An elderly husband and wife attended a free estate planning seminar conducted by a lawyer, hired the lawyer, and acted on his advice. In 1993, they transferred their home and other assets to a revocable trust. In 1995, they transferred $1.8 million in stocks and bonds to a family limited partnership. The assets transferred to the family limited partnership appear to have constituted a substantial majority of the wealth of the Korbys, and likely almost all of their liquid assets. It is not entirely clear from the case, but presumably the stocks were publicly traded and thus marketable securities. The revocable trust, which held almost all of their remaining assets,[83] was the 2% general partner, and the couple initially held the 98% limited partnership interest. Contemporaneously with the transfer of the assets to the family limited partnership, the Korbys gifted their 98% limited partnership interest

---

[79] The Tax Court has issued other opinions that are consistent with those discussed in this chapter, including Estate of *Jorgensen v. Commissioner*, T.C. Memo 2009-66; Estate of *Erickson v. Commissioner*, T.C. Memo 2007-107; and *Estate of Rosen v. Commissioner*, T.C. Memo 2006-115. For a case demonstrating how not to do family limited partnership planning, see Estate of *Hurford v. Commissioner*, T. C. Memo 2008-278; *see also* Wendy Gerzog, Hurford: *Family Limited Partnership Practice Pointers*, 122 Tax Notes 799 (2009).

[80] Thanks to Professor Carter Bishop of Suffolk University Law School for providing this figure.

[81] 408 F.3d 26 (1st Cir. 2005), *opinion amended*, 429 F.3d 294 (1st Cir. 2005), *cert. denied*, 547 U.S. 1178 (2006).

[82] 471 F.3d 848 (8th Cir. 2006).

[83] Under I.R.C. § 2038, the assets of the revocable trust would have been included in their estate.

to four irrevocable trusts for the benefits of their four sons, claiming a 46.61% discount on the gift for gift tax purposes.

Before their deaths, the family limited partnership made distributions to the revocable trust, as general partner, of about $120,000 in purported management fees. These distributions were used to defray the Korby nursing home and medical expenses, as well as to pay their taxes. This use of family limited partnership funds to pay personal expenses of the donors has proved fatal in other cases and was fatal here, particularly in light of the fact that the family limited partnership held the bulk of the Korbys' liquid assets. The Tax Court concluded that the payments were not management fees and that an implied agreement existed that after the assets were transferred to the family limited partnership they would continue to be available to the Korbys. This holding would generally require that the family limited partnership assets be included in the estate under I.R.C. § 2036(a)(1), unless the § 2036 exception applied. The Tax Court held that the section 2036 exception did not apply since Austin Korby essentially stood on all sides of the family limited partnership formation.

The Eighth Circuit affirmed these holdings of the Tax Court, noting that the Korbys did not retain sufficient assets to pay their ongoing expenses. The Eighth Circuit also stated that a transfer is typically not considered a bona fide sale when the taxpayer stands on both sides of the transaction, citing *Estate of Bongard*. It also concluded that for the transaction to be respected there must be some potential for benefits beyond estate tax saving, citing *Estate of Thompson*. Consequently, the family limited partnership assets were included in the Korbys' estates under I.R.C. § 2036(a)(1) (effectively mooting the gift).

In *Estate of Mirowski v. Commissioner*,[84] the Tax Court seems to have lightened up a bit. The court ruled in favor of the estate, holding that the decedent had the following legitimate and significant nontax purposes in forming a family LLC: "(1) Joint management of the family's assets by her daughters and eventually her grandchildren; (2) maintenance of the bulk of the family's assets in a single pool of assets in order to allow for investment opportunities that would not be available if Ms. Mirowski were to make a separate gift of a portion of her assets to each of her daughters or to each of her daughters' trusts; and (3) provision for each of her daughters and eventually each of her grandchildren on an equal basis."[85] It is noteworthy that the decedent had a long history of giving, that her death was unexpected, and that *Mirowski*, as a memorandum decision, did not receive the same level of court scrutiny as *Estate of Bongard*.

Finally, in *Estate of Miller v. Commissioner*,[86] the taxpayer was able to extract a partial victory. The decedent's husband had developed his own investment method and managed the family's investments. After the husband's death, the family in 2002 created a family limited partnership with a son as the general partner. The limited partners were the other three children and the decedent's wife as trustee of a QTIP.

---

[84] T.C. Memo 2008-74; *see* Wendy Gerzog, *Tax Court FLP Confusion:* Mirowski, 120 TAX NOTES 263 (2008).

[85] T.C. Memo 2008-74, at 81.

[86] T.C. Memo 2009-119.

Most of the family limited partnership's assets were marketable securities. The son worked about 40 hours per week managing the family limited partnership's investments according to his father's investment strategy. Later, in 2003, after her health deteriorated, the wife made several transfers representing most of her remaining wealth to the family limited partnership. Shortly thereafter she died.

The Tax Court held that the 2002 transfers fell within the bona fide sales exception to I.R.C. § 2036. The wife created the family limited partnership, the court concluded, for the management of her investments under her deceased husband's investment method. The existence of a long-established investment method likely allowed this family limited partnership of marketable securities to pass muster. As we have seen, family limited partnerships with marketable securities are generally very suspect. Further, the decedent was in good health at the time this family limited partnership was created and retained significant assets to maintain her lifestyle. The 2003 transfers, on the other hand, lacked a significant nontax motive, and were includable in the wife's estate.[87]

These cases generally demonstrate that use of family limited partnerships can be a viable part of an estate planning strategy with the right facts and the right planning. Most important is that some viable nontax purpose exists for creating the family limited partnership.

§ 14.06   READING, QUESTIONS AND PROBLEMS

A.   Reading

CODE:

    I.R.C. §§ 721, 704(e), 351(e), 262, 280A, 482, 731.

TREASURY REGULATIONS:

    Treas. Reg. § 1.704-1(e), 1.351-1(c).

B.   Questions and Problems

1. Mom and Pop equalize their portfolios in publicly traded securities then contribute their portfolios to NewFLP, LLC. NewFLP, LLC holds no other assets after the contribution and there is no plan or arrangement existing at the time of the contribution to sell any of the securities contributed. Will the contributions by Mom and Pop be treated as a transfer to a partnership that would be tax-free under I.R.C. § 721(b)?

---

[87] *See* Estate of Black v. Commissioner, 133 T.C. 340 (2009) (taxpayer win); Jorgensen v. Commissioner, T.C. Memo 2009-66 (taxpayer loss); Pierre v. Commissioner, 133 T.C. 24 (2009) (property rights initially determined under state law). *See also* Wendy Gerzog, *FLP in the* Black, 127 TAX NOTES 343 (2010); Estate of Turner v. Commissioner, T.C. Memo 2011-209; Wendy Gerzog, *FLP Loss, But* Crummey *Win*, 133 TAX NOTES 1139 (2011).

2. Mom and Pop equalize their portfolios in publicly traded securities then contribute their portfolios to NewFLP, LLC. As part of the same plan or arrangement, Janice, their daughter, also contributes cash equal to 10% of the assets of NewFLP, LLC determined immediately after the contribution. Will the contributions by Mom and Pop be treated as a transfer to a partnership that would be tax-free under I.R.C. § 721(b)? Would your answer change if there was a plan or arrangement existing at the time of the contribution of Mom and Pop's portfolio and Janice's cash to invest the cash in securities that replicate the portfolios contributed by Mom and Pop?

3. Mom and Pop equalize their portfolios in publicly traded securities then contribute their portfolios to NewFLP, LLC. NewFLP, LLC holds no other assets after the contribution and there is no plan or arrangement existing at the time of the contribution to sell any of the securities contributed. Immediately after the contribution to NewFLP, LLC, Mom and Pop each give 10% of their interest in NewFLP, LLC to their daughter Janice. Janice provides no services to, and contributes no capital to, NewFLP, LLC. However, the documents do not restrict Janice's ability to dispose of the interest; the documents require regular distributions to all members and Janice has a vote proportionate to her membership interest. Will Janice be respected as a partner of NewFLP, LLC for federal income tax purposes?

4. Lyle owns a condo in Orlando. He uses the condo two weeks a year, and rents it out as much as he can for the rest of the year. He lets his family use the condo whenever he has not rented it to a third party. In terms of the total usage of the condo, it tends to run three weeks to third parties, 6 weeks to family, and two weeks for himself. What portion of the expenses related to the condo may be deducted by Lyle? How does your answer change if Lyle charges his family fair market rent?

5. Mom and Pop equalize their portfolios in publicly traded securities then contribute their portfolios to NewFLP, LLC. NewFLP, LLC holds no other assets after the contribution and there is no plan or arrangement existing at the time of the contribution to sell any of the securities contributed. Immediately after the contribution to NewFLP, LLC, Mom and Pop each give 10% of their interest in NewFLP, LLC to their daughter Janice. Six years later, NewFLP, LLC redeems out Janice in exchange for a distribution in kind of 10% of the portfolio securities held by the company. The securities distributed out to Janice are distributed in proportion to their relative values in the portfolio of the company the day before the distribution. Do Mom and Pop recognize gain on the distribution under I.R.C. § 704(c)? Does Janice recognize gain on the distribution under I.R.C. § 737? Does Janice recognize gain on the distribution under I.R.C. § 731?

Chapter 15

DEATH OF A PARTNER

§ 15.01 INTRODUCTION

In Chapter 6, we discussed the potential step-up in the basis of partnership assets upon a partner's death if an election under I.R.C. § 754 has been made (as well as disposition of partnership interests, generally). In Chapter 7, we discussed the treatment of the retirement of a partner or the liquidation of a partnership interest (as well as partnership distributions, generally). In this chapter we review some of the general rules applicable on the death of a partner and focus on the special rules that are applicable to partners and partnerships when income in respect of a decedent is recognized.

§ 15.02 TERMINATION OF A PARTNERSHIP

I.R.C. § 708 provides that a partnership is considered as terminated only if: (i) no part of any business, financial operation, or venture of the partnership continues to be carried on by any of its partners in a partnership, or (ii) within a 12-month period there is a sale or exchange of 50% or more of the total interests in partnership capital and profits. Death of the partner does not ordinarily result in the termination of the partnership under I.R.C. § 708(b)(1)(B), because a disposition by gift, bequest, or inheritance is not considered a sale or exchange.[1] The death of a partner may result in the termination of a partnership under I.R.C. § 708(b)(1)(A) when the partnership is a two-person partnership. In such a case the death of the partner will cause the partnership to terminate unless the estate or other successor continues to share in the profits or losses of the partnership business.[2]

For example, suppose D and E are equal partners in a two-person partnership engaged in the wholesale produce business. Upon D's death, E purchases with cash, pursuant to a buy and sell agreement, and through the use of E's own funds, the decedent's interest in the partnership from his estate. Thereafter, the business is continued by E as a sole proprietorship. The sale of D's partnership interest to E results in the termination of the partnership under I.R.C. § 708(b)(1)(A) since the business is no longer carried on by any of its partners in a partnership.[3]

On the other hand, Treas. Reg. § 1.708-1(b)(1)(i) provides that upon the death of one partner in a two-member partnership, the partnership will not be considered as

---

[1] Treas. Reg. § 1.708-1(b)(2).

[2] Treas. Reg. § 1.708-1(b)(1)(i).

[3] Rev. Rul. 67-65, 1967-1 C.B. 168.

terminated if the estate or other successor in interest of the deceased partner continues to share in the profits or losses of the partnership business.

For example, A and B were equal partners in AB, a calendar year partnership. B died on January 1, 1983. Upon B's death, B's estate succeeded to B's interest in AB. The value of B's partnership interest as determined for federal estate tax purposes greatly exceeded the adjusted basis of B's share of partnership assets. During 1983, B's estate was taxable on its distributable share of partnership income. AB's partnership return for 1983 was filed on April 1, 1984. Although AB was a two-person partnership, the partnership does not terminate because the estate succeeds to the interest of the decedent.[4]

For these purposes, a deceased partner's successor-in-interest receiving payments under I.R.C. § 736 is regarded as a partner until the entire interest of the deceased partner is liquidated. Therefore, if a partner in a two-person partnership dies, and the partner's estate or other successor-in-interest receives payments under I.R.C. § 736, the partnership is not considered to have terminated upon the death of the partner, but terminates as to both partners only when the entire interest of the decedent is liquidated.[5]

Often partnership agreements will contain "buy-sell" provisions which allow or require the partnership interest to be sold upon the death of a partner. The manner of the sale may be in the form of a redemption by the partnership or a purchase of the interest by the remaining partners.

Ordinarily, the sale of a partnership interest by a partner owning 50% or more of the capital and profits interest of the partnership within a 12-month period will cause the partnership to terminate.[6] However, for the purposes of calculating whether the requisite 50% or more has been sold, liquidations of a partnership interest are excluded.[7] Thus, assume that A, B, and C are 20%, 20%, and 60% partners respectively in ABC. If C were to die, and if the partnership liquidated C's interest in the partnership, the partnership would not terminate under I.R.C. § 708(b). However, if a buy-sell agreement provides for A and B to each purchase half of C's interest, the partnership would have a sale or exchange of more than 50% of the interests in profits and capital, terminating the partnership under I.R.C. § 708(b).

§ 15.03   INCOME IN RESPECT OF A DECEDENT

I.R.C. § 691(a)(1)(A) provides that the amount of all items of gross income in respect of a decedent which are not properly includible for the taxable period in which the date of the decedent's death falls or a prior period, are included in the gross income of the estate of the decedent. (This assumes that, as typically would be the case, the right to receive the amount is acquired by the decedent's estate from the decedent.) I.R.C. § 691 does not actually contain a definition of income in

---

[4] Rev. Rul. 86-139, 1986-2 C.B. 95.

[5] Treas. Reg. § 1.736-1(a)(6).

[6] I.R.C. § 708(b).

[7] Treas. Reg. § 708-1(b)(2).

respect of a decedent. A definition is provided, however, by Treas. Reg. § 1.691(a)-1(b) which states:

> In general, the term "income in respect of a decedent" refers to those amounts to which a decedent was entitled as gross income but which were not properly includible in computing his taxable income for the taxable year ending with the date of his death or for a previous taxable year under the method of accounting employed by the decedent. . . . Thus, the term includes —
>
> (1) all accrued income of a decedent who reported his income by use of the cash receipts and disbursements method;
>
> (2) income accrued solely by reason of the decedent's death in case of a decedent who reports his income by use of an accrual method of accounting; and
>
> (3) income to which the decedent had a contingent claim at the time of his death.

In the partnership context, this definition has been modified by I.R.C. § 753, which provides that the amount includible in the gross income of a successor-in-interest of a deceased partner as the deceased partner's distributive share of partnership income under I.R.C. § 736(a) is considered income in respect of a decedent under I.R.C. § 691. The legislative history to I.R.C. § 753 indicates that Congress was intending to cause the I.R.C. § 736(a) payment to be income in respect of a decedent to the successor to the extent such amounts are attributable to the decedent's interest in the partnership's unrealized receivables and fees.[8]

In contrast with the somewhat narrower scope of the legislative history, the Regulations under I.R.C. § 753 provide that all payments coming within the provisions of I.R.C. § 736(a) made by a partnership to the estate or other successor-in-interest of a deceased partner are considered income in respect of a decedent under I.R.C. § 691.[9]

You may recall from our discussions in Chapter 7 that payments under I.R.C. § 736 may be comprised of several components. I.R.C. § 736(b) payments are generally payments for a partner's interest in partnership property. I.R.C. § 736(a) payments are either treated as a distributive share of partnership income if the payment is based upon partnership income or a guaranteed payment if the payment is not based upon partnership income. The Regulations under I.R.C. § 753 would require both types of I.R.C. § 736(a) payments to be treated as income in respect of a decedent.

Of course, if the estate continues as a partner in the partnership rather than withdrawing from the partnership upon the death of the partner, I.R.C. § 736 does not apply to the distributions that the partnership receives.[10] Instead, distributions during the period in which the estate or other successor continues as a partner

---

[8] H.R. Rep. 1337, 83d Cong., 2d Sess. 237 (1954).

[9] Treas. Reg. § 1.753-1(a).

[10] Treas. Reg. § 1.736-1(a)(1)(i).

would be treated under the normal rules under I.R.C. § 731.

The estate or other successor-in-interest of a deceased partner is also considered to have received income in respect of a decedent to the extent that amounts are paid by a third person in exchange for rights to future payments from the partnership under I.R.C. § 736(a).[11] Thus, the disposition of a right to receive income in respect of a decedent will itself result in income in respect of a decedent.

Payments to the estate of a deceased law partner that represent a share of profits attributable to work completed after his death on matters in process at the date of his death, and post-death partnership income were held to be income in respect of a decedent in *Estate of Riegelman v. Commissioner.*[12]

This rule may be illustrated with the following example:

A and the decedent B were equal partners in a cash basis business having assets worth $40,000 with an adjusted basis of $10,000. Certain partnership business was well advanced toward completion before B's death and after B's death, but before the end of the partnership year, payment of $2,000 was made to the partnership for such work. The partnership agreement provided that, upon the death of one of the partners, all partnership property, including unfinished work, would pass to the surviving partner, and that the surviving partner would pay the estate of the decedent the estate's share of partnership earnings after the date of death in the year of death plus $10,000 in each of the three years after death. B's estate's share of earnings after the date of his death was $1,000. Assume that the value of B's interest in partnership property at the date of his death was $20,000. It should be noted that B's estate's $1,000 share of earnings after the date of his death is not a separate item, but will be paid from partnership assets. Under the partnership agreement, A is to pay B's estate a total of $31,000. The difference of $11,000 between the amount to be paid by A ($31,000) and the value of B's interest in partnership property ($20,000) comes within I.R.C. § 736(a) and, thus, constitutes income in respect of a decedent.[13]

The payments by the partnership in this example have three components. First, the $1,000 share of earnings would be an I.R.C. § 736(a)(1) payment. The $10,000 in excess of B's share of partnership property and not based upon the income of the partnership would be an I.R.C. § 736(a)(2) payment. The $20,000 paid in respect of B's interest in partnership property would be an I.R.C. § 736(b) payment.

Generally, the mechanics of the Regulations under I.R.C. § 736 determine the amount that is paid for the deceased partner's interest in partnership property first. The excess of any payments over that amount are I.R.C. § 736(a) payments. The termination of the taxable year of the partnership in respect of the decedent should change the amount of partnership items included in the decedent's final year return, but, depending upon the accounting method of the partnership and how I.R.C. § 753

---

[11] Treas. Reg. § 1.753-1(a).

[12] 253 F.2d 315 (2d Cir. 1958).

[13] This example is based upon the example in Treas. Reg. § 1.753-1(c) modified to reflect that I.R.C. § 706 now requires the taxable year of the partnership to close with respect to the decedent on the death of a partner.

and I.R.C. § 736 are reconciled, it should not change the total amount that is treated as income in respect of a decedent.

If the partnership is on the cash basis method of accounting, items not received before the date of death will properly be in the estate's taxable year, rather than the decedent's final taxable year. However, if the partnership is on the accrual method of accounting, it is possible that items may appear in the final taxable year of the decedent if all events have occurred to make them fixed and determinable. Thus, an item that might otherwise be income in respect of a decedent in the estate's return may more properly be treated as included in the final year of the decedent depending upon the facts and circumstances.

It should be noted that this particular issue is reconciled within I.R.C. § 736(b). Although unrealized receivables are excluded from partnership property for the purposes of I.R.C. § 736(b) for partnerships in which capital is not a material income-producing factor, "unrealized receivables" are defined in this context by cross reference to I.R.C. § 751. I.R.C. § 751 only includes in unrealized receivable items that have not previously been taken into income by the partnership. Thus, an accrual basis partnership that takes an unrealized receivable into income prior to the death of a decedent should then include that unrealized receivable as property for the purposes of I.R.C. § 736(b).

One of the common ways that an estate may have income in respect of a decedent outside the partnership context is when the decedent entered into an installment sale prior to death.[14] When a partner who is receiving payments under I.R.C. § 736(a) dies, I.R.C. § 753 applies to any remaining payments under I.R.C. § 736(a) made to his estate or other successor-in-interest.[15] The Regulations under I.R.C. § 753 do not expressly deal with the situation in which a partner has retired prior to death and is receiving payments under I.R.C. § 736(b) at the time of death, but it is reasonable to presume that the analysis of such payments in the hands of the estate should be similar to the treatment of an installment sale that had occurred prior to the date of death.[16]

§ 15.04   CLOSING OF THE PARTNERSHIP YEAR

I.R.C. § 706(a) provides that, in computing the taxable income of a partner for a taxable year, the inclusions required by I.R.C. §§ 702 and 707(c) with respect to a partnership is based on the income, gain, loss, deduction, or credit of the partnership for any taxable year of the partnership ending within or with the taxable year of the partner.

Under I.R.C. § 706(c)(2)(A), the taxable year of a partnership closes with respect to a partner whose entire interest terminates (whether by reason of death, liquidation, or otherwise). The partnership taxable year will close with respect to the deceased partner, and the decedent and the new partner must each include their

---

[14] *See, e.g.*, Meissner v. United States, 364 F.2d 409 (Ct. Cl. 1966).

[15] Treas. Reg. § 1.753-1(a).

[16] I.R.C. § 753 does not establish the boundaries for the application of I.R.C. § 691 in the partnership context. *See* Woodhall v. Commissioner, TC Memo 1969-279, *aff'd*, 454 F.2d 226 (9th Cir. 1972).

proportionate shares of partnership income, loss, deductions, and credits in income.[17]

For example, B has a taxable year ending December 31 and is a member of partnership ABC, the taxable year of which ends on June 30. B dies on October 31, 2011. When B dies on October 31, 2011, the partnership's taxable year beginning July 1, 2011, closes with respect to him. Therefore, the return for B's last taxable year (January 1 to October 31, 2011) will include B's distributive share of taxable income of the partnership for its taxable year ending June 30, 2011, plus B's distributive share of partnership taxable income for the period July 1 to October 31, 2011. B's successor would include the distributive share for the portion of the partnership year after October 31, 2011.[18]

Treas. Reg. § 1.706-1(c)(2)(ii) provides that in the case of a sale, exchange, or liquidation of a partner's entire interest in a partnership,[19] the partner will include in the partner's taxable income for the partner's taxable year within or with which the partner's membership in the partnership ends, the partner's distributive share of items described in I.R.C. § 702(a), and any guaranteed payments under I.R.C. § 707(c), for the partner's taxable year ending with the date of such sale, exchange, or liquidation.

To avoid the expense of an actual closing of the books, which would presumably require all of the same types of calculations for the segment created by the death of a partner that one would normally expect to be made at the end of the full taxable year, many smaller partnerships and partnerships that have frequent changes of interests have adopted the proration method. The current Regulations provide that changes during a taxable year may, by agreement among the partners, be estimated by taking the partner's pro rata part of the amount of such items the partner would have included in the partner's taxable income had the partner remained a partner until the end of the partnership taxable year.

Prop. Treas. Reg. § 1.706-4(d) provides that by agreement among the partners a partnership may use a proration method, rather than the interim closing of the books method, to take into account any variation in a partner's interest in the partnership during the taxable year. Under the proration method, except for extraordinary items,[20] the partnership allocates the distributive share of partnership items under I.R.C. § 702(a) among the partners in accordance with their pro rata shares of these same items for the entire taxable year. In determining a partner's pro rata share of partnership items, the partnership is required to take into account that partner's interest in such items during each segment of the taxable year.

---

[17] *See* Treas. Reg. § 1.706-1(c)(3)(iv) & (vi) example 2.

[18] This is based upon Treas. Reg. § 1.706-1(c)(3)(vi), example (2). The example assumes a closing of the books method.

[19] The current Regulations do not provide for the partnership taxable year to close in respect of a partner that dies during the partnership taxable year unless pursuant to a pre-existing agreement a sale or exchange occurs upon the death of the partner. This is an anomalous vestige of the Regulations that were in effect at the time the statute was amended to clarify that the partnership's taxable year does close in respect of a partner that dies.

[20] Defined in Prop. Treas. Reg. § 1.706-4(d)(3).

In addition, Prop. Treas. Reg. § 1.706-4(d)(3) requires a partnership using the proration method to allocate extraordinary items among the partners in proportion to their interests at the beginning of the day on which they are taken into account. For this purpose, an extraordinary item is: (i) any item from the disposition or abandonment (other than in the ordinary course of business) of a capital asset as defined in I.R.C. § 1221 (determined without the application of any other rules of law); (ii) any item from the disposition or abandonment of property used in a trade or business (other than in the ordinary course of business) as defined in I.R.C. § 1231(b) (determined without the application of any holding period requirement); (iii) any item from the disposition or abandonment of an asset described in I.R.C. § 1221(1), (3), (4), or (5), if substantially all the assets in the same category from the same trade or business are disposed of or abandoned in one transaction (or series of related transactions); (iv) any item from assets disposed of in an applicable asset acquisition under I.R.C. § 1060(c); (v) any I.R.C. § 481(a) adjustment; (vi) any item from the discharge or retirement of indebtedness (for example, if a debtor partnership transfers a capital or profits interest in such partnership to a creditor in satisfaction of its recourse or nonrecourse indebtedness, any discharge of indebtedness income recognized under I.R.C. § 108(e)(8) must be allocated among the persons who were partners in the partnership immediately before the discharge); (vii) any item from the settlement of a tort or similar third-party liability; (viii) any credit, to the extent it arises from activities or items that are not ratably allocated (for example, the rehabilitation credit under I.R.C. § 47, which is based on placement in service); and (ix) any item which, in the opinion of the IRS, would, if ratably allocated, result in a substantial distortion of income in any consolidated return or separate return in which the item is included.

Treas. Reg. § 1.706-1(c)(2)(ii) provides that, under the proration method, the partnership's income and losses may be prorated based on the portion of the taxable year that has elapsed prior to the date upon which the partners' interests varied, or "under any other method that is reasonable." These other reasonable methods have become known as *conventions*.

The IRS issued a news release[21] announcing that partnerships using the interim closing of the books method were permitted to use a semi-monthly convention. Under a semi-monthly convention, partners entering during the first 15 days of the month are treated as entering on the first day of the month, and partners entering after the 15th day of the month (but before the end of the month) are treated as entering on the 16th day of the month (except to the extent that I.R.C. § 706(c)(2)(A) applies). The news release provided that, until Regulations were issued, partnerships that use the proration method were required to use a daily convention.

Prop. Treas. Reg. § 1.706-4(a)(1) would add a rule that for each partnership taxable year in which a partner's interest varies, the partnership must use the same method to take into account all changes in partnership interests occurring within that year.

---

[21] IR-84-129 (http://www.irs.gov/puv/irs-drop/ir-84-129.pdf) (Dec. 13, 1984).

The Proposed Regulations under I.R.C. § 706 do not attempt to coordinate the Regulations under I.R.C. § 736 or I.R.C. § 753, so certain questions will remain on the determination of amounts of income in respect of a decedent. As noted above, because the mechanics of the Regulations under I.R.C. § 736 determine the amount that is paid for a partner's interest in partnership property first, with the excess of any payments being treated as I.R.C. § 736(a) payments, the termination of the taxable year of the partnership in respect of the decedent should change the amount of partnership items included in the decedent's final year return, but it should not change the total amount that is treated as income in respect of a decedent. However, there is a potential for uncertainty as to the character of the income in respect of a decedent.

Changing the example used above in the discussion of income in respect of a decedent:

A and the decedent B were equal partners in a cash basis business having assets worth $40,000 with an adjusted basis of $10,000. Before B's death, the partnership sold a capital asset held over one year with a basis of $2,000 in exchange for a payment of $4,000. The proceeds of the sale were undistributed at the time of B's death, but have been included in the assets of the partnership described above. The income in respect of the sale of property was long-term capital gain to the partnership. The partnership agreement provided that, upon the death of one of the partners, the surviving partner would pay the estate of the decedent the estate's share of undistributed partnership earnings to the date of death in the year of death plus $10,000 in each of the three years after death. Assume that the value of B's interest in partnership property at the date of his death was $20,000. Under the partnership agreement, A is to pay B's estate a total of $30,000. The difference of $10,000 between the amount to be paid by A ($30,000) and the value of B's interest in partnership property ($20,000) comes within I.R.C. § 736(a) and, thus, constitutes income in respect of a decedent.[22]

Of the $10,000 that is treated as an I.R.C. § 736(a) payment, $1,000 is determined with regard to partnership income, and, thus, on first blush, would appear to be an I.R.C. § 736(a)(1) payment. Treas. Reg. § 1.736-1(a)(4) provides that payments, to the extent considered as a distributive share of partnership income under I.R.C. § 736(a)(1), are taken into account under I.R.C. § 702 in the income of the withdrawing partner and thus reduce the amount of the distributive shares of the remaining partners. If B's estate takes the item into account under I.R.C. § 702, it might suggest that the character of the item of income (capital gain) would flow through to the estate. However, if B's taxable year closed on B's death, B has already taken the capital gain into account in B's final return.

Although there does not appear to be any authority directly on point, it would appear that the better view would be that, once B has taken the capital gain into income, I.R.C. § 736 should not treat the payment as an I.R.C. § 736(a)(1) payment. Thus, the character to the estate would be ordinary rather than capital.

---

[22] This example is based upon the example in Treas. Reg. § 1.753-1(c).

§ 15.05 ADJUSTMENT TO BASIS

I.R.C. § 1014(a) provides that the basis of property in the hands of a person acquiring the property from a decedent or to whom the property passed from a decedent shall, if not sold, exchanged, or otherwise disposed of before the decedent's death by such person, be the fair market value of the property at the date of the decedent's death, or the alternate valuation date, if applicable.

I.R.C. § 1014(c) provides that I.R.C. § 1014 does not apply to property that constitutes a right to receive an item of income in respect of a decedent under I.R.C. § 691. Consistent with I.R.C. § 1014(c), Treas. Reg. § 1.742-1 provides that the basis of a partnership interest acquired from a decedent is the fair market value of the interest at the date of the partner's death or at the alternate valuation date, increased by the estate's or other successor's share of partnership liabilities on that date, and reduced to the extent that such value is attributable to items constituting income in respect of a decedent.

If a partnership files an election under I.R.C. § 754, I.R.C. § 743(b) provides that in the case of a transfer of an interest in a partnership by sale or exchange or upon the death of a partner, a partnership will increase the adjusted basis of the partnership property by the excess of the basis to the transferee partner of the transferee's interest in the partnership over the transferee's proportionate share of the adjusted basis of the partnership property.

Rev. Rul. 87-115[23] permits an equivalent basis adjustment under I.R.C. § 743 by both a lower-tier and an upper-tier partnership in the case of a transfer (by exchange or death) of an interest in the upper-tier partnership provided both partnerships elect to adjust the basis of partnership assets under I.R.C. § 754.

A coordination issue also exists between I.R.C. §§ 1014, 736, and 753 if the deceased partner was a general partner and the business of the partnership is providing services. I.R.C. § 1014 would theoretically take into consideration in determining the value of the partnership all assets of the partnership, including goodwill, resulting in a basis adjustment under I.R.C. §§ 1014 and 742. On the other hand, I.R.C. § 736(b)(3) may cause the payment for the deceased partner's share of goodwill to be an I.R.C. § 736(a) payment if goodwill is "unstated." Because payments for partnership property are generally not based upon the income of the partnership, the payment may well be an I.R.C. § 736(a)(2) payment. I.R.C. § 736(a)(2) payments are not reductions in basis, so the estate may end up with a capital loss. In addition, I.R.C. § 753 may require the estate to treat the payment as income in respect of a decedent because the payment is an I.R.C. § 736(a) payment. The issue becomes even more complex if an I.R.C. § 754 election is in place.[24]

---

[23] 1987-2 C.B. 163.

[24] Gary R. McBride, *Alice's Estate in the Wonderland of Subchapter K*, 122 TAX NOTES 971 (Feb. 23, 2009).

§ 15.06 READING, QUESTIONS AND PROBLEMS

A. Reading

CODE:

> I.R.C. §§ 61(a)(4), 706, 708, 736, 743, 753.

TREASURY REGULATIONS:

> Treas. Reg. §§ 1.706-1(c), 1.708-1, 1.736-1, 1.753-1.

PROPOSED REGULATIONS:

> Prop. Reg. §§ 1.706-1(c), 1.706-4.

B. Questions and Problems

1. Adanna and Bilal run a web-based app store delivering applications that they have designed. They run their store using an LLC. Adanna and Bilal each have a 50% interest in the capital and profits of the LLC. The LLC agreement provides that the LLC will be perpetual unless the members consent to dissolve the LLC. Bilal dies on June 30, 2011, halfway through the LLC's taxable year.

> a. If the LLC agreement provides that if either member stops working for the LLC the interest of the member who no longer works for the LLC is immediately forfeited without further action, has the partnership terminated on June 30 for federal tax purposes?

> b. If the LLC agreement provides that the LLC will redeem the deceased member's interest over a three-year period following the death of a member, has the partnership terminated on June 30 for federal tax purposes?

> c. If the LLC agreement provides that the estate of a deceased member becomes a member, but Bilal's estate sells its interest to Cayla on September 30, has the partnership terminated on June 30 for federal tax purposes? Has the partnership terminated on September 30 for federal tax purposes?

2. Using the facts of Question 1, if the LLC agreement provides that on the death of a member the LLC will redeem the deceased member's interest for one-half the value of the LLC's property plus one-half of the previous year's net income and the value of the LLC's property at the time of Bilal's death was $50,000 and the previous year's net income was $20,000, how much of the payment to Bilal's estate will be income in respect of a decedent under I.R.C. § 753?

3. Using the facts of Question 1, if (i) Bilal's estate succeeded to the ownership of the interest in the LLC, (ii) the net income of the LLC for the first six months of 2011 is $10,000, and (iii) the LLC has a net loss during the last half of 2011 of $20,000.

a. If the LLC uses the closing of the books method, what will Bilal's final return include as his distributive share of income from the LLC?

b. If the LLC uses the proration method, what will Bilal's final return include as his distributive share of income from the LLC?

4. Using the facts of Question 2 and assuming that the estate has no other interest in income in respect of a decedent from the LLC other than that determined under I.R.C. § 753, what would the estate's basis be in the LLC interest if the appraiser's determined that a 20% discount off of the LLC asset value was appropriate?

Chapter 16

S CORPORATIONS

§ 16.01   QUALIFICATION

Stepping out of tax law for a moment, there is no federal corporate law (or federal partnership or LLC law for that matter). An S corporation is a state-law corporation (or a state-law LLC that elects to be taxed as a corporation[1]) that meets certain requirements and makes an "S-election" filed with the IRS.[2] Although this filing with the IRS has an income tax effect, the nature of the entity as a corporation does not change for state law purposes.[3] Under I.R.C. § 1361, to make an S corporation election, a corporation may not:

1. have more than 100 shareholders,[4]

2. have anyone other than an individual, an estate, certain trusts,[5] or certain exempt organizations[6] as shareholders,

3. have a non-resident alien as a shareholder,

4. have more than one class of stock (although differences in voting rights are permitted),

5. be a financial institution which uses the reserve method of accounting for bad debt described in I.R.C. § 585,

6. be an insurance company,

7. be a foreign corporation,

8. be a domestic international sales corporation (or a former DISC), or

---

[1] This happens commonly. LLCs are often thought to have more modern "statutory architecture" than corporations. For example, a corporation commonly must have board meetings whereas an LLC may not be required to have member meetings by statute although the operating agreement may call for those meetings. This enables the member of the LLC to achieve, potentially, the best of both worlds by obtaining corporate-like protection from creditors without the corporate formalities, yet being taxed as an S corporation thanks to the check-the-box Regulations.

[2] A corporation is referred to as an "S" corporation because it is subject to Subchapter S of the I.R.C.

[3] The tax treatment of S corporations on a state level varies, and may require a separate election to be taxed as an S corporation (e.g., New Jersey).

[4] For purposes of counting shareholders, members of a family may be eligible to be treated as a single shareholder. I.R.C. § 1361(c).

[5] These trusts generally include grantor trusts and special trusts created to hold S corporation stock.

[6] An organization described in I.R.C. § 401(a) or I.R.C. § 501(c)(3) and exempt from taxation under I.R.C. § 501(a) may be a shareholder in an S corporation. I.R.C. § 1361(c)(6).

9.   have an I.R.C. § 936 election in effect (involving Puerto Rico and the possession tax credit).

The trusts that are treated as qualifying shareholders include a grantor trust, a trust that was a grantor trust prior to the grantor's death for the two years after the grantor's death, a testamentary trust for the two years after the stock is transferred to the trust, a voting trust, an electing small business trust (an *"ESBT"*), a qualified subchapter S trust (a *"QSST"*), and an individual retirement account (if the S corporation is a bank and the stock is held by the IRA on the date of enactment of the clause).[7]

A grantor trust, for these purposes, is a trust in respect of which all of the trust property is treated as owned by one individual who is a citizen or resident of the United States.

An ESBT is a trust all of the beneficiaries of which are individuals, estates, or exempt organizations that would qualify as shareholders and are described in I.R.C. § 170(c)(2), (3), (4), or (5).[8] No interest in an ESBT may be acquired by purchase. The trustee must elect for the trust to be treated as an ESBT. The result of the ESBT election is that the trust itself is subject to taxation subject to certain special rules.[9]

A QSST has a single-income beneficiary, during the life of whom the corpus may only be distributed to such beneficiary, and the income interest of whom terminates at the earlier of death or termination of the trust.[10] All of the income of the trust is distributed or must be distributed currently. The beneficiary of a trust must file a separate election for each S corporation whose stock it holds. The result of a QSST election is that the trust is treated as a grantor trust and the beneficiary is treated as the owner of the shares.

For the S corporation's first taxable year as an S corporation, in order for the S-election to be effective for the year in which the election is filed, a corporation must file the election on Form 2553 by the 15th day of the third month of the current tax year. Otherwise, the election will not take effect until the next tax year. For example, X, a C corporation, is a calendar year taxpayer. If X wishes to be an S corporation for 2012, it must have filed its election sometime during 2011 or on or before March 15, 2012. There is relief for late elections depending on the facts and circumstances.[11]

To be effective, all the shareholders must consent to the election.[12] Once made, the election remains effective until terminated. If the election is terminated, another election may not be made for five years.[13] There is, however, relief for inadvertent terminations depending upon the facts and circumstances.

---

[7] I.R.C. § 1361(c)(2).

[8] I.R.C. § 1361(e).

[9] I.R.C. § 641(c).

[10] I.R.C. § 1361(d).

[11] *See, e.g.*, Rev. Proc. 97-48, 1997-2 C.B. 521.

[12] I.R.C. § 1362(a)(2).

[13] I.R.C. § 1362(g).

There can be collateral effects. I.R.C. § 1363(d) provides that a C corporation which uses the last-in-first-out ("*LIFO*") method and elects S corporation status must, in its last taxable year as a C corporation, recapture the built-in gain residing in its inventory. The amount of LIFO recapture is the amount by which the inventory valued under the first-in-first-out method (lower of cost or market) exceeds its valuation under the LIFO method. Appropriate adjustment is made to the basis of the inventory to reflect the gain recognized. The additional tax is spread over four years.

§ 16.02 FORMATION

A contribution of property to a corporation in exchange for stock in the recipient corporation is tax free to the contributing shareholder if those persons who contribute property to the corporation collectively receive 80% or more of all classes of stock entitled to vote and at least 80% of the shares of all other classes of stock of the corporation.[14]

Example: Joe, Sally, and Kelley inherited BlackAcre from their mom. Because they are concerned about the individual liability associated with holding property in their own name, they contributed the title of the property to BlackAcre, Inc. in exchange for all of the common stock of BlackAcre, Inc. Absent other facts creating a different result, the contribution will be tax free to Joe, Sally, Kelley, and BlackAcre, Inc.

If property other than stock is received in addition to stock in a transaction that would otherwise qualify for tax-free treatment, gain is recognized to the contributing shareholder (but not in excess of the cash and other property received).[15]

Example: Joe, Sally, and Kelley own BlackAcre as tenants in common. They each have a tax basis in BlackAcre of $100 ($300 all together), but BlackAcre currently has a fair market value of $1,000. Because they are concerned about the individual liability associated with holding property in their own name, they contributed the title of the property to BlackAcre, Inc., which was formed by Ashley and Brent, in exchange for 85% of the outstanding stock of BlackAcre, Inc. Prior to the contribution of BlackAcre, BlackAcre, Inc.'s sole asset was $150 in cash. Simultaneously with the contribution of BlackAcre, $50 in cash is distributed to each of Joe, Sally, and Kelley.

Although contributions of property to corporations are generally tax free when the contributing shareholders receive at least 80% of the stock of the corporation, because Joe, Sally, and Kelley received $50 at the same time as the contribution, Joe, Sally, and Kelley will each recognize gain in connection with the contribution in an amount equal to the cash distributed to them. Since Joe, Sally, and Kelley each received $50 and the potential gain in regard to each of their contributions was greater than $50 (85% of the stock has a value of $850. $850 + $150 = $1,000. $1,000 ÷ 3 = $333. $333 − $100 = $233 of potential gain), each of them will recognize $50 of gain.

---

[14] I.R.C. § 351(a) applying the control test of I.R.C. § 368(c).

[15] I.R.C. § 351(b).

However, the tax-free treatment just described does not apply to a transfer to an investment company. *See* § 14.01.B.

An S corporation cannot have a second class stock,[16] though differences in voting rights are permitted.[17] As a general matter, each shareholder must have the same distribution and liquidation rights. Accordingly, it is very important to review the governing documents of the corporation to make sure there are no differences with respect to distribution and liquidation rights (i.e., each shareholder has the same economic rights). The governing documents include, but are not limited to, the by-laws, buy-sell agreements, corporate charter, and stock holder agreements.

§ 16.03 OPERATION

In general, no federal income tax is paid by an S corporation. Each shareholder reports on his or her tax return his or her pro rata share, based on stock holdings, of the items of income, gain, loss, deduction, or credits of the S corporation, whether or not any actual distribution is made to such shareholder.

Income and losses of an S corporation generally flow through and are taxed to or deducted by the shareholders, retaining the character they had in relation to the S corporation. A shareholder's stock basis is increased by his or her share of income and decreased by his or her share of losses.[18] Under I.R.C. § 1366, a shareholder's loss deduction is limited to the shareholder's basis in his or her stock and the basis of any debt owed by the corporation to the shareholder.[19] As is true with all "flow-through" entities, the income (or loss) of an S corporation is not always reported to its shareholders as a single net amount. Instead, items of gross income and deduction are segregated if the nature of the item could affect the determination of an individual shareholder's tax liability.[20] As is true with all tax partnerships, items of income, deduction, and loss that can have a variable effect on shareholders must be stated separately. Other items are combined.[21]

A C corporation may convert into an S corporation if the S corporation qualification requirements are met. After the conversion, however, the S corporation may have to pay a corporate-level tax in limited situations in addition to the shareholder-level tax. Under I.R.C. § 1374, an S corporation recognizes a corporate-level gain and must pay the highest applicable corporate rate on the disposition of assets, including a liquidation of the corporation. This section applies for 10 years from the date the C corporation made the election to convert into an S corporation.

The amount upon which the S corporation must pay a tax for during this 10-year period is the "net recognized built-in gain." The amount of net recognized built-in gain taken into account for any taxable year is limited to the net unrealized built-in

---

[16] I.R.C. § 1361(b)(1)(D).

[17] I.R.C. § 1361(c)(4).

[18] I.R.C. § 1367.

[19] The at-risk rules of I.R.C. § 465 and the passive loss rules of I.R.C. § 469 apply at the shareholder level.

[20] I.R.C. §§ 1363(b)(1), 1366(a)(1)(A).

[21] I.R.C. §§ 1363(b)(1), 1366(a)(1)(A).

gain over the net recognized built-in gain for prior periods after the S election. Net unrealized built-in gain means the amount by which the fair market value of the assets of the S corporation as of the effective date of the S election exceeds the aggregate adjusted bases of the assets at that time. Thus, this tax only applies to assets owned by the former C corporation immediately before the effective date of the S election and does not apply to after acquired assets. The purpose of this tax is to preserve the repeal of the *General Utilities* doctrine (i.e., that C corporations are subject to two levels of tax).

I.R.C. § 1362(d)(3)(A)(i) provides that an election by a corporation under I.R.C. § 1362(a) to be an S corporation will terminate whenever the corporation has Subchapter C earnings and profits at the close of each of three consecutive taxable years and has gross receipts more than 25% of which are passive investment income.

I.R.C. § 1375(a) imposes a tax on an S corporation if for the taxable year the S corporation has Subchapter C earnings and profits at the close of such taxable year and gross receipts more than 25% of which are passive investment income. The tax is imposed at the highest corporate tax rate on "excessive net passive income."

The term "passive investment income" is defined both for purposes of I.R.C. §§ 1362 and 1375 in I.R.C. § 1362(d)(3)(C). The term "passive investment income" means gross receipts derived from royalties, rents, dividends, interest, annuities, and sales or exchanges of stock or securities (gross receipts from such sales or exchanges being taken into account only to the extent of gains therefrom).[22] Net passive income is passive income minus directly associated expenses.[23] Excess net passive income generally is an amount which bears the same ratio to the net passive income for the taxable year as the amount by which the passive investment income exceeds 25% of gross receipts bears to passive investment income.[24]

§ 16.04 DISTRIBUTIONS OF CASH AND OTHER PROPERTY

In general, distributions of cash by an S corporation are not separately taxable to the shareholders except to the extent the distributions exceed the shareholders' respective bases in their stock. However, a distribution of cash by an S corporation that was a former C corporation may result in dividend income to the shareholders if the distribution is treated as being out of the C corporation earnings and profits.[25]

Distributions of appreciated property by an S corporation follow the same rules as distributions of appreciated property by a C corporation. In other words, the corporation is treated as selling the property at a price equal to the fair market value of the property distributed and the shareholder is treated as receiving a

---

[22] I.R.C. § 1362(d)(3).

[23] I.R.C. § 1375(b)(2).

[24] I.R.C. § 1375(b)(1).

[25] I.R.C. § 1368(c).

distribution equal to the fair market value of the property distributed.[26] This income, like other S corporation income, flows through to the shareholders, increasing their stock bases.[27]

§ 16.05   SALE OF SHARES IN AN S CORPORATION

The basis of a shareholder in his or her stock will be determined initially by reference to the initial capital contribution made by her. His or her tax basis will be increased by: (a) further capital contributions, (b) her distributive share of the S corporation's taxable income, and (c) her distributive share of items of income, the separate treatment of which could affect any shareholder's tax liability. A shareholder's basis in the stock will be decreased (but not below zero) by (i) her share of the S corporation's distributions, (ii) her distributive share of corporate losses, (iii) her distributive share of loss and deduction, the separate treatment of which could affect any shareholder's tax liability, and (iv) her distributive share of any expense of the S corporation not deductible in computing its taxable income and not properly chargeable to capital account (i.e., political contributions, foreign taxes paid, certain life insurance premiums, interest on debts incurred or continued to purchase tax-exempt bonds).

In general, the gain on the sale of S corporation stock will be treated as long-term or short-term capital gain depending upon the holding period of the selling shareholder in the stock. In addition, if the S corporation owns any collectables held for more than one year, that portion of the gain on the sale of the S corporation stock will be treated as collectables gain (typically taxed under I.R.C. § 1(h) at a 28% rate) that equals the amount that the selling shareholder would have recognized in respect of the shares sold if the S corporation had sold all of its collectable assets immediately before the sale of the shares.

§ 16.06   LIQUIDATION OR REDEMPTION

The same tests apply to an S corporation as to an ordinary corporation in determining whether a stockholder or a stockholder's estate will receive capital gain or loss treatment on a complete redemption. If a distribution would be treated as a dividend for a C corporation, a distribution is generally treated as a dividend by an S corporation and its shareholders to the extent that the S corporation has earnings and profits held over from when the corporation was a C corporation (or acquired from a C corporation in a reorganization such as the merger of a C corporation into an S corporation).

In general, the liquidation of an S corporation through the distribution of appreciated property to its shareholders will result in gain being recognized to the corporation and passed through to the shareholders to the extent of the amount of appreciation in the property being distributed. Ordinarily, the shareholders will not recognize gain on such a distribution, other than the passed-through gain of the

---

[26] I.R.C. §§ 311(b), 301(b)(1).

[27] It should be noted that the gain is allocated among all the shareholders — not just the recipient shareholder.

corporation: the basis of the shareholders in their stock is increased by the amount of the gain recognized to the corporation.[28] This means that, at the time the shareholder receives property in liquidation, his or her basis in the corporation's stock will already reflect the market value of the property received.

However, if an S corporation (that was formerly a C corporation) liquidates within 10 years after its election to be treated as an S corporation becomes effective, the corporation will be taxed at the corporate level at the highest corporate tax rate on any appreciation which existed in its property at the time the S election became effective, in addition to passing the recognized income and tax liability through to the shareholders.[29]

§ 16.07   QSUBS

I.R.C. § 1361(b)(3)(A) provides that a QSub shall not be treated as a separate corporation, and all assets, liabilities, and items of income, deduction, and credit of a QSub shall be treated as assets, liabilities, and such items (as the case may be) of the S corporation. I.R.C. § 1361(b)(3)(B) defines a QSub as a domestic corporation that is not an ineligible corporation, if 100% of the stock of the corporation is owned by an S corporation, and the S corporation elects to treat the corporation as a QSub.

A taxpayer makes a QSub election with respect to a subsidiary by filing a Form 8869, Qualified Subchapter S Subsidiary Election.

Thus, a QSub is similar to a single member LLC in that both are disregarded entities. One difference is that a domestic single member LLC is a disregarded entity by default under the check-the-box regulations, but a QSub must file an election if it wishes to be disregarded. For that reason, many practitioners prefer single-member LLCs to QSubs.

§ 16.08   ADVANTAGES OF S CORPORATIONS

A.   General Benefits That Come from Being a Corporation

S corporations are permitted to engage in mergers, stock-for-stock exchanges, and certain other restructurings with other corporations on a tax-free basis.[30] If the consideration is all cash or debt, no advantage is generally obtained. However, if a portion of the consideration is equity and the acquirer is a corporation, an S corporation has much greater flexibility than a partnership in structuring the transaction so that the equity portion of the consideration is received without immediate taxation. If a partnership participates in a reorganization with a corporation, the equity portion would generally be immediately taxable unless the partners receive 80% of the equity of the corporation in the transaction.

---

[28] Some gain (or loss) may be recognized if there are differences between the inside bases of the corporate assets and the outside bases of the shareholders in the stock of the corporation prior to the liquidation.

[29] I.R.C. § 1374(a).

[30] *See* I.R.C. § 368.

B.   Possible Social Security and Medicare Tax Planning

S corporations offer their shareholder-employees a possible way to avoid some of the Social Security and Medicare taxes that would be payable if a partnership or LLC were used.[31] Currently, if a partnership or LLC is used, Social Security taxes are 12.4% of self-employment income up to a maximum, for 2011, of $106,800. Generally, Medicare taxes are 2.9% of self-employment income; there is no cap. Most income of a general partnership or LLC will be self-employment income. In the employer/employee context, normally the overall rate of Social Security and Medicare taxes is the same, but half is paid by the employer and half by the employee. Thus, both the employer and the employee pay Social Security taxes of 6.2% of employee's wages (up to $106,800 in 2011) and Medicare taxes of 1.45% of the employee's wages.

Many argue that general S corporation income that flows through to shareholder-employees does not constitute wages. By paying a shareholder only part of the S corporation's income as wages, it may be possible to limit the Social Security and Medicare taxes (in this context called "employment taxes" given the employer/employee relationship). This result is particularly relevant to Medicare taxes which, unlike Social Security taxes, apply without an income cap.

Example: Assume an S corporation has as its sole shareholder a successful orthopedic surgeon. The S corporation has $700,000 in income after all expenses except wages to the surgeon. It pays the surgeon wages of $200,000 on which a Social Security tax and a Medicare tax are assessed. After the salary deduction, the S corporation has taxable income of $500,000. This amount flows through and constitutes income to the surgeon under I.R.C. § 1366(a). Arguably, this flow-through amount is general income and not wages. If true, it will not be subject to the Medicare tax. The saving of 2.9% of $500,000, or $15,550, is not petty cash.

While some have questioned the legitimacy of this method,[32] it has been used for many years, and for some reason the IRS has not issued a ruling challenging the technique. Until 2010, the court cases have involved taxpayers who were "hogs." The taxpayers usually received none of the income as wages and tried to avoid employment taxes altogether. The hogs got slaughtered. Typically the courts held that all of the income of the S corporations was wages.[33]

---

[31] The following materials are in part reprinted from MARK SARGENT & WALTER SCHWIDETZKY, LIMITED LIABILITY COMPANY HANDBOOK with the permission of Thomson Reuters. Further reproduction of any kind is strictly prohibited.

[32] *See* Walter Schwidetzky, *Integrating Subchapters S and K, Just Do It*, 62 TAX LAW. 749 (2009).

[33] Nu-Look Design, Inc. v. C.I.R., T.C. Memo 2003-52, T.C.M. (RIA) ¶ 55,059, 85 T.C.M. (CCH) 927 (2003), *aff'd*, 356 F.3d 290 (3d Cir. 2004); Mike J. Graham Trucking, Inc. v. C.I.R., T.C. Memo 2003-49, T.C.M. (RIA) ¶ 55,056, 85 T.C.M. (CCH) 908 (2003), *aff'd*, 2004-1 U.S. Tax Cas. (CCH) 50,214, 93 Fed. Appx. 473, 93 A.F.T.R.2d 1626 (3d Cir. 2004); Specialty Transport & Delivery Services, Inc. v. C.I.R., T.C. Memo 2003-51, T.C.M. (RIA) ¶ 55,058, 85 T.C.M. (CCH) 920 (2003), *aff'd*, 2004-1 U.S. Tax Cas. (CCH) 50,203, 91 Fed. Appx. 787, 93 A.F.T.R.2d 1364 (3d Cir. 2004); Water-Pure Systems, Inc. v. C.I.R., T.C. Memo 2003-53, T.C.M. (RIA) ¶ P55,060, 934 T.C.M. (CCH) 934 (2003), *aff'd*, 2004-1 U.S. Tax Cas. (CCH) 50,214, 93 Fed. Appx. 473, 93 A.F.T.R.2d 1626 (3d Cir. 2004); Veterinary Surgical Consultants, P.C. v. C.I.R., T.C. Memo 2003-48, T.C.M. (RIA) ¶ 55,055, 85 T.C.M. (CCH) 901 (2003), *aff'd*, 2004-1 U.S. Tax Cas. (CCH) 50,209, 90 Fed. Appx. 669, 93 A.F.T.R.2d 1273 (3d Cir. 2004) (especially egregious); Superior

Many practitioners have reported instead using the approach described in the example, commonly paying as a wage the maximum amount of income subject to the Social Security tax. Until very recently, there was no case that addressed this method. Arguably, there now is such a case, *Watson v. United States.* [34] There, the taxpayer, Watson, formed an S corporation of which he was the sole shareholder. The S corporation was a partner in an accounting firm partnership. The other partners were also one-person S corporations. In 2002, Watson's S corporation received profit distributions of $203,651 from the partnership. In 2003, it received $175,470 in profit distributions. In each of those years, the S corporation paid Watson a salary of $24,000 per year, let the balance of the income "flow through" as nonwage income, and distributed it to Watson. The court concluded that Watson's salary payments and distributions were an effort to avoid federal employment taxes, and that the distributions to Watson were, in part, remuneration for services performed. Interestingly, the court did not conclude, as it might have, that all of the S corporation's income was subject to federal employment taxes. An expert witness testified that fair market value of Watson's services for the years in question was about $91,044 per year. Only the difference between that amount and $24,000 was held to be subject to federal employment taxes, interest, and penalties.

Watson does not sound the death knell for this technique. Iowa federal district courts are not the last word on tax matters. The salary the taxpayer took, while not de minimis, was quite small. Finally, and most important, the court looked not to the income generated by the taxpayer's services in calculating his employment income, but rather to what a third-party expert said the value of his services were worth. A significant amount of income generated by the taxpayer's services, about $110,000 in 2002 and about $85,000 in 2003, still avoided employment taxes.

In some ways, *Watson* provides an additional incentive to use the technique. The court's holding permits significant amounts of income earned through services to avoid federal employment taxes; taxpayers just cannot be too greedy. If *Watson* were the law of the land, query whether it would be worth it to the Service to litigate a case where salaries equal to the Social Security tax maximum were paid, since often the fair market value of services will be relatively close to that amount. Note that under the court's reasoning in *Watson*, at issue is not the fair market value of the taxpayer's own services, but those of an average, similarly situated taxpayer, whose services might be worth less than those of the taxpayer in question.

At this point, the future of the technique is uncertain. The Iowa court keeps the door open, indeed may open it wider for those taking substantial salaries. However, another court in comparable facts might conclude that all the income is federal

---

Proside, Inc. v. C.I.R., T.C. Memo 2003-50, T.C.M. (RIA) ¶ P55,057, 85 T.C.M. (CCH) 914 (2003), *aff'd*, 2004-1 U.S. Tax Cas. (CCH) 50,146, 86 Fed. Appx. 510, 93 A.F.T.R.2d 647 (3d Cir. 2004); Western Management, Inc, v. United States, 45 Fed. Cl. 543 (Fed. Cl. 2000); Joseph Radtke, S.C. v. United States, 712 F. Supp. 143, (E.D. Wis. 1989), *aff'd*, 895 F.2d 1196 (7th Cir. 1990); *see also* Joly v. Commissioner, 211 F.3d 1269, 2000-1 U.S. Tax Cas. (CCH) ¶ 50,315, 85 A.F.T.R.2d 1234 (6th Cir. 2000); Spicer Accounting, Inc. v. United States, 918 F.2d 90 (9th Cir. 1990); Charlotte's Office Boutique v. Comm'r, 121 TC 89 (2003), *aff'd*, 425 F.3d 1203 (9th Cir. 2005).

[34] 107 A.F.T.R.2d 311 (S.D. Iowa 2010); *see also* Renkemeyer, Campbell & Weaver, LLP v. Commissioner, 136 T.C. No. 7 (2011).

employment income, which would disallow the technique entirely. Further, fairly recently there was a bill introduced in Congress which largely would have shut this technique down. For now, caution is advisable.

The manner in which owners of S corporations may be able to avoid employment taxes is unique to this business form. In a limited partnership, it is often easier than in other business vehicles to separate returns on capital (not subject to self-employment taxes) from income from services (subject to self-employment taxes). For example, a limited partnership can be structured so that it allocates returns on capital to limited partnership interests and payments for services to general partnership interests. One person might hold both types of interests. That said, it is far more common to use S corporations rather than limited partnerships to reduce Social Security and Medicare taxes.

The Health Care and Education Affordability Reconciliation Act of 2010, starting on January 1, 2013, applies an additional 0.9% Medicare tax on earned income exceeding certain thresholds (generally these thresholds are $250,000 if married, filing jointly, and $200,000 for single taxpayers), providing an additional incentive to look for means to avoid federal employment taxes.

C. "Capital Gain Freeze"

Problem: A taxpayer holds appreciated real property he has held for years that currently qualifies as a capital asset. He would like to subdivide and develop the property and sell the lots. But lots held for sale in the ordinary course of a trade or business do not qualify as capital assets under I.R.C. § 1221, and all of the gain will become ordinary income. Is there a way to lock in the existing gain at long term capital gain rates (currently usually 15%), so that only the gain resulting from the development will constitute ordinary income? The answer is yes. What is needed is a sale to a related entity. It is usually not possible to sell the real property to a partnership (or an LLC classified as a partnership) before development and recognize capital gain, however, because I.R.C. § 707(b) treats the gain as ordinary income if the partnership and the seller are related. Related in this context means that the seller owns directly or indirectly (including via family members) more than 50% of the partnership. It is possible to lock in the initial gain at capital gain rates by selling the property to a related S corporation. The S corporation rules contain no analog to I.R.C. § 707(b). If the sale to the S corporation is made in exchange for promissory notes or other forms of debt, care should be exercised that the debt is not reclassified as equity, potentially violating the one class of stock rule for S corporations. Generally, this will not be an issue if the debt complies with the straight debt safe harbor rules of I.R.C. § 1361(c)(5), discussed below.

§ 16.09 DISADVANTAGES OF S CORPORATIONS

Subchapter S sets forth rigid eligibility rules for S corporations that require administration and cost burdens. For example, an S corporation must be a "small business corporation,"[35] which now means it cannot have more than 100 sharehold-

---

[35] I.R.C. § 1361(b)(1).

ers, all of whom must be individuals (only residents of the United States), estates, exempt organizations, or certain qualifying trusts. Failure to meet these eligibility rules will mean the corporation will be subject to tax as a regular C corporation.

Contributions of property to a partnership are tax free under I.R.C. § 721, and distributions are tax free under I.R.C. § 731. Contributions to an S corporation may only be tax free (assuming no boot) if the I.R.C. § 368(c) 80% control test is met. Distributions of gain assets are always taxable; loss inherent in distributed assets may only be recognized, if at all, in a liquidating distribution. I.R.C. §§ 311, 336.

In an S corporation, income and loss allocations may only be based on stock holdings. In other words, special allocations are not permitted.[36] In contrast, in a partnership, special allocations are permitted, subject to certain requirements.

Also, in an S corporation, corporate debt does not increase stock basis. Therefore, it may be more tax beneficial for shareholders to borrow funds personally and lend those same funds to the corporation. This may expose shareholders, however, to an unacceptable amount of personal risk.

There is no equivalent to a I.R.C. § 754 elections for corporations and, as a result, if the shareholder dies and his or her heirs take a fair market value basis in the stock under I.R.C. § 1014, there will be no corresponding step-up in basis of appreciated corporate assets. If the assets are sold at a gain, the income will flow through and be taxed to the inheriting shareholders even though the appreciation occurred before the decedent's death.

An S corporation may generally only have one class of stock. Two classes of stock may exist, however, if the only difference between them relates to voting rights.[37] Therefore, both voting and nonvoting stock can be used. With an S corporation, it is not possible to have a class of equity interests that is limited in its right to share in growth or liquidation, as is possible with a C corporation or a partnership. This can be an important factor, especially when management wants to give an employee a limited ownership interest or when parents want to give their children such an interest. S corporations may, however, issue "safe harbor debt." An instrument that qualifies under the safe harbor debt rules is not treated as a second class of stock even if the obligation would be treated as equity under general principles of federal tax law.[38] To meet the safe harbor, an obligation must be a written unconditional promise to pay on demand or on a specified date a sum certain in money if —

(i)   the interest rate (and interest payment dates) are not contingent on profits, the borrower's discretion, or similar factors,

(ii) there is no convertibility (directly or indirectly) into stock, and

(iii) the creditor is an individual (other than a nonresident alien), an estate, a trust described in I.RC. § 1361(c)(2), or a person which is actively and

---

[36] I.R.C. § 1366.

[37] I.R.C. § 1361(c)(4).

[38] Treas. Reg. § 1.1361-1(l)(5)(iv). For a general discussion of the traditional tests of debt and equity, see Carman & Bender, *Debt, Equity or Other: Applying a Binary Analysis in a Multidimensional World*, 107 J. Tax'n 17 (July 2007).

regularly engaged in the business of lending money.[39]

For all of these reasons, many practitioners prefer tax partnerships to S corporations. As we noted, above, however, there are exceptions.

§ 16.10   READING, QUESTIONS AND PROBLEMS

A.   Reading

CODE:

I.R.C. §§ 1361, 1362, 1363(a)-(c), 1366, 1367, 1368(a)–(e), 1371, 1373, 1374, 1375, 1377, 1378.

CASES:

Nu-Look Design, Inc. v. C.I.R., T.C. Memo 2003-52, T.C.M. (RIA) ¶ 55,059, 85 T.C.M. (CCH) 927 (2003), *aff'd*, 356 F.3d 290 (3d Cir. 2004); *Watson v. United States*, 107 A.F.T.R.2d 311 (S.D. Iowa 2010).

B.   Questions and Problems

1. If Jonathan currently runs an apartment building as a sole proprietorship, owning everything directly in his own name, but then decides to contribute the business and the property to an LLC of which he will own 100%, what has happened to the LLC from a federal income tax perspective on the contribution of the property to the LLC?

2. If Jonathan decides to bring Sarah in as the manager of the property, giving Sarah a 20% interest in the LLC, what has happened from a federal income tax perspective? Would you expect Jonathan to recognize any tax consequences on the transaction? Would you expect Sarah to recognize any tax consequences on the transaction?

3. If Jonathan currently runs an apartment building as a sole proprietorship, owning everything directly in his own name, but then decides to contribute the business and the property to an S corporation of which he will own 100%, has anything happened from a federal income tax perspective on the contribution of the property to the S corporation?

4. If Jonathan decides to bring Sarah in as the manager of the property, giving Sarah a 20% interest in the S corporation, what has happened from a federal income tax perspective? Would you expect Jonathan to recognize any tax consequences on the transaction? Would you expect Sarah to recognize any tax consequences on the transaction?

5. What if Jonathan first brings in Ingrid for a 50% interest in exchange for a contribution of $100, which is used to make improvements on the property. Then Jonathan and Ingrid bring in Sarah as manager in exchange for 20%. What has

---

[39] I.R.C. § 1361(c)(5)(B).

happened to the S corporation when Ingrid makes her contribution and receives an interest in the S corporation from a federal income tax perspective? Would you expect Jonathan to recognize any tax consequences on the transaction? Would you expect Ingrid to recognize any tax consequences on the transaction? Would you expect Jonathan and Ingrid to recognize any tax consequences on the issuance of the interest in the S corporation to Sarah? Would you expect Sarah to recognize any tax consequences on the transaction?

6. What if, instead of contributing $100, Ingrid owns the parcel next door and contributes the parcel she owns to the S corporation in exchange for a 50% interest. What has happened from a federal income tax perspective? Would you expect Jonathan to recognize any tax consequences on the transaction? Would you expect Ingrid to recognize any tax consequences on the transaction?

TABLE OF CASES

[References are to pages]

[References are to pages]

[References are to pages]

W

TABLE OF STATUTES

[References are to page numbers.]

[References are to page numbers.]

[References are to page numbers.]

[References are to page numbers.]

[References are to page numbers.]

[References are to page numbers.]

[References are to page numbers.]

INVESTMENT ADVISORS ACT OF 1940

Section

INVESTMENT COMPANY ACT OF 1940

OMNIBUS BUDGET RECONCILIATION ACT OF 1987

SECURITIES ACT OF 1933

TAX EQUITY AND FISCAL RESPONSIBILITY ACT

TAX REFORM ACT OF 1984

TREASURY REGULATIONS

Proposed Treasury Regulations

[References are to page numbers.]

[References are to page numbers.]

[References are to page numbers.]

[References are to page numbers.]

[References are to page numbers.]

[References are to page numbers.]

UNITED STATES CODE (U.S.C.)

Title: Section

TABLE OF SECONDARY AUTHORITIES

[References are to page numbers.]

BOOKS

CHIEF COUNSEL ADVICE

FEDERAL REGISTER

HOUSE REPORTS

[References are to page numbers.]

[References are to page numbers.]

[References are to page numbers.]

[References are to page numbers.]

INDEX

[References are to pages.]

A

[References are to pages.]

[References are to pages.]

[References are to pages.]

[References are to pages.]

G

[References are to pages.]

[References are to pages.]

[References are to pages.]

[References are to pages.]

[References are to pages.]

[References are to pages.]